HENRY JAMES

By the Same Author

BIOGRAPHIES:

The Life of Henry James

The Untried Years 1953
The Conquest of London 1962
The Middle Years 1962
The Treacherous Years 1969
The Master 1972

Penguin "Peregrine" Definitive Edition, 2 volumes, 1977

Bloomsbury: A House of Lions
James Joyce: The Last Journey
Henry David Thoreau
Willa Cather (with E. K. Brown)

CRITICAL WORKS:

Writing Lives
Stuff of Sleep and Dreams
The Modern Psychological Novel
Literary Biography
A Bibliography of Henry James (with Dan H. Laurence)

EDITOR OF:

The Diary of Alice James

Henry James: *Letters,* four volumes; *The Complete Plays; The Complete Tales,* twelve volumes; the Bodley Head James, ten volumes; *Tales of the Supernatural; Critical Essays,* The Library of America (with Mark Wilson), two volumes

Edmund Wilson: *Notebooks and Diaries* (three volumes)

John La Farge's portrait of the young Henry James. Newport, about 1861.

HENRY JAMES

A LIFE

LEON EDEL

1817

HARPER & ROW, PUBLISHERS, New York
Cambridge, Philadelphia, San Francisco, London
Mexico City, São Paulo, Singapore, Sydney

Designer: Sidney Feinberg

Library of Congress Cataloging in Publication Data

Edel, Leon, 1907–
  Henry James, a life.

  Bibliography: p.
  Includes index.
  1. James, Henry, 1843-1916—Biography.
2. Novelists, American—19th century—Biography.
I. Title.
PS2123.E353   1985   813'.4 [B]   85-42563
ISBN 0-06-015459-4

CONTENTS

ILLUSTRATIONS

☙

Frontispiece: John La Farge's portrait of the young Henry James. *(Courtesy of the Century Association)*

(Following page 178)

PREFACE

This one-volume life of Henry James is derived from my five-volume biography written between 1950 and 1971, published in the United States and Britain. Catharine Carver, the experienced editor who had earlier prepared four of the original volumes for the press, carried out the abridgment. I am deeply grateful to her not only for the way she has used the bright pencils of her professional skills to reduce a great mass of words to their present proportions, but also for her editorial wisdom and literary tact.

When she sent me the reduced text, I found myself revising, retouching, rewriting—in some instances entire chapters. The earlier portions of the biography had been written more than a quarter of a century ago. They required a certain amount of updating. But there was something more important I had to do: to keep constantly in mind the changes that have occurred in biographical writing and in social attitudes toward privacy and our sexual lives. These changes are profound. A younger generation, accustomed to the more unbuttoned ways of our age, no longer reads the literature of the past with the same eyes as the children who came after the gilded age. I refer to the candor which prevails, the freedom we now possess in writing lives to deal with the physical as well as cerebral side of men and women. In looking through the liberating windows of the "sexual revolution" we must recognize just how great have been the changes since the time—in my youth—when simple sexual innuendos led to the banning of *Jurgen;* when the realism of *Ulysses* became contraband; and the mid-century fought battles for *Lady Chatterley* and Edmund Wilson's *Hecate County*.

I am not trying to suggest that I have, in my revisions, gone in quest of a "sex life" or even a "love life" for Henry James: my data remains the same. What I have been able to do is to discard certain former reticences;

to take less advantage of certain "proprieties" I practiced out of respect for surviving members of the James family, the children of William James. I remember that at the time, when biographers gathered, they talked about "how much should a biographer tell?" Today a biographer can tell a great deal more than we allowed—the modern question is not one of permissiveness, but of ethics. No biographer can tell "everything," for modern archives are massive. Selection, taste, tact, and certain decencies still remain: and biographers will have to be judged by the skill with which they adhere to what we humanly want to know rather than load us with gossip and the modern bedroom. We are able to offer a more forthright record of personal relations, of deeper emotions and sexual fantasies, and need no longer wrap indiscretions and adulteries in Victorian gauze. My revisions have attempted to touch the passional life of the celibate James, and the nature of his celibacy, the negative expression of love in his early tales and novels and the growth of his mastery of it —given his strong puritanism. I have accordingly inserted some new passages and an inevitable amount of speculation—the stock-in-trade of all biographers.

Edmund Wilson argued with me at one time that Henry James was less "innocent" as a young man than I made him out to be. He had read Flaubert and the French naturalists, and the tales of Maupassant; he could hardly be called an "innocent," Edmund said. Since Wilson had a healthy sexual appetite, he was not ready to accept my evidence—and that of modern psychology—showing that some individuals do not necessarily "act out" their libidinal drives, but seek to sublimate them using the written word and sensual gratifications. And then James, we remember, argued eloquently in his great essay on Maupassant that man's "moral nature" and his reflective side were more distinctive than his sexual nature. But James also recognized that the nineteenth-century novel had pushed sex aside in the Anglo-Saxon world and not dealt forthrightly with "the great relation between men and women, the constant world-renewal." His very words suggest the language of his time and that side of his life is expressed in James's apologia for his character, Lambert Strether, in *The Ambassadors.* Strether meditates on the fact that it is possible to enjoy a great deal of imaginative experience without necessarily living through actual "adventures."

My new material in this volume and my insertions and rewritings shed light on various aspects of James's life—his homoerotic component, his transmuted passions, his latent prudery, his scrupulous avoidances and verbal barriers; the clumsy love-making of his early heroes tells us much about James's own limitations—as his revision of the solitary kiss in *The Portrait of a Lady* testifies. Not least there was his timidity before women, even though he was one of the most remarkable observers of the feminine "mystique."

I have incorporated other matters: my discovery that it was Ernest Hemingway who invented James's "impotence," which critics talked about during the 1930s and 1940s (I document this in my notes); and my finding a new and prime source for "The Turn of the Screw"—James's tale of horror and mystery which has been dramatized and televised and made into an opera. For almost fifty years critics chased sources for this tale, a chase whose end, I believe, we have now reached.

With these numerous renovations I think I can claim that this volume stands quite free of its predecessors: it is indeed the only complete one-volume life of Henry James which draws on all existing sources. The Carver abridgment, I should mention, was made from a 1669-page edition in two volumes published in Britain by Penguin in their "Peregrine" biographical series, but not in the United States. That edition, which in 1977 I called "definitive," contained a certain amount of new material and important earlier revisions which have been retained here.

Henry James was once asked by a Boston publisher to write a life of his friend James Russell Lowell. He declined, saying

> if a man has had a quiet life, but a great mind, one may do something for him; as one may also do something with him even if he has had a small mind and great adventures. But when he has had neither adventures *nor* intellectual, spiritual, or whatever inward history, then one's case is hard. One becomes, at any rate, very careful.

On the ground of his sedentary life and adventures, James fits the above description. He possessed however the "great mind," the profound "inward history" and a verbal power that places him with the greatest writers of the English language. His letters, like all he wrote, belong to literature. His sedentary life is well known—how he wrote for six or eight hours a day, dined out in the gilded Victorian houses and traveled his well-beaten paths in France and Italy. Alone among American writers, he enjoyed the friendship of Europe's greatest novelists and poets. Flaubert, Zola, Turgenev, Daudet, Maupassant, George Eliot, Browning, Meredith, Trollope, Robert Louis Stevenson, Taine, Renan—he had met them all, known some of them intimately, and written about them in his remarkable advocacy and practice of his fictional and critical genius.

Edgar Allan Poe, at the dawn of modern fiction, repudiated the idea (so beloved of critics) that "the book of an author is a thing apart from the author's self." Joseph Conrad, many years later, put this another way: "The writer of imaginative prose stands confessed in his works." And

James, in the same vein, told us that the artist is present in "every page of every book from which he sought so assiduously to eliminate himself."

I have read James's work for the assiduous and dedicated artist who in a less confessional age confessed himself in the subjects he chose, the characters he delineated, the situations he adumbrated, the revelations he gave us on every page of his imagination in action. James was our one fully-achieved literary artist—a Shakespeare of the novel, the least superficial and most psychological of our novelists. The present volume makes him available to a new generation of readers, and tells the full story of his remarkable career, his fecundity, and the radiance of his powerful artistry.

LEON EDEL
Honolulu 1985

PART ONE

The Untried Years

1843–1870

> To live over other people's
> lives is nothing unless we live
> over their perceptions, live over
> the growth, the change, the
> varying intensities of the same
> —since it was by these things
> they themselves lived.
>
> HENRY JAMES

INTERROGATION

OF THE PAST

☙

The Spectral Eye

The James family was founded in America by an Irish immigrant who arrived in the United States immediately after the Revolution. He was a Protestant from County Cavan, William James. His father had been a William, and among the thirteen children the immigrant fathered in the New World there was still another William, and also a Henry who in turn became the father of still another William and of a Henry, a philosopher and a novelist. The names had become dynastic symbols, as if the family were a royal line.

Family legend has it that the founder of the line, who was eighteen in 1789, when he set foot in the New World, brought with him a "very small sum of money," a Latin grammar and a desire to visit the fresh battlefields of the Revolutionary War. He found employment as a clerk in a New York store, and two years later was able to open his own establishment. In 1793 he settled in Albany, then a thriving frontier town of 5,000 inhabitants. He purchased land in upper New York State and in Manhattan; ventured into activities as diverse as banking and the manufacture of salt. He became a power on the upper Hudson; in due course the name of James was given to a street in Albany, another in Syracuse and to Jamesville, New York.

When he died on 19 September 1832, William of Albany left an estate valued at $3,000,000 to be divided among his eleven surviving children and his widow, Catharine Barber, who outlived him twenty-seven years. And he left them a legacy of rigid Presbyterianism against which the elder Henry James—father of the novelist—rebelled all his life. This son was punished in the will with an annuity of $1,250 a year. The will also invested the trustees with wide powers to supervise the lives of the heirs "with a view to discourage prodigality and vice and furnish an incentive to economy and usefulness." The children of William of Albany rose against this attempt of their father to police their lives from beyond the grave. They went to court, and the will was broken. In the division, the elder Henry James received property that yielded him about $10,000 a year. He found himself, as he remarked, "leisured for life."

The elder Henry James was the fourth son of William of Albany's third marriage, the first wife having died in childbirth and the second two years after her marriage. He was a sensitive boy, strong of limb and keen of mind. The father, preoccupied with his ever-growing business empire, found little time for his numerous progeny, save to exercise them in the rugged Presbyterian manner. The elder Henry later recorded his memories of Sundays in the Albany household in which the children were taught

> not to play, not to dance nor to sing, not to read storybooks, nor to con over our school lessons for Monday even; not to whistle, not to ride the pony, nor to take a walk in the country, nor a swim in the river; nor, in short, to do anything which nature specially craved.

"Nothing," the old man added ruefully looking back at his childish self —"nothing is so hard for a child as *not-to-do.*"

Yet the observant, outgoing little boy found compensations and solutions. When the senior Henry was ten—he later confessed to one of his sons—he used to stop every morning on his way to school at a shoemaker's shop near his father's house for a nip of raw gin or brandy. The ritual was renewed in the afternoon. If it was a way of being a manly little fellow among his schoolmates, it was also a way of defying God the Father who had created dull Sundays and the other father who, in that Albany household, was virtually a god.

The son pictured William of Albany as a stern and uncompromising parent. "I cannot recollect that he ever questioned me about my out-ofdoor occupations, or about my companions, or showed any extreme solicitude about my standing in school." Nor does his mother seem to have filled the gap. "I was never so happy at home as away from it," he recalled. In the house in North Pearl Street competition with his brothers and sisters was intense; there the two fathers—the busy corporeal William of Albany and the invisible Almighty—kept him under their eye and *not-to-do* echoed through the rooms. The dark, silent night, for the small Albany boy, "usually led in the spectral eye of God, and set me wondering and pondering evermore how I should effectively baffle its gaze." There spoke a man who all his life felt himself spied upon. To baffle the detective gaze of a suspicious Calvinist Deity, to find a benign and friendly God, this was to be the troubled quest of Henry James Senior.

Venturing into the world of nature, the boy could at least provision-ally shake off the vocal prohibitions of home. "The dawn always found me on my feet," he wrote when he was old, but could still recall the rapture of pursuing "under the magical light of morning the sports of the river, the wood or the field."

There came a day however when the dawn did not find him on his feet. He was thirteen and attending Albany Academy. One of the boys' favorite pastimes was balloon-flying. The power was supplied by air heated by a ball of tow saturated with spirits of turpentine. One day some of the turpentine splashed over Henry's pantaloons. The balloon rose, caught fire; the ball dropped, the boys swooped down upon it. A sharp kick sent the flaming mass through the window of a nearby stable. Quick to realize the danger, Henry rushed into the barn and climbed to the hayloft. In stamping out the ball of fire his turpentine-soaked trousers were ignited.

The burns he suffered were severe. In one leg "a morbid process in the bone" set in which "ever and anon called for some sharp surgery." When the boy left his bed long months after the accident he had lost his right leg. It had been amputated above the knee. For two years on his back he had been face to face with the spectral eye. No longer able to pursue the sports of the river, the wood or the field, he was wedded, henceforth, to the pavement or wherever an artificial limb could take him.

During this time, however, he discovered that both his father and mother were not as unmindful of his existence as he had believed. He remembered his mother, candle in hand, sleep-walking to his bedside, covering his shoulders, adjusting his pillow, "just as carefully as if she were awake." He recalled his father's agony, standing by his son while the surgeons did their work. He would have remembered William of Albany as an "indifferent parent" if the accident had not revealed "his tenderness to me . . . so assiduous and indeed extreme as to give me an exalted sense of his affection."

The original struggle with his father was never resolved. If he felt himself belatedly appreciated, he also felt increasingly that there existed between man and the God of his father "a profound natural enmity." The thoughtful boy had time, during those months, to daydream and to read, and to develop a feverish mental life, and with it a vigorous, aggressive eloquence, a mordant wit, as if some fragment of the knife that had pierced his bone had remained in his mind.

When the dismembered young man found himself, at the end of his adolescence, erect again, facing the world on a solitary leg, he entered Union College, Schenectady, in 1828, in conformity with William of Albany's wishes. There he asserted his recovered manhood by becoming a spirited young blade. He indulged freely in un-Presbyterian luxuries: cigars, smart clothes, books of an undevout character, oysters. William of Albany had always kept loose change for the household expenses in a drawer of his dressing-table, and when Henry, at seven or eight, had incurred expenses at a confectioner's shop down the street he relieved himself of his debt by two or three times borrowing freely "without any thought of making restitution." When he ran up debts, however, at Schenectady, there was no convenient drawer into which he could plunge his hand. Instead, he quite simply gave his creditors drafts on his opulent parent, who wrote angrily to a friend that Henry had

> so debased himself as to leave his parents' house in the character of a swindler etc. etc. . . . . a fellow from Schenectady was after him today for 50 to 60 dollars—(in a note I understand) for segars and oysters.

All this, William of Albany concluded, would certainly "lodge him in a prison." The elder Henry ran away to Boston instead. There he found a position as a proof-reader, lodged himself comfortably, and enjoyed the society of the city's first families, by whom he was cordially received. And although he later established a truce with Albany and went back to Union College (he graduated in 1830), Henry neither completely placated his parent nor made peace with his own troubled spirit.

The death of his father only exacerbated his emotional problems: he now had a comfortably filled purse, yet did not know where to turn. Seeking to understand his misgivings over religion and to comprehend his relationship with God, the elder Henry gravitated in 1835 to the Princeton Theological Seminary—almost as if to do penance to the ghost of his father. The gesture of submission did not last long. How could so intense a rebel accept religion, conformity, blind belief? And yet the conviction of God's supernatural being "was burnt into me as with a red-hot iron." He abandoned his theological studies, he settled in New York, he married and became a father; but he remained troubled, as one who had never found quite what he was looking for—nor known quite what he sought. In 1843, when his second son—the subject of this biography—was only six months old, he took his family abroad to England. There, in one horrible hour, came the crisis foreshadowed in all the years of his conflict. After that came revelation.

Vastation

It came (in the image used by his son years later in a story) like some beast in the jungle that had long crouched within him for the spring. The elder Henry James had spent the winter in and out of London, and by the spring of 1844 had settled his family in Frogmore Cottage, in Windsor

Great Park. His health was good, he was in cheerful spirits, he was interested in his work, a study of the Book of Genesis. One day, towards the end of May, he ate a good meal and remained at the table after his wife and boys had left it. The afternoon was chilly and there was a fire in the grate. He gazed contentedly into the embers, relaxed, his mind skirting a variety of thoughts. Suddenly he experienced a day-nightmare. It seemed to him that there was an invisible shape squatting in the room, "raying out from his fetid personality influences fatal to life." A deathly presence had stalked from his mind into the house. Or was this again the sense of being spied upon, this time the spectral eye of the Devil?

He recognized that "to all appearance it was a perfect insane and abject terror, without ostensible cause"—but it was terror nevertheless. "The thing had not lasted ten seconds before I felt myself a wreck; that is, reduced from a state of firm, vigorous, joyful manhood to one of almost helpless infancy." Wanting to run like a child to the foot of the stairs and shout as if calling for his mother, or to the roadside to "appeal to the public to protect me," he did neither. He remained motionless, "beat upon by an ever-growing tempest of doubt, anxiety and despair," until he was able to struggle to his feet and confide the "sudden burden of inmost, implacable unrest" to his wife.

He consulted eminent physicians. They told him he had overworked his brain and urged upon him open air, cheerful company, a water-cure. The elder Henry obeyed; he went to an English watering-place, where the waters did not help but where he was struck by the pastoral beauty of the countryside; and we find him wishing himself a sheep grazing on a "placid hillside." Later he muses on the "heavenly sweetness in the soul of a patient over-driven cab horse, or misused cadger's donkey." He thus sought identity with the animals, the lowly subdued and passive servants of man.

The amputation had been a physical ordeal when the boyish frame could triumph over the shock. The second experience, twenty years after the first, was a collapse of mental well-being. He discovered that he no longer wanted to study the Scriptures. Evil, to put it in theological terms, in that shape that squatted invisible, had come to reveal to him that he must not question the word of God but await the Truth of Divine Revelation. The terror of defying Fathers and escaping spectral eyes was finally too much for him. Suffering from nervous exhaustion after years of inner doubt, he chose the one escape possible: return to the innocence of childhood. The time had come to make his peace with the gods, household and universal, so that he should have to conciliate neither. Within him the will to live, the will to manhood, eventually triumphed over the disintegrating forces of a divided self.

The revelation came in unexpected form through the medium of a mother-like figure, a Mrs. Chichester, who lived in the vicinity of the watering-place. One day this lady asked the elder Henry James what had brought him to seek a water-cure; he poured out the story of his visitation in all its horror. She listened attentively, and then told him he was, in her view, undergoing

> what Swedenborg calls a *vastation;* and though, naturally, you yourself are despondent or even despairing about the issue, I cannot help taking an altogether hopeful view of your prospects.

James inquired about Swedenborg—he had never read him. Mrs. Chichester explained that the *vastation* was, in Swedenborgian thought, one stage in the regenerative process of man—awakening, purgation, illumination—and that a new birth for man was the secret of Divine Creation and Providence. The elder James journeyed post-haste to London and purchased two of Emanuel Swedenborg's works—*The Divine Love and Wisdom* and *The Divine Providence.*

He said later that his heart divined even before his intelligence seized the truth he found in Swedenborg. The Swedish mystic provided the ailing man with a kind of mental healing that strengthened and saved him and altered the course of his life. As James formulated it himself: "I had no doubt that this being or self of mine ... came originally as a gift from the hand of God; but I had just as little doubt that the moment the gift had left God's hand ... it became as essentially independent of him in all spiritual or subjective regards as the soul of a child is of its earthly father." And independence of his earthly father was what he needed to effect his cure, even though his father had been dead for more than a decade.

With the discovery of Swedenborg the senior Henry "passed rapidly into that grateful infinitude of recognition and application which he was to inhabit for the rest of his days." He began to lecture and give of himself in brilliant talk, in friendship and at times in an almost ecstatic devotion to his family. He could now remake the God of his father—and by the same token his father, too—in his own image. He could *be* his father. In this manner he found a God that corresponded to his own expansive spirit.

Henry James had found the New Heaven. In Charles Fourier he found the "scientific insight" for the new life on earth. Fourier's "practical" social science could in a sense be read as complementing the doctrine of Swedenborg. Man made in the image of God had God-given instincts. To inhibit them, as civilization did, was to violate the will and the intention of God. "Every appetite and passion of man's nature is good and beautiful, and destined to be fully enjoyed," James wrote in consonance with

Fourier, whom he began to read while he was still recovering from the *vastation*.

Fourier's ideas had taken firm hold in America in those early decades of the nineteenth century. In 1846, the French social thinker had an estimated 200,000 followers in the United States. His proposals to establish communal societies, social units from which competition might be banished and an harmonious social order achieved, constituted an enlargement of the very ideas which the Transcendentalists at Concord were preaching—the fuller realization of Man.

As with Swedenborg, the elder Henry adapted Fourier to his needs. These doctrines sufficed for a lifetime. His last book, published three years before his death, reflected this marriage of Society and God; it bore the title *Society the Redeemed Form of Man and the Earnest of God's Omnipotence in Human Nature*. Evil for him were the constraints which civilization put upon the individual; they prevented him from fulfilling his God-given destiny, since the individual owes all he has to his inheritance and to the society in which he is born. "Make society do its duty to the individual, and the individual will be sure to do his duties to society." With this the elder James had supreme confidence that God would not fail man in his hour of need.

His life after his return to America was no longer an exhausting battle with himself, although his mercurial temperament remained unchanged. A growing family of four boys and a girl testified to his fertility, and now his writings began to multiply. He published them at his own expense. They never reached a wide public. They contain evidence of a continual self-questioning and an unfinished search for inner harmony; they reflect the welling up of emotion that sometimes clouded logic and reason, yet they constitute a body of religio-social thought essentially "Jamesian" with the stamp of the father's individual rhetoric. His style at its best is pithy, enthusiastic, good-humored; yet it is recondite.

He lectured, he indulged in polemic, he even had a few disciples. He was universally respected and became a local celebrity among the elite of New York and New England. Through Emerson he came to know the Transcendentalists—Margaret Fuller, William Ellery Channing, Bronson Alcott. Thoreau called on him when Henry Junior was in his cradle. He had a host of transatlantic Swedenborgian friends, most notable of these being J. J. Garth Wilkinson, a London doctor and writer. James was considered a genial and eminently likeable man. Emerson said he had a "serenity like the sun," and Thoreau found him "patient and determined to have the good of you."

The elder Henry James was an unusually affectionate man. He began always by liking; but often the great of his time, from their position of authority, seemed to him like gods, fathers, dictators, and hidden hostilities in his nature would escape from the tip of his tongue or his pen. Even the benign Emerson was not spared. Henry James could see him as "a soul full of doors and windows"; he could call him, also, a "man without a handle." Bronson Alcott, with whom he had sharp verbal tilts, was once informed that he was "an egg, half-hatched." He had seen Carlyle as "an artist, a wilful artist"; yet on renewed acquaintance, the Scotsman was "the same old sausage, fizzing and sputtering in his own grease."

A man who could caricature with so free a hand had a compelling need to trim his fellow mortals to the measure of himself. "My intelligence is the necessary digestive apparatus for my life," he once said, and indeed the regenerated Henry James fed hungrily upon all that came within his purview. His contemporaries felt that he lived too much by his intelligence; and there remained something rather ineffectual about him —he could lecture on art, on property, on democracy, on theology, but he remained fundamentally aloof from the core of action. Thus he never interested himself in the details of Fourier's planning, embracing only his ideas on the brotherhood of man and exalting his general principles. The elder Henry continued to lead an inner life, sallying forth among men, but returning quickly to his hearth to be at his greatest ease next to his wife who mothered him as she mothered her offspring.

Henry James was married, four years before his *vastation*, to Mary Robertson Walsh, sister of a fellow-student at Princeton Seminary. The Walshes were a prosperous family, as stoutly Presbyterian as the Albany Jameses. They were descended from Hugh Walsh, an Irishman of English extraction who came from Killyleagh, County Down, in 1764 and settled at Newburgh, New York, and from a Scotsman, Alexander Robertson, who arrived in the United States on the eve of the Revolution and attained civic prominence in Manhattan. Mary Walsh and her younger sister Catherine would sit in the family parlor at No. 19 Washington Square and listen to the strange and vivid eloquence of the young Albany scion, as he expounded his unorthodox religious views; both girls were charmed and spellbound. In due course he proposed to the elder sister and was accepted. Catherine Walsh became a member of the James household, lived and traveled with her sister's family and was in every way a second mother to the James children if not a second wife to the elder Henry.

In later years, in talk with Emerson, the elder James told him that on seeing Mary Walsh "the flesh said It is for me, and the spirit said It is for me." So successful was he in weaning Mary Walsh from orthodoxy that she consented to a civil ceremony, performed by the then Mayor of

New York, Isaac Leggett Varian, on 28 July 1840. The bride was thirty, her husband twenty-nine.

They did not set up house immediately. There were spacious family houses in Albany and New York to accommodate the newly married. They spent some time near Catharine Barber James. Then they moved briefly into No. 5 Washington Square, and thereafter lived at the Astor House, the great new hotel of Manhattan of that day. Here the first son was born in January of 1842, and it was probably this which prompted the elder Henry to seek a more permanent home. He purchased No. 21 Washington Place—a brick house a block off the Square, near Greene Street—for $18,000 from his younger brother, John James. By March the family was installed. That month the elder Henry met Ralph Waldo Emerson for the first time and, it is said, brought him home to see the new-born babe, named William after the grandfather.

A year later, directing Thoreau how to find him in Washington Place, Henry James described the street as running from the Square to Broadway, "flanked on one corner by the university and on the opposite by a church." In this home, within a stone's throw of these symbols of organized religion and systematized scholarship—from which he was always to remain aloof—was born, on 15 April 1843, "another fine little boy," as the father proudly announced to Emerson. "Tell Mrs. James," Emerson replied, "that I heartily greet her on the new friend, though little now, that has come to her hearth."

Keystone of the Arch

Mary James, the wife and mother, moves with so quiet a step and for so brief a space through the pages of her son's copious memoirs that we glimpse only a phantasmal form and catch only a distant echo of her voice—as if it were drowned in the clamor of her children and the undisciplined eloquence of her husband. The senior Henry spoke of her "sleepless" sense of justice, and Henry Junior described as "soundless" her "all-saving service and trust." Her daughter Alice spoke of her "selfless devotion." "She was our life, she was the house," Henry Junior wrote in his notebook just after her death. He added, "she was the keystone of the arch."

To have been the "keystone" of the James family arch required strength and firmness and an ability to control and weather high emotional tempests. This Mary James appears to have been able to do all her life. She was a strong woman, strengthened by the worship of her husband and the love of her four sons and daughter, who accepted her not only as their devoted mother but also as the exalted figure of their father's veneration.

Mary James seems to have governed with a certain grace and a quiet unperturbed dignity. Her domain itself was, however, far from quiet. An account of meal-time in the James household, when the boys were in their teens, gives us a picture of the turbulence that could prevail: Garth Wilkinson makes a remark and is challenged by his younger brother Robertson. Henry Junior emerges from his silence to defend Wilky. William joins in. Finally the father seeks to act as moderator. Ralph Waldo Emerson's son Edward, who described this scene, went on to say that the voice of the moderator

> presently would be drowned by the combatants and he soon came down vigorously into the arena, and when in the excited argument the dinner knives might not be absent from eagerly gesticulating hands, dear Mrs. James . . . would look at me, laughingly reassuring, saying "Don't be disturbed, Edward; they won't stab each other. This is usual when the boys come home."

A photograph of Mary James, taken two years before her death when she was seventy, shows a woman in the characteristic pose of resigned elderly maternity: the hands are folded, the lips pursed to a single, hard line. The nose is prominent, the eyes are keen, the forehead is high. Her countenance suggests a purposeful, strong-willed and determined woman. Again, we glimpse her in middle life in a few casual words set down by William James in a letter: "Mother is recovering from one of her indispositions, which she bears like an angel, doing any amount of work at the same time, putting up cornices and raking out the garret-room like a little buffalo."

During the early years of the marriage the family tore up its roots continually. In addition to moves between New York and Albany there were two trips to Europe, major undertakings at that time, with sojourns in England, France and Switzerland. Mary James always had domestic help, and took an American nursemaid with her to Europe when the children were small. She also engaged French maids, governesses, tutors. In addition, she was aided by her sister, the "Aunt Kate" of Henry James's letters and memoirs. Her lot as mother was eased considerably by her husband's comfortable means; but there were always responsibilities and worries, illnesses and accidents.

Despite these cares there were the compensations of a busy maternal life: she took justifiable pride in her growing children; she was surrounded by affection; she participated in her husband's dream of a Heaven on Earth. Her novelist son described her as always sitting on the steps of her husband's "temple" of Swedenborg, catching the "reverberations of the inward mystic choir." Apparently the reverberations sufficed. The father once said that his wife had not been "intellectually speaking" a "liberal education" to him—but, he added, "she really did arouse my heart."

In her later years Mary James wrote every Sunday morning to her scattered sons, dispensing brief factual reports of the local happenings in Cambridge, interlarding counsel with concern about health and with affectionate platitudes. It was doubtless such platitudes that prompted Lilla Cabot Perry to speak of Mary James as being "the very incarnation of banality" and to refer to the "poky banality of the James household." The letters are fluent but literal, the spelling not always certain, the formulations homely, prosaic, the handwriting precise, sharp, thin. "God bless you my darling boy and help you to be manly and generous in your intercourse with one another and with all about you." "All are well— Father has gotten over his sleeplessness and Aunt Kate is flourishing." "Deal honestly with yourself and with us, and try and observe closely what effect perfect rest has upon you, and act accordingly."

Not all her letters had such a homely air. She could smother Henry with maternal solicitude and denounce William, during his prolonged period of ill-health, as a too-articulate hypochondriac. "The trouble with him is that he *must express* every fluctuation of feeling and especially every unfavourable symptom," she wrote to Henry. "He keeps his good looks, but whenever he speaks of himself, says he is no better. This I cannot believe to be the true state of the case." She tells her second son shortly after he has settled in London that what is lacking in his life is the affection she could give him were he at home; "your life must need this succulent, fattening element more than you know yourself." Since she cannot be with him in England, she offers him the familiar motherly counsel that he take a wife: "You know Father used to say to you, that if you would only fall in love it would be the making of you." Or she might simply complain, "Another mail dear Harry, and no letter. I am trying not to be anxious."

There was something strong-yet-yielding, firm-yet-soft about Mary James. She could voice opposition to her children's ideas or plans, yet if in turn she was firmly resisted, she could yield with confusing promptness. She was inconsistent in her firmness; and this firmness itself was in contradiction to her husband's theory that children should be "free and uncommitted." A parental tug-and-pull upon the emotions of their offspring that was alike irrational and anxiety-provoking gives a deep significance to Henry James's remark in later years that in childhood "we wholesomely breathed inconsistency and ate and drank contradictions."

In retrospect Henry was conscious of "our sense of her gathered life in us and of her having no other." He also describes his mother as the "so widely open yet so softly-enclosing lap" of his father's "liberties and all our securities." Thus in the junior Henry's picture the mother envelops the family, the children are taken up in her softness and she becomes all-encompassing. "She *was* he, *was* each of us," he wrote after she had been dead thirty years. Both Henry and William James, who talked often of their father in later years, had little to say of their mother. And when Henry came to write of his parents in *Notes of a Son and Brother* he gave her only a few ambiguous paragraphs. His nephew, William's eldest son, inquired into the reason for this; the answer was: "Oh! my dear boy—that memory is too sacred."

The memory undoubtedly was "sacred." Yet the brief passages concerning the mother in the autobiographies reveal to some extent Henry James's difficulty in seeing her as she really was. He asks questions, he wonders, he justifies, but mainly he idealizes. She makes her sole appearance as a "pipeline" or conveyor of "Father's ideas" to her son—ideas he held himself "little framed to share." It was the way in which she listened to her husband that gave them some meaning for Henry Junior. He pictures Mary James as a support "on which my father rested with the absolute whole of his weight." She listened with the "whole of her usefulness" and also "the whole of her tenderness." She had a "complete availability."

Henry Junior saw his father as living only by his mother. After his mother's death, the father was incapable of going on without her: "he passed away or went out, with entire simplicity, promptness and ease, for the definite reason that his support had failed." However much Henry Senior was an individual in his own right, robust and essentially active, what struck the small boy was his dependency. He gives us a vivid glimpse of a little parental drama, as he watches from the window of the 14th Street house the departure of his parents for one of his father's lectures. At the carriage door, by the light of the street lamp, the father produces from a coat-tail pocket his lecture notes and shakes them in the face of his companion. Earnest and confident, she makes sure that the father has forgotten nothing.

It was the father who, at Christmas, weakened and gave his children a snatched view of the packaged gifts, making them promise not to tell their mother. It was to the father that little Alice wrote: "We have had two dear letters from you and find you are the same dear old good-for-nothing homesick papa as ever." His homesickness was but one of the established family jokes. Henry Junior remembered that "we all used brutally to jeer at him; and I doubtless as hard as the rest." William James participated in such occasions as well. Once when the father was at work on one of his abstruse volumes, he sketched the frontispiece for it: a picture of a man flogging a dead horse! The household pleasantries, however bright and funny, had a painful directness.

Before little Henry's observant eyes there was this ever-present picture of ambiguity and reversal of relation: a father strong, manly, yet weak and feminine, soft and yielding, indulging his children at every turn; and a mother, strong, firm, but irrational and contradictory. The future novelist accepted the queenship of his mother and her authority; it was less easy to understand the strange light in which a reversal of parental roles placed the father. The portrait Henry James drew of his father in *Notes of a Son and Brother* sixty years later reflects the ambiguity a child would experience in discovering the male parent in such a situation. Behind a warm show of affection, reflecting conscious feelings toward the senior Henry, we catch these uncertainties.

He could not give his father a paternal identity that conformed with the identity of other fathers. The senior Henry seemed unlike them in more respects than that of his missing limb. Other boys could describe their fathers as merchants, doctors or lawyers. Henry's father listed no occupation for himself in the New York directory until 1854-55 when he finally inserted "author" after his name. Henry James makes no allusion in *A Small Boy* to his father's amputated state, save as "a grave accident in early life." In *Notes of a Son and Brother,* however, he equates the lameness with his father's inability to be a large literary success. He describes the elder Henry's prose but criticizes him for a style which "affected me as somehow too philosophic for life, and at the same time too living . . . for thought." And he decides that there is a relationship between his father's crippled state and his apparent vagueness and lack of reputation. "The two acceptances melt together for me—that of the limits of his material action, his doing and enjoying, set so narrowly, and that of his scant allowance of 'public recognition.' "

From the daydreams recorded in his notebooks, from his tales, from his observations in the memoirs, we can fathom the effect on the young Henry of this view of the parental relationship which remained with him throughout his life. At some stage the thought came to him that men derive strength from the women they marry, and that conversely women can deprive men both of strength and life. Men used women, were propped up by them and sometimes could not go on living after they were dead. Women could control the lives of men, and this he believed had happened to his father. A father demanded the mother's complete attention. Similarly, women could command the abject worship of men.

This led to further considerations. What happens to anyone who gives himself to another? To love—was not that self-renunciation? Did not the mother give all of herself? Is the man therefore a threat to the woman in a love relationship? (It was clear enough to Henry that the woman could be a threat to the man.) Would the man collapse and become weak (like the senior Henry) if he ever allowed himself to love a woman? To be a man and to take a woman for wife—was that not something to be feared? Mary James was strong—the father revealed this by all his words and deeds—and when she died the sacred fount from which the father had derived life and strength was dried up.

Henry James did not reason in this fashion, but these equations emerge as fictional themes: and in particular what we might call the "vampire theme," elaborated in a number of his works, early, middle and late, recording the observed reality of his father's subservience to his mother and the perhaps less consciously observed fashion in which she in turn took strength from him. In the short novel of James's fifty-seventh year, *The Sacred Fount*, the theme attains its full morbidity: an acute and hyper-sensitive observer spends a week-end in a country house studying what he believes to be the way in which couples deplete one another. From *Roderick Hudson* to *The Ambassadors*, and in the tales, the situation is repeated: the observer is obsessed by the relationships between people, as if the little Henry, looking at his father and mother, and the ever-present Aunt Kate, never quite grasped what occurred between them.

Fear of women and worship of women: the love-theme plays itself out in striking fashion throughout Henry James's work. And usually love, in these fictions, is a threat to life itself. In a list of names he set down in his notebooks when he was fifty, James included that of "Ledward," and then, as was often his custom, he improvised several variants, Ledward-Bedward-Dedward-Deadward. This appeared to be a casual rhyming of led-bed-dead. It was, in effect, a highly condensed statement of the themes of many of his works. To be led to the marriage bed was to be dead.

Henry James accordingly chose the path of safety. He remained celibate.

Mere Junior

The male child born in 1843 in Washington Place was named Henry after the father, even as his elder brother had been named William after the grandfather. For the next forty years he was destined to be known as Henry James Junior. All his works, up to and including *The Portrait of a Lady*, carried the Junior label on their title-pages. Throughout his life Henry volubly protested against the parental failure to let him have a distinctive name and (by the same token) an identity of his own. As later generations of Jameses carried on the dynastic confusion, he pleaded with vehemence against the conferring of "that unfortunate *mere* junior" upon a "helpless babe." He argued that the name given to a child can affect his whole life.

As late as 1882, the year of the elder Henry's death, the father and son
were being taken for one another, since they both wrote and published
and on occasion appeared in the same table of contents of the *Atlantic
Monthly.* It was not, however, the confusion of names that really agitated
the novelist. Some sons are proud to bear their father's given name.
Deeply emotional reasons as well as practical ones are reflected in his
acute feelings. Foremost among these was his struggle in that family of
competing egos to find his own identity. William's name recalled the
long-dead Albany grandfather. Garth Wilkinson James, born after Henry
in 1845, honored the English Swedenborgian. Robertson, the youngest
boy, born in Albany in 1846, was named after the maternal grandfather.
Henry alone had a shared name.

Readers of Henry James's novels and tales can discover at every turn
the writer's predilection for second sons. Sometimes he kills off elder
brothers or turns them into villains; sometimes his hero is an only son,
usually with a widowed mother. He confers on them an ideal fatherless
and brotherless state. For Henry, life in the James family was a state of
inexhaustible younger brotherhood, as if William "had gained such an
advantage of me in his sixteen months' experience of the world before
mine began that I never for all the time of childhood and youth in the
least caught up with him or overtook him." William was

> always round the corner and out of sight, coming back into view but at
> his hours of extremest ease. We were never in the same schoolroom, in
> the same game, scarce even in step together or in the same phase at the
> same time; when our phases overlapped, that is, it was only for a moment
> —he was clean out before I had got well in.

The novelist's memoirs promptly establish the difference between
himself and his elder brother: it is the refrain of the autobiographies—
sometimes good-humored, sometimes a trifle mocking, but filled often
with self-pity and "abasement." The titles, *A Small Boy and Others* and
Notes of a Son and Brother, reflect Henry's need to put himself into the
forefront. What he described as "an attempt to place together some par-
ticulars of the early life of William James" emerged as autobiography.
It is Henry who is the Small Boy; and by the end of the volume that boy
has reached his teens, while the account of William remains to be written. A second volume became necessary. Once again Henry takes the
foreground. *Notes of a Son and Brother* are Henry's notes. He argued that
the only honest picture he could give of William and his father was in
the light of his own observation and relationship to them. But the terms
in which he talks of his father, a mixture of admiration, mild indulgence
and depreciation, and his brother, a mixture of affection and praise always coupled with humility, tell a story the author never intended us to
know, nor was fully aware of himself.

We are confronted with brotherly competition at the start of *A Small Boy* when Henry is brought crying and kicking to the primary school in the Dutch House in Albany—that house which James affectionately describes in the opening of *The Portrait of a Lady*. Isabel Archer's revolt against attending school is not explained by her creator; but in *A Small Boy* he is quite clear why little Henry James, aged five or six, kicks and screams in front of the yellow-painted colonial structure. His rage is provoked by the discovery that William is there ahead of him, seated at his desk, serene and "in possession."

The infantile Henry rebelled; the adolescent sought equality when he and William were in Geneva. He attained it when he was able to attend the Academy where William had been enrolled ahead of him; then, during their young manhood, at Newport, he picked up pencil and paint-brush, seeking to emulate his senior who was studying art in William Morris Hunt's studio (William drew "because he could, while I did so in the main only because he did"). Later still, when William went to Harvard, Henry followed him.

The terms in which he describes his descent upon Harvard at twenty, written half a century later, show that the old rivalry persisted. "At Cambridge, of course"—and the "of course" denotes inevitability—"I was further to find my brother on the scene and already at a stage of possession of its contents that I was resigned in advance never to reach; so thoroughly I seemed to feel a sort of quickening savoury meal in any cold scrap of his own experience that he might pass on to my palate." He fed himself on "the crumbs" of William's feast and on "the echoes of his life." This indeed is the complete abasement of younger brotherhood. Henry does not stop there. He remembers that he wished to live, if only "by the imagination, in William's adaptive skin." He thus characterizes himself as unadaptive, aloof, lacking in William's social qualities, and expresses clearly what he has always wanted to be—his elder brother.

William had been taken first to the theater, while little Henry was left at home by the lamplight in a "vivid vigil" to imagine the stage and the actors and to nurse "my view of paternal discrimination." William presided authoritatively over boyish games. William put Henry in his place with "*I* play with boys who curse and swear!" when Henry proposed to accompany him. Henry didn't curse and swear. And the old man, remembering his elder brother's broad rebuke, looked sadly at his younger self and added: "All boys I rather found were difficult to play with."

William himself recalled later in life another occasion when Henry, combining authorship with attempts at drawing, sketched a mother and child clinging to a rock in the midst of a stormy ocean. Beneath the drawing he wrote: "The thunder roared and the lightning followed."

That Henry should put thunder before lightning was a meteorological blunder inviting high derision. William pounced upon the brother's work and tormented him to such an extent that Henry ran for maternal protection. William was punished, but the incident which ended in triumph for the younger brother emphasized the elder's overlordship. It may well explain, in part, the reticence with which Henry surrounded his literary efforts early and late. William would continue to the end of his life to be a sharp and aggressive critic of Henry's work.

Escape from the frustrations of his juniorhood lay for the young Henry James in books, in the imagination, in writing. He couldn't draw like William, but he could read books about art and artists. He couldn't be active, or felt that he couldn't, but he invented stories about himself doing some of the things his brother did. William could be impulsive, filling each moment with imagination translated into action. Henry, possessing an equal capacity for action, translated it into imagination. The small boy cultivated a quiet aloofness; nothing would happen to him if he withdrew and used his eyes and his mind in that arguing family. Inside the little mind great worlds were created, great achievements, great aggressions planned. He confessed late in life that his favorite fairy-tale in childhood was "Hop-o'-My-Thumb." Is he not the merest of mere juniors and yet the greatest of little adventurers? Youngest of seven boys, deserted with his brothers by his parents, he takes charge—becoming thus Senior instead of Junior—outwits the ogre, obtains possession of the Seven League Boots and ends up as the benefactor of his entire family, including his unhappy parents. It was not Hop-o's smallness alone that counted; it was that, being tiny, he conquered worlds. And Henry James, inexhaustible younger brother, making himself small and quiet among the other Jameses, turned into the depths of himself to fashion a fictional world based on the realities around him in which elder brothers are vanquished, fathers made to disappear, mothers put into their place.

Such daydream triumphs—and aggressions—had their concomitant fears and anxieties and guilts within the outwardly serene little boy. Yet in this fashion, electing the observer's role rather than the actor's, he was able to achieve individuation in his own highly personal way and to conquer. He came to be his mother's favorite son. He was called "angel." At the time of his parents' deaths he had achieved international celebrity; he had surpassed his elder brother who was to win renown some fifteen years after Henry's first novel was published. The victory within the family was complete. But beyond the family lay the outer world, hard and competitive, and it would have to be faced in a new struggle—to assert himself and his art.

Notes on a Nightmare

No chapter has greater fascination in the records of Henry James's childhood than the one in *A Small Boy and Others* in which the novelist describes his rambles in Paris with his brother and his first visits to the Luxembourg and the Louvre. He puts us back into the 1850s, pictures himself and William in tall hats and black gloves, wandering from the Champs-Élysées along the quays, past the bookstalls and print-shops to the rue de Seine; up that familiar street into the old rue de Tournon, leading to the Luxembourg, the seat of the Senate but also the museum of modern works of art. He remembers the cobbles of the rue de Tournon, then a little grass-grown, and "the high grey-headed, clear-faced, straight-standing old houses." The houses represented "style"; they looked down upon himself and William "with conscious encouragement." He was then twelve; William fourteen.

He remembers William always carrying a sketch-book and drawing people and objects which caught his eye. They pause in the Luxembourg before Couture's large canvas of the "decadent Romans," the picture of the hour; Henry remembers also seeing landscapes, and repeats the names of Troyon, Rousseau, Daubigny and Lambinet. He especially recalls William's deep admiration for Delacroix at a time when that artist was not yet widely known. And then he speaks of a painting involving two brothers, Delaroche's *Les Enfants d'Édouard,* the princelings in the Tower, and describes "the long-drawn odd face of the elder prince, sad and sore and sick." He remembers other paintings by this artist, always historical: "the headsman, the bandaged eyes and groping hands, of Lady Jane Grey" and the "noble indifference of Charles the First" while being insulted by the Puritan soldiers. He and William were undergoing an education in "style," but at the same time he reveals his own interest in pictures with a "story" in them. Power is mingled with the thought of style, and power seems to have supreme and tragic issue—the murdered Princes, the beheaded Lady Jane Grey and Charles I.

From this, he moves in his memoirs directly to the Louvre where the pictures, the palace itself, the sense of power and glory and style "overwhelmed and bewildered me." In the great gallery whose "magnificent parts"

> arched over us in the wonder of their endless golden riot and relief, figured and flourished in perpetual revolution, breaking into great high-hung circles and symmetries of squandered picture, opening into deep outward embrasures that threw off the rest of monumental Paris somehow as a told story, a sort of wrought effect or bold ambiguity for a vista,

and yet held it there, at every point, as a vast bright gage, even at moments a felt adventure, of experience,

he felt himself "most happily cross that bridge over to Style constituted by the wondrous Galerie d'Apollon." There he "inhaled little by little . . . a general sense of *glory*. The glory meant ever so many things at once, not only beauty and art and supreme design but history and fame and power, the world in fine raised to the richest and noblest expression." In his own mind he extends the idea of the Louvre's glories to his vision of "the local present fact, to my small imagination, of the Second Empire."

In the Paris of that Second Empire, the name of Napoleon was still heard everywhere—a Napoleon who represented, in a Europe in which he was but thirty-five years dead, the glory of a recent and heroic past. If in the Louvre—the Louvre of Napoleon, the Gallery of Apollo—Henry James found his initiation to Style, then Style remained associated for him with power. He asks himself how childhood imbibes the sense of such matters, speaks of the effect "of a love-philtre or fear-philtre which fixes for the senses their supreme symbols of the fair and strange." At this point Henry James, recalling his first vision of the Galerie d'Apollon, remembers "what a precious part it played for me" when he awakened many years later, in a summer dawn, "to the fortunate, the instantaneous recovery and capture of the most appalling yet most admirable nightmare of my life."

He is defending himself, in terror, against the attempt of someone to break into his room. He is pressing his shoulder against a door and someone is bearing down on the other side. Suddenly the tables are turned. Terror is defined. Nightmare is routed. It is Henry who forces the door open in a burst of aggression—and of triumph. Now he is no longer afraid. He experiences an extraordinary sense of elation. The figure had tried to appall him. But now it is appalled. The pursuer, the attacker, becomes the pursued.

> Routed, dismayed, the tables turned upon him by my so surpassing him for straight aggression and dire intention, my visitant was already but a diminished spot in the long perspective, the tremendous, glorious hall, as I say, over the far-gleaming floor of which, cleared for the occasion of its great line of priceless *vitrines* down the middle, he sped for *his* life, while a great storm of thunder and lightning played through the deep embrasures of high windows at the right.

For James the

> lucidity, not to say the sublimity, of the crisis had consisted of the great thought that I, in my appalled state, was probably still more appalling than the awful agent, creature or presence, whatever he was, whom I had

guessed, in the suddenest wild start from sleep, the sleep within my sleep, to be making for my place of rest.

With his fidelity to inner memory James proceeded to recall the component which perhaps caused him to speak of a "fear-philtre" as well as a "love-philtre." He recognizes the effect upon his perceptions of the great rooms of the Louvre; he sees them as "educative, formative, fertilizing" and "in a degree which no other 'intellectual experience' our youth was to know." The strange nightmare went back to his first visit in 1855 to the Galerie d'Apollon with his brother. The two boys had been entrusted to the family courier, Jean Nadali, as their guide and he remembers that, "appalled but uplifted," he clung to Nadali's arm. He then asks himself why there had been "under our courier's protection and in my brother's company" a sense of "alarm" as well as one of "bliss." "The bliss in fact I think scarce disengaged itself at all, but only the sense of a freedom of contact and appreciation really too big for one"; the "alarm" he decides was that of a boy receiving more impressions than he could absorb. And this brilliant chapter of memory and re-creation ends with his feeling that "the great premises" of the Louvre had served as the starting point for his lifetime adventure. He likens the experiences he has described to silver and gold threads perhaps "casually inter-woven" but into a very fine tissue. It sufficed that he had learned and lived and created, and he recognized the difficulty of unravelling the tissue.

The threads cannot be unravelled: old dreams become mere fables when divorced from the dreamers. Yet clear at least in the dream, in its first part, is the picture of himself as threatened—who can tell by whom? —the "mere junior" surrounded by admonishing governesses, a permissive father, an often stern ambiguous mother, above all a hyperactive elder brother. William seems to be with him, for the scene is set in the Louvre; and William has been sketching and studying and appreciating. The "sublime" synthesis links the Gallery of Apollo and the Paris of the new Napoleon. *Apollon* and *Napoléon*—pronounced in French, the names sound almost alike—Apollo representing the glory of art and Napoleon the symbol for "history, fame, power." But with this James recurrently uses the word "appalling" which strikes the note of fear and alarm. The three words encapsulate the emotions he conveys to us in his dream-narrative—the grandeur and nightmare of history, the mixture of heroism and terror, the love-philtre which can be death (when did love-philtres lead anywhere but to tragedy?) and the fear-philtre which is the fear of the overwhelmed small boy, clutching the arm of his guide, and amid historical glories keeping pace with his older brother.

The remarkable element in the nightmare resides in Henry's conquest of fear and the guilt of his aggression. As we read his description of the great chase along the gallery in the Louvre, amid thunder and lightning, as of Zeus, we remember Henry's saying of William, "I never for all the time of childhood and youth in the least caught up with him or overtook him." Then, at the end of his dream, as the older brother waves aside the art-viewing and street-wandering in Paris as non-educative, the younger brother incorporates these memories into the immediate "fact" of the Second Empire. The artist sees the panorama of his childhood as an exposure to history and to style, which is synonymous with glory; to beauty and art and fame and "supreme design," which become power and grandeur.

There is evidence that Henry James may have had this "dream-adventure," as he called it, in 1910 when he was himself old and ill and William was dying. It was a kind of gathering in of the essence of his life, the story of his art and his self-assertion in relation to his brother and the way in which he had conquered fear and family pressures. There was one difference between the dream and the facts of his life. In the wishful dream his conquest was achieved by direct counterattack, by pursuit. In his life it was he who fled; his conquests were by persistence, indirection, secrecy. Napoleon had used the sword. Henry James used a subtle pen. James left his homeland; his real home was the Galerie d'Apollon. By the power of created art, he achieved a victory over the "appalling" of life. On his death-bed, he would, in his final dictation, speak of the Louvre.

When he was seventeen, and the hours of his last youthful stay in the Old World had shrunk to but a handful, Henry James slipped from his bed on the fifth floor of his hotel (it bore appropriately the name of Hôtel des Trois Empereurs) in the rue de Rivoli. It was a September morning and from the balcony he looked out on the open Place du Palais Royal with its ceaseless swarming movement. Across the way loomed the new wing of the Louvre. Set into the great palace wall were the statues of Napoleon's young generals—Hoche, Marceau, Desaix. At that moment "what it somehow came to was that here massed itself the shining second Empire, over which they stood straight aloft and on guard, like archangels of the sword . . ." The moment of French history now mingled with personal history.

> It meant, immensely, the glittering régime, and *that* meant in turn, prodigiously, something that would probably never be meant quite to any such tune again: so much one positively and however absurdly said to one's self as one stood up on the high balcony to the great insolence of

the Louvre and to all the history, all the glory again and all the imposed applause, not to say worship, and not to speak of the implied inferiority, on the part of everything else, that it represented.

The Louvre again is Napoleon and his generals, and *gloire* and style —the supreme palace of the western world, "the most peopled of all scenes not less than the most hushed of all temples." It was the Temple of Apollo and the Palace of Napoleon and the Palace of Art which in the end "became mixed and interchangeable with the House of Life."

SCENES
FROM
A BOYHOOD

Picture and Scene

Henry James always said that his earliest memory was of the Place
Vendôme in Paris, with its column celebrating the victories of Napoleon.
He had been taken to England when he was six months old. France was
visited during the following year. This means that Henry's remarkable
"recollection" of the Place Vendôme dated from his second year.

As he set it down, he remembered he was still "in long clothes" seated
on his Aunt Kate's lap in a carriage opposite his father and mother; he
was "impressed with the view, framed by the clear window of the vehicle
as we passed, of a great stately square surrounded with high-roofed
houses and having in its centre a tall and glorious column." Was this the
loom of memory at work, weaving backward and forward among things
seen early and late? Whether the brilliant infant had really absorbed and
remembered so concretely we cannot know. What we do know is that his
awakening consciousness was first exposed to Europe. It was there that
he emerged from the cradle and began to assimilate the world around
him.

Henry James reached the age of recognitions and perceptions during
the period of his father's *vastation,* in a small cottage between the Great
and Little Parks at Windsor. "Willy and Harry," the senior Henry wrote
to his mother in Albany, "from the nursery windows may hold delightful
converse with the sheep and cattle browsing beneath." They also had the
view of the long broad meadows of the Park, "dotted with the noblest oaks
of England." The infant had been taken from the edge of cart-crowded
Broadway in New York across an ocean and had opened his eyes before
the august beauty of the English countryside at the very spot where it was
designed to regale the eyes of a British queen.

If the novelist's first glimpses of the world were European, his emerg-

ing consciousness caught hold, on native grounds, of another square, in
the city of his birth, which was to give its name to one of his best-known
works. In the early pages of *Washington Square* he allows himself a
striking autobiographical digression, almost as if he wanted to make
certain his own identity with that Square would be permanently established:

> It was here, as you might have been informed on good authority, that you
> had come into a world which appeared to offer a variety of sources of
> interest; it was here that your grandmother lived in venerable solitude,
> and dispensed a hospitality which commended itself alike to the infant
> imagination and the infant palate; it was here that you took your first
> walks abroad, following the nursery-maid with unequal step, and
> sniffing up the strange odour of the ailanthus-trees which at that time
> formed the principal umbrage of the Square, and diffused an aroma that
> you were not yet critical enough to dislike as it deserved. . . .

He is alluding here to his first walks, not "abroad" but in Manhattan,
from his maternal grandmother's home, to which the James family
briefly went on their return to America when little Henry was two and
a half. Mary James was then carrying her third child, born in New York
on 21 July 1845, and named Garth Wilkinson. A few months later the
father gravitated anew with his family towards his mother in Albany. He
resided at No. 50 North Pearl Street, a few doors away from Catharine
Barber James, who lived at No. 43, and from his brother Augustus and
his family, who lived at No. 47. Here the James family remained until
1847 and here Mrs. James gave birth to still another son, Robertson, on
29 August 1846. When Henry Junior in later years spoke of "infantile
Albany" he meant his third and fourth years spent near his grandmother
in a veritable settlement of Jameses.

All his memories of Albany had a flavor of peaches. There were
certain "capital peach trees" in the great expanse of garden behind the
grandmother's large old-fashioned house and the small boy required no
urging to do justice to them. For Isabel Archer in the early pages of *The
Portrait of a Lady* peaches and Albany are synonymous. In *A Small Boy*
James remembers mounds of Isabella grapes and sticky Seckel pears. But
ah the "peaches *d'antan*"!

> every garden, almost every bush and the very boys' pockets grew them;
> they were "cut up" and eaten with cream at every meal; domestically
> "brandied" they figured, the rest of the year, scarce less freely—if they
> were rather a "party dish" it was because they made the party whenever
> they appeared, and when ice-cream was added, or they were added to it,
> they formed the highest revel we knew.

In matters of food the small boy was inevitably less discriminating than his later fictional characters. He ate large quantities of ice-cream; he swallowed hot cakes and sausages and molasses on the hospitable porch of a neighbor, when the family was back in New York; doughnuts were consumed on Broadway when young Henry wasn't using his pennies for the more tempting fare offered at Barnum's Museum, and waffles "by the hundreds" were eaten after school. Later, on the Continent, there were to be the melting *babas* and criss-cross apple tartlets with other delights of the French pastry-shops. At seventy Henry seemed to be smacking his lips over his hearty boyish appetite.

He remembered more than the peach trees in Albany, although these always came first to mind: the swing on the covered piazza to the rear of his grandmother's house, the long garden sloping down to the stable, the library of William of Albany, full of books "with frontispieces" which the child climbed on a chair to take down, guided in his selection chiefly by the pictures; the "office" beyond the library with its musty smell and ancient pieces of furniture, and the school-house across the street from which came the "hum of childish voices repeating the multiplication table."

In 1847 the James family moved back to New York, and here Mrs. James gave birth on 7 August 1848 to her fifth and last child, a daughter, named Alice. After a brief residence at 11 Fifth Avenue in a house later razed to make way for the Brevoort Hotel, the elder Henry settled his brood in the then fashionable "uptown" residential neighborhood near Union Square —first in a rented house and then at No. 58 West 14th Street, near Sixth Avenue, in a building which he purchased. The New York of *A Small Boy and Others,* in which the future novelist roamed between his fifth and twelfth years, was largely the area between Sixth and Fifth Avenues down to Washington Square and up eastward to Union Square which, in that era, was enclosed by a high railing, had a fountain and was presided over by a solitary amateur-looking policeman. As the boys grew older there were excursions downtown to the theaters of Chambers Street or Park Place and walks up and down Broadway and the farther reach of 42nd Street beyond which everything was clearly suburban. This was the "old liquor-scented, heated-looking city, the city of no pavements," of mixed buildings, vacant lots filled with weeds, theatrical billboards and wooden fences. The squares were fenced, there were poplars in the important thoroughfares, and stray pigs and poultry wandered in the side-streets. The grass plots in front of City Hall were known as "the park."

The childhood of Henry James was spacious in home and in city, a world rich and various, wrapped in outward security and "floating in such a clean light social order." The house on 14th Street was large and well furnished—parlors front and back, a sunny library, a guest room, bedrooms for the four boys and for Alice, the maternal and paternal quarters, the attic in which theatricals were staged by the enterprising William, and servants' quarters as well as a large old-fashioned kitchen below stairs. In the front parlor there was a large painting of a Florentine view by Thomas Cole; the rear parlor boasted a Tuscany landscape by Lefèvre; between the two rear windows stood the bust of a Bacchante, her breasts imperfectly covered, which certain visitors pronounced rather "cold."

Henry remembered Mr. Emerson seated on the sofa in the rear parlor, "elegantly slim, benevolently aquiline." In the library one day he saw Mr. Thackeray who had come to America to lecture on the English humorists of the eighteenth century. Henry was dressed after the fashion of the time in a tight jacket adorned in front with a row of brass buttons; hovering near the door of the sun-filled room, he heard himself summoned by the enormous English gentleman: "Come here, little boy, and show me your extraordinary jacket." Thackeray peered through and over his spectacles alike at garment and boy. He then carefully explained to Henry that if he were to go to England he would be addressed as "Buttons."

Between the front parlor windows in the 14th Street home stood a piece of furniture which housed volumes of Gavarni's caricatures, a set of Béranger enriched by steel engravings, and the four tall folios of Joseph Nash's *Mansions of England in the Olden Time.* Here on winter afternoons, in the glow of a red fire, the small boy lay on his stomach on the drawing-room hearth-rug studying the Nash pictures; in Gavarni he delighted in the sturdy Frenchwomen who came to life on the page. And here he read *Punch.* All England seemed to unfold from its pages, but mainly London—the names of London streets and theaters, Kensington Gardens and Drury Lane, the sounds of Piccadilly seemed to be there, people riding in the Row, cabmen and costermongers, little pages in buttons, small boys in tall hats and Eton jackets, pretty girls in striped petticoats with their hair dressed in the shape of mushrooms.

The transition from pictures in books to pictures in galleries was made early. New York at the mid-century favored large canvases and bright colors—as large "as the side of a house and of a bravery of colour and lustre of surface that I was never afterwards to see surpassed." The first exhibition of Leutze's celebrated painting of Washington crossing the Delaware, in a "disaffected church" on Broadway, was an occasion never forgotten; the James family attended in force, taking the crosstown omnibus on 14th Street at an hour of the evening when Henry was usually in bed. There it was, the painting, with little Henry taking in "the sharpness of the ice blocks . . . the sickness of the sick soldier . . . the strands of the rope and the nails of the boots . . . above all . . . the profiled national hero's purpose," which seemed to be that of "standing *up,* as much as possible, even indeed of doing it almost on one leg." The Father of the Country was thus promptly identified with Henry's own father.

What is clear from these early memories is the extent to which "picture" entered into the experience of the young Henry; he was to link it to "scene," which he learned also as a boy to watch on the stage, and of which he was given an early view when his father took him to visit an uncle on his estate at Rhinebeck, on the Hudson. One evening at Linwood little Henry, then eleven, had the company of his cousin, Marie, a year older. She was an object of special interest because Henry had heard she was "spoiled." The James boys had never been spoiled. It gave her a romantic status; he only half understood the meaning of the term. His uncle, Augustus James, at a given moment remarked with some emphasis that it was Marie's bedtime. Marie objected. There was an emphatic rejoinder from Uncle Augustus. Marie appealed to her mother, and Henry heard these sharp words: "Come now, my dear; don't make a scene —I *insist* on your not making a scene!"

> The expression, so vivid, so portentous, . . . seemed freighted to sail so far; it told me so much about life. Life at these intensities clearly became "scenes"; but the great thing, the immense illumination, was that we could make them or not as we chose.

An Initiation

After pictures came books. Visits to the bookstore, "fondest of my father's resorts," were frequent. Even before he could read young Henry sniffed the fresh paper and the printer's ink—he called it the "English smell" because so many of the books were imported from England. The small boy learned to read early. He remembered that he accompanied his father one summer's day on a visit to the New York *Tribune* in Nassau Street, where the elder Henry usually called on his friend Horace Greeley. Someone handed his father a volume by Solon Robinson, a staff member of the paper. It was called *Hot Corn.* Little Henry promptly wanted to get his sensitive nose into the book but one of the men suggested that the volume, with its lurid pictures of New York slum life, wasn't for little boys. Henry Junior at seventy remembered the "soreness of the thought that it was I rather who was wrong for the book."

As a consolation he was given Maria S. Cummins's *The Lamplighter,* then enjoying great vogue, and it was suggested to him that this was a "grown-up" book. In his memoirs James implies that the small boy wasn't fooled, although he confessed that the moralizing tale of the little orphan adopted by the lamplighter received an "absorbed perusal." Something else happened, however, to give young Henry his real taste of what a novel could be.

One day when the family had fled the New York heat and was staying at New Brighton, on Staten Island, the elder Henry accompanied by Henry Junior took the boat to New York to do some chores. These included the usual visit to the bookstore where the father purchased a number of volumes, including a novel for the mother's reading. This book was handed to young Henry to carry. They made their way back to the boat and in the little cabin or sitting-room he turned the book's pages. It was called *The Initials* and was by a woman with the picturesque name of the Baroness Tautphoeus. "It came over me with the very first page," he later wrote, "assimilated in the fluttered little cabin . . ." that *"The Initials was* grown-up."

Jemima Montgomery, Baroness Tautphoeus, an Irishwoman who had married a Chamberlain to the King of Bavaria, was one of a group of English writers of the time who skillfully illuminated foreign manners for Anglo-Saxon readers. The first page of this novel has an atmosphere not unlike the first page of "Daisy Miller": a young Englishman named Hamilton has alighted at a Munich inn and is taking a sophisticated view of his continental surroundings. In a few minutes an "international" situation develops, a mysterious note, merely initialled, is delivered, and in due course Mr. Hamilton has met the proud German beauty Hildegarde and her sister Crescenz. What was a sentimental story of an orphan and a lamplighter compared to a tale, romantic and witty, set in the Bavarian Alps, containing a lurid suicide, a struggle of lovers against cruel fate, even a quasi-elopement in which, however, the hero observes all the niceties after registering the heroine at a Mainz hotel and being taken for her husband. "I will go at once across, and if there be any rooms to be had, not quite on the other end of town, I shall not return until morning." The precision of the "not quite on the other end of town" could only be an anticipation of the early writings of Henry James Junior.

James discovered that day on the New Brighton boat what real fiction could be, fiction sophisticated and written with a bright, facile charm,

> the history of the long-legged Mr. Hamilton and his two Bavarian beauties, the elder of whom, Hildegarde, was to figure for our small generation as the very type of the haughty as distinguished from the forward

heroine . . . I memorably felt that romance was thick round me—every-thing, at such a crisis, seeming to make for it at once.

The "romance" that took the small boy from fiction to a "scene" from life was his discovery that "lurking" in the same public cabin sitting-room were two little girls whom he recognized as the "Boon Children" of the New York stage, scheduled to perform that evening at the New Brighton Pavilion. Thus Henry, not quite the long-legged Mr. Hamilton, could fancy himself as being "in relation" with two beauties, not quite Bavarian. The Boon Children were weary and sleepy, and young Henry was fascinated yet somehow afraid. The girls were frightening in their assurance, their lack of interest in anything and anybody; they seemed "awfully detached and indifferent, indifferent perhaps even to being pinched and slapped, for art's sake, at home." Ever after, Henry James was to have a certain contempt for actors and actresses, whom he considered "self-exhibitionistic" creatures. This, however, did not dull his admiration for their art or his love of the theater.

Henry James's theatrical memories are a striking part of *A Small Boy and Others.* Its 400 pages cover only the first fourteen years of his life, yet one-eighth of these is devoted to a detailed recounting of nights at the play—pantomimes viewed in early childhood, old theatrical billboards with their lurid synopses of the plays and the picturesque names of the stage folk, excursions to the theaters of New York and later of London and Paris. He was eight when the curtain rose on what was to be a lifetime of theater-going.

James believed that his first play was *A Comedy of Errors.* The work was read to him during the day and he recalled the "sacred thrill" once inside the theater before a green curtain that refused to go up. "One's eyes bored into it in vain, and yet one knew that it *would* rise at the named hour, the only question being if one could exist till then."

Young Henry was taken to all the leading theaters of the time. At Burton's, in Chambers Street, he saw such familiar farces as *The Toodles* and *The Serious Family;* at the Broadway the super-spectacle of *The Cataract of the Ganges, or The Rajah's Daughter* (with a cataract of "real water") and the popular *Green Bushes;* at Wallack's the clever comedies of Dion Boucicault, *London Assurance* and *Love in a Maze.* He saw hastily cobbled-up versions of Dickens's novels, the very names of whose characters—the Scrooges and Pickwicks, Oliver Twists and Paul Dombeys—assured a full house. Henry remembered the actor Burton as "a monstrous Micawber" with "the entire baldness of a huge easter egg and collar-points like the sails of Mediterranean feluccas." Always there is the vivid recollection of the actors: Madame Ponisi, the Oberon of *A Midsummer Night's Dream*, "representing all characters alike with a broad brown face framed in bands or crowns or other heavy headgear out of which cropped a row of very small tight black curls"; Madame Céline Celeste "straight out of London" in *Green Bushes*, "whose admired walk up the stage as Miami the huntress, a wonderful majestic and yet voluptuous stride enhanced by a short kilt, black velvet leggings and a gun haughtily borne on the shoulder, is vividly before me."

In November 1853 Barnum mounted his production of *Uncle Tom's Cabin* at his Broadway theater, attached to the "Great American Museum," and here the boy saw the play for the first time with Emily Mestayer giving an intrepid and graceful performance of Eliza's flight across the ice. This was an abridged version with a happy ending. Later, Henry saw the full version in six long acts at the National—an evening particularly remembered because it happened to be the occasion of his first theater party. Comparing the two versions, he was certain the second Eliza was less dramatic than Miss Mestayer; but the ice-floes at the National seemed more genuine. He was absorbed as much by the junior audience as by the play. The little sophisticates had gone to *Uncle Tom's Cabin* with some detachment but found themselves swept along by the play's strong currents. It was initiation into social as well as aesthetic adventure.

. . . And Others

The United States at that time consisted for Henry James of "the busy, the tipsy and Daniel Webster." The "busy" were all around him— and there was no shortage of the "tipsy." He knew that people went to offices and stores (though his father never did) and that they made money —yet the process of making it other than by writing was forever a mystery to him. Early in life there came to him faint echoes of the Mexican War; he caught a glimpse of an uncle in uniform and later was introduced to Winfield Scott on Fifth Avenue. Then he remembered two uncles arriving at their Fifth Avenue apartment, just before the family moved into 14th Street, to announce excitedly to his father the triumph of the revolution of 1848 in France. Henry was six when the country reverberated to the discovery of gold in California, but the Jameses had their eyes turned towards Europe as the covered wagons moved westward. These major events had reality for the boy only as stories told by persons around him.

Beyond the perpetual circle of relatives he began to pay attention to an ever-widening group of callers—artists, writers, publicists—at his father's house. He remembered meeting Washington Irving on the steamboat to Fort Hamilton. Irving told his father that Margaret Fuller had been drowned with her husband and child off Fire Island during the storm of two days before. Gradually an atmosphere was constituted around the small boy and his brothers and sister, in which figured people doing things, men with reputations, a world of books, talk of art.

Closest to Henry Junior were the maternal and paternal relatives; they are the *Others* outside his immediate family in the title of his autobiographical volume. Mainly there are cousins on all sides, even as we find them later in his novels in groups and clusters, people one could or could not be "in relation with" and who are also "other." In *A Small Boy* he tells us that he was "constantly eager to exchange my lot for that of somebody else, on the assured certainty of gaining by the bargain." He is careful at the same time to explain that this was not "jealousy." His desire to be "somebody else" was the equivalent of a small boy's view, he said, of sweets through a plate glass window. Little Henry thus reduced himself to his favorite pastime of watching. He observed his relatives closely.

William of Albany's family had been large; and there were maternal relatives as well. They pass before us in a series of sketches and portraits; they constitute a "chronicle of early deaths, arrested careers, broken promises, orphaned children." The mother's relatives are all "strong" females, holding their men under their thumbs, from Great-Aunt Wyckoff, "an image of living antiquity," to Cousin Helen, his mother's cousin, with her "fine old New York ignorance and rigour." Cousin Helen's husband, described as a "dim little gentleman," a "spectral spouse," a "shade of nullity," "a blank," "a zero," and a "natural plati-tude," was "Mr." to his own wife. Henry frequently went to the 14th Street "other house" and saw Helen's husband in his shipboard pace from the street-end to the piazza at the back; he wore neckcloths that seemed to elongate his neck and was partially bald, with his hair standing up on both sides. The husband talked often of the grand tour he would some day make. Finally, after half a century, he sailed for England. The shock was too much for him. There was a "snap of the tense cord . . . he just landed and died." Cousin Helen also had charge of Henry Wyckoff, her brother, and of his ample fortune. She gave him a dime a day on the theory that he was "not to be trusted" with money.

There were other cousins and uncles who died almost before their lives began: Minny Temple, a bright Albany cousin known briefly to the small boy, but later destined to play a large role in his life; Gus Barker, another James cousin, cut down at twenty-one by a guerrilla's bullet during the Civil War. We capture him, during his brief bright life, through Henry Junior's eyes, clad in the uniform of the military school he was attending, "the most beautifully-made athletic little person"; and again without uniform, in fact without clothes, on a pedestal being drawn by William James in Hunt's studio at Newport. Henry kept William's sketch; presently, it was all that remained of the genial Gus.

There was Gus's brother, Bob Barker, with his promise as a sculptor; Johnny James, with a talent for music cut short by death; the four uncles, Augustus, John, Edward and Howard, the first presiding in grandeur over Linwood, the last three figuring as customers of Mrs. Cannon who sold ties, collars and the essence known in old New York as "Cullone," somewhere near Fourth Street (she also rented apartments "of an intimacy of comfort" with attendant ladies whose roles were unclear to the small boy); and there was the blond-bearded short-of-breath dandy Vernon King, with his European background and his untimely end at Richmond or Petersburg during the Civil War. His pro-Southern mother buried him at Newport under a stone that makes no allusion to his soldier's death.

The dimmest ghost of all perhaps was the memory of Aunt Ellen King James, "softly spectral" with ringlets, who died at twenty-six—when Henry was six. He remembered a call at her house in Elk Street, in Albany, the memory being fixed mainly by the fact that she had married Smith Thompson Van Buren, the son of a President of the United States. The visitable past of the James family could lead Henry even to the White House.

Theory of Education

In the history of literature and in the lives of a majority of the nine-teenth-century novelists, Church and School figure as twin institutions coloring their childhood and casting shadows, for good or bad, across the adult years. The era of *The Way of All Flesh* and Wackford Squeers left Henry James Junior relatively untouched. Although he was born in a house hard by a church and a university he grew up unencumbered by religion or formal education.

The elder Henry, remembering his joyless childhood, shrank from anything that would be "narrowing" for his children. A cheerful anarchy characterized the schooling of the little Jameses. And when his school-mates challenged, "What church do you go to?" little Henry was as bereft of an answer as he was when asked to name his father's profession. The elder Henry's reply was that

> we could plead nothing less than the whole privilege of Christendom, and that there was no communion, even that of the Catholics, even that of the Jews, even that of the Swedenborgians, from which we need find ourselves excluded.

To have all the churches and all the religions was really to have none. When at twenty Henry wrote from New York to T. S. Perry, his Newport friend, that he had filled two Sundays with the sermon of a Presbyterian preacher and visits to a revival meeting and to "a congregation of the new dispensation," he was taking his father's account of their universal church membership literally. His taste in church services was to remain ecumenical.

Church-going for Henry, whether in London or while paying country visits in later life, was essentially a social phenomenon rather than a religious experience. If he can be said to have had a personal religion, it was a mysticism compounded of meditation and communion with spirits and forces vaguely discerned yet acutely felt, in a dim intuitional "beyond." By middle life he had a series of shrines—the shrines of art, tradition, morality, his own religion of beauty and the "religion of consciousness"—a worship almost pagan, were it not so highly sophisticated; he invoked the "powers and forces and divinities to whom I've ever been loyal," including the guiding spirit of his writing-table, whom he familiarly addressed as *mon bon*—the unseen but felt power within him that was his creative god. This, combined with the curious private prayers he wrote out in his notebooks—more invocation to the special Jamesian Muse than prayer—constituted the "religion" of the novelist.

The absence of formal religion in Henry's upbringing did stimulate a curiosity about religious experience; he wondered, for instance, at the absence of clergymen in the James household, although he found them present in most English novels read as a boy; but he did have the vision of his father and the revolt against Calvinism. During his boyhood he was exposed at the most to his father's talk of Swedenborg, his diatribes against organized religion and an occasional Sunday reading of the Scriptures. He was exposed much more to religious *feeling* than to religion itself. In later years James complained that Daudet in *L'Évangéliste* not only did not understand Protestantism, but lacked any "natural understanding of the religious passion." That "province of the human mind," James added, "cannot be *fait de chic*—experience, there, is the only explorer." Through his father he had had this experience. The "religious passion," while generally absent from his novels, was not absent from his life, where it was constantly being translated, in full measure, into his art.

"School" was present in Henry's life with much greater regularity than Church. First there were the "educative ladies"—the long line that included a Miss Sedgwick, a Mrs. Wright (Lavinia D.), a Russian lady with an accent whose name was forgotten, a Mlle. Delavigne, who taught French, and a Mrs. Vredenburg, who maintained a summer school at New Brighton on Staten Island. Then, when he was ten, he was sent to the Institution Vergnès in lower Broadway, " a sordidly *black* interior." M. Maurice Vergnès was an old and rather irritable individual, or seemed so to the young Henry, and the school swarmed with small homesick Cubans and Mexicans who were "not to be vulgarly whacked—in deference, presumably, to some latent relic or imputed survival of Castilian pride."

In due course the elder James, always experimenting, removed William and Henry to the greater establishment of Mr. Richard Puling Jenks at 689 Broadway, where they were pupils during 1853–54—that is, during Henry's eleventh year. Mr. Jenks was a rotund, bald man with a *barbiche,* who nursed his ferule and whacked occasionally, although Henry had no recollection of ever being the recipient of so much attention. Mr. Coe was the drawing-master, tall, white-haired and affecting a great cloak. What impressed little Henry was that so tall an individual produced such miniature drawings, "as if some mighty bird had laid diminutive eggs." The writing-master, Mr. Dolmidge, "a pure pen-holder of a man," taught the boys how to make complicated flourishes. The school itself was recalled by Henry as a couple of "middling rooms, front and back, our close packing, our large unaccommodating stove, our grey and gritty oilcloth, and again our importunate Broadway." The stove scorched without warming and Henry wondered how he could have been put into a school with such a "deficiency of landscape."

In the following year, Henry recalled, they were moved to the establishment of "Forest and Quackenboss" at 14th Street and Sixth Avenue. Henry studied with a Mr. Forest or Forrest, a massive individual in a black dress-coat and white neckcloth, and found him "the driest of all our founts of knowledge." William had Mr. Quackenboss and was "lost on upper floors, in higher classes, in real pursuits."

Henry James Senior's theory of education was comparatively simple. He feared pedantry and rigidity; he had a horror of dogma and of moral judgments. His solution was to throw his sons into many schools and to let them find their own feet. He reasoned that there was Divine Truth in the world and this the children were bound to discover under Divine Guidance. This "theory" produced in young Henry the feeling that he had been given no standard by which to judge the facts of the life he saw around him. He felt himself forced, he reasoned much later, to pay attention to everything, and by this process could seek to bring order, reason and common sense into the world's chaos. The senior Henry gave him, he felt, no sense of values save to realize the value of *all* life and *all* experience. The novelist reasoned that this free-and-easy mode of education—or absence thereof—was the best thing that could have happened to him: it made him "convert"—everything had to be translated into his own terms and rendered in the light of his own inner resources.

Reflecting in his old age on the years he spent in the New York classrooms, James was struck by his isolation. The little boy was as shy in class as at home. He neither attracted attention nor was molested by his thoroughly down-to-earth schoolfellows. He gives the impression that he was perturbed by this, yet at the same time aware of the ground upon which he stood as a little observer of the human scene. "I lived and wriggled, floundered and failed, lost the clue of everything but a general lucid consciousness (lucid, that is, for my tender years) which I clutched with a sense of its values." This lucid consciousness enabled him to remember the appearance and the dress of his teachers, the smell of the classrooms, the aspect of bustling Manhattan in which he moved. He had an eye for detail, for picture, for scene—and sensual awareness from the first. He "converted." The small boy's imagination could make

> all pastors and masters, and especially all fellow-occupants of benches and desks, all elbowing and kicking presences within touch or view, so many monsters and horrors, so many wonders and splendours and mysteries, but never, so far as I can recollect, realities of relation, dispensers either of knowledge or of fate, playmates, intimates, mere coevals and coequals.

Far from indulging in a flight from reality, he achieved something that did not exist for his fellow-pupils.

Henry's conclusion was that "no education avails for the intelligence that doesn't stir in it some subjective passion and that on the other hand almost anything that does so act is largely educative." There remains indeed the significant fact that not all little boys possess a subjective passion.

The Thames and the Seine

Henry James the elder had been settled only a few months in the house on 14th Street when he began to speak of taking his family abroad. This time, however, he did not move precipitately. The project was discussed for six years. As early as August 1849, when Henry was six, the father wrote to Emerson about his boys and their education. The family had grown, the 14th Street house required enlargement, a country place was needed for the hot summers. "These things look expensive and temporary to us, besides being an additional care," the father wrote,

> and so, looking upon our four stout boys, who have no play-room within doors, and import shocking bad manners from the street, with much pity, we gravely ponder whether it would not be better to go abroad for a few years with them, allowing them to absorb French and German and get a better sensuous education than they are likely to get here.

Years later, Henry Junior, quoting from the letter in his memoirs, amended the last words to read "get such a sensuous education as they can't get here." In this way he sought to create the impression that his father's decision to go abroad was not an arbitrary act but one of necessity.

In 1851, the debate was still going on in the elder Henry's mind. "We are still talking of Europe for the boys," he wrote to his London friend Dr.

Wilkinson. Finally the decision was taken, and on 27 June 1855 the elder Henry marched aboard the S. S. *Atlantic* with his wife and five offspring and a French maid, Annette Godefroi. The great adventure, the "re-exposure" to Europe, was begun. Henry Junior was then twelve.

The "nostalgic cup," he wrote years later, "had been applied to my lips even before I was conscious of it," when he was "hurried off to London and to Paris immediately after my birth." The cup was about to be offered to him again, this time not to an infant kicking his feet on someone's knee in the Place Vendôme, but to a keen-eyed little product of Manhattan, alert to the wonders of the world.

The family disembarked at Liverpool on 8 July 1855 and forty-eight hours later Henry was sitting beside a coachman on a vehicle piled high with luggage and packed with his brothers and sister, gaping at the spectacle of London. The remainder of the stay in the capital was a memory only of a curtained four-poster bed in the Euston Hotel. Henry suddenly developed chills and fever, and remained in bed "with the thick and heavy suggestions of the London room about me . . . and the far-off hum of a thousand possibilities."

A few days later the James boys were on a balcony of the Hôtel Westminster in the rue de la Paix, looking at the Paris of the Second Empire. It was at this moment that Jean Nadali took Henry and William to the Louvre for their memorable first visit. The family did not linger long in Paris. They took the railway to Lyon where, at the Hôtel de l'Univers, Henry spent more time in bed. There was no railway between Lyon and Geneva, and the father engaged two travelling-carriages to complete the journey. They set forth with young Henry stretched out like some young princeling on an improvised couch, formed by a plank across two seats, and with an elaborate retinue—a costumed postillion, the black-mustached Nadali and the fresh-colored, broad-faced Mlle. Godefroi.

The capital event of this journey, as the carriages mounted and mounted, was a halt at the doorway of an inn in the cool sunshine. Propped among his pillows, Henry munched cold chicken and surveyed the scene. The village street was unlike any that he had ever observed: it was hilly and opened on a fresh, a significant, in fact an epochal, revelation: a castle and a ruin.

The only "castle" Henry knew was an elaborate villa with towers at New Brighton; and he had never before encountered a ruin. Below the slope he spied a woman at work, attired in a black bodice, a white shirt, a red petticoat, a pair of sabots, the first peasant he had ever seen. Here was a "sublime synthesis" of Europe for the future novelist: a castle (with a tower), a ruin, a peasant woman in sabots engaged in field labor. Memories came to little Henry of books, of lonely readings in 14th Street; now imagined scenes focused into reality. "It made a bridge over to more things than I then knew."

High on the road into Switzerland that day Henry James glimpsed the romance and the ruin of Europe, the contradictions of past and present, the symbols human and material of the old feudal order. This was more education than he had ever received in Broadway or Washington Square.

In Geneva the James family established itself during August of 1855 in an old house, the Villa Campagne-Gerebsow, sublet by an invalid Russian lady who assigned five or six rooms to her guests and kept a wing for herself. The grounds led to the junction of the Arve and the Rhône. There was a view of Mont Blanc. All this for ten dollars a week, the elder James triumphantly announced in a letter to the New York *Tribune*.

Henry was still spending feverish days in bed. William, Wilky and Bob were placed at a Swiss boarding-school, the Pensionnat Roediger at Châtelaine, where Henry was scheduled to join them upon his recovery. The elder Henry extolled the school in a second letter to the *Tribune* for having a playground as big as Washington Square and providing the young with gymnastic facilities; in subsequent letters he stressed the fact that the students were given a large measure of freedom on Sundays. Henry Junior recalled the polyglot character of the school, where a babble of English, French, German and Russian was constant. But the stay in Switzerland, begun with such parental enthusiasm, was soon curtailed. In fact, by the time the father's enthusiastic letters were appearing in the *Tribune* he was writing his mother that Swiss schools were "over-rated." He and his wife had concluded that "home tuition" would be best for the children.

Early in October the elder Henry decided to spend the winter in London. This time without a courier, but with a new Swiss governess, they clambered aboard the big postal coach between Geneva and Lyon, "vast, yellow and rumbling." It was wholly filled by the Jameses. Two days later they were in Paris. Then, late one evening, tired and hungry, they were in London, at the Gloucester Hotel close to Berkeley Square, where they ate cold roast beef, bread and cheese and washed it down with ale, while an exuberant father extolled the English scene: "There's nothing like it after all." They moved into a small house at No. 3 Berkeley Square and then, before their first English Christmas, into a furnished house in St. John's Wood, No. 10 Marlborough Place, where they had Dr. Wilkinson and his family as neighbors. "You have a home-feeling in London," the elder Henry wrote to his mother.

On 14 November 1855, an advertisement appeared in *The Times* of London. "To teachers.—The advertiser wishes to engage a tutor, by the month, for three or four hours a day, who is competent to give his boys instruction in Latin, and the ordinary branches of an English education. None but well qualified persons need apply. Address H. J., 3, Berkeley-square, between 5 and 7 in the evening." The father selected, from an overflow of candidates, a fresh-complexioned, long-legged, clear-eyed Scot with a tendency to trip over his legs. Robert Thomson (James spelled it Thompson in his memoirs) engaged rooms in Titchfield Terrace to be near his charges, and from morning until noon he taught them—exactly what, Henry could not remember. He recalled only that Thomson gave him as a reward a copy of Lamb's *Tales from Shakespeare;* that he pitched ball with the boys in the large garden of their house; and took them on long rambles—the length of Baker Street, the Tower, St. Paul's, the Abbey, not to speak of Madame Tussaud's. Nor was their French neglected. Mlle. Amélie Cusin, one of "a longish procession of more or less similar domesticated presences," carefully officiated over the family's use of the Gallic tongue.

The James boys haunted the Pantheon in Oxford Street studying the vast canvases of Haydon; they visited Marlborough House and looked at the works of Maclise, Mulready, Landseer, David Wilkie; Henry "gazed and gazed again" at Charles Leslie's *Sancho Panza and the Duchess.* They went also to the Royal Academy and saw the fresh flowering of the Pre-Raphaelites—exemplified in Millais's *Vale of Rest,* his *Autumn Leaves* and his *Blind Girl.*

Playgoing in London was an elaborate ceremony, a ride through foggy tracts of the town from St. John's Wood to the West End. The "momentous" event of their stay was Kean's production of *Henry VIII.* For weeks afterwards the James children sought to reproduce in water-colors Queen Katharine's dream-vision of beckoning and consoling angels. "The spectacle had seemed to us prodigious—as it was doubtless at its time the last word of costly scenic science." At the Olympic, Henry saw Tom Taylor's *Still Waters Run Deep* with Alfred Wigan; Charles Mathews he saw in *The Critic.* He remembered the nights at the Olympic in Wych Street, approached through squalid slums, an "incredibly brutal and barbarous" avenue to the make-believe of the theater.

For Henry the London people themselves offered a wide field of observation. He remembered in particular one evening, a return from the Continent to London with his father, a long ride in a Victorian four-wheeler westward from the station at London Bridge. It was June: the evening light lingered softly; there were swarming crowds. Henry caught a glimpse from the cab window, as a framed picture, of a woman reeling backward from a blow to the face given her by a man. There were "embodied and exemplified 'horrors' " in the streets—to use the word "horrors" and leave it at that, was to suggest *all* the horrors a reader wanted to imagine.

From the London of the 1850s to the Second Empire was a small jump—yet it was a progress to another world. St. John's Wood was abandoned in the early summer of 1856 in favor of the French capital, where they lived first in a house rented from an American; Henry remembered glassy floors, a perilous staircase, redundant mirrors, clocks, ormolu vases, brocaded walls, sofas and chairs in red damask. The James boys in due course were entrusted to Monsieur Lerambert, who was apparently as good a teacher as Robert Thomson, although more aloof. Lerambert was spare and pale; he wore a tight black coat and spectacles and had written a volume of meditative verse which the great Sainte-Beuve had sympathetically noticed. The boys spent long sleepy mornings in a pavilion on the Champs-Élysées, rendering La Fontaine into an English that was admired and commended by their parents.

In the afternoons there was the wonderful Mlle. Augustine Danse, "her of the so flexible *taille* and the so salient smiling eyes," to take them for walks along the Champs-Élysées, and to vouchsafe them "all information for the free enjoyment . . . of her beautiful city." This "most brilliant and most genial of irregular characters" was abruptly dismissed, however; someone hinted she had been an "adventuress." That made adventuresses interesting for Henry. He relished Mlle. Danse's Paris, where the eye could take in the Tuileries and the grandeur of the Arch while cafés and houses with gardens and terraces were to be discovered along the Seine in a kind of "dusty ruralism" that merged with the Bois. Beyond the Arch was the beginning of suburb, and the two lodges of the *octroi* stood guard on either side, suggestive of revolutions and restorations. The young Empress, "more than young, attestedly and agreeably *new* and fair and shining," was constantly to be seen riding in state.

Paris of that era had a "homely grace," and the Jameses set up their fireside for another winter abroad. By September 1856 they had left the plush house for an apartment at No. 19 rue d'Angoulême-St. Honoré (now rue de la Boëtie), with many windows from which Henry could survey the full flow of life of his quartier: the inevitable boulangerie, the crémerie, the épicerie, the écaillère or oyster-lady, the blue-frocked workers and stout or spare cabmen, the marchand de bois with his neat faggots and logs stacked around him.

In Paris the staunch little playgoers were reduced to the level of circuses—the perpetual Cirques d'Été and d'Hiver and the Théâtre du Cirque. The plays in the French capital were, as Henry put it, "out of relation to our time of life . . . our cultivated innocence." There remained

with him, however, the memory of a walk with some girl cousins who
had more ready access to the French theater than he had and who related
how many times they had seen Madame Doche in *La Dame aux Camélias*
and what floods of tears she made them weep.

During the autumn of 1856 Henry and William began the long walks
through Paris that led them to the Luxembourg and the Louvre. In due
course Monsieur Lerambert was dropped by the father in favor of a
Fourierist school discovered in the rue Balzac, the Institution Fézandie.
M. Fézandie was bald, with a melancholy eye and a delicate beard. The
school was frankly experimental; it was part *pension,* part class-room.
Elders of both sexes and of many nations were taught French side by side
with the children. Dictation was read to the mixed class by M. Bonnefans,
who was contemptuous of Americans and ridiculed their pronunciation
of the all-important word *liberté.* Bonnefans was a candid, if whispering,
"subversive," opposed to the monarchy and full of dark hints about police
spies; he would recite with bravado from *Le Cid*

Nous nous levons alors!

and in the process would move from a crouch to a leap. It was from
instructors such as these, as well as from the constant reading of French
novels, that Henry gained his extraordinary fluency in the French language.

The family moved into still another apartment in the spring of 1857,
this time at No. 26 rue Montaigne—a large and costly establishment
which required many servants. Mary James estimated her annual household expenses here at $2,200. That summer they went to Boulogne-sur-
Mer, where they set up house at 20 rue Neuve Chaussée. The town of
Colonel Newcome had a large English colony. Henry assiduously explored the waterfront, with its fishermen and boatmen, tramped over the
cobbles, visited the Napoleonic monument. He seems to have been a
regular customer at the English lending library, kept by a Mr. Merridew,
who supplied him with Victorian three-deckers. "Henry is not so fond of
study, properly so-called, as of reading," his father wrote that autumn.
"He is a devourer of libraries." We have no record of Henry's readings,
but his constant allusions to novels and novelists, letter-writers and biographers in his early criticism could be made only by one saturated with
literature, and especially fiction, both in French and in English.

There came a day in Boulogne—it was in September of 1857—when
Henry remained in his bed through the afternoon with the sounds of the
port floating in through half-open windows. As the light waned he was
conscious of being increasingly unwell. He tumbled out of bed to summon help and then knew only the "strong sick whirl of everything." "My
Harry has been very ill with typhus fever," the elder James wrote to a

friend. "He was for several days delirious, and he is now extremely weak and low." It was "the gravest illness of my life," as the novelist later wrote; he was in bed the better part of two months.

By the end of October, when Henry was convalescent, the Jameses moved back to Paris. Now, for the first time, the children heard whispers of financial difficulties. The elder James had taken his family abroad during a period of booming American prosperity, the era of railroad expansion. During the summer of 1857 loans began to contract under the effects of an unfavorable trade balance, rail stocks began to fall, a great insurance and trust company went bankrupt and a characteristic American "crash" was under way.

Its effect on the senior Henry was marked. "We have been very nearly sent home by these dreadful commercial disasters on the other side," he wrote to a friend on 2 November 1857. In Paris they were paying 800 francs a month for their elaborate apartment in the rue Montaigne; they would retrace their steps to Boulogne, where they could find adequate quarters for as low as 200 francs a month. Instead of a retinue of servants and tutors they would do with one or two, and the children could attend the local schools. Later that winter, when they were installed again in Boulogne, at No. 29 Grand-Rue, in smaller and less elegant quarters than those of the preceding summer, the elder Henry wrote to the same correspondent, "We *have* lost some of our income by the crash at home . . . I don't know where another year may find us."

For a while, still convalescent from his typhus, Henry was assigned a tutor at home, a Monsieur Ansiot, whom he described later as "a form of bland porpoise, violently blowing in an age not his own." For all his dreariness, M. Ansiot left something with his young pupil, a "working" sense of *le vieux temps,* a glimpse of a past world. Later, at the Collège Impérial, Henry found himself no longer a young aristocrat, privately tutored, but a member of a class made up of the sons of shopkeepers, artisans and fishermen. He remembered in particular the son of the local pastry-cook, a youth with a pug-nose named Coquelin, whom he would later admire on the stage of the Théâtre Français—the inimitable creator of Cyrano de Bergerac.

A winter at Boulogne sufficed for the parents. And the elder Henry was again fretting about his children's education, his chronic excuse for displacement. "I have no doubt from all I can gather," he wrote to his mother, "that our own schools are . . . much superior to the European schools." After that it was inevitable that the Jameses would turn westward again. Early in the summer of 1858—the depression in America was running its short-lived course—the family set sail, their destination, for the first time, New England.

Newport Idyll

They went to live in Newport, Rhode Island, then a quiet seaside perch to which the elder Henry James was drawn by the presence of his old friends Edmund and Mary Tweedy, foster-parents of his nieces, the Temple girls. "We are settled very comfortably at Newport for the present," the father wrote that summer. "Mary is very well," he went on, and the boys were

> as good as good can be, . . . and utterly abandoned to the enjoyment of their recovered liberty, boating and fishing and riding to their hearts' content. They have not fairly recommenced their studies.

After their sojourn by the Thames and the Seine, after the galleries, palaces, schools, *pensions* and theaters of the Old World, their return to America—or to the rim of America—was for the James boys a return to happy native conditions, the rediscovery of certain cousins now grown up like themselves, and the making of new and important friendships. Henry felt in later years that Newport was "the one right residence in all our great country." The old town with its crooked streets and small buildings, its wharves, its historic cemeteries, its associations with Bishop Berkeley, seemed to be a bit of Europe or a European outpost on the soil of America.

Newport was more: it was a corner of the eighteenth century that had lingered into the nineteenth. It possessed in the 1850s a "quaint shabbiness." It had a landscape and a seascape; it had, indeed, some of the characteristics of the European watering-places, and for the little James pilgrims, freshly returned from far-away lands, it served as an ideal stepping-stone to reconciliation with their homeland. The town had an active social life; there was a colony of artists and a vast summer population: old-fashioned streets echoed to the footfalls of attractively dressed young men and women. There was, above all, a constant vision of land and sea, more sea than land, with walks to be taken along moss-clad rocks and over sand-choked grass and the ocean a constant companion. In his late book *The American Scene* there is almost a rhapsodic note as James comes to Newport after a fifty-year interval and remembers "far-away little lonely, sandy coves, rock-set, lily-sheeted ponds, almost hidden, and shallow Arcadian summer-haunted valleys with the sea just over some stony shoulder: a whole world that called out to the long afternoons of youth." The afternoons were long indeed.

For Henry James the place was to have always a "shy sweetness," and one suspects that the words betrayed his own state of feeling. His roots, pulled up when they were tender, from the banks of the Hudson, here found new and fresh American earth. In Europe, during these years of his emergence into young manhood, he had been able to make only casual friends; how could he do more in the capricious moves from place to place and school to school? The James boys had been "all along perfectly starved on their social side." Newport filled a serious gap in Henry's life; for museums and galleries, books and theaters and lonely European promenades he could substitute at last important human ties.

Two friendships formed by Henry James at Newport embraced letters and art and exerted a deep and enduring influence. Thomas Sergeant Perry was perhaps the first and closest friend; two years younger than Henry, and also a second son, he lived even more than the future novelist in a world of books. John La Farge, the painter, was seven years older. He proved to be an extraordinary mentor, sensitive and devoted, especially during the later phase of Henry's Newport residence. Both Perry and La Farge nourished Henry's mind and spirit at a crucial time.

Perry's father was a son of Commodore Oliver Hazard Perry, and a nephew of Commodore Matthew Calbraith Perry, who opened Japan to the west. Young Perry was precocious and passive, with a tendency to substitute books for action; James described him as a great lumberjack of the library, felling volumes and sets of volumes as if they were trees in a forest. The Redwood Library (whose name may have suggested the lumber-image) was the pride of Newport, with its fifty-foot-long reading-room, and more than 100 paintings on its walls. It was not the Galerie d'Apollon, but it was a haven for the literary Henry.

"Sargy" Perry met the James boys in June or July of 1858, shortly after they had settled in Newport. His diary discloses how often he and Henry were together, in and out of school. The latest educational institution to which Henry was committed was the Berkeley Institute, headed by the Rev. William C. Leverett, curate of Newport's Trinity Church, who was addicted as much to delivering orations as to coming to grips with the concrete. "H.J. in his books speaks without enthusiasm of his school studies," Perry recalled, "but he and I read together at Mr. Leverett's school a fair amount of Latin literature. Like Shakespeare he had less Greek."

John La Farge was of French descent, a Catholic of ample means and wide horizons. His father, like Henry's grandfather, had amassed a Hudson Valley fortune in real estate, and he had been brought up in the same compact old New York as the future novelist. Like Henry he had lived in Paris but with the difference that in the capital he had glimpsed the literary élite, and could speak of Sainte-Beuve, Baudelaire, Flaubert and the Goncourts with a certain familiarity. La Farge shared with Henry the latest copies of the *Revue des Deux Mondes* as they arrived in their salmon-colored wrappers. He took Henry on long rambles across the rocks. And he filled the afternoons with a full measure of talk, and more than this, ideas.

Perry too remembered their walks. Near Lily Pond they talked one day of Fourier. Another time they were full of their reading of Ruskin; Henry devoted himself to the "conscientious copying of a leaf and very faithfully drew a little rock that jutted above the surface of Lily Pond ... We read the English magazines and reviews and the *Revue des Deux Mondes* with rapture."

The first part of the Newport idyll lasted from early 1858 until the autumn of the following year. By September 1859 Henry James Senior was writing:

> I have grown so discouraged about the education of my children here, and dread so those inevitable habits of extravagance and insubordination which appear to be characteristic of American youth, that I have come to the conclusion to retrace my steps to Europe, and keep them there a few years longer.

Abroad the children went again with their undaunted parents. To the novelist, in his old age, these restless crossings of the Atlantic seemed to testify eloquently to a lack of purpose in his father. It was artistically more satisfying, in writing his reminiscences, to keep the family in Europe for a full five years and then return them, once and for all, to America. In 1913 he explained his reasoning to his nephew Henry, who noted:

> Uncle H. evidently has a very lively consciousness of his father's vacillations and impulses—as if the possibility of going home or going to Europe, going from one place to another, were always in the air and often realized to the disturbance of his, Uncle H.'s, equanimity.

To T. S. Perry the novelist confessed that he suppressed the 1859 journey to Europe in *Notes of a Son and Brother* to avoid giving the impression that his father was "*too* irresponsible and too *saccadé* in his generous absence of plan and continuity."

On 8 October 1859 the Jameses were in New York, and Henry was writing to Sargy: "You see by the date that this is our hour for sailing ... I can scarcely sit still to write this and feel myself thinking much more of what I leave behind than what I expect to find ... Goodbye to you and every body and every thing! Yours very truly H. James Jr."

The Rhône and the Rhine

Once again the Jameses turned their faces eastward. The steamship *Vanderbilt* made the crossing in eleven days of unrelieved bad weather. They landed at Le Havre and spent two days in Paris revisiting familiar places. Five days after landing they were in Geneva.

The James family had gone abroad in 1855 "with an eye to the then supposedly supreme benefits of Swiss schooling," and had ended up by the Thames and the Seine. Now, four years later, they retraced their steps to the city of Calvin and of Rousseau. Henry and Mary James took rooms in the Hôtel de l'Écu at the edge of the rushing Rhône. The two younger sons were placed in the Pensionnat Maquelin just outside Geneva, William enrolled at the Academy, which later became the University of Geneva, and Henry was dispatched to the Institution Rochette—a preparatory school for engineers and architects.

The Institution Rochette was selected, and apparently with Henry's concurrence, because it was the best school in Geneva other than the Academy and the Gymnasium, neither of which he was qualified to enter. There is no evidence that the parents intended to make either an architect or an engineer of their second son. As Henry puzzled it out towards the end of his life, they had "simply said to themselves that I read too many novels, or at least read them too attentively—*that* was the vice." Moreover, they had "got me in a manner to agree with them." At the Rochette school he found himself among students whose goals were far removed from literature; he was called upon to study mathematics, and his brave attempt to make some sort of showing was "mere darkness, waste and anguish." He considered himself inferior to others in not being able to attack geometry and algebra. He was determined to overcome the inferiority. It was a hopeless battle. Henry withdrew or was withdrawn "not even as a conspicuous" but "only as an obscure, a deeply-hushed failure."

In his letters to Perry, Henry kept up a bold front, assuring him repeatedly he was getting on "very well." But by Easter he had dropped all subjects at the Institution Rochette except German, French and Latin, and had arranged to sit in at a number of courses at the Academy instead. His bitter-sweet year in Geneva ended with his thus achieving a certain level of equality with his elder brother.

Geneva itself, as he described it later, was "a strongly-featured little city, which, if you do not enjoy, you may at least grudgingly respect." It had no galleries, museums or interesting churches, but it did possess a natural beauty; there were "liquid sapphire and emerald" in the surface of Lake Leman, and the "divinely cool-hued gush of the Rhône beneath the two elder bridges." The town itself presented a sordid aspect that nevertheless fascinated Henry when he first explored and described it to Perry with uncommon skill and concreteness: "Such dingy old streets and courts and alleys, black with age some of them are, steep and dirty, such quaint old houses, high and sombre."

From his letters to Perry we can reconstruct his day-to-day existence that winter. Henry rose at six-thirty in the dark; he breakfasted alone in the Hôtel de l'Écu. By eight, in the dawning light, he has reached the school. Four hours later he walks back for lunch. He is at his school bench again an hour later. At five he returns to the hotel. He dines; he studies till bedtime. And so it goes, from Monday to Saturday, with a half-day off on Thursday. During the Thursday afternoon he reads, he idles, he looks out of the hotel window, he explores the shops, he walks around the edge of the lake. He is very much alone. His brothers are scattered. He doesn't make friends with his schoolmates; he, an English youth and a young Russian are the sole foreigners. He talks to his fellow-foreigners.

Towards the end of the winter there seems to be a little more social life. "I go twice a week to a dancing school," he tells Perry,

> and seldom have I seen a more hideous collection of females than I do on these occasions. They all sit on benches ranged along one side of the room and the cavaliers stand up against the wall on the opposite side— for a fellow to sit down on one of their benches would be a most heinous crime. . . . I learned to dance because at the parties here that is the sole amusement,

and the young American with the ever-hearty appetite adds characteristically, "they do not even have supper but hand round little glasses of syrop and 'helpings' of ice-cream about twice as large as a peach pit!"

He is now liberated from his rigorous educational schedule; he has time for newspapers and magazines. The new *Cornhill Magazine,* edited by Thackeray, has arrived and he reads it avidly. He is studying French literature and Natural Philosophy at the Academy. He listens to H.-F. Amiel, vaguely aware of him as a "mild grave oracle." With a bow to science he studies anatomy. "I went the other day in company with half a dozen other students to see a dissection at the Hospital," he tells Perry. "The smell was pretty bad, but I am glad to say that I was not in any way affected by the thing." William is invited to join a Swiss student organization for "brotherhood and beer." He takes his younger brother with him to a village near Lausanne, where they drink, smoke German pipes and sing. The students swear allegiance with a great "swilling down of beer, of grasping of hands, of clashing of rapiers, and of glorious deep-mouthed German singing."

Despite the ups and downs of this winter, Henry has been quietly scribbling. Wilky, writing to Perry, reports seeing "some poetical looking manuscripts lying on the table, and himself looking in a most authorlike way." William had been reading aloud satiric odes to his sister Alice and other members of the family, and Wilky observes, "The only difference there is between Willy and Harry's labours is that the former always shows his productions while the modest little Henry wouldn't let a soul or even a spirit see his." Perry questioned Henry about his literary efforts and was told: "A fearful vengeance awaits Wilky's foolhardy imprudence in disclosing, as he did, my secret employment." But the young writer does not deny it. Perry having asked him what "style of work" he is cultivating, he volunteers readily, "I may reply that to no style am I a stranger, there is none which has not been adorned by the magic of my touch." And he begins his next letter with an extravagant imitation of the Eastern romances he has been reading. "The morning broke! High in the vast unclouded vault of Heving rode the Awb of Day, chasing before it the fleeting clouds that enshroud the slumber of men." And so on. Of his studies that spring Henry remembered that he read Livy and Virgil, Schiller and Lessing, and that he was "almost happy" with M. Toeppfer, with whom he read Racine and who described for him Rachel's playing of *Phèdre,* her entrance "borne down in her languorous passion by the weight of her royal robes—*Que ces vains ornemens, que ces voiles me pèsent!*"

The Swiss spring was at hand and Henry practiced swimming in the deep blue lake-water and enjoyed the Alpine views; he wandered along the verdant hedges, stopped to peer at the iron gateways up long avenues of trees leading to châteaux. Family plans called for a summer at Bonn and a stay at Frankfort. Before going to Bonn, William and Henry went on a week's walking-tour through the mountains. They crossed the Mer de Glâce, went to the Canton du Valais by way of the Tête-Noir, and from Martigny, with the aid of a guide and a mule, they climbed the St. Bernard. At the celebrated Hospice they are received by one of the Fathers, given warm slippers, hot broth and mutton, and sleep on mattresses "apparently stuffed with damp sand." Henry visits the morgue where the bodies of those found in the mountains are placed. "As they cannot be buried they are stood around the walls in their shrouds and a grim and ghastly sight it is. They fall into all sorts of hideous positions, with such fiendish grins on their faces! faugh!"

On the following day they go to Loèche-les-Bains and walk over naked and rugged terrain down narrow steep zigzags, ending their trip at Interlaken. There they meet, as scheduled, other members of the family, and travel on with them to Frankfort, sampling the hot springs and witnessing the gambling at Wiesbaden.

At Bonn, in July 1860, Henry and Wilky were installed in the *pension* of a Dr. Humpert, Latin and Greek professor, situated at No. 190 Bonngasse, near the birthplace of Beethoven. William was housed with a Herr Stromberg. It was the elder James's wish that his sons should acquire a working knowledge of German during the coming weeks. He and his wife took rooms for themselves and Alice in a large mansion looking across the river at the Seven Mountains.

Henry found himself in characteristic Germanic surroundings. The Herr Doktor's family was composed of his wife, her sister, and his son Theodore. There were also five young German boarders aged six to fourteen. The sister, Fräulein Stamm, reminded Henry of Hepzibah Pynchon in *The House of the Seven Gables,* always wiping hock-glasses and holding them up to the light and bearing long-necked bottles and platters of food through the "greasy rooms" of the house. Fräulein Stamm wanted to know whether there was a king in America; her knowledge of his homeland was based, Henry discovered, on a reading of expurgated adaptations of Fenimore Cooper. Life, he found, was a round of German "conversation" centering on the stereotyped amenities *Haben Sie gut geschlafen?* and *Wie geht's?* Henry made excursions, to nearby Godesberg and to the Drachenfels across the Rhine; there were picnics and walks on the Venusberg in the early morning, and the pursuit in German orchards of pears, cherries and plums. He didn't learn much German, devoting most of the summer to a laborious translation of *Maria Stuart,* after being taken by his father one night in Bonn to see Adelaide Ristori in the play ("the vulture counterfeiting Jenny Wren" was the elder's verdict).

They had been at Bonn only a few days when the elder Henry James took an important decision, which his second son promptly and exuberantly communicated to Perry. "I think I must fire off my biggest gun first. One-two-three! Bung-gerdee bang bang ... !!! What a noise! Our passages are taken in the *Adriatic,* for the 11th of September!!!!!!! We are going immediately to Newport, which is the place in America we all most care to live in." William James, after much inner debate, had confided to his father that he didn't want to be a scientist, as his parent had hoped. He felt his vocation to be that of a painter and he wanted to study with William Morris Hunt, who had a studio in Newport. The elder Henry re-expressed his misgivings about artists and writers. William argued with him: "I am sure that far from feeling myself degraded by my intercourse with art, I continually receive from it spiritual impressions the intensest and purest I know." That summer at Bonn William was striking a blow not only for himself; he was, in effect, leading a family revolt against further wanderings and an education that reflected too much parental indecision.

The father wrote to a friend on 18 July 1860, the same day that Henry wrote to Perry.

> The welfare of the other youngsters will, however, be as much con-
> sulted by this manoeuvre, I am persuaded, as Willy's. They are none of
> them cut out for intellectual labours, and they are getting to an age,
> Harry and Wilky especially, where the heart craves a little wider expan-
> sion than is furnished it by the domestic affections. They want friends
> among their own sex, and sweethearts in the other; and my hope for their
> own salvation, temporal and spiritual, is that they may "go it strong" in
> both lines when they get home.

We smile as we read that "none" of the boys was cut out for intellectual labors; but the elder Henry was right in perceiving—at long last—that his children were starved for the companionship of their American peers.

The decision taken, the father promptly left Bonn ("where he can neither understand nor make himself understood," William wrote to Perry), and was joined in Paris by his wife and Alice, Robertson and Aunt Kate. They installed themselves in the Hôtel des Trois Empereurs to await the September sailing, while the other three sons completed their period of study at Bonn. If the senior Henry deplored Henry's addiction to novels, he nevertheless sent him copies of *Once a Week,* which had begun to appear a few months earlier. William, reporting on life in Bonn, described Henry as working "pretty stoutly" and resisting all week the temptation to read the periodical. In another letter the eldest son announces, "We are going to put Harry through a slashing big walk daily." In August Henry himself wrote to his mother in a vein of filial amiability, describing the epistolary activities of his brothers, who "are so free in their communications that I begin to suspect they simply despatch you blank sheets of paper, for what they can find to say about Bonn to fill so many pages is to me inconceivable."

Punctually on 1 September the three boys made the twelve-hour train journey from Cologne to Paris in a first-class carriage. They shared it with a French lady's maid, valet and coachman, "who chattered by the hour for our wonderstruck ears." They gave Henry a glimpse in their talk on the one hand of "servile impudence" and on the other of the life of the French upper classes. During the day Madame la Marquise

> came on occasion and looked in on us and smiled, and even pouted,
> through her elegant patience; so that she at least, I recollect, caused to
> swim before me somehow such a view of happy privilege at the highest
> pitch as made me sigh the more sharply, even if the less professedly, for
> our turning our backs on the complex order, the European, fresh to me

still, in which contrasts flared and flourished and through which discrimination could unexhaustedly riot.

The Jameses sailed on the *Adriatic* on the 11th, were in New York on the 23rd and a few days later Henry was pacing the sands of Newport with Sargy Perry. The "nostalgic cup" had been filled to the brim. His European adventure of childhood and young adulthood was at an end.

Palette and Pen

For their second and longest phase in Newport, the elder Henry James settled his family in a rented house at No. 13 Kay Street, near the Edmund Tweedys. They lived here until the spring of 1862, and then in a large stone house at the corner of Spring Street and Lee Avenue. The youthful diary of Thomas Sergeant Perry gives glimpses of their activities. 2 January 1861: "Went with Harry James to the 40 Steps . . . Went after dinner with Jno [La Farge] and Willie J. to the Point." 3 January: "Down town then with Harry J. Met Willie and with him to Belmont's." 4 January: "In the morning down street with W.J. . . . dined at the Jameses." Saturday 5 January: "Down street again with H.J." And so the life went, a constant series of excursions "down street" and to the scenic points in Newport. On Sunday 6 January: "H.J. came to church with me in the morning," and then Perry boxes with Willie till 1 P.M. On Monday he and Henry go to the Redwood Library. On 13 January a significant entry: "To the Jameses. Introduced to and to walk with their cousins, the Miss Temples." Mary and Edmund Tweedy, having lost their three children, had taken into their home the four orphaned Temple girls, children of Catherine Margaret James, the elder Henry's favorite sister, and Colonel Robert Emmet Temple. Mrs. Tweedy, always referred to by Henry as "Aunt Mary," was a daughter of Colonel Temple by a first marriage.

William lost no time in starting to paint, and Henry "under the irresistible contagion" followed him to the studio of the American master William Morris Hunt. Apparently for the moment there was no thought of further schooling. Hunt had been a pupil of Couture; he had studied later with Millet in Barbizon. In Newport he was the artist to his fingertips, the flowing beard, the velvet jacket, the scarlet sash. At his studio on Church Street, filled with plaster casts and canvases, William, not yet twenty, worked upstairs with twenty-five-year-old John La Farge and Theodora Sedgwick, youngest sister of Mrs. Charles Eliot Norton. Henry remembered sitting alone in one of the grey cold lower rooms, trying to draw by himself, and day-dreaming that his copy of a plaster cast of the uplifted face of Michelangelo's *Captive,* seen in the Louvre, might attract the attention of the master. He felt that he was entering the temple of art "by the back door" but remained on the threshold.

One day he crossed the threshold. Wandering upstairs, he discovered his handsome young cousin, Gus Barker, standing on a pedestal, "divested of every garment." It was Henry James's first "glimpse of 'life' on a pedestal and in a pose." The spectacle settled matters for him then and there. The students were working in pencil and charcoal. Henry watched closely. His brother's ease in reproducing the figure astonished him. There was no point, he decided, in seeking to emulate such skill. Henry James pocketed his drawing-pencil and picked up his pen.

It is difficult to say whether James's decision to return to his own pasture was as deliberate and as vivid as he makes it out to be in his memoirs. What we know is that he found someone who took him seriously as a writer. John La Farge was not only willing to talk to him about books and about writing; he listened; he bestowed, in effect, paternal sympathy, for he was older and knew the world.

The painter was an attractive figure, riding on a chestnut mare across shining Newport sands, emerging in cool white from top to toe, or wearing his artist's velvet jacket. Henry posed for him willingly. The portrait he did at this time sets the young Henry in sharp profile against an opaline background, in dark attire, austere, almost priestly. The colors recall a stained-glass window—indeed, La Farge became a master of this medium. He was to invent opaline glass; he developed a deep interest in architecture and in aesthetics; his interest in stained glass and cathedrals set his friend Henry Adams upon the exploration of Mont St. Michel and Chartres.

For Henry James La Farge opened "more windows than he closed." He let Henry daub, but encouraged him and even pushed him to write. He gave Henry the sense of a young man who feels secure, "a settled sovereign self." And as Henry talked with him, he felt surer of himself. Above all, the painter introduced Henry to the world of Balzac, and Henry read him with such attention that years later, on reopening *Eugénie Grandet,* "breathlessly seized and earnestly absorbed" under La Farge's instruction, he was "to see my initiator's youthful face . . . look out at me between the lines as through blurred prison bars."

La Farge also introduced Henry to the short stories of Prosper Mérimée; the future novelist found himself "fluttering deliciously—quite as if with a sacred terror—at the touch of 'La Vénus d'Ille.'" He remembered that La Farge prodded him into translating Mérimée's tale of the ghostly Venus. He sent it to a New York periodical, "which was to do me the honour neither of acknowledging nor printing." La Farge was the first to spur Henry to a constructive writing effort and to insist that once his manuscript was completed, he do something with it. Perry testified that Henry went on to translate Alfred de Musset's *Lorenzaccio* and introduced into it scenes of his own. It was obvious that the youth needed no urging; what he did need was appreciation.

Henry James was in America in 1910 when John La Farge died at seventy-five; and he was in Boston when a large commemorative exhibition of La Farge's work was held. The novelist, then sixty-seven, looked upon landscapes that suddenly "laid bare the very footsteps of time." As he stood there his mind wandered back to one incident which he recounted in his *Notes* with such evident pleasure that it reveals, more than anything else, the depth of the Newport—and the La Farge—attachment.

La Farge had "proposed to me that we should drive out to the Glen, some six miles off, to breakfast, and should afterwards paint—we paint! —in the bosky open air." After partaking of coffee and griddle-cakes that were "not as other earthly refreshment" at the neat hostel in the "umbrageous valley," La Farge arranged his easel and canvas, palette and stool, while Henry "at a respectful distance" arranged his. He wondered, in recalling the incident, why it had been remembered and why it had "really mattered." It did indeed matter, he told himself, because there was "in the vagueness of rustling murmuring green and plashing water and woodland voices and images" the hovering possibility that "one's small daub might incur appreciation by the eye of friendship." "This indeed was the true source of the spell, that it was in the eye of friendship, friendship full of character and colour, and full of amusement of its own, that I lived on any such occasion."

James's debt to La Farge must not be measured in terms of "influence." He lived in the "eye of friendship"—and it was a painter's eye. La Farge had appeared in his life at a significant moment. The "sovereign" self, the breakfasts near the Glen, the walks with La Farge and Perry, and other memories were to remain and merge with Balzac and Mérimée and Musset, to form what Henry James meant when he spoke of the "time of settled possession" and the "pure Newport time." These were the richest hours of his young manhood, on the eve of national disaster.

An Obscure Hurt

The Southern guns opened up on Fort Sumter on 12 April 1861, and on 15 April—Henry James's eighteenth birthday—Lincoln issued his first call for volunteers. Presently T. S. Perry was noting in his Newport diary: "April 27: We made bandages all evening." "April 28: After breakfast we all rolled bullets."

Bandages and bullets! Abruptly the evidence of struggle confronted the young Henry James and his generation as the four epic years began. The paradise of paternal optimism and cheerfulness in which the Jameses had been reared, the free ranging through countries, schools, books, galleries, was now at an end. On the brink of manhood Henry and his brothers found themselves at the edge of the abyss, almost within earshot of the guns and in conflict whether they should go out and face them. Yet with the abrupt dawn of insecurity and grief, there was also the drama of war. The James boys run to the Armory to see the militia off. They are at the wharf to see the troops go by. And they see the ships returning, filled with the wounded.

After Fort Sumter came the moment when the North and South took a deep breath; then followed the Northern march on Richmond and in July the first battle of Bull Run. By then the North knew that the struggle would be difficult and perhaps long. The youths in Newport took their usual walks that summer; they watched the soldiers; they read the newspapers. In mid-July Henry and Sargy Perry went on a walking-tour in New Hampshire, climbing Mount Lafayette and Mount Washington and returning a week later to Newport, tired, cheerful, penniless. Perry noted: "At and with Harry James to the Lily Pond. Lay on the grass and talked." The idyllic life could, for the moment, still go on. One afternoon the two young men went "to a vast gathering of invalid and convalescent troops, under canvas and in roughly improvised shanties" on the Rhode Island shore, at Portsmouth Grove. There Henry talked with the men, strolled with them, sat by the improvised couches "of their languid rest." He drew from "each his troubled tale," and emptied his pockets for them of whatever cash he had. In his memories he identified the image of himself on this occasion with Walt Whitman, "even if I hadn't come armed like him with oranges and peppermints."

In September William entered the Lawrence Scientific School at Harvard, abandoning his study of art almost as abruptly as he had begun it a year earlier. Wilky and Robertson, then sixteen and fifteen, had been put to school at Concord the previous autumn. Henry was left alone at Newport with his parents, his sister and Aunt Kate. He proposed to his father at this time that he also should go to Harvard. The senior James brushed the suggestion aside, saying it was "wholly unpracticable," and Henry stayed on, marking time while around him young men were springing to the colors. Temperamentally unsuited for soldiering, unable to endure violence, he had long ago substituted close observation of life for active participation. Now he faced the social pressure (for there was no draft) to take the field in direct assault upon brother Americans. The senior Henry was not particularly helpful. While public sentiment pulled in one direction he pulled in the other, telling a correspondent very early in the struggle, "I have had a firm grasp upon the coat tails of my Willy and Harry, who both vituperate me beyond measure because I won't let them go." The elder Henry's letters suggest that both Henry and William, at various times, entertained plans to participate in the nation's struggle. Compulsory service was not instituted by the Lincoln administration until March 1863; and even then a young man had the option of finding a substitute or simply paying $300, which would exempt him from service.

Long before this, however, apparently in the spring of 1861, Henry James had suffered, as he tells us in *Notes of a Son and Brother,* a "horrid even if an obscure hurt" whose effects "were to draw themselves out incalculably and intolerably." The hurt occurred during "twenty odious minutes" and became part of the "huge comprehensive ache" of the country at war, so that

> there were hours at which one could scarce have told whether it came most from one's own poor organism, still so young and so meant for better things, but which had suffered particular wrong, or from the enclosing social body.

With this prelude he tells how during a Newport fire, "jammed into the acute angle between two high fences," in an awkward position, he and others managed to make "a rusty, a quasi-extemporized old engine" work sufficiently well to help put out what James characterized as a "shabby conflagration." He does not describe the injury he then received, but says that he tried to "strike a bargain" with his ailing condition, and spent much time in bed or on a couch on the theory that rest would help. Also he did not mention it to his family. Since, however, it did not mend, he finally confided his trouble to his father and received prompt and sympathetic attention. Early "that summer," he goes on to say, he accompanied his father to Boston "for consultation of a great surgeon, the head of his profession there." The eminent surgeon treated Henry to a "comparative pooh-pooh." And Henry felt, ruefully, that he had to reckon on the one hand with his pain and on the other "with the strange fact of there being nothing to speak of the matter with me." He accordingly resolved to act as if there wasn't—though he continued to suffer for many months. He decided once again that he would propose to go to Harvard. This time his father agreed.

This is all Henry tells us of the "obscure hurt." The time sequence as he gives it is confused. If the accident occurred as he says at the "same dark hour" as the outbreak of the Civil War—that is, in the "soft spring of '61" —then the visit to the doctor "that summer" must have taken place in 1861. But "that summer" becomes, at the end of the account, the summer of 1862. The other details are meager; and they bristle with ambiguities. The hurt is "horrid" but it is also "obscure." It is a "catastrophe" but it is in the very same phrase only a "difficulty." It is a passage of history "most entirely personal," yet apparently not too personal to be broadcast to the world in his memoirs. It is "extraordinarily intimate" and at the same time "awkwardly irrelevant." James gives no hint of the kind of hurt he suffered, although at various times during his life he complained of an early back injury, which he usually dated as of 1862. In some way he seems to have felt that by vagueness and circumlocution he might becloud the whole question of his non-participation in the Civil War. But his elaborate euphemisms had an effect not unlike that of the unspecified "horrors" of "The Turn of the Screw." His readers were ready to imagine the worst. Critics in the 1920s tended to see a relationship between the accident and his celibacy, his apparent avoidance of involvements with women and the absence of overt sexuality in his work. As a consequence there emerged a "theory" that the novelist suffered a hurt during those "twenty odious minutes" which amounted to castration.

The most logical explanation of James's blurring of the date of the hurt is that it served to minimize his failure during the first six months of the war to volunteer with the other young men. Had the injury occurred in April or May of 1861, it is doubtful whether he would have climbed mountains in New Hampshire with T. S. Perry during July.

Fortunately Perry provides a specific date for the incident, writing in a letter of 1914 that "the fire at West Stables was in the night of Oct. 28, '61," a full six months after Fort Sumter.

The contemporary records of the fire are detailed. A high wind blew through Newport on the night of 28 October, and some time between 10:30 and 11:00 a blaze was discovered in the large stable of Charles B. Tennant at the corner of Beach and State Streets. In a few minutes the entire stable was in flames; amid the screaming of horses, an alerted town rushed to give aid and to see the spectacle. The wind carried the fire to an adjoining stable, and the flames threatened a newly-built residence. By the time the fire-fighters had brought Engine No. 5 down to the Tennant stable there was little hope of saving it. Four horses perished and a number of vehicles were destroyed, as well as substantial quantities of hay and grain.

The No. 5 engine had stopped en route at the Redwood Reservoir only to discover that the hose was not long enough to reach the scene of the fire. The engine accordingly was brought farther down and two wells in the neighborhood were pumped dry in rapid succession. In the meantime the fire had begun to spread in the second stable; horses and carriages were removed to safety, while a stream from other cisterns was directed on the house, which also caught fire. A small carpenter's shop was gutted and the fire-fighters tore down another dwelling, directly in the path of the flames. It was 1 A.M. before the fire was put out and the firemen ordered home. The loss from the "shabby conflagration" was estimated by the press at $7,000. There were no reports of any persons suffering injuries.

Three days after the fire, on 31 October 1861, Perry's diary testifies to the fact that Henry was well enough to travel. "Thursday, Oct. 31 [1861] At recitation in morning. Harry has gone to Boston." A letter from William to the family after Henry returned to Newport speaks of the "radiance of H's visit" to him on this occasion. Henry remained for a long weekend. On 5 November Perry's diary says: "At school. Harry's before 12," and on the next day Henry walked with his friend to Easton's Point.

James's date of the summer of 1862 for the visit to the eminent surgeon seems accurate. However limited medical knowledge may have been in that era, it is quite clear that there would have been no "pooh-pooh" had the surgeon discovered a groin injury or a hernia. The "obscure hurt" was obscure indeed.

Some years after the Newport fire, when he was twenty-five, Henry James published in the *Atlantic Monthly* a short story entitled "A Most Extraordinary Case," about a Civil War veteran who survives the conflict without physical injury but is stricken by illness at the end. The nature of the disorder is not disclosed; the attending physician tells him, "You

have opposed no resistance; you haven't cared to get well." An affectionate aunt takes Mason, the veteran, into her home to care for him. Staying
with her is a beautiful niece, with whom Mason falls in love; he gives her
no intimation of his feelings. When he discovers that the niece has been
wooed successfully by his own doctor he has a relapse. "It's the most
extraordinary case I ever heard of," says the doctor as his patient dies.
"The man was steadily getting well."

The extraordinary case was as mystifying to the doctor as the obscure hurt was to Henry James. He was clearly unaware of the subjective
elements which conditioned and at the same time obscured his hurt, as
when he asserts that "what was interesting from the first was my not
doubting in the least its [the obscure hurt's] duration." This was a pre-
judgment which the doctor in Boston did not in any way endorse.

Fire had a particular meaning in the life of the James family. A fire
in a stable had an even more special meaning. The senior Henry's cork
leg had been the symbol through all Henry Junior's life of what could
happen to someone who becomes involved in putting out a stable fire. It
was an enduring injury. We can therefore speculate that from the moment Henry hurt himself in circumstances analogous to those of his
father, he felt his hurt too would have a long duration.

That there was an unconscious identification with the father at the
moment of the accident is borne out by the account set down in old age.
Describing his hurt—at one point he speaks of it as a "lameness"—as
keeping "unnatural" company with "the question of what might still
happen to everyone about me, to the country at large," James saw these
"marked disparities" as "a single vast visitation." The words evoke for us
that other word, almost a portmanteau version of *vast* and *visitation*—
Henry James at the last could claim that, like his father, he also had had
his *vastation*.

In 1867 William James speaks of having "that delightful disease in
my back, which has so long made Harry so interesting. It is evidently a
family peculiarity." Henry was still experiencing his back-ache in middle life. Edmund Gosse remembered that early in the 1880s he called on
James in London and found him stretched on his sofa. James apologized
for not rising to greet him, explaining that "a muscular weakness of his
spine obliged him, as he said, 'to assume the horizontal posture' during
some hours of every day, in order to bear the almost unbroken routine of
evening engagements. I think," Gosse added, "this weakness gradually
passed away, but certainly for many years it handicapped his activity."
In 1902 James mentions, in a letter, a photograph of himself taken at
Newport: "I remember (it now all comes back to me) when (and where)
I was so taken: at the age of twenty, though I look younger, and at a time
when I had had an accident (an injury to my back), and was rather sick

and sorry. I look rather as if I wanted propping up."

The evidence points unquestionably to a back injury—a slipped disc, a sacroiliac or muscular strain—obscure but painful as such injuries can be. That the hurt was exacerbated by the tensions of the Civil War seems quite clear. Mentally prepared for some state of injury by his father's permanent hurt, and for a sense therefore of continuing physical inadequacy, Henry found himself a prey to anxieties over the fact that he might be called a malingerer, and had a feeling that he was deficient in the masculinity being displayed by others of his generation on the battlefield. This is reflected in all his early stories and contributed to the Hemingwayan fantasy that James "castrated" himself.

Yet even if we did not have the evidence of his activities immediately after the fire, or his repeated assertions, the novelist's physically active later life and his monumental production would in themselves undermine the legend. He rode horseback, fenced, lifted weights (to fight off corpulence), took long daily walks and was an inveterate traveler; he spent hours daily at his desk; he combined literary labor with a crowded and intricate social life. There was nothing of the eunuch about him either in appearance or inaction. Henry James himself, we suspect, would not have used the word eunuch so freely, as he did on occasions, to describe bad and unproductive writers, had he been physically one himself.

The Younger Brothers

In Concord, where the major accents of Abolition had sounded, Garth Wilkinson and Robertson James now heard the more violent accents of the war. In 1862 Wilky, then seventeen, turned his back on school and sought a place in the Northern Army. A few months later Bob followed him.

The war emphasized a widening gulf between the four brothers that had been the result of their difference in age. Bob, in particular, had for some time "strained much at every tether," Henry observed. He considered himself a foundling in the family; he talked of running off to sea. The war offered him a ready alternative. The two boys' enlistment was a reflection of a youthful desire for action, freedom, adventure, and a response to strong anti-slavery sentiment to which they had been exposed both at home and at Concord; it was also a leap to manhood and the sudden achievement of a superior position in the family hierarchy.

The younger brothers sent vivid and excited letters from the field and gave Henry a continuing picture of the life of the soldier and the life of action. He remembered visiting Wilky when he was in the 44th Massachusetts at Readville and marveled that "this soft companion of my

childhood should have such romantic chances and should have mastered, by the mere aid of his native gaiety and sociability, such mysteries,
such engines, such arts." Presently Wilky joined the dramatically-con-
stituted 54th Massachusetts, the first regiment of colored troops, headed
by Colonel Robert Gould Shaw. They marched out of Boston on 28 May
1863 "to great reverberations of music, of fluttering banners, launched
benedictions and every public sound."

On 1 July 1863, as the battle of Gettysburg was being fought, Henry
paced restlessly in a Newport garden, "neither daring quite to move nor
quite to rest . . . This *was,* as it were, the War—the War palpably in
Pennsylvania." Before the month was out the war was experienced in the
James household. There had been a courageous assault by the Negro
regiment on Fort Wagner in Charleston Bay with the guns of Sumter
playing on them. The 54th withdrew after two-thirds of its officers and
nearly half its men had been shot down or bayoneted within the fortress
or before its walls. Shaw had died, leading his men, and Wilky James, his
adjutant, had received a wound in his side and a canister ball in his
ankle.

Wilky probably would have been among the dead had not a rescuing
hand intervened. Reported missing in the struggle at Charleston was
Wilky's closest friend in the Army, Cabot Russell, whose father promptly
went in search of his son. He did not find him, but he discovered Wilky
among the wounded and brought him north by boat to New York and
thence to Newport, where, one August day in 1863, he appeared at the
James residence with the wounded youth on a stretcher. They carried
Wilky in, placing the stretcher just inside the door of the house. There
he lay for days. The doctor ordered that he should not be moved. In Henry
James's first signed story the bringing home of the young hero from
battle is described, much as it occurred at Newport: "Death is not thinner, paler, stiller." A sketch made by William at this moment shows
Wilky almost as one dead—open-mouthed, leaden-eyed, his cheeks
sunken and his face covered with the stubble of his beard.

Wilky's recovery was slow, but he pulled through and with a fine
show of strength returned to the field in 1864, rejoining his own regiment
to participate in the entry into Charleston. He was present when the
American flag was hoisted over Sumter.

In the meantime Robertson had been made a lieutenant in the 55th
Massachusetts. While Wilky was recovering, he was at Morris Island
building earthworks and mounting guns in the Southern heat with rebel
shells playing on the troops. He suffered so serious a sunstroke during
Seymour's raid on Florida that he was recommended for discharge. Instead, as soon as he had recovered, he took a staff post in the cavalry, and
later returned to his regiment before Charleston. He participated in a

heavy fight and made an heroic charge that earned him a captaincy. The 55th later was the first body of Northern troops to enter Charleston.

Thus the younger brothers stepped into the bright and lurid light of war for their brief hour—and it turned out to be their only hour. Life after the Civil War was for them a long and painful anticlimax. Imbued with the cause for which they had fought, Wilky and Bob set out to be plantation owners in Florida with paid Negro labor. They struggled valiantly, risked their lives, lost large sums of money advanced them by their father, and finally gave up. The rest of Wilky's brief life was a series of efforts to find a place for himself in a disjointed America; sociable, as always, improvident, he drifted finally westward, worked as a railway clerk and died before he was forty after a period of prolonged ill-health. Robertson lived into our century, a brilliant, erratic individual, gifted, witty, deeply unhappy. He worked for a railroad for a while; he tried to paint, he wrote verse, he traveled; he experienced a series of religious conflicts much like his father—for a while he found solace in Catholicism, then he rebelled against the Church's authority and turned to the family religion, Swedenborgianism. There were periods of heavy drinking and guilt. He died in the same year as William, 1910, and Henry, mourning him, spoke of the "vivacity of his intelligence, the variety of his gifts" and the "easiest aptitude for admirable talk, charged with natural life, perception, humour and colour, that I have perhaps ever known."

A Particular Divergence

The doctor's pooh-pooh had offered Henry James neither cure nor the awkward solace of invalidism. He felt acutely that he had to "make some show of life . . . when everyone was on the move." The younger brothers were gone; William was in Cambridge. And now his boon companion Sargy Perry was about to enter Harvard. This was clearly no time to stay at home. In September 1862 Henry accordingly journeyed from Newport to Cambridge and registered in the Harvard Law School.

Thus at nineteen the young cosmopolite, who had lived in New York, in London, in Paris, found himself at last in that city which the consummate Brahmin, Dr. Oliver Wendell Holmes, with a Bostonian complacency and civic pride that Henry was later to satirize, had characterized as "the thinking centre of the continent." The words *rustic, rural, provincial* figure always in Henry James's picture of New England. He found Boston a "rural centre even to a point at which I had never known anything as rural"; one felt there the "breath of the fields and woods and waters . . . at their domesticated and familiarized stage." New York might be described as "vulgar" and "homely," but the Puritan capital, with its plodding horse-cars and the afterglow of the great snowfalls, reflected "the higher complacency": it was New England "unabsorbed and un-reconciled"—and also "the most educated of our societies without ceas-ing to be that of a village."

For all his saturation with Back Bay life and Cambridge over the next six years, James could never reconcile himself to the gentility of the Brahmins, or the manner in which New England considered culture to be an arduous duty rather than a joy of life and of civilization. Yet within this environment he considered hostile to major creative art lay the associations of his "untried years," old personal memories that had marked the launching of a career, *his* career. In the end his pictures of Cambridge and Boston are suffused with a kind of redeeming affection and tenderness. New England became a part of Henry James even though he resisted it.

"I wish," Henry had written to Perry from Bonn, two years earlier, "al-though I've no doubt it is a very silly wish, that I were going to college." In his old age it seemed "odd" to him that he should have wanted to go, and odder still that he should have elected the study of law. Law, never-theless, appears to have been for him the only acceptable alternative in 1862. Harvard was then a college of 1,000 students and thirty teachers. Nothing approaching "liberal arts" existed. The law was the one field which seemed eminently "practical." It represented "life" and the "world." In reality it was the avenue of least resistance for a shy, observ-ant young man who asked only to be just "literary."

Henry lodged with William for a few days after his arrival in Cam-bridge until he found, in Winthrop Square, an old house with "everything in it slanting and gaping and creaking." His sitting room commanded a view of distant hills, and in an alcove there was a large desk where "even so shy a dreamer as I . . . might perhaps hope to woo the muse." William was close at hand, to be sought at will; T. S. Perry was as always a familiar companion. But now Henry had Boston and Cambridge to ex-plore, and the privacy of his room to which he could return to watch from his window the flushed sunsets and the cloud scenery.

Harvard's setting at this time was entirely rural. In a matter of min-utes the student could find himself walking past little meadows and scrubby little orchards, encountering crooked little crossroads and study-ing solitary dwellings on long grassy slopes under tall New England elms "with their shingled hoods well pulled down on their ears." "Europe" had faded and was supplanted by a rustic and homespun scene studied by the earnest young man with penetrating eyes, who had become a cosmopo-lite without ever having been a provincial.

Henry joined William at meals three times a day at Miss Upham's

board in her house at the corner of Kirkland and Oxford streets. Maison
Upham, under the elms, was a "veritable haunt of conversation." There
was a major subject, the continuing war. Henry sat beside William, who
was brightly communicative, always ready to help "the lame dog of con-
verse over stile after stile." There was little need to do this, for opposite
sat Harvard's Chaucerian and collector of ballads, Francis J. Child,
round-faced, cherubic, filled with discourse about the conduct of the war,
his talk a "darting flame" when it came to the North's transatlantic
enemies. Among the others at the table was a young theological student
named Salter, with dark moustache and pointed beard, who looked like
an old Spanish portrait and who was New England at its "sparest and
dryest," and at the same time at its wittiest.

If Henry went conscientiously to the lectures in Dane Hall in the
mornings—and he marveled at the extent to which he faithfully attended
—it was because, he later felt, he could exercise his observer's role to his
heart's content. Sitting in the rear of the auditorium, in the dusky half-
smothered light coming from low windows, he sought to fix "the weight,
the interest, the function" of his fellow-Americans. He wanted to get to
know the "types." The law students at Harvard appeared to be standard-
ized and homogenized New Englanders, their very names redolent of the
area—Wentworth, Lathrop, Pickering, Young, Kirkland, Sargent. Curi-
ously enough, however, with the exception of Salter, who was William's
friend, and not a law student, Henry does not single out any New England
classmates for the vivid sketches of his young contemporaries which are
woven into his memoirs. It was a classmate designated as G. A. J., who
reached "westward, westward even of New York and southward at least
as far as Virginia," whom we identify as George Abbot James (not however a descendant of William of Albany), who was marked by Henry from
the first "for a friend and taken for a kinsman"—sole member of the
Harvard law class whose friendship the novelist retained in later life.

Only once during the year does Henry James seem to have stepped
out of his observer's role in the law school. The Marshall Club staged a
moot court and Henry agreed, or was assigned, to represent the "defend-
ant" in an arbitration suit. He found himself in "a perfect glare of publicity" which frightened him into virtual silence. The opposing counsel won
the case with ease. Henry retired in deep discomfiture. He had not studied his law books with any assiduity and, aside from this brave display
of himself before his class, his connection with Dane Hall remained "as
consistently superficial as could be possible" to one who was so "restlessly perceptive."

He went on long lonely rambles in Cambridge and Boston; he sat in
Gore Hall reading Sainte-Beuve, whom he discovered during that year;
he wandered occasionally into other classrooms, and on certain dark

winter afternoons listened to James Russell Lowell discoursing on English literature and Old French, the lamplight illuminating the bearded
face and expressive hands of the stocky Yankee.

Henry was in Boston at the height of the Abolition fever. On New
Year's day 1863 he made his way, through milling crowds, to the Music
Hall, where an excited multitude celebrated Lincoln's Emancipation
Proclamation with an uncommon Bostonian show of emotion. On the
crowded platform was the old family friend, Mr. Emerson, tall and spare,
reading his "Boston Hymn" in ringing tones.

There was a less historic evening when Henry traveled into Boston
to see Maggie Mitchell in *Fanchon the Cricket,* derived from a novel by
George Sand. Miss Mitchell had played the part up and down the United
States, and yet there was nothing stale about the charm she exercised
upon the young law student. He returned entranced to his room in Winthrop Square and wrote the actress a letter from which she should
"gather the full force of my impression." Maggie reciprocated, sending
him an autographed "acting edition" of the play.

The impression stimulated him to much more than a "fan" letter. He
sat down at his desk in the alcove "to enroll myself in the bright band of
the fondly hoping and fearfully doubting who count the days after the
despatch of manuscripts." His first piece of independent writing deemed
fit for publication dealt with a play and an actress. We do not know
whether this spontaneous piece of drama criticism was ever published.
But sometime between his departure from Harvard in 1863 and the appearance of his first unsigned criticism in the autumn of 1864, the young
writer found his literary feet and took the path from which he would
never stray.

Was this the turning-point in Henry James's life? Many years later,
he told himself, "I must then, in the cold shade of queer little old Dane
Hall, have stood at the parting of my ways, recognized the false steps,
even though few enough, already taken, and consciously committed myself to my particular divergence." James's recollections of his Harvard
year contain no mention of a conscious choice between law and letters.
He drifted into the law school and he nowhere mentions how or when he
drifted away from it. Dane Hall may not have marked a "turning-point"
so much as the turning of a corner. There were to be no more "false
steps."

Ashburton Place

The Civil War, as with all wars, was a time of terminations—and
beginnings. The Abolitionist cause had engaged common sympathies.
Men had laid down their lives to defend it; with it nineteenth-century

New England touched its highest note of compassion and humanity. In intellectual Boston the war marked the era of "radicalism" and a return to old conservative virtues.

The younger Henry James, at twenty-one, found life in the Back Bay full of interest. For him, too, the period was one of terminations and beginnings. Despair engendered by war and ill-health now gave way to a feeling of hope and elation. When the senior Henry and his wife moved to No. 13 Ashburton Place in Boston, from a Newport that had become too lonely for them, William and Henry were returned to the family hearth. The house, of red brick, was as substantial as Boston itself. Henry had a large green-shuttered room on the third floor overlooking the Place, and here he was able to establish his working relationship with "the small inkpot in which I seemed at last definitely destined to dip." In Ashburton Place Henry heard the news of Grant's victories and the surrender at Appomattox. Here—on his twenty-second birthday—the shrill cry reached him of an outraged and grieving America standing at the bier of the assassinated President. And here, in these same surroundings, he one day counted the first earnings of his pen, a dozen greasy dollar bills.

When the young literary aspirant arrived on the Boston scene in 1864 —as distinct from the collegiate scene in Cambridge of the previous year —the *Atlantic Monthly* was seventeen years old and the *North American Review* almost fifty. The *Atlantic* was under the editorship of James T. Fields, a friendly, hospitable and benevolent individual, deeply attached to his mission of publisher. Fields was a collector of literary relics, autographs, rare editions, and at his house by the Charles he and his wife maintained a salon in which were received the élite of the literary and artistic world from both sides of the water. They were host to Dickens and to Thackeray, to every distinguished visitor who came to Boston and to all the Brahmins; and it was not long before the young Henry found himself welcomed as a writer of promise, having Sunday supper opposite the celebrated Mrs. Stowe, who had a "nonchalance of real renown" to the eyes of a youth seeking renown. It was Fields who, in due course, published Henry James's first fiction in the *Atlantic.*

The young outsider could only, at this stage, stand in the shadow of the celebrities of Boston and Cambridge—none save Mrs. Stowe were novelists—who by the end of the Civil War were reaching comfortable middle-age and had become New England oracles as well as men of letters. Oliver Wendell Holmes, the "autocrat" and wit, was fifty-five when the Jameses appeared in Boston. Longfellow was fifty-seven, and Lowell forty-four. Fields, their publisher, was forty-seven. The New England élite fell roughly into two classes: the men who, like Emerson and Thoreau, had built a philosophy in communion with the out-of-doors, and the urban Brahmins, sons and grandsons of clergymen, whose creativity was fed by the creativity of the past. They still tended to preach. The recently dead Hawthorne alone among the writers had expressed, for Henry James, the passive, haunted, imaginative side of the transplanted Puritan.

The youngest of the Brahmins in 1864—he was thirty-seven—was Charles Eliot Norton, son of a celebrated Biblical scholar, a friend of Ruskin, an art scholar, a lover of Italy. His home, Shady Hill, like Lowell's Elmwood was a Cambridge landmark. There in his long library, he worked on his translation of Dante and carried out his "civilizing" mission, an apostle of Old World culture in the New World.

In 1864 Norton and Lowell undertook to rescue the middle-aged *North American Review* from the staleness into which long-established periodicals often decline. And on 30 July of that year Henry James addressed to the editors from Ashburton Place a two-sentence letter. "Gentlemen," he wrote, "I take the liberty of enclosing a brief review of [Nassau W.] Senior's *Essays on Fiction* published in London a few months ago. Hoping that you may deem it worthy of a place among your Literary Notices, I remain yours respectfully Henry James Jr."

The letter written, Henry left to spend the summer at Northampton, Massachusetts, in that era a comfortable health resort. He later spoke of the place, when he put it into the opening pages of *Roderick Hudson,* as the "only small American *ville de province* of which one had happened to lay up, long before, a pleased vision." The town has since grown, but when Henry visited it in 1864—he prolonged his stay there from early August to December—it was a small New England settlement, with broad country streets and old white houses framed by box hedges and set off by high elms. Situated near an elbow of the Connecticut River, it provided him with a place of relaxation and rest, where he could take a "water-cure" and be near woods and rocks, red cedars, pines, "beauty sufficient for an artist not to starve upon it," as he said in his preface to *Roderick.* The choice of Northampton in James's first important novel was deliberate and autobiographical, as nearly all his choices of scene were. In this town Henry James, the American artist, was driving his pen in a more professional fashion than ever before; it would be therefore a fitting town in which to launch his fictional artist, Roderick Hudson, and to impart to him those thoughts about the role of the creator in American society which Henry pondered as he walked beneath the lofty elms.

Nine days after dispatching his critical manuscript to the *North American Review* he had his answer. The article was accepted—accepted with a show of enthusiasm and a prompt demand for more. He replied that he would enjoy writing other literary notices if the books came "within my narrow compass." His notice of Senior's essays was

published in the October issue of the *Review,* and the January issue
contained three of his reviews, all of them unsigned.

During December 1864 Henry went out to snowbound Cambridge in
response to an invitation from Norton and spent a memorable half-hour
with him in his library at Shady Hill. The friendship formed that day
was to endure for years and to embrace Norton's immediate family and
his sisters as well. It is doubtful whether it ever became intimate. Charles
Eliot Norton was a dry, self-contained, demanding individual; but a deep
respect was there and the common ground of their love for the cultural
riches of the Old World. Always, the American art scholar remained for
Henry the man who had opened to him one of the first doors to the world
of letters. The *North American Review* paid him $2.50 a page; his first
review netted twelve dollars. He had a sense of being launched, the first
member of the family of the elder Henry James to have taken a step
towards earning his way.

The book review which had received such prompt acceptance dealt
with the art of fiction. What its readers did not know was that the anonymous writer was not talking of fiction in a vacuum. He had published at
least one tale and was writing others soon to see print.

The essay is distinctly young and yet singularly mature. Its youth is
proclaimed by its dogmatism, its attempt to demolish in cutting phrases,
its forced mannerisms; yet the casual reader of 1864 would have been
impressed by the remarkable range of the writer's reading and his original ideas on the art of the novel. Fiction, the writer affirms, is a reflection
of life; "even the most photographically disposed novels address pre-
eminently the imagination"; the public must be approached from its own
level and not be preached at; fiction must become "self-forgetful," not
seek to instruct or to edify. Men and women must be represented as they
are, as motivated living creatures, not puppets.

In Boston, at twenty-one, Henry James was approaching fiction more
consciously and with greater deliberation than any American novelist
before him; the need to put the house of fiction in order and the need for
precept, canon, codification, is clearly in evidence. In his early unsigned
notices he lectures such writers as Miss Prescott and Miss Alcott on the
need to create living characters, give them "a body, a local habitation, a
name." He advises the novelists to read Mérimée, to learn from the pages
of Balzac how to set a scene and launch a drama, and to study the realism
of George Eliot. The novelist must not describe, he must *convey;* characters once launched must *act* in certain ways consistent with their personality; the artist must not finger his puppets as a child besmudges a doll,
he must endow them with their individuality and with life.

Whatever doubts and hesitancies Henry had about his personal abilities he had none whatever about how fiction should be created. He re-

views *Felix Holt* and forgives George Eliot her "clumsily artificial" plots because she delineates character, possesses human sympathy, poetic quality, microscopic observation, morality, discreet humor and exquisite rhetoric. As he nears his twenty-third birthday he reviews Dickens's *Our Mutual Friend* with a sense that his early idol has written himself out; Henry had seldom read "a book so intensely *written*, so little seen, known, or felt," and concludes that Dickens knows men rather than *man* and that "it is one of the chief conditions of his genius not to see below the surface of things." As such he is the "greatest of superficial novelists." The young critic is not intimidated by greatness. What is important for him is his search for a viable theory of fiction.

This theory was derived not only from his close reading of novels, but from a long saturation with French literature, largely through the medium of the *Revue des Deux Mondes.* A young man who had been carefully reading Sainte-Beuve and Taine was equipped with serious critical tools; and a young man who had read—and studied—the minor French novelists as well as the major, from Balzac to George Sand and Flaubert, inevitably had standards of form, of style, of grace, of subtlety, that did not exist in the as yet brief history of American criticism. The young Henry James had more theory in his head and a wider embrace of European models than any novelist then writing in the United States—and he had not yet written a novel himself.

He was, however, assiduously writing fiction. It has always been assumed that Henry James made his debut as a critic and then as a writer of short stories. In reality the reverse occurred. "The Story of a Year," the first story to which he signed his name, had a significant anonymous predecessor. In March 1864, a full year before this tale appeared, Henry wrote to Perry that the printer's devil had been knocking at his door. "You know," he wrote, "a literary man can't call his time his own." A few sentences later he proposes that he use Perry's mail address for correspondence with the *Atlantic* editors about a story. "I cannot again stand the pressure of avowed authorship (for the present) and their answer could not come here unobserved." So there had been "avowed authorship." And a letter written by a Newport neighbor of the Jameses enables us to identify what was Henry James's first published but unsigned tale.

On 29 February 1864 Mrs. George De Kay wrote to her son Charles, then at school:

> Miss Elly Temple has just come in looking very fresh and pretty—Henry James has published a story in the February Continental called a Tragedy of Errors. Read it. Smith Van Buren forbade Elly to read it! which

brought a smile of quiet contempt to Harry's lips but anger and indignation to those of Miss Minnie Temple.

Smith Van Buren was exercising an uncle's prerogative over one of his orphaned nieces. For perhaps the first—and certainly not the last—time in his literary career, Henry James stood accused of writing stories unfit for young girls to read. The February 1864 issue of the *Continental Monthly,* a journal devoted to literature and national policy, contains a twelve-page tale, unsigned, entitled "A Tragedy of Error." It is clearly from the early pen of Henry James Junior.

The tale begins in the best manner of a French romance: "A low English phaeton was drawn up before the door of the post office of a French seaport town. In it was seated a lady, with her veil down and her parasol held closely over her face. My story begins with a gentleman coming out of the office and handing her a letter." The lady gives the gentleman her parasol to hold, lifts her veil to show "a very pretty face" and "such persons as were looking on at the moment saw the lady turn very pale."

Hortense Bernier has learned from the letter that her husband is returning. She must act, for she has taken a lover in his absence. She has "half a mind to drown myself," she tells Louis de Meyrau, but ends by making a pact with a brutal boatman to drown her husband instead. The boatman will meet the arriving vessel beyond the breakwater and offer to row her husband ashore. It will be simple to do away with him en route.

> "Is he an old man?"
> Hortense shook her head faintly.
> "My age?"
> She nodded.
> *"Sapristi!* it isn't so easy."
> "He can't swim," said Hortense, without looking up; "he—he is lame."
> *"Nom de dieu!"* The boatman dropped his hands.

Hortense has not counted on her lover deciding on his own course of action. He goes aboard the ship in the early dawn to greet the husband, only to discover that Bernier has already had himself rowed ashore. He finds a waiting boat, however, and asks the boatman to take him to the Bernier house. "You're just the gentleman I want," says the boatman. Hortense, pacing nervously in her garden, utters a cry when she sees "a figure emerge from below the terrace and come limping toward her with outstretched arms."

Thus in the earliest of Henry James's stories a limping husband is married to a woman capable of strong and determined action—even to the point of seeking to destroy him. The plot embodies the lameness of Henry's father and we are asked to assume that the lover, who is not lame, also cannot swim. But the narrative is lively, the talk vivid, and little touches at every turn show how precociously the young writer had studied his craft. The characterization of boatman, lover and the heroine herself is skillful. Louis de Meyrau's hard-headed egotism is revealed in his first remarks; we know he will be of no help to Hortense. As for the distracted wife, she is the first of a long line of "bad heroines," capable of murder, yet exciting our sympathy.

There are other such foreshadowings in this first tale. Again and again it is not James who sees what goes on but someone else: "although to a third person it would have appeared," "a wayfarer might have taken him for a ravisher escaping with a victim." On the way to the boat Hortense walked "as if desirous to attract as little observation as possible ... yet if for any reason a passer-by had happened to notice her ..." The third person, the observer, the wayfarer, the onlooker, the passer-by— and their testimony is presented objectively to the reader. There was conscious method in the narrative. The young man who talked of the art of fiction had the glimmerings of a design and a ruling theory.

Henry James had sailed confidently into Charles Eliot Norton's study as a critic. The publication of "The Story of a Year" seems to have been attended by greater difficulties. In March 1864, Henry told Perry he had been rewriting "that modern novel I spoke of to you. . . . On the whole, it is a failure, I think, tho' nobody will know this, perhaps, but myself . . . it is a simple story, simply told. As yet it hath no name." He was sending the tale to the *Atlantic Monthly* and asking the journal "to send their letter of reject, or accept" to Perry. In October, while staying at Northampton, Henry received word from his friend that an answer had come, for he replied to him, "I suppose I ought to be thankful for so much and not grumble that it is so little. One of these days we shall have certain persons *on their knees* imploring for contributions." And he draws a sketch of a man representing the *Atlantic Monthly* kneeling before a haughty bearded individual. The letter suggests that there has been a qualified acceptance, either a request for a certain amount of rewriting or an encouraging rejection. From the drawing it would appear that by his twenty-first year Henry James had begun to grow the beard which he was to wear, after the fashion of the time, for the next thirty-five years. Its acquisition coincided with the decision of Henry's hero in "The Story of a Year" to "crop my head and cultivate my chin."

Henry doesn't tell us what year this is the story of, but General McClellan's picture figures on the heroine's table beside that of the hero;

the hero is wounded on the Rappahannock River in Virginia, where young Gus Barker was shot down by a guerrilla in 1863, and this, it would seem, was the year James was writing about. The three figures in the foreground of the tale were to reappear in many forms in James's later fiction—the determined mother, her ward or protégée or relative, and the young son in love, unsure of himself, fearing to assert himself, and if he does, paying for assertion by personal disintegration. Mrs. Ford, the hero's mother, seated sewing, bites the end of her thread as if "executing a human vengeance" when her son John discloses to her his engagement to Elizabeth. The hero gives up the fight even before he goes off to war; he is certain he will die. He wants his engagement to be a secret, but he doesn't keep it from his mother. John Ford is brought back to his mother's door, like Wilky James, wounded in battle. He has no desire to live. Lizzie, sitting at his bedside, is unaware that he sees her not as flesh but as stone. "He lay perfectly motionless, but for his eyes. They wandered over her with a kind of peaceful glee, like sunbeams playing on a statue." In most of Henry James's early stories loved women are compared to statues. Only later does he become aware, if not of their flesh, at least of their heart and mind.

In December 1864 Wilky James wrote from the front, "Tell Harry that I am waiting anxiously for his 'next'. I can find a large sale for any blood and thunder tale among the darks." "The Story of a Year" appeared in the March 1865 issue of the *Atlantic Monthly*. The senior Henry wrote to Wilky that it was "considered good" and that he was sending him a copy, "so you can see his name in print." Henry was launched, and just how successfully he could measure when there appeared at Ashburton Place a handsome, vigorous man, an Irishman, named Edwin Lawrence Godkin. He had arrived in New York in 1856 after serving in the Crimean War, and by 1865, at thirty-four, had thoroughly identified himself with America and its future. He was convinced that the time was ripe for the launching of a weekly publication which would reflect the changing times and particularly the pressing problem of the freed slaves. He gained the sympathies of Norton and other Bostonians and raised enough capital for immediate needs. In July 1865 the *Nation* began its long and illustrious career.

The purpose of Godkin's call at Ashburton Place was to enlist the services of the two Henry Jameses on behalf of the new publication. Vol. I, No. 1 contains unsigned reviews by both father and son—Henry Junior reviews a novel by Henry Kingsley and Henry Senior Carlyle's *Frederick the Great.* From then on the junior Henry was a consistent writer for the *Nation,* first of reviews, later of travel sketches, all of these unsigned. For a brief period he was an informal staff member in New York, still later the *Nation*'s informal correspondent-at-large in England; his connection with the journal can be said to cover almost half a century. The *Nation* was never an important source of income to the writer: nevertheless, in having access to its pages, James became, in effect, a significant commentator for his countrymen on the latest books and pictures, occasional theatrical developments and trends in literature abroad, as well as a purveyor of tidbits of political intelligence.

James's early acceptance as a writer was a distinct piece of good fortune in giving him assurance and recognition. Had he found himself in a society less receptive, or in a time when old periodicals were not being overhauled and new ones created, he might have had to face a much greater measure of discouragement than was his lot. As it was, he made his literary début in a fashion devoid of frustration and distinguished in every way.

Heroine of the Scene

In 1884, while writing a letter to the editor of the *Atlantic Monthly,* Henry James made a series of slips of the pen. He was promising to write a serial for the following year and instead of 1885 he wrote 1865 at three different points in his letter. That the year 1865 had an emotional importance for him is corroborated by the exclamation recorded in his notebook late in life, "Ah, the 'epoch-making' weeks of the spring of 1865!"

That spring was indeed epoch-making: in the national life the end of the Civil War and the discharge upon the North of the great veteran army; in Henry James's private life, the year of his official début as a writer of fiction. It was also the year in which William James departed with a scientific expedition to the Amazon. At one stroke Henry was freed of the anxieties engendered by the war; and at the same time he found himself elevated, at least temporarily, into the position of the elder brother, clear of the lingering sense of being subordinate and supervised. He knew well his own role and purpose.

The new-found freedom bursts through the lines of memory: "I literally came and went, I had never practised such coming and going." He paid repeated visits to Newport, spending happy days with John La Farge, who had married the sister of his friend Perry. He spent enthralling hours in Lawton's Valley, a short ride from Newport, with the "Boston Muse," Julia Ward Howe; he visited, also at Newport, the Edmund Tweedys. At the Tweedys' lived the four Temple sisters, and in particular Mary (Minny) Temple, the younger, who had begun to assume an important place in Henry's life. He also went "in particular, during summer weeks to the White Mountains of New Hampshire, with some repetition." He went there, though he does not tell us so in *Notes of a Son and Brother,* for the same reason that he gravitated to the Tweedy house in Newport.

Minny Temple spent the summer of 1865 in the White Mountains.

In 1865 Minny was twenty, "a young and shining apparition," slim, graceful, with a "wonderful ethereal brightness of presence." She was always interested in those around her; she always had questions and looked for answers; she had a fund of wit and a striking face—large eyes, an upturned nose, full lips, large but not unattractive teeth. She talked with a charming toss of the head and walked with the "long, light and yet almost sliding steps" which Henry James imparted to several of his heroines. She remained for him always a dancing figure, possessing more humanity "than any charming girl who ever circled round a ball-room." In the end she became for him "a disengaged and dancing flame of thought."

She might have had her flirtatious moments, but for a girl addicted to the ballroom she had a serious mind. She attracted young men who could not be satisfied by a pretty face alone. She was courted, or at least admired, at this period, by a future philosopher, a future novelist, a future Supreme Court Justice and a future professor of law. In those Civil War years they were simply "promising" youths drawn to Minny Temple's presence, making her, as Henry put it, "the heroine of our common scene." "Most of those who knew and loved, I was going to say adored, her . . ." Henry wrote in his memoirs. Henry *adored* Minny, and the word explains why in the retrospect of half a century he spoke of her alternately as angel and human. He remembered her on the one hand as graceful and quick, "all straightness and charming tossed head," and on the other as having "noble flights and such discouraged drops." To have flights one must have wings. It is not strange that in these circumstances he embodied his ultimate memory of Minny in *The Wings of the Dove.*

Among the young men back from the wars was the junior Oliver Wendell Holmes, a young law student William James had met at Harvard, who became an intimate of Henry as well. Thrice wounded in the conflict, Holmes was now sitting in Dane Hall under Henry's old professors. The future Supreme Court Justice was two years Henry's senior and a good deal more at ease socially, in particular with young women. "Harry never lets up on his high aims," Wendell later wrote to William James, admitting that *he* often did. Wendell was singularly pleasing to young ladies.

Henry had arranged his visit to the White Mountains for the end of July 1865 and he invited Wendell to join him. He set Minny Temple room-hunting for them but with the summer influx she could find only a single room, "the only one in the place, high or low—far or near. This," Henry exuberantly informed Wendell, "the wretch who owned it refused to furnish with two beds; but she took it and when we get up there we can pull his own out from under him." On 1 August they traveled together up the coach road into the mountains, to North Conway. Holmes brought with him another young man fresh from the wars, a bearded fellow-student, already a friend of Minny's, John Chipman Gray, destined to become one of Harvard's most distinguished jurists.

In *Notes of a Son and Brother,* without divulging the identity of Holmes or Gray, James paints a scene of "the fraternizing, endlessly conversing group of us under the rustling pines." They talked of "a hundred human and personal things," and he felt the talkers constituted "a little world of easy and happy interchange, of unrestricted and yet all so instructively sane and secure association." In 1905, when James returned to this scene, he saw it as "the near . . . the far, country of youth." The woods were a "sacred grove," a place "prepared for high uses, even if for none rarer than high talk." Forty years before, in similar woods and on similar meadows, he had walked with his Temple cousins and here, not far from Mount Washington's paternal face, had taken place a little drama, divided neither into scenes nor acts, and wholly without climax, that nevertheless touched off in Henry's mind stories to be relived early and late at his writing-desk.

The drama resided largely in his mind. For what happened at North Conway during that August of '65 was simply that two young Civil War veterans, perhaps still in uniform, and Henry, gallantly attended the Temple girls, devoting themselves particularly to Minny. Henry, however, felt himself in a very special relationship to the veterans. The bronzed, muscular young men had come back full of stories and were "swamping much of the scene as with the flow of a monster tide." And while he presented himself as "the dreaming painter of things" seeking to absorb some portion of this common fund of history, Henry felt himself once more on a footing of inequality among his fellows. Every uniform, every swordbelt and buckle, suggested a life of action that could never be a part of his life.

Here then was Minny in earnest or witty talk with Lieutenant-Colonel Oliver Wendell Holmes Jr., and Judge Advocate John Chipman Gray Jr., while Henry, the "mere junior," the civilian stay-at-home, looked on from the outer rim of talk. The heroine was there but the would-be hero was eclipsed; "the interesting pair," Wendell and John, had a "quantity of common fine experience that glittered as so much acquired and enjoyed luxury—all of the sort that I had no acquisition whatever to match." He could only rejoice that his friends had so much to show to Minny, such "brilliant advantage," even if he had "none of my own" to offer. His was the consolation of the observer; the "emanation the most masculine" came from the veterans of the Civil War.

It is doubtful, however, whether Henry would have acted otherwise, even if there had been no young men present to admire, to love, to adore

Minny. Naturally shy and tending to hover in the background of any social situation, Henry in reality wanted only to worship Minny from a quiet and discreet—and we might add, safe—distance. He was too reticent and emotionally withdrawn to be an ardent wooer—to woo at all— too intellectual to accept romance on its own sentient terms; and he lived in an era when, particularly in his world, there was much greater reticence between the sexes. Henry James was in love, but it was love of an inner sort, a questioning love, unvoiced, unavowed.

True love is best by silence known. And such silence can have in it a component of fear. Henry James feared women and worshipped them. He hesitated to express his feelings lest he be turned away. For him women could be as chaste and beautiful—and unattainable—as Diana; or else they were another kind of huntress, harsh and predatory, literally dedicated to the chase—the chase of a husband—and thus to be fled.

Minny was not only a bright-burning flame, or Diana, chaste and beautiful. Her very name, Mary, was his mother's; she was a kinswoman and she had a capacity, similar to Mary James's, for being all charm and simplicity while holding back certain feelings; she could "relate" winningly to those around her with the familiar toss of the head and at the same time draw down a curtain of inscrutability. "Heroine of the scene" she was for him, and the very word "heroine" suggests the extent to which he exalted her. Some time later Henry wrote to William: "Every one was supposed, I believe, to be more or less in love with her," and, while in this letter he denied that he was, he added, "I enjoyed *pleasing* her almost as much as if I had been. I cared more to please her perhaps than she ever cared to be pleased."

Evidence of Minny's role as an object of his affection is transparently written into a short story, "Poor Richard," which James published during the next year. It appeared in the *Atlantic Monthly* in three installments in 1867. Its biographical interest resides in the central situation—that of a wealthy young heroine loved by three men, a Captain, a Major and Richard Clare, a stay-at-home. While neither of the military men appears to resemble Holmes or Gray, the civilian hero is endowed with the feelings of Henry James. He suffers from a deep sense of inadequacy, and is conscious of his "insignificance" in the presence of the military suitors.

> His companions displayed toward their hostess that half-avowed effort to shine and to outshine natural to clever men who find themselves concurring to the entertainment of a young and agreeable woman. Richard . . . writhed and chafed under the polish of tone and the variety of allusion by which the two officers consigned him to insignificance.

The eloquence as well as minuteness with which Henry describes poor Richard's feelings have the vividness of personal experience. Richard expresses his love for the heroine, Gertrude, but later loses interest in her when she accepts the mendacious Major.

Midway through the story Richard comes down with typhoid, an illness Henry James was well qualified to describe. The other officer, the Captain, who has loved Gertrude in silence—in Henry's fashion—has gone off to the wars and been killed; and when Richard recovers his health he finds that Gertrude, who has really loved the Captain, is now ill. "I've got my strength again," Richard exclaims, "and meanwhile you've been failing." The Jamesian "vampire theme" is here enunciated for the first time. Henry had linked himself to Minny as he had seen his father linked to Mary James. If she was the "heroine of the scene," then he could not be the hero. One or the other had to give way in Henry James's ambivalent equation.

5

THE

COMPLEX

FATE

Jacob and Esau

In the Old Testament, Esau and Jacob are twins, born but a few minutes apart, the first of the two a cunning hunter, the second a stay-at-home son, beloved of the mother. One day Esau, driven by hunger, sells his birthright for a mess of Jacob's pottage. Later their father, Isaac, old and near-blind, calls upon his eldest son to bring him venison and to receive the paternal blessing. But while Esau hunts for the game, Jacob, at the urging of his mother, deceives his father, usurps his brother's place, and receives the blessing. Then Esau, returning, weeps: "He has supplanted me these two times. He took away my birthright and behold, now he hath taken away my blessing."

William James came back from Brazil in March 1866 and resumed his medical studies, spending that summer as an intern in the Massachusetts General Hospital. Henry spent an uncomfortable summer at Swampscott, on Massachusetts Bay, twenty miles north of Boston. He read a great deal and wrote very little, recording in his notebook that he was "miserably stricken by my poor broken, all but unbearable, and unsurvivable *back.*" In the autumn the brothers were reunited under the family roof, which was moved from Ashburton Place to 20 Quincy Street, a large comfortable house, facing the Harvard Yard. This was to be the last home of the James family.

Now it was William James, the vigorous and active elder brother, who fell into a series of illnesses—back-aches, like Henry's, insomnia, eye-trouble, digestive disorders—a general state of exhaustion, nervousness and depression, the symptoms of which were to continue for several years. In the spring of 1867 he interrupted his medical studies and left for Germany in search of health and to profit by research in German laboratories and study of the language.

Henry, on his side, showed prompt signs of improvement after William's departure. "I have felt quite strong since you sailed," he wrote his brother in May 1867; and their mother wrote to William that "Harry does you the compliment of choosing the same cloth for a summer suit as you had last year." It was almost as if, in the absence of the elder brother, Henry could step into his clothes—don, like Jacob, the raiment of Esau —and be, in role and in dress, the firstborn.

With Henry's improving health came resumed literary activity. He was so productive during the months of William's absence that he earned $800 by his pen. William on his side seems to have been troubled over his own inability to contribute to, rather than use, the family's resources. In September of 1867, in Berlin, he tried his hand at a book review, sending it to Henry for revision and possible publication. "I feel that a living is not worth being gained at this price," he wrote. "Still," he went on, "an' but ten beauteous dollars lie down on their green and glossy backs within the family treasury, in consequence of my exertions, I shall feel glad that I have made them." It is significant that here, as in other letters, William is concerned not so much about literary achievement as by the fact that he, as well as Henry, could "draw a revenue" from writing. He wrote a few reviews and articles under his brother's aegis and editing, but did not pursue this type of writing for long.

In the autumn of 1868, after eighteen months abroad, William returned from Europe. Henry promptly ceased to publish. His back-ache revived; he could bring himself neither to read nor write. Apparently the observation Henry had made about his new-found freedom, on William's departure for the Amazon, had become a pattern. When his elder brother was away, Henry could expand and flourish. The moment William returned, the inhibiting forces in their relationship reduced Henry to inaction and even illness.

Mary James, faced with two ailing sons, tended to exacerbate rather than ease the hidden psychological tensions. She might fuss over Henry's aches and pains, to which the household was quite accustomed, but William's sudden acquisition of analogous symptoms she considered with a singular lack of sympathy. Henry had taken illness with a kind of fatalistic resignation that made him easy to live with; the pronouncedly active William could be neither fatalistic nor resigned. He experienced his fluctuations of mood with a lack of reticence and a voluble protest.

There was not much open rivalry between the two brothers. On the surface there was love and affection between them, and mutual respect as well as close intellectual sympathy. But below the surface of the conscious and adult relationship, the old brotherly equations of childhood underwent a significant change. In 1866 a very important, and to William disturbing, reversal of role had occurred within the James family. Henry, the mocked and derided junior of old, emerged as the only one of the four brothers who had his goal clearly in view and was proceeding towards it in a straight line. William, on the other hand, appeared to be without fixed purpose. Returning from South America, where he had believed himself to be the focus of family interest, he discovered that Henry was in the center of the scene, exciting admiration and approval as a promising young man of letters. Jacob had supplanted Esau. It seems however that William experienced the supplanting more than Henry. The latter deeply loved his elder brother, and envied his power of assertion. The satisfaction he now derived came from a developing individuation; at bottom his struggle—like William's—was with his parents. They had tried to force a kind of twinship on the two, to treat them as equals. They would now have to recognize they dealt with distinctly differing personalities.

In 1867 Henry, in a letter to William, mentioned he had received "overtures" from the *Nation,* perhaps the offer of an editorial post. All we know is that the "overtures" were turned down. A year later Charles Eliot Norton asked him to become an editor of the *North American Review;* the post held promise of regular earnings. Yet Henry unhesitatingly declined. There seems to have been no self-questioning, no doubt. He had made up his mind what his career would be, and was not allowing himself to be deflected. When moments of decision came he made the right choice, perhaps because he consulted only his inner self. He never yielded to the false whispers of the immediate and the external. And because he had such deep underground sources of observation, training, knowledge and imagination and such faith in them, he moved implacably forward in spite of delays occasioned by his mode of life, uncertain health and parental pressures.

However, he showed a strange inertia by remaining in the family home, looking enviously on while William and Wendell Holmes and Sargy Perry successively went abroad. "Can Cambridge answer Seville?" queries Henry when Perry writes to him from Spain. "Can Massachusetts respond unto Granada?" Apparently it could at least voice envy. "Bedbugs? Methinks that I would endure even them for a glimpse of those galleries and cathedrals of which you write." Why then did Henry James linger in Quincy Street long beyond the time when most young men leave home to make their own way in the world? In a sedentary young man it was perhaps understandable that he should hesitate to alter the established course of his life. It required no effort to allow the days to glide by and to accept all the home-comforts provided by his mother. Yet it is clear that for Henry this existence was boring. The young man who looked eagerly across the sea to the literary world of London and Paris spoke of life in Quincy Street as being "about as lively as the inner

sepulchre." Yet these were his horizons from 1866 until 1869—his twenty-
third to his twenty-sixth years: the writing-desk, the book, the occasional
play, the rare and usually disappointing social call, the journey by horse-
car from Cambridge to Boston.

Was he a fledgling who took longer than most to try his wings? Was
he a Jacob satisfied to dwell in tents and brew his literary pottage rather
than roam afield? There is no doubt that he was waiting his turn to go
to Europe; his ample earnings were not yet sufficient to provide funds for
travel, and his father, with the younger brothers on his hands, and with
William to support abroad, does not seem to have been prepared at this
time to keep two sons in Europe simultaneously. The question indeed
would not present itself were it not for the tales Henry was writing
during this time.

Three tales were set down during William James's absence in
Europe and each resolves itself into a similar situation. The first deals
with the rivalry of two sisters for the hand of an Englishman who has
come out to make his fortune in the colonies. The younger sister wins
him, but dies in childbirth, having obtained a promise from her husband
that her trousseau, carefully locked away, will be kept for her daughter.
The elder sister is now able to supplant the younger. She marries the
widower and becomes the stepmother of the child, but she cannot put her
hands on her sister's fine clothes. Finally she obtains the key to the trunk
and opens the forbidden lock. Her husband finds her, at sunset, dead,
lying beside the satins, silks, muslins and velvet she will never wear. The
tale, "The Romance of Certain Old Clothes," written singularly enough
not long after Henry ordered a suit similar to William's, contains ghostly
punishment for sisterly identification and imitation, as well as usurpation. Henry had abundant guilt about his relation with his brother.

A second tale, also ghostly and melodramatic, moved the clash of
wills and struggle for self-assertion into a marital frame. "De Grey: A
Romance" tells of a young man whose bride defies an old family curse
which dooms her. She succeeds: but then discovers the curse has been
transferred to her husband. Her defiance is to be his death. James writes,
"As she bloomed and prospered, he drooped and languished. While she
was living for him, he was dying of her." Again there is guilt; and a fear,
too, that self-assertion can bring a loss of love. Henry was caught between
wanting to keep his brother's love and at the same time asserting his own
place in the family constellation. As his tale implies, what was bliss for
one was bale for the other.

The third tale in this sequence is the most powerful, and brings us
into the deeper realm of the homoerotic feeling that Henry must have
had for his brother William and which William sensed and feared. Taking Browning's poem "A Light Woman," James moved it into the mascu-

line world and titled his tale "A Light Man." Maximus Austin is the first
of James's narrators to tell a story unflattering to himself. He returns to
America from Europe penniless. His friend Theodore Lisle, who treats
him as if he were a brother, invites him to stay at the home of his
employer, a soft decadent wealthy eccentric, described as if he were a
homosexual. This man, Sloane, acts as a kind of father-mother to both
young men—and has indeed been the friend of the father of one and the
mother of the other. Maximus discovers that Sloane has made out his will
to Theodore. He plays on the old man's erratic—and erotic—affections.
The old will is destroyed. However, the would-be benefactor dies before
he can write a new one. Max thus deprives Theodore of what might be
considered his "birthright," but he fails to obtain it for himself. In this
tale the author's language is often sexually charged: and especially when
he is manipulating Sloane to change his will. Maximus experiences "a
desire to leap astride of his weakness and ride it hard into the goal of my
dreams." He wants to feel the human heart "throbbing and turning, and
struggling in my grasp, know its pants, its spasms, its convulsions, and
its final senseless quiescence." Aside from Henry's apparent unaware-
ness that he was using vivid libidinal language, the tale seems to imply
that the brotherly struggles in rivalry and self-assertion might defeat
their need to keep their provider placated—for it was the senior Henry
who could make possible their liberation from Boston and from one
another.

Had Henry usurped William's place in Quincy Street? Their roles
were undergoing a reversal. In a sense Henry was wearing William's
clothes, and he had stepped into William's shoes in the family in which
he had for so long felt himself to be in a subordinate role. The situation
was not unlike Henry's dream of the Louvre; there too the pursuer had
become the pursued. We may speculate that Henry's ambivalences kept
him anchored in Quincy Street—and not least his caution lest he might
have to "go it alone" in the competitive literary world. William James,
on his side, enjoying Europe, was experiencing feelings of guilt as well.
"It seems a sin to be doing such things while Harry is moping at home,"
he wrote in his diary. And in a letter to his sister he uses the language
of the Bible: "I somehow feel as if I were cheating Harry of his birthright." Thus the two brothers played out the drama of Jacob and Esau.
The curious thing was that both cast themselves in the role of Jacob.

Venus and Diana

The young man in Quincy Street held back from the world, and this
meant that he held back from women as well. He seems to have seen little
of Minny Temple during the Cambridge years. She was off at Newport,

or New York, or suburban Pelham, near New Rochelle, where she now lived, in a gay whirl of parties, dances and concerts. But the bright and shining flame of the heroine of his scene was flickering: she was wracked by cough and suffering occasional lung hemorrhages that subdued her dancing body and committed her to silence and rest. There is no evidence that Henry was aware of her condition; she was away in the distance, removed from him, a remote Diana, chaste and active, while Henry continued to hold himself aloof.

In Cambridge he saw a goodly number of women, saw them as creatures to be observed and chatted with at tea; and he formed a series of friendships with various spinsters, notably of the Norton entourage, that endured for many years. Of these, the friendship with Grace Norton, who was nine years older than himself, appears to have been the most enduring; something in her personality, and in her troubled spirit, evoked a response in Henry James and inspired him to write to her certain of the most felicitous letters of his middle years. Miss Norton seems to have poured out her troubles to Henry and received advice, comfort, solace from him. It was largely a pen friendship, for they were, for years, separated by the Atlantic.

A younger friend, intermittently at Cambridge and Newport, was Elizabeth Boott, who was also a friend of Minny Temple. She was the daughter of a widower, Francis Boott, an amateur composer of the elder Henry James's generation, who had lived long in Italy. Lizzie had grown up a graceful, well-tended American-European girl, shy, reserved, proficient in languages and dabbling in art and music. Henry was to see much of her at home and abroad and to enjoy her modest company. This was one of the few friendships of his life with a woman of his own age. However there is not a word in Henry's letters—which Lizzie carefully preserved—to suggest a closer intimacy.

In general Henry felt at Cambridge that the women he saw were "provincial, common, inelegant." They did not appeal to his fancy, he wrote Perry, but he did admit that "perhaps I am grossly insensible." Henry James could take the measure of his countrywomen with a clear sense of their attributes and shortcomings. He could describe them; he could reproduce faithfully their conversation and their manners; he might even try to give a picture of their minds; his intelligence could grasp them—but what were they? Fine pieces of statuary, yes, he could say that and did, likening them in his early tales to Venuses and Dianas and Junos, frozen in stone. They were, when they aroused feeling, or were encountered in the flesh, creatures of mystery and consequently of danger.

When Henry James wasn't writing stories of self-assertion, he wrote of the mystery of womankind, of young men trapped by wily females, of sad heroes betrayed, of curious men circling at a distance from the irrepressible *ewig Weibliche* of literary allusion. In his first acknowledged story the hero in his dying moments sees his fiancée as a statue, a sculptured goddess in a Greek temple. In his next story, "A Landscape Painter," the heroine is the "very portrait of a lady"—her name is Esther Blunt—who marries the hero for his $100,000 a year. He had thought he was being loved for himself. "It was the act of a false woman," the landscape painter blurts out when he discovers the truth. "A false woman?" Esther queries and then smiles: "Come, *you* be a man!" Just how dangerous woman in flesh (or even in stone) could be to man who felt himself deficient in masculinity we have seen from the vampire tale of "De Grey." In the French story that fascinated James, "La Vénus d'Ille," the statue of Venus, upon whose outstretched finger the hero has carelessly placed his engagement ring, comes crashing into the bridal chamber to claim her "fiancé" and crushes him to death. Lovers preyed upon one another, women preyed upon men; the supreme love of Venus could be all-destroying.

In another of James's tales, "Osborne's Revenge," the lawyer hero determines to avenge his dead friend Robert Graham, who committed suicide because of a broken heart. He seeks the acquaintance of the young woman, Henrietta Congreve, feeling a "savage need to hate her." To his surprise, he discovers she is a gentlewoman, of fine intelligence and feeling. The image he has compounded of her as a flirt and a vampire is false; in reality, she never jilted Graham and it was Graham who was over-attentive and volatile. She did not even know of his suicide and believed his death due to natural causes. The tale is that of a man seeking to understand a woman and discovering that he has been in error from start to finish. It speaks of a serious doubt: what if Henry's reading of women were wrong?

Each early tale reveals in its avoidances and hesitations and old-time formalities that Henry James was inexperienced in love, and his heroes do not know how to approach or talk to young women. He can describe —out of observed life—with closeness and humor; and he draws constantly on literature, out of the traditions of poetry and fiction. The love affairs, such as they are, prove ineffectual; the hero's masculinity seems always in question. The men are personally charming, confused, romantic. The young women are shrewd, practical and look like goddesses. In James's experience we can discover no affairs, no mistresses, no shy avowals, only touches of infatuation. We would have difficulty in placing him in a brothel or seeing him yield to some physical impulse. In the stories he seems to be unburdening himself of scruples and reticences. Forty years later his hero Lambert Strether, in late middle age, will confess "a man might have—at all events a man such as he—an amount of experience out of any proportion to his adventures."

William James, in a letter from Dresden of 24 July 1867, urged Harry to "read (if he wants to) an essay by Grimm on the Venus de Milo . . . and compare it with the St. Victor one. Both are imaginative rhapsodies, but how much solider the German! (if I remember right). It is worth reading, Harry." We do not know whether Henry read the Grimm essay; that of Paul de Saint-Victor was published in 1867 in a volume entitled *Hommes et Dieux,* which remained from then until the end of Henry James's life in his library. In the year before his death he scrawled his name on the flyleaf and below it affixed the dates "1867–1915." Saint-Victor endows the Venus de Milo with many qualities that must have evoked a response in Henry James.

> This is the Celestial Venus, the Venus Victorious, always sought, never possessed, as absolute as the life whose central fire resides in her breast. . . . There is not an atom of flesh in her august marble . . . she sprang from a virile mind nourished by the idea and not by the presence of the woman. . . . There are no bones in this superb body, nor tears in its blind eyes, nor entrails in this torso . . . Allow the charm to have its effect . . . rest at the foot of the august marble, as if under the shadow of an ancient oak. Soon a profound peace will course through your soul. The statue will envelop you in its solemn lineaments and you will feel as if you have been enlaced in its absent arms. It will elevate you quietly to the contemplation of pure beauty.

Saint-Victor's subjective reverie, however rhapsodic, corresponds to Henry James's dream of fair women as beings beyond flesh—immortal Venuses, chaste Dianas—translated into imperishable stone where they may be contemplated by the eye and the mind as goddesses. A woman of flesh and blood could be a source of grave anxiety and bewilderment. In stone—or in death—she could be felt as beauty pure. One could even allow oneself to be enlaced by her absent arms.

Venus, Diana—and Jezebel! There were many kinds of women in this world, and a man had to be on guard lest his inner feelings make him attribute qualities that in reality were not there; for women added to their worldly appearance embellishments, trickeries—and treacheries—that were at the same time elegance and luxury and civilizing attributes. When Henry James in October 1868 reviewed a trifling book entitled *Modern Women* in the *Nation,* he came to the conclusion that it was impossible to discuss and condemn modern women apart from modern men. Their follies were all "part and parcel of the follies of modern civilization." They also reflected "with great clearness the state of the heart and the imagination of men." This suggested that women existed as images in men's minds and as "patient, sympathetic, submissive" creatures willing to model themselves upon those very images. Henry James would learn to portray women not as men had fashioned them but as persons. Greater ease with them, and closer study, never banished however his primitive fear of womankind, a symptom of his own troubled sexuality.

The Terrible Burden

One day in September of 1867 in Cambridge, when Henry James was twenty-four, he wrote a long letter to his friend Perry, who was in Paris. In characteristic vein, he begins in French, then lapses into English. He lists his readings; he affirms that English literature is in reality a vast unexplored field, "especially when we compare it to what the French is to the French." In a confiding mood he writes that "Deep in the timorous recesses of my being is a vague desire to do for our dear old English letters and writers *something* of what Sainte-Beuve and the best French critics have done for theirs." And now the serious writer who was being published and noticed in New York and Boston begins to speak. He has no wish, he says, to imitate Sainte-Beuve, "a man of the past":

> we young Americans are (without cant) men of the future. I feel that my only chance for success as a critic is to let all the breezes of the west blow through me at their will. We are Americans born—*il faut en prendre son parti.* I look upon it as a great blessing; and I think that to be an American is an excellent preparation for culture. We have exquisite qualities as a race, and it seems to me that we are ahead of the European races in the fact that more than either of them we can deal freely with forms of civilization not our own, can pick and choose and assimilate and in short (aesthetically etc.) claim our property wherever we find it. To have no national stamp has hitherto been a regret and a drawback, but I think it not unlikely that American writers may yet indicate that a vast intellectual fusion and synthesis of the various National tendencies of the world is the condition of more important achievements than any we have seen.

He had had a vision during these solitary months in Cambridge, at the end of the long summer during which he had not budged from the paternal home: with remarkable prescience he had studied his native land and looked into himself and seen the future; for it was he who would deal "freely with forms of civilization not our own." James was determined from the first to be an American artist, determined to discover what his native land could offer his art. At the same time his ideal was that "vast intellectual fusion and synthesis" which was to become the melting-pot dream of later decades. What he could not foresee in the

Cambridge quiet of the 1860s was the great abyss that would open up between the tight little eastern society, which was the America of Henry James, and the floodtide of immigration and the industrial growth that followed the Civil War.

To Charles Eliot Norton he wrote, some time later, "Looking about for myself I conclude that the face of nature and civilization in this our country is to a certain point a very sufficient literary field. But," he added, "it will yield its secrets only to a really *grasping* imagination." And again to the same correspondent, "It's a complex fate, being an American, and one of the responsibilities it entails is fighting against a superstitious valuation of Europe."

The years of James's young manhood in Cambridge were filled with close and studious observation of the American life around him. He did not attempt to write of Europe until he could see it with adult eyes. His first thirteen tales—those to which he signed his name—deal exclusively with his homeland. He confined himself to the people of his particular world, those who lived the leisured cultivated life of Newport and Boston. His characters were either rich young men, dilettantes, artists, doctors, lawyers, unhappy Civil War veterans from the middle class, young heiresses, and in one instance a young gentleman farmer. His first novel, *Watch and Ward,* was set in Boston; later in the Balzac-Zola manner he "did" the city in a full-length work. The America and Americans he observed during the ten years between his adolescent return from Europe and his later journeys abroad remained with him all his life.

James was alive to the virtues and shortcomings of his countrymen; he considered himself an American artist-in-the-making—with one important difference. Unlike some of his fellow-artists, he brought to his observation the cultivated cosmopolitanism of his early years and his literary saturation. He could not accept his Americanism lightly; he had seen the world sufficiently to take nothing in it for granted. He had spoken of his "complex fate"; he was later to speak of it as a "terrible burden" which no European writer had to assume.

A Suburban Friendship

He talked of these questions, of America and Europe and of his writing, with a new-found friend during these Cambridge years—a man seven years older than himself who admired his work and encouraged it and was himself a writer freshly returned from a stay in Italy. This was William Dean Howells, who had just moved to Cambridge to become the assistant editor of the *Atlantic Monthly.*

In later years the legend grew that it was Howells who gave Henry his start in the world of letters. It was, as with all legends, partly true.

When Howells assumed his post at the *Atlantic* two of Henry's stories had appeared in it and a third had been accepted. Howells remembered that the first Jamesian tale to reach his desk was "Poor Richard," late in 1866. J. T. Fields had asked Howells whether the story should be accepted, and the new editor replied, "Yes, and all the stories you can get from the writer."

Norton and Lowell at the *North American Review* were older men; they published Henry, but could not become his intimates. Godkin and his staff were in New York, and Henry's relationship to the *Nation,* while close, was essentially that of a reviewer who supplies his copy and is paid for it; his relationship with a fourth journal, the *Galaxy,* begun in 1866, was formal. At the *Atlantic* J. T. Fields had accepted Henry James as a promising young man to be encouraged among imposing Brahmins. Now, however, William Dean Howells, himself a would-be novelist, full of the memories of his Venetian years (where he had been American Consul during the Civil War, the reward for a campaign biography of Lincoln), proved to be an editor who could also be a friend; he was young enough and close enough to Henry's generation to understand him and have deep faith in his art and his future. "Talking of talks," Howells wrote in December 1866 to Edmund Clarence Stedman, the New York banker-poet,

> young Henry James and I had a famous one last evening, two or three hours long, in which we settled the true principles of literary art. He is a very earnest fellow, and I think him extremely gifted—gifted enough to do better than anyone has yet done towards making us a real American novel. We have in reserve from him a story for the *Atlantic* which I'm sure you'll like.

The story was "Poor Richard." After it appeared Howells wrote to Norton that an adverse notice of the tale in the *Nation* made him feel unsure of Henry's public. The *Nation* critic wondered whether a character as loutish and belligerent as Richard would have "entertained a doubt as to his inferiority" in the presence of the two Civil War officers and the heroine. He also noted Henry's fondness "for handling delicate shreds of feeling and motives in the intricate web of character." This prompted Howells to observe that "James has every element of success in fiction. But I suspect that he must in a great degree create his audience"—a balanced and prophetic judgment.

Howells and James remained friends all their lives, in a relationship that was both professional and intimate. Their correspondence of almost half a century testifies to Howells's esteem from the first for his younger contemporary and an unswerving belief in his literary powers; there is, in some of his later letters, pride in Henry James's achievement and a genuine humility and awareness of his own narrower limits. They sent each other their novels. Henry always took pains to read and discuss Howells's work—and even on occasions to borrow suggestions from it. His strictures expressed always in the kindest terms his feeling of Howells's artistic limitations; he was candid, but in a gentle and generous way.

"I sometimes wish . . . for something a little larger,—for a little more *ventilation,*" he wrote to Howells in one instance while proclaiming that "the merit and the charm quite run away with the defect." When he read *A Hazard of New Fortunes* he wrote to his brother:

> I have just been reading, with wonder and admiration, Howells's last big novel . . . His abundance and facility are my constant wonder and envy —or rather not perhaps, envy, inasmuch as he has purchased them by throwing the whole question of form, style and composition overboard into the deep sea—from which, on my side, I am perpetually trying to fish them up.

On the following day he wrote to Howells himself: "The novelist is a particular *window,* absolutely—and of worth in so far as he is one"; and, he went on, "it's because you open so well and are hung so close over the street that *I* could hang out of it all day long. Your very value is that you choose your own street—heaven forbid I should have to choose it for you." The "usual imbecility" in fiction, he said, is that

> the reader never touches the subject and the subject never touches the reader: the window is no window at all—but only childishly *finta,* like the ornaments of our beloved Italy—this is why as a triumph of *communication,* I hold the *Hazard* so rare and strong.

The praise is subtle and confined to that which Henry could honestly praise. He is saying, ever so gently, that his friend's novel is limited, and implying that if it is a triumph of communication it is not necessarily a triumph of art.

The friendship between James and Howells was never more intimate than during its early years, when the two young men took suburban walks on Sundays to Fresh Pond, talking of their art and their ambitions, or when they sat, as they did one November day, in the thin pale sunlight, on the edge of a hotbed of violets at the Botanical Gardens, with Howells cheerfully punching his stick into a sandy path while the talk followed a spontaneous and meandering course. Howells could talk about Italian writers and about Italy, and then refer back to his native Ohio; he had had a childhood in a log cabin and had gone to work in his father's print-shop. Henry, the young patrician, could evoke old New York, and describe his innumerable relatives and his European boyhood. If Howells talked of Hawthorne, whom he had met, Henry talked of Balzac and of Sainte-Beuve, whom he had closely read. And if Henry submitted to the *Atlantic* two rather Hawthorne-like tales, we are led to suspect it was to meet Howells's preferences at this time for the romance, and not necessarily because he had himself fallen under the American novelist's influence.

George Moore once remarked that Henry James went abroad and read Turgenev while William Dean Howells stayed at home and read Henry James. The remark was unkind but in a sense true. Henry was cosmopolitan; Howells was provincial. Howells wanted above all, during his early years, to become a Boston Brahmin. On his first visit to the American Athens he had been treated with marked respect by Lowell, Fields and Holmes; the memory of that time, and of his talk with other Bostonians and the great Concordians, was kept green all his life. He was later to reach toward realism and to flirt earnestly with socialism; yet his reach had sharp limits and his flirtation was on the sentimental side. Henry had more rigorous, if more conservative, standards and more dazzling aims. Five years after meeting him, the young novelist could write —still from Quincy Street—to Charles Eliot Norton:

> Howells is now monarch absolute of the *Atlantic* to the increase of his profit and comfort. His talent grows constantly in fineness but hardly, I think, in range of application . . . He has little intellectual curiosity, so here he stands with his admirable organ of style, like a poor man holding a diamond and wondering how he can wear it. It's rather sad, I think, to see Americans of the younger sort so unconscious and unambitious of the commission to do the *best.* For myself the love of art and letters grows steadily with my growth.

This was not only a candid evaluation of a literary friend: it was the expression also of Henry's own ambition and passion—to do the *best,* to surpass himself, to grow, to escape from the present into the future, to take as his models in his art those who had in his time come as near attaining what he deemed to be perfection. Henry was supremely confident that, when *he* found himself holding the diamond of his style and art, he would know what to do with it.

6

THE
PASSIONATE
PILGRIMAGE

𝒯

Departure

In later years Henry James remembered how quiet the house had been when he called to say good-bye to Minny Temple. She entered the old spacious parlor with her swift sliding step and her old free laugh. She was slight, erect, thin, almost transparent. He remembered ruefully that he thought her delicate appearance "becoming."

En route to Europe, he had journeyed in mid-February of 1869 to Pelham to bid farewell to his cousin. He told her his plans. He would go to England, then to the Continent, perhaps to winter in Paris or to push southward to Italy, where he had never been. They agreed it was "wholly detestable" that he should be voyaging off while she was staying behind. The doctors had talked to her about another climate. Perhaps the cousins would meet next winter in Rome.

They talked of writers. Minny had come to have "an overpowering admiration and affection"—so she said—for George Eliot. Did Henry intend to meet her? She would like very much to see that woman. They parted gaily. Perhaps they *would* see each other soon abroad. He would write.

"Harry came to see me before he sailed for Europe," Minny wrote to John Gray. "I am very glad that he has gone, although I don't expect to see him again in a good many years."

The Banquet of Initiation

He stepped ashore from the steamer, the *S.S. China,* at Liverpool on a windy, cloudy, smoky day, Saturday, 27 February 1869. The black steamers were knocking about in the yellow Mersey under a low sky that almost touched their funnels. There was the promise of spring in the air

and "the solemnity of an opening era." By the time he had brought his
luggage to the Adelphi Hotel in a hansom, it was two o'clock. In the
deserted coffee-room he drank his tea and ate his boiled egg and toasted
muffin, folding and refolding the crisp copy of *The Times,* much too
excited to notice its contents. The damp dark light floated in from the
steep street; a coal fire glowed in the room's obscurity. "The impressions
of my boyhood return from my own past and swarm about my soul," he
wrote home a few hours after his arrival. "I enjoy these first hours of
landing most deeply."

He slept soundly that night, exhausted by his voyage, the excitement
of arrival and the afternoon in Liverpool. He had planned to go to Chester
on Sunday, but he overslept. When he arose he found the rain coming
down monotonously upon the gloomy shut-up city; he snatched a hurried
breakfast and caught the London train.

Arriving at Euston Station at dusk, Henry engaged a four-wheeler
into which his luggage was piled and rode through the town to Morley's
Hotel in Trafalgar Square. "What terrible places are these English hotels!" he exclaimed in a letter to his mother. There was, however, a warm
fire in the coffee-room and the heavy mahogany furniture gleamed in its
light. In his room the large four-poster bed was lit up luridly by the
bedroom candle. For the moment he felt homesick, although he may
have been exaggerating for the benefit of Quincy Street.

The mood passed quickly enough. He sallied forth early next morning, purchased a pair of gloves, went down to the City, probably to take
care of his letter of credit, and "all history appeared to live again." He
took a walk along the Strand, dallied before the shop-windows, resisting
the temptation to buy everything. London, old and new, the city of boyhood memory, and of history, and of mid-Victorian reality, assumed an
air of magnificence, a grand tone it was ever to have for him in spite of
its slums and squalor, its dirt and darkness. He imagined it as a great
Goliath, and this suggests that he must have thought of himself as a
young David. He was to conceive of cities, and London in particular, as
places to be besieged, conquered, possessed.

Charles Eliot Norton was in London with his wife and his sisters
Grace and Jane. Norton introduced Henry to a young Englishman named
Albert Rutson, who told him there were furnished rooms available below
those he occupied. Within three or four days of his arrival Henry had
transported his luggage from Morley's to No. 7 Half Moon Street, just off
Piccadilly. He had dark rooms on the ground floor decorated with litho-
graphs and wax flowers. He could hear the din at the end of the street,
and as he stared into the fire "a sudden horror of the whole place" came
over him. His rooms seemed "an impersonal black hole in the huge
general blackness." He would rather "remain dinnerless, would rather

even starve than sally forth into the infernal town, where the natural fate of an obscure stranger would be to be trampled to death in Piccadilly and his carcass thrown into the Thames." This sense of powerlessness in the face of London made him wish he were in Quincy Street "with my head on mother's lap and my feet in Alice's!"

Henry may have feared at first to venture out for dinner, but presently he found himself resorting with some regularity to the Albany—the name could not have been a happier one for the grandson of the first William James—a small eating-house in Piccadilly. It had compartments as narrow as horse-stalls, and the feeders sat against the high straight backs of the wooden benches so close to one another that they seemed to be waving their knives and forks under their respective noses as they ate their mutton chops. Every face in the establishment was a documentary scrap, every sound was strong to the ear, and the scene that greeted him there was as definite as some of the Dutch paintings of low life.

The first phase of Henry's pilgrimage was in the fullest degree, as he put it, "a banquet of initiation." If his senses fed on London, he also discovered how sociable England could be when it was host to a cultivated young American provided with unusual credentials. The note of hospitality was struck with great promptness in his own lodging when young Rutson invited Henry to breakfast with him upstairs. There the American discovered a fellow-guest, the Hon. George Broderick, son of Lord Midleton, like Rutson bewhiskered in the Victorian fashion. They ate fried sole and marmalade and Henry was questioned closely about President Grant's new Cabinet—but he was at a loss to offer any tidbits of American political intelligence.

Two or three days after settling in his lodgings, Leslie Stephen, then thirty-seven, called to invite him to lunch. They had met in Boston; Stephen was a fellow contributor to the *Nation.* Jane Norton also was a guest at the lunch, and in the afternoon Stephen took his American visitors by the London underground to the Zoo in Regent's Park. In the evening Henry dined with the Nortons, and went with them to University College, to hear John Ruskin lecture on Greek myths.

Another day he goes with Norton to call on William Morris in Queen Square. Morris, short, burly, corpulent, carelessly dressed, loud-voiced, says no one thing that Henry can remember, yet all he utters shows good judgment. Above all Henry is enchanted by Morris's wife. "O ma chère," he writes to Alice, "such a wife! *Je n'en reviens pas*—she haunts me still." A "tall lean woman in a long dress of some dead purple stuff, guiltless of hoops (or of anything else, I should say)," she is a figure "cut out of a missal—or out of one of Rossetti's or Hunt's pictures." They stay to dinner. Then Mrs. Morris, suffering from toothache, stretches out on the sofa with a handkerchief over her face while Morris reads an unpublished poem about Bellerophon, "a legend of prodigies and terrors . . . around is all the picturesque bric-à-brac of the apartment . . . and in the corner this dark silent medieval woman with her medieval toothache." Later Henry visited Rossetti's studio, in "the most delicious melancholy old house at Chelsea"; at this time he also met Edward Burne-Jones, destined to become a warm friend.

A few days after meeting Morris, he dined at Denmark Hill with the great defender of the Pre-Raphaelites, John Ruskin. To his mother he described him as "scared back by the grim face of reality into the world of unreason and illusion," where he wandered "without a compass and a guide—or any light save the fitful flashes of his beautiful genius." Again at Ruskin's, it was the women-folk who interested him; but what he enjoyed even more than Ruskin's two nieces was a portrait by Titian —"an old Doge, a work of transcendent beauty and elegance such as to give one a new sense of the meaning of art."

He dines often with the Nortons, not so much because of Norton himself, but because the Norton women are friendly and congenial. One day he goes with Susan, Norton's wife, to lunch with the Darwins and for a memorable stroll through Holwood Park. He visits the British Museum to see the Elgin Marbles; he visits the Kensington Museum and on a grey raw day he takes the penny steamer and rides on the Thames. He goes to Hampton Court and Windsor, Richmond and Dulwich; he inspects towers and temples and cathedrals; he strolls endlessly through the National Gallery, finding Titian's *Bacchus and Ariadne* "one of the great facts" of the universe. One afternoon, as he studies the painting, he becomes aware of a little man talking vivaciously with another man beside him—the little man with astonishing auburn hair "perched on a scarce perceptible body" Henry promptly recognizes as the author of *Atalanta in Calydon.* "I thrilled . . . that I should be admiring Titian in the same breath with Mr. Swinburne—that is in the same breath in which *he* admired Titian and in which I also admired *him.*"

Henry was in the "best of health and spirits," he wrote to his mother after a month of this busy London life. He was exaggerating somewhat; in reality, he had begun to suffer from a recurrent and debilitating costiveness which he attributed to over-indulgence at London eating-houses. In deference to his sluggish condition he went, in early April, to Malvern and took up residence in the therapeutic establishment of Dr. Raynor. The regimen there consisted of a cold bath on rising, a walk to "get up a reaction," breakfast at eight-thirty, another bath at noon, followed by another reactionary walk. Dinner was at two, and at five Henry took a running sitz-bath. Tea was at seven; an early bedtime was prescribed.

The baths do not seem to have been particularly helpful, and Henry enjoyed most of all the walks over the sloping pastures of the Malvern hills. It was April and the whole land had burst into spring. As he walked to get his "reactions," he carried a sketch-book; for the first time since his Newport days with La Farge, he sketched hills and trees and spreading willows.

Henry spent three comparatively sedentary weeks at Malvern and then decided that what he really needed was "plain, physical movement." He accordingly visited Raglan Castle, Monmouth, Tintern Abbey and Chepstow; he went to Worcester by coach, to Gloucester and to Newport; he spent a day at Tewkesbury. He visited Salisbury and Ely, Blenheim and Winchester. At Oxford, bearing letters from Leslie Stephen and the Nortons, he dined in Hall at Christ Church, and at Lincoln was the guest of the rector, Mark Pattison, and his young wife, who was in riding-habit and inclined to use slang of which Henry disapproved. He wondered whether an English woman could be emancipated "except coldly and wantonly."

Deeply stirred alike by their architecture, their quiet and their summer-term beauty, he wandered through the Oxford colleges. He lingered by New College's ancient wall; he spent a dreaming hour or two in St. John's spacious garden; he walked in Christ Church meadow. In the college gardens, Henry wrote, he wanted to lie on the grass "in the happy belief the world is all an English garden and time a fine old English afternoon."

The little English tour lasted three weeks, after which Henry returned to London. Writing to Quincy Street, he reported his improved health and mentioned, among other things, that the trip had cost him £60—a largish sum for a somewhat limited journey. Quincy Street was startled and disturbed. William promptly wrote on behalf of the elder Henry to say that "it seems a pity to let such a sum go in a single escapade." Worried lest his parents should think him improvident, Henry wrote a long and troubled letter to his father.

> To have you think that I am extravagant with these truly sacred funds sickens me to the heart and I hasten insofar as I may to reassure you . . . As to the expenses of my journey, in telling that tale about the £60 I acted on gross misinformation. I was circulated for nearly three weeks and spent less than £25, seeing a very great deal on it.

He had spent during his eleven weeks in England £120, distributed among five weeks in London, three at an expensive water-cure and three in traveling. It covered the purchase of considerable clothing and articles of permanent use, but "very little trivial, careless or random expenditure," except perhaps a large amount of cab-hire. "I have treated you to this financial budget," he added, "as a satisfaction to myself rather than because I suppose you expect it." He did not want his enjoyment of travel to be diminished by "constant self-torturing as to expense." In a word, he wanted a little more family faith in his ability to act responsibly.

In a letter to William, he spoke of a need to lay the foundations for an education in the great works of painting and sculpture "which may be of future use to me." He also had to make the most of the opportunity to visit the great cities and historic places on the Continent. "I shall hang on to a place till it has yielded me its drop of life-blood," he said. "In this way I hope to get a good deal for my money and to make it last a long time. How long I know not. When it is gone I shall come home," and he added, "a new man." He still had £867 in his letter of credit.

In London that spring, he kept his promise to Minny Temple. "I was much interested in your account of George Eliot," she wrote to him. Another account, of 10 May 1869, written for Henry's father, records the impression the novelist made on him:

> She is magnificently ugly—deliciously hideous. She has a low fore-head, a dull grey eye, a vast pendulous nose, a huge mouth full of uneven teeth and a chin and jawbone *qui n'en finissent pas* ... Now in this vast ugliness resides a most powerful beauty which, in a very few minutes, steals forth and charms the mind, so that you end as I ended, in falling in love with her. Yes behold me literally in love with this great horse-faced blue-stocking. ... Altogether, she has a larger circumference than any woman I have ever seen.

On this first occasion, although agitated over the illness of one of G. H. Lewes's sons, George Eliot was cordial and communicative. In her black silk dress and the lace mantilla attached to her head, with the low-falling thickness of her dark hair, she was "illustratively" great—there was grace in her anxiety that day and "a frank immediate appreciation of our presence." He counted it the "one marvel" of his stay in London—that he should have been admitted to her distinguished presence.

The Dishevelled Nymph

England, he wrote to his family, had been "a good married matron." Switzerland, where he spent the summer, was a "magnificent man." Italy, which he reached late in the autumn of 1869, he found to be a "beautiful dishevelled nymph," whom at regular intervals all his life he was to pursue.

When, in mid-May, Henry crossed the Channel to rediscover the Continent, Boulogne looked as if he had left it yesterday, only it seemed much smaller. In Paris, where he stayed for a day while waiting for the train to Switzerland, he enjoyed the magnificence of the new boulevards; but they were too monumental and certainly, for Henry's Cambridge taste, over-lit at night. Too much "flare and glare." Between noon and night Henry visited the Salon and strolled through the eternal Louvre. "Oh the tumult and the splendour," he exclaimed to his mother, "the headlong race for pleasure—and the stagnant gulf of misery to be seen in two great capitals like London and Paris."

After this, Switzerland was calm, cool, quiet. Geneva was still the city of his youth. Henry took long walks over familiar boyhood paths, visiting Coppet, with its memories of Madame de Staël, and the Ferney of Voltaire. For a time he settled at Glion in a hotel-*pension* on the mountainside, above the castle. Finding himself fit and strong, he began to tramp through Switzerland, as he had done in his youth. "I feel," he wrote on 12 July 1869 to William, who was still ailing at home, "as if every walk I take is a burning and shining light for your encouragement." A month later at Lucerne he was glowing with a sense of well-being.

His mother now suggested that perhaps a winter in Paris, or even Germany, as William urged, might be more frugal (and sensible) than a winter of "recreation" in Italy. But Henry's mind was made up. "The only economy for me," he wrote, "is to get thoroughly well and into such a state as that I can work." A winter in Italy would "help me on further than anything else I know of." In thinking of the proposed Italian sojourn as "an occasion not only of physical regeneration but of serious culture too (culture of the kind which alone I have now at twenty-six any time left for)" he found "the courage to maintain my proposition even in the face of your allusions to the need of economy at home." Whereupon Mary James went to an opposite extreme. "Take the fullest liberty and enjoyment your tastes and inclinations crave, and we will promise heartily to foot the bill. Italy will be just the place for you; and do not, I pray you, cramp yourself in any way to hinder your fullest enjoyment of it."

By mid-August, at Lucerne, Henry had had his fill of Switzerland. "What was Switzerland after all? Little else but brute nature, of which at home we have enough and to spare. . . . I pined for a cathedral or a gallery." Thus muses his narrator in a story written shortly afterwards which catalogues his life at Lucerne.

One morning at the beginning of September, he marked his luggage "Milan" and took the steamboat at Lucerne. He approached Italy across the Alps partly by coach and partly on foot. Crossing the Devil's Bridge high on the long monotonous St. Gothard road, he tramped over the Simplon and down the winding highway thirty-three miles to the frontier town of Iselle and into Italy, "warm and living and palpable," the Italy of the Romantics. To William a few days later, he wrote of "that mighty summer's day upon the Simplon when I communed with immensity and sniffed Italy from afar."

His impressions were new and he had a sense of strangeness in that land where the late summer lingered in the north and the soft landscape wrapped him in enchantment. He came to Maggiore and Como, and paused at Cadenabbia on Como's shore, "the pink villas gleaming through their shrubberies of orange and oleander, the mountains shimmering in the hazy light like so many breasts of doves, the constant presence of the melodious Italian voice." He could not surrender completely to the "Spirit of the South," but "I nevertheless *feel* it in all my pulses."

He is in Milan, in the brooding heat, before Leonardo's *Last Supper.* "I have looked at no other picture with an emotion equal to that which rose within me as this great creation of Leonardo slowly began to dawn upon my intelligence from the tragical twilight of its ruin." He goes to the Certosa of Pavia, the Carthusian monastery south of Milan. And then, unhurried, he turns the pages of Italy's early history . . . Brescia, Mantua, Verona, Vicenza, Padua, a chain of towns constituting his avenue to Venice, shabby, deserted, dreary, unclean, into which the sun pours fiercely, dead little towns yet how full of the past! Henry sat in the cafés and walked about with his Murray and his Baedeker—and in his pocket *La Chartreuse de Parme.* He is reading Stendhal for the first time. At Verona in the Caffé Dante, in the Piazza dei Signori, he lingers three nights running until midnight, experiencing the scene: the slender brick campanile, the white statute of Dante, the ancient palace—wherever he turns in Italy he finds "a vital principle of grace," whether it is in the smile of a chambermaid or the curve of an arch. And at every step he feels "the aesthetic presence of the past" and gathers "some lingering testimony to the exquisite vanity of ambition." It was as if this hot Italian sun and these dark shadows created by the venerable stones of old buildings alternately warmed and cooled his American blood, so that feeling could first melt and then be poured into the crucible of the intellect. The young intellectual from Quincy Street had become quite suddenly a sentimental and impassioned traveler.

He came into Venice toward the end of a mid-September day when the shadows began to lengthen and the light to glow. He caught the distant sea-smell, glimpsed the water, the domes, the spires, and then the brown-skinned white-shirted gondolier swept him through the water amid slimy brick, battered marble, rags, dirt, decay. It was not, however, Venice in its details, but Venice in its totality that fired his imagination. With Ruskin in his pocket he walked or floated through the city; he explored church and palace; he discovered Veronese, Bellini, Tintoretto. He devoted many hours to contemplating the latter's two Crucifixions and writing William long letters about him. "I'd give a great deal," Henry burst out, "to be able to fling down a dozen of his pictures into prose of corresponding force and colour." He admires Bellini and goes to out-of-the-way churches to look at his work. Each of his pictures seemed to Henry "a genuine act of worship."

The mere use of his eyes in Venice was happiness enough. Even the children, clamoring for coppers from the tourists, playing "on the lonely margin of a decaying world, in prelude to how bleak or to how dark a destiny," were remembered. It was a melancholy city—in a sense the most beautiful of tombs. However, gondolas spoilt one (he wrote William) for a return to common life. James's first stay in Venice lasted a fortnight. He frequented the cafés and studied the people; he went to the Lido—then a very natural place, with only a rough lane across the little island from the landing-place to the beach—and dined on the wooden terrace, looking at the sea. At the Academy he glimpsed the Bronsons, of Newport, not yet residents of Venice; Mrs. Bronson was destined to become his closest American-Venetian friend.

Early in October he traveled to Florence by easy stages, Padua to Ferrara, Bologna, the Parma of Stendhal, finally Firenze, in that time of the year when the sun is still hot, the evenings cool and the city's aspect softly jeweled in riverine and mountain setting. Florence caught his fancy as no other city in Italy. The Tuscan palaces with their pure symmetry had for him the nobility of Greek architecture; there was less romantic shabbiness here than in the Lombardian and Venetian towns, and when it did occur, as in the group of old houses on the north side of the Arno, between the Ponte Vecchio and the Ponte Santa Trinità, it was, in the yellow light with mellow mouldering surfaces, "the perfect felicity of picturesqueness." Henry spent his mornings at the Uffizi or the Pitti; he went on his regular walks; he explored the churches, the squares, the cafés, as in the other towns and cities. He accompanied Charles Eliot Norton on a villa-hunt: and confessing that Florence had its gloomy aspects, he nevertheless found in its architecture "a charm inexpressible, indefinable."

In the Tuscan city he had casual encounters with fellow-countrymen, known and unknown, as when he

> fell in with a somewhat seedy and sickly American, who seemed to be doing the gallery with an awful minuteness, and who after some conversation proposed to come and see me.... I anticipate no wondrous joy from his acquaintance.

William had asked Henry how the English compared with the Americans, and Henry replied, of the latter:

> There is but one word to use in regard to them—vulgar, vulgar, vulgar. Their ignorance—their stingy, defiant grudging attitude towards everything European—their perpetual reference of all things to some American standard or precedent which exists only in their own unscrupulous windbags—and then our unhappy poverty of voice, of speech, and of physiognomy—these things glare at you hideously.

This passage has often been quoted as evidence of James's intolerant and snobbish attitude towards his fellow-countrymen in Europe. Yet in the same letter Henry went on to say,

> On the other hand, we seem a people of *character*, we seem to have energy, capacity and intellectual stuff in ample measure. What I have pointed at as our vices are the elements of the modern man with *culture* quite left out. It's the absolute and incredible lack of *culture* that strikes you in common travelling Americans.

As an artist and social satirist, James drew his Americans as he found them in those European galleries and streets, cathedrals and cafés, along the well-beaten nineteenth-century tourist paths—and often the satire hurt.

Early in October, in Florence, Henry's health, which had shown constant improvement, took a turn for the worse. It was again not the backache, but the constipation which had led him earlier to Malvern. On 16 October 1869, he wrote to William, then the newest of new M.D.s, a letter describing his symptoms and his sufferings and the treatment he received from an Irish doctor practicing in Florence. A week later he began to ponder curtailing his trip and returning to Malvern to take the waters.

Reduced to a pathetic state, he dragged himself about Florence uncomfortable in body, unhappy in mind and deeply disturbed at the prospect of having to leave Italy in a renewed search for health. On 26 October he wrote William that his condition was "unbearable." He posted the letter and began an easy stroll, through the Roman Gate and into the country. Three miles beyond the gate he came to a hillside; on its summit he perceived a Carthusian monastery resembling a medieval fortress and "lifting against the sky, around the bell-tower of its gorgeous chapel, a kind of coronet of clustered cells." It was but five minutes of uphill climb to reach its lower gate, past a clamoring group of beggars thrusting their stumps of limbs at him. He gained admission and inspected the great proportions of the church, designed by the primitive painter Andrea Orcagna. He visited the subterranean oratories and the funeral vaults, he looked at the dwellings of the monks in the great pillared quadrangles, lying half in the sun and half in the shade. The little chambers were cold and musty; the view, beyond the Arno and the clustered towers of Florence, magnificent. A second letter of the day to William shows a great calm, the descent of an inner peace. "On coming out," Henry wrote to his brother, "I swore to myself that while I had life in my body I wouldn't leave a country where adventures of that complexion are the common incidents of your daily constitutional: but that I would hurl myself upon Rome and fight it out on this line at the peril of my existence."

The weather had turned cold and there was much rain. He took reluctant leave and in the bleak dawn of 30 October 1869 he reached the Eternal City.

The letter Henry James wrote to William that evening after his first solitary day in Papal Rome was an ecstatic outburst, a page of exuberant rhetoric, as if he had to inscribe the emotion of the moment for posterity —which indeed he did. Fully conscious of his literary powers, he could not resist "writing" a subject to the hilt the moment he put pen to paper. His letters home were destined, moreover, for an invisible recipient who would read them later in the American setting—himself. "They will serve me in the future," he told his family, "as a series of notes or observations—the only ones I shall have written." On this evening in Rome Henry wrote:

> At last—for the time—I live! It beats everything: it leaves the Rome of your fancy—your education—nowhere. It makes Venice—Florence— Oxford—London—seem like little cities of pasteboard. I went reeling and moaning thro' the streets, in a fever of enjoyment. In the course of four or five hours I traversed almost the whole of Rome and got a glimpse of everything—the Forum, the Coliseum (stupendissimo!), the Pantheon, the Capitol, St. Peter's, the Column of Trajan, the Castle of St. Angelo— all the Piazzas and ruins and monuments. . . . Even if I should leave Rome tonight I should feel that I have caught the keynote of its operation on the senses. I have looked along the grassy vista of the Appian Way and seen the topmost stone-work of the Coliseum sitting shrouded in the light of heaven, like the edge of an Alpine chain. I've trod the Forum and I have scaled the Capitol. I've seen the Tiber hurrying along, as swift and dirty as history! . . . In fine I've seen Rome, and I shall go to bed a wiser man than I last rose—yesterday morning.

James would come to see Rome less ecstatically, as a muddy provincial city in which papal power was shrinking even while he was visiting it. But he caught it at the last moment of its old splendor—the romance of antiquity aside. "A leaf out of the Middle Ages," he wrote as he saw the Pope arrive at a church opposite his hotel, surrounded by cardinals and ambassadors. He remembered the Vatican draped in scarlet, the scarlet coaches of the cardinals, the *monsignori* in their purple stockings followed by solemn servants, the sobriety of the papal newspapers, the traces that Lords Spiritual still presided by divine emanation over the rites of mere humans.

Secular Rome, and above all antique Rome, touched Henry more profoundly. The Pantheon loomed out of its centuries with a "delicacy" of grandeur; it seemed to him more worshipful than the most mysterious and aspiring Gothic. St. Peter's was a "first-class sensation"; but the Protestant side of Henry James turned away to admire the statue of Marcus Aurelius at the Capitol. As between "that poor sexless old Pope" and the imperial Aurelian legs astride the splendid horse "swinging in their immortal bronze," Henry James cried out to Quincy Street, "Here at last was a *man!*"

His health improved during his first weeks in Rome, almost as if the stimulus to his mind and senses ministered to physical well-being. He systematically visited all sections of the Holy City, churches, sculptures, ragged columns, ancient stones, shabby princely old palaces—and then "the great violet Campagna." He was regularly at the Vatican museum; he spent hours in the Colosseum, then still filled with earth and flowers. He watched the parade of priests, and the French troops supporting the Pope against the Risorgimento during these last crucial months of that historic drama—troops soon to be diverted, at the first cannon-burst of the Franco-Prussian War. He visited the graves of Keats and Shelley in the Protestant Cemetery, with its grey pyramid inserted into the sky on one side and the dark cold cypresses on the other.

"I see no people, to speak of, or for that matter to speak to," he wrote home. Towards the end of his Roman stay, however, he met some members of the American colony, including the American sculptor William Wetmore Story, "very civil and his statues very clever." In December he went to Naples and wandered sadly among the excavations of Pompeii. For Christmas he returned to Rome, having made up his mind by this time that he would curtail his Italian journey. He was still unwell. On 27 December, the day before he left Rome, he went to San Pietro to bid farewell to Michelangelo's statue of Moses, and decided that of all the artists who had wrought in Italy he was the greatest. His energy, positiveness, courage, marked him as a "real man of action in art." For one whose ambition was to be such a man, the figure of Moses, leader of men, could speak eloquently. In describing the figure to William, however, and stressing its "health and movement," Henry was to a degree accentuating his own wish for similar health and strength—and power.

Next day he took the train for Assisi, and had there "a deep delicious bath of medievalism." He went on to Perugia and Siena and thence to

Florence, to which he bade a farewell of much greater intensity than he had thought possible. "The whole affair," he said, speaking of his decision to leave Italy in a letter to his father written when he reached Genoa,

> was brutally and doggedly carried through by a certain base creature called Prudence, acting in the interest of a certain base organ which shall be nameless. The angel within me sate by with trembling fluttering wings watching these two brutes at their work. And oh! how that angel longs to spread these wings into the celestial blue of freedom and waft himself back to the city of his heart . . . Last night I spent—so to speak —in tears.

The city of his heart was Florence.

As he turned his face toward the winter sleet and drizzle of England, he was deeply depressed. He regarded his decision as an act of courage, "the deliberate, cold-blooded, conscious, turning of my back on Italy." It required a great will to turn one's back upon a dishevelled nymph.

Minny Temple

The dream that they—Henry and Minny—might meet in Rome had been only a dream. The months during which Henry had been discovering Europe were months of serious illness for Minny. Of this Henry appears to have been unaware. He continued to have hopes of meeting her. Twice in September 1869 he asked his mother: "What of Minny Temple's coming to Italy?" "Is Minny coming abroad?"

In the weeks after Henry's departure for Europe, Minny had frequent lung hemorrhages. The doctors knew little that could help. They prescribed quiet to that dancing spirit and she went to bed, at Pelham, at Newport or in Philadelphia, wherever she might be among her numerous relatives. Then, when she felt better, she would start a new cycle of visits, sleigh-rides, concerts, dances—followed by an inevitable relapse. Her letters to John Chipman Gray (some of them printed in *Notes of a Son and Brother*) speak of "my old enemy haemorrhage," and she tallies them for him: she had had "seven big ones" on one occasion and several smaller. "I can't stop them." The voice is unresigned, helpless yet full of courage. "I mean to beat them yet." She speaks freely of death, laughs at it with the free laughter of her twenty-three years.

Her letters to Henry James are written with the same candor as those to Gray. "I have had no more interesting news so far to give you but of my repeated illness, so I thought I would spare you," she writes from Newport in June of 1869. "My darling Harry," she writes, and parenthesizes, "You don't mind if I am a little affectionate now that you are so far

away, do you?" She tells him that his last letter "reached me while I was
in the very act of having the third haemorrhage of that day, and it quite
consoles me, for them."

> I am most happy to know that you are well and enjoying yourself. If you
> were not my cousin I would write and ask you to marry me and take me
> with you, but as it is, it wouldn't do. I will console myself, however, with
> the thought, that in that case you might not accept my offer, which would
> be much worse than it is now.

Had he seen George Eliot? "Kiss her for me. But from all accounts, I don't
believe that is exactly what one wishes to do to her. If I were, by hook or
by crook, to spend next winter, with friends, in Rome, should I see you,
at all?" And so she continues, in a half-flirtatious tone, with a slightly
forced euphoria and an abundance of misplaced commas. She signs herself "always your loving cousin Mary Temple."

Two months later, at Pelham, she writes, "Think, my dear, of the
pleasure we would have together in Rome. I am crazy at the mere
thought. It would be a strange step and a sudden for me to take. . . . I would
give anything to have a winter in Italy. We must trust in Heaven and wait
patiently." She doesn't post this letter until a week later when she adds,

> The evening I wrote you I was enchanted with the project, but the next
> morning I was disenchanted. I am really not strong enough to go abroad
> with even the kindest friends. I have been ill nearly all week with a kind
> of pleurisy, which makes me clearly perceive that it would never do for
> me to be ill away from home, on the bounty of strangers for my nursing,
> See'st thou?

During the summer of 1869, Henry's mother reported that "Minny
writes that she gets up at 6 o'clock every morning and takes a lesson in
drawing. Perhaps she is beginning to work out her own salvation." But
Minny wasn't working out her salvation at this particular moment: she
was trying quite simply to *live,* even if the process meant early rising for
the sake of art—although we suspect that it was not exclusively for art's
sake that Minny was up at six. She was spending sleepless nights. Yet she
continues her rounds of visits. Her last letter to Henry is dated from
Pelham, 7 November 1869. She had spent some days in Quincy Street and
read some of Henry's letters to William and to his father.

> To think that you should be ill and depressed so far away, just when
> I was congratulating myself that you, at all events, were well and happy,
> if nobody else was. Well, my dearest Harry, we all have our troubles in
> this world—I only hope that yours are counterbalanced by some true
> happiness, which Heaven sends most of us, thro' some means or other.
> I think the best comes thro' a blind hanging on to some conviction, never

mind what, that God has put deepest into our souls, and the comforting
love of a few chosen friends.

In Cambridge, she had much light banter with William James, of
whom she was deeply fond. On 5 December William wrote to Henry, "M.
Temple was here for a week, a fortnight since. She was delightful in all
respects, and although very thin, very cheerful."

Henry had written to Minny that gondolas reminded him of her (the
"sliding step"?) and in her letter from Pelham she wrote,

> My dear, I hope you may henceforth *live* in gondolas, since gondolas
> sometimes make you think of me—so "keep a doin' of it" if it comes
> "natural" . . . I feel much better now-a-days. Good-bye, dear Henry—
> "words is wanting" to tell you all the affection and sympathy I feel for
> you. Take care of yourself, write soon. God bless you. Your loving cousin,
> Mary Temple.

Affectionate these letters are, a mixture of tenderness and inconse-
quential chatter. They are not love-letters. The letters to Gray are, in a
reticent way; longer and more detailed, they are the communications of
a serious young lady to a serious young man. She wonders whether she
is "hopelessly frivolous and trifling," or does this mean that she really
doesn't *believe,*

> that I have still a doubt in my mind whether religion *is* the one exclusive
> thing to live for. . . . In fine is it the meaning and end of our lives, or only
> a moral principle bearing a certain part in our development?

She goes to hear Phillips Brooks preach and doesn't find an answer. He
didn't touch the real difficulties. "I wonder what he really does think
about it all," Minny writes, "and whether he ever feels the reaction I feel
about Thursday, which is sure to follow the enthusiasm and confidence
made by his eloquence and earnestness on Sunday. Tomorrow will be
Saturday, and I shall be glad when Sunday comes to wind me up again."

The time was coming when no amount of winding would help. It was
now near the end of January 1870, and Minny was exhausted. The doctors
are giving her morphine in the hope that it will help her sleep. It only
makes her ill. "I am sometimes tempted to take a drop of 'pison' to put
me to sleep in earnest," she confesses.

"I had a long letter yesterday from Harry James from Florence—
enjoying Italy but homesick," she writes to Gray. The letter was apparently written during Henry's brief pause there as he was England-bound.
In the middle of February, Minny left Pelham for Manhattan in a state
of great fatigue and weakness to consult Dr. Metcalfe, an important
specialist. He told Minny her right lung was weaker than her left, which
was quite sound, and that if she kept up her general health she might

fully recover. He had known a case ten times worse get entirely well. He recommended a trip to Europe, "so this last is what I am to do," she told John Gray, "if I am not dead before June."

She sat on the piazza at Pelham bundled up on this February day scribbling her long letter in pencil.

> If I begin to be indifferent to the result I shall go down the hill quickly. I have enough Irish blood in me rather to enjoy a good fight.
> I feel the greatest longing for summer, or spring; I think I would like it to be always spring for the rest of my life.

After Henry James had his last look at Florence, he traveled with an aching heart to Genoa, where on 14 January 1870 he wrote a long, affectionate and philosophical letter to his father, who had apologized for sermonizing his son. Henry rejoined, "Don't be afraid of treating me to a little philosophy. I treat myself to lots." And he went on to tell him of his regret at leaving Italy. Three days later he was at Mentone. From there he went the following day by carriage to Nice. He visited Monte Carlo and watched the play at the gaming tables; for a while he toyed with the idea of staking a napoleon "for that first time which is always so highly profitable." Discretion triumphed; he turned instead to study the "nobler face of the blue ocean."

On 27 January he was in Paris. He went to see *Frou-Frou* with Desclée at the Gymnase, and for the first time he visited the Théâtre Français where he saw a play by Molière. He spent hours at the Louvre, he dined modestly, he returned in the evenings to the Théâtre Français and read late into the night by the fire in his hotel. He would have liked to linger in Paris—"I should have learned *bien des choses* at the Théâtre Français." He recrossed the Channel via Boulogne and went to the Charing Cross Hotel, where he promptly re-acclimated himself by dining in the coffee-room off roast beef, brussels sprouts and a pint of beer.

On 5 February, in a letter from London, he gave his mother an accounting of his year's expenditures. He had been in Europe almost eleven months and had drawn £379 of the £1,000 his father had put at his disposal. He had not been extravagant, he said; though "My being unwell has kept me constantly from attempting in any degree to rough it. I have lived at the best hotels and done trips in the most comfortable way." Nevertheless, he had run through almost £400, and this seemed to him a large sum. Everything would depend now on how things went at Malvern. If he didn't feel better he would return home.

Four weeks passed and he was writing to William from Malvern. He was obtaining plenty of "gentle emotions from the scenery," but had found no intellectual companionship among his fellow-patients at the thermal establishment. The women, particularly, struck him as plain, stiff, tasteless in "their dowdy beads and their linsey woolsey trains."

"Nay, this is peevish and brutal," he wrote. "Personally (with all their faults) they are well enough. I revolt from their dreary deathly want of—what shall I call it?—Clover Hooper has it—intellectual grace—Minny Temple has it—moral spontaneity."

The name of Minny, and the present tense, slipped easily from his pen as he wrote his letter in his rapid hand. The date of the letter was 8 March 1870. On this very day Minny's tired, sick lungs had drawn their last breath in the quiet house in Pelham, where little more than a year before Henry had said the good-bye to her that was destined to be their last.

"The Wings of the Dove"

The heroine—the "very heroine of our common scene"—was dead at twenty-four, and Henry, contemplating the cold green landscape of Malvern through his tears, found himself trying to face the irreversible truth. Minny was *"dead*—silent—absent forever . . . While I sit spinning my sentences she is dead." He received the news on 26 March from his mother and replied to her on the same day. "I have been spending the morning letting the awakened swarm of old recollections and associations flow into my mind—almost *enjoying* the exquisite pain they provoke," he wrote. He experienced a feeling of "absolute balm in the thought of poor Minny and *rest*—rest and immortal absence." Life on a footing of illness and invalidism would have been impossible for that disengaged dancing flame.

It had come as a violent shock. "Your last mention of her condition had been very far from preparing me for this." He scribbled the thoughts as they came to him. "Oh dearest Mother! oh poor struggling suffering *dying* creature!" He wanted all the details of her death, the last hours, the funeral. "I have been raking up all my recent memories of her and her rare personality seems to shine out with absolute defiant reality. Immortal peace to her memory!"

When he had written himself out, he took a long walk, and gradually the thought of her disappearance became familiar. He wished they could have met in Europe; he would have liked to tell her many things, to take up the talk where they had left off at Pelham. He strolled across the fields; the landscape assented stolidly enough to death, "this vast indifferent England which she fancied she would have liked. Perhaps!"

He returned to his room and picked up his pen again. He had written in the first part of his letter, "It comes home to me with irresistible power, the sense of how much I knew her and how much I loved her." He now added: "It is no surprise to me to find that I felt for her an affection as deep as the foundations of my being, for I always knew it."

The letter to Mary James, written in the first moments of grief, reflects his immediate shock. The eloquent letter he wrote three days later to William is long, self-conscious, rambling and repetitive, the fruit of meditation and inner contradictions. He had written to his mother, "Twenty years hence—what a pure eloquent vision she will be," and now he reiterated, as if talking to Minny, "Twenty years hence we shall be living with your love and longing with your eagerness and suffering with your patience." Minny alive was a creature of flesh and blood to be loved; and also, for Henry, a threat, as women were; Minny dead was an idea, a thought, a bright flame of memory, a statue—Diana!—to be loved and to be worshipped in complete safety.

The letter to William culminates in a passage describing what Minny had meant to Henry James—"she *represented,* in a manner, in my life several of the elements or phases of life at large—her own sex, to begin with, but even more *Youth,* with which, owing to my invalidism, I always felt in rather indirect relation." He reflected sadly on

> the gradual change and reversal of our relations: I slowly crawling from weakness and inaction and suffering into strength and health and hope: she sinking out of brightness and youth into decline and death. It's almost as if she had passed away—as far as I am concerned—from having served her purpose, that of standing well within the world, inviting and inviting me onward by all the bright intensity of her example. She never knew how sick and disordered a creature I was and I always felt that she knew me at my worst. I always looked forward with a certain eagerness to the day when I should have regained my natural lead, and our friendship on my part, at least, might become more active and masculine. This I have especially felt during the powerful experience of the past year.

At the end of the letter he repeats: "I can't put away the thought that just as I am beginning life, she has ended it."

This thought is the key to Henry's feelings at the moment of Minny's death. What he had observed from his earliest years and later recorded in his fiction had now become in his mind (for so he articulated it) a part of his own life—"the gradual change and reversal of our relations." But what *had* been his relation to Minny? What transparent mental link had he forged with the image of his cousin to arrive at the equation that her loss was his gain? It was almost as if, in his mind, he had already imagined himself betrothed to her or even married. He was drawing up his eternal balance-sheet of love and death as he had observed it, in which either the man or the woman, or both, were victims of a love relationship.

He said that twenty years hence Minny would be "a pure eloquent vision." She began to figure in Henry's short stories and novels long before the day when, a quarter of a century later, he made his first notebook entry for *The Wings of the Dove,* on "the situation of some young creature . . . suddenly condemned to death." Seven years after Minny's death Henry wrote a curious tale, "Longstaff's Marriage," published in *Scribner's Monthly* in 1878. The heroine is named Diana— Diana Belfield—and she is as beautiful as the chaste huntress, with a "tall, light figure . . . a nobly poised head . . . frank quick glance . . . and rapid gliding step"; like the huntress she is "passionately single, fiercely virginal." Wintering at Nice with her companion, Agatha Gosling, she finds herself being observed daily on the promenade by a young Englishman whose name she discovers to be Reginald Longstaff. He is clearly a worshipper of Diana—but from a safe distance. He makes no effort to speak to her or to be introduced to her. One day, however, he does summon the courage to speak to her companion. He tells Agatha he is a dying man, and asks her to tell Diana after he is gone how much he loved her.

When Longstaff's serving-man comes to announce that his master is dying, not of consumption but of love, Agatha urges Diana to go to see him, out of pity. She finds Longstaff in bed, gravely ill. He makes an extraordinary proposal: nothing less than a deathbed marriage so that Diana may inherit his possessions, "lands, houses, a great many beautiful things." In exchange he would have "a few hours in which to lie and think of my happiness."

Diana is not unmoved by his plea. However, she has a down-to-earth reflection: "Suppose, after all, he should get well." Longstaff, overhearing this, moans softly and turns his face to the wall. Diana leaves. "If he could die with it," she observes coldly, "he could die without it."

Two years pass and she summons Agatha to her. "Will you come abroad with me again? I am very ill." One day in Rome, in St. Peter's, Diana glimpses a healthy and completely recovered Longstaff. "So you were right," Agatha tells Diana. "He would, after all, have got well." Diana replies: "He got well because I refused him. I gave him a hurt that cured him." Longstaff is clearly no longer interested in Diana. She, however, is now in love with him, and dying. She sends for him. He agrees to marry her on her deathbed. Unlike Longstaff, she does not recover. Love—and marriage—have been fatal to her.

What is striking in the tale is that Longstaff is afraid to express his love in the first instance, and that fear is a component of his illness. From the moment that Diana rejected him—from the moment that she had made it clear the relationship must remain that of a man to a statue— Longstaff no longer felt himself threatened. So Henry's reiterated expression in his letter to William, that Minny had become a memory, a thought instead of a fact, an image, "a steady unfaltering luminary in the mind," was in reality an expression of relief that his cousin had permanently been converted into a statue, an object to be contemplated, appreciated and even loved—through the opaque glass of memory; and this without the uncomfortable feeling that he ought to do something about his ambivalence. Minny's death, much as it brought deep personal grief and a sense of irreparable loss, brought also, in this curious buried fashion, a concealed emotional catharsis.

Minny alive had been a constant reminder to Henry of his inarticulateness and his fear of asserting himself. Minny gradually sinking into decline could renew his strength. Dead, Minny resided within the walls of his mind. He did not have to marry her and no one else could, neither John Gray, nor William, nor Wendell, none of the clever young men who surrounded her at Conway or in the ballrooms of New York. Minny was now permanently his, the creature of his imagination.

She became, nine years after her death, the heroine of *The Portrait of a Lady.* The hero of that scene, Ralph Touchett, dies of consumption (again a reversal of roles), but not before he has watched Isabel Archer —the name suggests a kinship with the archeress Diana—play out the drama of her life and make a mess of it. "Poor Minny! how much she was not to see!" Henry had written to his mother. In the novel Henry gave his heroine a chance to see the world and live out her dreams and disillusion. Isabel goes from Albany to England, to Italy, and sees all that Minny might have seen; she has much of the happiness Minny might have had. Courted by three lovers strangely parallel to those in "Poor Richard," one disqualified by invalidism, she chooses a fourth and ruins her life.

In the years between *The Portrait* and *The Wings of the Dove* there was a curious story, a pot-boiler, "Georgina's Reasons," in which a girl named Mildred or Milly Theory dies of consumption. Though Milly Theory is a pale shadow of the future Milly Theale, once again Minny's ghostly figure had passed across Henry's desk. She returned finally at the turn of the century, to be converted into the ultimate flame-like creature of his fiction. The theme of *The Wings,* the reverse of that of *The Portrait,* was the fictional rendering of Minny's actual ordeal.

"Death, at the last, was dreadful to her; she would have given anything to live." And when Milly Theale, the "dove," has folded her wings, Kate Croy and Merton Densher confront one another. Milly's money makes possible their long-deferred marriage. Kate, however, is no longer sure of Densher.

"Your word of honour that you're not in love with her memory."

"Oh—her memory!" Densher exclaims.

Kate makes a high gesture. "Ah don't speak of it as if you couldn't be ... *Her memory's your love. You want no other."*

So it was with Minny Temple and Henry James.

Return

Henry James recrossed the Atlantic in the spring of 1870, eager to be home. Fifteen months had elapsed since his visit to Pelham, the most crowded and dramatic months of his life. Minny had been laid to rest in Albany Rural Cemetery, and Henry seems to have observed the prescription of his letters: a little decent grief, "a sigh of relief—and we begin to live for ourselves again."

At Malvern, in the first days after receiving the news of Minny's death, he had had a bad relapse. His back-ache returned, and he rushed to London to consult a specialist. Dressing the balance between remaining abroad and returning home he decided that the most economical road to recovery lay through Quincy Street. In London a meeting with his Aunt Kate, who had been traveling abroad, provoked an acute fit of homesickness. They sailed on 30 April, on the *Scotia.* By the time he reached Cambridge—on 10 May—he was so much improved that Dr. William James, who examined him, pronounced him "tough and stout."

For the moment Henry sought some point of re-attachment to the old scenes. He had a sense of lost time and of pressure to get back to his work. A few days after his return, writing to Grace Norton, who was still abroad, he proceeded to Italianize Harvard.

> Here I am—here I have been for the last ten days—the last ten years. It's very hot: the window is open before me: opposite thro' the thin trees I see the scarlet walls of the president's *palazzo.* Beyond, the noble grey mass —the lovely outlines, of the library: and above this the soaring *campanile* of the wooden church on the *piazza.* . . . Howells is lecturing very pleasantly on Italian literature. I go to the lecture room in Boylston hall; and sit with my eyes closed, listening to the sweet Italian names and allusions and trying to fancy that the window behind me opens out into Florence. But Florence is within and not without.

The year in Europe had worked its spell: and Henry could announce to Miss Norton, "When I next go to Italy it will be not for months but years." In the meantime there were contrasts and comparisons to be made between the Old World and the New, tales to write out of his journeys, and the question of his career. He had tasted enough of Europe to want to see more of it: ill-health and the money anxieties of Quincy Street had interrupted his course. What was to follow now was a period of careful exploration of New England and then a renewed and longer experience of Europe.

When he was writing the closing words of *Notes of a Son and Brother,* almost half a century later, Henry James said that he and William felt the death of Minny Temple to be "the end of our youth." He qualified this in *The Middle Years,* where he likened youth to a continuing "reluctant march into the enemy country, and the country of the general lost freshness."

If in 1870 one phase of his youth seemed at an end, another was about to begin; a great fund of freshness had not yet been lost. By trial, by error, by the happy accidents of nature and the long ordeal of endurance, the artist had been formed, a quiet, pondering, sovereign being, with a great, strange, passionate gift of expression wedded to gifts of observation and insight. "Mysterious and incontrollable (even to oneself) is the growth of one's mind," he wrote to William. "Little by little, I trust, my abilities will catch up with my ambitions."

They were catching up more rapidly than he knew. The fledgling years, the untried years, were at an end. The long ordeal of the war, the struggle for health, Minny's death, "the whole infinitude" of pain, "door within door," had been experienced. "I have in my own fashion learned the lesson that life is effort, unremittingly repeated."

Now, before him, stretched the broad new decades, the years of saturation and maturity.

PART TWO   Years of Saturation

_____

                                      1870–1875

The great thing is to be *saturated*
with something—that is, in one
way or another, with life; and I
chose the form of my saturation.

HENRY JAMES

1

A

SEASON IN

CAMBRIDGE

The Precious Wound

In the spring of 1870, after returning from his "passionate pilgrim-age" abroad, Henry James settled down at No. 20 Quincy Street in Cambridge. It was a little like being born again. He looked anew at the Cambridge horizons—the Harvard elms, the friendly verandahs of Kirkland Street, the horse-cars in Harvard Square, the cows grazing in the lot beyond the Common. To this he was reduced, after the campaniles and cathedrals, the glimpses of pagan and papal Rome, the theaters of Paris, the studios of the Pre-Raphaelites. The Harvard Yard, fenced with gran-ite posts as if to keep animals from straying in, possessed none of the mystery or beauty of the Oxford colleges with their thick walls and clois-tered privacy. For a young cosmopolitan, whose only desire was to be "literary," the parochialism of Cambridge and the sparseness of the New England scene represented intellectual and sensual starvation.

He had little in common with his Cambridge coevals; they had had their grand tours and were happy to be starting their careers on Ameri-can soil. Writing to Charles Eliot Norton, who was still abroad, he alludes to his loneliness in Cambridge, as artist, as well as gregarious human being: "If it didn't sound weakmindedly plaintive and fastidious, I would say I lacked society. I know no 'nice men'—that is, passing few, to con-verse withal." William Dean Howells and his old Newport friend T. S. Perry were his sole literary company; but Howells was now busy at the *Atlantic Monthly,* and could only occasionally resume his old walks and talks with his friend. Henry complained there was little to do, little for his eyes to rest upon—"When I go to Europe again, it will be, I think, from inanition of the eyes." Sometimes he would be bidden to feasts in honor of celebrities and find himself among the Cambridge and Boston wor-thies: as when Cambridge fêted that "clever writer" Bret Harte. But

"Cambridge society is a little arid," Henry remarked to his friends in Europe. "My dissipations have been in Boston chiefly."

The journey from Cambridge to Boston by horse-car took him over the long, low bridge that seemed to crawl on staggering posts across the Charles River. If he looked back, his view was of "the desolate suburban horizon, peeled and made bald by the rigour of the season." It was all "hard, cold, void"—boards and tin and frozen earth, sheds and rotting piles and railway-lines across puddles. Years later Henry could still describe minutely his exploration of the down-at-heels South End of the city.

In the streets around Boston Common the scene was sufficiently animated: the shop-fronts glowed through frosty panes, the bells of the street-cars were heard in counterpoint with the cries of newsboys in the cold air; and behind large plate-glass windows the interiors of the hotels, with their marble-paved lobbies, revealed their life in the white gaslight glare. The illuminated playhouses to which Henry resorted seemed seductive behind swinging doors of red leather or baize, flanked by posters and photographs of actresses. He reached out in his "dissipations" for anything that might offer an evening's relief from ennui. He ventured into private meetings and seances, demonstrations of mesmerism, speeches by ardent young reformers or discourses by lady editors advocating new religions, listening attentively to their flow of ready-made oratory. Or he might make his way to the central haven of culture, the Music Hall—high, dim, dignified, with its great and somber organ overhanging the bronze statue of Beethoven. Henry James had long ago exhausted the city's nocturnal life.

"My year in Europe," he writes to Grace Norton in the autumn of 1870,

> is fading more and more into an incredible past. . . . I feel my European gains sinking gradually out of sight and sound and American experience closing *bunchily* over them as flesh over a bullet—the simile is apropos! But I have only to probe a little to hear the golden ring of that precious projectile.

He had received a lasting wound; and his ache was the ache of having been free on an old and picturesque continent. Sometimes he called his wound a virus; sometimes it became a poison. His most characteristic image was that he had been fed "too prompt a mouthful" of the fruit of the Tree of Knowledge. Why, he was to ask himself, had it left "so queer a taste" during all his early years of travel with his family on the Continent? In old age, he wondered at the "infinitely greater queerness" which he had experienced on his return from his first adult journey abroad.

The "queerness" was the stark contrast between his two worlds, and his dilemma: for however much he belonged to New York and Boston, his "home" seemed even more now to be Europe. When William, years later, after a term abroad, spoke of America's "scraggy aspects," Henry told him:

> I tasted of that intensity once and forever when I returned from Europe in May 1870—and determined, in the deadly days, on my future life. I felt then, as I felt after subsequent returns, that the only way to live in America was to turn one's back on Europe; that the attempt to *mix* them is a terribly comfortless business.

And ultimately, in his old age, when his sister-in-law urged him to return to America to receive care and family affection, his response was "Dearest Alice, I could come back to America (could be carried back on a stretcher) to *die*—but never, never to live." He added, "when I think of how little Boston and Cambridge were of old ever *my* affair, or anything but an accident, for me, of the parental life there to which I occasionally and painfully and losingly sacrificed, I have a superstitious terror of seeing them at the end of time again stretch out strange inevitable tentacles to draw me back and destroy me."

During his two years in Cambridge Henry James wrote not only a series of tales, but a short novel, eight travel sketches, two dramatic sketches, seven book reviews, and three art notices—and counted himself "wantonly idle." Following the course of the Franco-Prussian War, he told Grace Norton that he was so busy reading newspapers "that I largely manage to forget that I am doing no work of consequence." He held a large part of his desire to return to Europe to be "morbid"; he reasoned that "I should be very much less subject to it, if I were engaged here in some regular and absorbing work."

This was a further element of the "queerness." The literary life, in a busy America, seemed to Henry an idle life. His fellow-citizens were creating industry and building railroads, or were preoccupied with the law or even with metaphysics. In the Cambridge society, trying to live by his pen and earning his meager supply of dollars, Henry seemed confined to his room with his blank sheets of paper, and largely to female society. His repeated refrain was that the profession of literature seemed out of harmony with his American environment.

The Exquisite Provincials

Idle though he might seem, James did not allow himself to be crushed by his recurrent nostalgia for Europe, nor lulled into inaction by his melancholy. He was barely resettled in Quincy Street in the early summer of 1870 when he persuaded the *Nation* to accept a series of travel articles from his pen—pictures of Rhode Island, Vermont, New York. It was an opportunity to earn some ready money; it was also a way of convincing the *Nation* how lively a travel writer he could be—especially if he were in Europe.

There was, however, a deeper prompting. He would be "haunted and wracked," he told Grace Norton, if he returned to Europe with a "thankless ignorance and neglect" of his homeland. He would therefore "see all I can of America and *rub it in* with unfaltering zeal." His tour consisted of a month in Saratoga, where he drank the waters and "cunningly noted many of the idiosyncrasies of American civilization"; a week at Lake George; a fortnight at Pomfret, where his parents were on holiday; and a fortnight at Newport.

James's *Nation* articles offer us a good account of what he saw and how he traveled. His view of the American landscape in all its wild richness is that of a man who appreciates it best when it has been tamed. James spoke of the "complete absence of detail" as he crossed Lake George and explored Burlington and Ticonderoga; or of the surroundings of Saratoga, "no white villages gleaming in the distance, no spires of churches, no salient details. It is all green, lonely, and vacant." The foreground, more often than not, was bleak and nondescript: a wooden building, a saw-mill, a high black chimney, all "as transient and accidental as the furniture of a dream." There spoke the traveler who had looked upon the stones of antiquity—the *historical* picturesque.

The describer of scenery however was also an observer of manners. As he sits on the large piazza of his hotel in Saratoga, he notices the overdressed mothers and their young daughters idly circling in the broad noonday: "at any hour of morning or evening, you may see a hundred rustling beauties whose rustle is their sole occupation." The men, lounging about the hotels, feet and cigars tilted up, "are not the mellow fruit of a society which has walked hand-in-hand with tradition and culture; they are hard nuts, which have grown and ripened as they could. When they talk among themselves, I seem to hear the cracking of the shells."

At Concord he spent "a couple of days with Mr. Emerson," as he reported to Grace Norton—"pleasantly, but with slender profit." The visit was a private matter, not chronicled in the *Nation.* He was invited because Emerson remembered his letters written during his European wanderings, which the elder James had brought to Concord. Henry saw his father's friend in his homely surroundings. If the young writer had been looking at characteristic American landscape in recent weeks, he found himself here in the one town outside the beaten path of American material triumph where the "landscape of the soul" had been contemplated always in close harmony with nature. Hawthorne was six years dead; Thoreau eight. It was as if they still lived, as if the great moment in the town's history had not yet passed.

Again and again James would use the word "exquisite" in speaking of Emerson and Hawthorne. They were both "exquisite geniuses." He spoke of them also as "exquisite provincials." He was to wander later with Emerson in the Louvre and the Vatican. "But his spirit, his moral taste, as it were, abode always within the undecorated walls of his youth." The Emersonian innocence, the exquisite provinciality of it, touched James deeply. Life had never bribed Emerson to look at anything but the soul. And the young realist, busy looking at the visible things of life and at human behavior around him, pondered this. That Emerson had considered Hawthorne's novels "not worthy of him" was a judgment extremely odd: "How strange that he should not have been eager to read almost anything that such a gifted being might have let fall."

In Cambridge, later, James read the newly published French and Italian journals of Hawthorne. Reviewing them for the *Nation* early in 1872, he remarked that they "show us one of the gentlest, lightest and most leisurely of observers, strolling at his ease among foreign sights in blessed intellectual irresponsibility, and weaving his chance impressions into a tissue as smooth as fireside gossip." The words "intellectual irresponsibility" express James's vision of Hawthorne in Europe. The truth was that the older writer looked at things "as little as possible in that composite historic light which forms the atmosphere of many imaginations." He assented to nothing he could not understand. "We seem to see him strolling through churches and galleries as the last pure American—attesting by his shy responses to dark canvas and cold marble his loyalty to a simpler and less encumbered civilization." Henry James would never be able to stroll through the churches and galleries of Europe with quite the same purity, the same air of innocence—or of ignorance.

During this time James had ample leisure in which to ponder his ambiguous state. He could look at Europe with American eyes, and he knew that he looked at America often as if he were a European. The international mind seemed to him an accident of nature. When it did happen, one had to make the best of it: "There comes a time when one set of customs, wherever it may be found, grows to seem to you about as provincial as another; and then I suppose it may be said of you that you have become a cosmopolite."

James came to see himself in the ironic light of the story of Eden. America was his lost paradise and his had been the "fortunate fall." "Very special and very interesting," he was to write of "the state of being of the American who has bitten deep into the apple of 'Europe' and then been obliged to take his lips from the fruit."

The Dispossessed

In a passage of reminiscence set down when he was fifty-five Henry James spoke of his Cambridge period as a time of "brooding exile." He imagined himself as having been like "dispossessed princes and wandering heirs" deprived alike of kingdom and inheritance. The kingdom, he believed, was the Europe of his *Wanderjahr*—where he wanted to be; the inheritance was his matured vision of the transatlantic world, which he could contemplate now only from the ruralism of Quincy Street and Harvard Square.

The phrase about dispossessed princes and wandering heirs echoed a remark dropped by the narrator in James's early story "A Passionate Pilgrim," written at the beginning of his Cambridge "exile." To the "pilgrim" of the story, in the grounds of his ancestral home in England, the narrator says: "Here you can wander all day like a proscribed and exiled prince, hovering about the dominion of the usurper." And in another story of this time, "The Madonna of the Future," the hero speaks of Americans as being the "disinherited" of art. Dispossession, disinheritance, exile, usurpation—James's heroes in these stories think of themselves as deprived of their birthright, turned into spiritual (and actual) wanderers, unable in their new strange state to enter into possession.

In the first tale Clement Searle, the sensitive New Yorker who makes the pilgrimage, has found himself out of place in America. He is one of those old-time "claimants," who believes he still has a right to his ancestral property in England. But when the owner of the Elizabethan manor house, the pilgrim's remote English kin, discovers Clement's design, he and the narrator are ordered from the house. The pilgrim has sought to possess something that in reality belongs to others. He wanders into delusion, and dies at Oxford of a delirious fever, killed by an excess of sensibility, of spiritual "dispossession."

In the second tale, written when James was once more in Europe, an American painter in Florence has passed twenty years dreaming before a large canvas that is to be the epitome of all the madonnas that ever were, the very ideal of the maternal, in its highest spiritual form. It is this painter, Theobald, who proclaims to the American stranger he has met in the moonlight beside the Palazzo Vecchio, "We are the disinherited of Art. We are condemned to be superficial!" He says, "the soil of American perception is a poor little barren, artificial deposit," and he adds, "We lack the deeper sense. We have neither taste, nor tact, nor force."

"You seem fairly at home, in exile," rejoins the narrator, "and Florence seems to me a very pretty Siberia." He goes on to say that "nothing is so idle as to talk about our want of a nutritive soil, of opportunity, of inspiration and all the rest of it. The worthy part is to do something fine!"

Theobald discloses his dream of a "madonna of the future." He has met the Italian madonna-type; he has sketched her, studied her, loved her. But he has not produced his masterpiece. When the narrator remarks, quite casually, that his model has lost her youth, it is as if he gives the painter a mortal blow. Serafina is, in truth, middle-aged, and fat. She "had made twenty years pass as a twelvemonth." The artist turns his face to the wall. Like Clement he dies in a raging fever. His masterpiece is "a mere dead blank, cracked and discoloured by time." In his last moments he mutters: "While I fancied my creation was growing, it was dying." He has lived with an obsession and clung to a sterile past.

On the surface, these tales of the Cambridge period embody the novelist's debate between America and Europe. On a deeper level they picture Henry's double exile—his sense of being an outsider at home, his fear of being an outsider in Europe. He knew himself to be a prince who had taken possession of his domain in Europe, and tasted the joys of personal freedom. But by the familiar hearth he was once again the wide-eyed little Harry James, observed and observant, who had to defend his status within the James family. If the story of the painter in Florence, worshipping an eternal mother, and that of the pilgrim clinging to an unattainable family past were told on a fanciful and imaginative plane, there were other tales, cruder and less imagined, which take us close to the inner life of No. 20 Quincy Street.

One of these was called "Master Eustace." The mother in this tantrum-packed tale, a widow, has treated her only child as if he were a lover, and also as an "heir-apparent." She liked to lean her head on his shoulder, and "resting in this delicious contact," would "close her eyes in a kind of tremor of ecstasy." Small wonder that Master Eustace also experiences ecstasy, as well as a sense of complete possession. He leaves for his grand tour of Europe; and on his homecoming, finds that his mother has married an old and loyal friend. His rage explodes in speeches such as James must have heard upon the New York stage during his childhood: "Am I a man to treat in that fashion? Am I a man to be made light of? Brought up as a flower and trampled as a weed! Bound in cotton and steeped in vitriol!" Eustace's outrage is that of a husband who has an unfaithful wife, rather than that of a son whose mother has sought happiness in a new marriage. The drama is resolved in a pistol-flourish, and the mother's death of heart-failure. Dispossession is complete.

So Henry, returning from his grand tour, discovered distinct changes in the climate of Quincy Street. He might still be the preferred son of his mother, the old-time "angel" of the family, but Quincy Street had grown accustomed to his absence. The elder brother had remained at home, in comfortable possession. Into a second tale Henry projected his fraternal attachments and animosities. "Guest's Confession" is a tale of two brothers, the elder a successful man with a vengeful disposition, and the younger a sensitive and artistic individual. Edgar, the elder brother, is also a hypochondriac, "a miserable invalid, . . . perpetually concerned with his stomach, his lungs, and his liver." The younger brother has been courting a young woman he has met at a summer resort. Edgar arrives and discovers that the girl's father is a man who once defrauded him in a business deal. He forces the older man to kneel in public and confess his business sins, giving no thought to the fact that he is ruining his brother's chances with the girl.

"Was I, after all, so excessively his younger brother?" the suitor muses. The story shows that he was. And while Edgar bears only superficial resemblance to William James, the fraternal struggle described in this tale offers vivid illustration of Henry's submerged feelings.

"The Great American Novel"

For Henry James, spending his days in Cambridge in what he deemed to be a state of sinful idleness, the logical solution seemed to be to write a novel which would establish his fame, earn him some money, make possible perhaps a return to Italy. Unmistakable hints had appeared in his *Nation* travel sketches. Arriving at Newport, which he found substantial and "civilized" after Saratoga, he reflected: "I can almost imagine a transient observer of the Newport spectacle dreaming momentarily of a great American novel."

Henry's dream apparently was not momentary. By the time the Saratoga and Newport seasons of 1870 were at an end, the writer had submitted three parts of a five-part work of fiction to J. T. Fields, Howells's superior at the *Atlantic Monthly*. He hoped Fields would content himself "with my assurance that the story is one of the greatest works of 'this or any age.' " This may have been his little joke: it is of a piece with his daydream of the "great American novel." To Norton he wrote in a less exuberant vein. The subject was "something slight; but I have tried to make a work of art."

Watch and Ward emerged demurely in the pages of the *Atlantic* as the story of an effete young Bostonian, who wears lavender gloves and consoles himself for failure in love by adopting a twelve-year-old girl. Roger Lawrence nourishes the private hope that Nora Lambert, on attaining womanhood, will marry him: he will have thus married, so to speak, his own carefully-raised daughter, without incurring the risk of incest. But his cousin, the Rev. Hubert Lawrence, a worldly clergyman, shows unusual interest in the young lady; and Nora's own cousin, the penniless Charles Fenton, also pursues her in the hope of a substantial dowry. Henry has been unable to stray from picturing family relations: the brothers of "Guest's Confession" are converted in this novel into Roger, the man of sentiment, and Hubert, the religious-worldly type. In the end Roger wins his wife—after arousing her pity by a prolonged illness. Once again a "heroine of the scene" is surrounded by suitors who possess traits of the significant figures in James's childhood, with himself as the unassertive and self-doubting aspirant. But this time he gives himself the victory.

Conceived as a study of Boston manners, *Watch and Ward* deals rather with the *moeurs* of Quincy Street. Indeed there is no painting of the Boston scene; at every turn we are aware, however, of the relationships among the characters. James moves into a further phase of dispossession. The rejected Roger entertains James's dream of fair women: and the ideal woman, this time, will be secured from rivals by an act of previous possession. If "Master Eustace" showed strong sensual feeling between a mother and a son, the relationship between Roger and Nora has a more overt element of sexuality, but how conscious James was of this is a moot point. Both the serial and book versions—published eight years apart—contain a passage in which Roger wonders after adopting Nora whether at the worst a little precursory love-making would do any harm: "The ground might be gently tickled to receive his own sowing; the petals of the young girl's nature, playfully forced apart, would leave the golden heart of the flower but the more accessible to his own vertical rays." This is a curious passage to come from an inveterate reader of French novels. Another and better-known passage describes Nora, in *déshabille* at bedtime, bringing her watch to be wound, with Roger's key proving a "misfit" and Hubert Lawrence's rather more successful, even though "some rather intimate fumbling was needed to adjust it to Nora's diminutive timepiece." A large innocence seems to reside in the imagery of these passages.

Watch and Ward found a public in the *Atlantic,* but long before it had run its course Henry must have realized that his amused hopes for it had been exaggerated. He was to republish it in book form in 1878 only because of expediency and for purposes of copyright. It was "pretty enough," he remarked after revising it; still it was "very thin and as 'cold' as an icicle."

Alice

The young heroine of *Watch and Ward* reflected, to a considerable degree, James's discovery on his return from Europe that his only sister, Alice, some four years his junior, had arrived at charming—if nervous and high-strung—womanhood. At twenty-three she was gentle, almost sedate; her eyes were large and candid; she had a broad brow, a strong mouth, a straight nose, and a certain strong facial resemblance to her novelist brother and her father.

Five men, four brothers and a father, loomed in her childhood and youth. The father and the two elder brothers had always bestowed upon her elaborate mocking gallantries, but one gathers that life in the nursery was an endless battle. When her two younger brothers, Wilky and Bob, did not ignore her, they subjected her to the usual petty indignities which small boys heap on sisters. She remembered a trip in an open carriage to the outskirts of Boulogne-sur-Mer, when she had been seven or eight, and "the anguish, greater even than usual, of Wilky's and Bob's heels grinding into my shins." Outside the nursery, life proved deceptive and ambiguous. Certain female figures—Aunt Kate, her mother, governesses—hovered over her, admonitory, critical, disciplinary. The elder Henry smothered her often with clumsy affection, while the older and more distant brothers, Willie and Harry, petted—and teased. William sends his love to the "cherry-lipped, apricot-nosed, double-chinned Alice," and wishes she would sass him "as of yore"; the mother refers to Alice's "sweet, loving chaffing" of their father.

The girl's attachment to her father was strong; and it was transferred to her brother Henry. Since he was the quiet one, among the children, he probably constituted less of a threat to her selfhood than the lively William, or the boisterous shin-kicking younger brothers. Alice learned her share of wit and sarcasm and the aggressive disguises of humor. She cultivated the robust attitudes of mind of her male siblings. But, as the brothers move out into the world, and she finds herself isolated, we begin to see the melancholy beneath the chaffing, the desperation in the "sassing."

"In our family group," James was to write, "girls seem scarcely to have had a chance." The time came when Alice James sat with folded hands and cultivated a Victorian composure, the mask of modest dress and quiet demeanor concealing intensities of feeling. She sat and waited —waited as the young women of her time did—for the liberation that matrimony might bring. When no cavalier came for her, she lapsed progressively into the familiar invalidism of so many of her Victorian sisters. In 1868—when she was twenty—she suffered a nervous prostration. For the next ten years she was recurrently ill, with periods of recovery. Her second nervous collapse occurred in 1878. After this she was frequently ill. Doctors treated her for ailments that seemed to them emotional and neurasthenic. They prescribed massage, cold water treatment, ice and electric therapy, "blistering," Turkish baths. This was the best that medicine could do for Alice James. Like Henry James, his sister had her "obscure hurt."

Her first illness is vividly recalled in her journal. She envisaged it as a fight "simply between my body and my will."

> As I used to sit immovable reading in the library with waves of violent inclination suddenly invading my muscles, taking some one of their myriad forms such as throwing myself out of the window or knocking off the head of the benignant pater as he sat with his silver locks, writing at his table, it used to seem to me that the only difference between me and the insane was that I had not only all the horrors and suffering of insanity but the duties of doctor, nurse, and straitjacket imposed upon me too.

Alice's memory of her illness a decade later was of "that hideous summer of '78 when I went down to the deep sea, and its dark waters closed over me, and I knew neither hope nor peace." When she was better, her mother wrote that "She is able now when driving to take the reins herself, and has done so for an hour and a half at a time. She always enjoyed this very much." Alice's pleasure in holding the reins suggests how much she would have relished some kind of control of her existence. This she was never to have. When she did become independent, she no longer had the power to use her freedom.

She frankly talked to her father of suicide. Was it a sin for her to feel "very strongly tempted"? He replied that he did not believe it sinful, if she wished to escape from suffering. He gave Alice (as he wrote to his youngest son) his fatherly permission to "end her life whenever she pleased," exhorting her only to "do it in a perfectly gentle way in order not to distress her friends." The elder Henry James had in this simple fashion made his daughter aware that she might be mistress of herself. Alice told him, after considering his answer, that "now she could perceive it to be her *right* to dispose of her own body when life had become intolerable, she could never do it." And indeed, although she was to undergo intolerable suffering, she never took the final step that would have brought her peace.

The Painter's Eye

A reader of Henry James's early melodramas, with their rage-filled soliloquies, might understandably show a preference—as indeed his brother William did—for his book reviews and art notices. These are the work of a cool, competent, witty appreciator of the arts. His touch is light, and there is tidiness of formulation, orderliness of thought, quiet authority. He finds a "deplorable levity" in Disraeli's fiction and a "great deal of small clevernesses." The fictions of Gustave Droz, one of the last novelists of the Second Empire, delight him. They have French precision of thought and statement, the "old Gallic salt of humour." For Taine's classic work on English literature James is all admiration. Taine, however, is "a stranger to what we may call the intellectual climate of our literature." A reader of these reviews is constantly aware of being in touch with a curious, ranging, logical mind. It is empirical; its interest lies in places and persons, in generalizations about peoples, not in abstract ideas. Henry James is concerned above all with things his eyes can rest upon.

Towards the end of 1871 Howells asked James to serve as an occasional art reviewer for the *Atlantic Monthly.* He knew that he possessed what John La Farge called "the painter's eye," a rare virtue in a man of letters. Through a wedding of the visual sense and verbal power he dominated and used his other senses.

In accepting the task, James predicted his work would soon collapse for want of material. His articles appeared with agreeable consistency for three months—January to March 1872. They were unsigned. After a lapse of two months one further article appeared. He dispatched from London an account of the showing of the Wallace Collection at Bethnal Green, and wrote a few more pieces of art criticism for the *Atlantic* when he returned to Boston two years later; but he never made of this part of his critical endeavor a very prolonged or consistent effort. In all, there are extant about sixty papers on art and artists.

One marvels, in these pieces, at the assurance and ease of the young American observer. James's precision and precocity may be judged in the way he shows us Sir Noel Paton's *Christ the Great Shepherd*—in two sentences: "Christ is walking through a rocky country with a radiance round his head, and a little lamb in his arms towards whom he gently bends his face. The little lamb is very good." Or the realism of Meissonier's *Battle of Friedland:* the best thing in this picture, the young art critic wrote, was "a certain cuirassier, and in the cuirassier the best thing is his clothes, and in his clothes the best thing is his leather straps, and in his leather straps the best thing is the buckles." Or Leighton's nudes, of which he remarked that their texture "is too often that of the glaze on the lid of a prune-box; his drawings too often that of the figures that smile at us from the covers of these receptacles."

James was not, as modernity defines it, an "art critic." His "painter's eye" never carried him into technique or "painterly" feeling. He was slow in assimilating the Impressionists, and he was inevitably bewildered by the post-impressionists in his old age. It took him a long time to appreciate Whistler, of whom he first said, "his manner of painting is to breathe upon canvas."

Art-making, art-watching, art-collecting is to be found in twenty-five of James's first thirty stories. Among his novels, his famous "portrait" of a lady includes the most scathing characterization in literature of an art-dilettante who is the lady's husband. He writes *Portraits of Places, Transatlantic Sketches:* his pen seems to be also a brush.

The art criticism in Henry James is that of the genius who uses pictures to feed his own art; his was a visual sense that, in the end, came to regard pictures as life itself, to feel that artifacts, whether the work of a goldsmith or a master of the brush, spring from human resources and are intended for human uses. He could describe a picture with such exactness and brilliance that we forget that the description is often as critical as it is descriptive. But the picture for him was not only canvas and paint; it was feeling and memory, history, ambition, power, conquest.

Escape

Late in the summer of 1871 Henry James visited Canada briefly, from Niagara to Quebec, writing articles once more for the *Nation.* His little tour began with a boat-trip—from Toronto across Lake Ontario; he studied Niagara and rhapsodized for his readers in the manner of one of his own untutored Americans in his tales—"it beats Michelangelo." His observations of Quebec were happier. Here at least was evidence of an older culture, instead of nature in the raw.

The city reminded him somewhat of the Boulogne-sur-Mer of his childhood. He grasped quickly the nature of the French-Canadian society, "locked up in its small dead capital, isolated on a heedless continent, and gradually consuming its principal, as one may say—its vital stock of memories, traditions, and routine." Evenings in Quebec, he thought, might be as dull as Balzac's scenes of provincial life. James walked in the market-place and listened to the *patois* of the farmers; one of them spoke to him "with righteous contempt of the French of France. 'They are worth nothing; they are bad Catholics.'" In these words, and with his searching scrutiny, Henry James caught the unchanged note of French Canada.

Early in 1872 he began to hint in his letters that he had some hope of getting to Europe: it was still "absurdly vague," he told Elizabeth Boott, but he was determined to cross the ocean "by hook or by crook in the late summer or early autumn." Sometime between the beginning of that year and May, when he sailed, he was able to convince the *Nation* that he could write a usable series of European travel articles for the journal; and he obtained from his father an advance of money for the trip, which he hoped to pay back by literary earnings.

What aided him was the feeling in the James family that it was time for Alice to be given the advantage of foreign travel already enjoyed by William and Henry. The devoted Aunt Kate offered to go as her companion; and it was settled that Henry would act as escort to the womenfolk. The plans were broad, and the itinerary would depend upon Alice's ability to support fatigue. Henry hoped that if all went well they might, at the end of the summer, dip into Italy for a month.

One day that spring Henry walked to Shady Hill, to attend the funeral of Susan Norton, Charles Eliot Norton's wife. She had died in February, in Dresden, and Norton, in Europe with his young children, had not been able to accompany the body home. On 6 May 1872 James, writing to Norton and describing the burial, sought to comfort his correspondent. He urged Norton to allow himself to "feel" to the fullest his loss and pain. One had to stand face to face with "the hard reality of things." Henry added that he presumed to speak to his friend in this fashion "out of my own unshaken security." At the end of the letter he mentioned casually that his departure for Europe was but five days off.

Henry James had had his season in Cambridge. His own spirit again and again had tested "the hard reality of things." Now his trunk was packed, and his own design was clear. He would stay abroad as long as he could, to show whether his pen could accomplish in Europe what it had failed to do in America—give him freedom and independence. This, he was now well aware in his "unshaken security," he could not obtain in Quincy Street.

2

TRANSATLANTIC
SKETCHES

Brother and Nephew

It was as brother and nephew, rather than as writer for the *Nation,* that Henry James sailed for Europe in May 1872. Escorting Alice and his Aunt Kate seemed a modest price to pay for going abroad. They crossed on the *Algeria,* a sturdy Cunarder which brought them to Liverpool in a little over eight days. On arrival in England Henry booked an October return for his companions on the same ship.

They went first to Chester and its Roman ruins, favorite starting-place for many an American tour, then on to Lichfield and Warwick, North Devon and Salisbury; they passed through the rich farmland of the Shakespeare country and, reaching Oxford, wandered from college to college and garden to garden. In London they spent only a week; in Paris just long enough to visit Norton and his children at St. Germain-en-Laye and to see a play at the Théâtre Français. While the ladies rested, James visited the burnt-out ruins and barricades of the recent Commune. They took an overnight train to Geneva and presently were settled at Villeneuve, on Lake Leman, in the Hôtel Byron, near the castle of Chillon. The stay in Switzerland was designed as a breathing-spell from train and coach, a gain of coolness and quiet.

At the Hôtel Byron they met, by pre-arrangement, their loyal friends, the Bootts, Francis and his daughter Elizabeth. Assured of sociable companionship, Henry looked forward to several weeks of Swiss tranquillity. However, a period of torrid weather set in; and, after a week at Villeneuve, the Jameses and the Bootts moved to Grindelwald, at 3,400 feet, partly in the belief that Alice needed a more bracing climate. In a letter from there, the brother and nephew confessed that "the romance of travel—of *tables d'hôtes,* strange figures and faces, and even of Alps—soon rubs off." Nevertheless he had been able to distill the romance into four pieces for the *Nation,* the record of their sight-seeing in England. He had also climbed the Faulhorn, an eight-hours' trudge, and was pleased to discover that "my old Swiss legs, such as they are, haven't lost their cunning."

From Grindelwald the Jameses went alone by slow carriage to Meyringen, and finally to the Grisons, where they put up at a hotel at Thusis. Now the air was too bracing for Alice, and she took to her bed in a state of nervous exhaustion, the first of three such occasions at high altitudes when she became ill and had to be nursed and comforted. "Alice has tested stiff mountain air to its condemnation," Henry wrote to Quincy Street. She had need of the "human picturesque."

After Thusis, Henry lost no time in moving his companions to Berne, where they rejoined the Bootts in an old-fashioned hotel amid "a large entourage" of Bostonians. He was glad enough to be in a city again. He confessed in one of his *Nation* articles that he relished "a human flavour in his pleasures" and felt that there was a more equal intercourse between man and man than between man and mountains. The Jameses enjoyed Berne, and set out cheerfully for Italy on 26 August, limiting their tour to northern Lombardy and Venetia, with the promise of a return to coolness in the Austrian Tyrol.

Once they had negotiated the Mont Cenis tunnel, old sensations made Henry aware how intense had been his 1869 experience of Italy—the balcony, the Venetian blind, the cool floor, the speckled concrete; the Castello in Turin's square with its shabby rear and its pompous front; the brick campaniles in the mild, yellow light; the bright colors, the soft sounds—it was the eternal Italy and also his personal Italy. In Milan they inspected the cathedral; they paused at Lake Como, and devoted four dreamy days to Venice. The mosquitoes kept them awake at night, but in the daytime they lived in gondolas and found coolness on the lagoons and in the churches. They ate figs and went every night to Florian's for ices. An afternoon at Torcello was "a bath of light and air—colour and general luxury, physical and intellectual."

Austria-bound, they paused at Verona before going on to Innsbruck. Henry found Germany "uglier than ever" by contrast with Italy. Munich was "a nightmare of pretentious vacuity," Nuremberg only a little better, and Henry was prepared to trade a thousand Nurembergs for "one ray of Verona." Toward the end of the German trip he was convinced—so he wrote from Heidelberg—that he should "listen to the voice of the spirit —to cease hair-splitting and treat oneself to a good square antipathy."

In Paris again, at the Hôtel Rastadt, in the rue Neuve St. Augustin, they found the old family friends the Tweedys, Edmund and "Aunt" Mary, with whom they dined almost daily. Henry, Alice and Grace Norton had an evening together at the theater. The sister and aunt were occupied with visits to dressmakers and milliners, dispatching parcels and trunk-packing. "Alice has just shewn me a ravishing bonnet," the brother tells Quincy Street, "which will certainly, next winter, be the wonder and envy of all Cambridge."

The brother and nephew was loyal to the end. He crossed the Channel with his charges, paused briefly in London, escorted them to Liverpool and saw them aboard the *Algeria.* He could now begin his career abroad in earnest.

The Sentimental Tourist

Quincy Street had been carefully prepared for the news that Henry was remaining in Europe. Five of his travel sketches had appeared in the *Nation;* "Guest's Confession" was published that autumn in the *Atlantic,* and during his brief stay in London he had taken Alice to see the Wallace Collection, to write another of his art pieces for Howells. "A decent little sum" was thus due to him from the magazines. "You have learned, by my recent letters," he informs William, "that I mean to try my luck by remaining abroad. I have little doubt that I shall be able to pull through."

It would be economical to remain in Paris for a while; his destination, however, was Italy. One reason was that the *Nation* had a Paris correspondent, but none in Rome. Having explained this, he asked permission to draw on his father's letter of credit intended for his and Alice's tour. The elder Henry agreed. He proposed that the magazines send their payment for his son's articles directly to him. He would thus be Henry's banker as well as his literary agent. "It is the best plan," Henry replied, little realizing that this would keep him tethered to Quincy Street. "I shall do very well without ruining you."

Henry James's travel sketches in the *Nation* readily won a public, for Howells presently was asking him for similar articles for the *Atlantic;* and the *Galaxy* in New York, which had printed some of James's tales, was quite prepared to publish his essays. He thus broadened his market at this crucial moment, and gave himself the material foundation for a continuing stay abroad.

From Quincy Street his brother William kept up a running fire of praise and criticism. He complained of Henry's "over-refinement and elaboration." Henry had to cultivate directness of style. "Delicacy, subtlety and ingenuity, will take care of themselves." William confessed, however, that he had been surprised at the number of persons who were reading his brother and liking what he wrote.

In his travel sketches James proceeded from a very clear conception of this kind of writing. The observations of an intelligent traveler were worth recording, he believed, even when the experience was confined to the beaten track. He was aware also that the travel writer must keep the reader within a certain angle of vision. Although he designates himself in the *Nation* as "our old friend the sentimental tourist," he is above all "an observant American." His vision may be cosmopolitan, but he tries to use his eyes on behalf of his domestic readers. During his walks he seeks the "fine differences in national manners" as well as the "foreign tone of things."

There is considerable method in James the traveler. His attention is divided between the works of nature and the works of man: his concern is with the works of man—the flow of life into art, the flow of art into life. Descriptive prose by now comes easy to him: he can evoke Devon's flora and fauna with a few brushstrokes—the embankments of moss and turf, the lace-work of trailing ground-ivy, the solid walls of flowering thorn and glistening holly. But he also likes to get the reader out of the fields and into the towns and cities. He is in Berne and has "the vision of a long main street, looking dark, somehow, in spite of its breadth, and bordered with houses supported on deep arcades, whereof the short, thick pillars resemble queerly a succession of bandy legs, and overshaded by high-piled pagoda roofs." His eye is always for the architecture, for the buildings by which man has asserted himself. In Milan the cathedral may have its shortcomings but "it is grandly curious, superbly rich." Henry hopes he will never grow too fastidious to enjoy it, even though the great columns have little refinement of design, "few of those felicities of proportion which the eye caresses, when it finds them."

The Jamesian eye is a caressing eye. Life is not immobile; it is all a flowing scene. In Turin he pauses before Van Dyck's portrait of the children of Charles I: he thinks of the young ones not as images on canvas but as living babies; "you might kiss their hands, but you certainly would think twice before pinching their cheeks." In Venice, at Torcello, he meets a group of urchins not on canvas, one of whom has a smile "to make Correggio sigh in his grave."

In Venice he greets a young American painter in the piazza, an encounter foreshadowing the opening scene of "The Madonna of the Future." He constructs with his eyes what should have been that painter's world: his mornings in "the clustered shadows of the Basilica"; afternoons in church or campo, on canal or lagoon; evenings in the piazza feeling the languid sea-breeze throbbing "between the two great pillars of the Piazzetta and over the low, black domes of the church." Henry would have liked to spend all his days in the decaying city.

A Parisian Autumn

He had returned to London after bidding farewell to his sister and aunt and he remained long enough to replenish his wardrobe. "Oh, the grimness of London! And, oh! the cookery of London!" He recrossed the Channel with relief. In Paris he regained his old room at the Hôtel Rastadt and settled contentedly into it for the remainder of the autumn. Its window framed a pleasant view of roof-tops. He wrote in the mornings, walked in the afternoons, and in the evenings dined out, usually on a *rosbif saignant* washed down by English ale. Then he went to the theater or simply returned to his room to read quietly by his fire.

He had led a "madder and merrier" life in Cambridge, he remarked to his parents; as yet, the waiters in the restaurants were his chief society. However, if he was not meeting the French, he at least had no lack of American society. There were times when Cambridge seemed to have settled by the Seine. The Nortons had come and gone, the Tweedys had just left for Rome, but the Lowells were in the Hôtel Lorraine, near the Quai Voltaire, in the company of John Holmes, brother of the autocrat of the breakfast table. Henry felt that Lowell, with all his reputation and advantages, was really indifferent to the world. Instead of moving in Parisian literary circles, "here he is living in the heart of Paris, between his Cambridge wife and his Cambridge friend." They made "a little Cambridge together."

Henry had had only a nodding acquaintance with Lowell at home. Now they struck up a "furious intimacy." It had begun when Norton asked James to take a message to Lowell; the next day Lowell returned the call and "we went out to walk and tramped over half Paris and into some queer places which he had discovered on his own walks." In later years James was never to cross the Seine on rainy winter nights without recalling his old sociable errands to the Left Bank. He would have preferred to meet French writers and to make French friends; failing this, Cambridge-by-the-Seine mitigated solitude.

One evening in mid-November 1872 James arrived at the Hôtel Lorraine to find that Concord had joined the Parisian Cambridge. Ralph Waldo Emerson and his daughter Ellen were in Lowell's sitting-room; they were pausing briefly on their way to Italy and Egypt. Emerson seemed still to remember Henry's art letters, for he proposed that they visit the Louvre together. This they did on the morning of 19 November. Some weeks earlier Henry had paid a visit to the museum with Norton and had written home that "he takes art altogether too hard for me to follow him." Emerson, he found, did not take it hard enough. "His perception of art is not, I think, naturally keen; and Concord can't have done much to quicken it." Nevertheless, he was pleased that he appreciated the splendors of Paris and of the Louvre. Even when Emerson had nothing to say, "his presence has a sovereign amenity." Some years later James recalled the occasion:

> I was struck with the anomaly of a man so refined and intelligent being so little spoken to by works of art. It would be more exact to say that certain chords were wholly absent; the tune was played, the tune of life and literature, altogether on those that remained.

Emerson was unworldly; Norton was cold; Lowell touched James deeply —"the oddest mixture," as he was to say, "of the lovable and the annoying, the infinitely clever and the unspeakably simple." On the surface the two men seemed hardly compatible. Lowell at fifty-three was a homespun Yankee, a lover of the American vernacular who also much preferred Cambridge to the Champs-Élysées. But he was, James wrote, the American of his time "most saturated with literature and most directed to criticism." James smiled gently at Lowell's pugnacious parochialism. "I don't feel as if I should ever get anything very valuable out of him," he remarked on meeting him a year or two after their walks in Paris. Nothing valuable for his work, but he got an extraordinary degree of acceptance of himself and the loyalty of a robust friendship.

That autumn of 1872 they took ten-mile walks together. They browsed in bookshops and along the quays, Lowell driving great bargains with the antiquarians. If he was bookish, he was, in the Parisian streets, "the least pale, the least passionless of scholars." His company could be shared without experiencing overtones of moral ravage or inner conflict. A broad daylight cheerfulness surrounded the poet. "No situation could be dull for a man in whom all reflection, all reaction, was witty."

Lowell's wit made Paris agreeable for James during a November and December otherwise rain-washed and dreary. "*Two whole months* of uninterrupted rain," he wrote to his sister; and yet he lingered while Rome beckoned. He was still walking, play-going, Louvre-going, reading and writing. Christmas of 1872 was approaching when Henry began to uproot himself from his little room in the Hôtel Rastadt.

On 18 December he took his cab to the railway station. It was evening and the boulevards were filled with holiday-makers. He wondered whether it wasn't a mistake to leave. The journey to Turin took twenty-four hours. He rested for a day, then went on to Florence. During the evening of 23 December, Henry was once again—after three years' absence—in the Eternal City.

3

ROMAN

HOURS

A Roman Winter

After the glittering boulevards of Paris, the Eternal City seemed a sleepy *ville de province.* Putting up at the Hôtel de Rome, in the middle of the Corso, Henry went out immediately into the narrow, crooked streets. They were dark and empty. He climbed the Spanish Steps and turned into the Via Gregoriana. All was silent and deserted. At No. 33 he knocked, and a few minutes later was being greeted affectionately by Mary and Edmund Tweedy in a charming little crimson drawing-room. Edmund had been ill with gastric fever, but was mending. They wanted Henry to stay with them, but that would have made him feel the world was a small place indeed.

He awoke next morning to perfect weather. Rome glittered in the winter sun. He called on Lizzie and Francis Boott, and stayed with them for dinner on Christmas Eve. On Christmas Day he dined with the Twee-dys, and drove with Aunt Mary to St. Peter's in her open carriage. During the succeeding days, while Tweedy was convalescent, James became Mary's escort; when she wasn't driving to the butcher's and the baker's, they visited churches or drove out over the old and the new Appian ways.

There were signs of change in the Eternal City since his visit to Papal Rome in 1869. The Pope was no longer to be encountered, sitting in the shadow of his great coach with uplifted fingers. Instead, as James passed the Quirinal, there was King Victor Emmanuel in person, with a single attendant, receiving petitions from a group of men and women. Italy, Henry noted, still had its full measure of beggars and children pleading for coppers with their fine eyes and intense smiles.

He found it pleasant to sit coatless at the window of his large room in the hotel, while the January sun poured in. Or he took his daily walk, often alone, but sometimes with Francis Boott, down back streets from the Corso to the Capitol, past the low Capitoline hill and the meager quadrangle—which made Roman history seem so shrunken—to emerge on the other side at the Forum, where the new régime had launched excavations. As yet only an immense stretch of pavement was laid bare, studded with broken pedestals. Henry liked to lean on the railing with the idlers. He found it odd "to see the past, the ancient world, as one stands there, bodily turned up with the spade."

And so on around to the Colosseum, to gaze on Rome present and past, pagan and Christian, medieval and modern, and the contrast between bright light and mouldering cruel ruin. He took this particular walk one day when the Roman carnival had filled the Corso with masked revelers. As the hubbub died away in the distance, he found himself strolling up a steep byway on the Palatine hill, from just behind the Arch of Titus. At the end of this path stood the little church of St. Bonaventure, with a modest façade. Lifting the leather curtain, James found himself in a small poor whitewashed interior. Before an altar decorated with muslin flowers was a solitary priest—a young, pale, kneeling figure, who gave him a sidelong glance as he entered. He watched the priest visit the altars in turn and kiss the balustrade beneath each one. While the Carnival was creating tumult in the city, here was one figure kneeling for religion. Planted there, his face pale with fasting, his knees stiff with praying, the young priest seemed a stern satire on the thousands in the streets. Here was the religious passion, "the strongest of man's heart." Among the "churchiest churches" in Europe—those of Rome—James reflected that the man-made houses of God formed the constant background of a great human drama. In the streets of Rome, he felt himself a part of this centuries'-old grandeur.

As for the Roman social scene, to which the Tweedys introduced him, his first fears were that he was falling into a Cambridge-by-the-Tiber, analogous to what he had witnessed by the Seine. On his third evening in Rome he went to a party given by a friend of the Nortons, at which he met Sarah Butler Wister, of Philadelphia, daughter of Fanny Kemble, the celebrated actress. Mrs. Wister invited him to her "at home," two nights later, where he was introduced to "the terrific Kemble" herself. Sarah Wister, in Rome with her husband and son, took an immediate fancy to Henry James. Strikingly handsome and possessed of a magnificent head of hair, she was "literary," a woman of ideas, and had much of her mother's energy and force. With a promptness that took James by surprise, she invited him to accompany her the next day to the French Academy in the Villa Medici.

They went instead to the Colonna gardens, where they wandered among "mossy sarcophagi, mouldering along heaven-high vistas of ilex" and "lingered at the base of damp green statues." Henry was distinctly charmed. "A beautiful woman who takes you to such a place and talks to you uninterruptedly, learnedly, and even cleverly for two whole hours is not to be disposed of in three lines," he told his mother. But he hasn't time to tell her more. He must be off to the "Cambridge Greenoughs, confound 'em. I have not come to Rome for Cambridge tea fights." He added, "The chapter of 'society' here—that is American society—opens up before me."

It did, more largely than he had imagined. The presence in Rome of an eligible and charming literary American bachelor became known almost immediately. The Terry household in the Odescalchi Palace had two marriageable daughters; the Storys, also with a marriageable daughter, were no less hospitable in their vast apartment in the Barberini. Presently Henry is attending musical and theatrical evenings in "the rival houses of Terry and Story." At Mrs. Wister's he meets Mrs. Charles Sumner, separated from her political husband; he encounters the lively Alice Bartlett and the haunting Elena Lowe; and there are the Bootts, with their circle of friends. He complains, but he surrenders himself wholly to American society and the "sovereign spirit" of the city. He meets American artists in palaces and studios; he makes excursions to visit scenes of antiquity and takes part in picnics, the food and wine laid out on the warm stones of ruined temples. He spends days at Frascati and "ineffable hours" at the Villas Mondragone and Aldobrandini, lying on the grass at the foot of ilexes. Returning from his rambles, he finds friendly doors opening wide to him on all sides.

James knew that certain of these doors, in villas and palaces, had opened wide fifteen years before to a distinguished American predecessor, and there were moments when he distinctly felt himself following the footsteps of Nathaniel Hawthorne. The little group of artists and amateurs of Hawthorne's day had grown in the intervening years. American painters and sculptors continued to come abroad. And in Rome, too, as Hawthorne had shown, there were subjects for novelists as well.

With the artists came also the dabblers and the dilettantes. And then in the American colony there were men and women who simply enjoyed the soft climate of Rome, in preference to the harsher one they had abandoned, and who gave themselves over to the simple pleasures available in the ancient city.

James, from the first, was prepared to enjoy these pleasures. He liked nothing better, at an evening party, than to find an agreeable corner, next to an agreeable and attractive woman. He thrived more on people than on scenery. He tended, however, to emphasize the emptier side of this society to Quincy Street. Cambridge, after all, was expecting him to be industrious. He feared that his social relaxation might seem, if not sinful, at least wasteful to his mother and father. "Every week I hope 'society' is over—but it spurts up again," he writes home. He confesses, however, that "I have deliberately taken all that has come of it and been the gainer." Later he was to speak of "the incomparable *entertainment*" of Rome in "manners, customs, practices, processes, states of feeling." "Entertainment" of this kind was the very stuff of life for a novelist; and Henry was seeing how transplanted Cambridge and Boston moved against a grandiose background. Were they not all dancing to good music —and in the noblest ballroom in the world?

The Two Palaces

Henry's playful allusion to "the rival houses of Terry and Story," as if they were Montague and Capulet, singled out in the American colony two artists who lived in old princely palaces and vied with one another in entertaining Americans. The Storys were housed in splendor, an apartment of more than forty rooms, in the Palazzo Barberini, on the slope of the Quirinal. The Terrys were in a lesser palace, in rooms on the second floor of the Odescalchi in the Piazza dei Santi Apostoli, opposite the Colonna Palace. Both the Barberini and the Odescalchi had been built from designs by Bernini; and while the effect of grandeur went with an effect of gloom, the Barberini could rejoice in brightness of façade and an almost modern gaiety.

As Henry climbed the stairs leading to the small door of the right wing, he could hear the splash of the Barberini fountain. He passed, on one of the landings, the bas-relief of a Thorwaldsen lion. The modest doorway, with the name "W. W. Story" inscribed on it, swung open into grandiose reception rooms, where since the middle of the century this American from Salem and Cambridge had been host to former American Presidents, writers, painters, and Roman nobility, secular and ecclesiastical.

The lawyer turned sculptor was a genial host; "talk was his joy and pleasantry his habit." He was animated and gay, with a faculty for humor and mimicry: he was interested in ideas, in people—in everything. His Roman memory was long. Severn, Landor, the Brownings, Thackeray, Tennyson, Hawthorne, General Grant, a row of Cardinals and British prime ministers, had paid homage to him in his palace. Pope Pius IX, on seeing Story's statue of Cleopatra, had paid the cost of transporting it to the London Exhibition of 1862, where it captured the Victorian imagination and made Story famous. On visiting Story's studio in the Via San Nicolo di Tolentino, James found the sculptor "in the midst of an army of marble heroines . . . not altogether unsuggestive of Mrs.

Jarley's waxworks." To Charles Eliot Norton he wrote: "I have rarely seen such a case of *prosperous* pretension as Story. His cleverness is great, the world's good nature to him is greater." Mrs. Henry Adams, visiting the same studio at this time, exclaimed: "Oh! how he does spoil nice blocks of white marble."

In the more modest Odescalchi Palace Luther Terry lived with his wife, sister of Julia Ward Howe and widow of the sculptor Thomas Crawford. There were three Crawford children, the two marriageable daughters, Annie and Mimoli, and the son Marion, destined for popular fame as a writer of romances. Terry, a rough-bearded, lonely man, had left his native Connecticut at twenty, and spent the rest of his life in Italy. His studio at 23 Via Margutta pleased James: it was situated in a squalid house, in a squalid street, promising gloom within, yet had a pleasant first-floor court, a sort of hanging garden, open to the sky, out of which opened the large studio. Terry showed James a painting called *The Artist's Dream,* another *The Vision of St. John—*"the queerest old survivals of the American art of thirty years ago. It is an agreeable curiosity to see their author sit and look at them seriously and expound his intentions and yet be on the whole a sensible man of the world." Americans visiting Rome purchased pictures from Luther Terry as "a grateful memorial" of pleasant sociabilities, suggesting that a certain charm of "salesmanship," genial and without Story's flamboyance, animated their host. The charm was also one of background. The Odescalchi Palace, built of stone and brick round a colonnaded court, had high rooms with coffered ceilings. In the notable Magenta Room, with its panels of pink brocade, the ceiling was vaulted, and painted with a grapevine trellis on a background of burnished gold. The presiding genius of the Terry household was Annie Crawford, who "has every gift," Henry wrote home, but was "as hard as flint and I am pretty sure she will never have an adorer. He will have to be a real lion-tamer." Indeed, Annie married Erich von Rabe, a Junker baron with a dominating will, an estate in Prussia and violent anti-English prejudices.

In addition to Story's pretentious statues and Terry's mediocre paintings, Henry saw the imitative art of other Americans who had come to Rome in the earlier years. At the Storys' he met Harriet Hosmer, whom fifteen years before Hawthorne had described as "bird-like" and her work as "quietly impressive." In middle age she struck Henry as "a remarkably ugly little grey-haired boy, adorned with a diamond necklace"; but she was better, he imagined, than her statues. He called at the studio of Eugene Benson, a few doors from Terry's in the Via Margutta; a friend of the elder Henry James, Benson never lost his devotion to the classical mode. Henry pronounced his landscapes "careful, and conscientious, but very uninspired." Edward Darley Boit and his teacher, Frederic Crown-inshield, he also met, and he called on an elderly lady artist, Sarah Free-man Clarke, a friend of his father's and of Emerson's, who had once studied with Washington Allston.

He was most at home in the studio of Lizzie Boott, where she painted "little tatterdemalion Checcos and Ninas—with decidedly increasing ability." He told his sister of finding Lizzie one morning in her studio, "*en tête-à-tête* with one of the very swell models—a wondrous youth in a sheepskin jacket and bandaged legs and flowing curls and the most pictorial complexion." Lizzie had learned to paint at an early age, and threw herself into her painting with an intensity that far exceeded her talents.

There was one other artist on whose fate James meditated in later years. This was J. Rollin Tilton of New Hampshire. Like Story he lived in the Barberini, but in a more modest corner. James described Tilton as "a very queer genius. He is great on sunsets and does them (and all sorts of aerial luminosities etc.) very well." But he was "the most blatant hum-bug in his talk you ever heard." James scrutinized his paintings of Italian and Egyptian landscapes, and wondered at Tilton's one moment of fame in London, when his work was recognized by the Academy. Then he fell from sight, his "reputation sadly, publicly, permanently unfinished." He was still another type of an American artist-failure in Europe.

Although James's letters from Rome mention only these artists, it is clear that he encountered others and studied them closely. What kind of artist could an American be in a foreign environment, he seems to have asked himself—an environment as congenial and as soft as Rome, which conspired to make him lazy or imitative; or pretentious, like Story; or mediocre, like Terry; or plodding, like Benson; or inspired but unprofes-sional, like Tilton. What if an artist arrived in this environment with a vaulting ambition (such as Henry's) and felt within himself the stirring of greatness?

The time was to come when Henry would seek to answer these ques-tions. In Rome, in 1873, he looked with a critical eye upon the American artists. They worked and abandoned themselves to their momentary ex-periences while the novelist sought to read the lessons of their careers. They would serve both as example and warning to himself.

James encountered another sort of example that winter in Rome. One day he entered the Caffè Spillmann, on the Via Condotti, and observed an English family at lunch—a mother, a father, and a little girl. The father had characteristic Victorian side-whiskers, a large sensitive mouth, a broad-lined brow. The face was serious and captivating. James recognized it at once. A decade earlier he had walked through the New

Hampshire woods with his young cousins, declaiming the verses of this man. Among the earliest of his published reviews had been a notice of *Essays in Criticism.* In Matthew Arnold the young Henry James had found an intellectual kinsman, an Englishman with a continentalized intelligence like his own.

On the evening after James's glimpse of Arnold at Spillmann's, he found himself face to face with him in one of Story's tapestried rooms. There was no doubt about it: Arnold had a powerful visage, but James, looking into it, found it was not as "delicately beautiful" as he might have hoped. The critic's manner was easy, mundane, even "somewhat gush-ing." What seems to have set James off particularly was the "little glass he screwed into one eye." With this chattering Englishman with a mono-cle Henry had, as he wrote, "first and last a little small talk." The note was almost rueful. "He did nothing to make it *big,* as my youthful dreams would have promised me." To Norton he wrote: "He is not as handsome as his photographs—or as his poetry. But no one looks handsome in Rome —beside the Romans."

James had so admired Matthew Arnold, he wrote long afterward, that he had supposed that "to encounter him face to face, and under an influence so noble, would have made one fairly stagger with a sense of privilege." The sense of privilege had to be postponed. In the Barberini it was "as if, for all the world, we were *equally* great and happy, or still more, perhaps, equally nothing and nobody; we were related only to the enclosing fact of Rome." That "enclosing fact" concealed in it the mem-ory of a monocle.

Roman Rides

One day toward the end of January 1873, Henry James hired a horse and rode out of the Porta del Popolo to the Ponte Molle (Ponte Milvio), where the Tiber flowed between its four ecclesiastical statues. He had never been much of a horseman, but he knew how to stay in the saddle. The day was mild, the air filled with a mellow purple glow. As he rode, the beauty of the landscape, the sense of movement, the feeling of power —and of control—took possession of him.

From that moment he gave to the Campagna a generous share of his Roman days. "I can stick on a horse better than I supposed," he wrote to Quincy Street. Presently he was galloping in the grassy shadows of aque-ducts and tombs and taking ditches as if he were a huntsman. Riding doubled his horizon; he could pass with ease from one Roman picture to another. He hired a horse by the month and justified the expense to his mother by explaining how good it was for his health.

The Campagna was at its best on mild winter days, "when the bril-

liant air alone suffices to make the whole landscape smile." Detail and
ornament varied from week to week. Henry liked to gaze at sun-cracked
plaster and indoor shadows. He stared into gateways of farms, with their
moss-coated stairways climbing outside a wall. On the homeward
stretch, in waning light, he would rein up by an old tavern and buy a
bottle of *vino bianco* or *vino rosso.* The tavern often had a yard, with a
pine-wreathed arbor casting shadows on the benches. He could sit with
his feet in the dirt and think that in February, in snow-blown Cambridge,
his feet would be seeking the warmth of the parlor hearth-rug.

More often than not, Henry did not follow the highway. He liked to
ride along the newly disinterred walls of Rome, gazing with contemplative eyes on ancient stones "in which a more learned sense may read
portentous dates and signs—Servius, Aurelius, Honorius," the wall-build-
ers, the architects of empire.

Servius, Aurelius, Honorius—James caught from the ancient stones,
from the great arches and the towering aqueducts, that emanation of
grandeur and that echo of *imperium* which he had known from his
youth, when he had lived under the Second Empire of France. The very
names he now plucked from the chiseled stones were those of the great,
the imperial time. He could identify himself with Servius the wall-
builder; or Aurelius the Stoic conqueror; or Honorius seeking to shore up
Rome against decline; and reflect, with the irony of a poet and a dramatist, upon the incongruous in these ancient stones in which pagan and
Christian elements were now mixed timelessly with those of a benevolent bourgeois monarchy. For him ancient stones meant grandeur rather
than decay. Before the tomb of the Valerii, to which he rode one day, he
could muse that it was "strange enough to think of these things . . .
surviving their immemorial eclipse in this perfect shape and coming up
like long-lost divers from the sea of time." He found a "peculiar fascination" in things recently excavated. All these relics spoke to Henry "of the
breadth of human genius."

If James admired the Roman relics as symbols of the endurance of
art and of the nature of "glory," he also experienced a profound uneasiness in their presence. Power was acceptable to him only in some at-
tenuated or disguised form, as he had known it behind the mask of
resignation of his mother; and in the disguises he himself had assumed
when he gave himself a motionless observer's role, or when he could play
omniscient author in the lives of his characters while finding ingenious
technical devices to conceal his omniscience. Unadulterated power had
all the frightening qualities of open assault. The equestrian statue of
Marcus Aurelius at the Capitol had been, when he looked at it in 1869,
"totally admirable." It spoke for power masked with kindness. Matthew
Arnold had seen in the pagan statue a "portrait most suggestive of a

Christian conscience." This mildness in an Emperor who had indeed shrunk from violence—while being committed to it—gave Henry pause.

His travel essays and his letters to Cambridge show Henry's sense of power in his new-found freedom, allied with his relish for the strength and dominion reflected in his Roman surroundings. But his deepest anxieties created by this may be discerned in two tales written during these months, which sprang directly from his Roman rides and his exploration of ancient things.

In "The Last of the Valerii" a Roman Count, a kind of sleepy, dreamy, well-fed Donatello, marries a young American girl. A statue of Juno is disinterred in the grounds of the villa, and the sleepy-eyed Conte Valerio falls in love with it. He neglects his wife and ultimately abandons himself to worship and pagan blood-sacrifice. "When a beautiful woman is in stone, all he can do is to look at her," the little Roman excavator remarks to the distraught American girl. She takes the hint. The Juno is quietly and secretly buried again. The young daughter of the Puritans has exorcised pagan evil—and triumphed.

The second tale, "Adina," describes a shepherd, Angelo Beati, asleep in the Campagna, as James had one day seen such a man, "with his naked legs stretched out on the turf and his soft peaked hat over his long hair." He is discovered by two Americans, a classical scholar named Scrope and his friend, a proper Bostonian. Scrope notices that the shepherd clutches in his hand a discolored object: he drags it from him, and when Angelo awakens, throws a few coins at him. The object appears to be some ancient jewel. Scrope spends days learning how to clean it. One midnight, in high elevation, he brings to his companion a beautiful topaz, carved with a laurel-crowned imperial figure and bearing the words *Divus Tiberius Caesar Totius Orbis Imperator.*

Emperor of the whole world! The topaz was carved for Tiberius, the campaigner in Gaul, Armenia and Germany, the conqueror of the Illyrians. In a long speech, Scrope boasts of his own conquest of the centuries in recovering the imperial symbol. He gives the stone to his young American fiancée, Adina Waddington. She regards it as evil and refuses to wear it. Moreover, Adina has been attracted to the young shepherd, who trails the American about Rome claiming he has been cheated. One evening Adina breaks off her engagement to Scrope; the next morning she climbs out of her window and runs off with Angelo. "She's better than the topaz," he says. Scrope, in due course, pauses on the bridge of St. Angelo and commits the stone to the muddy Tiber. As with the Juno, the past is restored to the past—but in this instance Scrope's love is not restored to him.

James seems to be saying in these tales that the past can be dangerous to love and to life. Things buried for a millennium lose none of their baleful force when restored to the light of day. Much that lay uncovered in Rome fascinated James; yet clearly, by the testimony of his tales, he felt that the living—in order to go on living—consorted with it at their peril.

Henry James had arrived at his first clear statement of one of his major themes: the corruption to be found in Europe by a still innocent America. The tales of the Juno and the topaz contain a sense of shock Henry experienced in discovering how close civilization can be to paganism. On another level they suggest also his intuitive understanding that he would have to bury his personal past, the past of Quincy Street, and make his way in a disengaged present. The happy meeting-ground of puritan and pagan could be precisely the ground of art. An artist could permissibly enjoy the pleasures of his senses—the very throb of Rome— and aspire to greatness without fear of punishment. In Quincy Street Henry had to be reticent. Abroad, on horseback, he could be resolute— and he could *feel* "imperial," experience the glory of his dream of the Louvre.

Five Women—and a Sixth

"I am now," Henry boasted in a letter to his parents, "in the position of a creature with *five* women *offering* to ride with me." There is a distinct swagger here, a suggestion to Quincy Street that its young writing son is a social success in Rome. There were indeed five ladies—two married, one about to be divorced, two eligible for marriage—who welcomed the company of Henry James Jr., of Cambridge, Mass.

First there was Mrs. Sumner. Before her brief marriage to Senator Charles Sumner, she had been the widow of William Sturgis Hooper of Boston. She was thirty-five—five years older than Henry—slender and stately and with a high-bred manner and aristocratic reserve. In Rome, she was awaiting her divorce from Sumner. "I have seen a good deal of late of Mrs. Sumner and adore her," Henry wrote to his father. When Henry announced that he "adored" a woman, it was sufficient sign that he was in no danger of "involvement." Mrs. Sumner (who was to be known after her divorce as Mrs. Alice Mason) had force and presence. During that winter Henry rode often with her and with her friend Alice Bartlett with whom Mrs. Sumner shared an apartment in the Via della Croce.

Second on James's list to his family was Mrs. Edward Boit, wife of the painter. If she "offered" to ride, it seems certain that the young man did not accept the offer. "I shall fight shy of Mrs. Boit who, I believe, is an equestrian terror." But Henry was extremely fond of her from the first— "a decidedly likeable little woman—bating her giggling." Later he remembered her as "always social, always irresponsible, always expensive, always amused and amusing."

The third lady was Mrs. Wister, and with her James rode often, sometimes alone and sometimes in the company of her husband. She inspired no "terror," but she was not "easy." "I went out the other day with Mrs. Wister and her husband. They led me rather a dance, but I took four ditches with great serenity and was complimented for my close seat. But the merit was less mine than that of my delightful little horse." Mrs. Wister, married to Dr. Owen Jones Wister of Philadelphia, was eight years older than Henry. She had grown up separated from her mother, for the fiery Mrs. Kemble had abandoned her husband Pierce Butler, the Southern gallant and slave-holder, and was in England during the Civil War. This winter, reunited, mother and daughter both had their brief salon in Rome before returning to America.

Alice Bartlett, "that mighty maiden," posed no romantic problems. "I feel," Henry wrote after a gallop in her company, "very much as if she were a boy—an excellent fellow." During the spring James came every three or four days to the Via della Croce to improve his Italian by reading Tasso with her. Alice Bartlett was as much a friend of Lizzie Boott as of Mrs. Sumner, and Henry was to see her often during the next five years.

Last of the five was Lizzie Boott. She was the most Europeanized of his riding companions and the one he knew best. James had spoken of her on occasion as "homely," but photographs and paintings show a chiseled, refined charm, a bland beauty. She was warmly American in spite of her markedly European manners. Lizzie became a cherished image in James's life, the "Cara Lisa" of his letters, a link with Italy, and the center of a drama of which he would be a fascinated as well as a troubled spectator. "As Lizzie depends upon me," he wrote to his father, "I shall be chiefly her companion." And so they rode together often, joined sometimes by Miss Bartlett.

There was a sixth woman. She did not offer to ride with Henry; indeed she does not seem to have been particularly interested in him. This may have contributed to his interest in her. She attracted him by her beauty, her remoteness, her air of quiet intelligence—her mystery. Elena Lowe, daughter of a Bostonian named Francis Lowe, seemed to float in an air of melancholy, yet she carried herself with pride and distinction. Henry spoke of her as an "intensely interesting personage." In March 1873 he writes to his father that he calls occasionally "in the dusky half-hour before dinner" on a girl who is "sweet and very clever," named Miss Lowe. "She is very handsome, very lovely, very reserved and very mysterious, not to have many adorers. But I am not yet regularly enlisted as one of them."

In April Henry Adams and his wife passed through Rome and James dined with them. Present on one occasion was Miss Lowe, "beautiful and sad." A few weeks later he writes to Mrs. Wister that he has seen Miss Lowe once or twice, "though I have tried oftener." In August Henry records that Miss Lowe is the subject of wagging tongues. He met the sad beauty at Assisi, "attended by the painter Bellay," and heard afterwards that "it was a case for a more suggestive word" than *attended.* A year later, he writes to Mrs. Wister that he has read of Miss Lowe's marriage at Venice to a "reputable British gentleman," a consul. "Happy man," and Henry adds, "So much for Bellay." James thought Miss Lowe's marrying a British consul "a little of a prosy performance." But he had misread the paragraph in *Galignani's Messenger,* which announced the marriage of Elena Lowe to Mr. Gerald Perry, son of Sir William Perry, retired British consul, and of the late Geraldine de Courcy, sister of Lord Kingsale. Miss Lowe seems to have placed herself in good society.

In Elena Lowe and her "mysterious" qualities Henry had found an image for the heroine of his first important novel. Again and again in that novel Christina Light is portrayed as an enigma and a "riddle." He was to find Christina sufficiently attractive and mysterious to revive her in a second novel, as the Princess Casamassima.

A Study in Mauve

Henry James's recurrent complaint to his family was that in Rome he lacked male companions. Neither Story nor Terry nor the younger artists could provide the stimulating literary talk of Lowell in Paris; or Howells in Cambridge; or his brother William in his own home. In these circumstances James looked to his women friends for intellectual companionship. Mrs. Boit certainly did not provide this, nor Lizzie Boott; Alice Bartlett and Mrs. Sumner were "both superior and very natural women, and Mrs. Sumner a very charming one, but they are limited by a kind of characteristic American want of culture." And he added: "Mrs. Wister has much more of this—a good deal in fact, and a very literary mind, if not a powerful one."

From the first however he seems to have been of two minds about her. He tells his father that she has "fierce energy in a slender frame," rides, walks, entertains, has musical rehearsals, and "is very handsome into the bargain"—but "she isn't easy." To William he writes that in a certain light, and at certain moments, with her hat on, she bears "a startling likeness to Minny Temple"—but the likeness, he adds, is all in the face. This suggests some of the appeal she had for him. From Henry's mother came warnings. "Mrs. Wister is too conscious of her own charms to be very dangerous I am told—but beware!"

Henry James had no need of such advice where handsome women

were concerned. Nevertheless, it is quite clear that he saw more of Mrs. Wister than he admitted. She was charming, clever, lively—yet always not "easy." It was Henry who felt uneasy. He saw himself somehow "involved" with a married woman. Sarah Wister brought to the surface unknowingly the conflict between his need to be passive with women and yet to assert himself as a man. The artist in him told him to live dangerously, to invite passion, to feel and act. The reasonable self, the well-conditioned conscience, echoed his mother's "beware."

Henry James kept a notebook while he was in Rome; he used passages from it in an article in the *Galaxy* which he reprinted in *Transatlantic Sketches.* In describing some of his Roman excursions he referred to his companions by their initials. When he revised the book for Tauchnitz in 1883, he wrote to Mrs. Wister saying that she would "recognize an allusion or so" in his Roman pieces. "Enjoy them and forgive them according to need. You will see—I had to make up for small riding by big writing."

> *December 30* [1872]. I went yesterday with Mrs. W. to the Colonna Gardens—an adventure which would have reconverted me to Rome if the thing were not already done . . .
> *February 12th* [1873].—Yesterday with Mrs. W. to the Villa Albani. Over-formal and (as my companion says) too much like a tea-garden; but with beautiful stairs and splendid geometrical lines of immense box-hedge . . .
> *Middle of March.*—A ride with Mrs. W. out of the Porta Pia to the meadows beyond the Ponte Nomentana—close to the site of Phaon's villa where Nero, in hiding, had himself stabbed. It was deeply delightful—more so than one can really know or say. For these are predestined memories and the stuff that regrets are made of; the mild divine efflorescence of spring, the wonderful landscape, the talk suspended for another gallop.

Mrs. Wister had proved a challenging companion. She asked questions; she invited James to join her in appreciating art, experience, history; to have ideas on a hundred subjects while being gallant, attentive, devoted. The Roman notebook suggests that the friendship had deepening roots and underlying intensities for Henry, heightened by a sense of the place and the "divine efflorescence" of the spring. When the moment of parting came toward the end of March, and Dr. and Mrs. Wister and their son Owen (the future novelist) turned their faces toward Philadelphia, Henry told his father, "I took her last ride with her away and away under the shadow of the aqueducts. She is most broken-hearted to exchange Rome for Germantown." Henry may not have been as broken-hearted, yet a distinctly romantic moment in his life had come to an end.

Some months later, when he was living in an inn at Bad Homburg, he wrote a story which embodied his experiences as a young unmarried man enjoying the friendship of a married woman. Perhaps it was his memory of the purple Campagna, the scarlets and lavenders and violets of Rome, the perpetual lavender satins and purple velvets worn by Mrs. Kemble, or even the name Wister itself, with its evocation of lilac wistaria—at any rate he named the story "Madame de Mauves."

Euphemia Cleve, a convent-bred American girl, nourished from her early years on those love-romances which stirred the blood of Emma Bovary, has married the young, dissipated Baron de Mauves. When Longmore, the American hero of the tale, discovers her she is already an unhappy, rejected woman, deeply hurt by her husband's infidelities and aggressively determined to endure them. Longmore thinks he loves her. They walk along garden paths and shady woods at St. Germain-en-Laye (like those of the Villa Medici). For a moment Longmore dreams of taking Euphemia away. But he wavers. He is in conflict. Euphemia's defenses are formidable; but they are never put to the test.

The Baron de Mauves, throughout the story, has been more than a complaisant husband. He has urged Longmore to make love to his wife; it would remove her from her high moral throne. Of this Euphemia is aware. Her puritanism stands firm and her fidelity becomes her instrument of revenge. When his wife closes her door to him, the Baron cannot tolerate the frustration, and Henry James asks his readers to believe that in his despair the hedonist blows out his brains. Longmore, back in America, is moved at first to rush to Euphemia; but something holds him back. He "has become conscious of a singular feeling,—a feeling for which awe would be hardly too strong a name."

James's two preceding tales—those of the recovered statue and the restored topaz—had treated evil and corruption as inexorable historical forces, in an atmosphere bordering on the supernatural. In "Madame de Mauves" evil is embodied in the Baron de Mauves, the representative of "Europe," but now as part of everyday life. The tension is less the result of extremes and of shock than of human ambiguities. At the end of the story one feels that the Baron, whatever his moral laxities, had a decidedly rigid wife. On the other hand Longmore too is "difficult." He cannot bring himself to act. "Women were indeed a measureless mystery," Longmore ponders—even as his author had pondered, in looking upon Elena Lowe, or in praising and canceling out his praise of Mrs. Wister. In "Madame de Mauves" Henry expressed his ambivalence "whether it was better to cultivate an art than to cultivate a passion"—as if he had to separate the two.

Sarah Wister saved Henry James's letters. They are propriety itself,

though charged with friendship and memory. "Never, never have I forgotten," he wrote to her, "how some of the most ineffaceable impressions
of my life were gathered . . . fifteen years ago in your society." In a tale
written almost twenty years after their springtime in Rome, an elegant
trifle called "The Solution," James seems to be setting down in the description of the charming Mrs. Rushbrook a sketch of Mrs. Wister as he
had known her:

> She had a lovely head, and her chestnut hair was of a shade I have never
> seen since . . . She was natural and clever and kind, and though she was
> five years older than I she always struck me as an embodiment of youth
> —of the golden morning of life. We made such happy discoveries to-
> gether when I first knew her: we liked the same things, we disliked the
> same people, we had the same favourite statues in the Vatican, the same
> secret preferences in regard to views on the Campagna. We loved Italy
> in the same way and in the same degree . . .

For James, Rome, Mrs. Wister and the rides in the Campagna had been
indeed "the golden morning of life"—and it was tinted mauve.

A Personal Timetable

"The days follow each other in gentle variety, each one leaving me
a little more *Roman* than before," Henry James wrote home that spring.
He abandoned himself wholly to the enjoyment of the new season; he
rambled in the Borghese Gardens, and rode with Mrs. Sumner and with
Miss Bartlett who had three horses and placed one at his disposal. One
day he escorted Emerson—homeward bound from his Mediterranean
journeyings—to see the Vatican sculptures, much as he had escorted him
a few months earlier through the Louvre. He found him "as lovely as
ever, serene and urbane and rejuvenated by his adventures." The Henry
Adamses arrived; James had known the historian during his Cambridge
months, and now found him "improved." Mrs. Adams, the former Marian
(Clover) Hooper, seemed to have had her "wit clipped a little"—but he
supposed she had "expanded in the affections."

The warm weather made his hotel room stuffy, and James moved
into a little fourth-floor apartment in the Corso—No. 101—where he had
a *loggia* with a view of roof-tops and two comfortable rooms. His landlord
sold Catholic images in a shop in the basement and lived with a large
family in a curtained alcove down the hall from his tenant.

Henry had hoped to settle down now to less desultory writing; however he complained of his lassitude. "Lingering on here in these lovely
languid days of deepening spring," he wrote to Mrs. Wister, "I felt as if
I were standing on some enchanted shore, sacred to idleness and irre-

sponsibility of all kinds." But not too irresponsible, for he wrote to Quincy Street: "The other day, I became THIRTY—solemn fact!—which I have been taking to heart."

He had been writing for ten years and he had not yet published a book. His months in Rome however had shown him that he stood firmly planted in his career. There is a kind of serene confidence in his letters when he speaks of what he is doing and what he will do. He is a little unhappy that he has not written more; but what he is really "taking to heart" is the question of what kind of artist he is to be, and how he is to arrange his artist's life. For the rest, if Quincy Street still tugs at the silver cord, he is learning how to resist. He has been discovering the meaning of freedom: he is learning belatedly to feel comfortable in the world.

And the world appreciates him. Only the other day Norton had written from London that Ruskin was delighted with Henry's comments on Tintoretto in the *Nation.* "You may be pleased from your heart," wrote Norton, "to have given not merely pleasure, but stimulus, to a man of genius." Ruskin wished Henry James Jr. had been appointed Slade Professor of Fine Arts at Cambridge rather than Sidney Colvin.

Henry has misgivings as to the value of art criticism—indeed of all criticism. What he really wants to do is to write prose fiction. "To produce some little exemplary works of art is my narrow and lowly dream," he tells Grace Norton: "They are to have less 'brain' than *Middlemarch;* but (I boldly proclaim it) they are to have more *form.*"

The sense of a personal schedule which he will follow, regardless of the schedules of Quincy Street, is strong in his letters. His father had sounded out a Boston publisher and offered to pay for the printing of a volume of Henry's tales; Henry replied that he was not ready for this. He is prepared to wait until he has written some new stories. "What I desire is this," he tells his mother, "to make a volume, a short time hence, of tales on the theme of American adventurers in Europe, leading off with the 'Passionate Pilgrim.' I have three or four more to write." And he knows what his second book will be:

> I shall write a few more notes of travel: for two reasons: 1° that a few more joined with those already published and written will make a decent little volume; and 2° that now or never (I think) is my time.... I doubt whether, a year or two hence, I shall have it in me to describe houses and mountains, or even cathedrals and pictures.

These replies demonstrate the extent to which Henry James had taken the measure of himself and his opportunities. He might be thirty, and his apprenticeship might be long. But he had his own time-table.

For Henry James, the question of money was quite another matter—a rather ticklish matter—perhaps because his father abandoned finances to his mother, and left it to her to discuss them in detail with her son. Henry drew regularly on his letter of credit. But through his arrangements to have the magazines pay his father rather than himself, Quincy Street became Henry's personal banker, and he was increasingly held accountable to his family for his expenditure—and, as it seemed, for his life—abroad.

"What are you living on, dear Harry?" Mary James wrote.

> It seems to me you are living as the lilies, and feed like the sparrows. But I know too that you toil and spin and must conclude that you receive in some mysterious way the fruits of your labour. We have been all along under the impression that your publishers were to send your money to us, and as nothing has come, and nothing has been drawn by the Bankers since Nov. 1st, it is quite a mystery to me.

Henry reassures her. He isn't starving. He had drawn on his letter of credit before leaving Paris. There are inevitable delays in payment by magazines. Life in Rome is moderately expensive: at the hotel he paid seventy Italian francs ($14) a week for service, breakfast, beefsteak, potatoes, fires and light. His only "serious expense" had been his riding. He pays $50 a month for a horse, or a little more than $2 for a single long ride. "But this," he explains, "is so substantial a pleasure and profit that I can manage it."

His mother's next letter announces that $250 had been received in Quincy Street for five pieces in the *Nation.* Early in May Henry set down in two columns the balance sheet of his Roman sojourn:

Drawn by me since Dec. 18th		Paid and to be paid father on my account.		
Paris	£ 30	From	*Nation*	$250
Rome	20	"	*Nation*	75
"	20	"	*Atlantic*	60
"	40	"	*Galaxy*	30
"	20		*N.A.R.*	75 (?)
	130	"	*Galaxy* (for story I think I asked $150)	
= $650 *in gold* (I suppose not more than) $575 at most in paper.				150
			Atlantic (for story forthcoming)	
		"		100 *at*
$575			$640	least

He hoped to reach the stage where payments from the magazines would come in "like revenue." Then as if to make certain, he verifies his figures and discovers that his total should have been $740. Maternal pressure, perhaps, was not conducive to good arithmetic. At any rate, the final balance was sufficiently reassuring. He had paid his way according to his own plan.

June was approaching. The heat was not yet intense; nevertheless there was a "peculiar quality" in the air. James needed something more bracing. In the "loving mood of one's last days in Rome" he went to St. John Lateran forty-eight hours before setting forth on his travels. A sirocco was blowing. Rome for the moment had become the mouth of a fiery furnace. Henry contemplated the façade with its robed and mitred apostles, bleached and rain-washed by the ages, rising in the air like strange snow-figures in the hot wind. He crossed the square to the Scala Santa— the marble steps brought to Rome from the praeterium in Jerusalem— and studied them through a couple of gilded lattices. Impious thoughts crossed his mind: the steps seemed oriental or Mohammedan.

James said his farewells at the rival palaces. He dined with the Terrys *en famille* and his last evening in Rome he spent with Story, who, in his large cool Barberini rooms, usually remained until July. They parted almost affectionately. As he packed his bags, Henry seemed to experience a reluctance not unlike that which he had felt half a year before when he was on the point of quitting Paris. In his Roman notebook he wrote, "One has the sense of a kind of passion for the place, and of a large number of gathered impressions." Many of these, he said, were "intense, momentous," but they had come in such profusion that he did not have the time to sort them out. "As for the *passion,* we needn't trouble ourselves about that. Sooner or later it will be sure to bring us back!"

Years later he would wonder whether Rome hadn't been "a rare state of the imagination," a Rome of words made by himself, "which was no Rome of reality." Enchanting things could doubtless also happen by the Thames, the Seine, the Hudson—even the Charles—but somehow he did not "thrill at their touch." The Roman touch had the ultimate fineness. "No one who has ever loved Rome as Rome could be loved in youth wants to stop loving her," he wrote—almost fifty years later.

William

While Henry was in Rome tasting for the first time the happiness of self-possession and freedom, William James remained in Quincy Street exposed to an imprisoning emotional climate. He enjoyed his father's talk up to a point; his mother was attentive and solicitous, but in a rather uncomfortable way. She was impatient with William's self-absorption. The family surroundings renewed the conditions—back-aches, head-aches, eye trouble, loss of appetite—which had long troubled him. For thirteen years—from his twenty-third year to his thirty-sixth, when he finally left home—his life was marked by recurrent lapses in health and spirit. He was like a mountain-climber who triumphantly scales a peak, only to be terrified by the height he has dared to ascend. The culmination of his medical studies ministered in no way to self-esteem. He seems to have had no thought of setting up in practice. It was at this time that William "touched bottom." He wondered whether he would ever bring himself into any harmonious relation "with the total process" of the universe.

We know that William was profoundly involved with both his parents: and his later preoccupation with the emotions and memories of amputated persons may have been prompted by his sense that during these years he had been as crippled emotionally as his father had been physically. The record he set down in *The Varieties of Religious Experience* of an "hallucination" seemed almost a repetition of the "vastation" recorded by the elder Henry James. William's account also included a shape—summoned, however, from actual memory, and therefore not hallucinatory, or as horrible as the shape that his father experienced. It was

the image of an epileptic patient whom I had seen in the asylum, a
black-haired youth with greenish skin, entirely idiotic, who used to sit all
day on one of the benches, or rather shelves against the wall, with his
knees drawn up against his chin, and the coarse grey undershirt, which
was his only garment, drawn over them, inclosing his entire figure.
. . . *That shape am I,* I felt potentially.

And William, late in life, went on to describe how every morning he
awoke with a "horrible dread at the pit of my stomach, and with a sense
of the insecurity of life that I never knew before, and that I have never
felt since."

An anxiety as prolonged and recurrent and as overpowering could
stem only from a personal dilemma. What William looked for was a cure
for his soul-sickness (and his bodily ailments) for which his fellow medical doctors—as he well knew—had no remedy. Like his father he seems
to have found a partial answer in a book. Reading the essays of Charles
Renouvier, he was struck by the French philosopher's definition of free
will—"the sustaining of a thought *because I choose to* when I might have
other thoughts." This was not unlike the senior Henry's discovery of the
meaning of Selfhood in Swedenborg. It was also like Alice's recognition
that she did have a choice over the fate of her body. From this, William
was to write in his diary: "My first act of free will shall be to believe in
free will."

But the ghosts that haunted him were not prepared to depart at the
summoning of a belief; he found no solution for almost another decade.
He began his teaching at Harvard in 1872, as instructor in physiology, and
in the spring of 1873 the elder Henry James could report to his son in
Rome that William was getting on "swimmingly." But if he was doing
"swimmingly" in March, this could only mean that he would probably
have a sense of drowning shortly thereafter. President Eliot offered him
a renewal of his appointment and asked him to teach anatomy, with the
prospect of a permanent post. William's first impulse was to decline. He
changed his mind and accepted. Then he changed his mind again, for he
resisted the teaching of anatomy. By the end of May he began to toy with
the idea that he might take the year off, and escape to Europe. In a letter
to his brother he broached the subject of joining him.

Henry was in Switzerland when he replied. He suggested that William might find Rome interesting; the place, he said, offered more resources for recreation than elsewhere in Europe. Henry's letter contains
no attempt to influence William in one direction or another.

William did not reach an immediate decision. For two months he
debated, amid fits of despondency and languor, whether to keep his $600-

a-year job at Harvard or to take leave in pursuit of health. "Poor fellow," wrote his mother to Henry on 1 July 1873,

> I wish it was possible for him to learn to live by the day, and not have to bear today the burden of coming months and years. He says the question of being able to do the work that lies before him next winter, and indeed his whole future career, weighs so heavily upon him that it keeps him from rallying.

In July William was still saying that to go abroad would be a "desperate act." By August Henry had decided what William's decision would be, for he asked him to bring to Europe certain of his books and some American toothpaste and candy. On 2 September William could announce to Henry that "the die is cast! The six hundred dollars' salary falls into the pocket of another! And for a year I am adrift again and free. I feel the solemnity of the moment, and that I *must* get well now or give up."

William sailed for Europe on 11 October 1873. He paused briefly in London, devoted two days to Paris, and then traveled on to Florence, the appointed meeting-place of the brothers. He arrived towards midnight and went to Henry's hotel—the Hôtel de la Ville. Henry was asleep. William did not awaken him. Instead he went to his room and before retiring wrote a brief letter to his sister: "The Angel sleeps in number 39 hard by, all unwitting that I, the Demon (or perhaps you have already begun in your talks to distinguish me from him as Archangel), am here at last. I wouldn't for worlds disturb this his last independent slumber." William was going to bed with a light heart—and "the certainty of breakfasting tomorrow with the Angel."

Angel and Brother

Henry had left Rome late in May of 1873; he visited the hilltop towns from Perugia to Florence as he had promised himself. Then he fled the Italian summer to Switzerland. After a stay in Berne, he crossed into Germany and settled at Bad Homburg, where he spent ten weeks. He strolled in the evenings and listened to fussy band-concerts. Forty years later he could recall "a dampish, dusky, unsunned room, cool, however, to the relief of the fevered muse, during some very hot weather." The place was so dark that he could see his way to and from his inkstand only by keeping the door open. As well as his tale of "Madame de Mauves," he wrote travel pieces, and read Turgenev in a new German translation. He was feeling better. "I have for two years been so well," he told William, "and have now in spite of everything such a standing fund of vigor, that I am sure time will see me through."

Early in October he returned to Italy through Switzerland and by coach over the St. Gothard. By this time he knew that William was on his way to Europe. He found Florence oppressively hot and delivered over to mosquitoes. He accordingly went to Siena, where in an article for the *Atlantic* we find him indulging in what was to become a characteristic mannerism of his travel writings—that of imparting a voice to houses, palaces and monuments. "We are very old and a trifle weary," the houses in Siena say to him, "but we were built strong and piled high, and we shall last for many a year." Into the midst of these colloquies between Henry and the Old World his elder brother intruded, bringing his unsentimental wit to bear upon the sentimental traveler. He brought with him also old obscure childhood memories. For in a sense William would be reasserting his characteristic role, and Henry would again shrink into his younger brotherhood.

From Henry James Jr. in Florence to Henry James Sr. in Cambridge, 2 November 1873:

> I wrote to you a week ago, telling you of Willy's being on his way to me —and I had hardly sent my letter when he arrived. He had travelled very fast, stopping only one day in Paris, in his impatience to reach me. A compliment to me! . . . He is very much charmed with Florence and spends a great deal of time in going about the streets and to the galleries. He takes it all as easily as possible, of course, but he already manages to do a good deal and has made a beginning which augurs well for the future.

From William James in Florence to Mr. and Mrs. Henry James in Cambridge, 9 November 1873:

> First—of the angel. He is wholly unchanged. No balder than when he quit; his teeth of a yellowish tinge (from the waters of Homburg, he says); his beard very rich and glossy in consequence he says of the use of a substance called Brilliantine of which he always keeps a large bottle on the table among his papers. . . . The "little affectations" of which Mother spoke I have not noticed. He probably fears me and keeps them concealed, letting them out when foreigners are present. He speaks Italian with wonderful fluency and skill as it seems to me; accompanying his words with many stampings of the foot, shakings of the head and rollings of the eye sideways, terribly upon the awe-struck native whom he addresses. His manner with the natives generally is very severe, whereas I feel like smiling upon them.

This was William James's first journey to Italy and the first time the two brothers had been united on European soil for nearly fifteen years. Henry felt at times as if Quincy Street had descended into his private world.

William fretted constantly. He wanted to be "settled and concentrated."
He looked upon the beauties of Florence and the past of Rome with a
jaundiced eye, feeling "like one still obliged to eat more and more grapes
and pears and pineapples, when the state of the system imperiously
demands a fat Irish stew, or something of that sort." William apparently
could not accept Italy as it was, and enjoy it with his senses. He told
Henry he feared the "fatal fascination" of the place. It seemed to be
taking "little stitches" in his soul. He was too impatient and restless to
be completely refreshed. He had been eager to go abroad. He was just as
eager, shortly after his arrival, to return home.

He had before him, moreover, the constant spectacle of his younger
brother's industry. Henry spent his mornings at his writing-table; William's presence in Florence was not allowed to change this daily schedule. Only when his work was done was Henry ready to lunch with his
brother and explore the artistic and human resources of the city.

Occasionally, in James's "Florentine Notes," we capture glimpses of
his companion, as he carries out his inspection of Fiesole, or visits the
castle of Vincigliata, or ponders the pictures in the Pitti as they "jostle
each other in their splendour" and "rather fatigue our admiration." William is "the inveterate companion" or "my irrepressible companion" or,
in one instance, "W—," who remarks on looking at Santa Croce: "A trifle
naked if you like but that's what I call architecture, just as I don't call
bronzed or marble clothes statuary." One gains the impression that perhaps the happiest hours spent by the two brothers were during these
rambles. They could commune on the common level of painting—that
art in which William had first thought he had a vocation; and they could
be again, briefly, the boys who had wandered in their teens along the
quays of Paris and in the salons of the Louvre.

The Apennine winter descended in full force. William complained
of the cold and wanted to move to Rome. Henry was at this moment quite
happy by his Tuscan fireside; nevertheless, he felt he should accompany
his brother and guide him in the city he had made his own earlier that
year.

The brothers arrived in Rome during an evening in early December.
The air was mild; there was a moon. When they were settled in their
hotel, Henry led William to the Colosseum and the Forum. They looked
upon the clear, silent arena, half in shadow, half in moonlit dusk, with
its great cross half-way round. The old stones cast strange shadows.
Henry seems to have been, as usual, delighted with the sad beauty of the
ruins. Writing to his father he reported that William "appreciated it
fully." William, however, had not wanted to dampen Henry's romantic
ardor. His version to Quincy Street expressed a deep revulsion which
seized him on the site where Christians had shed their blood. It was like

a nightmare. If Henry had not been with him, he said he would have fled "howling" from the place.

Rome weighed heavily on William James. He felt the decay, the mouldering paganism, the atmosphere of "churchiness"; it heightened his New World sense of justice and democracy to the point of belligerency. Henry reported that the artist side of William finally confessed to Rome's "sovereign influence." He enjoyed "under protest," however, the very melancholy of antiquity which charmed his brother.

The brothers had taken rooms at the Hôtel de Russie, a quiet, fashionable hostelry near the Piazza del Popolo. But Henry discovered that the little apartment in the Corso of his Roman springtime was vacant and moved in, leaving William alone at the hotel—he seems to have felt they needed to be free of one another. As in Florence, William spent his mornings in solitary sightseeing, while Henry worked. At lunch-time he went to a café in the Corso, and there awaited Henry who "comes in with the flush of successful literary effort fading off his cheek." Continuing in his characteristic vein of caricature, William assures his sister that he is dining frugally, and saving his dollars, even to total abstinence from liquor, "to which Harry, I regret to say, has become an utter slave, spending a large part of his earnings in Bass's Ale and wine, and trembling with anger if there is any delay in their being brought to him."

Rome had never seemed more delightful to Henry James. After the freezing temperatures of Florence, he basked in the sunshine on the Pincio; he had fraternal company in comfortable doses; he took afternoon walks and drives, introduced William to the sociable drawing-rooms in the two palaces. For Henry—so he told his father—there was the "especial charm of seeing Willy thriving under it all as if he were being secretly plied with the elixir of life."

This idyllic life did not last, as it might have, into the soft spring. At Christmas William was seized with chills and fever. Fearing malaria, he promptly took a train back to Florence. Henry reluctantly followed him there, a day or so later. He found his brother in good medical hands, dosing himself heavily with quinine, and already distinctly improved.

Henry felt an intense frustration. To Grace Norton he wrote that he had been "jerked away from Rome, where I had been expecting to spend the winter, just as I was warming to the feast, and Florence, though very well in itself, doesn't go so far as it might as a substitute for Rome. It's like having a great plum-pudding set down on the table before you, and then seeing it whisked away and finding yourself served with wholesome tapioca." Two days after writing this letter, Henry suddenly fell ill. He had a splitting headache and a bronchial cough and fever. William brought in a nurse to attend him. The fever abated after three nights and

only the headache remained. William could discern no special cause for
the illness; he described it to Quincy Street as "an abnormal brain fever."
Henry spoke of it as "a strange and mysterious visitation, it would be
hard to say just what it was."

It seemed once again, as in the time of their youth, that the Angel and
his brother could not long remain in each other's company without experiencing a certain amount of physical and moral discomfort. Henry's
headache could have spoken for the vexation and frustration expressed
in the letter to Grace Norton, that unvoiced helplessness of rage of his
early childhood, when he had to accommodate himself to his elder
brother's active life. Each brother brought to this meeting his old boyhood self. William in Italy could be quite simply a headache for Henry;
and the latter a chronic irritation to William.

The elder brother did not linger. He was impatient to be home and
he cut short his stay as soon as Henry was on the way to recovery. Early
in March he sailed from Bremen. Quincy Street had nourished a hope
that William would bring the lingering literary son back with him, but
Henry had no desire to quit Europe. His illness, he wrote, seemed to have
"cleared him up," he felt better than ever and he wanted to take "a more
contemplative and ceremonious leave" of the Old World. He wished to
"hang on" for three or four months longer. Spring was coming, and he
would remain in Florence. "I confess," he informed Quincy Street, "I
shall leave Europe without alacrity."

The Fork in the Path

William James returned to Quincy Street towards the end of March
1874. Cambridge seemed shrunken and small, and he now understood
better what Henry meant when he spoke of the "provinciality" of Boston.
When he encountered Howells he told him that he had "a newly-quick-
ened sense of the aridity of American life." Henry wrote home amusedly:
"I tremble for future days when I learn from Willy that even he finds
Cambridge mean and flimsy—he who used to hanker so for it here."

Willy's mood was temporary. In due course he wrote a letter designed
to warn Henry of the dangers of repatriation. "It is evident," he wrote,
"that you will have to eat your bread in sorrow for a time here." Was
Henry "ready to make the heroic effort?" William asked.

It is a fork in the path of your life, and upon your decision hangs your
whole future. This is your dilemma. The congeniality of Europe on the
one hand plus the difficulty of making an entire living out of original
writing and its abnormality as a matter of mental hygiene—the dreari-

ness of American conditions of life plus a mechanical routine occupation
possible to be obtained, which from day to day is *done* when 'tis done,
mixed up with the writing into which you distil your essence.

William was saying that Henry could not support himself by his writing
and would be wise to take a job when he came home—something Henry
had long ago determined not to do. There was also the general fact,
recognized by Henry, that in America, more than elsewhere at the time,
to be a writer was to accept the way of loneliness and isolation; and
William had said that writing was an "abnormality," that is, not quite an
active, manly, healthy way of existence. Summing up, William told
Henry that if he was not prepared to face a three-year "slough of de-
spond" he would do well to remain abroad.

There seems to have been in William James throughout his life a
certain blindness to the laws of art that dictated his brother's life. He had
seen Henry joyously engaged in the act of writing and doing this religiously every day, without understanding the meaning of such dedication. Far from "abnormal," this seemed to Henry the most "normal"
thing he could do. He never felt better or stronger than when he had
completed a morning's work. Henry was always to refuse to be bound by
the expediencies advocated by his elder brother. And he felt none of the
urgency William expressed about his future.

He chose not to reply to his brother directly. "Tell Willy," he wrote
to his mother, "I thank him greatly for setting before me so vividly the
question of my going home or staying." He was aware that he was reaching a crossroads in his life, but he shrank, he said, from William's apparent assumption that a return to America at this time was "to pledge
myself to stay forever." He was quite prepared to return "on stern practical grounds." He could find "more abundant literary occupation by being
on the premises," and in this way he would relieve his parents of their
"burdensome financial interposition." He did not intend to bother too
much about that future of which William spoke. "The present bids me
go home and try to get more things published."

There was indeed a "fork in the path" before Henry James, but it was
not the one envisaged by William. The magazines had begun to compete
for his works. His travel pieces in the *Nation* had created a demand for
them in the *Atlantic* and the *Galaxy*. And his efforts to find more outlets
for his stories now began to bear unexpected fruit. Howells wrote asking
James not to send any of his short stories to *Scribner's Monthly*. They
were trying to lure away the *Atlantic* contributors. James, however, had
just sold a story to *Scribner's*. He told Howells the *Atlantic* would simply
be unable to print all the stories he was capable of writing. He promised,
however, that he would always give the *Atlantic* his best.

Meanwhile the editor of *Scribner's,* Dr. Josiah Holland, had written to the elder James in Quincy Street, proposing that Henry do a serial for his magazine. The father replied, without consulting his son, that he would do his best to persuade Henry to write the novel. He also mentioned that it was his opinion that his son's gifts did not lie in the realm of fiction. "His critical faculty is the dominant feature of his intellectual organization." He hastened to add, however, that his son did not agree with this estimate.

Apprised of Holland's proposition, Henry saw at once, what his father had failed to recognize, that there was a singular value in having two magazines competing for his work.

> I am pretty sure the *Atlantic* would like equally well with *Scribner* to have my story, and I should prefer to appear there. It must depend upon the money question, however, entirely, and whichever will pay best shall have the story.

Holland had proposed $1,000 for the serial. Henry decided he would ask $1,200 from the *Atlantic,* that is, twelve installments yielding $100 a month. If the *Atlantic* declined, he was ready to take the $1,000 from *Scribner's.* Howells sent him a contract, giving him the option of terminating his serial before it had run to twelve numbers. James signed it; he said he wished above all "to write close, and avoid padding and prolixity."

"My story is to be on a theme I have had in my head a long time and once attempted to write something about," he told Howells.

> The opening chapters take place in America and the people are of our glorious race; but they are soon transplanted to Rome, where things are to go on famously. *Ecco.* Particulars, including name (which, however, I'm inclined to have simply that of the hero), on a future occasion.

"I shall immortalize myself: *vous allez voir,*" he told his family. He also announced that he would delay his return to Cambridge. A summer in Europe would speed the writing of his novel. "I perfectly perceive the propriety of getting home promptly to heat my literary irons and get myself financially and reputationally on my legs. I have long tacitly felt it; but the moment for action has come."

The Palpable Present

Henry James's course was now clear. He would remain in Florence until summer, then travel northward. He planned to sail late in August. This would give him margin for a few more travel sketches as well as a running start on his serial.

During early April, while he awaited final word from Howells, he broke his Florentine stay for an excursion to Leghorn; then he went to Pisa, Lucca and Pistoia. He could not face doing a large piece of work in a small hotel room, and on his return moved into an apartment at 10 Piazza Santa Maria Novella. It consisted of a sitting-room and balcony, two bedrooms, a scullery and a china cupboard, and cost $25 a month. "Blessed Florence!" he exclaimed to Alice. "My literary labours will certainly show the good effect of my having space to pace about and do a little fine frenzy."

When he was not writing, he took long walks, and paid calls. "Nothing particular happens to me and my time is passed between sleeping and scribbling (both of which I do very well), lunching and dining, walking and conversing with my small circle of acquaintance," he wrote to his mother. Florence decidedly was not Rome. Henry missed the full sense of the Italian spring he had so richly experienced the previous year. Against the rugged walls of the Strozzi Palace, however, flowers stood in sheaves, and he had pleasant strolls in the Cascine. James Russell Lowell turned up for a few days and they renewed their friendship of two years before. "I feel as if I know Lowell now very well," he wrote home.

One afternoon he went to a party in the Villa Castellani on the hill of Bellosguardo. Lizzie Boott had spent her adolescence in a wing of the Villa—one of those large Italian residences which afford space and coolness and, in this case, a superb view of Florence. To Lizzie, then in America, Henry wrote: "It was an enchanting day, the views from the windows were lovely, the rooms were perfumed with a wealth of spring flowers—and the whole thing gave me a sense that it might yet be strangely pleasant to live in that grave, picturesque old house." He added prophetic words: "I have a vague foreboding that I shall, some day."

The writer of thirty-one, who sat in his large shabby room in the Piazza Santa Maria Novella during the Florentine spring of 1874, working on his first important novel, was quite different from the troubled Henry James of four years before who had hurriedly written *Watch and Ward* and hoped it would make his name in American literature. He had always had a sense of his destiny; and now he worked with confidence, drawing his material out of the past decade of his life—the days he had spent in Northampton, just after the end of the Civil War; the days he had spent in Rome a year before—and out of his inner vision as artist.

In his travel sketches and literary reviews, during his slow process of development, he had taken possession of a personal philosophy that would forever guide him. It stemmed from a saturation with certain aspects of life and of literature, and a happy synthesis of the two—and from his constituted personality: the way in which he had learned to look steadily at—and accept—whatever life might bring into his orbit. In one of his travel sketches he spoke of "that perfectly honorable and legitimate instinct, the love of the *status quo*—the preference of contemplative and slow-moving minds for the visible, the palpable, measurable present—touched here and there with the warm lights and shadows of the past."

A year earlier he had written to Charles Eliot Norton, "I regard the march of history very much as a man placed astride of a locomotive, without knowledge or help, would regard the progress of that vehicle. To stick on, somehow, and even enjoy the scenery as we pass, is the sum of my aspiration." James, on his locomotive of history, offers a vision of a comparatively happy observer and artist; the reality in which he had been placed by fate fascinated him to such a degree that the task of observing and recording it from various points of appreciation and ironic judgment proved sufficient for a lifetime.

The models to whom James turned were writers like himself who had been able to arrive at a large view—Balzac, in his "palpable, provable world," teeming with life; Thackeray, most certainly, when he pictured his *Vanity Fair,* and showed his characters acting themselves out in it; George Eliot, with her strong intellectual grasp of experience. To these predecessors James could now add a contemporary, Ivan Sergeyevich Turgenev, a writer with whom he had great affinity, both in his psychological turn of mind and in the aristocracy of his temperament. In the article he had just written about him, he saluted Turgenev as "the first novelist of the day."

Describing Turgenev, James seems to be describing himself. Turgenev was "a story-teller who has taken notes"; his figures were all portraits; "if his manner is that of a searching realist, his temper is that of an earnestly attentive observer"; he had "a deeply intellectual impulse toward universal appreciation." No matter how he shifted his point of view, his object was constantly "that of finding an incident, a person, a situation, *morally* interesting." Speaking of his relation to Russia, James finds that "M. Turgenev gives us a peculiar sense of being out of harmony with his native land—of his having what one may call a poet's quarrel with it." Americans could appreciate Turgenev's state of mind, he said, and if they "had a native novelist of a large pattern, it would probably be, in a degree, his own."

A passage in this essay reveals the stage James had reached in his personal philosophy at the moment he began *Roderick Hudson.* In it he used the old image of life as a moral and spiritual struggle, something not to be defied, or argued with, but to be coped with and mastered. Revolt, he implies, is futile. "Life *is,* in fact, a battle," he wrote. "Evil is insolent and strong; beauty enchanting but rare; goodness very apt to be weak; folly very apt to be defiant; wickedness to carry the day; imbeciles to be in great places, people of sense in small, and mankind generally, unhappy." He continued:

> But the world as it stands is no illusion, no phantasm, no evil dream of a night; we wake up to it again for ever and ever; we can neither forget it nor deny it nor dispense with it. We can welcome experience as it comes, and give it what it demands, in exchange for something which it is idle to pause to call much or little so long as it contributes to swell the volume of consciousness. In this there is mingled pain and delight, but over the mysterious mixture there hovers a visible rule, that bids us learn to will and seek to understand.

In literary terms this could be taken as the manifesto of a novelist who was to consider himself, and to be considered, one of the new realists in American fiction. It implies also the explorer of spiritual values in human conduct. The battle he chose to observe was the struggle within society for values and standards, for devotion to greatness of mind in art and in the imagination. By his embrace and stoic acceptance of reality, James lifted his work into the realm of psychological truth. For he was a solipsist; he believed that each human consciousness carries its own "reality," and that this is what art captures and preserves.

The novelist whose pen was now tracing the history of the passionate and irresponsible Roderick Hudson among the artists of Rome was impervious on the whole to the great scientific strains of his century. James had not only read but had met Darwin in 1869; the new science, however, and the debates about determinism, was to take on particular meaning for him only later in its literary manifestations, in the *naturalisme* of Zola. The word "measurable" in James's view of his immediate world was to acquire in his creative life certain distinct accretions of meaning: he was to place that which was "visible" and "palpable" within the window of a given point of view—that is, his characters' angles of vision by which they observed and measured the world around them. For James metaphysics could have meaning only when translated into art. In the James household religious and philosophical discussion belonged to his father and his brother; this was perhaps reason enough for Henry to go in search of other—of aesthetic—ground. Intellectual though he was, he gave a primary place to "felt life."

At some point, fairly early, James had recognized something else: that he had not "lived" in the way of the great artists. He had known neither the turbulences of Balzac nor the brothels of Flaubert; and he had not smelled Baudelaire's "flowers of evil." He had had an intellectual and aesthetic—and highly puritanical—upbringing. In "Madame de

Mauves" his young American, after encountering a woman like Mrs. Wister, asks himself whether "it is better to cultivate an art than to cultivate a passion." The phrasing suggests James's dilemma: he seemed to think one could not enjoy both; passion, as his tales had shown, was dangerous and life-threatening. Years later he would return to his question in another way. Lambert Strether would tell himself "a man might have—a man such as he was—an amount of experience out of any proportion to his adventures." The imagination could supply the adventures. Literature could supply the materials. So could intimate observation. The games of sex and society were visible in all drawing rooms.

Today we might wonder whether James acted out his capacity for tenderness towards men—but in his catalogue of life homosexuality could be as frightening as women. Sex was frightening—because passion was frightening. It would diminish his masculinity. James's avoidances and omissions sprang out of high fantasies subjugated by civilization. Control, guilt, anxiety—some such bundle was James's inheritance and he overcame it, as his works would confess, by inquiring into states of being and the truths of "felt life." Such life could be found also in man's acquisitive side: the quest for power, expressed in artifacts, paintings, sculptures, household goods, antiques, worked silver and gold, shining stones brought from the depths of the earth, great tapestries and murals, the decoration of the body. All this spoke for human history; all existed in the records of man's imaginings set down in literature. Like Shakespeare, who used the works of others, James would seek to make literature out of literature; the novel would be his art as the poetic drama was Shakespeare's. Poetry made true everything a great writer imagined. James looked at tales of other writers and said to himself, "How would I tell such a story?" And he retold them. Creation became criticism. Literature became James's pigments out of which new tales were written, even as artists had repainted one another's paintings. This would be James's "figure in the carpet."

He wrote his first large novel with great care and he recognized that he was concerning himself more with the life of the intellect and of the emotions than with the life of action. It was a novel in which passion proves fatal. In a letter that summer to Mrs. Wister he told her that he was reliving some of his Roman experiences. He prophesied with complete accuracy what would be criticized in his book. "The fault of the story, I am pretty sure," he said, "will be in its being too analytical and psychological, and not sufficiently dramatic and eventful; but I trust it will have some illusion for you, for all that. *Vedremo.*"

"I am still lingering on here in Florence—one of the few survivors of the winter colony," James wrote to his mother in June 1874. The hot weather had come; the piazza glared white in the noonday sun and seemed to scorch the eye; loungers took their siesta half-naked, flat on their faces, on the paving-stones. He darkened his rooms and stayed on. In the morning he took walks and sought the coolness of the churches; he lunched early and spent the long hot hours of the afternoon in his room, working. His novel was proceeding "not very rapidly, but very regularly, which is the best way."

Four days after describing to his mother his way of coping with the Florentine weather, James fled. A great heat wave had descended upon the city. He went to Ravenna for a day, long enough to study the tomb of Dante and visit the two-storeyed dwelling in which Byron had lived. Pushing on to Milan, he found that even the cavern-like cathedral offered inadequate coolness, and he sought the higher altitude of Monte Generoso near Como. "In spite of the temperature," Henry wrote to William, "I have been lacerated at leaving Italy." He made for Switzerland, via the Splügen. The thought of renewing acquaintance with Bad Homburg made him "deadly sick." He stopped therefore in Baden-Baden, settling in the Hôtel Royal. The place was "coquettish" and "embosomed in a labyrinth of beautiful hills and forest walks." Besides, he wrote to his father, "Turgenev lives here, and I mean to call on him." He did knock on Turgenev's door, only to discover that the Russian was at Carlsbad in Bohemia recovering from a bad attack of the gout. James had sent him his article some weeks earlier; and Turgenev wrote from Carlsbad that it was "inspired by a fine sense of what is just and true; there is manliness in it and psychological sagacity and a clear literary taste." The Russian added, "It would please me very much indeed to make your acquaintance as well as that of some of your compatriots," and he gave James his permanent address in Paris in the rue de Douai.

Henry's days in Europe were now numbered. He spent some five weeks in Baden-Baden—"the dullest weeks of my life," he told Mrs. Wister—and then announced to Quincy Street that he had booked his passage. "Be sure about Sept. 4th to have on hand," he wrote to his mother, "a goodly store of tomatoes, ice-cream, corn, melons, cranberries and other indigenous victuals." He would spend the autumn completing *Roderick Hudson.* Then he would try his fortunes in New York. "I have no plans of liking or disliking, of being happy or the reverse; I shall take what comes, make the best of it and dream inveterately, I foresee, of going back for a term of years, as the lawyers say, to Italy."

James left Baden-Baden in early August, and then by a Rhine journey entered Holland, where he spent some days paying tribute to the "undiluted accuracy of Dutch painters," and relishing that country's "harmonies of the minor key." In Belgium he gave much attention to Rubens—a painter who, he said, "throws away his oranges when he has given them but a single squeeze." He had paid what was to be his only visit to the Low Countries, and with his articles on them his European journey—his book of transatlantic sketches—could be ended.

He sailed from England on a slow Boston Cunarder, the *Atlas,* encountering on board his old friend Wendell Holmes who was newly married. Our next glimpse of him is in a letter written by Mary James to her youngest son, Robertson, at Prairie du Chien:

> Harry has come home to us very much improved in health and looks. When he came in upon us from his voyage in a loose rough English suit, very much burnt and browned by the sea, he looked like a robust young Briton. He seemed well pleased to be home at least as yet.

To the same brother Henry gave testimony of his feelings a month later:

> My arrival is now a month old, first impressions are losing their edge and Europe is fading away into a pleasant dream. But I confess I have become very Europeanized in feeling, and I mean to keep a firm hold of the old world in some way or other.

"Roderick Hudson"

Roderick Hudson was the longest and, as James later said, most "complicated" subject he had yet undertaken: that of a promising young sculptor from Northampton, Massachusetts, who is befriended by an amateur of the arts and taken to Rome to pursue his studies. He shows ready proof of his genius. Pledged from the first to marry his American cousin, he nevertheless falls in love with a great and ultimately unattainable beauty in Rome, and is consumed by his passion. He ceases to create and his disintegration is rapid. The moral of the story seems to be that love and passion are fatal to art.

The opening sequence in Northampton is a skillful variation on familiar Quincy Street problems. Roderick is a second son, unsure of himself in the world, but unlike his creator bereft of a father and elder brother. He is given a new father-brother in the art patron, Rowland Mallet. Adopted by him, he is taken abroad not only to fulfill himself but also to fulfill Rowland's hopes for him. What saves the Northampton part of the story from the clumsiness of the earlier tales is the clarity with which James pictures the artist's dilemma in the small American town. In a few scenes he makes us feel its limitations and the dull future before the gifted young man.

In Rome, Rowland and Roderick wander about very much as Henry and William had recently wandered, Roderick's riot of emotion constantly tempered by Rowland's stuffy sobriety. The young sculptor embraces Europe with intensity. He tries, both in garb and manner, to shake off his parochialism, and project himself into other and more dramatic centuries. Rowland sees him as a "nervous nineteenth-century Apollo."

Roderick's first statues are paternal and maternal—Adam and Eve. He also wants to do a Cain and nourishes the ambition of embodying Beauty, Wisdom, Power, Genius, even Daring, in marble. However, his fear of failure is intense. "What if the watch should run down and you should lose the Key?" he says. "What if you should wake up some morning and find it stopped—inexorably, appallingly stopped? The whole matter of genius is a mystery."

We meet a group of artists, through whom James pictures the various types he had encountered in Rome. Gloriani, the professional opportunist, possesses some of Story's humbug, but he has much candor, intellectual liveliness and the courage of his convictions. In comparison with him, Roderick is distinctly the inspired genius. He is the romantic artist of tradition, the artist who "lives dangerously"; and the difference between him and Gloriani is, in part, his new-world freshness, his openness to experience. We watch him gradually substituting a life of excess for the placid horizons he has abandoned.

Rowland's observation of Roderick is that "the poor fellow is incomplete." This is true; and it is Rowland who, in a sense, completes him. He possesses the cool measuring mind, the dispassionate heart, which Roderick needs—but also rejects. It is as if James has abstracted the incandescence of his genius and placed beside it his decorous, cautious, restrained self, or his mother's warnings beside his own desires. Rowland Mallet is thus the watchdog of his own spirit. He is literally a watcher, for we see the greater part of the story through his eyes. But he is also Roderick's other self. James seems to be asking an unanswerable question: how can the artist, the painter of life, the recorder, the observer, stand on the outside of things and write about them, and throw himself at the same time into the act of living? How become involved in life—and remain uninvolved? It was as if a wall of glass stood between Henry James and his desires. The glass at least permitted him to look at life.

James was sufficiently a Rowland to realize that he could never be a Roderick. Instead of acting out his passions he could invest his characters with them. In this novel the *feeling* self had to die. It was too great a threat to the rational self.

Into the life of Roderick Hudson, during his early days in Rome, there walks Christina Light, with her poodle, her grand manner, her shifting moods. The daughter of an American adventuress and an Italian Cavaliere, she has been brought up unaware of her illegitimacy. Christina is a strong woman capable of cruelty, yet redeemed by certain moments of honesty, and her awareness that she is the plaything of forces she cannot change. Her final act—her marriage to Prince Casamassima—is carried out under her mother's coercion. She is never wholly a free agent. She carries with her the sadness of her grandeur and all its futility.

Christina Light was the great success of *Roderick Hudson.* Created as a foil to Roderick's cousin Mary Garland, representing corrupt Europe as Mary represents innocent New England, she testified in her success to the traditional fascination which evil exercises on the Puritan soul. It was inevitable that she should be all color and vividness, while Mary is prosaic and dull. James had needed this contrast. But there were in the work certain chilly passages which its contemporary critics shrewdly discussed. James's friend Mrs. Wister, in an anonymous notice of the novel in the *North American Review,* gave full recognition to the maturity of the prose and the auspicious character of Henry James's emergence as a full-fledged novelist. But her final words on the book must have given Henry pause: "All it lacks is to have been told with more human feeling."

A New York Winter

The Roman novel began its course in the *Atlantic Monthly* in January 1875, and *A Passionate Pilgrim,* James's first volume of tales, came out on 31 January. J. R. Osgood published it and paid him a royalty. During this month of his début as a novelist and man of letters, James set out to "try New York" and discover whether it might serve as a place in which to live and work.

In his six busy months in the city of his birth, he seems almost literally to have sat at his work-table day and night and "scribbled," as he put it, in a kind of rage of endeavor to see how much he could earn. In addition to the $100 he was receiving each month from *Roderick,* he managed to earn another $100 from miscellaneous writing, largely for the *Nation.* At the same time he saw his second book, *Transatlantic Sketches,* through the press—it was published on 29 April—and made arrangements to bring out *Roderick Hudson* in book form at the end of the year. For the time being, however, once he had completed *Roderick,* he ceased wholly to write fiction. He published only one tale during 1875. The *Nation* paid him anywhere from $10 to $35 for a review, depending upon its length. He had to read three or four books and write about them to earn as much as he could gain from a single travel article. His New York stay proved that it was better economy for him to live in Europe.

One of his problems in Italy had been his loneliness: his loneliness, that is, as a writer who would have liked to know colleagues and who wanted the company of men instead of the perpetual female society to which he had been exposed. He desired that company, he said, "because it would, I am sure, increase my powers of work." He did not find it in New York. Manhattan seemed to confine him in the world "uptown" while all its activities went on "downtown" in the world of business. Seated for several months "at the very moderate altitude of Twenty-Fifth Street" Henry felt himself alone with the music-masters and the French pastry-cooks, the ladies and the children. There was "an extraordinary absence of a serious male interest."

On arriving in New York from Cambridge early in January, James had found two rooms at 111 East 25th Street between Lexington and Fourth Avenues. The Madison Square neighborhood at 23rd Street and Fifth Avenue was within easy walking distance. His sitting-room was small, but sufficiently comfortable, with a fireplace, and he apparently had next to it a hall-bedroom. On leaving his domicile Henry could see, eastward, the "fantastic skeleton" of the elevated railway, which smothered the avenue "with the immeasurable spinal column and myriad clutching paws of an antediluvian monster."

The articles he carried to the *Nation* office at 5 Beekman Street show the range and variety of his reviewing. The journal's editor was still E. L. Godkin, now a power in American journalism. His flourishing weekly, with its 10,000 circulation—substantial for that era—was prepared to publish James on books, art exhibitions, theaters. The book-review department was in the hands of Wendell Phillips Garrison, son of William Lloyd Garrison, the abolitionist. Godkin's assistant was an old friend, Arthur G. Sedgwick, of the Cambridge family into which Norton had married. The novelist occasionally dined with him "at theatrical chop houses," and boasted to Howells of being "a naughty bohemian." "I feel vastly at home here and really like it," he wrote shortly after settling in Manhattan. He added, however, *"pourvu que ça dure."* Later he spoke of this winter as "bright, cold, unremunerative, uninteresting."

Of the seventy notices and articles James wrote during 1875, thirty-nine appeared in the *Nation* during his six months' residence in New York, two in the *Atlantic* and one in the *Galaxy.* Garrison seems to have given him free choice of the books that came into the office. He preferred travel, literary essays, biographies of New England worthies, anything relating to America and Europe. He eagerly took all French subjects. But he reviewed also such works as *Ismailia,* a narrative of an expedition to Central Africa for the suppression of the slave trade. His reviews are light and humorous; they have authority; some could be called scholarly, although the imagination of the literary creator frees them from any suggestion of pedantry. What Henry brought to them was his taste for the flavor as well as the substance of any work he read. He has occasion to refer to Emerson's "magnificent vagueness," and another time observes that "in the day of Mark Twain there is no harm in being reminded that the absence of drollery may, at a stretch, be compensated by the presence of sublimity." Of Stopford Brooke's essays on theology in the English poets he remarks that "he rather too readily forgives a poor verse on the plea of a fine thought." And so his pen races along, cheerful, easy, carefree, imparting to the readers of the *Nation* accounts of Dr. Livingstone's journals, the life of the Prince Consort, the story of a missionary bishop, Taine on Paris, Augustus Hare on Rome—and all with a spontaneity which did not reflect the sheer pressure of production in 25th Street.

His inspection of the New York theaters, as reflected in his *Nation* articles, was not edifying. The playgoing public saw few American plays; it received rather "an Irish image, a French image, an English image" in the tinkered dramas brought from overseas. Nor did the American plays at the Fifth Avenue Playhouse demand much intellectual effort. Seeing a concoction called *Women of the Day,* which he described as "ghostly, monstrous, a positive nightmare," Henry regretted that audiences in America did not indulge in the old-fashioned freedom of hissing.

Of the five art notices contributed to the *Nation* during this period, one, "On Some Pictures Lately Exhibited," contains a spirited defense of art criticism:

> It may be very superficial, very incompetent, very brutal, very pretentious, very preposterous; it may cause an infinite amount of needless chagrin and gratuitous error; it may even blast careers and break hearts; but we are inclined to think that if it were suppressed at a stroke, the painters of our day would sadly miss it, decide that on the whole it had its merits, and at last draw up a petition to have it resuscitated.

He proceeded—as he invariably did—to give a good example to the *Nation* readers of what a perceptive and schooled eye, supported by aesthetic feeling and strong verbal skill, could do in the observation of pictures. Notable particularly during this year was his praise for the work of Frank Duveneck, a painter who had trained himself in Munich and who was attracting attention in Boston and New York. James discovered certain Velázquez qualities in his portraits: he would "take it hard," he said, if Duveneck failed to do something of the first importance.

The New York winter was cold but there was much brilliant sunshine; and the spring was a mixture of rain and snow. James would take the elevated train uptown and walk over to the long narrow tract of Central Park. There was a "raw delicacy" in the April air; and in spite of the Park's rockwork grottoes and tunnels, its pavilions and statues, "lakes too big for the landscape and bridges too big for the lakes," he at least got some feeling of the vernal season.

Spring brought back memories of Rome. These had been revived a few weeks earlier by a visit to Butler Place in Philadelphia, the home of Mrs. Wister, where the recollections of their Roman days had seemed vivid amid the winter snows. Mrs. Kemble was living in York Place, near her daughter, and James called on her one morning. He remembered the sunny drawing-room, the morning fire, the "Berlin wools" she was wearing, the way her spectacles were placed on her nose, and her rich English tones as she read, as only she could read, certain passages from Edward FitzGerald's translation of a Calderón play.

Mrs. Wister introduced Henry to her New York friend, Florence Lockwood, whose Manhattan home provided him with excellent conversation; "a remarkable woman," he wrote to Mrs. Wister, perhaps too tense, and too *in*tense, but "so singularly lovely that a *tête-à-tête* with her is a great bliss." By June, when the hot weather came, Henry felt that his New York experiment had given him the answers he needed. He might have tried to write fiction instead of book reviews, and eventually earned an adequate living. But the New York scene offered him few themes compared with those which he found abroad. His choice had really been made from the first. Many years later Logan Pearsall Smith suggested his decision was a foregone conclusion: "In speaking of New York he said that it was impossible to have a picturesque address there, and he told me that he had gone back to New York to live and be a good American citizen, but at the end of a year he had quietly packed up his few belongings and come away."

The one piece of fiction written by Henry James during his winter in Manhattan was an allegory entitled "Benvolio." It was to be his only venture into this form. Allegory, he remarked later, is "apt to spoil two good things—a story and a moral, a meaning and a form." "Benvolio" however had neither story nor moral; it was a *jeu d'esprit,* a fairy-tale James set down one day in 25th Street, and its meaning is not difficult to discover.

Benvolio, a young-man-about-town, is "more than twenty-five" but not yet "thirty-five"—in other words he is Henry James's age. He lives in two chambers in a city; one of them offers him a view of the great square and its teeming life; the other, his bedroom, resembles a monk's cell, and looks out on a quiet garden. He is a man of fashion; he sports an intaglio, or "an antique Syracusan coin," in his cravat. He is equally capable of putting on a "rusty scholar's coat" and braving the daylight without ornament. He is a man of peace, named for Romeo's friend who tried to keep the Montagues and Capulets from brawling with one another. This Benvolio tries to keep the two sides of his nature from brawling: not that they are really at war. On the contrary: he thinks he should make up his mind between the life offered him by a certain Countess, a life of great extravagance and much amusement, and the life he enjoys with Scholastica, daughter of a Philosopher into whose garden he looks from his bedroom window. The Philosopher, like Henry James's father, or his brother William, thinks the young man best fitted for philosophy, and spends his time discussing the Absolute and the Relative with him. But Benvolio, when he is with the Countess, is inclined to write brilliant comedies rather than philosophical disquisitions.

We do not have to look far to see what the two women represent. The Countess is the world, and the world is Europe—when indeed did America have Countesses? And Scholastica is the good studious life seen in the modest unimaginative terms of Quincy Street. Or she might well be also that side of Henry James which could function as critic and drudge, as he was doing in New York, when his inner being craved the freedom of Europe, the liberty to write as he pleased.

America or Europe? The life of the teeming square, or the life of the monastic cell? There is no resolution. When Benvolio is away from the Countess, and when Scholastica, feeling rejected, flees to the Antipodes, Benvolio misses them both and leads "an extremely fretful and unproductive life." When he resumes his life with Scholastica, he is productive again, but his poems are "dismally dull." Benvolio seems to be both critic and creator, and is quite content to alternate between the two.

It was precisely by such alternation, by the vision of the two great worlds between which he shuttled, the Americans in Europe, the Europeans in America, the polarities of the parochial and the cosmopolitan, that Henry James was to live. And he led always that double life of Benvolio: he courted Europe, and he never forgot America.

What strikes the reader in James's fantasy is the fact that the two personages dwelling within Benvolio, although quite different, nevertheless manage to enjoy peaceful co-existence. Benvolio is happy when he looks out on the square and lives with the Countess; he is no less happy when he contemplates the garden and Scholastica. This suggests that in certain fundamental areas James was an individual without conflict. He saw the world as it was and pursued his aims without hesitation. At the end of his stay in New York, he did not find himself in any particular dilemma. He had known from the first that he wanted to live in Europe. It was, as he had said of his *Atlantic* serial, purely a question of money. The writing of "Benvolio" was probably his way of settling the matter in his mind.

He returned to Cambridge in mid-July of 1875, knowing that his first two books were receiving good reviews and having an honorable sale. Howells had launched *A Passionate Pilgrim* with superlatives: "In richness of expression and splendour of literary performance," he wrote, "we may compare him with the greatest, and find none greater than he." Other critics did not go to such extremes; they recognized the qualities of the style, but found flaws in Henry's characters. The reviews of *Transatlantic Sketches* were more complimentary; the *Nation* did remark however that Henry, as a traveler, not only discussed the objective scenery but also put into his writing the "scenery of his own mind."

Particularly encouraging was the news that in three months the travel book had sold almost 1,000 copies. Henry had thus finally taken hold of a literary place in America: and he had the assurance that his third book would be published by the end of the year. The question to be resolved was how, and in what circumstances, he could now take his leave of Cambridge and re-cross the Atlantic. The best thing he could imagine was to go abroad and "try Paris" as he had tried New York. Moreover he had already discussed with the *Galaxy* an idea broached some time before by William James, that he should write a series of essays on the important French novelists. Paris would be the best place to do this.

At this moment, poised between his winter's grind in New York and the thought of Paris, James wrote the first of these essays—his first major literary essay. The definitive edition of Balzac's works had recently appeared in twenty-three volumes; and re-reading the novels and tales he recaptured his fascination with "the first of the realists": "the things he invented were as real to him as the things he knew." Having just published his first novel in his thirty-second year, James alludes to the fact that Balzac had spent a decade trying to write novels before he had learned the world.

> Walter Scott, Thackeray, George Eliot, Mme. Sand, waited till they were at least turned thirty, and then without prelude, or with brief prelude, produced a novel which was a masterpiece. If it was well for them to wait, it would have been infinitely better for Balzac.

Thus the American novelist who had also waited. The autobiographical overtones of this passage, and of the passages in which James describes Balzac's money needs, suggest that Henry had thought of himself as a Balzacian scribbler during those weeks in 25th Street in which he had turned himself into a writing-machine.

There was a consistent reference back to Balzac in all that he was to do. Planning once again a transatlantic leap, what more natural than to test the land and city of Balzac, to be himself like one of Balzac's young men from the provinces—even if from the American provinces—arriving in the great metropolis, there to conquer not with a sword but with a tireless pen? But how was he to do this? What he needed above all in

Paris was some foothold, some regular means of writing that would furnish him his needed revenue, as the *Nation* had done in New York.

The answer, as he later recorded it in his journal, "loomed before me one summer's day in Quincy Street." He had met in New York John Hay, who had been an assistant secretary to Lincoln, and was now an editorial writer for Whitelaw Reid, publisher of the *New York Tribune.* To Hay, Henry wrote, on 21 July, that he had "a tolerably definite plan of going in the autumn to Europe" to establish himself for a "considerable period" in Paris. "I should like, if I do so," he said, "to secure a regular correspondence with a newspaper." It would be non-political, wholly concerned with manners, habits, people, books, pictures, the theater, perhaps travel sketches in rural France. The *Tribune* had, as James knew, a correspondent in Paris—the Frenchman Arsène Houssaye—who was writing the kind of sketches he envisaged, but he felt he could do these from an American point of view. Hay promptly sent a memorandum to the publisher urging that James be engaged—"you know his wonderful style and keen observation of life and character." Hay proposed that Houssaye be dismissed at the time of James's going abroad with the explanation that the labor of translation created extra difficulties for the paper.

Whitelaw Reid saw the force of this argument. He was inclined to offer $20 a letter instead of the $25 James asked; this Henry accepted. With $60 or $80 monthly from the *Tribune* he could live comfortably in Paris and augment his income by writing fiction. He asked the *Atlantic* to advance the $400 due on the four remaining installments of *Roderick Hudson.* His father agreed once more to back his needs with a letter of credit. Thus armed, he bade farewell to his family, and sailed on 20 October for Liverpool on the *Bothnia.*

There were gale-winds and the Cunarder tumbled and tossed during its ten-day voyage. James discovered that Anthony Trollope was on board and had some talk with him. He was struck by his "plain persistence" in writing every day, no matter how much the ship rocked. Trollope had "a gross and repulsive face and manner, but appears *bon enfant* when you talk with him. But he is the dullest Briton of them all." In the evenings the British novelist played cards with Mrs. Arthur Bronson of Boston.

On 31 October, a Sunday, James stepped off the boat-train in London and went to Story's Hotel in Dover Street, off Piccadilly. On Monday morning, to get his land-legs, he walked up Piccadilly and into Hyde Park. In the afternoon he sat down and wrote to Quincy Street, to the entire family, to "Dear People All." The exclamatory opening sentence would do for all the ensuing decades: "I take possession of the old world —I inhale it—I appropriate it!" He had made his choice: he had consummated his adventure. No conquistador, planting a flag of annexation, could have sounded a note more genuinely triumphant.

Henry James Jr., aged eleven,
with his father.

Mary Walsh James, HJ's mother,
in middle life.

Henry James at sixteen, Geneva.

Henry James in the period after his
"obscure hurt," aged seventeen.

William and Henry James, Newport, 1860. Apparently posed in imitation of
Titian's *Man with Glove* in the Louvre. "There is a great Titian at the
Louvre—*l'homme au gant;* but I, in my gloved gentleness, shall run him
close" (HJ to Mrs. Frank Mathews, 18 Nov. 1902).

From HJ's sketchbook, near Tewkesbury, Gloucestershire,
England, 8 April 1869.

Minny Temple at eighteen.

The American, cover of the pirated "yellowback" issue in England.

Henry James at Dover, 1884.

At the Villa Castellani, Bellosguardo, Florence, 1887: Elizabeth Boott Duveneck with her father, Francis; Frank Duveneck to the rear with Ann Shenstone, who had been Elizabeth's nanny.

Alice James in Leamington with Katharine Loring, 1889.

Constance Fenimore Woolson,
Venice, probably 1893.

The Palazzo Barbaro, Venice.

The poster for *Guy Domville*, December 1894.

Henry James at Dunwich, Suffolk.

Lamb House, Rye, Sussex, from the garden. The detached Garden Room
is on the right.

Max Beerbohm, "A memory of Henry James and Joseph Conrad conversing at an afternoon party, circa 1904."

Henry James with Cora Crane at a garden party in the
Brede Rectory, near Rye.

In front of the Palazzo Borghese,
Rome, 1899.

Henry James
and Mrs. Humphry Ward.

James and his gardener, George
Gammon, Lamb House.

Ellen (Bay) Emmet's unfinished portrait, 1900.

The Jameses at 95 Irving Street, Cambridge, 1905, in the garden—Peggy, William, Henry and Mrs. William (Alice).

The brothers, Henry and William, in Cambridge, 1905.

Henry James at St. Augustine, Florida, in 1906, with Mrs. Robertson James and her daughter, later Mary James Vaux.

Henry James and Molly Hooper Warner (Mrs. Roger S. Warner), a niece of Henry Adams.

A series of caricatures of HJ in the United States during his 1906 lecture tour.

The Master in an anxious moment.

Henry James's walking sticks at the Lamb House entrance.

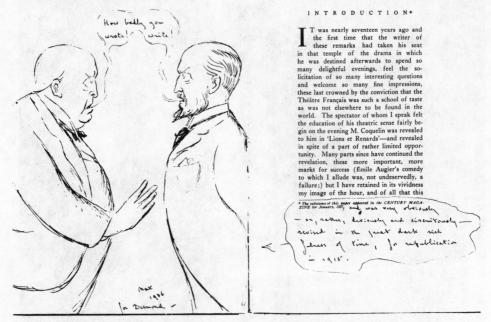

I T was nearly seventeen years ago and the first time that the writer of these remarks had taken his seat in that temple of the drama in which he was destined afterwards to spend so many delightful evenings, feel the solicitation of so many interesting questions and welcome so many fine impressions, these last crowned by the conviction that the Théâtre Français was such a school of taste as was not elsewhere to be found in the world. The spectator of whom I speak felt the education of his theatric sense fairly begin on the evening M. Coquelin was revealed to him in 'Lions et Renards'—and revealed in spite of a part of rather limited opportunity. Many parts since have continued the revelation, these more important, more markt for success (Émile Augier's comedy to which I allude was, not undeservedly, a failure;) but I have retained in its vividness my image of the hour, and of all that this

* The substance of this paper appeared in the CENTURY MAGAZINE for January, 1887, and was very obviously — or, rather, deviously and circuitously — revised in the great dark rich fulness of time, for republication in 1915.

Max Beerbohm's sketch for Desmond MacCarthy about Henry James's late revisions of his work.

"The Chariot of Fire"—Edith Wharton's Panhard with chauffeur
Charles Cook at the wheel, Teddy Wharton beside him and the Master
and Edith in rear (1907).

Edith Wharton in 1905 when HJ met her.

W. Morton Fullerton in Paris, 1907.

On a terrace at Cernitoio near Vallombrosa, 1907. The Master standing with
cigarette, Howard Sturgis (left) with the Edward Boits.

FRANK LESLIE'S NEW YORK JOURNAL,

Of Romance, General Literature, Science and Art.

New Series.—Vol I.—Part 2.   FEBRUARY 1855.   CENTS.

TEMPTATION.

Continued from page 12.

Now this was the very thing the gentleman did not choose to give.

"It is a mooted point," he replied, "whether the spirits of the dead ever are permitted to return to earth. Antiquity and history are both in favor of the supposition that they do. I need not remind you of the Witch of Endor."

"No, no! I have read of her in the Bible."

"Or the spirit which it is said appear[ed] just before the battle of Philippi, in fact speaker, "it is one of those question[s] balanced in the human mind, that in ni[ne] of ten we are guided by our impress[ion] than our reason."

The sexton seized his spade and be[gan]. The doctor saw that he was dissatisfi[ed].

"Do you comprehend what I have added.

"No," replied the old man. "Do you? to know what you thought about the m[an] you talk to me about the Witch of Endor[.]

CHAPTER XXXV

O thievish night,
Why shouldst thou, but for some felonious end,
In thy dark lantern thus close up the stars
That nature hung in heaven, and filled their *lamps*
With everlasting oil, to give due light
To the misled and lonely traveller?—MILTON.

IT is not to be supposed that Miles, who had been trained in the school of Peter Quin, would leave any means untried to discover the abode of Martha, whom he both hated and feared. Hated, for having subdued and humbled him—and feared, from the power which her knowledge of his crimes had armed her with.

Still it was not without considerable misgiving that he set himself to the task: it was necessary to proceed cautiously—for he knew that if his intended victim obtained the least clue to his proceedings, or entertained a suspicion of his design, she would keep no terms with him. Many men—bunglers in the trade of villany—would have commenced operations by setting on parties to watch; but Miles was too cunning for that: the information which he required he determined to obtain himself.

MIKE AND PETER QUIN IN THE CHURCHYARD.

PART THREE

The Conquest of London

1875–1881

I have an inalienable mistrust of
the great ones of the earth and
a thorough disbelief in any security
with people who have no imaginations.

HENRY JAMES

Ivan Sergeyevich

In New York one could not have a picturesque address. Henry James's now was 29 rue de Luxembourg, since renamed rue Cambon, which extends from the rue de Rivoli to the Boulevard des Capucines. In 1875 it was still composed of large residences, with old high garden-walls. From the windows of his second-floor apartment he had a good view and he was to remember the particular light click of the passing cab-horses on the clear asphalt, and the hard music of hoofs when each morning a troop of cuirassiers charged down the street and into barracks on the Place Vendôme.

James had arrived in Paris on 11 November 1875. He was settled within the week and on 22 November he dispatched his first letter to the *Tribune.* And in the 15 November issue of the *Revue des Deux Mondes* he discovered a translation of his tale "The Last of the Valerii." His permission had not been asked; nevertheless it was almost as if his arrival were being trumpeted in France.

On the same day that he mailed to New York his first *Tribune* article, James made his way to Montmartre. Climbing its hilly streets, he found the rue de Douai, No. 50, a three-story house; he passed through a small front courtyard, and on entering was ushered into the presence of Ivan Sergeyevich Turgenev. He was to remember his meeting with the tall, white-haired Russian, and the large sofa, in the green room on the second floor, built to accommodate Turgenev's sprawling figure. There was a fine painting by Théodore Rousseau on one wall, a Corot on another, a bas-relief of Pauline Viardot, the singer, in whose house Turgenev was living. There were none of the odds and ends one expected in the rooms of a man of letters; no accumulation of papers; few books. James recalled however that Turgenev wrote little in Paris; he did most of his work during periods of withdrawal to his properties in Russia.

The Russian was uncommonly tall; his frame suggested brute strength. One could see in him the man of the out-of-doors, the sportsman, the hunter. He had a finely shaped head; his features were irregular, and yet there was beauty in the face; his expression, James was to write, "had a singular sweetness," and his eye, "the kindest of eyes, was deep and melancholy." His hair was abundant and straight; his beard, trimmed and short, was as white as his hair.

Turgenev had asked James to come between 11 and 1. He arrived at 11, met the Viardots; then for the next two hours the two writers discussed "a variety of topics." The novelist spoke English well, but rather "stiffly"; he had remarked that no language was comparable to the Russian. "He seemed very simple and kind," benign and gentle. James had come prepared to like him for his novels. He found a human being who was "adorable." Later he would discern flaws, particularly his "softness" and his passivity. However he took him as he was. Turgenev on his part received James as a mature *confrère,* with courtesy, interest and respect.

The meeting of American and Russian, divided by their years (James thirty-two, Turgenev fifty-seven), by geography, language and background, took place on the wide ground of cosmopolitanism and craft— their artistic temperaments, their sense of the great sprawling land-mass which each had left for the alien yet friendly soil of France. Large historical forces had been in motion behind them. Russian society, like that of America (as James observed), was in process of formation, and the Russian character was "in solution" in a sea of change such as existed also in the United States. Deep similarities might be found in their family history. Turgenev had had to contend with a tyrannical mother; Henry with a mother who concealed an iron grip. Both had emerged with a certain inner softness as well as an ability to "tune in" to the feminine consciousness. As artists, they had the power of creating the atmosphere of place and both knew how to see into the essences of personality. Both were "realists," that is their work has a certain historical and documentary as well as psychological value; both—above all—took a certain melancholy pleasure in their belief in renunciation and the man-made trappings of the social order. They were articulate spokesmen for all that was civilized in their two countries—that part of civilization both nations had "imported" from western Europe.

In meeting Turgenev, James discovered a man old enough to be his father and young enough to be his friend; a man of singular allure. He had the gentleness of the elder Henry James without his bristling qualities; and he accepted James as an artist, which his father never wholly did. A month after their encounter James wrote to Quincy Street: "I have seen him again several times, with unabated regard. He seems rather older and drowsier than I first thought him, but he is the best of men. He has twice called on me."

In his later memoir of his Russian friend James described the elation he used to experience after being with Turgenev. He always left him, he said, in a state of intimate excitement. This condition was like a man swinging a cane, leaping lightly over gutters, stopping for no reason at all, to look, with an air of being struck, into a shop window—where he actually saw nothing. What was this enchantment of talk which made Henry behave like a young man in love? Four occasions stood out, on which a meeting with the Russian brought him a supreme sense of artistic feeling and artistic spontaneity.

It was raining on the first such occasion, in the early months of 1876, when the American called at the rue de Douai. In the green room, Turgenev is sprawled on his sofa. He has been ill, with gout and then with bronchitis, but shows little sign of it in his talk. He is animated, responsive, reflective. He begins to tell how stories come to him. He never thinks of a plot. The germ comes in the form of some figure he has known, hovering and soliciting him. Before writing about this figure, Turgenev wants to know it intimately. He compiles its dossier, as if he were a detective; only when he knows its biography does he become aware of what it will do and how it will act. Starting with the figure, he invents, selects, pieces together, as James put it, "the situations most useful and favourable to the sense of the creatures themselves."

The Russian's testimony confirmed James in his own way of storytelling: he, too, began with his personages. That winter in Paris he still had the feeling that working in this fashion he was putting the cart before the horse; that plots, not people, were what he should be looking for. To have the man he regarded as "the first novelist of the day" reassure him gave new authority to his own methods, essentially psychological, in which the author sought constantly the truths of human behavior.

And so the long rainy afternoon passed—a vivid unforgettable afternoon—and Henry wrote to his brother that Turgenev "gave me a sort of definition of his own mental process, which was admirably intelligent and limpidly honest. This last is the whole man; and it is written in his face."

The second meeting occurred on another damp day in the rawness of the Paris winter. But the café in the Avenue de l'Opéra is new and bright, with large settees made for comfort and talk. James and his Russian friend linger over their noonday meal. Turgenev talks about Russia: he tells of curious visits paid him by émigrés; he describes nihilists he has known; he dwells on the "dark prospects of his native land," the anguish of struggle and revolt. When he is in this vein (James later observed) he is powerful, the splendid story-teller, "extraordinarily vivifying and stimulating."

By the third meeting, James, now a familiar, is invited to Madame Viardot's Thursday musicales, and to the family's Sunday evenings, devoted to simple sociabilities, mainly charades. There is something "strange and sweet" in Turgenev—the same Turgenev of the serious talk and the meditative manner—prancing and crawling on the floor, wearing old shawls and masks, "at his age and with his glories," as if he were a child. "Fancy Longfellow, Lowell, or Charles Norton, doing the like, and every Sunday evening!" James writes to Quincy Street.

The fourth meeting: It is April. James has met a young Russian, Paul Zhukovski, a dilettante painter, a good conversationalist, who is also a friend of Ivan Sergeyevich. Zhukovski invites Henry and Turgenev to dine with him, and turns up with a sympathetic Russian woman, the Princess Ourousov. At a little restaurant in the square in front of the Opéra Comique, Ivan Sergeyevich is jovial, prattlesome, entertaining. Henry delights in his mixture of wit and almost infantile naïveté. The evening seems scarce begun, however, before Turgenev leaves. He has faithfully promised Pauline Viardot he will be home by 9:30.

There would be other meetings, reunions in London and again in Paris, but these were the most precious of Henry's year in the French capital. He had seen certain aspects of Turgenev that revealed him as a lovable human being; James could not have enough of him. To be sure, the Russian had his weaknesses. He had an "expansive softness, a comprehensive indecision," like so many of his characters. Henry gossiped to his parents that Turgenev was Pauline Viardot's "slave"; the Viardots treated him as a *vache à lait* and made free and easy with his money. And the 9:30 curfew! Madame Viardot stood between James and more frequent meetings with the beloved Ivan Sergeyevich. He may have cut the silver cord of Quincy Street but he had for the moment fastened the dangling end to the rue de Douai.

In his later essay James remarked that Turgenev "to the best of my belief" ignored his, James's, writings, and "was unable to read them." He went on to say that the Russian

> cared, more than anything else, for the air of reality, and my reality was not to the purpose. I do not think my stories struck him as quite meat for men. The manner was more apparent than the matter; they were too *tarabiscoté,* as I once heard him say of the style of a book—had on the surface too many little flowers and knots of ribbon.

Nothing in Turgenev's letters suggests that he thought James's tales were not "meat for men." Turgenev had praised the "manliness" and "psychological sagacity" in James's early work. But one possible reason for Henry's self-abasement suggests itself. William James had often re-proached Henry for his "fancy" writing—the "knots of ribbon"—and the gallicisms sprinkled through his prose; his father praised his essays at the expense of his fiction. Accustomed to some note of criticism in those dearest to him, holding Turgenev dear, and sensing in him paternal and fraternal qualities, James endowed the Russian with the familiar elements of his own life. In setting him up as an authoritative figure he seems to have grouped him with the candid critics of Quincy Street.

Councils of the Gods

Three weeks after their first meeting, Turgenev took James to one of Flaubert's Sunday afternoons. In a letter a few days later to his friend Perry, James remarked with pride and irony, *"je suis lancé en plein Olympe."*

On that memorable Sunday in December 1875, when Henry and Ivan Sergeyevich climbed to the high end of the Faubourg St. Honoré and then mounted the five flights of stairs, it seemed to the American that he was indeed being transported to some Olympus. Flaubert opened the door himself. He embraced Turgenev as if he were receiving a beloved brother, and shook hands with his transatlantic visitor, greeting him in a timid, friendly way. The Frenchman was tall; his face was serious and sober; he had light-colored salient eyes. He wore what James described as a "long colloquial dressing-gown," with trousers to match.

The guests were ushered into a high small room that seemed "bare and provisional," save for a gilded and painted Buddha of considerable size on the chimney-piece. Here before his cheerful fire the author of *Madame Bovary* dispensed his hospitality. On this first occasion James met Edmond de Goncourt, fifty-three, a year younger than Flaubert, the busy survivor of the fraternal writing team: tall, slender, *type du gentil-homme français,* James said of him. He was also introduced to Émile Zola, thirty-five, author of *Thérèse Raquin* and the first volumes of his series of the Rougon-Macquart. "A very common fellow," was Henry's first impression.

On his second Sunday visit, in mid-January of 1876, James met Alphonse Daudet. Daudet was Zola's age; he had a black wispy bohemian beard and a visage that was—with his later physical sufferings—to be generally considered "Christlike." James's first impression of him was also negative. Later, too, he met Guy de Maupassant, twenty-five, a protégé of Flaubert's, who so far had published nothing.

On this Olympus, the gods were uncommonly talkative: disputing the art of fiction, gossiping about the latest scandals of Paris, discussing censorship, royalties, publishers, sexual adventures, the theater, politics.

No subject was sacrosanct. On one occasion Zola confided in a matter-of-fact way to the group that he was collecting all the *gros mots* of the language, the familiar talk of the working class, a veritable small dictionary of obscenities. His new novel, *L'Assommoir,* was starting its run in a magazine; he was being well paid for it; but the journal had received protests from provincial subscribers against the serial's indecencies and it looked as if publication would be suspended. The *cénacle* was stirred up; its opinion was that while this was a bore, it could only do the book good.

James seems to have visited the *cénacle* about once a month during his stay in Paris. With his real joy in the wit and intellectual power of the Flaubertians, he found them distinctly insular: Turgenev spoke English fluently, and Flaubert had mastered enough to read Shakespeare. Zola and Daudet, however, could not meet James on the ground of *his* language and literature, as he could on theirs; there was no doubt that the French men of letters were inclined to consider Paris as their all-sufficient country.

James was astonished how little respect these men had for the *Revue des Deux Mondes* and with what ease they dismissed certain of the minor novelists he had enjoyed and reviewed: Victor Cherbuliez, Gustave Droz, Octave Feuillet. Such writers, James was to say years afterwards, "were not even conceivable" in that room. On one occasion, when the name of Gustave Droz came up, Zola muttered that Droz's books were *merde à la vanille.* The matter troubled James a little; was this a failure in *his* literary taste, or simply the *brusqueries* of dogmatists? He alluded to it in one of his *Tribune* letters:

> A little school that dislikes every other school, but is extremely active and industrious within its own circle, is an excellent engine for the production of limited perfection . . . It is simply the old story that, either in politics or in literature, Frenchmen are ignorant of the precious art of compromise.

If James was being made welcome at the *cénacle* it was decidedly not on the strength of his tales which were appearing in the *Revue* during that winter (after the first, three more were published, in rather poor translations). "I have seen almost nothing of the literary fraternity," he was to write later that spring to Howells, "and there are fifty reasons why I should not become intimate with them. I don't like their wares, and they don't like any others." We must make large allowance for these complaints. The truth was that James greatly enjoyed himself among his young French peers and he saw more of them than he seemed to admit. For all their "narrowness" he cherished their memory.

In his memorial essay on Turgenev he stresses the elements in the rue de Faubourg St. Honoré which were important to him.

> What was discussed in that little smoke-clouded room was chiefly questions of taste, questions of art and form; and the speakers, for the most part, were, in aesthetic matters, radicals of the deepest dye. It would have been late in the day to propose among them any discussion of the relation of art to morality, any question as to the degree in which a novel might or might not concern itself with the teaching of a lesson.

The Victorian debate between art and morality did not concern them. "The only duty of a novel was to be well written; that merit included every other of which it was capable." This was the common ground on which James stood with these "deep-dyed radicals." And it was this that made him say, long after, that his year in Paris "was time by no means misspent."

In the little high room at the Faubourg's end James heard always many voices: but he did not go every Sunday to the *cénacle.* He preferred to see Turgenev by himself; and he wanted intimate talk with Flaubert. One mid-week afternoon towards the end of March 1876 he found the Frenchman alone. He sat with him a long time. Their conversation turned to French writers, and Flaubert gave Henry certain reminiscences of Théophile Gautier, who had been his intimate, and whom he preferred to Musset. *"Il était plus français,"* more generally French in the quality of his melancholy. Reaching for Gautier's volumes he began to read a poem. It dealt with old and yellowing portraits in oval frames, portraits of beauties faded and violated by time, yet clasping forever their withered century-old bouquets, a poem nostalgic and fragile in its artful sadness. *"J'aime à vous voir en vos cadres ovales,"* Flaubert read, slowly and in measured tones, *"Portraits jaunis des belles du vieux temps."*

Flaubert loudly declaimed the lines—he used to speak of his "bellow." The moment was filled with deep emotion for James. There was something extraordinarily tender in the way Flaubert showed his affection for his friend's delicate verses. James always vividly remembered this moment, when the author of *Madame Bovary* had read to him—to him alone—in the quiet little room in the old Faubourg. In his final essay on Flaubert thirty years later he devoted an entire page to the scene. The poem, he confessed—it is entitled "Pastel"—had been new to him; and since that time he had never been able to discover it in Gautier's works. This was perhaps a happy thing.

> But for the rhyme in fact I could have believed him to be spouting to me something strange and sonorous of his own. The thing really rare would have been to hear him do that — hear him *gueuler,* as he liked to call it.

There were other weekday occasions at Flaubert's when they talked alone, and sometimes on Sunday James was the first to arrive and had the writer to himself. He considered him "the most interesting man and strongest artist of his circle." *Madame Bovary* was a masterpiece, this he recognized. *Salammbô* was as hard as stone; *L'Éducation Sentimentale* was as cold as death. *Madame Bovary* alone had enough emotion to take off the chill of the other works. There was "something ungenerous" in Flaubert's genius, and James was to note that in all the French writer's letters there was no mention of "any beauty but verbal beauty."

He talked of Flaubert one day with Turgenev. The Russian said that Flaubert's great trouble was that he had never known a decent woman. He had passed his life exclusively *"avec des courtisanes et des riens-du-tout."* Neither of them apparently knew then of Flaubert's long-ago affair with Louise Colet; there is a genuine tone of surprise in James's later review of Flaubert's letters as he comes upon his correspondence with the energetic and opportunistic bluestocking. But in 1876, telling of his talk with the Russian, he writes to William: "In poor old Flaubert there is something almost tragic; his big intellectual temperament, machinery, etc., and vainly colossal attempts to press out the least little drop of *passion.*" There was however something human and even "august in a strong man who has not been able completely to express himself." Flaubert was "cold—and he would have given everything to be able to glow."

James's final verdict on him, set down in the intimacy of his journal, was that he was of "a powerful, serious, melancholy, manly, deeply corrupted, yet not corrupting nature. He was head and shoulders above the others, the men I saw at his house on Sunday afternoons." Exception made, of course, for Turgenev.

Parisian Life

That winter Henry James moved in a sort of cosmopolitan enclave within Paris—among Russians and Americans—but having only occasional glimpses of the French. He felt himself distinctly an outsider even though he had access, as artist, to the *cénacle*; indeed, this made him feel more of an outsider than ever. When summer had come, he could announce to Howells that he was "turning into an old, and very contented Parisian." But he added: "Of pure Parisianism I see nothing."

He was to say, years later, that the French are "the people in the world one may have to go more of the way to meet than any other." For one as curious as James and as interested in manners, this must have been a chronic exasperation. Godkin had given him a letter of introduction to the political correspondent of the *Nation,* Auguste Laugel, who

invited James often to his home. He had been secretary to the Duc d'Au-
male, and Madame Laugel obtained for James an invitation to a ducal
reception, where he met members of the Orléans family. He was much
amused by a corpulent Princess of Saxe-Coburg who gave him "a realizing sense of what princesses are trained to." The Laugels also arranged
dinners at which James met Ernest Renan and Émile Montégut, the
French critic of American literature. He liked Renan, but toward Montégut, "a Frenchman of the intense, unhumorous type," he developed an
acute personal dislike, so strong that he could no longer read him.

James complains constantly of being caught in concentric social
circles, but he makes the most of them. Through an American friend he
is invited to the salon of Montégut's patroness, the old Marquise de
Blocqueville, daughter of one of Napoleon's marshals. "She is a great
invalid, very corpulent, never leaves the house and has her head swathed
in long veils and laces à la sultane—but with the remains of beauty." The
French have a habit of not introducing anyone to anyone else, and James
complains that he wanders about among "a lot of people." He tells his
brother he will go again to her Monday at-homes, and "by keeping it up
long enough shall perhaps get something out of it."

The trouble with many of these salons was their addiction to music.
Henry had an unmusical ear. He hears assorted divas, tenors, string
quartets. At Madame Viardot's "I stood the other night on my legs for
three hours (from 11 to 2) in a suffocating room, listening to an interminable fiddling." When Pauline Viardot sang, however, as she now rarely
did, it seemed to him "superb."

Henry manages to meet assorted figures in the Parisian world. He
dines with the new Minister of Education, William Waddington, who has
an American wife; he meets the Duc de Broglie one day at the Long-
champs military review. He is introduced to the grandson of Jérome
Bonaparte, of the American branch of the family, a "fine-looking stupid
man." It is all a parade, a kind of reception line in which James shakes
hands with figures as they pass. There is French wit and French incisive-
ness in the air all about him. He remains nevertheless simply one of the
audience.

Most vividly remembered of all these ephemeral encounters will be
his visits to a certain house in the rue du Bac, whose windows overlook
a formal garden. He has gone there with a letter from Fanny Kemble, and
met the eighty-three-year-old Madame Jules Mohl. Her memories go
back to Madame Récamier, and to Chateaubriand, who died in the very
house in which she lives. Madame Mohl was Scottish; her maiden name
had been Mary Clarke. She had conducted one of the last of the Romantic
salons. It was this "little old woman, with her grey hair in her eyes,
precisely like a Skye terrier," who told James an anecdote he was to

allude to later, of how the eighty-year-old Madame Récamier, after her lover was dead, had said with adorable grace, "I don't want to seem pedantic, but I wish for nothing now but virtue."

Henry saw little purpose in cultivating "the American village encamped *en plein Paris,*" but it cultivated him. He found Mrs. Mason there when he arrived (she who had been Mrs. Sumner), "a most comfortable creature, especially for so handsome a woman." Mrs. Wister's friend, Mrs. Lockwood, passed through the capital and Henry saw much of her. He also renewed acquaintance with Mrs. Charles Strong, of New York, the former Eleanor Fearing, whom he had met in Rome in 1869. Mrs. Strong, a Catholic convert, had "a spark of the *feu sacré,* an ability to interest herself and *s'enthousiasmer* which is sincere and pleasing." He went with her to the opera; he liked to have idle talk with her. Among the unmarried, James met that spring one woman at whom he looked very carefully. He described Henrietta Reubell in April 1876 as being twenty-seven or twenty-eight, "extremely ugly, but with something very frank, intelligent and agreeable about her." He went on: "If I wanted to desire to marry an ugly Parisian-American, with money and *toutes les élégances,* and a very considerable capacity for development if transported into a favouring medium, Miss Reubell would be a very good objective. But I don't." By now he seems to have made up his mind that he would never marry; he had nevertheless entertained the fancy. Etta Reubell's home at 42 Avenue Gabriel was to be a cherished foyer in the coming decades.

James was most at home in the household of the Edward Lee Childes, friends of the Nortons, whose intimate dinners he found pleasant and sophisticated. He liked the alertness and vivacity of Mrs. Childe, the former Blanche de Triqueti. "I call in the afternoon and find Mme. Lee Childe in black velvet by her fire (she is a very graceful, elegant and clever Frenchwoman) with old decorated counts and generals leaning against the mantelpiece." James would like to have a tête-à-tête with her, but her fireside is always pre-empted.

Perhaps the strangest of James's American friendships that winter was with the physicist, astronomer and logician, Charles Sanders Peirce, who was swinging pendulums at the Observatory. Learning from William James that Henry was in Paris, Peirce called upon him, took him to dinner; and the two presently fell into the habit of meeting at regular intervals. William was much amused, and told his brother he must find Peirce an "uncomfortable bedfellow, thorny and spinous." But Henry found him more gentle and urbane than he had known him to be in Cambridge. And his novelist self studied Peirce's sense of dislocation in Paris—his feeling that French scientists treated him indifferently; his tendency to live luxuriously, wear extravagant clothes, employ a secretary, yet lead a life of "insupportable loneliness and sterility." Later, when he was summarizing his Paris winter in his journal, James wrote: "I saw a good deal of Charles Peirce that winter—as to whom his being a man of genius reconciled me to much that was intolerable in him."

The French seemed inaccessible; and James had hardly come abroad to pay calls on Americans. He was happiest, therefore, with the cosmopolitan Russians. In addition to being received in the rue de Douai he became a familiar in the Faubourg St. Germain home of Madame Nikolai Turgenev, widow of "the William Lloyd Garrison of Russia," who had died in 1871. James found these Turgenevs, mother and grown children, "an oasis of purity and goodness in the midst of this Parisian Babylon." Ivan Sergeyevich and these remote relatives of his, and "a young man whose acquaintance I have lately made, give me a high idea of the Russian nature—at least in some of its forms." The young man was Paul Zhukovski. James and the bearded soft-eyed Russian, with his great fondness for the music of Richard Wagner, had liked each other from the first.

Zhukovski had the manners of an aristocrat and the ardor of a romantic. Orphaned son, by a German mother, of the famous poet and translator Vassili Zhukovski, tutor to the Tsar, Paul had been brought up at the Russian court, dandled by empresses and princesses. In his young manhood he had lived in Venetian palaces. His large Parisian studio and apartment were filled with Italian treasures. An amateur painter, Zhukovski was exhibiting two large canvases that spring in the Salon. James studied them and decided that if Paul Zhukovski was "one of the flowers of civilization," he would also never be anything "but a rather curious and delicate dilettante." He appreciated his delicacy and enjoyed his company. "He is much to my taste and we have sworn eternal friendship," he told his sister. The two cosmopolitans—the American and the Russian—knocked about Paris a great deal together that spring.

James found the Princess Ourousov, Zhukovski's friend, attractive. She had dark hair, flashing dark eyes, a rather characteristic broad Russian nose. The daughter of a great Russian industrialist, Marie Maltzov had always moved among aristocrats and she had ended by marrying a prince. The family fortune dwindled, however, and she was living now "without princely splendour." In later years, in Paris, Maupassant frequented her salon; the young André Gide brought Oscar Wilde to meet her. James spoke of her being "as easy as an old glove." Her only fault, he told Quincy Street, was that "she smokes too much." Through the smoke-haze, however, James found a woman "of such liberal understanding and culture that conversation with her is a real pleasure."

His Russian friends, Henry told his father, "are quite the most (to me) fascinating people one can see." Moving among them, and among his compatriots, and gaining his glimpses of the French, the transatlantic visitor found himself abandoning certain Cambridge rigidities, taking life a little less hard, giving himself over to the simple pleasures of genial living.

Silk Purse and Sow's Ear

Henry James had told John Hay confidently that he would write entertaining letters from Paris for the *New York Tribune.* In his first letter, since he was fresh upon the scene, he chatted about the obvious: the aspect of Paris to a revisiting American, the pre-Christmas atmosphere, the subjects in the daily headlines. In a laudatory editorial, probably written by Hay, the *Tribune* promised an extended series of dispatches by James and spoke of him as "one of the best-equipped Americans who have crossed the Atlantic."

When the novelist read his first letter in print, he recognized that it was too general and too long, pitched "in too vague and diffuse a key." He also confessed, when the time came to write a second letter, that "I can think of nothing in life to put into the *Tribune.*" He took refuge in an exhibition of animal statuary, the decorations of the new opera, the renovation of the Odéon. He knew this was hardly the intimate Paris-from-the-inside type of letter that was wanted, but to be "chatty" about Paris and the Parisians was more than he could do.

"Subjects are woefully scarce," he complained to his mother in January; and to his father, two or three months later, he spoke of "a painful dearth of topics" — this when he had all Paris to write about, and a strong resurgent France recovering from the Franco-Prussian War and the Commune. James could and did exploit the theaters, the art shows, occasional books of general interest, newspaper controversies and the human interest in the effervescent political scene. And yet an acute helplessness pervades his *Tribune* letters. Try as he might, James could never speak in the journalistic voice.

The voice we hear in the *Tribune* letters is that of the artist. When all else failed him, and his *Tribune* pen lagged, he could fall back upon his aesthetic faculty:

> The huge towers of Notre Dame, rising with their blue-gray tone from the midst of the great mass round which the river divides, the great Arc de Triomphe answering them with equal majesty in the opposite distance, the splendid continuous line of the Louvre between, and over it all the charming colouring of Paris on certain days—the brightness, the pearly grays, the flicker of light, the good taste, as it were, of the atmosphere—all this is an entertainment which even custom does not stale.

This is the painter-observer at work with blue-grey, pearl-grey and flickering light; it is distinctly not newspaper reportage; nor was the wandering sentence suitable for journalism.

If a *Tribune* reader was willing to accept the literary tone, the unorthodox sentences, the substitution of color and atmosphere for hard fact, he could find his rewards, over and above the descriptive felicities. He could tour the salon of 1876 with the patience and vigor required in visiting this annual French display of miles of painted canvas; he could encounter works by Taine, Renan, Zola, Sainte-Beuve, carefully reviewed and analyzed; he could catch Henry James Jr. at a ball watching Johann Strauss conduct his waltzes; and on another occasion he would be present to hear Giuseppe Verdi lead his *Requiem*. James's *Tribune* articles are readable when he performs in his characteristic magazine vein; for the rest they are rather forced, and often on the dull side.

William James's comments reflected his awareness of his brother's problem: "Keep watch and ward lest in your style you become too Parisian and lose your hold on the pulse of the great American public, to which after all you must pander for support." But writing for the newspaper went against Henry's grain. To his father he wrote: "The vulgarity and repulsiveness of the *Tribune*, whenever I see it, strikes me so violently that I feel tempted to stop my letter." He could not, however, yield to this temptation: he needed the money.

His letters were passively received. The correspondence columns of the paper contain letters of praise for most of the *Tribune*'s other correspondents, but no praise and little blame for James. And Whitelaw Reid was to comment that other journals, which often quoted the newspaper, seemed oblivious of Henry's letters.

Six years later James recorded: "I wrote letters to the New York *Tribune*, of which, though they were poor stuff, I may say that they were too good for the purpose (of course they didn't succeed)." A truer statement was embodied in a tale in which the heroine confesses she has agreed to write London letters for a provincial paper; "I can't do them— I don't know how, and don't want to. I do them wrong, and the people want such trash. Of course they'll sack me."

The *Tribune* did not "sack" Henry; but ever after he was to speak as if it did. By midsummer, when he had written twenty letters and received the tidy sum of $400, he asked Whitelaw Reid for more money, $30 per letter. The publisher offered a compromise. Explaining that James's subjects were "too remote from popular interests," he proposed that he alter the character of his letters: make them shorter and "newsier," and that he space them more widely. "You must not imagine," Reid wrote, "that any of us have failed to appreciate the admirable work you have done for us." He added, however, the forthright statement: "The difficulty has sometimes been not that it was too good, but that it was magazine rather than newspaper work."

Reid touched James's professional sensitivity; and his concluding sentence had a peculiar and painful force. The terms also offered no ground for negotiation. If James was to receive the same amount for less work, this "less" had also to undergo a qualitative change—be more "newsy," informative, gossipy. The pen which answered the publisher was more incisive than it had ever been in the columns of the *Tribune.* "I know the sort of letter you mean," James wrote; "it is doubtless the proper sort of thing for the *Tribune* to have. But I can't produce it—I don't know how and I couldn't learn how."

> If my letters have been "too good" I am honestly afraid that they are the poorest I can do, especially for the money! I had better, therefore, suspend them altogether. I have enjoyed writing them, however, and if the *Tribune* has not been the better for them I hope it hasn't been too much the worse.

To his father he wrote that Reid "had stopped off my letters to the *Tribune*—practically at last—by demanding that they should be of a flimsier sort. I thought in all conscience they had been flimsy enough. I am a little sorry to stop, but much glad." He was ultimately to make a short story of the episode, "The Next Time"—"the idea of the poor man, the artist, the man of letters, who all his life is trying—if only to get a living — to do something *vulgar,* to take the measure of the huge, flat foot of the public . . . to make, as it were, a sow's ear out of a silk purse."

His own dilemma had not been comparable. He had simply ventured into an alien medium. The magazine world was quite prepared to accept him. He did say to Quincy Street shortly after resigning his journalistic chore: "You needn't commiserate me for my *Tribune* cessation; I don't miss the *Tribune* at all; I can use my material to better advantage." And he did.

"The American"

On reaching the French capital James found himself short of funds. He had drawn upon his father's letter of credit in London to pay for new clothes and for his installation in the rue de Luxembourg; his royalties from *Roderick Hudson* (published in Boston on 20 November 1875) were to be sent to his father to reimburse him. His fortnightly letters to the *Tribune* did not cover his rent; his fugitive reviewing and other writings would barely feed him. He needed about $150 a month. He was committed to the *Atlantic* for another novel, but a certain delay was necessary following serialization of *Roderick.* The only practical course was to start a new serial, as quickly as possible, in some other magazine. Having already had tentative talks with the editors of the *Galaxy,* he wrote to them from Paris on 1 December 1875 that he would "take for granted" that they would be "ready to publish, on receipt of them, the opening chapters of a novel," to be called *The American,* which he had begun sooner than expected. He planned to complete it in nine months; his price would be $150 an installment.

Transatlantic Sketches had yielded a royalty balance of $200 at the end of the year, and this money had gone directly to Quincy Street. On 24 January James received a letter from his mother accusing him of extravagance, and informing him that his autumn draft on his father had been "excessive and inconvenient." He replied that this had been a necessity of his situation. Paris was not cheap; but it was not as dear as New York, and he was certain that by the end of the year he would have a balance in his favor.

The effect of his mother's letter was, for the moment, to undermine James's sense of security. He could draw no further on his father; and he had to find ways to keep his pen busy. The *Galaxy* did not reply, and James stopped writing *The American.* Instead he hastily wrote two tales, "Crawford's Consistency" and "The Ghostly Rental," and sold them to *Scribner's* for $300.

Meanwhile Howells wrote to say he would take James's serial whenever he was ready to let him have it. Henry ruefully replied: "I took for granted that the *Atlantic* would begin nothing till June or July, and it was the money question solely that had to determine me." *The American,* he said, was the only subject "mature enough in my mind to use immediately. It has in fact been used somewhat prematurely; and I hope you find enough faults in it to console you for not having it in the *Atlantic*." He said, however, that if the *Galaxy* editors were not satisfied, or failed to meet his terms, he would ask them to forward the first installment to Howells. His price remained $150 a month for nine months.

Howells lost no time in offering to take *The American* if the *Galaxy* did not want it. James, on his side, laid down an ultimatum to that journal: "These then are my terms—$150 a number—to commence in *May* — and failing this to send the copy instantly to Cambridge." The editors of the *Galaxy* obliged. Howells scheduled the serial to begin in the *Atlantic*'s June issue.

The American was a firm, rapid stride on the part of Henry James into full literary maturity. He had told Howells he was writing the novel "prematurely." What he meant by this was that he was uncomfortably close to his materials; this novel, of all James's works, is written, as might be said, "off the top of his head." Yet he had long nourished the image of Christopher Newman. The old idea of a robust American confronting an aristocratic society could now be brought into James's new environment. He would write a novel about an American businessman and his siege of Paris, of Balzac's Faubourg St. Germain, of which he himself was having a passing glimpse.

He speaks in the novel of "those grey and silent streets of the Faubourg"—streets such as the rue de l'Université, where much of the novel's action takes place, the rue de Lille and the rue de Bellechasse—"whose houses present to the outer world a face as impassive and as suggestive of the concentration of privacy as the blank walls of Eastern seraglios." In James's time there were in these streets a great many fine old *hôtels,* with their wide gates and coachyards. James had hoped that some of these gates would swing open for him. His American, Christopher Newman, however, has a much higher hope—that of marrying into one of the Faubourg's old aristocratic families. He reflects, in a measure, some of James's frustration at not achieving entrance into this world in which, through saturated reading of French novels, he felt himself, in his imagination, to be an initiate.

Newman is thus an image of James's Parisian life of action, while at the same time being a mordant portrait of an American, whose qualities show the national character in all its forthrightness and innocence as well as in its predatory aspects. The Californian is in some respects "quiet"; he is "nice" in many ways. But there is in him a strong and vulgar streak of materialistic self-satisfaction which James understood from the first. If Newman is, as one critic observed, "a Californian boor," his boorishness resides not in his pretensions—decidedly superficial—to art or architecture; it is in the side of him which shows pride in being "self-made" and his belief that anything can be bought. Newman would seem to be that future paradox in the civilized world: the American who is hospitable to life's chances, yet is "committed to nothing in particular" save his own incredible self-assurance.

Christopher Newman begins with the belief that "Europe was made for him, and not he for Europe." He has acquired his pile of money; now he dreams of a wife; "there must be a beautiful woman perched on the pile, like a statue on a monument." She has, indeed, to be "the best article on the market." He has a prime conviction "that a man's life should be easy" and it is the ease of one who has had a continent to conquer, who has lost and made fortunes in leather, wash-tubs, copper. At the same time he possesses the morbid fear of idleness which colored James's days in Cambridge.

He does not wave the Stars and Stripes belligerently. However, with his wealth he carries a solid belief that his homeland is "the greatest country in the world" and that Americans "could put all Europe in their breeches pocket." When he is told that he has "a sort of air" of being thoroughly at home in the world he ascribes this to the privilege of being an American citizen. "That sets a man up." "You are the great Western Barbarian," he is told, "stepping forth in his innocence and might, gazing a while at this poor effete Old World and then swooping down on it." This is one side of Newman, thoroughly dissimulated, however, behind the energy, geniality and "drive" with which he moves through the book, impervious to all save his own anchored dollars and the sense they give him that he is free to do as he pleases.

James sketches an innocent Western Barbarian, but he shows us also the candor of Newman's innocence and the courage of his ignorance. The central irony of the book is that the American has not been corrupted by his gold; he is still one of "nature's noblemen" and, in the end, he can be as moral and therefore as noble as the corrupt Europeans. The truth is that the old Marquise de Bellegarde is simply a European version of Christopher Newman; she sits upon her aristocratic sanctity with the same tough possessiveness and assurance that Newman sits on his pile of dollars. In the struggle between the two, it is Newman who emerges the better Christian. When the woman he loves, or rather prizes (and wishes to take possession of as if she were a railroad or a mine), immures herself in a convent, Newman simply recognizes the realities: he has a chance to take his revenge, but he will not regain Claire de Cintré. And because the Bellegardes have been cruel to him is no reason for him now to be cruel to them. A good American, a shrewd businessman, does not indulge in waste effort.

It is a strong ending to the story, and it does impart to Newman an aura of distinction. The original readers of the novel did not experience this. They had read the *Atlantic* installments from month to month, in the fond belief that their author would give Newman the prize. Howells pleaded with him to do so. On the other hand Fanny Kemble, in the serenity of her old age, and speaking out of her transatlantic experience, expressed a fear lest he should put the marriage through. *"Voyons,"* James wrote to Howells, "they would have been an impossible couple." And he went on to argue that they would have had no place to live: Claire de Cintré would have hated New York, and Newman could not dwell in France; there would be "nothing left but a farm out West." Newman was confronted by an insuperable difficulty from which the only issue, as far as James could see, was forfeiture. If he had settled for "a prettier ending," he would have felt, he said, "as if I were throwing a rather vulgar sop to readers who don't really know the world and who don't measure the merit of a novel by its correspondence to the same."

In insisting that he was a realist, James overlooked the essential fact that he had written a romantic novel. His persons were real enough; their backgrounds were real; but the story of what happened to them moved across the borderland of the actual into the imaginary. It was not so much a question of throwing a sop to his readers as making the book true to itself; given the book's initial character, its ending was false. James was to recognize this in later years; he substituted a happy ending when he dramatized the novel. In his final preface he recognized that the Belle-gardes "would positively have jumped at my rich and easy American" and not have minded any drawbacks.

Why then did James insist on breaking off the marriage instead of seeking means to unite his lovers? We may speculate that having ruled out marriage for himself, he found it genuinely difficult to offer it to his heroes. James's tales of the artist-life invariably contain the admonition that marriage could only be a distraction, a form of servitude fatal to art. Identified with Newman as an active and independent individual, James shut up Claire de Cintré in the convent as he shut women away from himself. And in endowing Claire with weakness and inconstancy he underlined his sense of women's fickleness as well as his own fear of them.

Bernard Shaw was to say to James years later that an author can give victory to one side as easily as to another. Certainly this did not apply to tragedy. But in a comedy like *The American* Henry James did have the choice: his "determinism" (and fear of marriage) nevertheless prevailed.

It is doubtful whether James thought of *The American* as a comedy. He thought he was writing a Balzacian novel. "I suspect it is the tragedies in life that arrest my attention, more than the other things, and say more to my imagination," he wrote to Howells. Yet in *The American* James, for the first time, revealed to the full his grasp of the comedy residing in the contrasting manners of America and Europe. Earlier writers had barely sketched this American-European theme; none had possessed his kind of delicate humor.

The touch of comedy is present on almost every page of *The American*—save those which James gives over to unutterable gloom. The scenes between Newman and the aristocrats are nearly always on a plane of *double entendre:* the exchange of wit is constant, and quite often there is an element of mockery of which Newman is unaware. When Newman offers a recital of his life to the Bellegardes and tells them of his sisters' early marriages, he mentions that one of them had made a match with the owner of the largest india-rubber house in the west. "Ah," observes the Marquise, "you make houses also of india rubber." And young Madame de Bellegarde takes up the cue: "You can stretch them as your family increases." Newman finds this hilarious, wholly unaware that they are laughing at him. Or simply the casual remark of the Mar-quise de Bellegarde, when she first meets Newman: "You're an American. I've seen several Americans." To which Newman replies, "There are several in Paris." The comedy flows easily from the characters and from the situation in which James placed them.

Roderick Hudson had represented James's final dialogue with Quincy Street, a last tug at the silver cord. He had made his choice, and his story of Christopher Newman was symbolic of his own stepping-forth into the world—as a new man. But the vivid personalities of Quincy Street, the conflict of its strong egos, remained. The differences with William emerge in *The American,* no longer in the complaining terms of the Cambridge time, but simply as hard fact. The unpleasant Marquis de Bellegarde, who is fifteen years senior to his brother Valentin, represents one extreme of ancient family feeling; by the same token, Valentin, another second son, is charming, ineffectual and doomed. Dominating the book is the matriarchal old Marquise, the archetypal mother-figure of James's work, in whose hands husbands are crushed or robbed of their manhood, or—as in this instance—even murdered.

Howells liked *The American* and decided that he would spread it through twelve monthly issues of the *Atlantic* instead of nine. James agreed to take the same price for the twelve as he had asked for the nine, since the amount of copy was unchanged. This would yield him $1,350. The novelist's livelihood was assured until the following year.

The novel's reception in America was mixed. It was, however, read more attentively, and aroused more discussion, than anything James had done before. The originality of the international theme was recognized and nearly all the critics were prepared to consider the work an important contribution to American literature. They were not yet prepared however—and this they said—to place James beside Hawthorne or Trollope or Dickens—or for that matter George Eliot.

In the Provinces

The time had come to say farewells. Turgenev was returning to Russia for the summer, hoping to finish *Virgin Soil.* James joined the Viardot household for charades once again on a Sunday evening, and then called on the novelist one morning and found him "more charming than I had ever seen him." A day or two later Turgenev joined James and Zhukovski at dinner and "was again adorable"—but once again he had to return to Madame Viardot at an early hour. Late in May, Henry went to Flaubert's last Sunday afternoon of the season. He had an hour alone with the author of *Madame Bovary,* after which he said his summer good-byes to the *cénacle.*

Zhukovski remained in the city for a while and James attended vari-

ous boring Wagnerian evenings at his studio. When the Bootts turned up
in Paris, James arranged a dinner-party for them. Zhukovski found Boott
"extrêmement sympathique" and thought he looked like one of Titian's
men; and Lizzie, to James's surprise, revealed great fluency in French.

He was still in Paris in July. It was hot and he frequented the cafés,
drinking beer, watching the crowds, dining in the Champs-Élysées under
the trees, beside ivy-colored walls. Or he would take a penny steamer to
Auteuil, eat fried fish at a *guinguette* on the river-bank, and return on
top of a horse-car. For a change he would dine in the Bois de Boulogne
and drive back through the woods at night in the cool air. "Your last few
letters," William wrote to him, "have breathed a tone of contentment and
domestication in Paris which was very agreeable to get." From Elmwood,
Lowell wrote: "Don't get to be too much of a Mounseer and come home
as soon as you can."

James had no thought of return. One day in late July he packed his
bags, reserved his apartment for the autumn, and took a boat down the
Seine, to Rouen, to Honfleur, to Le Havre. He finally settled at Étretat,
taking lodgings near the beach and his meals at the Hôtel Blanquet. He
bought himself a fishing cap and canvas shoes; he wore his old clothes;
and for a month he wrote peacefully, giving over his spare time to long
walks across the dunes. He found the Boston-Roman Edward Boits living
in an old house nearby, and went on excursions with them; once he
trudged ten miles to see the races at Fécamp, and admired the "plastic"
landscape of Normandy. Lying on the beach watching the French bath-
ers, James mused on the differences between French matrons and their
American sisters.

> I have never seen such richness of contour as among the mature *bai-*
> *gneuses* of Etretat. The lean and desiccated person into whom a dozen
> years of matrimony so often converts the blooming American girl is not
> emulated in France. A majestic plumpness flourished all around me—
> the plumpness of triple chins and deeply dimpled hands.

He went on to analyze the difference in manners between America and
France and the institution of the *jeune fille*—a subject that was to interest
him in years to come.

He would gladly have lingered at Étretat but he had promised the
Edward Lee Childes that he would visit them in their home near Montargis, in the Gâtinais. He found himself in an enchanting part of France.
His hosts drove him to the little castle in which they lived—on an island
just large enough to hold it, surrounded by three-foot-thick walls and a
moat. It looked operatic. There were garden flowers on the further bank
of the moat and James took long walks before eating massive country
breakfasts. He was taken to nearby Le Perthuis, the *maison de campagne*

in which Blanche Childe's mother lived, the Baronne de Triqueti, a robust woman of eighty. She had "the strength of an ox" and took a great
liking to the brown-bearded American, inviting him to stay with her.
After "the most heroic and succulent *déjeuner de province"* at the Baronne's, James decided that "under her roof I should have died in thirty-
six hours of an indigestion of game and melons." He liked Le Perthuis
with its grass plateau, bordered on one side by a short avenue of horse-
chestnuts and on the other by a dusky wood. Beyond the trees were the
steep russet-roofed yellow-walled farm buildings and a stretch of turf
where he watched the farm-servants play at bowls on Sundays.

Blanche Childe took him to visit the peasantry in their "queer little
smoke-blackened big-bedded, big-clocked kitchens," and everywhere
James was "charmed with the nature of the people—with their good
manners, quaintness and *bonhomie."* They had "the instinct of civility"
and a talent for conversation. He liked the women in particular: they
struck him as possessing "a stronger expression of the qualities of the
race" than the men.

At the end of August, he decided to visit south-western France. He
went directly to Biarritz but found it crowded and unpleasant. He retreated to Bayonne and stayed a week. Unseasonal rains proved depressing and James decided to return to Paris. Before doing this he crossed to
San Sebastian and enjoyed a brief glimpse of Spain. He studied a life-
sized Virgin in a church with a flamboyant façade and felt that she was,
as he said in his travel sketch, "the sentiment of Spanish catholicism;
gloomy, yet bedizened, emotional as a woman and mechanical as a doll.
After a moment I grew afraid of her, and went slinking away."

In Bayonne he found the Childes, whom he had visited so recently,
staying at a castle above the town, the Casa Caradoc. James was invited
to dine. And then, with the Childes, their hosts, and a couple of young
officers from the local garrison, he went once again to San Sebastian, to
see a bull-fight. He liked the spectacle. The ladies who sat beside him
often yawned, but never shuddered. He liked the toreadors as well, "yet
I thought the bull, in any case, a finer fellow than any of his tormentors,
and I thought his tormentors finer fellows than the spectators." A bull-
fight, he concluded, "will, to a certain extent, bear looking at, but it will
not bear thinking of." He never visited Spain again.

A Channel Crossing

Henry James returned to Paris on 15 September 1876 and discovered
that, despite his precautions, his apartment had been let. He was promised another, on the fourth floor, but would have to wait until it was
vacated. He accordingly took a room in Lowell's old hotel, and a few days

later moved outside the city, to St. Germain-en-Laye, where he worked quietly until he was able on 29 September to move into his rooms. He saw the Bootts off to Italy, and had a desire to go south himself. He had decided, however, that he would attempt a second winter in the French capital. In the high *salon* of his new quarters at 29 rue de Luxembourg, he worked on the final installments of his novel. The "thin, quick, quite feminine surface-breathing of Paris" provided the accompaniment to the sad ending of Christopher Newman's romance. In the last pages Newman, on an impulse, crosses the Channel to visit England. The same impulse now came to James.

He had for some months, in his letters home, shown signs of impatience with France. He had gone so often to the Théâtre Français, he said, that he knew its repertoire by heart. He had done with the French, he told his brother, "and am turning English all over." To his mother he wrote that autumn that he felt another six months of Paris would suffice. He no longer had his *Tribune* correspondence, which might have justified a continued sojourn. "There is nothing else, for me personally, on the horizon," he told Quincy Street, "and it is rather ignoble to stay in Paris simply for the restaurants." "I don't remember," he later recorded in his journal,

> what suddenly brought me to the point of saying—"Go to; I will try London." I think a letter from William had a good deal to do with it, in which he said, "Why don't you? — That must be the place." A single word from outside often moves one (moves *me* at least) more than the same word infinitely multiplied as a simple voice from within. I *did* try it.

Although his mind was made up early in November he remained for almost a month. He renewed his friendship with Zhukovski, the Princess Ourousov, and the Nikolai Turgenevs. He was delighted to see Mrs. Mason again. The Parisian weather was beautiful to the last. It was hard to leave. He retraced his steps to the rue de Douai and found Ivan Sergeyevich as he had often found him, stretched out on his sofa, with his gouty foot. The Russian was as affectionate as ever. He made James promise to write from London; he promised he would answer. *"Adieu, cher ami,"* the Russian said as they parted.

James had written a long article on Balzac before taking up residence in the French capital. Now, on the eve of leaving, he wrote another, a review of Balzac's letters, lately published. The story of Balzac's fierce dedication, his methods of work, his stubborn professionalism, his grandiose sense of *métier,* told for the first time in detail, fired James's imagination. As he prepared to cross the Channel he could say to himself that he had now fully mastered the lesson of Balzac. He too could possess, as artist, a kind of massive self-sufficiency; he too was not to be swayed from his course where his craft was concerned. Ambitious and resolute, James left Paris without regrets. He had "tried" New York. He had by now spent a full year in France. He was about to try London. He crossed the Channel —Boulogne to Folkestone—on 10 December 1876. In his journal a single sentence offers the best reason for his departure: "I saw that I should be an eternal outsider."

The Observant Stranger

Henry James fell into London during the winter of 1876 as if he had lived there all his life. "I took possession of it," he said; and it took possession of him. His lodging at 3 Bolton Street, Piccadilly, was two streets from Half Moon Street, where he had stayed in 1869. Although his windows on the first floor looked onto the street and he had a balcony, it could scarcely be said that he had "a view"; at best he could obtain a sideways glimpse of Green Park. He used to sit writing with a featureless, sooty, brown brick wall facing him across the way, the wall of a great house, Lord Ashburton's.

He moved into his lodging on 12 December, and the next morning awoke to his first domestic breakfast—bacon, eggs, slices from an "exquisite English loaf," cups of tea, served by a dark-faced maid with the voice of a duchess. "You may imagine the voluptuous glow in which such a repast has left me," he wrote to Alice. The season was dark and wet; the fog was "glutinous," and yet James experienced a contentment he had never known in Paris.

He took long walks in the rain. He brought home armfuls of books from Mudie's Library and read them by his fire. Sometimes it was so dark that he had to light his candles at noon. Whatever mood the dark and the fog induced, London, in spite of its "agglomerated immensity," became "home." It was "ugly, dusky, dreary, more destitute than any European city of graceful and decorative incident." Yet the light leaking and filtering from the cloud-ceiling turned harshness into softness, gave subtle tones to objects and buildings, created beautiful pictorial effects. London was certainly "not agreeable, or cheerful, or easy, or exempt from reproach," and yet, James added, "it is only magnificent." It was "the most complete compendium of the world." The human race was better represented in it than anywhere else. It was a veritable kingdom for a novelist.

Shortly after his arrival he made certain initial overtures to mitigate possible loneliness. He got in touch with a young Englishman named Benson, who had visited the James family in Quincy Street. Benson promptly invited him to lunch at the Oxford and Cambridge Club and introduced him to Andrew Lang. Henry called also on G. W. Smalley, the London correspondent of the *New York Tribune* whom he had met in Paris, and looked up a young English Jew whom he had met the previous summer at Étretat, Theodore Child, a graduate of Merton who wrote for the *Pall Mall Gazette.* Child invited Henry to lunch with him at the Arts Club on Christmas Eve 1876. James had hitherto known few Jews: he conceived of them as outlandish, with beaked Shylockean noses and Fagin-like beards: the handsome Child did not fit the stereotype. He was lively, literary, aesthetic. They distinctly liked each other.

If these sociabilities promised well for London, that Christmas was perhaps the loneliest of Henry's life. The holiday fell on a weekend and he spent three solitary days in a tightly-shut city with blank streets and wet vistas of sooty bricks. But as soon as the festivities were over, he found himself the object of traditional English hospitalities. A lady he had met at Smalley's invited him to a "heavy London dinner, composed of fearful viands and people I didn't know." He was invited also to the home of a Mrs. Pollock, who had heard from the Smalleys that he was in London. She had read him in the *Atlantic Monthly.* "Who she is I haven't any idea," he wrote home; but he goes out of pure civility, to discover himself in the home of the distinguished jurist and his wife, the future Sir Frederick and Lady Pollock, who would remain his friends during all his London years. At still another dinner he meets Sir Charles Dilke, a rising political figure, and discovers their common interest in French literature. He dines in due course with the Andrew Langs, "a very nice fellow with a pleasant graceful mind and a great facility and understanding." Dinner leads to dinner. "I am getting quite into the current of London life," Henry wrote to Quincy Street. He had been in England barely six weeks.

As he began to see London interiors and the comfortable side of the Victorian world, he could not help contrasting them with the raw London through which he often walked late in the evening after dining out. There were too many gin-shops, "too many miserable women at their doorsteps; too many, far too many, dirty-faced children, sprawling between one's legs." And one dark night, against the dismal background of fog and sleet, James came upon "a horrible old woman in a smoky bonnet, lying prone in a puddle of whisky." The vision struck him as symbolic. "She almost frightened me away," he wrote. He had seen poverty and squalor in many forms in France and Italy, but it had a certain out-of-door picturesqueness. In London it became "the hard prose of misery." Strolling at Easter into a crowded Westminster Abbey, he was driven away by an odor that "was not that of incense."

The crude state of poverty in London gave Henry pause. He was struck by "the rigidly aristocratic constitution of society; the unaesthetic temper of the people; the private character of most kinds of comfort and entertainment." The Victorian world was carefully organized to preserve —to reinforce—respect for traditional institutions. This was one way of maintaining national stability. To a member of America's upper middle class, where society was in a state of flux, England's codes and rules, and its stratified class structure, proved a revelation. The thought occurred to James that in a nation in which personality was repressed to such an extent, there had to be some safety valve. Where had the Britons placed the "fermenting idiosyncrasies" that had been corked down? "The upper classes are too refined," James was to write, "and the lower classes are too miserable." The judgment may have seemed to him in later years too summary, too unsubtle. His revising pen altered it to "The better sort are too 'genteel,' and the inferior sort too base." This might be the measure of the distance he was to travel from Bolton Street into the life of England's leisured class.

James would become the historian of "the better sort." But he was not to lose sight altogether of the Hogarthian London of this early time. He was to ask himself, during ensuing years, what life would be like to one who had not had his own singular good fortune: for him the doors of London opened "into light and warmth and cheer, into good and charming relations." Yet the place "as a whole lay heavy on one's consciousness." He walked a good deal, "for exercise, for amusement, for acquisition and above all I always walked home at the evening's end." And he added: "One walked of course with one's eyes greatly open."

James's observation of poverty and high life in England was that of an intellectual and a humanitarian; it was not that of a reformer. He had called himself in his earlier English articles "the sentimental tourist." He called himself now "the observant stranger," having no desire to change his status of outsider, even though he was to become identified with much of English life. As an "observant stranger" he could describe without necessarily passing judgment; he could also compare; he could —as he was about to demonstrate—satirize Americans with the same ease as the English. But he had no desire to be a satirist. His forte was irony. To his friend Perry he confessed that in his English sketches he had withheld a great many impressions. "One can't say everything when one is settling down to enjoy the hospitality, as it were, of a country."

To Grace Norton he was to write on 7 July 1878:

In one sense I feel intimately at home here, and in another sense I feel —as an American may be on the whole very willing, at times, very glad, to feel—like a complete outsider. There are some English institutions and idiosyncrasies that it is certainly a great blessing to be outside of. ... I have learned a good deal about British manners and the British mind (thinking on the whole finely of the latter and meanly of the former)— and they no longer have any terrors—or even perplexities—to me. There are times indeed when I seem to myself to carry all England in my breeches pocket.

Again and again he spoke of liking London as "a big city and a regular basis of mundane existence." "It was, in fine, dear Charles," he wrote ultimately to his friend Norton,

a very happy inspiration of mine, two years since, to come to London to live; so thoroughly have I attached myself to its mighty variety and immensity, so interesting do I find the spectacle of English life, so well do I get on, on the whole, with people and things, so successfully, on the whole, do I seem to myself to assimilate the total affair.

He had a real tenderness for the "personal character of the people. It seems to me many times the strongest and richest race in the world—my dream is to arrive at the ability to be, in some degree, its moral portrait-painter."

The tales James wrote during the first year of his residence in England, no less than his essays, testify to his accuracy of observation. Only a man who had "successfully" assimilated the total affair could write stories which foreshadowed as well as depicted the manners and customs of international society. And it was with the same accuracy that, at the end of his first year in Bolton Street, he wrote a prophetic letter to his brother William. He had been dining out, and had listened to army men indulging in "the densest war talk" over the possibility of England's involvement in the Russo-Turkish war. He himself believed, he went on to tell William, that England would keep out of war because

the nation as a whole, looking at the matter deliberately, have decided that mere prestige is not sufficient ground for a huge amount of bloodshed. This seems to me to indicate a high pitch of civilization—a pitch which England alone, of all the European nations, has reached.

And then came the prophecy:

I have a sort of feeling that if we are to see the *déchéance* of England it is inevitable, and will come to pass somewhat in this way. She will push further and further her non-fighting and keeping-out-of-scrapes-policy, until contemptuous Europe, growing audacious with impunity, shall put upon her some supreme and unendurable affront. Then—too late—she will rise ferociously and plunge clumsily and unpreparedly into war. She will be worsted and laid on her back—and when she is laid on her back will exhibit—in her colossal wealth and pluck—an unprecedented power of resistance. But she will never really recover as a European power.

By the time 1914 came he had probably forgotten his prediction: and in our own time we can look back at the Battle of Britain and see how Henry James, more than half a century before, understood and spoke—almost in Churchillian cadences—of the deepest nature of the people in whose midst he made his home.

A More Spacious Existence

Between the time of his first solitary Christmas in 1876 and the Easter of 1877, Henry James firmly established himself in the London world. Early in February 1877 John Lothrop Motley, nearing the end of a busy life as historian and diplomat, called on his fellow-countryman in Bolton Street to tell him that he had put him on the honorary list of the Athenaeum. James would thus have temporary access to a club which gathered under its substantial roof in Pall Mall the nation's eminent men of letters, philosophers and churchmen. At the Athenaeum he could not only dine sociably at the end of a long day's writing, but he had the use as well of a fine library and occasion to meet certain of his transatlantic peers. The club admirably extended his sense of home; it was, so to speak, a luxurious annex to his lodgings.

Remembering his Thackeray, Henry relished describing to his sister the dignitaries sprawling or reading their papers—"all the great chairs and lounges and sofas filled with men having afternoon tea—lolling back with their laps filled with magazines, journals, and fresh Mudie books, while amiable flunkies in knee-breeches present them the divinest salvers of tea and buttered toast." The London club was to become for the bachelor of Bolton Street a necessity, a means by which he gave himself a more spacious existence. He could meet and make friends; he could entertain fellow-writers and reciprocate certain hospitalities; it was a place as fundamental to his existence as the old coffee-houses had been to an earlier London.

Unfortunately his access to the Athenaeum had its term. For some time he went to the Travellers', thanks to Charles Milnes Gaskell and Frederick Locker; and for a good while to the St. James's, haunt of young diplomats. In all he was guest in seven London clubs before his election to one he could call his own. Before he had been six months in England, however, he was put up for the Reform, the club of the country's liberals in the political and literary walks of life. It could not boast as many celebrities as the Athenaeum, its near neighbor in Pall Mall, but it was one of the best clubs in the capital, and materially "the most comfortable corner of the world." James was elected in May 1878. "*J'y suis, j'y reste* — forever and a day*," he announced triumphantly to his father and drew £42 on his letter of credit to pay his entrance fee. He told his sister that his election had "doubled my 'selfhood,' as Father would say," and added, "bookless and houseless as I am, it is a great blessing."

Another kind of London club opened its doors to him when he was invited to one of Lord Houghton's legendary breakfasts. Henry Adams had sent James a letter of introduction to Richard Monckton Milnes, Lord Houghton, but the breakfast invitation arrived before James had a chance to use the letter. Monckton Milnes had written verses as a young man and had been Keats's first champion. In Parliament his speeches had been too literary. In 1877 the "bird of paradox" was sixty-eight, a little rusty but still as eager a collector of celebrities for his breakfasts as he was of rare volumes and erotica.

By Lord Houghton's standard, then, Henry James could consider himself a celebrity—or on his way to becoming one. The breakfast groups could hardly be said to resemble Flaubert's *cénacle;* fame rather than dedication to art seemed the fundamental criterion. However, they were occasions for pleasant talk, high gossip and a kind of extended fellowship among a variety of "personalities." There is a note of world-weariness in Henry's account to William of the first breakfast he attended—a bare twelve weeks after settling in London—as composed of half a dozen men "all terribly 'useful-informationish,' and whose names and faces I have forgotten." But he is bidden again by Lord Houghton to another gathering, the Cosmopolitan, a kind of "talking club, extremely select," and here he encounters, amid a little knot of parliamentary folk, his fellow-passenger of two years before, Anthony Trollope.

James found Lord Houghton to be "very kind and paternal" and

> a battered and world-wrinkled old mortal, with a restless and fidgety vanity, but with an immense fund of real kindness and humane feeling. He is not personally fascinating, though as a general thing he talks very well, but I like his sociable, democratic, sympathetic, inquisitive old temperament.

By the time James wrote this he had passed from being a breakfast guest to being a dinner guest and to visiting Lord Houghton in the country, at Fryston Hall. At one dinner he encountered Tennyson, Gladstone, and the excavator of Troy, Dr. Heinrich Schliemann. James sat next but one to Tennyson, whom he described as swarthy and scraggy and less handsome than he appeared in his photograph. The Bard talked exclusively of port wine and tobacco; "he seems to know much about them, and can

drink a whole bottle of port at a sitting with no incommodity." James
continued:

> Behold me after dinner conversing affably with Mr. Gladstone—not by
> my own seeking, but by the almost importunate affection of Lord Hough-
> ton. But I was glad of a chance to feel the "personality" of a great political
> leader . . . That of Gladstone is very fascinating—his urbanity extreme
> —his eye that of a man of genius—and his apparent self-surrender to
> what he is talking of, without a flaw.

In very little time Henry James found himself considered not merely
an "item" in Lord Houghton's celebrity collection, but a personal friend.
The "collector" asked James for an introduction to Turgenev and Flaubert. The American suggested Turgenev might introduce Lord Houghton
to Flaubert. He also wrote to Flaubert, asking the French novelist to
introduce Houghton to Zola, whom he wanted particularly to meet. To
Lord Houghton he explained that Flaubert was "the only one of *ces messieurs* with whom I established personal relations," adding he was certain "the others won't do me the honour to remember me."

That first year of his residence in London, James remained in the city
until midsummer and then discovered the pleasures of country visits.
Henry Adams had urged him to stay with his friend Charles Milnes
Gaskell, and when he received the invitation he gladly went to Wenlock
Abbey, a ruin in Shropshire, partly restored and modernized, where he
spent several pleasant days. He enjoyed the sensation of stepping from
the medieval stone gallery, where the monks used to pace, into a modern
drawing-room. On accepting another invitation, to visit friends in Warwickshire, James found himself in a great house, in an immense park
where there were grazing deer and massive ancient oaks, and where he
mingled with some fifteen friendly guests. Still in Warwickshire, he
stayed with the Carters (Mrs. Carter being a sister of James's Parisian
friend Eleanor Strong) at "The Spring," near Kenilworth. The place was
small and charming, and across the lawn, from the drawing-room window, James looked straight at the romantic mass of Kenilworth Castle.
He began his visit by going to a party at the old rectory and dancing all
evening with shy, rosy Warwickshire maidens. "The women dance ill,"
he told Lizzie Boott, "but they are soft and clinging."

An Autumn Journey

While *The American* was appearing serially in the *Atlantic,* James
continued to support himself by fugitive writing. He sold ten articles
during that year to the *Galaxy,* for which he received $1,200. He was also

able to place three articles for the first time in *Lippincott's,* and these, with his usual writings for the *Nation,* brought his earnings for 1877 to about $2,500. With the prospect of a serial for the *Atlantic* in 1878, he felt at ease financially and was able to plan a trip to the Continent. He wanted above all to revisit Italy.

Before he crossed in the autumn, the novelist gathered together his French essays and sent the manuscript to the firm of Macmillan, which had expressed an interest in publishing him in England. He had not thus far brought out a book or published an article in the country now his home, although certain of his volumes had been imported into England and in a few instances reviewed in a temperate if condescending way. He was, in other words, largely unknown. In the United States he had built up a reputation by a long process of periodical publication, and during the past two years by the appearance of two novels, his tales and his travel book. There existed thus for James a serious problem: what sort of début should he make in England, where he would, so to speak, come before the reading public "cold." He no longer considered *Roderick Hudson* suitable for such a début; he felt he could do much better. He apparently was not sure that *The American,* just out in Boston and New York in book form, was good enough; it had been written too hastily. A volume of essays could not injure his reputation as a writer of fiction—and he could then prepare a proper and bold entry into English literature. Deciding with characteristic deliberation to appear in England not as a novelist but as a critic of novelists, and not as a writer of tales or of travel but as an authority on French literature, especially on French realism, he deposited a manuscript titled *French Poets and Novelists* at the offices of the Macmillans, and left for the Continent.

First there was Paris. The city glistened in the September sun. James looked at the French people with new pleasure. They were alert, bright, vivacious. When he returned to the Café Riche on the boulevard for his breakfast, the *garçon* remarked that Monsieur had been away a long time, led him to his favorite table and brought him his usual newspaper. James noticed the familiar faces of certain habitués, sitting over their drinks or their dominoes. He was prompted to compare them with the gentlemen he saw in the London clubs. In London he could discern a majestic social order massed behind the clubmen. What was behind these Frenchmen was probably not adapted for exhibition.

He was in no hurry to reach Italy. He found a couple of shabby rooms off the Champs-Élysées, in the Avenue d'Antin, where he could do his daily writing. His first act was to inform Ivan Sergeyevich of his arrival. Turgenev had kept his word; he had corresponded with James. His warm and affectionate letters were filled with melancholy over the Russo-Turkish war. *Virgin Soil* had been a failure in Russia; one had even heard the word *fiasco* mentioned. James had reviewed the French translation in the *Nation,* and praised it while recognizing that it was not the best of Turgenev. The Russian wrote to him: "Something was lacking in this last work which a spirit of such fine perceptions as yours must have discerned: a sense of freedom. I wrote always under a cloud."

When he learned of James's arrival Turgenev sent a note in his rather stiff English: "I am very glad that you are in Paris and very desirous to see you. In my present state of mind I rather avoid to see human faces—but you are naturally an exception." They breakfasted at Bignou's, in the Boulevard des Italiens. Turgenev talked incessantly of the Turkish war. He expected total collapse on the part of the Russians, but doubted whether military defeat would result in an uprising of the Russian people. The Tsar could with impunity "do absolutely what he chooses with them." All this gave Ivan Sergeyevich sleepless nights and dreadful visions.

James saw Turgenev several times, visiting him in his chalet at Bougival on the Seine, next to the summer home of the Viardots. On one occasion the two novelists lunched with the Nikolai Turgenevs. On the whole, "Russians, just now, are depressed and depressing company," James told Quincy Street. He dined with Theodore Child, now Paris correspondent of the *Daily Telegraph;* he saw Mrs. Kemble on her way to London from her usual Swiss summer; and during this visit he became a closer friend of Henrietta Reubell, whom he had liked from their first meeting in 1876.

He went as always to the theater. One evening he saw at the Théâtre Français a play he had seen several times before: *Le Demi-Monde* by Dumas *fils,* and came away with a feeling of "lively irritation." James found it very difficult to swallow the morality of the piece, one of those characteristic nineteenth-century dramas exploring the fate of a "woman with a past." The heroine seeks to marry a respectable young man; the young man's friend, whose mistress she has been, is determined to prevent the match, and is quite prepared to tell a lie so as to make the woman compromise herself. James, walking the lamp-lit streets after the theater, found himself wondering whether an English audience would consider this kind of conduct gentlemanly and fair. Might he not give another turn to the situation? What if an American lady—say with a long list of divorces—tried to crash her way into British society? What if a British matron sought to uncover the American woman's past? Would an American gentleman tell? James did not know it that September in Paris, but he had found the plot for one of his most amusing "international" comedies, "The Siege of London."

Early in October he took the train to Turin, lingered briefly, and proceeded to Florence. He made his way to Bellosguardo, to see Francis and Lizzie Boott in the Villa Castellani. Frank Boott showed his age; Lizzie remained charming, busy, artistic. They were "a most friendly, lovable, pure-minded, even touching couple." Boott had taken his baby daughter abroad in 1847, after the death of his wife, Elizabeth Lyman, and that of their infant son, and had reared her in Italy as if she were a hot-house flower. Now his devotion to his daughter was "more intense and absorbing than ever and his unremitting attention to every stroke that she draws or paints, half-touching, half-amusing." This was the first time James had had an opportunity to see the quiet life of the father and daughter on Bellosguardo, its limited nature and their constant industry.

He left his hotel by the Arno daily, to climb the steep and winding way to the villa along a narrow road bounded by mottled, mossy garden walls. He spent long afternoons on the sunny terrace, or sauntered along it by a moon that threw shadows on the buildings below in the softly-scooped hollow of the hills. It was charming entertainment for a week, to walk about and look at the villas: Montauto with its tower, where Hawthorne had lived; the Brichieri, associated with Mrs. Browning; to wonder at the height of the cypresses and the depth of the loggias. He walked home in the fading light noting the glow of the sunset on westward-looking walls. In imagination James found himself renting each villa. And yet there seemed to be something melancholy in the place. The fanciful stranger could only murmur to himself: "Lovely, lovely, but oh, how sad!"

In Rome he found a little apartment in Via Capo le Case, No. 45, the "rather ragged and besmirched establishment" of a Cavaliere Avvocato Spinetti. His rent was modest and the rooms were flooded with sunlight. On his first evening he made his pilgrimage to the Colosseum. The place seemed shrunken and prosaic. As for the American circle of three years before, Story was in Boston and the Terrys had had financial reverses. "Rome has changed and I have changed," he told Quincy Street. A few days later, however, he was writing to Grace Norton: "The old enchantment, taking its own good time, steals over you and possesses you, till it becomes really a nuisance and an importunity." He had hoped to get some work done; the sunshine and the atmosphere drew him constantly out of doors. He saw Alice Bartlett; the Bootts arrived from Florence to spend the winter in the Holy City; and five weeks slipped by.

Before leaving Rome James recaptured the old pleasure of riding in the Campagna—the golden atmosphere, the violet mountains, the flower-strewn grass, the lonely arches crowned with wild weeds and crumbling in the sunshine. His previous rides had been in the springtime. Riding now in the autumn he found certain differences: there were other kinds of flowers—the faded fields were made rosy, for instance, by "little pink autumnal daisies."

It may have been while they were galloping over the daisies of the Campagna, or one evening while they were together with the Bootts, that Alice Bartlett had occasion to mention an episode which had occurred in Rome during the previous winter. A simple and uninformed American woman had been trailing through the hotels of Europe with a young daughter, "a child of nature and freedom." The girl picked up, with the best conscience in the world, a good-looking Roman "of a rather vague identity," who was serenely exhibited, and introduced, in the Victorian-Roman-American society. Miss Bartlett seems to have furnished few details. There had been some social setback, some snub administered to the innocent girl. Henry's pencil made a brief record of this seemingly trivial anecdote.

One of the first things that confronted him on his return to England, on all the railway book-stalls, was a pirated edition of *The American,* the cover showing a tall Christopher Newman and a Claire de Cintré rather more blonde and less dignified than she was ever intended to be. These were the days of piratical publishing, and James knew he would receive not a penny from the sale of this popular edition. Moreover, the volume was "vilely printed" and carelessly edited; whole paragraphs were omitted. Nor was he happy to receive from Germany, however flattering, a pirated translation of the same novel, with a happy ending substituted for his own. Quite clearly it was time for him to take hold of his affairs, not only in England but on the Continent.

What James did not see was the confidential report which John Morley had written for the Macmillans on *French Poets and Novelists.* The essays were sensible and refined, Morley wrote, free from narrowness and prejudice, and served their turn as fugitive criticism. "Of charm, delicacy, finesse," he said, "they have none. They are prosaic to the last degree, and *as criticism* not at all interesting." The book might have some slight sale; nevertheless, Morley did not believe it would make a deep literary mark. "The style wants *cachet* and distinction, and the method wants depth and subtlety." He called it "honest scribble work and no more."

The Macmillans decided to bring out the book in spite of Morley's adverse report. They recognized that James was a productive writer, and if *French Poets and Novelists* would not make money, it would nevertheless place him under their wing. There had actually been no book in English as important as this on the new French writers. Moreover, the dry, high-minded Morley was insensitive to style. When the book came out early in 1878, a qualified reviewer, George Saintsbury, pronounced the papers on George Sand and Balzac "admirable" and astutely pointed to resemblances between Turgenev's work and James's.

Bundles of proofs of the volume had awaited James in Paris and he spent ten days reading them—and paying visits. He had an opportunity to see Turgenev several times—"very bad with the gout." He felt himself "better friends with him than ever." He re-crossed the Channel just before Christmas 1877.

Fanny Kemble had asked him to join her at Alveston Manor House, Stratford-on-Avon, at the home of her daughter. He arrived on Christmas Eve and we glimpse him, in a letter of Mrs. Kemble's, as "our dark-bearded, handsome American friend," helping to trim the tree in the nursery. The picturesque house, with its big fires and its hangings of holly and mistletoe, provided a distinctive final setting to a remarkable year in James's life—the happiest and most "lived" year yet. He had found an anchorage in London. *The American* was in its second edition in the United States; Tauchnitz had just bought it for a Continental edition. *French Poets and Novelists* would be out in February and Macmillan was already asking for simultaneous serialization, in *Macmillan's Magazine,* of his next *Atlantic* novel. He faced the coming year with great confidence.

Daisy

"My London life flows evenly along, making, I think in various ways, more and more a Londoner of me," Henry James wrote to William at the end of January 1878.

> If I keep along here patiently for a certain time I rather think I shall become a (sufficiently) great man. I have got back to work with great zest after my autumnal loafings, and mean to do some this year which will make a mark. I am, as you suppose, weary of writing articles about places, and mere potboilers of all kinds; but shall probably, after the next six months, be able to forswear it altogether, and give myself up seriously to "creative" writing. Then, and not till then, my real career will begin. After that, *gard à vous.*

There was a strange insight here into the calendar of his life. For what came to pass was that James wrote "Daisy Miller" during that winter. It was accepted by mid-April for the *Cornhill Magazine*—the journal of Thackeray and Trollope—and was published within six months. After that Henry James was to be considered by the world "a (sufficiently) great man."

Almost the first thing he had done after returning from the Continent to his fireside in Bolton Street was to write the tale suggested by Miss

Bartlett's anecdote of the American girl who was snubbed in Rome. The story reads today—has always read—as if it had flowed spontaneously out of the tip of his pen; it has a fine lucidity and a vividness of detail; ironic laughter echoes between its lines until it reaches its final, gently-sketched scene of pathos. There is no lingering, no explaining; the story moves objectively with quiet incident to its conclusion.

James first submitted the tale to the editor of *Lippincott's* in Philadelphia, who returned it without comment. James was not certain why, and he found the absence of comment grim. He accordingly asked a friend (perhaps Leslie Stephen) to read the story; the opinion he got was that the editor had probably rejected it because he considered it "an outrage on American womanhood." James himself was not convinced; he thought that perhaps the story was simply too long. At any rate he submitted it to Stephen for the *Cornhill,* it was accepted "with effusion," and James made his bow for the first time in an English magazine in the June and July 1878 issues. The story was pirated immediately both in New York and in Boston, and when Harper's brought it out as a pamphlet it sold 20,000 copies in a matter of weeks. James's royalties were negligible. The tale was destined, however, to be "the most prosperous child" of Henry's invention. All unaware, he had written a small masterpiece.

"Daisy Miller" had a subtitle: James called it "A Study," to suggest that he had written the equivalent of a pencil sketch on an artist's pad, rather than a rounded work. Later he said it was because of "a certain flatness" suggested in the very name of his heroine. And indeed the slightness of the story has made a later generation wonder why it should have proved so attractive. A modern reader, unrehearsed in the history of manners, might wonder at the social fuss which occurs merely because an American girl "dates" an Italian.

The story begins in Vevey at the Trois Couronnes, where the Europeanized American, Winterbourne, meets in the garden of the hotel the little American boy Randolph, and presently his sister. Her name is Annie P. Miller but everyone calls her Daisy. She has a bright, sweet, superficial little visage; her features are eminently delicate. "There isn't any society," she claims in describing her experiences in Europe and she adds, "I have always had a great deal of gentlemen's society." Her misfortune is that she does not know the European definition of a gentleman.

Later that year, in Rome, Winterbourne—through whose eyes we continue to see her—meets Daisy again. She has acquired a charming Italian; his name is Giovanelli. He has a mustache and is attentive; he does not hope to marry her, but he enjoys her company, and she is pleased to have a "gentleman" dance attendance on her, as her boy-friends did in Schenectady. It never occurs for a moment to Daisy that she is the subject of gossip, and that her behavior violates European codes; that young girls simply do not go about without a chaperon. Even when she is snubbed in Mrs. Walker's crimson drawing-room she does not comprehend the meaning of the gesture.

Winterbourne wonders whether this bright, young, admirably turned-out example of the new American generation is "honest" or frivolous, innocent or depraved. A true Jamesian male, he never quite makes up his mind. When he encounters Daisy and Giovanelli rambling late in the evening in the Colosseum he believes his worst suspicions are confirmed. Daisy catches the Roman fever and dies of it; and in the Protestant cemetery Winterbourne and Giovanelli exchange the remarks which are, so to speak, her epitaph. "She was the most beautiful young lady I ever saw, and the most amiable," says Giovanelli—whose name expresses youth and irresponsibility—and, he adds, "she was the most innocent." Winterbourne, whose name expresses the chill Daisy complained of in him, can only stare at the grave and decide that Miss Miller would have "appreciated one's esteem."

If the tale of the girl from Schenectady is now a piece of superseded social history, "Daisy Miller" remains a remarkable story; it has a spare economy, a quick painting of background and a chaste narrative, a summary sketching of American ignorance confronting American rigidity in Europe. It remains also the prototype of the "international" story. Henry was to write more important and more brilliant tales, but "Daisy Miller," like its name, still blooms among his works, "the little tragedy," as he explained to a lady who wrote to him, "of a light, thin, natural, unsuspecting creature being sacrificed as it were to a social rumpus that went on quite over her head and to which she stood in no measurable relation."

The story, as literary history knows, was an extraordinary success, but not the *succès de scandale* which legend attributed to it. There was nothing in the public reaction to warrant any suggestion of "outrage." On the contrary, Daisy was distinctly liked by many American readers. She was a girl of spirit, a "child of nature and of freedom." The vogue set off by Daisy continued for a long time afterwards: she became a perennial figure—and "a Daisy Miller" was to be a much-used descriptive phrase whenever some particularly charming, forward young lady from America showed up in Continental surroundings.

James had discovered "the American girl"—as a social phenomenon, a fact, a type. She had figured in novels before, in Trollope, for example, but never had she stood in fiction so pertly and bravely, smoothing her dress and asking the world to pay court to her. The rustling young ladies on the verandahs at Saratoga, the busy beauties of uptown New York, the graceful, idle females of Newport, suddenly became James's large subject; and all by the simple turn of exhibiting them in their finery as in all the stages of their timidity or insolence, their doubt or their triumph —at the moment of their encounter with Europe and their refusal to yield their heritage of American innocence and ignorance. American women in all their variety passed before James: the timid, the adventurous, the self-made, the divorcée in search of respectability, the heiress in search of a princedom, the demure maiden in the European *pension* engaged in an earnest quest for "culture" and self-betterment—and always there was the chase for the husband. What was new for the Europeans was the general freshness and innocence of these products of the new society, their spirit of conquest, their belief in themselves and their ability for self-improvement: above all the strange new egalitarianism, which nourished the legend that an American could do anything. These new-comers to the ancient civilization came from an order of wealth rather than of aristocracy; and James's picture of them contained a large measure of affection even while he played his delicate irony over them.

James was to tell many years later how in Venice one day a lady-friend observing two young American girls had spoken of them as "Daisy Millers." A second lady in the gondola remarked that *these* crude creatures were the real Daisies, about whom James had *not* written, and that the one he had created was a distortion, because he endowed her with form and prettiness and pathos and bathed her in the beautiful light of his own imagination. James was prepared to agree. "My supposedly typical little figure was of course pure poetry, and had never been anything else; since this is what helpful imagination, in however slight a dose, ever directly makes for." She was, as we say today, "archetypal."

A Question of Irony

By the time "Daisy Miller" appeared in the *Cornhill* during mid-summer of 1878, Henry James, writing with speed and assurance, had posted to Howells all four installments of the serial he had promised him a year earlier—a short novel narrated in 100 pages of the *Atlantic Monthly*. *The Europeans* reversed the "international situation," to which James was, for the time, committed; instead of taking Americans to the Continent, he transferred two Europeans to America, to the Boston of 1840, even as in his next tale he placed a British peer and his friend in midsummer Manhattan and Newport.

The Europeans began its run in the *Atlantic* in July 1878, the very month in which "Daisy Miller" was beginning its long vogue, and it further increased James's popularity. Written in the same clear ironic prose, the short novel possessed the compact beauty of "Daisy"; it was a light and humorous satire. Henry was saying with a touch of caricature that the puritans of New England's "silvery prime" possessed no *joie de vivre.* Mr. Wentworth, the head of his clan, looks "as if he were undergoing martyrdom, not by fire but by freezing," and he welcomes his European relatives not through any human sense of hospitality but solely as an "extension of duty."

"What a pleasant house!" observes the European-American, Felix, on entering the New England dwelling. "It's very clean! No splendours, no gilding, no troops of servants; rather straight-backed chairs. But you might eat off the floors, and you can sit down on the stairs." Yet the inhabitants of this bright establishment are sad; they "take a painful view of life." "Nothing makes them happy. No one is happy here."

There are fine atmospheric touches in *The Europeans:* the horse-cars, the sunsets, the Boston streets, the steel-engravings of religious mottoes on the walls—all painted as in clear watercolors. James made up for his unhappy ending of *The American* by giving Howells more marriages than he had asked for—no less than three—but he remained true to himself: the important marriage of the story does not take place. Mr. Acton, the congenial New Englander who has traveled in the East and is not altogether parochial, cannot bring himself to propose to Felix's sister, the interesting and glamorous Eugenia; like Winterbourne in "Daisy," he is not sure she is an "honest" woman.

James did not take *The Europeans* very seriously, nor did he intend it to be anything more than the light ironic comedy he made of it. When it came out as a book in the autumn of 1878 it found a large public both in London and in Boston. Certain Boston reviewers, among them T. W. Higginson, murmured at James's imputation of parochialism in the Boston way of life. But in Madrid the new American minister to Spain, James Russell Lowell, chuckled over the novel. He had grown up with Mr. Wentworth's generation, and he wrote to James, "You revived in me the feeling of *cold furniture* which New England life has often *goose-fleshed* me with [so] that I laughed and shivered at once."

As 1878 drew to a close James wrote one more tale. This was "An International Episode," his story of Lord Lambeth on Broadway and in Newport, his offer of marriage to a young American bluestocking and her rejection of him. James placed great store by his idea of having a young girl from Massachusetts reject a British peer, and the tale underlines the bad manners of certain members of the British aristocracy and the democratic feeling of the American girl. There had been, perhaps, a little too much laughter at Daisy Miller's expense in England, and James did not want to appear in the invidious role of a satirist to the English world of Americans abroad. His suspicions were borne out when Mrs. F. H. Hill, in a review, accused James of caricaturing the British nobility and of putting language into its mouth which it would never utter. Since he had met the lady socially, James, on this occasion, replied, defending himself in particular against Mrs. Hill's charge that in describing the manners of the two rude English noblewomen he was expressing a view of English manners in general. "One may make figures and figures," he declared, "without intending generalizations—generalizations of which I have a horror." And then, he went on,

> in such a matter, the bother of being an American! Trollope, Thackeray, Dickens, even with their big authoritative talents, were free to draw all sorts of unflattering English pictures, by the thousand. But if I make a single one, I am forthwith in danger of being confronted with a criminal conclusion—and sinister rumours reach me as to what I think of English society.

To his mother he wrote:

> It seems to me myself that I have been very delicate; but I shall keep off dangerous ground in future. It is an entirely new sensation for them (the people here) to be (at all delicately) *ironized* or satirized, from the American point of view, and they don't at all relish it.

Whatever the reflections of his readers, Mrs. Hill's review was more than a straw in the wind. James had the sense at last of the power of the writer whose image of society becomes the mirror in which society looks at itself. He had come to England two years before comparatively unknown and had moved with the silence of an observer through the English scene. Now he was a literary lion, an authoritative voice, a recognized artist.

His third Christmas in England was a far cry from the first in Bolton Street, or even the second with Mrs. Kemble. This time he went into Yorkshire to be the guest of Charles Milnes Gaskell; and to greet the new year at Lord Houghton's. It was "a hideous part of England—the Yorkshire manufacturing country, which is blighted and darkened by smoke and cinders, and the presence of a dreary population." Gaskell drove him in a sledge through the deep snow to Bretton to call on Lady Margaret Beaumont, "a drawling, lisping fine lady enclosed in her great wintry park and her immense, dusky, pictured, luxurious house," and Lord Houghton took Henry to visit the old Duchess of Somerset, a one-time "Queen of Beauty," and now "a dropsical, garrulous old woman." The "bird of paradox" was charming as usual, and at dinner Henry listens with delight to endless anecdotes told by his fellow-guest, Mrs. Procter, which he retails late in the evening to his sister Alice "in the hope of affording you a little innocent amusement."

The new year is coming in over the frosty land. "It is just 12 o'clock —1879. My blessing on it for all of you. I hope you are having a reasonable winter—here it is a very different affair from the two last and the York-shire climate has given me back the chilblains of infancy. Love to dear parents, from your *devotissimo.* H. James jr."

A Position in Society

Among the witnesses of Henry James's social conquest of London were William Jones Hoppin, First Secretary of the American Legation in London, and Ehrman Syme Nadal, Second Secretary. Mr. Hoppin was sixty-three, a successful lawyer and a man of means; he had been nomi-nated to the post by the new administration of President Hayes and had arrived in the British capital a few weeks before Henry James. A bache-lor with an interest in the arts, he had found the idea of descending on London in the Indian summer of his life appealing. Mr. Nadal, the Sec-ond Secretary, was a Virginian, twenty years younger than Mr. Hoppin. He had served in the London legation at the beginning of the seventies, returned to New York to be a journalist, and was now resuming his diplomatist's career. The two Secretaries had distinctly different temper-aments; the only thing they shared, over and above their responsibility to their position, was an ambition to succeed in British society.

Mr. Hoppin, although a man of wealth, had carefully resigned from all his financial posts before coming abroad; and while he could have afforded a large establishment he took a modest place and engaged only a housekeeper. Having a long legal experience, he performed his duties punctiliously. Nadal later described his elderly colleague as "a cultivated and very agreeable man, about as good a type of American gentleman as it would be possible to find."

Mr. Hoppin would not have been flattered, since he considered Mr. Nadal a lightweight; the journal he kept during the decade he lived in London abounds in his irritated sense of his colleague's laxities. It was true that Nadal contented himself with doing as little work as possible. His *Impressions of London Social Life,* published in 1875, and his later volume of reminiscences, reflect his superficial and amiable view of society. Henry James, who had reviewed the first book during his winter of work in Manhattan, described it as "gentlemanly"; but Nadal's obser-vations seemed to James "vague and ineffectual." Mr. Nadal was a little more assertive than Mr. Hoppin, but not disagreeably so. Mr. Hoppin, on his side, felt that his years, his social and diplomatic position, could always speak for him. He seemed, therefore, a trifle shy.

Early in 1877, when Mr. Hoppin had been in London but a few months, he met Lord Houghton, who gave Mr. Hoppin a card to the discussion club, the Cosmopolitan, to which James had also been invited. On a Sunday evening in March Mr. Hoppin directed his footsteps to 30

Charles Street, Berkeley Square, a large gloomy house which had served as a studio for the painter George Frederick Watts. Mr. Hoppin entered, found that Lord Houghton was not yet there, and was persuaded by the doorman to take off his coat and hat and mount the stairs. In a large barnlike studio with an immense mythological picture on the side wall, six or seven gentlemen were seated round the fire. None rose; no one noticed Mr. Hoppin. "This was characteristically English," he wrote in his journal. He marched about, looked at some of the pictures, and when Lord Houghton did not show up descended the stairs.

Another gentleman was just arriving. He was rather short, stocky and dark-bearded. He introduced himself as Henry James, an American. Hoppin remounted the stairs with him. James knew one of the men, Edward Dicey, and introduced Hoppin. Presently Lord Houghton arrived and "everything thenceforth was smooth and easy."

James and Hoppin met again at the St. James's Club on 6 January 1878, and Mr. Hoppin's account of the occasion reads:

> I dined there last evening for the first time. Henry James, the author, was there, who had been introduced by Nadal, and I joined table with him. Nothing remarkable in the talk—I think that men [who] live by writing for the magazines on current topics seldom ventilate their choice ideas. They keep them to be fresh in the market. The dinner was not so good as I had expected.

Perhaps Mr. James did not care to ventilate his "choice ideas" to Mr. Hoppin; for Nadal later noted that "James talked incessantly and with the originality and somewhat of the authority of those who read aloud to you their thoughts out of their own mind. His talk was very alert and eager."

Nadal and James had met at the American Legation during the Fourth of July reception of 1877, four months after the novelist's first encounter with Hoppin. Nadal recorded: "A rather dark and decidedly handsome young man of medium height, with a full beard, stood in the doorway and bowed rather stiffly, as if he were not to be confused with the rank and file of his compatriots. I was at once struck by his appearance." He is introduced and when he discovers that James lives in Bolton Street mentions that he had had rooms there when he first came to London, at No. 6. Henry invites him to come and see him. Nadal remembers that the door was opened by a slender dark young woman. James explains that she is not a servant but a relative of the landlady. "She's an English character," he explains. "She isn't a lady and she isn't a woman; she's a person." He was always discussing English class distinctions, Nadal noted, and made a point of saying he was a foreigner.

Nadal's memories of James seem circumstantial, and reasonably authentic. Nevertheless Henry James, like Mr. Hoppin, would have considered Mr. Nadal a superficial reporter. To his sister Alice he described "the little second secretary of legation" as "a most amiable nature but the feeblest and vaguest mind, and socially speaking, a perfect failure here —though he is not aware of it and it doesn't seem at all to have embittered him. He is a wonderful specimen of American innocence."

Unlike Nadal, Hoppin knew that he was a failure in London society and it did make him bitter. In the second year of their acquaintance, after the 1878–79 Season, Mr. Hoppin was prompted to write in his journal a little essay that stemmed from James's remarking to Hoppin that he had dined out that winter no less than 140 times. Mr. Hoppin had been crushed: "This great success of James leads me to inquire," he wrote, "how it is that some people succeed so well here while others constantly fail. I class myself decidedly among the failures."

Nevertheless Mr. Hoppin was determined to understand the Jamesian success and to explain it to himself:

Henry James is good looking, has good manners, but more than all, he is a popular author. People read his books and their curiosity is piqued to know him. I don't think he talks remarkably well. I believe he keeps his most piquant ideas for his novels—but he has that dash of cynicism which is in fashion. There is nothing that pleases a woman so much as to hear some spicy ill-natured *Wort* about her best friends. A kindhearted man who is naturally disposed to like people—to admire beauty —to find out who is becomingly dressed—has no chance at all in companion with an ill-natured growler who growls in an original tone.

In his talk with James about society and social success in London, Nadal gained the impression that the novelist did not want to be "in smart English society because he really preferred the company of smart people. It was rather that he did not like to feel that he was shut out from that or any other kind of company." He told Nadal that he wanted "to be taken seriously" by the English. This was a phrase he often used. He particularly detested "that excluded feeling."

One day Nadal spoke critically of certain Americans who had pursued social success in London and had been snubbed. Nadal had disapproved of their attempt: he saw no reason why they should have exposed themselves to rudeness at the hands of London's social leaders. Henry James's reply was perhaps the most significant of all that Nadal set down: "I don't agree with you," James said. "I think a position in society is a legitimate object of ambition."

In France James had but walked the periphery of society; in London in 1878 and 1879 he was presently swept into its center. It was a gradual and almost imperceptible process: one call led to another, one dinner to another, until he was constantly dining out. At first he accepted invitations to luncheon; very soon, however, he had to take precautions against being drawn into the morning and afternoon leisure of the upper classes. Only his evenings were dedicated to the pursuit of his "legitimate ambition." It was he who in reality was pursued—pursued to the point that, after a year or two, he tended to flee London or to frequent it during the "dead season." For the time, however, he gave himself over to the social process with the same systematic care he had exercised in the planning of his professional career. To dine out 140 times, as, by the count of his engagement-book and Hoppin's record, he did during the winter of 1878–79, to have had the stamina to face so many evenings of talk—not all of it good talk, by any means—so many heavily loaded tables, so much "stuffy" Victorian formality, was some kind of test of endurance. James thrived on it.

He was in a sense launched by G. W. Smalley, who, as the principal American newspaperman in London, was able to make his home into an Anglo-American meeting ground. Here James sat down to dinner with Mr. Froude, the historian and biographer, Mr. Kinglake, whose book of Eastern travels had enchanted him during his adolescence, his fellow-American Mr. Motley, and with Mr. Browning. Kinglake, sitting beside him, was "a most delicious, sweet, old man, as urbane and deferential as Emerson." Browning, however, at sixty-five a hardened diner-out, was a bit of a shock. He was "no more like to Paracelsus than I to Hercules," and to Howells James said he was "a great chatterer, but no Sordello at all."

During these early London years James came to see many walks of English life, reflected in detail in his correspondence with Quincy Street. There was first of all the fascination of meeting writers whom he already knew intimately through their works. Browning was but one instance. He meets Walter Pater at the home of the Hertzes, German Jews living in a pleasant house in Harley Street. Pater is "far from being as beautiful as his own prose," and though James chats with him he does not tell Quincy Street what they chatted about. George Meredith he encounters at a dinner in the home of the Positivist, J. Cotter Morison; he finds Meredith "a singular but decidedly brilliant fellow, full of talk, paradoxes, affectations, etc. but interesting and witty, and of whom, if he didn't live in the country, I should see more."

At the home of Madame du Quaire he meets Matthew Arnold for the first time since their encounters at the Barberini. "I cannot get over a feeling of pleasure that he writes just as he does; even his limitations have a practical excellence." Later at W. E. Forster's he meets Arnold's entire family and sits next to the eldest daughter, "as pretty as an American girl and chattering as freely."

Then there is the Thackeray-Stephen-Ritchie circle. The editor of
the *Cornhill* had been kind and hospitable. After the death of Stephen's
wife, the former Minny Thackeray, James finds him "rendered more
inarticulate than ever." He is fond of Thackeray's surviving daughter,
Anne, now Mrs. Richmond Ritchie: she is "lovable and even touching"
in her "extreme good nature and erratic spontaneity." He is invited to the
home of the famous Victorian dilettante Charles Hamilton Aïdé, "an
aesthetic bachelor of a certain age and a certain fortune, moving apparently in the best society and living in sumptuous apartments." Here he
meets George Du Maurier, "a delightful little fellow." They will become
close friends. Early in his dining out he re-encounters Trollope, "a very
good genial ordinary fellow—much better than he seemed on the steamer
when I crossed with him." He meets the talkative poetaster and civil
servant F. T. Palgrave, remembered for that substantial symbol of his
era, *The Golden Treasury.* Palgrave—"the biggest talker in England or
the world"—takes a great liking to James, and frequently visits him in
Bolton Street in the morning on his way to his office in Whitehall, thus
breaking into the novelist's working hours.

Not all the dinners James goes to are pleasant. An evening at Frederick Locker's—the writer of light verse and bibliophile—proves deadly
dull, the other guests either speechless or disagreeable, James listless
with a horrible cold, the Lockers trivial, and the room freezing. But if this
can happen on one evening, there can be others when a pleasant incident
colors the stuffiness of the diners and the dinners.

He meets British science in the person of T. H. Huxley, "a delightful
sympathetic man" to whose home he is invited, a "pleasant, easy, no
dress-coat sort of house" in St. John's Wood, in Marlborough Place, where
James had lived as a boy.

> Huxley is a very genial, comfortable being—yet with none of the
> noisy and windy geniality of some folks here, whom you find with their
> backs turned when you are responding to the remarks that they have
> very offensively made you.

He meets the British soldier, embodied in the personality of Sir Garnet Wolseley—in a great house in Portman Square, filled with Queen
Anne bric-à-brac "to a degree that quite flattens one out." Here he finds
"plain women, gentlemanly men etc. Sir Garnet is a very handsome,
well-mannered and fascinating little man—with rosy dimples and an eye
of steel: an excellent specimen of the *cultivated* British soldier."

He meets editors and publishers as a matter of course; and in certain
houses, less rigidly Victorian, the stage folk are beginning to be received.
There are cosy dinners at the home of Mrs. Rogerson—Christina Stewart
Rogerson—one of London's more informal hostesses, who compensates
for her homeliness by her dark skirt and white shirts of the finest linen

with stiff cuffs and links, and Highland shoes with large silver buckles. It will be chronicled that James said of her: "If she had been beautiful and sane, she would have been one of the world's great wicked women." At her table the novelist meets his fellow-countryman, James McNeill Whistler, "a queer but entertaining creature," whom he has sharply criticized in certain of his anonymous accounts of the London galleries published in the *Nation.* Whistler invites James to one of his Sunday breakfasts in Chelsea. "He is a queer little Londonized Southerner and paints abominably," Henry writes home. "But his breakfasts are easy and pleasant, and he has tomatoes and buckwheat cakes." He would later revise his opinion of Whistler's work.

Elsewhere he meets Frederic Leighton, the Holman Hunts, Thomas Woolner the sculptor, "good plain conceited fellow," and Samuel Lawrence, "the artist who did your bad portrait in the dining-room," he tells his father, "a very kind, soft little man: who, when I told him he had done my father's portrait, said that was what every American told him."

Henry James looks with curiosity at certain Englishmen, fortunate in all the circumstances of their life, and yet limited by their fortune to a kind of passive elegance, and the superior forms of amateurism and conformity. Thus he has close observation of Henry Adams's friend Charles Milnes Gaskell, "an originally good fellow, depraved by snobbishness, over-many possessions and position giving him all sorts of opportunities for taking himself and his luxuriant appurtenances with praeternatural seriousness."

James Bryce, author of the famous work on the Holy Roman Empire, calls on the novelist in Bolton Street and takes him to Oxford as his guest during Commemoration. Bryce always talks well and is "distinctly able." However James sees him as belonging to the class of "young doctrinaire radicals (they are all growing old in it) who don't take the 'popular heart' and seem booked to remain out of affairs. They are all tainted with priggishness—though Bryce less so than some of the others."

Bryce later takes James to Cambridge, to Trinity, to dine with a group of Oxford and Cambridge men. The dinner is dullish, but the guests include Sir Charles Dilke, who takes James fraternally by the arm and walks him over Cambridge and "all its lovely picturesqueness." James decides that "in detail, I think, it beats Oxford; though inferior in *ensemble.*"

He studies Dilke closely, finding him "very skilful and very ambitious," another "specimen of a fortunate Englishman"

> born, without exceptional talents, to a big property, a place in the world, and a political ambition which—resolute industry and the force of social circumstances aiding—he is steadily *en train* to realize. And withal, not a grain of genius or inspiration.

Pure political ability such as Dilke's did not appear to James to be "a very elevated form of genius."

This was James's panorama of London dinner tables; there came a time when he wrote to his sister Alice (it was in May 1879) that his dinners were falling "into a sort of shimmering muddle" in his memory. There was one he had given himself, at the Reform Club, to a small and select circle, John Cross, Edward Piggott, Andrew Lang and Mowbray Morris: "the thing was pleasant and the dinner was good." He went on: "I am trying to think over my other dinners, but for the life of me I can't remember half of 'em." "If you dine out a good deal in London," he wrote to William, "you forget your dinner the next morning—or rather, if you walk home, as I always do, you forget it by the time you have turned the corner of the street. My impressions evaporate with the fumes of the champagne." The moment of surfeit had come.

At the beginning of his life in London he had told Lizzie Boott, "My personal life is much less *thin* than on the Continent." Now he spoke of his "excess of opportunities"—"I have too much material—in the way of observation I lay it in at the rate of a ton a day, and already am much embarrassed for storage room."

He had reached the point where he might still be a foreigner, but he no longer felt he was a stranger. "I am living here too long to be an observer," he writes to Grace Norton on 8 June 1879:

> I am sometimes really appalled at the matter of course way of looking at the indigenous life and manners into which I am gradually dropping! I am losing my standard—my charming little standard that I used to think so high; my standard of wit, of grace, of good manners, of vivacity, of urbanity, of intelligence, of what makes an easy and natural style of intercourse!

He quickly adds however that his words about his "standard" must be taken with a grain of salt: "The truth is that I am so fond of London that I can afford to abuse it—and London is on the whole such a fine thing that it can afford to be abused!" He continued to abuse London, to abuse the Season, to complain about the social pressures—and went on dining and visiting and observing.

The Objective Genius

The year 1878 had been Henry James's *annus mirabilis*. The new year, whose arrival he welcomed amid the snows of Yorkshire, saw the establishment of his fame on both sides of the Atlantic. He lost no time, now that his name was known in England, in bringing out those novels which had already appeared in America. In the history of authorship few novelists have seen through the press so many books in a single year. "An International Episode" came out in America at the end of January 1879. In England in February James brought out three tales in two volumes, "Daisy Miller," "An International Episode," and "Four Meetings." In March the English edition of *The American* appeared; in May a completely revised version of *Roderick Hudson*. In August he began a six-part serial in *Scribner's*, entitled *Confidence*, which came out in book form in December on both sides of the Atlantic. Meanwhile some of his earlier stories appeared in London as *The Madonna of the Future and Other Tales* in October. His study of Hawthorne for the English Men of Letters series was published in December.

This was not all. He managed, in the midst of this activity, to write the tale of "The Pension Beaurepas" for the *Atlantic*, "The Diary of a Man of Fifty" for *Harper's*, and "A Bundle of Letters"—a tale written in Paris, which he was persuaded to print in Theodore Child's small English-language newspaper, the *Parisian*. The tale was pirated in America within a matter of weeks. In the absence of copyright James had no legal redress.

He was showing in his daily life a Balzacian fertility; and with it a precision of prose that seemed to belie the rapidity of his writing. When Quincy Street became worried lest he be exhausting his physical powers, he replied: "I am as broad as I am long, as fat as a butter-tub and as red as a British *materfamilias.* On the other hand, as a compensation, I am excellently well! I am working along very quietly and steadily, and consider no reasonable show of fame and no decent literary competence out of my reach."

He was a much-discussed author, a literary lion. What disturbed him was that his financial returns were not keeping pace with his reputation. "I have got a good deal of fame and hope some day to get a little money," he wrote to his friend Perry. And to his brother: "My reputation in England seems (considering what it is based on) ludicrously larger than any cash payment that I have yet received for it."

His royalties were small; but he commanded larger sums from the magazines. He had sufficient money to live at ease and to travel; and he possessed a great serenity. When his parents expressed concern lest he be embittered by the British criticism of "An International Episode" his reply was:

> I honestly believe that it would be impossible to be less at the mercy of common criticism than I. I know too perfectly well what I intend, desire and attempt, and am capable of following it in absolute absence of perturbation. Never was a genius—if genius there is—more healthy, objective, and (I honestly believe) less susceptible of superficial irritations and reactionary impulses. I know what I want—it stares one in the face, as big and round and bright as the full moon; I *can't* be diverted or deflected by the sense of judgments that are most of the time no judgments at all.

This was to be his attitude towards criticism during all his years of success.

The Bachelor of Bolton Street

James had long ago made up his mind he would not marry. It was not so much a matter of making up his mind, as of following his inclination: given his difficulties with younger women, and his comfortable relationship with elderly widows and old ladies, he saw no reason why he should change his pleasant celibate status for one that might prove a threat to his art and his personal sovereignty. "I am too good a bachelor to spoil," he wrote to Grace Norton. "That sounds conceited—but one may be conceited in self-defence."

By remaining a bachelor James could live modestly; instead of having to find a house, or a large apartment, he could for the present remain in his little rooms in Bolton Street. He was in the heart of London. His routine of life was as simple as his establishment. He rose usually after a sound sleep, having taken a long walk before going to bed. He began work without breakfast. He would eat a substantial mid-morning *dé-*

jeuner; and he would write sometimes for five or six hours after that. At the end of his work-day he paid calls, went to tea, or during free evenings turned to his club to read the newspapers before his solitary meal. After dinner he would chat with fellow-clubmen, or read in the library, or write letters. He dealt with a voluminous correspondence—there was Quincy Street, and his continental friends, and the usual social "twaddle" in answer to invitations. There was also his business correspondence, for he took care of all his publishing arrangements.

London was particularly delightful to the bachelor when he could be solitary; after so much social intercourse he enjoyed the "dead season," during which Society moved to its country houses and estates. James liked the quiet that descended on the city. At night he could hear the creaking boots of the lonely policeman passing along Bolton Street; and in the morning the sharp double-tap of the postman bringing the usual deluge of mail. He enjoyed the routine irruptions of the domestics into his rooms bringing him his tea and bread-and-butter, or his chop and potatoes. Life was never dull for a bachelor absorbed in his work and in his world as James was. If he felt lonely he walked in the park; there was always something to look at and to study; and by this time he seems to have had enough friends at whose door he could knock of an evening.

Of these friends, three old women in London society, full of the world and its ways, took their special places in Henry James's bachelor life: places more important than those of the younger women he constantly met. The longevity and experience of the three—he once said that their combined ages amounted to about 250 years—made them objects of the deepest interest to him. They were also high-spirited, witty, full of old stories; and they were imperious and demanding. Writing at the time of George Eliot's marriage to John Cross, a man much younger than herself, James told his mother: "Old women are marrying young men, by the way, all over the place. If you hear next that Mrs. Kemble, or Mrs. Procter, or Mrs. Duncan Stewart is to marry *me,* you may know we have simply conformed to the fashion. But I will ask your consent first." When he wrote this Mrs. Kemble was seventy-one, Mrs. Procter eighty-two and Mrs. Duncan Stewart eighty-three.

For James, Fanny Kemble was "the first woman in London." She was also "one of the consolations of my life!" Thirty-two years older than the novelist—and in fact one year older than his mother—Fanny Kemble became one of his great attachments. In the 1870s she was still sufficiently active to accompany James to art exhibitions and on occasion to the theater—where she was usually unrestrainedly demonstrative, weeping profusely or exclaiming violently, over memories of her own career. She possessed great strength of character and of will; and a blazing artistic temperament. She was a volcano in eruption, Henry said, or "like a straight deep cistern without a cover, or even, sometimes, a bucket, into which, as a mode of intercourse, one must tumble with a splash." Sometimes he compared her to the Alps.

Such a temperament made for constant surprise; more often than not it gave rise to the dramatic. Mrs. Kemble was capable, for instance, of saying that G. H. Lewes looked as if "he had been gnawed by the rats—and left." As a rule James did not like actresses and the "mountebank" side of their art. Mrs. Kemble however was an actress with a strong aversion to the stage; and who had, in spite of this, mastered it; she brought to her art an intelligent competence as well as a remarkable personality. And she remained, until she was a frail old lady, a powerful presence, a great histrionic voice possessed of a beautiful utterance. Proud of spirit, she gave James a vision of female grandeur that surpassed all others in his experience. "My sublime Fanny," he said of her. He responded to her "human largeness" and she brought out in him all that was most filial and charming. "I think of you almost as if you belonged to me," she wrote to him.

Mrs. Procter—Anne Benson Procter—had known almost everyone of importance during the nineteenth century. She had stories of Shelley and Keats, Byron, Coleridge, Wordsworth, Southey, Landor. James considered her "the best talker I have met in England." Fanny Kemble called her "the queen of newsmongers," but James wrote that "She abounds so in reminiscences and in *esprit* that one of her speeches chases another from one's mind. She has known literally every one." Her memory went back to the time of Napoleon and to personalities who belonged to the eighteenth century. James's final tribute to her was: "She was a kind of window in the past—now it's closed there is so much less air."

In a posthumous profile of her G. W. Smalley observed that Mrs. Procter had masculine qualities—energy, decision, abruptness, "clear ideas of what she wanted and how to get it." Like Mrs. Kemble she possessed an overbearing side to her nature. She was nearly eighty when Henry met her, and it got to be a little joke between them that he would some day marry her. "I expect soon," he wrote to his mother, "to hear that I am engaged to Mrs. Procter *aetat* eighty-two. I have indeed proposed to her several times, but she seems to think she can do better. As poor old William Hoppin, the American Secretary of Legation here, age sixty-seven or so, was lately reported to be about to espouse Mrs. Duncan Stewart, who is eighty-three or so, you will see to what an advanced period people here are assumed to keep up their interest in life."

Mrs. Duncan Stewart wore voluminous capes of old lace and black velvet. She was said to have been the natural daughter of an earl; brought up in a convent in France, she had married Duncan Stewart, a merchant, and had lived for years in Liverpool. Her daughter Christina was the Mrs. James Rogerson to whose home James was frequently invited. The mother, widowed in 1869, settled in London, in small rooms at 101 Sloane Street, where she gave pleasant luncheon parties. She had known Washington Irving and Leigh Hunt and counted Disraeli among her friends. In his notebooks, three years after Mrs. Stewart's death in 1884, James sketched the tale which became "A London Life": "There must be an old lady—like Mrs. Duncan S.—only of rank—a genial, clever, worldly, old-fashioned, half comforting, half shocking old lady." The forthright Lady Davenant in the tale is "full of life, old as she was, and had been made finer, sharper and more delicate, by nearly eighty years of it." She expects a great deal of attention; she has firm opinions and is capable of strong quick sympathies.

Like the other two old ladies, Mrs. Stewart possessed a certain hardness and sharpness. Her letters to Mr. Hoppin, which the latter preserved, are brief, amusing, flirtatious. She chides him for neglecting her; she points out that Mr. James does not neglect her. One gains a sense of a demanding woman with a rough fund of witty attack and a sharpness of tongue, when the occasion warranted.

"I constantly hear," the novelist wrote to his mother in 1880, "that I have been 'very attentive' to numerous spinsters and widows, and also that many of my well-wishers think that I should be 'so much happier' if I would only marry." His sentence might have been amended to read "elderly widows and spinsters of a certain age." That he was attracted to older women because they offered him the polished surface of London wit and cultivation, and their long social histories, is understandable in an insatiable student of manners. His inveterate choice of women who were strong and domineering and had in them a streak of hardness, sometimes even of cruelty, was probably because such qualities were distinctly familiar: Mary James and his Aunt Kate had been quite as hard, firm and sovereign.

The race of formidable and sometimes terrifying female power-figures: the Mrs. Gereths, Madame Merles, Kate Croys, in James's novels, women seen ambivalently as destructive and yet admirable, he created without recognizing wholly that they embodied certain traits of the older women in his life. His experience of the manipulating, maneuvering, meddling woman had been always with the elderly female. When he encountered certain spinsters closer to his own age, he tended to subject them to the play of his often-irresistible charm; and then was astonished to discover that they were not merely as receptive as the older ladies—they also expected an offer of marriage.

Finally, when he came to younger women, the full contradiction asserted itself: they were charming, they were sometimes beautiful, soft, clinging, intense, and James could only ask himself, as he asked of his image of the "beautiful, mysterious, melancholy, inscrutable" Elena Lowe—could they really be trusted? A tale he wrote immediately after "Daisy Miller," "The Diary of a Man of Fifty," expresses his bafflement. It is the story of a middle-aged man returning to Florence, where, a quarter of a century before, he had turned his back on a difficult woman, whom he had decided he could no longer trust. Now he meets a young man in love with this woman's daughter, and thinks his old experience is being re-enacted. "You admire her—you adore her," he tells the ardent young lover, "and yet secretly you mistrust her." The young man tries in vain to persuade him that the circumstances are different. The marriage does take place—and the narrator wonders whether he had really been right or whether his old suspicions had been ill-founded.

During this time, when he could easily laugh at the possibility of his marrying the Mrs. Kembles and Mrs. Procters of the London world, James wrote to Grace Norton (another version of this sort of woman): "I am unlikely ever to marry." He had become used to his unmarried state, and "an amiable bachelor here and there doesn't strike me as at all amiss, and I think he too may forward the cause of civilization."

There was no doubt that the bachelor of Bolton Street forwarded civilization's cause: his wit and charm were the talk of London. And yet the affluent trappings of the Victorian social order, the amusing drawing-room sallies of the ancient ladies or Henry's interest in the "heroines of the scene"—now the Anglo-American scene—reflected also his enclosed and guarded libido, the preserve of family innocence and American puritanism, overlaid with the façade of Victorian London. The young women he feared and admired distanced him from physicality; love and affection were reduced to the words in his novels. Isabel Archer, we recall, fled from any suggestion of a passionate kiss; Christina Light inspired but gave little passion. And we remember Olive Chancellor's hatred of men and Madame de Vionnet's (much later) spinning her fine gold of artifice around the bewildered Lambert Strether. Women were fenced away from Henry and he had neither the drive to sort and pick nor the daring to pursue: observation sufficed. So too he looked away from the underground sex of the Victorians—except when it became a scandal headline in the papers. For the young Oscar Wilde he would show contempt; for the ardent invert John Addington Symonds, simply amused irony. To be sure he had young male friends: but here too all was coolness and reserve. He liked the little Jewish journalist, Theodore Child, who kept all his letters; these show an easy freedom in mocking the more relaxed sexuality of Zola or Daudet, through a prism of Anglo-Saxon condescension. French naturalism was "dirty"; and there was too much talk of the brothel. Even Henry's fascination for the expansive Zhukov-ski, Turgenev's friend, would melt when he discovered the Russian's friends who belonged to Richard Wagner's gay entourage. As for the male relations in his novels—Roderick and Rowland, Newman and Va-lentin—these are more decorous than physical, even boyish and a bit adolescent. The adult enjoyment of sex is slyly introduced with literary reference—but here we must not insist on the evidence, for James could not write about any kind of sex in the "family" magazines of America. What is clear is that society gave Henry all the human warmth he seemed to want at this time. Like his sculptor Roderick, whose Roman evenings in society resemble very much Henry's later Mayfair evenings, James had channeled himself in the cultivation of his art—an art, how-ever, carefully disengaged from disturbing passions.

Strangely enough the light-weight Mr. Nadal had an accurate per-ception of this. He remarked years later that James proved attractive to women of all ages because he was genuinely distinguished, and "pos-sessed an inscrutability which piqued their interest and curiosity." More important still, women liked him, said Nadal, for his sympathetic and delicate discernment of their own qualities. "He seemed to look at women rather as women looked at them. Women looked at women as persons; men look at them as women. The quality of sex in women, which is their first and chief attraction to most men, was not their chief attraction to James." This is what enabled him to draw them in his fiction with both detachment and intimacy.

Visits

There was no way of getting to know the English better, James felt, than by seeing them "through their great invention of country-house life." The upper classes in England depended on country visits in order to "get at each other," an indispensable complement to the fugitive con-tacts of London. Periodically James embarked on a round of such visits. During his first years he enjoyed their novelty and their variety; he wel-comed the break they offered in the rhythm of his London days. With time, he became discriminating; but this was only after he had been surfeited, and had, in the process, seen many corners of England.

In the autumn of 1878 he made his first trip to Scotland, to stay with Sir John Clark. The weather was splendid, the hospitality generous, the company "inoffensive," and James wrote with rapture of the breezy moors, the brown and purple hills, the rich mixture of autumn mist and sunshine. He had never before been on the moors and for three days he had a feast of them. He made a trip to a ruined castle on horseback and returned stiff and sore from his hours in the saddle, only to go to a ball and dance polkas half the night. Lily Langtry, the great beauty, was present and James watched her in a highland reel with young Lord Huntly, a very handsome fellow in a kilt who leaped, romped and reminded Henry that ancient Caledonian "barbarism" still lurked among the Scots.

There was a visit of a different order, to Eggesford Manor, in North Devon, the house of Lady Portsmouth.

> The place and country are of course very beautiful and Lady P. "most kind"; but though there are several people in the house (local gentlefolk, of no distinctive qualities) the whole thing is dull. This is a large family, chiefly of infantine sons and daughters (there are 12!) who live in some mysterious part of the house and are never seen. Lord P. is simply a great hunting and racing magnate, who keeps the hounds in this part of the country and is absent all day with them. There is nothing in the house but pictures of horses—and awfully bad ones at that.

Lady Portsmouth takes Henry for a drive in her phaeton through lovely Devonshire lanes. In the evening the nursery *corps de ballet* comes into the gallery with governesses, and dances cachuchas and minuets "with the sweetest docility and modesty." The next day the weather turns bad, and Henry sits alone "in a big cold library of totally unread books, waiting for Lord Portsmouth, who has offered to take me out and show me his stable and kennels (famous ones)." Writing home, James says he will try to get away the next day. "I don't think I could stick out a Sunday here."

Then there was Lord Rosebery, destined to be one of the last of Victoria's prime ministers. James enjoyed his hospitality on a number of occasions, watching his political career and his rise to power with unabated interest. Late in the autumn of 1880 he was invited by Lady Rosebery to Mentmore, the great house built by her father, Mayer Amschel Rothschild, in 1851. His fellow guests included John Bright, the idol of Birmingham and champion for many years of the middle class in Parliament, and Lord Northbrook, the last Liberal Viceroy of India. Henry spent a good part of the time, as he wrote to Quincy Street, listening to the conversation of Bright, who "gives one an impression of sturdy, honest, vigorous, English middle-class liberalism, accompanied by a certain infusion of genius." He reminded Henry a good deal of "a superior New Englander—with a fatter, damper nature, however." Meeting the M.P. on a later occasion in Oxford, when Bright related to him at length the plot of "a splendid novel" by General Lew Wallace—doubtless *Ben-Hur*—James decided that Bright's "culture," as he told Grace Norton, was "so narrow, his taste so bad, and what remains of his intellect so weak," that he "wondered greatly that a 'great statesman' should have coexisted with such limitations."

At Mentmore, as James wrote his letter home, the guests were at tea in a vast hall "where an upper gallery looks down like the colonnade in Paul Veronese's pictures and the chairs are all golden thrones belonging to the ancient Doges of Venice." James had withdrawn from the glittering scene "to commune with my mammy." As he is meditating by his fire "on the fleeting character of earthly possessions," the footman arrives and lays out his things.

> You may be interested, by the way, to know that Lord Rosebery said this morning at lunch that his ideal of the happy life was that of Cambridge, Mass., "living like Longfellow." You may imagine that at this the company looked awfully vague, and I thought of proposing to him to exchange Mentmore for 20 Quincy Street.

Lord Rosebery's diary of 29 November 1880 quotes James as saying, "I mean to write a great novel before I die, Lord Rosebery, but I do not mean to be in a hurry." And Rosebery adds, "he tells me he is thirty-five and has made up his mind not to marry."

It was after this visit that Mr. Hoppin recorded in his journal for 12 December 1880 a conversation with Henry James in which James described "the luxury and elegance at Mentmore as something fabulous." But, wrote the First Secretary,

> James thinks there is a great drawback in making a country visit. Although we hear a great deal to the contrary, a guest must give up much of his personal independence. To be obliged to be agreeable morning, noon and night for several days is a great task upon one's spirits—if not one's intellect. It is better that we should never go into society excepting when we are in a mood for it and when we can show ourselves at the best.

Another Christmas (1880), and this time James is a guest at Government House in Devonport, on the edge of Plymouth Sound, the official residence of General Pakenham, commanding officer of the military district. His wife, a former American belle, is now intensely Anglicized. The day after Christmas James is conducted over a man-of-war, one of the old-fashioned big line-of-battle ships at anchor there, and breakfasts with the officers in the wardroom. Mrs. Pakenham urges James to stay for the big New Year's ball. Henry begs off. He would be lost, he feels, in a wilderness of redcoats. He goes instead to the Clarks', who are in Cornwall for the winter, and is driven by Sir John to Penzance and then to Land's End. The morning is soft and moist. He stands meditatively watching the winter Atlantic heaving gently round the outermost point of old England. After that he is happy to recover his fireside in Bolton Street.

A Dinner at the Reform

In June 1879 occurred an occasion, modest enough, and yet one of those evenings that James was later to remember with deep pleasure. This time it was he who was the host. There had come from Paris a brief note from Ivan Sergeyevich written in his elegant and quaint English. He was leaving Paris for Oxford; the university "does me the unexpected honour of making me a D.C.L." The "promotion," he said, would take place on 18 June: in a week. On his way back he had "the greatest desire of seeing you, myself." He proposed "a quiet dinner."

James was overjoyed at the prospect of seeing his Russian friend again, and this time it seemed to him that he should forgo the pleasure of the intimate dinner. Instead he proposed to dine Turgenev at the Reform to fête the honorary degree, the first ever given by Oxford to a novelist.

The group that gathered round the table at the Reform Club on 20 June seemed more philosophical and political than literary—but then Turgenev had given James very little notice. He invited W. R. S. Ralston, Turgenev's translator; a familiar from Cambridge, the philosopher John Fiske, who had turned up in London; J. Cotter Morison, the Positivist; John Cross (who was to marry George Eliot a few months later) and Mowbray Morris, of *Macmillan's Magazine.* James Bryce and young Hugh Arnold-Forster (ultimately Secretary for War under Balfour) joined the party later in the evening.

"It was all extremely pleasant, dear Ivan Sergeyevich being at his best and most charming, which is not saying little," James wrote to his mother. "His simplicity and sweetness are as great as his wit and intelligence, and his conversational powers are flavoured (excuse the culinary expression) by the most captivating *bonhomie.*"

At Oxford, the novelist had received his honor in the company of John Ruskin and Sir Frederick Leighton. Turgenev was delighted with the gift made to him of the gown he had worn at the ceremony. It would serve admirably for Sunday charades at Madame Viardot's.

Celebrities

Turgenev was Henry James's touchstone for the English novel. Writing to W. E. Henley, he pointed out that the Russian was the exact opposite of Meredith. Turgenev didn't care a straw for an epigram or a phrase;

Meredith—a mannerist, a coquette—cared enormously. Turgenev wasn't a whit literary, but simply human and moral. So too, in thinking of George Eliot, James observed that she was a philosopher, while Turgenev was a poet. The Russian cared for the aspect of things; she for the reason of things.

James nevertheless looked with high affection upon George Eliot. He hoped that he would meet her again. There had been the one brief occasion, in 1869, when Grace Norton had taken him into the presence of the overpowering lady while a son of G. H. Lewes was writhing on the floor in the next room in a fit of pain and Lewes himself had gone to the apothecary for morphine. Now that he was a Londoner, James embraced the first possible occasion to pay his respects to the author of *Middlemarch*.

Early in April 1878 John Cross invited him to a dinner at the Devonshire Club at which Lewes was present. James found the older man "personally repulsive, but most clever and entertaining." Lewes remembered James's 1869 visit, and "asked me to come back, which I shall do." He did—probably on 21 April 1878—and reported to William:

> The Leweses were very urbane and friendly, and I think that I shall have the right *dorénavant* to consider myself a Sunday *habitué*. The great G.E. herself is both sweet and superior, and has a delightful expression in her large, long, pale, equine face. I had my turn at sitting beside her and being conversed with in a low, but most harmonious tone; and bating a tendency to *aborder* only the highest themes I have no fault to find with her. Lewes told some of his usual stories, chiefly French.

James's anecdote of a later encounter with the Leweses is well known. Taken by a hostess, Mrs. Greville, with whom he was staying in Surrey, to visit the couple in their house nearby on a drenching afternoon, he found the bland and benign George Eliot standing beside a fire in a chill desert of a room with the master of the house guarding an opposite hearthstone, and both conveying to James's keen observation that if they greeted them with a show of warmth they "should more devoutly like it when we departed." James and his companion left shortly after, and Lewes, seeing them to their carriage, suddenly rushed back into the house and brought out a couple of blue volumes Mrs. Greville had lent to the household. "Ah, those books—take them away, please, away, away!" Henry recognized ruefully that the two blue volumes were *The Europeans*—and that neither George Eliot nor Lewes apparently had in the least "connected book with author."

Lewes died shortly afterwards; and George Eliot married John Cross. She was sixty; he was twenty years younger. When word reached James, he wrote to Cross on 14 May 1880 to congratulate him on an occasion in which he felt, as he said, "all the cordiality of mankind mingling with my individual voice. Don't let this mighty murmur drown my feeble note." George Eliot lived but a few months longer. To his mother Henry wrote that her death was all the sadder in that "she, poor woman, had begun a new (personal) life: a more healthy, objective one than she had ever known before."

A few days later he paid his respects to Cross. He was received in the novelist's "beautiful little study they had just made perfect" and sat in the chair George Eliot used to occupy.

> Cross said that her memory and her absolute exemption from the sense of fatigue, were more amazing the more he knew her. He, poor fellow, is left very much lamenting; but my private impression is that if she had not died, she would have killed him. He couldn't keep up the intellectual pace—all Dante and Goethe, Cervantes and the Greek tragedians. As he said himself, it was a carthorse yoked to a racer: several hours a day spent in reading aloud the most immortal of works.

To James's vision there had been two elements in George Eliot—the "spontaneous and the artificial." It was almost as if within her there were also the carthorse and the racer: the carthorse wrote *Romola,* so to speak, and the racer *Middlemarch.* Her spontaneous side enabled her to observe life and to feel it, and then she was at her best; when she tried to feel "views" upon life, she became a burden to her story-telling.

On the day after their visit in the downpour to George Eliot and Lewes, when his two blue volumes had, in a manner, been hurled after him, the loquacious and eccentric Mrs. Greville took James to call on still another celebrity living near her Surrey cottage. They were expected at Aldworth, and Alfred Tennyson suffered from no lapse of memory about the identity of his visitor, whom he had met at Lord Houghton's.

When they had lunched, the Poet Laureate was urged to read a poem. They went upstairs to his study. One of the great poems of Henry's youth had been *Locksley Hall* and this was the poem he asked for. Tennyson growled it from its noble cadenced beginning through its full length: it wasn't Flaubert's *gueuler,* but it was a continual monotonous vocalization. James sat at a rain-sheeted window and asked himself whether this was really he, and whether this was the Laureate. He wanted to pinch himself when he remembered the emotions this poem had aroused in him in his youth at Newport. He felt none of the vibrations now. "Why in the name of poetic justice had one anciently heaved and flushed with one's own recital of the splendid stuff if one was now only to sigh in secret

'Oh dear, oh dear'?" The author lowered the whole pitch: he took "even more out of his verse than he had put in."

"I went to lunch with Tennyson," Henry wrote to Charles Eliot Norton,

> who personally is less agreeable than his works—having a manner that is rather bad than good. But when I feel disposed to reflect that Tennyson is not personally Tennysonian, I summon up the image of Browning, and this has the effect of making me check my complaints.

James held Browning in high esteem; and if at moments he was depreciatory, he was to recognize, when he recalled the contrasting figure of the Laureate, that the scales were weighted in favor of Browning: "One of my latest sensations was going one day to Lady Airlie's to hear Browning read his own poems—with the comfort of finding that, at least, if you don't understand them, he himself apparently understands them even less. He read them as if he hated them and would like to bite them to pieces."

Browning was "loud, sound, normal, hearty," a presence "bustling with prompt responses and expected opinions and usual views." In his personal delivery of the fruits of his genius he tended to harshness; however, "the result was that what he read showed extraordinary life." James had had quite another image of Tennyson. He had supposed him to possess all the fine flush of his own youth. That day at Aldworth he learned "what a Bard consisted of"—as he learned earlier in Browning something of the nature of "involvement"—in life and in poetry.

Compatriots

Henry Adams and his wife Marian, once Clover Hooper, arrived in England during the early summer of 1879, and sought out Henry in Bolton Street. James had seen very little of them since their meetings in Rome six years before. The Adamses settled in furnished rooms, two streets away, in Half Moon Street, and Henry got into the habit of dropping in to see them. He took them to a Sunday afternoon at the Grosvenor Gallery and introduced Clover to Mrs. Duncan Stewart—"delighted my dear in Americans," the veteran lady told Clover, "they are all so charming." The generalization was rather wide, but James came to agree where it concerned his old-new friends, formerly of Cambridge, now of Washington.

There was, however, a fundamental opposition of temperament between the two Henrys. For Henry Adams the past, history, was a means by which he attempted to unravel the riddles of man and the personal New England riddle of himself. For Henry James the past was part of man's imagination; he saw it as a vast accumulation of creative aware-

ness applicable to a palpable present. Adams was trussed up in the rigidities of ancestry and upbringing and was always struggling to be free. For
James, life was an act of joyful and imaginative curiosity; for Adams it
was a gloomy questioning of personal experience that he could not reconcile to the eternal flux of history. At the end the novelist was to speak of
Adams's "rich and ingenious mind," his "great resources of contemplation, speculation, resignation." "Henry is very sensible, though a trifle
dry," was James's comment on the historian during this period. He
added: "Clover has a touch of genius."

James had always liked Clover Adams. Long ago he had spoken of
her "moral spontaneity." Now he had occasion to see how sharp, how
cutting she could be; how she subjected everything that came under her
view to a mordant and often highly humorous aggressivity. She had an
abundance of wit: and an intense Americanism. Europeans were people
to be judged, appraised and usually condemned. "Mrs. Adams," Henry
wrote to Grace Norton, "in comparison with the usual British female, is
a perfect Voltaire in petticoats."

The Adamses, after a trip to France and Spain, returned to London
for the winter of 1879–80 and we catch glimpses of them in various great
houses, or entertaining in their own pretty house, which they took for the
season, at 22 Queen Anne's Gate. James saw much of them. On a Sunday
afternoon, 22 February 1880, Adams, writing to Henry Cabot Lodge, records: "Harry James is standing on the hearthrug, with his hands under
his coat-tails, talking with my wife exactly as though we were in Marlborough Street." What the Adamses offered James was the American
companionship for which he longed in London. "The Henry Adamses are
here," he told Lizzie Boott, "very pleasant, friendly, conversational, critical, ironical." He had sat up with them till one o'clock that morning
"abusing the Britons. The dear Britons are invaluable for that."

The Adamses were "not at all crazy about London." When in the
autumn of 1880 the time came for their departure, James wrote, again to
Grace Norton:

> One sees so many "cultivated Americans" who prefer living abroad that
> it is a great refreshment to encounter two specimens of this class who
> find the charms of their native land so much greater than those of
> Europe. In England they appear to have suffered more than enjoyed, and
> their experience is not unedifying, for they have seen and known a good
> deal of English life. But they are rather too critical and invidious. I shall
> miss them much, though—we have had such inveterate discussions and
> comparing of notes.

Even as these *confidants* were leaving, a turn of the wheel brought
to London the charming elderly Yankee who had made bright James's

autumn in Paris eight years before. Lowell had been shifted from Madrid to the Court of St. James. During his London years Lowell's friendship with James deepened into an affectionate and enduring intimacy, built upon their common Americanism and their common foundation of literary allusion.

James discovered soon enough that if the importunities of English society ceased at certain times of the year, in the "dead season," there arrived at such times on Britain's shore—and on his doorstep—many of his strenuous compatriots. There were days when he gave himself over entirely to entertaining old American friends, acquaintances of his brothers, Albany and New York relatives, and a continuing procession of literary pilgrims. If he had said to William that he always had his eyes on his native land, his native land, more often than not, had its eye on him.

Among the earliest of his visitors after fame had come to him was a Boston lady who thought herself descended from Scottish royalty and who, accordingly, conducted herself as if she were a Queen. Her motto, on the seal she ultimately designed, was *C'est mon plaisir.* Isabella Stewart Gardner came abroad early in 1879 with her husband, and presently Henry James was telling her how to find her way to Burne-Jones's studio and hoping "to see you often—if you will allow me." The novelist's relationship to the regal Mrs. Gardner was handled with the same firmness and ingenuity that governed all his dealings with exalted—and self-exalted—personages. He quite fell in with Mrs. Gardner's wish to be treated as if she were royalty. He was prepared always to be the most humble of her courtiers—but his tone was that of *noblesse oblige.* His letters are masterpieces of epistolary persiflage, written as if he were flourishing a plumed hat before her and making formal obeisance. And yet he very carefully maintained a kind of distance designed to show Queen Isabella that it was he who was bestowing favors. "Look out for my next big novel," Henry wrote in one of his earliest letters to her. "It will immortalize me. After that, some day, I will immortalize you."

Isabella found this exhilarating, and James had his fun. He could rail at her in the privacy of his notebooks, see her as one of the tide of transatlantic "barbarians" over-running Europe, carrying off shiploads of spoils—while at the same time he penetrated the façade and understood that Isabella's acute queenship concealed a certain shyness and timidity, a certain unsureness that no real Queen would have. There were times when he was less patient. "Mrs. Jack returns to Paris tomorrow," he wrote to Henrietta Reubell. "She is not a woman, she is a locomotive—with a Pullman car attached."

During the summer and autumn of 1879 James went sight-seeing with Mrs. Gardner on both sides of the Channel. On one occasion in Paris

the Boston Gardners and the Washington Adamses, accompanied by the
novelist, dined at a *café chantant* in the open air and went to the Cirque,
after which they ate ices at a wayside café. The experience could not
have been lost on James: an imperious "Queen" juxtaposed with a "Voltaire in petticoats" in a setting such as Manet painted. Isabella took her
place in the pattern of Henry James's days and years, and fixed her image
in his work: for if one of his great themes was the chase of the American
girl for the husband, another was the chase of the wealthy American for
the artifacts of Europe.

4

PORTRAIT

OF

A LADY

A *"Divorce"*

William James was married in July 1878 to Alice Howe Gibbens, a short sturdy brown-haired Bostonian, fresh-faced and practical, a school teacher who had, like the Jameses, lived in Europe. When he informed his younger brother of his engagement, Henry replied "I had long wished to see you married; I believe almost as much in matrimony for other people as I believe in it little for myself—which is saying a good deal."

His next letter was considerably less cordial. The couple had decided on a prompt marriage and Henry did not receive the exact date of the wedding until after it had taken place. He now wrote with strange diffidence: "I have just heard from Mother that you have decided to be married on the 10th ult. [he was actually writing after that date] and as I was divorced from you by an untimely fate on this occasion, let me at least repair the injury given you, in the most earnest words that my clumsy pen can shape, a tender bridal benediction." The reference to his "clumsy pen" and the curious use of the word "divorced" suggests that some troubled feelings had been stirred in Henry. What those feelings were we would not know had he not written, in the ensuing weeks, a novel called *Confidence* dealing with a marriage which separates two intimate friends. The genesis of the story moreover suggests a strong spasm of jealousy and even hate, including a fantasy of homicide. James recorded it in his notebooks on 7 November 1878, three months after William's marriage. The William persona in the story was to murder his wife and "the violence of this denouement does not I think disqualify it." By the time Henry completed *Confidence* he had tossed out the melodrama and substituted a drawing-room comedy of love, marriage, intrigue, jealousy—a series of implausibles and absurdities after the manner of a French farce. What brought it off was Henry's gift for easy persiflage and his ability to move his characters about Europe and America—from Baden-Baden to Normandy, from Paris to New York. In *Confidence* Henry's first fantasy was to reclaim for himself his brother William. He was patently jealous of the young bride and for complex psychological reasons. It was not that William was rejecting him. William had pushed him away ever since their childhood when he had plainly told Henry he was too much of a sissy to play with boys like himself who curse and swear. The drama, as critics have suggested, resided now in the struggle of the two brothers, after half a lifetime of "twinship," to achieve their individuation.

Henry had always been so deeply identified with William that he sometimes could not distinguish himself from his brother: they had a kind of "oneness" that we can observe in the case of Thoreau and his brother John, in which the identifying brother reacts to every mood and every tone of his sibling. Henry and William had been reared as if they were twins, although they were fifteen months apart: they had shared the same nursery and had led the same lives in their childhood. Again and again Henry later spoke of the extent to which he felt he was William and wanted to live in his "adaptive skin." Our best evidence is to be found in the surviving manuscript of *Confidence,* in which Henry constantly mixes up his two characters, calling them by each other's name. The two are the typical intimates of James's early tales—the scientific active male is here called Gordon Wright (William was supposed to be always "right") and Bernard Longueville is his artistic and aesthetic friend. James constantly confuses their names: he writes Gordon for Bernard, and Bernard for Gordon. He predicates a situation in which Gordon, wishing to marry, absurdly asks Bernard to pass judgment on the girl who has won his affections. That girl is named Angela, a feminization of Henry's pet name in the family—the much-derided "Angel" of William's early mockeries. *Confidence* contains in this way the masculine-feminine of Henry, embodied in Angela, and the twinship of Henry and William, embodied in the confusions we find in the manuscript and in the vagaries of the plot.

The situation is complicated when Bernard discovers he has fallen in love with Angela—that is, the Henry persona falls in love with the feminine version of himself. We have here a series of complex gambits, in which Henry seeks to disentangle himself—as William had to do also —from the fraternal symbiosis. In the end, Gordon Wright is reconciled to the wife James originally planned to have him murder; and Henry brings off his own marriage—to his androgynous self. A distinct rite of passage is buried in the psychological and sexual content of *Confidence,* one of James's minor works by which, in later years, he set little store. The crucial rhetoric is spoken near the end of the book by Gordon Wright.

The William character expresses Henry's deepest feelings—"It's horrible, most horrible, that such a difference as this should come between two men who believed themselves . . . the best friends in the world. For it is a difference—it is a great gulf and nothing will ever fill it up."

The gulf remained. It had always been there—but Henry had hitherto overlooked it because he had invested so much of his love in his brother; and this would never change. He loved him to the day of his death in spite of their rivalries, quarrels and chronic differences.

The year 1878—the year of "Daisy Miller" and of William's marriage —was distinctly a crisis year in the lives of the two brothers. Both now moved into their separate lives. Henry had made a start when he settled in Europe and sought fame as a writer: but he still clung to his love for his brother. William now had signaled him that he loved someone else, the woman he made his wife. In marrying, after ten years of depression and hypochondria, he at last settled into his career as philosopher and psychologist. The aesthetic Henry remained a problem to his brother— "his whole way of taking life has so little in common with mine," William would write to his wife. Henry's hedonism and his androgyny suggested a possible homosexuality that deeply disturbed the elder brother. What William could not have understood was that Henry's libidinal "investment" in himself as elder brother probably precluded identification with the gay world. Henry remained as faithful to his love for William as he did to his idealized love for their cousin Minny Temple. By taking a wife, William unknowingly opened the way for Henry to face his own androgynous nature. The novelist seemed ready now to accept the feminine side of his artist self. *Confidence* demonstrates this; and indeed, this slight novel leads into *The Portrait of a Lady*.

A Storm in the Provinces

William's marriage had touched hidden feelings in Henry. Now, in the renewed selfhood of the elder brother, there re-emerged his traditional challenges to the fraternal relation. He had to deal with Henry's recent literary successes and he did so with his invariable directness and aggressivity. He attacked the slightness of *The Europeans* and objected to the ending of "Daisy," which seemed to him frivolous. He asked for greater "fatness and bigness" in Henry's stories. To the author of these works, flushed with his considerable success, William's observations seemed as ill-founded as they were ill-timed. He felt that William tended to take such works "too rigidly and unimaginatively." William, he observed, seemed to think that "an artistic experiment was a piece of conduct, to which one's life were somehow committed." Henry added: "I don't trust your judgment altogether (if you will permit me to say so) about *details;* but I think you are altogether right in returning to the importance of subject. I hold to this very strongly."

Henry James's sense of having been set aside—with critical violence—in his brother's life would however have had little consequence beyond his minor novel serialized in *Scribner's,* which yielded him $1,500. But it was followed by another occurrence, of a larger public nature. He had completed his book on Hawthorne for the English Men of Letters series. Macmillan set it up rapidly and published it in the midst of Henry's fictional successes. The book proved extremely popular among British readers. They liked its quiet tone, its wit, the authority and brilliance of James's pictures of the New England of Hawthorne's time.

Hawthorne had not been out long before James realized that he had profoundly irritated his American reviewers. He was attacked in both Boston and New York for adopting a "foreign" attitude toward Hawthorne, and for his emphasis on the parochial quality of New England life in Hawthorne's day. The American critics for the first time began to suggest that James was losing his native point of view by his continued residence abroad. The tone of the book, and certain of his formulations, evoked a sharp, if characteristic, outburst of chauvinism. James argued that America had been bare of society and history when Hawthorne came upon the scene. Finding no rich social fabric, such as English novelists could draw upon, the romancer tissued his work out of haunted Puritan memories of New England. In depicting the America of the earlier part of the century, James enumerated the things "absent" from American life in Hawthorne's time which existed for British novelists:

> No sovereign, no court, no personal loyalty, no aristocracy, no church, no clergy, no army, no diplomatic service, no country gentlemen, no palaces, no castles, nor manors, nor old country-houses, nor parsonages, nor thatched cottages, nor ivied ruins; no cathedrals, nor abbeys, nor little Norman churches; no great Universities, nor public schools—no Oxford, nor Eton, nor Harrow; no literature, no novels, no museums, no pictures, no political society, no sporting class—no Epsom nor Ascot!

The listing, while accurate enough, seemed depreciatory. It little mattered that Hawthorne himself, in his preface to *The Marble Faun,* had spoken of "the difficulty of writing a romance about a country where there is no shadow, no antiquity, no mystery, no picturesque and gloomy wrong, nor anything but a commonplace prosperity, in broad and simple daylight, as is happily the case with my dear native land." Taken out of context, the passage does make James sound as if he were advocating adoption by the United States of those very British institutions which America had abjured.

Even James's friend Howells was critical. In an anonymous review in the February 1880 issue of the *Atlantic,* the editor expressed delight in certain of the chapters, but to James's enumeration of the things absent from American life, he rejoined, "we have the whole of human life remaining, and a social structure presenting the only fresh and novel opportunities left to fiction, opportunities manifold and inexhaustible."

James judged Howells's review "handsome and friendly," and told him that the *Hawthorne* had been "a tolerably meditated performance." He admitted that he had used the word "provincial" too many times and also pleaded guilty to overworking the word "dusky." As for his enumeration of "absent" things, he went on, "It is on manners, customs, usages, habits, forms, upon all these things matured and established, that a novelist lives—they are the very stuff his work is made of." In saying "we have the whole of human life remaining" Howells was begging the question. There was that much less of life when there were fewer institutions and fewer works of civilization.

James was first bewildered and then hurt by the storm he had raised in America. He shrugged it off as "a very big tempest in a very small teapot"; nevertheless it made a deep impression on him. Thanking his friend Perry for a favorable review, James wrote in April 1880: "What a public to write for!—what an inspiration in addressing them! But let us hope they are not the real American public. If I thought they were, I would give up the country."

In the end he shrugged the matter off as "the clucking of a brood of prairie hens." However, America—like his brother—had suddenly made him feel cast aside. His work had been spurned and abused at the very moment when he seemed to be harmoniously attaining all his aims. The tempest blew itself out; but the weight of fraternal—and national—disapproval, in which his friendly editor had joined, left a certain amount of wreckage in its wake. Superimposed upon the wounds of his boyhood, the reception of his *Hawthorne* brought James to a turning point in his development which was reflected immediately in his work.

The Frail Vessels

The change which occurred had been quietly symbolized by the fact that the "Angel" was Angela in *Confidence.* From this moment James began to write novels about heroines instead of about heroes. There were, to be sure, certain later exceptions: as with Hyacinth Robinson in *The Princess Casamassima* or Lambert Strether in *The Ambassadors;* but from now on the female protagonist took possession of the Jamesian scene. Years afterwards he was to ponder this and to attempt to explain what he had done. Musing on George Eliot's words, "In these frail vessels is borne onward through the ages the treasure of human affection," James proceeded to justify his major studies of the female sensibility, his insistence, at the heart of his own work, upon the heroine rather than the hero. "Frail vessel," however, was hardly applicable to James's strong and egotistical young women. They possess not a little of his own power, will and strength in imposing themselves upon the world. James, at any rate, argued that a novelist—a novelist like himself—did not necessarily have to deal with the life of action. He could, through characters such as Isabel Archer or Milly Theale, record the fascination of mental and emotional experience—make the contemplation of such experience as exciting "as the surprise of a caravan or the identification of a pirate."

Confidence was completed during the summer of 1879. Everyone seemed interested in what Henry James would do next. He had promised that he would write a "big" novel. Compared to his lighter works, he told his parents, this work would be "as wine unto water," and from this point the novel, destined to become *The Portrait of a Lady,* is spoken of in the family letters as the "wine-and-water novel." It was with the intention of starting this work in earnest that James went to Paris in the early autumn of 1879, on his way to Italy.

The study of Hawthorne was completed that September at 42 rue de Luxembourg, a few doors from the house in which he had passed his memorable winter, three years before. On the day the last sentences were written he went out to celebrate the occasion with Mrs. Gardner. The Henry Adamses were also in Paris, on their way to Spain, and James saw them almost daily. Certain of his English friends turned up as well, and he acted as their cicerone. He found them quite as provincial as his American friends. Hamilton Aïdé, the amiable dilettante, arrived, and James took him to Bougival to see Turgenev. The Russian was "delectable as ever, though a little gouty."

Later in the autumn Ivan Sergeyevich joined him in town for what had become their traditional *déjeuner.* Zhukovski was in Naples, and Henry planned to see him there. However, early in December, as he was about to leave for Florence, a raging blizzard covered all Europe. At the height of the storm Henry sat snugly in his hotel, in the rue Neuve St. Augustin, whither he had moved with the advent of the cold, and wrote in a single sitting his light tale of American and European manners, "A Bundle of Letters," which he gave to Theodore Child to publish in the *Parisian.*

For Child, the novelist reviewed the newly published *Nana,* and while in the French capital he seems also to have written his long reviews of the correspondence of Sainte-Beuve and of Delacroix—reviews which show how much authority he had gained since his Paris residence. They are not only vigorous in their close analysis of the qualities of the writers; they demonstrate how much more receptive he was to their nature as artists. James had long mastered the art of generalization. There is now however a greater use of aphorism, of sharpened epigram. "In the arts," he writes, "feeling is always meaning." And he speaks of Saint-Beuve's search in his biographical studies for "the seam as it were between the talent and the soul." If on the one hand James seems to toss these profundities at readers with a light gesture, he seems to invite them on the other to give close attention to his seeded paragraphs.

In the review of *Nana* he complained, in the best Victorian manner, that the novel was simply "unclean"; nevertheless he has much praise for the solidity and the strength of Zola himself. He is prepared to allow him his subject: indeed his complaint is that Nana is not quite human and that there is an absence of humor in the book. Humor, he suggests, might have served as a disinfectant.

The cold winter and the heavy snows caused James to postpone his trip to Italy and the beginning of his wine-and-water novel until spring. He recrossed the Channel amid heaving wintry seas, and was happy to find himself again by his Bolton Street fire. Moreover he was writing a new short novel, and was deeply absorbed by it. He called it *Washington Square.*

Fathers and Daughters

He had apparently begun *Washington Square* while he was on the Continent, intending it to be a short story, and hoping to send it to the *Atlantic.* Early in 1880 he wrote to Howells that "I tried to squeeze it down for you, but it was no use." He sold it finally to the *Cornhill,* and *Harper's New Monthly Magazine* in America—the first time James achieved simultaneous serialization on both sides of the ocean. Both journals used illustrations by George du Maurier.

Washington Square was based on an anecdote told James by Mrs. Kemble, a small item of her family history. Her brother had jilted an heiress when he discovered that her father would disinherit the girl. This simple story is told without varnish, and with an unsparing economy; and while James began by focusing on the jilting of the girl, he ended with a brilliant picture of a father's clumsiness in dealing with his daughter's love and his crude failure to spare her feelings. It is a perfect piece of psychological realism, and with its four characters, the father, the daughter, the lover and a romantic foolish meddlesome aunt, achieves a considerable degree of intensity and pathos. Although he has made her rather simple and plain, James's sympathies are clearly with the daughter, Catherine Sloper. And in terms of his recent life she is an image of himself as victim of his brother's—and America's—failure to understand either his feelings or his career. Dr. Sloper would appear to be still another of James's fictional re-creations of his brother: the William who could love him and also spurn him. In the end it is Catherine who can spurn her lover, when he returns years after, still possessed of a faint hope that he can acquire the benefits of her fortune. She, however, can neither forget nor forgive. Among the endings of James's novels there is none more poignant than when Catherine, her interview with the middle-aged Morris Townsend over, picks up her morsel of fancy-work and seats herself with it, "for life, as it were."

In the intensity of the narrative, the short scenes, the heightened dialogue, the clash of wills, *Washington Square* showed the mastery James had now attained. The novel is concerned above all with a struggle for power, a will to freedom, and the refusal of a simple soul to bow before the domineering spirit of another. James was to treat again and again of the relationship between fathers and daughters, but *Washington Square* remains at once the simplest and most dramatic—and most American—handling of the subject, framing an eternal drama of a certain kind of family life in a Square that was both a personal and an historical symbol of American upper-class life. The novel testified also to the destructive power of a materialism untouched by the imagination.

Washington Square was completed between James's visit to Paris, during that rude winter, and his departure for Italy in the spring of 1880. In the same interval Henry dined out strenuously, visited friends, and laid his plans for the large novel which he had been wanting to write for the past three years. When *The American* was still appearing in the *Atlantic,* he had outlined for Howells his plan to do "the portrait of the character and recital of the adventures of a woman—a great swell, psychologically a *grande nature*—accompanied with many 'developments.' " But Howells could not take a large novel on the heels of *The American,* and James had been side-tracked into writing certain of his international tales. He had made a beginning of his novel, however, and the delay enabled him to conclude better arrangements for its publication; by the middle of 1879 it was agreed that he would start his *Atlantic* serial during 1880 and run it simultaneously in England in *Macmillan's Magazine.*

"I must try and seek a larger success than I have yet obtained, doing something on a larger scale than I have yet done," he told Howells. "I am greatly in need of it—the larger success." Macmillan now had six of his books in print, though the royalties thus far seemed pitiably small. Chatto & Windus, to whom he had offered *Confidence,* had been willing to publish that novel on favorable terms; but then the Macmillans, fearing they might lose their author, sent an advance against future royalties, which for the moment mollified him. Negotiating from a position of strength, he made stiff terms for his big novel. The *Atlantic* was to pay him $2,500 and *Macmillan's* £250. He estimated that he would receive in all $5,000 by the end of the serialization. *Confidence, Hawthorne* and *Washington Square* had yielded him about $4,000. Early in 1880, when T. S. Perry offered to write an article on James's works to date, James told him to wait for the novel he would do that year. "It is from that I myself shall pretend to date—on that I shall take my stand." To Howells he announced that he had found his title—*The Portrait of a Lady.*

With the old fragment of his work in progress in his writing portfolio, and provided with ample funds, James left London for Italy. He took ship on 22 March 1880, spent two or three days in Paris, and arrived in Florence on the 28th. He put up at the Hôtel de l'Arno, in a room with a window on the river yellow in the spring sun; he spread his writing materials on his work-table—but he was not yet ready to start. He needed a holiday.

The "gentle and pure-minded" Bootts had wintered in Florence proper but were in the process of re-installing themselves in the thick-walled Castellani, in the big rambling apartment on the ground floor, where Lizzie had her studio beside the rough terrace with its view of the Val d'Arno. Lizzie now appeared to James rather elderly and plain, but happy in her indefatigable industry. "She seems to spend her life in learning, or rather in studying without learning, and in commencing afresh, to paint in someone's manner," wrote James. Her newest painting master was the burly Frank Duveneck, whom Lizzie had persuaded to move from Munich to Florence. Duveneck, a rough-and-ready "child of nature and of freedom" from Kentucky, had learned his craft decorating altars in Catholic churches all the way to Canada. At the Academy in Munich, he had carried off prize after prize. James considered his work strong and brilliant; it had about it a "completeness" he would not have suspected from some of his things he had seen earlier in Boston and New York.

Aside from his painting, the uncouth, vigorous and good-natured Duveneck seemed the strangest person in the world to be in the constant company of Lizzie Boott, product of a careful education and a sheltered life. They were a curious group, the father, the daughter and the painter, and James was to watch the evolution of Lizzie's love affair with her bohemian teacher with the interested eyes of a friend—who was also a novelist.

A Neapolitan Episode

James was restless in Florence and he decided, a few days after arriving, to take a ten days' run to Rome and Naples and fulfill his promise to visit Paul Zhukovski. On his way to Naples James paused for a few days in Rome and found the city much changed—new streets, horse-cars, a hideous iron bridge over the Tiber—all "so many death blows to the picturesque."

What happened at Posillipo, in the environs of Naples, we can only guess. In Paris Zhukovski had appeared to the novelist as a charming and romantic dilettante; now he saw him as a rather weak and dissolute hero-worshipper and perhaps became aware he was homosexual. Richard Wagner was spending that year at the Villa Ungri, a short distance from Zhukovski's villa, and the Russian was all for James's meeting Wagner at once. The American, however, demurred. He had no desire to meet "the musician of the future," believing such a meeting would be futile—he spoke too little German, and Wagner spoke neither English nor French. The Russian spoke of Wagner as the "greatest and wisest of men," and confided to Henry that it was his ambition to go and live at Bayreuth so as "to take part in the great work." James doubted whether Zhukovski would do this, since he seemed such an eternal dabbler.

James left Posillipo after three days and drove from Castellammare to Sorrento. There, in a hotel on the edge of the sea, looking out onto the Bay of Naples, with Vesuvius "smoking his morning pipe," he felt himself again in tune with the world. Writing to Grace Norton with this scene before his eyes, he told her that "the manners and customs of a little group of Russians" he had just been observing "were about as opposed to those of Cambridge as anything could well be." He had found the Naples museum more interesting than the "vileness" of the humanity of Posillipo.

The group of Russo-German sensualists in the Wagner entourage had shocked James. There is no record of later meetings with Zhukovski. The Russian did follow Wagner to Bayreuth, and became, in the three remaining years of the composer's life, a member of his inner circle. Zhukovski painted the sets for *Parsifal,* and contributed to the Wagner legend by painting the picture of the "Holy Family" at Wahnfried, with Wagner's daughters as angels and himself as a figure in the background.

Late in life Zhukovski and James established touch again and a long, effusive, affectionate letter from the Russian remained among James's papers. It tells us little. He had been, for his brief moment, one of those with whom the novelist had thought he might found a lifetime friendship. James had to recognize that he had been mistaken.

Fenimore

During the stormy winter of 1879-80 there had come to Europe an American authoress who had published many sketches in the magazines, a narrative poem entitled *Two Women* and a volume of tales, *Castle Nowhere.* Constance Fenimore Woolson, a grand-niece of James Fenimore Cooper, was a dainty lady of thirty-nine, with a clear complexion, an alert manner and the bearing of a gentlewoman. Arriving in London, she had taken rooms in Clarges Street, adjoining Bolton Street. She had with her a letter of introduction to Henry James Jr., which she presented at No. 3 Bolton Street, but James was in Paris. Soon the cold and damp made her seek the warmer climate to which she was accustomed. She had been living for some years in Florida. She crossed to the Continent at about the time that James was returning to London, after the big snow in Paris.

The letter of introduction had been given to Miss Woolson by James's cousin, Minny Temple's sister, Henrietta Pell-Clark, of Cooperstown, New York. The authoress wanted to meet James because she had read him, admired him, studied him, and enthusiastically reviewed him in the anonymous "Contributor's Club" of the *Atlantic.* New England-born, she had grown up on the shores of Lake Erie and knew the flora and fauna of America. Distinctly "regional," her northern sketches imbibed both the tradition of her great-uncle and the spirit of Bret Harte and they had proved generally popular. When circumstances took her to the South of the reconstruction, her imagination was captured by a society reconstituting itself after the fratricidal war, the garrison life, the run-down plantations, the wretched houses. She went to the war cemeteries. She talked to Negroes and made notes on their dialect. She took lonely walks at the end of hot days on the edge of rice-fields, skirting swamp-lands and observing the death-in-life of the South. She made the region hers as she had done the Lake country. Now she was preparing a volume of tales of the South, *Rodman the Keeper,* for the press.

Miss Woolson had come to know Europe through the writings of Henry James. As she neared her forties she faced the world unmarried and alone, but she had her power of lonely sustained work, and a sufficient income from her writings. She would go to Henry James's Europe. Her friends John Hay and William Dean Howells encouraged her.

Europe, that winter, was as snowbound as her Lake country. The cold drove her to the Riviera. Here in the bright sunshine she settled into the Hôtel des Anglais at Mentone, a quarter of a mile from the Italian frontier. She spent her mornings in her room writing a novel, *Anne,* that was to bring her a wider public still, and the afternoons in sightseeing and local excursions. She also wrote poems. One called "Mentone" begins, "Upon this sunny shore / A little space for rest." In its second stanza she spoke of "a little space for love."

Henry James returned to Florence at the end of April 1880 and re-installed himself in the Hôtel de l'Arno. There he began *The Portrait of a Lady,* or rather worked over the "aching fragment" he had already written. He was late in getting started and rather than crowd himself wrote to Howells and to *Macmillan's* asking to begin the serial in October instead of August as had been arranged. To his sister Alice he wrote that he was at last leading a quiet life, although Florence was "a place where one is liable to tea-parties." He added: "I have to call, for instance, on Constance Fenimore Woolson, who has been pursuing me through Europe with a letter of introduction from (of all people in the world!) Henrietta Pell-Clark."

When James finally paid his respects to Miss Woolson at her *pensione* on the Lung'Arno, he found a trim woman, her hair carefully braided and piled in rings at the back of her head, leaving a pair of delicate ears to the view. A fringe of hair concealed a high forehead. Miss Woolson had an oval face, questioning eyes, a straight nose and a wide mouth. She listened intently, and James noted that she seemed to be hard of hearing. "Constance is amiable," he wrote to Quincy Street, "but deaf, and asks me questions about my works to which she can't hear the an-swers." Actually he discovered that her deafness was confined to one ear. Little that he said was lost upon her.

In ordinary circumstances James would have limited his amenities to his countrywoman. However, her interest in his work, her bearing, and her sense of her own literary position quite disarmed him. Perhaps, too, he was still feeling his disillusion with Zhukovski and it was pleasant to find a new admirer. Lizzie Boott, who always devoted much time to James when he was in Florence, was preoccupied with Duveneck. There seemed, after all, small danger of his becoming too interested in an earnest, provincial, middle-aged, deaf woman who was trying very hard to learn the meaning of art and was clearly discomposed by the nudity of the statues. They did much sightseeing together, and James quite forgot his usual reserve: he turned on the full power of his charm for this American woman.

If Miss Woolson had given up hope of marriage, she must now have begun to wonder a little about the prompt and kind attentions of the aloof bachelor, three years her junior. James was all decorum and distance; nevertheless he showed endless patience; and he seemed delighted to be her cicerone and escort. Their interest in one another seems to have served as a kind of mutual flattery. Thus, against a background of old palaces and the glories of Renaissance art, was formed one of the strangest friendships in American literary history, and one of the most secretive. Constance Fenimore Woolson—Fenimore as he was to call her—became one of those friends in James's life whom he considered "a private resource," and to whom he was always loyal, in his distant way.

"Florence," Fenimore wrote to a friend shortly after meeting James,

> is all that I have dreamed and more; here I have attained the old-world feeling I used to dream about, a sort of enthusiasm made up of history, mythology, old churches, pictures, statues, vineyards, the Italian sky, dark-eyed peasants, opera-music, Raphael and old Michael, and ever so many more ingredients—the whole having, I think, taken me pretty well off my feet! Perhaps I ought to add Henry James. He has been perfectly charming to me for the last three weeks.

She described him. He had a "beautiful regular profile," a brown beard and hair, and large light-grey eyes, from which, she wrote, "he banishes all expression." His manner was "very quiet, almost cold." From this time on, in certain of Miss Woolson's tales, a Henry James character makes his appearance, with Henry's style of beard and his build, and always with grey *expressionless* eyes—eyes that refuse to commit themselves, one might say.

By the end of that summer Miss Woolson had written and published a tale called "A Florentine Experiment," in which she incorporated a certain number of James's observations on Florentine art. "He delivered quite an epic upon Giotto's two little frescoes in the second cloister of Santa Maria Novella," she wrote in this tale, and

> he grew didactic and mystic over the round Botticelli of the Uffizi and the one in the Prometheus room at the Pitti; he invented as he went along, and amused himself not a little with his own unusual flow of language.

James was an easy improviser. He did have a certain awareness of Fenimore's feelings, for he wrote to his Aunt Kate on 3 May 1880, "This morning I took an American authoress [on] a drive—Constance Fenimore Woolson, whose productions you may know, though I don't. . . . Constance is old-maidish, deaf and 'intense,' but a good little woman and a perfect lady." He added to his aunt: "I hope your spring is genial, without being (like Miss Woolson) intense."

At another time James might have been more wary of such intensity. It is abundantly present in "A Florentine Experiment" in which an American heiress, believing the Henry James character to be in love with another woman, trifles with his affections. The "experiment" is hers; it stems from her belief in his masculine arrogance and conceit, which she is quite prepared to deflate. What the tale overlooks, understandably, is the heroine's own large measure of conceit as well. There is evidence enough to show, in what she was to write to him, that Fenimore aspired to the style, the manner, the mastery of Henry James. She was to try, during the ensuing decade—her final "phase"—to write international stories, after the manner of the man to whom she became attached, and with whom she now felt herself, on some strange deep level, to be competing. Henry must have sensed this. It is to some such appeal to his constituted nature that we may attribute his long and continuing friendship with Fenimore—one of the few relationships in his life in which his eyes may be said to have been partially sealed. Insight was to come only in the long aftertime.

A Band of Egotists

When Henry James bade farewell to Florence—and to Fenimore— late in May or early in June 1880, he had in his portfolio the first installments of *The Portrait of a Lady.* This time his copyright would be safeguarded: the serial was to begin in October in England and a month later in America. Moreover, he now had the advantage of working from proofs supplied by Macmillan, and would not be dispatching raw manuscript to Howells.

In his journal-summary of this period he wrote:

> I returned to London to meet William who came out in the early part of June, and spent a month with me in Bolton Street, before going to the Continent. That summer and autumn I worked, *tant bien que mal,* at my novel. . . . I had a plan of coming to America for the winter and even took my passage; but I gave it up. William came back from abroad and was with me again for a few days, before sailing for home. I spent November and December quietly in London, getting on with the *Portrait,* which went steadily, but very slowly.

William's sudden trip abroad had been to obtain a change and a rest: he was still prone to nervous fatigue and eye-trouble. The brothers had not seen each other since 1875. In the interval the novelist had found his place in life, and William had become a husband and father. Henry reported to Quincy Street that he found him little changed, "all his vivacity and brilliancy of mind undimmed." Yet there remained in him, Henry felt, "more of nervousness and disability," than he had supposed, "and I can't get rid of the feeling that he takes himself, and his nerves, and his physical condition too hard and too consciously."

Henry sought to offer William the amenities of London, and did give a small dinner for him at the Reform Club. Otherwise his efforts to draw him into his own social orbit failed; the elder brother found England "oppressively social." On reaching the Continent he wrote to Quincy Street that his brother "as he grows older," seemed "better suited by superficial contact with things at a great many points than by a deeper one at a few points." No one reading the fruits of Henry's contact with the human scene, the social fabric (hardly "things at many points"), would today use the word "superficial."

His brother's visit this time was but a ripple in James's generally contented life and work in London. Nevertheless William had barely left for the Continent when Henry was reporting to his mother that he was recovering from "one of those wretched sieges of pain in my head which I have had so often and which are so unprofitable." He also informed Quincy Street that he would not be returning to America that autumn as he had planned. It seemed to him the wiser course to remain abroad until his novel should be complete, and then give himself a total holiday at home. He was to get a great deal of money for *The Portrait,* "and therefore I wish to carry it on quietly and comfortably—the more so as I have just been correcting the opening proofs and that they seem to me very good."

The Portrait of a Lady, the third of James's large studies of the American abroad, was twice as long as either *Roderick Hudson* or *The American.* James began with the thought that his Isabel Archer would be a female Christopher Newman. Indeed this may be why he named her Isabel, for the Queen who sent another Christopher faring across the ocean. And Isabel Archer embodies a notion not unlike that of Isabella of Boston, with her motto *C'est mon plaisir.*

Like her male predecessors, Roderick and Christopher, Isabel goes abroad a thorough provincial, with her "meagre knowledge, her inflated ideals, her confidence at once innocent and dogmatic, her temper at once exacting and indulgent." James presents her to us as a young romantic with high notions of what life will bring her; he speaks of her "mixture of curiosity and fastidiousness, of vivacity and indifference," of her "combination of the desultory flame-like spirit and the eager and personal creature of her conditions." And he adds: "She treated herself to occasions of homage."

The allusion to her "flame-like spirit" suggests that Isabel is an image of James's long-dead cousin Minny Temple, whom he would describe in the same way. But if Isabel, with her eager imagination and intellectual shortcomings, has something of Minny in her make-up, she has much of Henry himself. He endows her with the background of his own Albany childhood, and when he sends her to Europe and makes her into an heiress, he places her in a predicament similar to his own. James was hardly an "heir"; but his pen had won him a measure of the freedom which others possess through wealth. In posing the questions: what would Isabel do with her new-found privileges? where would she turn? how behave? he was seeking answers to the transcendentalism of Concord: his novel is a critique of American "self-reliance."

Isabel presently finds herself with a series of suitors. The first, the American Caspar Goodwood, has a "disagreeably strong push," insists "with his whole weight and force." He is monotonously masculine; and if Isabel finds his sheer sexual force attractive it is also terrifying. For her, passion, or sex, is not freedom. Her second suitor is the British Lord Warburton, a fine upstanding liberal without too much imagination, one of the types Henry had met at his club or in country houses. He inspires a different kind of fear in the young American.

> What she felt was that a territorial, a political, a social magnate had conceived the design of drawing her into the system in which he rather invidiously lived and moved. A certain instinct, not imperious, but persuasive, told her to resist.

Social position, in a word, was also not necessarily freedom.

"I'm very fond of my liberty," Isabel says early in the book, and she says also "I wish to choose my fate," quite as if the ultimate choice were hers. But as Henrietta Stackpole, the energetic and rather meddlesome newspaperwoman, reminds Isabel: "You can't always please yourself; you must sometimes please other people."

At this stage James's heroine is still full of hopes and dreams. Asked to define her idea of happiness she offers a vision of a journey into the unknown—"A swift carriage, of a dark night, rattling with four horses over roads that one can't see." However, the young lady from America does try very hard to see, at every turn, the roads before her. And what she discovers is that even in daylight on a clear highway it is possible to take a wrong turning.

Isabel's wrong turning occurs without her knowledge, when she meets Madame Merle (the *merle* is a blackbird), a woman of a certain age, worldly-wise and accomplished, an American expatriate of long standing, who has the appearance of freedom and insouciance to which Isabel aspires. In Florence, Serena Merle introduces Isabel to another American expatriate, who lives with his young daughter in a thick-walled villa on Bellosguardo. James had spoken of Francis Boott and Lizzie as "figures in an ancient, noble landscape," and Gilbert Osmond and his daughter Pansy are such figures. Osmond, however, bears no resemblance to Boott, the open, generous, naïve and easy-laughing amateur of life. James gives him the same intelligence and the same piercing sarcasm as Catherine Sloper's father in *Washington Square;* he is capable of the same coldness to his daughter's feelings. But he is infinitely more malign, and his will to power is infinitely greater than Dr. Sloper's.

Osmond expresses one side of Henry James himself—a hidden side: he is what James might under some circumstances have become if he allowed snobbery to prevail over humanity, and arrogance and egotism over urbanity and his benign view of the human comedy. James put into Osmond his own high ambition and drive to power—the grandiose way in which he confronted his own destiny—while at the same time recognizing in his evil character the dangers to which such inner absolutism might expose a limited being like Osmond. In him, the drive to power ended in dilettantism and petty rages. The same touch of megalomania had given James unbounded creativity.

Isabel and Osmond are then, for all their differences, two sides of the same coin, two studies in egotism—and a kind of egotism which belonged to their author. For Isabel, generous high-minded creature though she is, in pursuit of an abstraction she calls "freedom," insists that she has found it in Osmond. When she marries him she believes that it is she who brings powerful elements into the union; possessed of her wealth, "she would launch his boat for him; she would be his providence." This is indeed an exalted notion of her role, and it suggests the role she assigned to Osmond. In the end they cannot suffer each other. Osmond tries to bend Isabel to his will. She cannot be bent. Each insists on supremacy. The impasse is complete.

James had written into this work his legitimate aspiration to freedom, and his covert drive to power hidden behind compliance, docility and industry. In the largest sense, egotism and power—not love—are the real subjects of *The Portrait of a Lady.* How was one to possess the power and presumption of one's genius and still be on good terms with oneself and the world? Above all, how enjoy one's freedom and not make mistakes in the exercise of it? Beyond the unhappiness—the mistake—of Isabel's marriage lies the revelation that she has been the victim of a carefully-laid plot: that Madame Merle had been the mistress of Osmond; Pansy is their child; and the marriage had been arranged by the wily blackbird to endow Pansy with Isabel's fortune.

It is possible to see in this light that Isabel's rejection of Goodwood and Warburton went beyond the mere sense of their threat to her freedom. Isabel speaks for a society in which a woman might claim full equality; she speaks also for a kind of Emersonian ignorance of evil. She had looked upon one aspect of herself in Osmond and had fallen in love with it. He had done the same in looking at her. The other image, that of Osmond's selfishness, and his "demonic imagination," belong in all probability to James's "buried life," some part of which he concealed even from himself, but which emerged in the writing of this character.

In the end one feels that Isabel's disillusionment, the damage to her self-esteem and the crushing effect of her experience reside in the shock she receives that she should have been capable of so great a mistake; and in her realization that instead of being able to maneuver her environment, as her freedom allowed, she had been maneuvered by it. Moreover Serena Merle and Gilbert Osmond are Americans; long divorced from their native soil, they have been corrupted by Europe. They conceal a world of evil unknown to Isabel. America had ill-prepared her for this. Thus are woven into the novel certain fundamental elements of America's myth: an ideal of freedom and equality hedged with historical blindness and pride; a self-interest which often takes a generous form; a sense of hurt when this generosity is discerned by others as a wielding of power.

When he had sent off his early installments, James received worried letters from Howells. The editor suggested that Isabel was being over-analyzed; and that the figure of the American newspaperwoman, Henrietta Stackpole, was overdrawn. "In defence of the former fault," James replied, "I will say that I intended to make a young woman about whom there should be a great deal to tell and as to whom such telling should be interesting." Indeed, he was to consider the book's finest passage to be Isabel's self-analysis after she perceives the relationship between Madame Merle and Gilbert Osmond.

As for Miss Stackpole, Henry told Howells that she was not "I think really exaggerated—but 99 readers out of a 100 will think her so: which amounts to the same thing. She is the result of an impression made upon me by a variety of encounters and acquaintances made during the last few years." One such encounter was with a young woman from Cambridge, a Miss Hillard, whom William sent to him shortly after Henry had moved to London. Writing to William on 28 June 1877, Henry says:

> I have got to go and see your—excuse me I must say—accursed friend Miss Hillard, who has turned up here and writes me a note every three days, appointing an interview. I do what I can; but she will certainly tell you that I neglect her horribly. Do you admire her, particularly? She is, I suppose, a very honourable specimen of her type; but the type—the literary spinster, sailing-into-your-intimacy-American-hotel-piazza type —doesn't bear somehow the mellow light of the old world.

On the back of this letter, William wrote: "Do you notice the demoniac way in which he speaks of the sweet Miss Hillard?" In a letter a few days later James added, "She is a good girl: her faults are that she is herself too adhesive, too interrogative and too epistolary." Henrietta Stackpole, with all her forthrightness, good humor, meddlesomeness, and 100-per-cent Americanism, is completely characterized in *The Por-*

trait in an interchange between Isabel and Ralph Touchett. "She's a kind of emanation of the great democracy—of the continent, the country, the nation," Isabel says. And her cousin replies: "She does smell of the Future —it almost knocks one down."

The Portrait of a Lady established itself as a work of high literary art, one of the best-written novels in English in its evocation of American and European backgrounds, its rhythmic narrative pace, the easy flow of its episodes and its psychological insight into its characters. It introduced into a Europe that was reading Flaubert, Turgenev, Tolstoy and Zola a distinctly American heroine—a modern woman whose fate did not necessarily depend on marriage and sex, but on her freedom of choice. The great European heroines were victims of their condition in society. James showed a new and liberated "Americana," without minimizing the kinds of problems she had to face.

Isabel's portrait hangs in the gallery of the world's classical fiction. She holds her head high; she possesses a great pride, and there is a fierce shyness in her steady gaze. The gallery in which James placed her had on its walls paintings of other women who, like Isabel, had never literally "lived"; they were creatures of the printed word. And yet all had taken on a life of their own—Becky Sharp, Dorothea Brooke, the Lady of the Camellias, Jane Eyre, Anna Karenina, Emma Bovary. And Isabel Archer, who seems actually to have resided in Albany, and ultimately in a palace in Rome, retains her uniqueness among her European sisters.

The painting is exquisite. Every touch of the artist's brush has been lovingly applied to his subject who, as a grand-daughter of the Puritans, has something of their rigidity in her bearing, and not a little of their hardness of surface. She looks down at us out of American "transcendentalism," in the freshness of her youth—and the strength of her innocence and her egotism.

Venice

Early in 1881, with *The Portrait* scheduled to run through the magazines until autumn, Henry James found his novel so far advanced that he could seek once again the light and air of Italy. This time he chose Venice. He crossed on 10 February. As usual he gave up a few days to the Paris way-station, staying at the Hôtel Continental, and paying three longish calls, in particular, to Turgenev's gouty couch. "He seemed and looked a good deal older than when I saw him last; but he was as pleasant and *human* as ever." He saw Henrietta Reubell, now firmly fixed in the circle of Parisian friendship, the Laugels, the other Turgenevs. The Edward Lee Childes gave a dinner in his honor. Once again James was struck by the "lightness and brightness of the French conversational tone." Twelve days sufficed. "In Paris, I suspect, it is always the little Parisian horizon," he wrote home, and took his train southward.

He was in Marseilles on 24 February eating a big bowl of *bouillabaisse,* "a formidable dish, demanding a French digestion," in a restaurant opposite the Château d'If. At San Remo he spent three congenial weeks. "I worked there capitally," he was to remember, "and it made me very happy. I used in the morning to take a walk among the olives, over the hills behind the queer little black, steep town." Then he would return to his inn, eat his *déjeuner* and settle down to three or four hours of writing. In the fading light he would take another walk, dine, go to bed early and read until late.

On 16 March he was in Genoa for a day. In Milan, where he spent ten days, he worked industriously. The place was cold and he knew no one. Arriving in Venice he finds it cold and dreary and after a few days he leaves for Rome. On the way he stops in Florence for his customary visit to the Bootts. Lizzie was in Spain, traveling with a group of artists; she wrote urging him to join them. He was tempted. However he had no time for new adventures: *The Portrait* had to be finished.

In Rome he stops at the Hôtel de Russie. It is wet and cold, and he has a violent attack of lumbago and a bad headache. Fenimore has settled in the Holy City for the time being; she speaks, at a later date, of "a tea-table, with the same spluttering little kettle you saw in my sky-parlour at Rome." From his journal account Henry seems to have been interested in another lady:

> Toward the last part of April I went down to Rome and spent a fortnight—during part of which I was laid up with one of those terrible attacks in my head. But Rome was very lovely; I saw a great deal of Mrs. V. R.: had (with her) several beautiful drives. One in particular I remember; out beyond the Ponte Nomentana, a splendid Sunday.

"Mrs. V. R.," always alluded to by her initials, or as the "Rensallina" in his correspondence, was probably the widowed Mrs. Philip Livingstone Van Rensselaer, who lived for many years abroad. A short, dumpy woman, she seems first to have charmed Henry by her energy and liveliness; later, in London, she bored him. During her Italian years James believed her to be searching for a husband, and his Roman headache may have been a consequence of finding himself caught in a crossfire between two demanding women, Fenimore and Mrs. V. R.

James's stay on the Riviera and in Rome was the prelude to a memorable visit to Italy. As he had taken possession early of Rome, later of Paris and finally of London, so now—and for all his life—he took possession of the city of the Doges in its grandeur and decay. Venice was one of the greatest topographical love affairs of James's life. A dead city on the Adriatic teeming with modern life, it was "as changeable as a nervous woman and you know it only when you know all the aspects of its beauty." And again, "you desire to embrace it, to caress it, to possess it; and finally a soft sense of possession grows up and your visit becomes a perpetual love affair." Henry had never written of any woman in this erotic way.

He found rooms, "dirty apartments with a lovely view," on a fourth floor at 4161 Riva degli Schiavoni, near the passage leading off to San Zaccaria. Straight across the lagoon, before his windows, rose the great pink mass of San Giorgio Maggiore. "It stood suffused with its rosiness . . . the bright sea-light seems to flush with it, and the pale whiteish green of lagoon and canal to drink it in." From his windows, with an opera-glass, he studied the gondolas and ships. No ballet was more beautiful than the rhythmical movement of arm and oar on every side. There was always the same silhouette—the long black slender skiff, moving yet seeming not to move, with the grotesquely-graceful figure on the stern which had "the boldness of a plunging bird and the regularity of a pendulum." The view from his windows was *una bellezza:* "Here I wrote diligently every day and finished, or virtually finished, my novel."

He would rise in the morning and have an early breakfast at Florian's. Then he would go to the Stabilimento Chitarin for his bath. Refreshed, he would stroll in the coolness looking at pictures, watching the street-life, idling away the hours until it was time for his *déjeuner,* which he would take at the Caffè Quadri. After this he would return to his rooms and work till five or six o'clock. A quarter of a century later he was to remember how again and again in the "fruitless fidget of composition" he responded to the human chatter coming up to his windows from the Riva, and wandered over to see whether "out in the blue channel, the ship of some right suggestion, of some better phrase, of the next happy twist of my subject, the next true touch for my canvas, mightn't come into sight." Venice was an invitation, constant and repeated, to idleness—and yet he worked.

His writing done, he would go out on the water in a gondola for a couple of hours. In the evenings he would stroll about, stop at Florian's, listen to the music in the Piazza; and two or three nights a week he would visit Mrs. Bronson. His fellow-passenger during the memorable crossing of the Atlantic, when he had sailed to embrace the Old World, had fixed herself in an old Venetian house, Ca' Alvisi, where she had a waterside salon whose most distinguished members were Robert Browning and Henry James. Casa Alvisi was directly opposite the Baroque church of Santa Maria della Salute. In a city of palaces, it was a small house indeed: this is what Mrs. Bronson liked about it. Everything seemed in the right proportion.

The former Katherine De Kay of New York had a vivid and lively personality. Her affectionate portrait is sketched, one seems to see, as Mrs. Prest in "The Aspern Papers." The novelist complained during these early weeks that her *milieu* was too American for his taste. Nevertheless his testimony to its geniality is to be found in the closing sentences of the essay he wrote on Venice for the new *Century* magazine:

> If you are happy you will find yourself, after a June day in Venice (about ten o'clock), on a balcony that overhangs the Grand Canal, with your elbows on the broad ledge, a cigarette in your teeth and a little good company beside you. The gondolas pass beneath, the watery surface gleams here and there from their lamps, some of which are coloured lanterns that move mysteriously in the darkness.

And if the serenading is overdone, he adds, "you needn't suffer from it, for in the apartment behind you—an accessible refuge—there is more good company, there are more cigarettes."

Late in May, James came upon an unexpected companion. "Tell William," Henry wrote to his father, "his old friend Herbert Pratt has turned up here and I have seen a good deal of him. He is a queer, but almost delightful, creature and entertaining through all the strange eastern lands he has seen."

If James was cosmopolitan in the sense that he could alternately be a western European and an American, or both at the same time, Pratt was the embodiment of the graceful American wanderer, the perpetual poetic hobo. Apparently a man of some means, he was at ease in all lands and he seems to have carried his good nature and his guitar wherever he went. William had met him at medical school, where Pratt was completing his studies interrupted by service in the Civil War. He had done a little postgraduate study in Vienna and Berlin, and had set up in practice at Denver. From 1874, and for the next forty years, he was a wanderer upon the face of the earth. James would have liked to be as foot-loose, without responsibility, and taking life as it came. Herbert Pratt, he wrote in his journal, "used to talk to me about Spain, about the East, about Tripoli, Persia, Damascus; till it seemed to me that life would be *manquée* altogether if one shouldn't have some of that knowledge." And James added: "He was a most singular, most interesting type, and I shall certainly put him into a novel. I shall even make the portrait close and he won't mind." He did so, as Gabriel Nash in *The Tragic Muse,* eight years later.

One evening Pratt took Henry to a queer little wineshop, frequented largely by gondoliers and *facchini,* where they drank some excellent muscat wine. On another evening he took James to his rooms overlooking the Rialto. The night was hot. The cry of the gondoliers came up from the Grand Canal. Pratt took out some Persian books and read extracts from Firdusi and Saadi. "A good deal might be done with Herbert Pratt," the novelist said to himself in his journal.

There were other diversions. "Mrs. V. R." came out from Rome, and James went with her one day to Torcello, and to Burano, where the children assailed him for coppers and pursued the gondola into the sea. Henry took away an impression of bright-colored hovels, stagnant canals, young girls with splendid heads of hair, fishermen mending their nets. It was altogether a happy time and James recaptured his old faculty for experiencing and enjoying the picturesque which had faded during his long months in Bolton Street. In June he took a brief recess for five days and wandered in Vicenza, Bassano, Padua. Three of these days were spent at Vicenza, where a letter to Grace Norton records his impressions. James had sat the previous evening in the city's square. The place was flooded with moonlight. The Vicentini strolled on the big smooth slabs of the piazza, and the tall slim campanile seemed to lose itself in the brightness of the night. He had been recalling his 1869 visit and "was pleased to find that on the whole I have not quite lost my 'sensibility.'"

To Grace Norton James confessed that he had "fallen deeply and desperately" in love with Venice: "the rest, the leisure, the beauty, the sunsets, the pictures." Before he left the Adriatic city the heat had become intense. The days and the nights were now impossible. "I left it at last," Henry wrote in his journal, "and closed a singularly happy episode; but I took much away with me."

When he consulted his memories he had, as Proust was to have after him, colors before his eyes, iridescence, little corners rather than images of the great Square. "I simply see a narrow canal in the heart of the city —a patch of green water and a surface of pink wall. The gondola moves slowly; it gives a great smooth swerve, passes under a bridge, and the gondolier's cry, carried over the quiet water, makes a kind of splash in the stillness." The old pink wall seemed to sink into the opaque water. Behind the wall was a garden, out of which the long arm of a June rose flung itself as a spontaneous ornament. On the other side of the small waterway was a great shabby façade of Gothic windows and balconies— on which dirty clothes were hanging—and there was a cavernous door opening from a low flight of slimy steps. It was hot and still. That garden, the rose, the gondola, the general Venetian color and imagery melted together a decade later into "The Aspern Papers."

PART FOUR

The Middle Years

> . . . youth is an army, the whole
> battalion of our faculties and our
> freshnesses, our passions and our
> illusions, on a considerably
> reluctant march into the enemy's
> country, the country of the general
> lost freshness . . .
>
> HENRY JAMES

TERMINATIONS

Rediscoveries

In his room in the Brunswick Hotel in Boston, late in November of 1881, Henry James found himself seated one day in front of a marble-topped table, writing in a fat scribbler he had purchased some months before in London. The walls of his room were white and bare; they shone at night in the flaring gaslight from a chandelier of imitation bronze, which emitted a hissing brightness. There was too much glare, too much scorching air from the heating system. James had learned to accommodate himself to a fireplace and to candlelight; to adjust temperature and illumination to his needs. Nothing seemed adjustable in his hotel room. He was lonely and homesick. This act of writing in the fat scribbler was a way of transporting himself out of his immediate American environment back to London—or to Venice. For what James was setting down was a long retrospective summary of his six years abroad; a survey of his traveled cities and country visits, his new friendships and his Continental resources.

"Here I am back in America after six years of absence," he wrote, "and likely while here to see and learn a great deal that ought not to become mere waste material." He was glad that he had returned. He had needed to see his family, to revive the "sense of the consequences that these relations entail." "Apart from this," he added, "I hold it was not necessary I should come to this country."

"My choice," he wrote,

is the old world—my choice, my need, my life. There is no need for me today to argue about this; it is an inestimable blessing to me, and a rare good fortune, that the problem was settled long ago, and that I have now nothing to do but to act on the settlement. . . . My work lies there—and with this vast new world, *je n'ai que faire.* One can't do both—one must choose. No European writer is called upon to assume that terrible burden, and it seems hard that I should be. The burden is necessarily greater for an American—for he *must* deal, more or less, even if only by implication, with Europe; whereas no European is obliged to deal in the least with America.

The statement was prophetic. And it was, as James himself saw, the statement of a novelist in search of subjects larger than those offered him by the sparse American scene. "My impressions of America I shall, after all, not write here." And he added, "Heaven forgive me! I feel as if my time were terribly wasted here!"

When James left Venice five months earlier, he had gone to Lake Como and then to Switzerland. He went to Lucerne to visit Mrs. Kemble, but she had gone to Engelberg; he followed her to that "grim, ragged, rather vacuous, but by no means absolutely unbeautiful valley." One day he climbed the Trübsee toward the Joch Pass. "The whole place was a wilderness of the alpine rose—and the alpine stillness"; the beauty of the high cool valley revived for Henry memories of his old Swiss days.

After Switzerland he had returned to London to meet his sister, who had come abroad accompanied by a Boston friend, Katharine Loring, a hearty woman who seemed to derive a genuine satisfaction in using her own vitality and strength to make life easier for her sickly friend. James recognized that Alice had become deeply attached to Miss Loring and seemed happy in her company. The novelist spent a few days with his sister at Richmond, but she had her own itinerary and was scheduled to sail for Boston before Henry would be ready to leave. He accordingly departed to pay a series of visits while the final chapters of *The Portrait* were at the printer's. He visited the Anglicized American banker Russell Sturgis and his wife at their luxurious country house in Leatherhead; he twice visited the Roseberys at Mentmore and on one of these occasions had Gladstone as a fellow guest. He went to his publisher's, Frederick Macmillan, at Walton-on-Thames and spent a week in Somerset at Midelney Place, the Lady Trevilian's. Then, as his sailing date approached, he had gone to Scotland, to Tillypronie, Cortachy, Dalmeny, Laidlawstiel. He remembered the drive from Kirriemuir to Cortachy, and his arrival in the twilight before the great lighted pile of the castle, where Lady Airlie, hearing the wheels of the vehicle on the gravel, "put her handsome head from a window in the clock-tower," asked if this was indeed Henry James, and wished him a bonny good-evening.

Now, sitting in the uncomfortable hotel room, writing and remembering, James was confronted by things far removed from such pleasures. He had crossed the October Atlantic on the steamer *Paris* by the

St. Lawrence route, disembarked with the mails at Rimouski and then spent two days getting connections to Boston. In Quincy Street, his mother struck him as tired and shrunken; his father was infirm and more lost than ever in his self-composed world. James made friends at once with William's wife—the second Alice in Quincy Street—and with William's little boy: "the little Henri-trois," his uncle dubbed him. He saw Howells immediately; his friend had just resigned the *Atlantic* editorship, succeeded by the bland, sociable Thomas Bailey Aldrich. He saw his old friend T. S. Perry. He began to pay calls on Mrs. Gardner. He spent evenings with Grace Norton. He journeyed to Newport to see the Tweedys.

But he was restless. His removal from Quincy Street to a Boston hotel had been designed to give him a feeling of his Bolton Street privacy. He wanted to resume his work, but he found the hotel hostile to literature. Early in December he went to New York, where he stayed with Edwin Godkin at 115 East 25th Street, in the same neighborhood in which he had passed his book-reviewing months of 1875. Manhattan was hospitable to its literary son—*The Portrait of a Lady* had just come out and had proved immediately popular. "I have been three weeks in New York," James recorded in his journal, "and all my time has slipped away in mere movement." To Grace Norton in Cambridge he wrote: "I have seen many persons—but no personages; have heard much talk—but no conversation."

James went back to Quincy Street for Christmas. His younger brother Wilky, increasingly an invalid, came from Wisconsin to be with the family, and with the exception of Robertson, the youngest son, the James family was briefly reunited. But when Christmas was over James did not linger in Cambridge. He returned to New York to attend "a gorgeous flowery banquet" given by Whitelaw Reid, whose Paris correspondent he had been. Here he met the just-retired Secretary of State, James G. Blaine. From New York he went to Philadelphia to pay a visit to Mrs. Wister and her husband. And from Germantown he went on to Washington. This was his first visit to the capital.

The Dome and the Shaft

In *The Bostonians* James was to make one of his ladies ask whether anyone had heard of "that little place," Washington, and to add that "they invented it" while she had been abroad. James seems to have had this feeling as he stepped from the train one morning early in January, and looked at the single dome of the Capitol and the single shaft which then dominated the scene. The first thing the novelist did, after settling in the two sun-filled rooms Henry Adams had reserved for him at 720 15th

Street, was to take a solitary walk to the Capitol. With a critical eye he appraised this great American dome. False classic, white marble, iron, stucco. And yet it had a grand air. He went into the rotunda. It was a little like entering a railway station. There were no functionaries, no officers, no uniforms, no doorkeepers—not the least spot of color such as one found in the European seats of government. He was to make a character remark that "this isn't government by livery"; however it is clear that James would have liked some livery in the vast expanse of marble, some relief from the ubiquity of spittoons.

The spittoons would recede, works of art would take over; but this was not, in effect, to change the artistic complexion of the place. James's first feeling, which he concealed, was that the Capitol was "repulsive." Later he was willing to concede that it embodied a kind of New World concept of space and air, of dominion and of power created *de chic.* What he felt in 1882 was that there wasn't in Washington "enough native history, recorded or current, to go round."

The city had two faces for James. There was official Washington, "the democratic substitute for a court city," and there was social Washington, harboring a society well organized, with its own codes and standards, that seemed bent on excluding Senators and Congressmen from its houses rather than admitting them. There seemed to be passages of national life in which "the President himself was scarce thought to be in society."

Society seemed to operate in the foreground, and it used official Washington as a backdrop. James wondered how the foreign diplomats, facing the phenomenon of a capital that differed from, rather than resembled, other capitals and other societies, could cope with their task of "penetration and discretion." The story which he began at this time, "The Point of View," is the most sharply critical of any he ever wrote about his homeland. His vision of Washington was much influenced, however, by the spacious drawing-room at 1607 H Street, and the tart reflections of his friend, the "Voltaire in petticoats."

"Thursday, Henry James put in an appearance; that young emigrant has much to learn here," wrote Clover Adams to her father on 8 January 1882.

> He may in time get into the "swim" here, but I doubt it. I think the real, live, vulgar, quick-paced world in America will fret him and that he prefers a quiet corner with a pen where he can create men and women who say neat things and have refined tastes and are not nasal or eccentric.

"I shouldn't wonder if the place were the most agreeable of our cities," James wrote to Grace Norton.

The pleasant thing here is the absence of business—the economy-empty streets, most of them rather pretty, with nothing going on in them. I am making the best of everything—so much so that I feel at moments as if I were rather holding my nose to the grindstone.

To Henrietta Reubell he wrote: "Enormous spaces, hundreds of miles of asphalt, a charming climate and the most entertaining society in America." And to Godkin: "I have seen a good many people, chiefly under the influence of the Adamses, and find the social arrangements, and the tone of conversation, very easy and genial."

The Adamses constituted themselves James's guides and evaluators of all he reported from his social rounds. Mrs. Adams paraphrased scripture to her father to describe the novelist's predicament—"And a certain man came down to Jerusalem and fell among thieves . . . and they sprang up and choked him." To which she added: "Henry James passed Sunday evening at Robeson's and dines tomorrow with Blaine." On his side James wrote to Godkin that the Adamses disapproved of the company he was keeping, "though I notice that they are eagerly anxious to hear what I have seen and heard at places which they decline to frequent. After I had been to Mrs. Robeson's they mobbed me for revelations; and after I had dined with Blaine, to meet the President, they fairly hung upon my lips."

The Robeson of whom the Adamses disapproved was Congressman George Maxwell Robeson of New Jersey. He and his wife were about to attain much notoriety, sponsoring Oscar Wilde during his visit to the capital. The press talked largely of Bunthorne-Wilde. "The newspapers haven't got scent of Henry James yet," Mrs. Adams observed, and he managed to keep out of their way. However he called on Wilde as a matter of courtesy. "Oscar Wilde is here—an unclean beast," he wrote to Godkin. He told Mrs. Adams he found him "a fatuous cad." But then James had admitted to Oscar he was homesick for London, and Oscar adroitly implied that this was rather provincial of him. "Really! You care for *places?* The world is my home."

The dinner to which James G. Blaine invited James, to meet the twenty-first President of the United States, Chester A. Arthur, was an elaborate occasion, attended also by the British Minister, the Governor of California, Generals Sherman and Hancock, and others of what the press called "a small and noted company." Henry James Jr. was described as "that eminent novelist and anglicized American." Henry observed the President's "well-made coat and well-cut whiskers," and after dinner enjoyed an intimate chat with him about various members of the James family whom President Arthur had known in Albany. Arthur "evidently believed me to be the son of Uncle William [the Rev. William James, elder brother of Henry's father]," Henry wrote to his mother, "and wouldn't be disillusioned." To Mrs. Gardner James wrote that he thought the President "a good fellow—even attractive. He is a gentleman and evidently has that amiable quality, a desire to please."

At the end of January the novelist was enjoying himself sufficiently to plan to remain another month. He was finding the capital "genial and amusing." On 27 January, however, his brother Robertson wrote from Cambridge that their mother had suffered an attack of bronchial asthma. On Sunday morning the 29th James wrote to her saying that it was "impossible almost for me to think of you in this condition, as I have only seen you hovering about the bed of pain, on which others were stretched." Late that evening, while he was dressing to go to a party, he received a telegram from William's Alice: "Your mother exceedingly ill. Come at once." There was no train until the next morning. Distraught and anxious, James rang the bell of the Adamses at 11 P.M. to inform them of his impending departure. He took the morning train to New York, and by that time Clover Adams had received an answer to a telegram she had sent to Boston. She knew—what he did not—that his mother was no longer alive.

An Exquisite Stillness

Thirty-six hours later, in the early snow-reflected light, James entered the north room of the house in Quincy Street where his mother lay in her shroud. Mary James had died quite suddenly the evening of the 29th, as she sat in the closing dusk with her husband and her sister. She had been recovering from the asthma. Her heart had simply stopped, in her seventy-first year.

Henry found her now "as sweet and tranquil and noble as in life." He later said he had never known how tenderly he loved her till he saw her lying there that morning. His death-vigil was lonely—and triumphant: lonely, in that he had always felt a special tie between himself and his mother, as her favorite son; triumphant, in that he seemed to feel that with her death he came into full possession of her. In life he had had to share her with his father, with William, with his younger brothers and sister. Now, in the depths of his memory and imagination, she belonged to him. This was why, when he wrote the long elegiac passage in his journal, commemorating all that his mother meant to him, he spoke of these "hours of exquisite pain."

His father and sister Alice, by the time he talked with them, had begun to reconcile themselves to this break in their lives. Both were "almost happy." Wilky arrived the next morning a matter of hours before the funeral, from Wisconsin; Robertson had been in Quincy Street while

Henry was in Washington. For the first time in fifteen years—and for the last—the four sons and the daughter of Mary James were together under the family roof.

That Wednesday dawned clear and cold. The snow-shroud was deep, the air brilliant and still. In the bright frosty sunshine the sons of Mary James carried their mother to her temporary resting-place in a vault in the Cambridge cemetery. In the spring a site would be chosen for the grave.

A few days after the funeral Henry moved from Quincy Street into Boston. "I wish to remain near my father," he wrote to a friend. "I do not wish however to be in Cambridge." He found "bare and ugly" rooms at 102 Mount Vernon Street on Beacon Hill, where he reconstructed, as best he could, the conditions of Bolton Street. On the day after he moved into these rooms—9 February 1882—he wrote a long passage in his journal on his mother's death, describing her as the "keystone" of the James family arch. The passage is eloquent in its self-conscious grief, and it reflects Henry's complete idealization of his mother:

> She held us all together, and without her we are scattered reeds. She was patience, she was wisdom, she was exquisite maternity. Her sweetness, her mildness, her great natural beneficence were unspeakable, and it is infinitely touching to me to write about her here as one that *was*.

He felt as if an "eternal stillness" had settled around him. It was "but a form of her love. One can hear her voice in it—one can feel, forever, the inextinguishable vibration of her devotion."

He went on to speak of her continued restlessness, her preoccupation with her children, her loyalty to her husband. "Summer after summer she never left Cambridge," he noted.

> The country, the sea, the change of air and scene, were an exquisite enjoyment to her; but she bore with the deepest gentleness and patience the constant loss of such opportunities. She passed her nights and her days in that dry, flat, hot, stale and odious Cambridge, and had never a thought while she did so but for father and Alice.

But there had been many summers spent away from Cambridge—in New England coastal resorts and Canada. Moreover Alice had been seriously ill in recent years, and this, as much as the father's increasing infirmities, had kept his parents in Cambridge. In her death as in her life Henry made himself his mother's champion against a kind of family oppression.

Mary James had been the central figure of all his years, and so she would remain. The strange thing was that on a deeper level of feeling, which he inevitably concealed from himself, he must have seen his

mother as she was, not as he imagined and wanted her to be. She is
incarnated in his fiction not as the fragile self-effacing and self-denying
woman he pictured in his filial piety, spending her last strength for her
children. The mothers of Henry James, for all their maternal sweetness,
are strong, determined, demanding, grasping women—Mrs. Touchett or
Mrs. Gereth, Mrs. Hudson or Mrs. Newsome. They are neither ideal nor
ethereal.

"All those weeks after Mother's death," wrote James, "had an exquisite
stillness and solemnity." He kept his London hours. In the mid-morning
he would walk across the Common and have his breakfast at Parker's.
Then he would return to his rooms and write until four or five o'clock.
In the gathering winter twilight he would walk to Cambridge, "over that
dreary bridge whose length I had measured so often in the past," a mile
of wooden piles. He had the horse-cars for company. Four or five times
a week he would dine in Quincy Street with his father and sister. Then
he would return to Boston in the clear American starlight. "It was a
simple, serious, wholesome time. Mother's death appeared to have left
behind it a soft beneficent hush in which we lived for weeks, for months,
and which was full of rest and sweetness."

His work interested him. He chose, during this period, to write not
the fiction to which he was addicted, but a play, the harbinger of his later
siege of the theater. It seemed to him that the success of "Daisy Miller"
in the magazines and as a book could be duplicated on the stage. In New
York he had had some preliminary negotiations with the Mallory brothers, who owned the new Madison Square Theatre, and it was for them
that he converted his celebrated tale into the concreteness of a dramatic
action. To do this he had to invent new "business": Daisy had to survive;
and she would marry Winterbourne. Eugenio, the courier, became the
villain, and the foreign lady in Geneva an *intriguante* such as James had
often seen at the Théâtre Français.

The Mallorys' manager found the play "beautifully written" but distinctly too literary. "It had too much talk and not enough action," he said.
Thus ended James's first struggle—the first of a series—with theater
managers. He had his play privately printed; then he made an effort to
get it accepted by the Boston Museum Theatre, and offered it to London
managers. The verdict was always the same, and James finally sold it to
the *Atlantic,* for $1,000. During this period he also roughed out a first act
for a drama founded on *The American,* planning there also to substitute
a happy ending for Newman and Claire. The collapse of the "Daisy"
negotiations led him to put it aside.

The story he had begun in Washington lay unfinished in his portfolio, and play-writing filled in the time very well. It was like working out an elaborate puzzle. The dramatic form seemed to him "the most beautiful thing possible," but "the misery of the thing is that the baseness of the English-speaking stage affords no setting for it." When his play was written he carried his script to Mrs. Gardner and read it to her, during two long evenings. He had, so to speak, his private performance at the Court of Isabella.

Between bouts of homesickness for London and small Boston sociabilities James managed to decrease the distance to his May sailing date. A letter to William J. Hoppin asks for "a little parcel of London items." How was Mrs. Duncan Stewart? What was the latest news of her daughter, Mrs. Rogerson? He missed London, "the full extent of my devotion to which I didn't know until I had put the ocean between us." He told the First Secretary of Legation that when he next arrived at Euston Station, "I shall fall down and kiss the platform." To Mrs. Kemble he wrote that he smiled with derision at her suggestion that he might be "weaned" from "my London loves and longings by remaining over here." He was within a month of sailing. "My father is much better than he was a month ago, and will not listen to my making any 'sacrifices' for his sake."

Some time before he sailed his father and Alice took a small house in Boston, in Mount Vernon Street. The big house in Quincy Street was too large for them. William had established his own home and the elder Henry and Alice wanted something smaller and more intimate. James saw them comfortably installed and was ready to sail with an easy conscience. Almost the last thing he did before his departure was to attend another funeral. On 27 April the bells of Concord tolled the death of Ralph Waldo Emerson, and James made the familiar journey three days later to pay his respects to the benign figure of his childhood. Regular and special trains brought a large congregation; others came in wagons and on foot to pay tribute to "the principal gentleman in the place." As a public funeral James found it "curious, sociable, cheerful," a popular manifestation, the most striking he had ever seen provoked by the death of a man of letters.

On the day before he sailed, his father wrote a long letter to him:

> My darling boy, I must bid you farewell. How loving a farewell it is, I can't say, but only that it is most loving. I can't help feeling that you are the one that has cost us the least trouble, and given us always the most delight. Especially do I mind Mother's perfect joy in you the last few months of her life, and your perfect sweetness to her. I think in fact it is

this which endears you so much to me now. I feel that I have fallen heir to all dear Mother's fondness for you, as well as my proper own, and bid you accordingly a distinctly widowed farewell.

Henry was now his father's "angel" as he had been his mother's. And the old man repeated: "A lingering goodbye, then, dearest Harry, from all of us! and above all from your loving Father."

Season of Malaise

Henry James crossed the Atlantic on the *Gallia* in eight days. He left the ship at Cork, to get a glimpse of the land of his father's father. He spent a week in Ireland and found the cities filled with constables and soldiers; otherwise he saw little but green fields and dirty cabins. If he had had any idea of turning his Irish visit into copy he abandoned it. On 22 May he was back in Bolton Street. Reclining on the sofa and awaiting him was an unexpected guest, his youngest brother Robertson. On his desk was a pile of invitations. The city seemed oppressive, big, black and "actual," and while he reverted to it with "a kind of filial fondness" everything somehow seemed changed. He was restless, he was bored. The death of his mother had, for the moment, drained life of all interest. Much of his visit to his homeland had been like a dream—"a very painful dream."

His nostalgia for London seemed to have evaporated as well. He went through the motions of participating in the Season, yet the London social world, into which he had plunged with such eagerness three years before, seemed to him "a poor world, this time." At the end of a brief journal note, he remarked: "I have gone in too much for society." To make matters worse he found himself invaded by editors and friends. At various times that summer Howells and his family, Osgood, Aldrich, Charles Dudley Warner, John Hay, Clarence King, whom he met at this time, were all in London, not to speak of certain ladies to whom James was indebted for hospitality: Henrietta Reubell; Mrs. Boit with her "merry laugh"; Mrs. V.R.; Mrs. Wister. In this "bewilderment of conflicting duties and pleasures" James was fretful. "All summer I had been trying to work," he wrote in his journal; and he also notes that "the evenings had become dull." Even his election to a second Pall Mall club, the Athenaeum, where he had been proposed by Leslie Stephen, seemed now routine; a process of disenchantment had begun.

To make Henry's restless summer complete, William had suddenly decided to apply for a year's leave from Harvard and was coming over to meet some of his fellow psychologists in Europe. Early in September the novelist found himself on his way to Euston Station to meet his brother's boat-train. Strangely, William had chosen to take this leave a few months after the birth of his second son (who had been named William after his father and great-grandfather). He had done the same thing two years before, after his firstborn had arrived—it was as if the presence of infancy in his house was more than he could bear. Perhaps the new child, like the firstborn, may have touched some chord of early memory in William and awakened an old anguish, that of little rivals invading *his* nursery—as Henry had done long ago. To his brother it seemed that William's timing was unfortunate. He wrote openly to his sister-in-law: "Abandoned by your husband, you seem to me, dear Alice, very greatly to be pitied, and I assure you that I think of you with tender sympathy."

As William descended from the train at Euston Station he gave high proof of his temper to his brother:

> My!—how cramped and inferior England seems! After all, it's poor old Europe, just as it used to be in our dreary boyhood! America may be raw and shrill, but I could never live with this as you do!

William's eldest son, reconstructing this vigorous monologue many years later, remarked that his father was always under the spell of Europe when he was in America—and was "most ardently American when on European soil." The account continues: "The effect on Henry can better be imagined than described. Time never accustomed him to these collisions, even though he learned to expect them." Henry usually ended by rushing William off to his Continental destination—which was what he did this time, two days later.

James's season of malaise was reflected in his fiction. In Bolton Street he completed the tale he had begun in Washington—"The Point of View"— and its picture of American life captures in a critical light the glittering weaknesses of the American democracy. Although set forth in the opinions of foreign visitors to New York and Washington, whose letters he created with craft and cunning, the "point of view" is unmistakably James's own. What he found was a country in which egalitarianism was diluting individuality; in which a thinness of history and a smallness of national experience had to be reconciled with a continental grandeur and a national sense of space and freedom. The repatriated American gentlewoman complains that "there is no respect for one's privacy, for one's preferences, for one's reserves." The lady at Newport remarks on the liberties given—and taken—by American youth.

> The girls are not shy, but I don't know why they should be, for there is really nothing here to be afraid of. Manners are very gentle, very

humane; the democratic system deprives people of weapons that everyone doesn't equally possess. No one is formidable . . . There are no brilliant types; the most important people seem to lack dignity.

The emerging picture is of an easy democracy that breeds an easy mediocrity, in an atmosphere of advancing material civilization and chattering women.

A British M.P. surveys that civilization good-naturedly, comments on
the luxurious trains, and on the people, visits the schools and finds it
extraordinary how many persons "are being educated in this country;
and yet, at the same time, the tone of the people is less scholarly than one
might expect." The expatriated American aesthete complains at the absence of variety—"Everyone is Mr. Jones, Mr. Brown; and everyone looks
like Mr. Jones and Mr. Brown. They lack completeness of identity; they
are quite without modelling." The French Academician sees the women
as engaged in a chase for a husband, and American literature contains
"no form, no matter, no style, no general ideas." The books seem written
for children and young ladies. His conclusion is that America is "the last
word of democracy, and that word is—*flatness.*" But James gives the final
word to the Americans and largely to Marcellus Cockerell, who has had
his fill of Europe. It is from his letter that Clover Adams culled the
epigram most pleasing to herself, as it was to most Americans. "We are
more analytic, more discriminating, more familiar with realities. As for
manners, there are bad manners everywhere, but an aristocracy is bad
manners organized."

The tale was published late in the year in the *Century Magazine.*
Henry had predicted to his father that it would "probably call down
execration on my head," and it did. James was accused of being too
severe in his treatment of the American national character. The tale
tended to confirm the public image of the novelist: he was a chronic critic
of the land of the brave and the free. James knew how "to play the harp
of fiction," said one reviewer, but, he added, his harp didn't have enough
strings. These remarks inevitably made Henry feel that Americans were
thin-skinned.

His disenchantment with English society emerged in a tale originally designed as a contrast between Anglo-American and French morality. In 1877 he had found it impossible to swallow, in Dumas's *Le Demi-
Monde,* the denunciation of the heroine "with a past" by a very moral
young man who had been her lover. In "The Siege of London," which he
gave to Leslie Stephen for the *Cornhill,* an American adventuress, Nancy
Headway, wants to elbow her way to respectability in spite of her multi-
ple divorces. She sets her cap for a stolid English baronet, Sir Arthur
Demesne, under the observing eyes of a sophisticated American, rather

like James himself. The lengths to which the mother of the baronet, Lady Demesne, goes to find out about Nancy's past embarrass and finally irritate the American. The tale is written in a vein of high comedy and its morality is the reverse of the French play. Nancy gets her nobleman; and the American "tells" only when he knows it is too late to change anything. In reality this tale is James's farewell to London society. He seemed to feel now that it was not much of an achievement to get into it—"poor world" that it was—indeed that anyone could do so with a little honest effort, as witness the case of Mrs. Headway, a roaring success on the strength of her quaint Americanisms and her bold manner.

Perhaps James also felt the English had taken him up not because he had good manners and was a gentleman, but simply because they found him "entertaining." In his essay on "Du Maurier and London Society," which he published a few months later in the *Century,* he praised Du Maurier, whose cartoons in *Punch* held up "a singularly polished and lucid mirror to the drama of English society." And he wondered whether the conquest of London had been really worth while after all. Philistines were philistines, on either side of the Atlantic; the artist was doomed always to be an outsider anywhere in the world. Pondering Du Maurier's satire of aesthetes, James concludes that the English were simply not an aesthetic people:

> They have not a spontaneous artistic life; their taste is a matter of con-
> science, reflection, duty, and the writer who in our time has appealed to
> them most eloquently on behalf of art has rested his plea on moral stan-
> dards—has talked exclusively of right and wrong. . . . there is always a
> strange element either of undue apology or of exaggerated defiance in
> their attempts at the cultivation of beauty. They carry on their huge
> broad back a nameless mountain of conventions and prejudices, a dusky
> cloud of inaptitudes and fears, which casts a shadow upon the frank and
> confident practice of art.

Art seemed to have no place, either in an industrially expanding America bent on equalizing everything, or in an England where the "conventions and prejudices," not to speak of "inaptitudes and fears," made James feel as if he were a freak of nature, or some curiosity, to be wined and dined and patted on the back without ever being truly appreciated or understood.

After he got William off to the Continent Henry paid a few country visits, and then crossed the Channel in mid-September to do a specific chore. A Harper editor had suggested that he write a travel book about France, and though Harper later backed out, James sold the book to Osgood. As *A Little Tour in France,* it was to serve successive generations in the

château country and the Midi. Before starting his tour he paid his customary visit to Turgenev at Bougival, this time finding him seriously ill.
They had some good talk nevertheless.

James devoted all October 1882 to his "little tour." He began at Tours,
the birthplace of Balzac. Here he spent a week, joining Mrs. Kemble and
Mrs. Wister who were holidaying there. Mrs. Wister had her young son
Owen with her. James admired the châteaux, and the country around
Tours was "as charming as the essential meagreness of the French landscape will allow it to be." Leaving Tours and the Kemble-Wisters on 8
October, he first traveled a small circle—Angers, Nantes, La Rochelle
and Poitiers; then he went to Bordeaux, Toulouse, Carcassonne, Narbonne, and Montpellier, and finally into the heart of Daudet's Midi—
Nîmes, Tarascon, Arles, Avignon; after which he curved northward to
Orange, Mâcon, Beaune and Dijon.

By mid-October, when he was in the Midi, he wrote to William, who
was in Venice: "I pursued my pilgrimage through these rather dull
French towns and through a good deal of bad weather, and all my desire
now is to bring it to a prompt conclusion. It is rather dreary work."
Decidedly the French provinces were not Italy. He experienced a revival
of interest, however, when he came to the Roman towns; and certain of
the cathedrals, as always, deeply absorbed him. In Avignon the Rhône
was in flood, and he was pleased to get out of its watery streets and make
a straight line for Paris. The account he wrote of his little tour is much
less personal than his other travel writings, much more strictly a guidebook. The material did not possess the "human picturesque," but the
book still has great charm. It suffered perhaps from the lack of his former
freshness and from an underlying mood of fatigue and depression, over
which, however, his characteristic good nature still prevailed.

November had come when James traveled back to Paris. He put up
at the Grand Hotel and recognized once again that the city had "a little
corner of my complicated organism." The pleasantest coincidence was to
find John Hay at the same hotel. James had never known him well, but
he respected him highly. With Hay was his friend Clarence King, author
of the major governmental survey of American mineral resources, and
friend of Henry Adams. Like Adams, James admired King's wit, his energy, his ceaseless interest in the world around him. The three breakfasted together, roamed the boulevards, prowled in shops. "King is a
charmer," James wrote to Howells. "He charmed all the bric-à-brac out
of the shops." After his solitary journey in the Midi it was a delight to
come upon such congenial fellow Americans.

He had exchanged notes with Ivan Sergeyevich, who continued to be
ill, and on 17 November went again to see him at Bougival, where the
Russian had remained much later than usual, attended by doctors,

among them the eminent J. M. Charcot. James was astonished at the change in his friend. His towering figure was stooped, his great frame shrunken. But he was as *accueillant* as ever. "He had been ill, with strange, intolerable symptoms, but he was better," James later wrote, "and he had good hopes." Neither knew, that day in November, what cruel months lay ahead. Ivan Sergeyevich had cancer of the spine.

After a period of complete immobility the Russian had begun to go out again, and on that afternoon he had to go into Paris. Ordering a carriage, he asked James to ride with him into the city. For an hour and a half, as they drove through the thickening dusk, James had his beloved friend to himself. Turgenev talked constantly, in English, and never better. When they reached the city James left the carriage at an exterior boulevard. There was a little fair going on in the chill November air, under the denuded trees. The nasal sound of a Punch and Judy show somehow became mixed with his farewell at the window of the carriage. Then the vehicle rolled away. He would not see his friend again.

A Blessed Farewell

James had hardly returned to London when word came from his sister and aunt that his father was rapidly declining and had not long to live. William was in Paris attending Charcot's celebrated clinics at the Salpêtrière. The brothers agreed that Henry should sail for home, and William would come to London and stay in Bolton Street while awaiting further news. Henry obtained passage on the *Werra,* from Liverpool, leaving on 12 December. The ship reached New York on Thursday, 21 December, and waiting for Henry at the dock was a letter from Alice written the day before. "Darling Father's weary longings were all happily ended on Monday at 3 P.M. The last words on his lips were 'There is my Mary!' " The funeral would be on Thursday morning. "There seemed no use in waiting for you, the uncertainty was so great."

His father, then, had been buried that very morning while his steamer was pulling into New York harbor. James reached Boston at eleven that night and was met at the station by his brother Robertson. In Mount Vernon Street Alice was resting. Aunt Kate, however, was up and they talked into the morning.

The elder Henry had died as he had lived, with an unflagging moral optimism; although his physical strength had failed him, he had turned his sickroom into a place of joy. He announced that he had entered upon the "spiritual life" and thereafter refused all food. The doctors spoke of "softening of the brain," but all the evidence indicates that until his last hours he was in possession of his faculties. He lay facing the windows and refused to have them darkened. He slept a great deal. He was told

that Henry was on his way. The news gave him pleasure, but he showed
no signs of impatience—save to die. Toward the end Aunt Kate heard him
say "Oh I have such good boys—*such* good boys!" Asked about funeral
arrangements he said (Aunt Kate wrote this down):

> That here is a man who has always believed in the only true spiritual life,
> a direct intercourse with God—and who leaves it as his dying wish that
> men should know and understand that all the ceremonies usually ob-
> served in births, marriages and funerals are nonsense and untrue.... [He
> further said] that he did not believe in individual salvation, but in the
> free personal intercourse of all men with God.

In long letters to William, conveying to him all the details as he
gathered them, Henry said the father's passing had been "most strange,
most characteristic above all, and as full of beauty as it was void of
suffering." In the house in Mount Vernon Street, there was the silence of
death. Alice, in a state of collapse, had been taken by Katharine Loring
to the Loring home at Beverly. Henry, deprived of his last glimpse of his
father, developed one of his debilitating migraines and was ill for four
days. Aunt Kate, sole survivor of the paternal group, sat in silent meditation in the parlor. She repeated again and again that the father had
"yearned unspeakably" to die. "I am too tired to write more," Henry told
William, "and my head is beginning to ache." He added: "All our wish
here is that you should remain abroad the next six months."

On the last day of the year 1882 Henry James walked through the deep
snow of the Cambridge cemetery to where the previous spring a family
plot had been selected on a small rise in the land. Here the mother had
been committed to the earth. Now, in the silence of the Sunday morning,
he looked at the new grave, cut in the cold ground ten days before. The
elder Henry lay very close to his wife. At some point during this visit the
son took a letter from his pocket and began to read it aloud into the wintry
air, addressing it to the graves.

What Henry read was a letter written by William to his father on 14
December, just after the elder son had arrived in Bolton Street. It had
reached Cambridge the day before, too late by a fortnight for the man for
whom it was destined. Substituting his own voice and presence for that
of his brother, Henry now communicated it to the dead.

" 'Darling old Father,' " Henry read,

> We have been so long accustomed to the hypothesis of your being taken
> away from us, that the thought that this may be your last illness conveys
> no very sudden shock. You are old enough, you've given your message to
> the world in many ways and will not be forgotten; you are here left alone,

and on the other side, let us hope and pray, dear, dear old Mother is waiting for you to join her. If you go, it will not be an inharmonious thing. Only, if you are still in possession of your normal consciousness, I should like to see you once again before we part.

And William continued:

In that mysterious gulf of the past into which the present soon will fall and go back and back, yours is still for me the central figure. All my intellectual life I derive from you; and though we have often seemed at odds in the expression thereof, I'm sure there's a harmony somewhere, and that our strivings will combine. What my debt to you is goes beyond all my power of estimating,—so early, so penetrating and so constant has been the influence.

Recognizing that he had at various times given his father trouble, and expressing the belief that in his own paternal role he would learn to understand his father's paternity, William ended:

. . . it comes strangely over me in bidding you good-bye how a life is but a day and expresses mainly but a single note. It is so much like the act of bidding an ordinary good-night. Good-night, my sacred old Father. If I don't see you again—Farewell! a blessed farewell!

Henry replaced the letter in his pocket. He was certain, he told his brother, that the elder Henry had heard him "somewhere out of the depths of the still, bright winter air." And he also said: "As I stood there and looked at this last expression of so many years of mortal union, it was difficult not to believe that they were not united again in some consciousness of my belief."

Now the son and brother could turn from the dead to the living. As he walked back, he stopped at William's house and sat with his brother's wife and her two children, admiring the new infant William, "a most loving little mortal." In writing to his brother, Henry again enjoined him not to come rushing home. Everything was being taken care of; moreover there was nothing William could do, since the elder Henry's last will and testament had named his second son executor. For the time at least, Henry, the quiet "angel," assumed legally the administration of the James family affairs. Jacob had indeed supplanted Esau—and Esau at this moment was in a far-away land.

Son and Brother

Henry James the elder left an estate valued at $95,000. It consisted of more than $80,000 worth of land, houses and stores, in Syracuse, New York, yielding seven per cent after taxes and maintenance, or about

$5,000 a year. The remainder, largely money derived from the sale of the Quincy Street house, had been invested in prosperous railway stocks and bonds, with a yield per annum of $3,500. These latter were willed to Alice and provided adequately for an invalid spinster of that time. The estate was to be divided among the three brothers William, Henry and Robertson. Garth Wilkinson James, the improvident and happy-go-lucky son, was omitted from the will because he had received his inheritance in advance. For some years he had been a constant drain on his father. Only a short time before, on declaring himself bankrupt, he had been given $5,000.

Wilky however was seriously ill; he had a rheumatic heart and other complications. He was crushed by his debts, and he had a wife and children in Milwaukee. Henry, from the outset, took the position that the will was "unfortunate," and proposed a re-division into four equal parts. Robertson and Alice voted with Henry, but William, thinking of his two sons, wrote from abroad that he was not at all certain such a re-division would be equitable. He proposed re-division into fifths. He also worked out an elaborate breakdown into sixteenths, according to the population of the James family groups. But Henry had already moved for equal division, assuming William would agree.

William's first impulse was to book passage for home early in February. A lively correspondence ensued in which Henry threw all his weight into convincing William he must stay abroad. He pointed out that William would have no place to stay in Cambridge, since part of his house had been sublet, and although he could be accommodated in Boston at the Mount Vernon Street house, in the small guest-room where Aunt Kate had stayed, "I won't offer to give up Father's room, because I lately made you a present of my rooms in London." And Henry argued there would be "a painful want of *form*" in William's returning to Cambridge "prematurely"—especially after having remained away during his father's illness and death.

William replied that Henry was meddling in his affairs; however he cancelled his passage, and after further negotiation a portion of the estate was set aside for Wilky's family, in a trust fund, with the net consequence that William and Henry would each receive about $1,300 a year.

Henry traveled to Milwaukee in a temperature of twenty below zero and a blinding blizzard for direct talks with the younger brothers, and later visited Syracuse to inspect the properties, located on James Street. William came home in March and Henry made over to him the general handling of the estate. His own income, he announced, was to go entirely to Alice—"She assures me that she will have no occasion to use it—will save it and invest it for my benefit etc. But I wish her to have it, to cover all the contingencies of her new existence." Henry James would continue to live by his pen.

He drove his pen on Beacon Hill during these months, and ventured forth for walks in the snowy streets. He was to evoke, in a charming tale, "A New England Winter," written some months later, the familiar aspect of the long straight avenue airing its newness in the frosty day, with its individual façades, the large clear windows of the curved fronts facing each other "like candid, inevitable eyes." James became thoroughly familiar with the Boston winter-scene—

> The denuded bushes, the solid pond, the plank-covered walks, the exaggerated bridge, the patriotic statues, the dry, hard texture of the Public Garden for its foreground, and for its middle distance the pale, frozen twigs, stiff in the windy sky that whistled over the Common, the domestic dome of the State House, familiar in the untinted air, and the competitive spires of a liberal faith.

In Washington Street, on a winter's afternoon, he trod the slushy thoroughfare, past the crawling horse-cars, the thronging pedestrians, the "sisterhood of shoppers" laden with satchels and parcels. Every fifty yards there was a candy-store. Behind the plate-glass, behind counters, were pale, delicate, tired faces of women, with polished hair and glazed complexions. He was struck by the "numerosity" of the women folk; there was a "deluge of petticoats." Henry felt he was in a city of women, a country of women, and it was this that determined him in the selection of the subject for his next novel.

"I feel strangely settled here for the present," he wrote to his publisher in London, "and shall probably remain for the summer." It was clear to him that he would not return again to America for a long time; there was no further reason for doing so. "My sister and I make an harmonious little ménage," he wrote, "and I feel a good deal as if I were married." It was the last holding-together of the family, and Henry, in his father's room, and Alice, presiding over the house, must have felt as if they were re-embodying their parents. But he nevertheless noted the extent to which Alice leaned upon her powerful friend, Katharine Loring. Miss Loring had quite taken over the foreground of Alice's life and entered into her daily well-being and her nervous prostrations. Alice had described her friend shortly after meeting her as having "all the mere brute superiority which distinguishes man from woman, combined with all the distinctively feminine virtues. There is nothing she cannot do from hewing wood and drawing water to driving runaway horses and educating all the women in North America." James was to observe this relationship closely. One might say that the figure of Olive Chancellor in

The Bostonians had appeared upon the novelist's very doorstep.

James's productivity during the months he spent in America—in spite of family preoccupations—was impressive. But, as after his mother's death, he did not do much new work. He saw through the press the dramatized *Daisy Miller* and he put together for J. R. Osgood a volume containing three tales, "The Siege of London," "The Pension Beaurepas" and "The Point of View." He assembled a volume of miscellaneous travel papers to which he gave the title *Portraits of Places,* including also his old papers on Saratoga, Newport and Quebec, which, he reminded both his American and English readers, had "only the value of history." Thirteen years had brought many changes.

James reviewed all his American publishing arrangements and pledged himself to produce a novel and a series of tales, giving Osgood not only the serial and American book-rights but the English rights as well, for which he would receive more money than he could realize by direct sale to Macmillan. The English publishing house, on its side, at this time proposed to Henry the issue of a small inexpensive pocket edition of his principal novels and tales. James welcomed the idea. Over and above the pleasure of having a collective edition on the British market, he felt that this would give him an opportunity to establish his new identity on the title-page, to get rid of the Henry James "Jun. or Jr."—the "mere junior"—now that his father was dead.

The Macmillan edition was published late that year, in a series of fourteen attractive blue-bound volumes which sold for one and six apiece, and the full set for a guinea. Four volumes were devoted to the miscellaneous tales, grouped as closely as possible according to theme; James could not altogether carry out his plan for these groupings because some stories were shifted in the interest of uniform volume-size.

In addition to seeing this edition through the press, James completed the greater part of his French travel sketches for Aldrich, and wrote the first of the series of tales he had promised Osgood. This was "The Impressions of a Cousin": the story, set in New York, in which an executor defrauds a young heiress, drew on his recent responsibilities in the family affairs.

He was much more in the public eye during this winter than the previous year. This was due, in some measure, to a laudatory article about him which Howells had published the previous autumn in the *Century Magazine,* asserting that it was James who was "shaping and directing American fiction." The article was part reminiscence and part criticism. Now that he was no longer James's editor Howells could allow himself the liberty of expressing in public all the praise he had been obliged hitherto to bestow in private. He discussed in some detail James's gift for creating character, and also said that a reader could find in Henry

James's writings "a perpetual delight" in his way of saying things. The effect of these observations was not altogether what Howells expected. To some critics it seemed as if he were "puffing" the work of his friend; and in England certain journalists accused Howells and James of constituting an "American Mutual Admiration Society"—this in spite of the fact that James had never written about Howells save an anonymous review of an early novel.

James had been approached three times to give a reading in public, and finally he yielded. This was before a Boston women's "Saturday Morning Club," where he read from a section of his little tour in France. The newspapers reported that the rooms were crowded "by people of taste and fashion." James, introduced as the "Thackeray of America," read in a monotonous manner, but the matter "more than made amends." At the conclusion of the reading he was given a bouquet of white daisies surrounded by leaves of the plant known as "dusty miller."

He made one other appearance: at a meeting of the American Copyright League in New York, James asked for the floor. "For ten or fifteen minutes," wrote Lawrence Hutton, he talked

> in a manner absolutely to the point and carrying much weight. He made as great an impression as a speaker as he had ever made as a writer; and for the first time, after a long residence abroad, he was brought into intimate contact with the men of his own guild in his own country.

He was in New York on 15 April 1883, in the city of his birth—and it was his fortieth birthday. Contemplating the advent of this year, he had written in his journal the previous autumn:

> I shall be forty years old in April next: it's a horrible fact.... I must make some great efforts during the next few years ... if I wish not to have been on the whole a failure. I shall have been a failure unless I do something *great!*

In the meantime there remained almost half a year before he could see his way to returning to England, since he wanted to stay for a while longer with Alice. The record of these months is filled with small detail. He visited Washington and was pleased by its aspect in the spring. He saw his friends the Adamses again. He was much preoccupied with Wilky, whose health had taken a turn for the worse; in Mount Vernon Street Henry sat up nights with him, giving him what aid he could during his heart attacks. He paid calls as usual on Mrs. Gardner, and he saw much of his old friend Grace Norton.

Miss Norton was going through a bad phase at this time, a certain strain with her brother, a sense of isolation, and James wrote to her always with great gentleness and good humor. Since he could no longer write the letters of a son to his mother, he had found in Cambridge someone to whom he could offer filial feeling—someone closer to him intellectually than his mother had been. To Grace Norton he wrote a letter which embodies the very heart of his philosophy and his attachment to reality—a kind of simple stoicism based on looking neither backward nor forward:

> I don't know *why* we live—the gift of life comes to us from I don't know what source or for what purpose; but I believe we can go on living for the reason that . . . life is the most valuable thing we know anything about and it is therefore presumptively a great mistake to surrender it while there is any yet left in the cup.

Repeating his frequent warning to his correspondent not to give herself too much to the world's woes and to the grief of others, he tells her: "Don't melt too much into the universe, but be as solid and dense and fixed as you can." And with this, his admonition was that Miss Norton adopt his own kind of doggedness: "Don't think, don't feel, any more than you can help, don't conclude or decide—don't do anything but *wait.*"

> Sorrow comes in great waves—no one can know that better than you— but it rolls over us, and though it may almost smother us it leaves us on the spot and we know that if it is strong we are stronger, inasmuch as it passes and we remain. It wears us, uses us, but we wear it and use it in return; and it is blind, whereas we after a manner see.

A darkness, such as she was passing through, he said, was *only* a darkness—not an end, not *the* end.

James wrote this letter to Miss Norton within a month of his return to England. He took passage on the *Servia,* leaving Boston on 22 August; he filled in the intervening hot days by padding about in a state of undress in the Mount Vernon Street house. Wilky had left for Milwaukee to rejoin his family. Henry must have known that this was their final parting. Alice spent the summer in a rest-home in Jamaica Plain, where her brother occasionally visited her. He saw little of William, who went off to the mountains with his family.

In a later story, "The Patagonia," James describes what must have been his general feelings on the empty summery Beacon Hill. The Boston houses on the eve of his sailing were dark in the August night; Beacon Street seemed a desert. The club on the hill alone emitted light from its cylindrical front, and the sound of billiard-balls clicking within suggested the servants were passing the time in the empty place. The heat was insufferable. He thought with joy of the freshening breeze he would have on board ship. The crossing was uneventful, and on 29 August he arrived in Liverpool, where he stayed until 1 September. He had been but

forty-eight hours in Bolton Street when word reached him that Ivan
Turgenev had come to the end of his sufferings at Bougival.

One by one the fixed landmarks of his life were vanishing. James followed with intense emotion the newspaper accounts of the final rites for
Turgenev: the ceremonial at the station in Paris when the Russia-bound
coffin was placed on the train, and the farewell orations of Ernest Renan
and Edmond About on behalf of the writers of France. It was with a
rendering of Renan's noble words that James began his own tribute in
the *Atlantic,* written little more than a month later:

> Turgenev received by the mysterious decree which marks out human
> vocations the gift which is noble beyond all others: he was born essen-
> tially impersonal. His conscience was not that of an individual to whom
> nature had been more or less generous; it was in some sort the conscience
> of a people.

But if Renan spoke of Turgenev as impersonal, and if now it seemed in
Russia the grief of the nation and the funeral pomp lifted Ivan Sergeyevich out of the range of familiar recollection, James set down, for the
Atlantic, the "personal" Turgenev: a simple record of his meetings with
the Russian writer, his many recollections of him, his whole-hearted
devotion to his work. "Intolerable pain had been his portion for many
months before he died," Henry wrote. "His end was not serene and propitious, but dark and almost violent. But of brightness, of the faculty of
enjoyment, he had also the large allowance usually made to first-rate
men, and he was a singularly complete human being."

At the request of the *Century* he translated for its November 1883
issue Daudet's reminiscences of Turgenev: this he did anonymously.
Thus in two leading monthlies of America the passing of the Russian
genius was eulogized through the agency of Henry James.

He had barely posted his tribute to the *Atlantic* when he found himself writing a private tribute of quite another sort. Wilky was now dead
in Milwaukee at thirty-eight, the third member of the James family to die
in two years, and the first of the children. He had never had good health
after his precocious service in the Civil War. When Henry got word that
his younger brother was on his deathbed, he drew from among his
possessions the little pencil drawing William had made many years before, after Wilky had been carried home wounded from the assault on
Fort Wagner. Sitting in Bolton Street Henry looked a long time at this
drawing of the stricken rough-bearded soldier. The time of the war came
back to him. "It was taken," he wrote to Lizzie Boott, "at a moment when
he looked as if everything was over. I say to myself as I look at it that it
probably represents the dear boy now." With the aid of the past Henry

sought to visualize the present. "Peace be to his spirit," he wrote to Lizzie, "one of the gentlest and kindest I have ever known."

And so Henry James buried his dead. Now he was once more in his lodgings in London at his large work-table by the Bolton Street window. He had said good-bye to his parents in their graves on the Cambridge hillock, to his younger brother, dead before his time, and to the great Turgenev. The house on Quincy Street was no longer fixed in the orbit of his days. His return to Europe was like a new beginning of the career he had begun nearly a decade before.

The Lost Freshness

Henry James's first impulse on his return to London from America was to search for a house. His old lodgings at No. 3 Bolton Street now seemed to him small, dingy, impermanent. His short stay at his sister's on Beacon Hill had given him a feeling of greater space and comfort. Now that the Quincy Street house had passed into memory, he needed such a mooring in England. He started his search in St. John's Wood, where the James family had lived in the 1850s. Presently he found a house in Elm Tree Road that seemed ideal; a painter had lived in it. The studio was now converted into a noble dining room; the place was commodious; the garden was charming.

The various ladies with whom he discussed his plans for domestication assumed at once that he was planning to marry. But he wrote to Grace Norton:

> I shall never marry; I regard that now as an established fact. . . . Singleness consorts much better with my whole view of existence (of my own and of that of the human race), my habits, my occupations, prospects, tastes, means, situation "in Europe," and absence of desire to have children—fond as I am of the infant race.

And reflecting on his bachelor state, and the blessings of living in a section of London within walking distance of his clubs and the theaters, James had a "sudden sense of being very well off where I am"—and broke off negotiations for the house. His Bolton Street rooms might be shabby but he had called them home for a long time.

This brief flurry of house-hunting, which occurred within a month after James's return, was symptomatic. At forty he had made a further march into the country of "the lost freshness." England was now his true home; he was no longer an "observant stranger." And though he often felt the oppressive largeness of the city, he believed London to be the right place for him to live. It was a matter of "learning to live there differently from what I have done hitherto."

One of the ways would be to restore the sense of "permanency" Quincy Street had given him, to find ultimately a more comfortable and spacious home. The other was to break away from London "society," and to go into it only at moments of his greatest ease. And so instead of superficial contacts with the British upper classes, Henry James began to form friendships of a more significant kind—with members of his own class, the writers and artists of London.

His friendship with George Du Maurier was a deeply attaching one. He found "something in him singularly intelligent and sympathetic and satisfactory." He liked walking to Hampstead from Piccadilly on a Sunday evening and sitting on a particular bench on the Heath with Du Maurier where their conversation could roam over Anglo-French subjects with an ease and affection that never diminished. The marriages of the Du Maurier sons and daughters and the career of Gerald Du Maurier on the stage commanded his interest and loyalty.

He liked the high-minded Mrs. Humphry Ward and her husband, who was an editor on *The Times.* Her novels had in them no sense of art, but James always wrote to her about them and lectured her on the craft of fiction. He was at home in the Ward house in Russell Square and on easy terms with the Ward children. It was the same at the George Lewises' in Portland Place—Lewis being one of the great Victorian solicitors whose home was open to the arts.

His friendship with Edmund Gosse, at first casual (Henry thought him amiable but second-rate), became one of the most literary-gossipy friendships in Victorian annals. Gosse was gifted: he had made his way by charm and ability from a lowly post in the British Museum to become translator to the Board of Trade. Later he would be Librarian of the House of Lords. An indefatigable bookworm, he wrote easy and pleasant literary essays, and critical and biographical studies of some importance. James found Gosse an endlessly amusing companion. He helped to break the solitude of some of his dinners at the Reform or the Athenaeum. Gosse had his finger in almost every literary pie in London. He knew the secrets of the literary generation; he was an artful exchanger of confidences. If James praised a certain book he quietly passed the praise along to the author; if an author praised James, Gosse discreetly communicated the praise. He made an art of flattery and a political craft of gossip. In the bourgeois sociabilities of his home in Delamere Terrace, as well as in the later confraternity of the Royal Society of Literature, he and James were faithful companions for the better part of four decades.

Thus by degrees James began to find substitutes for the lost anchorage of Cambridge. He might have more speedily achieved some form of contentment had not the life of the entire decade in England undergone a marked change. The Victorian calm was being shattered by Irish dynamiters, anarchist violence, and the deep unrest of England's workers, in their starving despair of the early 1880s. "Nothing *lives* in England today but politics," James wrote. "They are all-devouring, and their mental uproar crowds everything out." During the phase of his re-settlement in the British capital there were moments when he felt distinctly as if he were upon a heaving and boundless sea, without a rudder to steer him into a friendly port.

It was clear to James that the day of his little "international" tales was virtually at an end. He could still write them, but he believed he had worked that vein to exhaustion. He was moreover bored: and if "Pandora" and "Lady Barberina" of this time still have the old power, the undimmed perception of international manners, they represent a terminal point. "Lady Barberina" (with its built-in allusions to British equestrianism implicit in the title's reference to the Barbary horse, the name Canterville, the country house of Pasterns, Dr. Feeder, Lady Beauchemin and such phrases as *pied-à-étrier*) is also a study of Anglo-American marriages and a contrast of transatlantic manners and hierarchies. In effect James was saying that he would be bored if he had to live in New York; and that he, too, would flee to London, never to return.

James turned in this way to new subjects. His novel of Boston, promised to Osgood, delayed for more than a year, had to be written; and after that he harbored in his imagination a long novel on London—actual London—that would mark his total removal to the Old World.

Castle Nowhere

James had not seen Constance Fenimore Woolson since the spring of 1881, when he had visited her apartment in Rome; she had remained on the Continent during his absence in America and had written him long —very long—letters. Now, however, in the autumn of 1883, she arrived in the British capital, a bare month after James unpacked his bags in Bolton Street. In her letters she had spoken of spending the winter in Algiers. She always said that she needed warmth and sunlight. Nevertheless James reports to Lizzie Boott on 14 October 1883 that "Costanza has just arrived in South Kensington," and six months later that "the Costanza is handy, in Sloane Street, and is to remain, I believe, until August." Fenimore herself recorded in a letter of October 1884 that she had been in England for a full year.

In later years Miss Woolson and Henry James agreed to destroy each other's letters; however, four of her letters to the novelist, belonging to the period of his two trips to America, accidentally survived. Their inordinate length—the four total approximately fifteen thousand words—reveals Miss Woolson's propensity to pour herself out to James. Full of self-pity at her foot-loose state, she had titled an early volume of her tales *Castle Nowhere;* for this itinerant *littératrice,* wandering among the Continental cities to places far removed from the Western Reserve and the American South, felt herself alien and solitary. At the same time she reminds James of her own rooted Americanism. The tone of her letters, above all else, is one of depression and of a touching loneliness—a middle-aged woman reaching out to a man younger than herself for a friendliness which she had glimpsed during those long-ago weeks in Florence, and which absence threatened to efface. "You are never in Italy," she writes, "but always in America, just going; or there, or just returned. How many times have I seen you in the long months that make up three long years? I don't complain, for there is no reason in the world why I should expect to see you." Fenimore complained in the very act of not complaining.

Again and again in her letters, under the guise of discussing and criticizing James's writings, Miss Woolson seems to be saying to him that he is cold, disinterested, does not understand women—does not understand how a particular woman, say Miss Woolson, feels.

> I have been thinking about all this work you have undertaken [she is now writing from Venice in May 1883]; and I have wished that I could send you a message across the ocean—a spoken one. . . . In one of the three novels,—or if that is impossible, in one of the shorter stories—why not give us a woman for whom we can feel a real love? There are such surely in the world. I am certain you have known some, for you bear the traces —among thicker traces of another sort.—I do not plead that she should be happy; or even fortunate; but let her be distinctly loveable; perhaps, let some one love her very much; but, at any rate, let *her* love very much, and let us see that she does; let us care for her, and even greatly. If you will only care for her yourself, as you describe her, the thing is done.

If you will only care for her yourself. This was the deepest argument of the letters, which return perpetually to the same theme. She had met Mrs. Bronson in Venice, and when that lady told Miss Woolson that it was to her balcony James alluded in his article on Venice, when he spoke of smoking a cigarette at the end of the day and watching the traffic on the Grand Canal, Fenimore has a little spasm of jealousy. She ends the letter: "The lagoons, the Piazzetta, the little canals all send their love to you. They wish you were here. And so do I. I could go in a gondola, you know, and see you on Mrs. B's balcony. That would—be something. Goodbye."

There was also in the letters a strong competitive feeling. Fenimore was a dedicated writer; and she aspired to some of the greatness of her friend. On the one hand she proclaimed her inability to do the kind of writing he did; on the other she conveyed to him the helplessness to which this reduced her. She remembered well, she told him, how she had talked to him in Florence, of the problem of making a clean copy of her stories; and how he had answered, "Oh, *I* never copy." On a mute gesture from Fenimore he had added: "Do you think, then, that my work has the air of having been copied, and perhaps more than once?" She wrote: "I think I made no direct reply, then. But I will, now. The gesture was despair—despair, that, added to your other perfections, was the gift of writing as you do, at the first draft!"

In one of her letters she suddenly fears she is not being a very literary correspondent, and in the process gives us a hint of the way in which he wrote to her:

> If I were clever, I should always bear in mind the fact, that when I have written to you many sheets, I have received a short note in reply, beginning with some sentence as this: "Dear Miss Woolson. One doesn't answer your letters; one can't. One only reads them and is grateful;" and this followed up by three very small pages (in a very big hand) in which no allusion is made to anything I have said, the "faithfully" of the signature occupying the room of several of my sentences. Then, when I have written you a short note myself, I have received from you a charming letter in reply, eight pages long, and not such a very big hand either, and the "faithfully" even put across the top or side of the first page instead of being relied upon to fill the half of the last!

This is an accurate picture of Henry's epistolary strategy. On the other hand she tells him: "Your letters are better than you are." And then the praise: "The best part of you is your incorruptible and dignified and reasonable modesty and your perfectly balanced common sense. It is such a comfort that you have them."

For, if she could not give full expression to her feelings for her correspondent, she could do so freely for his work. When her enthusiasm led her to the man—and she felt that she might overstep the bounds of reticence—she promptly took refuge in praise of his writing. Thus, after describing her rooms in Venice she has a fantasy of James's coming to tea:

> There is a very nice sofa here, placed just at the angle that commands the beautiful eastern view. And there is a tea-table, with the same sputtering little kettle you saw in my sky-parlour at Rome. If you could come in now, and rest a while (till time to go to the next dinner-party), I would make you some of the water which you consider "tea." And you would find at least the atmosphere of a very perfect kindness. You say you "fall

back" upon my "charity," feeling that it is "infinite." You can safely fall back; for infinite it is. Only charity is not precisely the word. Call it, rather, gratitude. This isn't for you, personally—though of course you have to be included: it is for your books. You may be what you please, so long as you write as you do.

In a sudden burst of emotion, she tells him that "the deepest charm" of his writings is that "they voice for me—as nothing else ever has—my own feelings; those that are so deep—so a part of me, that I cannot express them, and do not try to; never think of trying to." She concludes by telling him—she who had written of "Castle Nowhere"—that his writings "are my true country, my real home. And nothing else ever is fully —try as I may to think so. Do you think this is quite an assumption, or presumption?"

This identification of her feelings with his, her home with the very heart of his created work, cannot have been lost upon James. In the same letter she offered him a gift; certain ancient Greek coins she had had mounted as tie-pins. She remembered that Benvolio had worn a Syracusan coin; and that she had seen James wearing "six rings on one hand." Would he accept the gift? He could choose any one of three—a coin bearing an owl, one with the head of Bacchus and one with the shield of Boeotia. Apparently James chose the Bacchus. At any rate a photograph, front-face, of his later years shows a coin-pin in his cravat.

Only at one moment in these long and pleading missives does Fenimore seem to be on the verge of an outburst, some break in her self-control. She had spoken of returning to America. "It is all very well to hold out the prospect of 'talking it over' against an Italian church-wall," she writes. "As to a 'church-wall,' there has never been but that one short time (three years ago—in Florence) when you seemed disposed for that sort of thing." And voicing her complaint about his long absences she remarks, "Don't put in those decorative sentences about 'Italian church' walls."

And so Fenimore took up her residence in England (it seems clear) to be near the man whose writings were her "real home." In the letter in which she speaks of having been in England a year she mentions that she has seen only Dover, Canterbury, Salisbury and London itself; and during that year we know that her visit to Dover coincided with James's stay there at the end of the summer, and that from Salisbury they went together to Stonehenge, on 7 September 1884. We also know that one evening he encountered her at a theater to which he had escorted Mrs. Kemble; and since he had a better seat he introduced her to Mrs. Kemble and gave Fenimore his place.

Only the Bootts knew of her existence in his life, or of the cautious intimacy that had grown between them. However, the Howellses during the previous year had seen something of Miss Woolson in Florence, and writing from Paris in February 1884 to his former editor, James said: "Miss Fenimore Woolson is spending the winter there [in London]. I see her at discreet intervals and we talk of you and Mrs. *you.* She is a very intelligent woman, and understands when she is spoken to; a peculiarity I prize, as I find it more and more rare."

The Besotted Mandarins

During the nine years that had elapsed since his visits to Flaubert's *cénacle* James had made no attempt to revive his friendship with Daudet, Zola or the elderly Edmond de Goncourt. In mid-winter 1884-85—on 2 February—James crossed the Channel for a brief holiday, long promised to himself. One of the first things he did after putting up at the fashionable Hôtel de Hollande, in the rue de la Paix, was to search out his French colleagues. He did not try to reach them directly; he seems indeed to have thought that they would not remember him. In Gallic fashion James resorted to an intermediary: his friend Theodore Child, by now a well-established journalist and editor, thoroughly at ease in the Parisian world of letters.

On the third day of James's stay, Child sent a note to Edmond de Goncourt inquiring whether he could bring the American novelist to call on him in Auteuil. Goncourt received them the next morning, in the house where he and his brother had lived together for so many years. We know very little of this visit. In James's report to various persons that they had had a talk, he offered a single reminiscence, a remark made by the survivor of the fraternal team, that there had been a "great deal of crawling into bed and playing the truant" in the daily life of Flaubert. The remark suggests, however, that the saturnine Goncourt was sufficiently expansive and anecdotal. A few evenings later James saw Goncourt again, this time at Alphonse Daudet's.

Daudet, responding cordially to Child's note that James was in Paris, invited the two and promised a cup of tea and "a dozen persons—Goncourt, Zola, Coppée, Loti the sailor—*la haute gomme littéraire,*" that is, the "swells" of current French literature. From Child's account we know that when he and James were ushered into Daudet's modest apartment, on a fourth floor overlooking the Luxembourg Gardens, Zola and Daudet at once recognized the American. "Why," Daudet exclaimed, "I have known you 150 years!" James proceeded to compliment Daudet on "all those *trouvailles* of phrases and epithets" in his work, and Daudet, twirling the points of his silky beard, his eyes sparkling behind his glasses, launched into a discussion of the burden of writing, the need always to say things in a new way.

Something of the old magic of the *cénacle* seems to have been recov-

ered by James that night as they discussed Flaubert's favorite subject—
the search for the *mot juste,* the attempt to use prose as a plastic medium.
On the next day (13 February 1884), Henry James described their talk to
T. B. Aldrich, editor of the *Atlantic.*

> The torment of style, the high standard of it, the effort to say something
> perfectly in a language in which everything has been said, and re-said
> —so that there are certain things, certain cases, which can never again
> be attempted—all this seems to me to be wearing them all out. . . . Daudet
> spoke of his envy and admiration of the "serenity of production" of Tur-
> genev—working in a field and a language where the white snow has as
> yet so few footprints. In French, he said, it is all one trampled slosh—one
> has to look, forever, to see where one can put down his step. And he
> wished to know how it was in English.

The evening at Daudet's had profoundly impressed James. To Howells
the novelist wrote:

> I have been seeing something of Daudet, Goncourt and Zola; and there
> is nothing more interesting to me now than the effort and experiment of
> this little group, with its truly infernal intelligence of art, form, manner
> —its intense artistic life. They do the only kind of work, today, that I
> respect; and in spite of their ferocious pessimism and their handling of
> unclean things, they are at least serious and honest.

But to Child, he commented that there was a "Chinese quality" to the
existence of his French contemporaries. It was "mandarin." They lived
in an enclosed world, and studied "warts rather than the beauties of
man" and his creations. And in a letter to his brother five years later,
after another visit to Paris in which he listened to French writers and
their talk: "Chinese, Chinese, Chinese!" he exclaimed. "They are
finished, besotted mandarins and Paris is their celestial Empire."

James could not swallow "naturalism" whole. *"Ces messieurs,"* he wrote
to Child, "seem to me to have lost the perception of anything in nature
but the genital organs." James found Daudet sympathetic; and they became warm friends. For Zola he acquired an ever-increasing respect. To
his friend T. S. Perry, James wrote: "Zola's naturalism is ugly and dirty,
but he seems to me to be *doing something*—which surely (in the imaginative line) no one in England or the United States is, and no one else
here." And again: "Zola has his faults and his merits, and it doesn't seem
to me important to talk of the faults. The merits are rare, valuable,
extremely solid." "I have read a good deal of naturalism," James wrote
to Mrs. Humphry Ward as his visit to Paris neared its end.

James's mind was now working on the lessons of the naturalists even as he had long ago studied the lesson of Balzac. He was abandoning the "international" theme. His new novels would "do" Boston and London as Zola had done his Paris, and was to do the coal-mines—by descending into the very heart of his subject. James's fortnight in Paris—extended into a month—proved much richer than he had anticipated. It had brought him back to the fundamentals of his career, after the long American interval and the unsettled London return.

Prodigies and Disciples

There was another side to Henry's visit to Paris. He called on the Princess Marie Ourousov and had an intimate talk with her about Turgenev's last days. He visited Mrs. Charles Strong, and saw the Auguste Laugels, who were friends also of Henrietta Reubell. Above all James spent many hours in Miss Reubell's salon at 42 Avenue Gabriel, and saw much of her friend Mrs. Boit, now living in Paris. Henrietta Reubell remained the same genial, shrewd spinster, with her bright red hair, her high laugh, her lorgnette, her original mind. She moved in a world of writers, painters, pictures, studios. She numbered Whistler and Oscar Wilde among her friends, and was loyal to both. She permitted, in her drawing-room, "anything but dullness and ill-manners."

James often alluded to a particular alcove of her little parlor, where on a particular sofa, under a golden canopy, he and Miss Reubell would have their intimate gossipy *tête-à-têtes* in a perpetual cloud of smoke. There always seemed to linger in this alcove "the fragrance of all the cigarettes that have been smoked out in discussion of the pleasant things of Paris."

It was in the entourage of "the tall Etta" and her friend Mrs. Boit that James met the young American prodigy of painting, John Singer Sargent. He already knew his work and had stood in admiration before the striking picture of the young Boit daughters which Sargent had done a year before. The painter was now a mere twenty-seven. A tall, athletic, ruddy-complexioned, dark-haired and dark-bearded man with vivid grey-blue eyes, he was quiet, cultivated, sedate: in marked contrast to the rough-and-tumble bohemians of art, or the dilettantes. The novelist was promptly and powerfully attracted to him.

The two had so much in common that they must have seemed to each other, in certain respects, mirror-images. Continentalized from their earliest years—Sargent even more than James—innate aristocrats with a penchant for society and the *beau-monde* (and taking many of their subjects from it), possessing a dignity and distinction that commanded respect wherever they went, dedicated to their art, capable of extraordinary assiduity, they were counterparts in their different mediums. If

James had a more subtle mind, and Sargent a greater naïveté, this merely echoed the differences often to be found between a writer and a painter. James was much more strongly intellectual than Sargent; and both had in them a vestigial stiffness of the American puritan.

Sargent took James to his studio at 41 Boulevard Berthier and showed him his large painting of Madame X. This was the portrait of Madame Gautereau which was to have a *succès de scandale* in the Paris salon a few weeks later. James only "half-liked it." But he was impressed by the talent that had produced it. And he was worried by this excess of skill in one so young. "His talent is brilliant," he wrote to Lizzie Boott, "but there is a certain incompleteness in it, in his extremely attaching, interesting nature a certain want of seriousness." He added that Sargent's future was "the most valuable thing he has to show." James was to see that future, and it was for him "a knock-down insolence of talent and truth of characterization, a wonderful rendering of life, of manners, of aspects, of types, of textures, of everything."

Within a month after he said good-bye to Sargent in Paris, James welcomed him to London. Sargent's reputation at that time was almost wholly French, and James argued the time had come for him to cross the Channel permanently—as he himself had done. Since Sargent was a stranger to the British capital James gave him "a push to the best of my ability." It was a strenuous push indeed. On Saturday, 28 March 1884, Henry took him to an exhibition of the works of Sir Joshua Reynolds and then to the National Gallery. The next day, Sunday, the novelist conducted Sargent through ten artists' studios to see pictures just going into the spring Academy exhibition; and that evening he entertained him at a dinner at the Reform Club to which he invited half a dozen friends, including Edward Burne-Jones.

Among the studios they visited were those of John Everett Millais and Sir Frederick Leighton, President of the Royal Academy. The novelist was immensely struck by the wealth and power of Millais and Leighton, "the gorgeous effect of world prosperity and success" they revealed. "I suppose," he wrote to Grace Norton, "it is the demon of envy—but I can't help contrasting the great rewards of a successful painter, here, and his glory and honour generally, with the so much more modest emoluments of the men of letters."

The English art critics, as well as some of his fellow painters, among them Burne-Jones, at first felt Sargent to be crude and too startling in some of his effects. Within a year, however, the American painter had settled in England, in Whistler's old house in Tite Street, Chelsea—as it proved, for life.

The spring and summer of 1884 were filled with "interruptions and distractions," easy sociabilities and the Season, amid the pressure of

James's heavy writing commitments. He seems to have worked steadily from March until August, despite the fact that nearly all his American friends were in London; and a cholera epidemic along the Mediterranean brought Continental friends as well. Along with seeing old and less old friends—Osgood and Norton, John Hay and Clarence King, Mrs. Strong from Paris, Mrs. Gardner, fresh from a world tour, Mrs. Mason—James formed two new friendships during these weeks. These were with members of the younger literary generation of France and England—two writers who promptly dedicated their books to him.

To his rooms in July Sargent brought a rather flabby-looking Frenchman, Paul Bourget. James remembered having read his *Essais de psychologie contemporaine,* which he had judged "almost brilliant." Bourget was thirty-two but looked twenty-eight: a small, rather sturdy man, for all his softness, with long tapering hands and searching eyes. He was on obviously good terms with his tailor.

Bourget wrote *Cruelle Énigme* that summer. It made him famous in France; and he attached himself to James as a disciple. But James cared little for what Bourget wrote, regarding his plots as factitious and his "psychology" as increasingly superficial. It was Bourget the conversationalist that he found interesting. He dined the Frenchman at the Reform, introduced him to Gosse, made him his guest at the Athenaeum. James judged him "too much of a dilettante," but found him a sympathetic and attractive being with a "brilliant little intelligence," and "one of the most charming and ingenious talkers I ever met."

"Bourget est tragique," James wrote to a mutual friend, *"mais est-il sérieux?" Cruelle Énigme* bore a rather flowery dedicatory epistle, which suggests what their friendship meant to the French writer. It was inscribed to the "memory of the time when I was beginning to write it and which was also the time when we became acquainted." "I am greatly compromised here by the dedication of Bourget's novel," James told Child, "the story being so *malpropre.* But I admire much—not the story, but the ability of it."

The second friendship, less intimate and personal, was with Violet Paget, an Englishwoman of twenty-seven, who had lived most of her life in Italy and who had lately published, under the name of Vernon Lee, volumes entitled *Euphorion* and *Belcaro.* She and James met in various London homes and James described her as "a most astounding young female." *Euphorion* was "most fascinating and suggestive, as well as monstrous clever. She had a prodigious cerebration." Tall, angular, with slightly protruding teeth and peering near-sightedly through her glasses, Miss Paget seemed the traditional man-like bluestocking. James paid her marked attention, was helpful, curious, encouraging. He little realized how closely Miss Paget listened and to what extent he was involving the young writer in the emotions of a friendship that was on his side wholly "objective." The first warning sign came when Miss Paget decided that she would dedicate her novel *Miss Brown* to him. He could hardly refuse. But he was cautious.

Reading her works James must have had second thoughts. There was something too sharp, too penetrating, in this inexhaustible young woman's mind. He wrote to her with delicate irony, saying it frightened him to have "the honour of an invocation however casual," and added: "Please hint that you offer me *Miss Brown* only to encourage me!" The irony escaped Miss Paget. Her inscription was literal: "To Henry James I dedicate, for good luck, my first attempt at a novel." When the novel reached him, James realized the danger of a too ardent admiration. The book was raw and violent; there were too many recognizable persons. This embarrassed him. He postponed thanking Vernon Lee. Months passed. When he finally sat down to write a letter, he was abjectly apologetic, feeling he returned admiration with discourtesy:

> You have proposed to yourself too little to make a firm, compact work —and you have been too much in a moral passion! That has put certain exaggerations, overstatements, *grossissements,* insistences wanting in tact, into your head. Cool first—write afterwards. Morality is hot—but art is icy!

Speaking of her characters, James told her that

> *life* is less criminal, less obnoxious, less objectionable, less crude, more *bon enfant,* more mixed and casual, and even in its most offensive manifestations, more *pardonable,* than the unholy circle with which you have surrounded your heroine. And then you have impregnated all those people too much with the sexual, the basely erotic preoccupation: your hand was over-violent, the touch of life is lighter.

Miss Paget seems at the time to have paid attention to James's criticisms, and to have recognized their value and authority. She also looked sharply and critically at the novelist, and his "absolute social and personal insincerity and extreme intellectual justice and plain spokenness."

Atmosphere of the Mind

The summer came and James was still in London—hot, tired, restless, uneasy. "Infinitely oppressed and depressed," he wrote in his notebook on 6 August 1884, "by the sense of being behindhand with the novel —that is with the *start* of it, that I have engaged, through Osgood, to write for the *Century.* " He had not yet found a title for it. It was known for the moment only as *Verena.* Osgood was to pay a flat fee of $5,000 for the book-rights for a specified period. James knew he had driven a good bargain. Moreover he had come to terms with the *Atlantic* for a second novel, for 1885–86, for which he would receive $15 a page, or about $350 a month.

He remained in London that summer to write two tales for the New York *Sunday Sun* and its syndicate. "It is a case of gold pure and simple," he wrote to Perry. The first of these tales was "Georgina's Reasons," a strange unmotivated sensational story, written in the belief that this was what newspaper readers wanted. He based it on an anecdote Mrs. Kemble had told him—of a woman in society who married a naval officer in secret, gave birth to his child secretly, as if it were illegitimate, and disposed of it to foster-parents. James's heroine then remarries, and her husband, back from a long voyage, is faced with the dilemma of denouncing her, or of accepting the possibility of bigamy for himself. Two other figures in the story—the sisters Kate and Mildred Theory, Mildred dying of consumption—will return to James's imagination later: Kate and Milly, with the man later named Densher, will enact the drama of *The Wings of the Dove*.

The second tale written for the *Sun*, "Pandora," was told with great charm through the eyes of a young German diplomat bound for America. Pandora Day, whom the diplomat first meets on board ship, a counterpart to Daisy Miller, is a kind of "self-made" American girl. Her parents have totally abdicated. When the President of the United States, attending a party in a splendid Washington home (very like that of the Henry Adamses), has a chat with Pandora, she obtains from him a post in the diplomatic service for her fiancé. The amazed German feels he has full documentation on the resilience and daring of American young women. James by now possessed a fluent mastery of this type of story—the arrival in New York, the Washington interiors, the social rise of Pandora, every step seen through the Germanism of Count Vogelstein, is told with a concreteness of data, and the lightest kind of irony. The tale was as critical of "permissiveness" and American institutions as James's other international stories. What many of James's readers could not appreciate was his boundless good humor; they experienced the humor as depreciatory.

When these tales were sent off, James settled himself in Dover, in the Marine Parade. The Channel twinkled under his windows and he had almost an entire lodging-house to himself. "I have gone in for privacy, *recueillement* and literary labour," he told Miss Reubell. He had never allowed himself so slim a margin before starting a serial. Bourget came from London, and they sat on Henry's little balcony smoking cigarettes and looking across the Channel. James spent six or seven productive weeks here, put himself back into tune with his work, and returned to Bolton Street in late September with his novel well-launched. By 1 October he had sent Richard Watson Gilder the first installment of *The Bostonians* for the *Century.*

Before leaving London James had written a comparatively short but substantial essay, to which he gave the title "The Art of Fiction." It was partly a response to a lecture, "Fiction as One of the Fine Arts," delivered the previous April at the Royal Institution by Walter Besant, a prolific Victorian novelist. The burden of Besant's argument was that novel-writing should be classed with the arts of poetry, painting and music, taught as the laws of harmony are taught in music or perspective in painting, and awarded honors and prizes as were the other arts. With much of this James had no argument; but he could not accept Besant's dictum that a novel should possess "a conscious moral purpose." Nor could he agree that a lady novelist who lived in a quiet village might not write fiction about garrison life, or that young novelists from the lower classes ought to refrain from launching their characters in high society. The truly imaginative novelist, James said, knew how to guess the unseen from the seen, "to trace the implication of things, to judge the whole piece by the pattern."

For the rest, James argued that the novel, far from being "make-believe," actually competes with life, since it records the stuff of history. The core of his essay contained a defense of the novel as a free and elastic form, which made it difficult to prescribe "what sort of an affair the good novel will be." It would always be a personal impression of life; and its value would be greater or less "according to the intensity of the impression." It was all very well for Besant to say one should write from "experience."

> What kind of experience is intended, and where does it begin and end? Experience is never limited, and it is never complete; it is an immense sensibility, a kind of huge spider-web of the finest silken threads suspended in the chamber of consciousness, catching every air-borne particle in its tissue. It is the very atmosphere of the mind; and when the mind is imaginative—much more when it happens to be that of a man of genius—it takes to itself the faintest hints of life, it converts the very pulses of the air into revelations.

James denied a *conscious* moral purpose to the novel. The province of art was "all life, all feeling, all observation, all vision," and the critic should not prescribe which subjects were valid and which were not. The critic's concern was solely with what the novelist did with his material. Recalling his talks with his French *confrères,* James reached the conclusion that a novel invariably conveyed "the quality of the mind of the producer" and that "no good novel will ever proceed from a superficial mind." "The Art of Fiction," published in *Longman's Magazine,* remains a brilliant individual manifesto, written with elegance and grace: never had the case for realism in fiction, and for the novel as social history, been put in the English world with such force, nor "experience" defined with so much psychological understanding.

One remark in the essay caught the eye of an invalid at Bournemouth, a novelist who had been having severe lung hemorrhages and who did most of his writing in bed. Discussing reality in fiction, James had alluded to *Treasure Island* as a success, remarking: "I have been a child, but I have never been on a quest for buried treasure." Robert Louis Stevenson promptly wrote still another essay on the subject: "A Humble Remonstrance" appeared in *Longman's* two months after James's paper. To the particular remark about *Treasure Island* Stevenson rejoined that if James had "never been on a quest for buried treasure, it can be demonstrated that he has never been a child." A novel could not compete with life, he argued. It had to be "make-believe." Fiction, Stevenson said, simplified some "side or point of life," and stood or fell by its "significant simplicity." Life was "monstrous, infinite, illogical, abrupt, and poignant," whereas a work of art was, in comparison, "neat, finite, self-contained, rational, flowing, and emasculate."

James had met Stevenson in 1879, during the "Daisy Miller" period, when he found him, as he told Perry, "a pleasant fellow, but a shirt-collarless bohemian and a great deal (in an inoffensive way) of a *poseur*." They had never had occasion to develop this acquaintance, Stevenson being much out of England. But when his article on the novel appeared, James wrote to thank him for many of the things he had said—"the current of your admirable style floats pearls and diamonds." His own pages in *Longman's,* he explained, represented only half of what he had to say. "Some day I shall try and express the remainder. The native *gaiety* of all that you write is delightful to me," and all the more so, he added, since he was aware how ill Stevenson was.

Stevenson replied that his own efforts were modest beside James's. As for their differences, "Each man among us prefers his own aim, and I prefer mine; but when we come to speak of performance, I recognize myself, compared with you, to be a lout and slouch of the first water." Being ill, he liked visitors; he invited James to come to Bournemouth, where he would put him up and offer him "a fair bottle of claret." These were the overtures to a strong and enduring friendship.

The Two Invalids

When Henry James returned to London from Dover, he knew that his sister would shortly join him. A letter to William of 5 October 1884 mentions that "Alice's advent here is by this time (in prospect) a familiar idea, though I feel naturally a good deal of solicitude about it." Her sailing date had not yet been set. With both her parents dead and with Katharine Loring available only at certain times, Alice had been leading a lonely life in Mount Vernon Street. Miss Loring had a sister, Louisa, with weak lungs; she could not therefore give undivided attention to Alice. But she was bringing Louisa abroad, and Alice, rather than remain alone in Cambridge, decided to journey with her friends.

The ill-health and dependency of Alice posed serious problems for James. They had talked of some sort of joint domestic arrangement; with her invalidism this seemed out of the question, but as her one bachelor brother, he felt a responsibility for her. "I have quite escaped, as yet, being alarmed by Alice's now impending advent," he wrote to Grace Norton. "I *may* be wrong, and it *may* wreck and blight my existence, but it will have to exert itself tremendously to do so." She was not even coming to visit him, he said. She was simply coming to Europe and

> there is no question of her living with me. She is unspeakably undepend-
> ent and independent, she *clings* no more than a bowsprit, has her own
> plans, purposes, preferences, practices, pursuits, more than anyone I
> know, has also amply sufficient means, etc. and, in short, even putting her
> possible failure to improve in health at the worst, will be very unlikely
> to tinge or modify my existence in any uncomfortable way.

Nevertheless Alice's illness, by its very nature, had its clinging side. At Liverpool, where he met her ship, James found his sister in one of her fits of nervous prostration. She had to be carried off on a stretcher. Louisa Loring seemed in much better health than Alice, who was "more infirm than I expected," Henry reported to Aunt Kate.

After some observation James discovered that his sister was markedly jealous of Louisa. She wanted Miss Loring for herself. Katharine Loring was taking Louisa to Bournemouth on the very next day and James first thought Alice would be taken there as well; but Miss Loring's sister was, on her side, in a high state of nerves. Miss Loring tactfully suggested that Alice's arrival at the health-resort be postponed. After some days James brought Alice from Liverpool to London and installed her with her maid at 40 Clarges Street, near his own lodgings. By this time the drama was clear: Louisa Loring and Alice James were engaged in a fierce subterranean competition for the nursing and attention of the stalwart Katharine. Whenever Katharine had to be with Louisa, Alice sooner or later developed alarming symptoms. James would send an anxious telegram, and Miss Loring dashed to the rescue. Alice's symptoms then subsided. At the same time James observed that even when the crisis was over, Alice insisted on remaining in bed so long as Miss Loring was available to care for her.

James finally took his sister to Bournemouth in January 1885, when it became clear that Louisa Loring was on her way to recovery. The British doctors meanwhile gave Alice a thorough examination. They could find nothing organically wrong and they ended by treating her as neurasthenic. So long as Miss Loring was with her, Alice had no particular need for Henry. But he promised her he would spend the spring in the seaside resort: it would be a good place to work and to avoid the London "Season."

The novelist moved to the seaside in late April, when Miss Loring went to London with her sister. The greater part of *The Bostonians* had been written, and he was clearing the ground for *The Princess Casamassima.* He took rooms on the ocean, three minutes' walk from where Alice was staying, with her nurse and a maid. Once or twice a day he would drop in for a twenty-minute visit. Bournemouth he found wholly uninteresting, "of an almost American newness and ugliness." He enjoyed the view, however, especially of the Isle of Wight. In the afternoon, and sometimes in the evening, he became a regular caller at Skerryvore, where he spent hours in happy talk with another Bournemouth invalid, Robert Louis Stevenson.

Stevenson was thirty-five, seven years younger than James; he had all the activity and make-believe of a boy in constant search of adventure. Disabled physically, he remained extraordinarily prolific. He suffered little pain, and seemed to have a rare capacity for pulling himself back, again and again, from the brink of death. Stevenson received James with boundless affection and much ceremonial. Mrs. Stevenson, American and older than her husband, treated her fellow-countryman with a certain awe and respect: the two transformed what might have been for James a lugubrious stay in Bournemouth into a pleasant literary and social way of life.

The Stevensons lived in a house on the brink of the Alum Chine or gulley, a two-story structure of yellow brick with a blue slate roof, overgrown with ivy. They had renamed the place Skerryvore, after the great lighthouse built by the novelist's ancestor. In the blue room hung a Venetian mirror which James had given them. Here Stevenson would sit at the end of the table rolling cigarettes in his long fingers. He wore bohemian velvet jackets; sometimes when it was cold he would drape himself in a maroon-colored shawl, like a Mexican poncho. A passionate energy possessed his slight frame.

Stevenson wrote lively verses dedicated to Henry. But when he published them James felt, with embarrassment, that privacy had been violated. Two of the poems lead, in their moment of climax, to the entry of Henry James into Skerryvore—suggesting perhaps how much his daily coming was awaited. In one, celebrating the gift of the Venetian mirror, the mirror is speaking:

Now with an outlandish grace,
To the sparkling fire I face
In the blue room at Skerryvore;
Where I wait until the door
Open, and the Prince of Men,
Henry James, shall come again.

"My only social resource," James wrote to Howells,

is Robert Louis Stevenson, who is more or less dying here. . . . He is an interesting, charming creature, but I fear at the end of his tether; though indeed less apparently near death than he has been at other times.

Stevenson seemed to consort on such amiable terms with the constant presence of death that this gave an additional measure of intensity to the friendship. He would live for another decade; and when he departed for the South Seas their correspondence took on the charm and spontaneity of their personal meetings. The tone of communication on both sides continued to be one of deep affection. It was at Skerryvore in 1886 that Stevenson gave James a copy of *Kidnapped,* inscribing it "And I wish I had a better work to give as good a man."

James's closeness to Alice during these weeks gave him a clear picture of certain of her problems. Early in May there was "a cataclysm," James told Aunt Kate, when Miss Loring's presence was required. Katharine then announced that she would, in a month or two, return to Alice "for a permanency," and release Henry. Louisa's weak lungs seemed cured, and, said James, Katharine's being with Alice "may be interrupted by absences, but evidently it is the beginning of a living-together, for the rest of such time as Alice's life may last."

Henry felt that there was no alternative but to accept gratefully Miss Loring's willingness and generosity although he was not convinced that the relationship was a good one. Alice took too much joy in being cared for by her friend. There was however nothing anyone else could do. "There is about as much possibility of Alice's giving Katharine up," he told his aunt,

as of her giving her legs to be sawed off. She said to me a few days ago that she believed if she could have Katharine *quietly* and *uninterruptedly* for a year, "to relieve her of all responsibility" she would get well. Amen! She will get well, or she won't, but, either way, it lies between themselves. I shall devote my best energies to taking the whole situation less hard in the future than I have hitherto.

A solution had been found for a deeply complicated and painful situation. Louisa Loring did make a complete recovery and her elder sister increasingly confined herself to Alice. The novelist was liberated to pursue his work. But he was to continue to have Alice on his mind, and he frequently hesitated on her account to take trips away from England. She held him by her invalidism in a delicate moral bondage. "Henry the Patient," Alice was to call him, and she recorded in her journal in March 1890: "I have given him endless care and anxiety but notwithstanding this and the fantastic nature of my troubles I have never seen an impatient look upon his face or heard an unsympathetic or misunderstanding sound cross his lips."

Alice James rarely left her bed after her arrival in England. She refused to risk a return voyage to America, and during the seven years that remained to her she wrested from the hovering Miss Loring and the loyal brother a full amount of attention and love which, in some large way, she felt had been denied her during an earlier period of her existence.

A Very American Tale

In *The Bostonians* Henry James wrote the most considerable American novel of its decade. For all its compulsive detail, there is no other novel of such value and distinction to place on the bookshelf of the late nineteenth century; yet the editors of the *Century,* where the ill-fated book ran through thirteen months, said they had never published a serial which had encountered such an awesome silence.

The first notation for the book was made on 8 April 1883 when James was in Boston, and in setting it down he spoke of it in the past tense—as if the novel were already written. "I wished to write a very *American* tale, a tale very characteristic of our social conditions, and I asked myself what was the most salient and peculiar point in our social life. The answer was: the situation of women, the decline of the sentiment of sex, the agitation on their behalf." Another notation is a single word, "Reformers," scrawled across the flyleaf of the *Correspondence of Thomas Carlyle and Ralph Waldo Emerson.* The page-number attached to it refers us to a passage in a letter of Emerson's: "We are all a little wild here with numberless projects of social reform."

Later, as his book took shape, James was to discover that the subject was "less interesting and repaying than I had assumed it to be." Perhaps he knew Boston too well; and the theme was clearly uncongenial. A kind of nagging hand seemed to tug at his pen; the fluid style of the international tales was replaced by heavy Balzacian detail. Each scene was described with an exhaustive minuteness. A kind of uncontrollable prolixity is everywhere. James had intended to tell his story as a six-part serial, of the length of *Washington Square.* He had nothing to gain by more than doubling its length save the dubious satisfaction of bringing into being a weighty 950-page manuscript.

The Bostonians is a strange instance of a writer of power so possessed by his vital material that he loses his mastery of it. Something in the very nature of the story, the deep animus James felt for certain aspects of Boston life, took possession. In the end James recognized this. He excluded the novel from the New York Edition. He admitted that it was "too diffuse and insistent—far too describing and explaining and expatiating." His readers of that time agreed. Yet today the book's social documentation has an historical interest, and the women's liberation movements of our century have given the novel a new actuality.

The drama of *The Bostonians* resides in a struggle for possession not unlike the drama of Katharine Loring, her sister, and Alice James. Olive Chancellor, a wealthy, chilly, unyielding Boston intellectual, simmers in chronic anger over the subservience of women to men. Encountering a young and inexperienced girl named Verena Tarrant, who possesses a strange histrionic oratorical gift, she recognizes in her the instrument she lacks. It occurs to Olive that she should adopt this girl; she would impart noble thoughts and noble aims to her; make her the sounding-box of the American feminist movement.

James intended the story to be "a study of one of those friendships between women which are so common in New England." Modern critics have tended to regard the novel as portraying a lesbian attachment; but in terms of James's time, and Boston morality, it is more accurate to see the relationship in its overt nature. The focus of the story is on Olive's fierce possessiveness; the drama is her struggle to keep Verena from marrying Basil Ransom, a weak, easy but also powerfully possessive Southerner, a remote relative of hers. The conflict between Olive, all rectitude and flaming feminine politics, and Ransom, determined to place Verena in the kitchen and the nursery, has in it elements of strong human drama and high comedy. James, however, has little respect for either of his contending personages. It is their struggle for power which he finds fascinating; they are ruthless, self-seeking, blind to the feelings of others, aware only of their own needs. Olive wants to make Verena a projection of herself; Ransom is sufficiently of the post-war South still to believe that some persons should be enslaved by others.

Had *The Bostonians* been written with James's usual economy and the same wit as *The Europeans,* he would have created something close to the "great American novel" of which he had dreamed in his youth. What he created instead was a series of vignettes; and certain pages valuably critical of American institutions—the invasion of privacy by the press, the meddlesome character of Boston reformers, the general tawdriness and banality of certain aspects of American life of the time.

The print in the *Century* was hardly dry on the early chapters of the novel when James received word from his Aunt Kate, from James Russell Lowell (now back in Cambridge after the end of his term as minister in London) and from his brother William that he had lampooned a much respected Boston reformer, Elizabeth Peabody, the elderly sister-in-law of Hawthorne, whose good works and crusading zeal were famous. "It is a pretty bad business," William wrote, and Henry showed some perturbation over this remark. He pleaded not guilty. At best he had thought of Miss Peabody's spectacles on the bridge of her nose when he had described his character Miss Birdseye—"the whole moral history of Boston was reflected in her displaced spectacles."

Henry told William that he had not seen Miss Peabody for twenty-five years, and that he had always had the most casual observation of her. "Miss Birdseye," he said, "was evolved entirely from my moral consciousness like every person I have ever drawn." He had wanted to describe "an old, weary, battered and simple-minded woman," so as not to be left open to the charge of treating all the reformers "in a contemptuous manner." In subsequent installments he enlarged Miss Peabody's heroism, and William, when he read the completed volume, withdrew his criticisms and praised it, but felt that it was overdrawn. Neither he nor anyone at the time noticed the close relationship between the names of the real-life character and the fictional lady. A "bird's eye" is indeed a "pea-body." Henry James had perhaps imitated life more than he himself allowed.

A few weeks before he had begun the writing of this novel James composed a short story, "The Author of 'Beltraffio,' " published in the spring of 1884 in the *English Illustrated Magazine.* The tale had its origin in James's hearing from Edmund Gosse that the wife of John Addington Symonds intensely disliked his writings. James did not know at the time that Symonds's homosexuality was the real issue. But he clearly had some divination of it and made his tale a subtle and poisonous narrative of Mark Ambient's struggle with his wife for possession—body and soul —of their exquisite little boy. The mother's morbid fear that Dolcino will be contaminated by what she sees as evil in his father's art causes her to perform the act of Medea. She fails to summon medical help when the child falls ill, and Dolcino dies.

This tale of a struggle for possession heralded the struggle in *The Bostonians.* It seemed as if Henry James were back in some dim passage of childhood or youth in which he had felt himself identified with a powerful mother, whose strength is so often represented in the stories, and at the same time with the image of his maimed father. The disappearance of the home in Quincy Street, the now permanent absence of a Cambridge hearth, is probably the single deepest emotion out of which *The Bostonians* sprang. The paradox was that while James intellectually was holding up a satirical mirror to the city of his youth, another and younger self within him seemed to plead almost tearfully that nothing be altered. In the final scene, in which Ransom insists that at this crucial moment Verena must make her choice, there is an urgency and a shrillness that may bespeak the author's own piercing anxiety. In *The Bostonians* James wrote out the immediate anguish of the collapse of his old American ties, and coupled this with a kind of vibrating anger that Boston should be so unfriendly as to let him go. It incorporated as well Miss Loring's serene and full possession of Alice. In accommodating himself to his new London life, Henry was in some deep underworld of emotion reliving ancient and morbid states. This, we might speculate, lay at the bottom of his inability to discipline the material of his novel, and his need to drag it out beyond its prescribed length.

While the last chapters of *The Bostonians* were appearing, there occurred a serious financial crisis in Henry's affairs. His American publisher, James R. Osgood, went bankrupt. Osgood had five of Henry's books on his list, two early works, two volumes of tales and the impending Boston novel. Henry had not received a penny of the $5,000 promised him for the American, British and serial rights of that work. The novelist acted immediately to recover his various copyrights. He promptly sold the English rights in the novel to Macmillan, along with English and American rights to his next novel, and Macmillan ultimately took over the American book rights in *The Bostonians* as well.

James's advance against royalties from Macmillan did not approximate the sum promised him for his year's work. He could, however, expect a substantial sum from the *Atlantic Monthly* for his next work. He would have liked, on the strength of this, to proceed to the Continent. But he was for the moment tied to England by the necessity for "production" and by the silver cord—and the common humanity—that bound him to his suffering sister.

The Peacock and the Butterfly

One morning in early December 1884 the author of "The Art of Fiction" might have been seen standing in the damp and cold outside a dark and gloomy building on the edge of the Thames, well-known to Victorians as Millbank Prison. The prison's walls were bare and brown; the building had ugly pinnacles; its aspect was sad, stern, impersonal. It had housed—in its accommodation for 1,120 prisoners—almost a century of human misery.

Henry James, before the forbidding entrance, pulled hard at the bell. The gates slowly opened, and he was allowed to go into a kind of dimness, while behind him he heard the rattle of the keys and the slamming of the bolts. He was conducted through a stony court, up steep staircases, past circular shafts of cells, where he could see captives through grated peepholes. He edged past prisoners in the corridors, silent women, with staring eyes.

He was carefully conducted through the establishment in accordance with the arrangements he had previously made. He asked questions. But largely he looked—attentively and reflectively. "Millbank Prison," he was to write, "is a worse act of violence than any it was erected to punish." When he was outside again, in the common London day, it was almost as if he were being released from prison. In his rooms he wrote to T. S. Perry: "I have been all the morning at Millbank Prison (horrible place) collecting notes for a fiction scene. You see," he added, "I am quite the Naturalist. Look out for the same—a year hence."

By June 1885 he had sent off the first chapters—the prison sequence—of *The Princess Casamassima.* He had then come up from Bournemouth to London early in July to find a house for his sister and Katharine Loring.

They had agreed that Bournemouth could be abandoned. After a week's search, he found a cottage on Hampstead Heath which he took for two months. He was about to return to Bournemouth when "three French-men," as he wrote to Miss Reubell, "bearing introductions from Sargent and yearning to see London aestheticism," arrived. James was perhaps not the best guide to the aesthetes. But to do Sargent's introduction proper honor, he put off his departure and devoted Thursday and Friday, 2 and 3 July 1885, to entertaining them.

One of the visitors was the "unique extra-human" Count Robert de Montesquiou-Fezensac, as Sargent described him to James, well-known in Paris as the homosexual eccentric and dandy who had furnished Huysmans his character of Des Esseintes in *À Rebours.* A tall thin man, who described himself as looking like a greyhound in a greatcoat, he had upward-pointed and waxed moustaches, used make-up, cultivated exotic perfumes; his conversation and anecdotes were as artfully contrived as his manner of life. The Count was some twelve years younger than James, who found him, he remarked to Miss Reubell, "curious, but slight." The second visitor was Dr. Samuel Pozzi. Sargent had painted him in his red gown; a society doctor, a book collector, a cultivated con-versationalist, he was three years younger than James. The third of the visitors, a man in his sixties, Prince Edmond de Polignac, was an ama-teur musician of considerable personal charm.

On the first of the two days, James took Montesquiou to see *"tous les Burne-Jones et tous les Rossettis possibles."* On the second, he gave his distinguished visitors dinner at the Reform Club to meet the one painter in London the Count admired above all the others, James McNeill Whis-tler. He thus brought together a stylized French nobleman, a poetic ad-mirer of peacocks and an American master whose emblem on canvas was the butterfly. The peacock and the butterfly dazzled one another across the white table linen. Montesquiou described Whistler in avian detail—"a rare bird, his little eyes shining like jet pearls," his voice emitting "squeak-like words." Whistler ultimately painted Montesquiou as *grand seigneur*— he was related to most of Europe's royal families— in the elongated dandyism of black and grey we can see today in the Frick Collection. Montesquiou pleaded to be shown Whistler's "Peacock Room" —the fabled dining room in the home of a shipping magnate, with golden peacocks painted against intensities of blue on old Spanish leather. But Whistler was committed elsewhere that week-end and James had to be off to Bournemouth. The latter, however, agreed to make the visit possi-ble, writing that "on the whole nothing that relates to Whistler is queerer than anything else." Montesquiou in due course sent James an effusive thank-you note, to which James replied in French that England might seem to have a dull surface, but it was a mask—*"un masque trompeur des jouissances qui vous attendent."*

We now know that James had spent his two days with three of Proust's future characters. Montesquiou would become a model for the Baron de Charlus. Elements of Polignac apparently went into the fashioning of Bergotte, and of Pozzi into Dr. Cottard. A novelist of the nineteenth century had been consorting with the real-life characters of a novel of the twentieth.

34 De Vere Gardens

The Princess Casamassima is one of Henry James's most loosely written books. We may ascribe this in part to many interruptions, his fatigue after writing *The Bostonians,* his constant worry about his sister. During the summer of 1885 he installed her in Hampstead; and when she seemed comfortable in that environment he left for Dover, where he had worked so well before, and where he wrote steadily that summer.

In the autumn of 1885 he paid the first of what would be a series of visits to the village of Broadway, in Worcestershire. Here a group of American artists had gathered around the household of Frank Millet, originally an illustrator and now painting in oils. They shared a large studio—Millet, Edwin A. Abbey, Sargent who joined them, and certain English illustrators and painters as well—and here Sargent painted his celebrated *Carnation Lily, Lily Rose.* James was at ease with his "brothers of the brush," as he had been with John La Farge long ago. He explored the Cotswolds in a dogcart, walked to Chipping Camden, and became a fast friend of Millet whose "Yankee energy" he admired, and of Abbey.

Edmund Gosse, who visited the group on a later occasion, remembered James as the center of it. "Not much serious work was done," Gosse testified, "everything was food for laughter." He remembered a "rollicking day" rowing down the winding Avon, with much singing and Abbey twanging his banjo. James presided, "a sort of bearded Buddha, at the prow." Out of these visits grew James's series of articles on the American illustrators, later assembled in his small book *Picture and Text.* He disliked illustrations when they were intended for his stories; but he enormously liked the illustrators.

Early in the autumn of 1885 he re-visited Paris, saw certain of his old friends, including Mrs. Edward Childe, now dying of tuberculosis, whom he had visited at Montargis a decade earlier. He also saw most of his literary friends and at Bourget's met the Normandy novelist, Jules-Amédée Barbey d'Aurevilly, who had once known Beau Brummel. In October he was summoned back to Alice; she had had a neurasthenic episode. He recognized that he would have to keep himself always available.

He spent, after this, thirteen consecutive months in London, inter-

rupted only by occasional country visits. He felt he should see Alice
regularly. And his serial was exacting; he had left himself small margin
—he was never more than two or three installments ahead of the printer.
There was however still another reason, almost as compelling. Early in
December 1885 he announced that he had signed a twenty-one-year lease
for an apartment in Kensington, at 34 De Vere Gardens. His decision was
a measure of the perspective he had gained in the two further years in
Bolton Street after his parents' death. He had sought a house in St. John's
Wood in 1883 out of childhood memories. Now he was moving into the
neighborhood consecrated by Thackeray with a sense of its agreeable
"suburban" qualities and its proximity to the center of London life. For
a walker of James's propensities, the distance across Kensington Gardens, through Hyde Park, to Piccadilly offered salutary exercise after
hours at his desk.

His rooms in Bolton Street had been dark and small; now he would
have light, space and air in his fourth-floor flat in De Vere Mansions, a
substantial Victorian building. An enormous window, with the immensity of London spread below it, provided a place for his desk. There was
a sitting-room, in addition to his study, and a "grand salon" which served
also as a library; there was a comfortable bedroom, a guest-room, servants' quarters. Henry had the enjoyable experience for the first time
in his life of wandering in shops, looking for old pieces of furniture
and decorating his rooms to his taste. For his sitting-room he chose
Whistlerian blues and yellows, and in his salon the "richest crimson." A
month after his installation he told William the place was "perfection."
Presently he engaged a man and his wife—their name was Smith—on
board-wages, for £10 a month. Presently also he was able to have a long-
wanted pet—a dachshund—upon which he bestowed the name of Tosca.

James was finally domesticated in London. He no longer needed to
dine out. He could receive friends and reciprocate hospitality. And he
was sufficiently removed from the hubbub of Piccadilly to relish the
tranquillity of his neighborhood, with the green of Kensington Gardens
at the end of the street. In the year following James's installation, Robert
Browning acquired the house at No. 22, a few doors down, on the opposite
side of the street. For the remainder of Browning's life Henry had as
neighbor an author who had once deeply influenced him, and whom he
now regarded with a mixture of respect for his genius and surprise at his
worldliness.

During the early months of his residence in De Vere Gardens, James
testified to his permanent establishment in the heart of Britain by writing an essay on London, as he had years before written essays on Rome
and Florence and Venice. It is perhaps the best of the series, certainly the
most saturated with the "sense of place." He wrote of the city of his
adoption as a frank "London-lover." When he stood on the bridge over the

Serpentine, he found that the towers of Westminster, seen from the shining stretch of Hyde Park water, were no less impressive than those of Notre-Dame rising from their island in the Seine. He expressed his profound feeling for the metropolis whose grandeur he knew and whose poverty and suffering had come to be "a part of the general vibration." Following *The Princess Casamassima* and his establishment in his own apartment, the essay was his way of saying that he had at last taken root in the particular spot which communicated "the greatest sense of life."

Soon after he made the decision to move, James learned, during Christmas week of 1885, that his "Voltaire in petticoats"—the sharp-tongued and witty Marian Hooper Adams—was dead. She had been depressed ever since her father's death less than a year before; and she had swallowed some of the chemicals she used in her photography, knowing full well how speedily they would do their work. Clover's acute and morbid animus toward life had in the end been turned against herself.

"I suppose you have heard the sad rumors (which appear founded) as to poor Clover Adams's self-destruction," James wrote to Lizzie Boott, who had known Clover almost as long as he had. "I'm afraid the event had everything that could make it bitter to poor Henry [Adams]. She succumbed to hereditary melancholia. What an end to that intensely lively Washington *salon.*"

Clover Adams was linked with many of the novelist's old associations: his long-dead cousin Minny Temple; the spring-time in Rome, when he had dined at the Adamses' with Elena Lowe; and not least with the life in Washington which he had so much relished and depicted in "Pandora." If the novelist wrote at this moment to the stricken Adams, his letter has not survived; but, writing to Godkin some weeks later of "poor Mrs. Adams" who "found, the other day, the solution of the knottiness of existence," he said: "I am more sorry for poor Henry than I can say—too sorry, almost, to think of him."

Politics and the Boudoir

Alice James, that winter of 1885–86, was having the best and most animated time of her residence in England. She had moved with Katharine Loring into small furnished lodgings in Bolton Row after vacating the house on the Heath. Her guests were not numerous. Sometimes Mr. Lowell, when he was in London; Fenimore appears to have been welcomed; Mrs. Kemble and Mrs. Humphry Ward were among the others. "My sister is doing exceedingly well and keeping an American salon," James told Godkin. "She is much better, and if she should get better yet, and remain here, she would become a great social success, beating the British female all round." She startled him, he said, "by the breadth of

her *aperçus* and her intimate knowledge of English public affairs." Alice
was absorbed above all in the Irish question; it provided a generous outlet
for her bile, diminished her self-absorption; and expressed the essential
Irishness of her nature.

"We are up to our necks in the Irish question," Henry wrote to Grace
Norton. There were three changes of government during 1885–86 while
The Princess Casamassima was being serialized. Parnell, at the height
of his fame, was exercising his balance of power in the House of Commons with all his political genius. Gladstone had become for James a
"dreary incubus" mouthing platitudes; and in the midst of this Sir
Charles Dilke, a monument of respectability, who had been spoken of as
a possible successor to Gladstone, was named as co-respondent in a divorce case brought by the husband of Mrs. Donald Crawford, a reckless
society belle.

The political mores of the Victorians fascinated Henry; and the un-
masking of their sexual mores gave him a little more freedom in his
tales. He could say now more casually that Victorian ladies were not
always virtuous, and that Victorian gentlemen sometimes behaved like
cads. Dilke had befriended James during his early days in London, and
the novelist told Miss Norton that the scandal had a certain "low interest"
for him, since he had the "sorry privilege" of being acquainted with most
of the people who were closely and remotely involved. One of them was
his old friend, Christina Rogerson, daughter of Mrs. Duncan Stewart, at
whose home he had had many pleasant lunches and dinners. She was
one of two women—the other was Mrs. Mark Pattison—who had been
publicly involved with Dilke while "he meanwhile was 'going on' with
poor little Mrs. Crawford, who is a kind of infant," wrote James to Miss
Norton. "For a man who has had such a passion for keeping up appearances and appealing to the said middle class, he has, in reality, been
strangely, incredibly reckless." The "whole thing," he concluded, was "a
theme for the novelist—or at least for *a* novelist."

When it came to the Irish question, James did not share his sister's
belligerency. Ireland was a country "revelling in odious forms of irresponsibility and license." When Miss Norton wrote to say she thought the
Irish a "great people" James retorted:

> I see no greatness, nor any kind of superiority in them. . . . They have been
> abominably treated in the past—but their wrongs appear to me, in our
> time, to have occupied the conscience of England only too much to the
> exclusion of other things.

Earlier however he had written to his friend Perry: "If I had nothing else
to do I think I should run over to Ireland: which may seem strange to you
on the part of one satiated in his youth with the Celtic genius. The reason

is that I should like to see a country in a state of revolution."

The closest he had come to seeing a revolutionary setting had been that day, long ago, in Paris when he visited the barricades and ruins of the Commune. But one day in February 1886, before he had moved to De Vere Gardens, returning from Bournemouth where he had gone to pay a visit to Stevenson, he found Piccadilly littered with broken glass, and the mansions at the corner of Bolton Street boarded up. It had been a day of noisy rioting in the heart of London by the very unemployed for whom he was speaking in *The Princess.* This was not revolution; it was however still another great fissure in the decorous life of the English. James regretted missing the riot. But Fenimore, then in London, had been abroad in the streets and could supply an eye-witness account. Armed with her American innocence, and her deafness, she had wandered into Piccadilly from lodgings in Seymour Street. She heard distant noises and saw a mob hurry along the edge of Green Park in the direction of Hyde Park Corner. There were still groups of men, eight or ten in a group, clearly of the laboring class, moving about, and it began to dawn on her that she was the only woman in sight. Traffic was at a standstill. Further along she encountered broken glass and smashed shop-fronts. Fenimore cautiously picked up a cab in a side-street and persuaded the driver to take her home by a circuitous route. During the next couple of days a dark fog settled over the city as if to blot out the destruction. Describing the scenes to William, Henry told him there was "immense destitution" everywhere. Nevertheless he felt that the usually orderly British populace would not riot again in the near future. The episode had sufficiently illustrated the "topical" character of his new novel.

By the spring of 1886 Alice had decided she would spend the summer in Leamington. The move was made at the end of May; Miss Loring escorted her to her new quarters and spent a month with her. Alice seemed quite content and urged Henry not to make the long journey to visit her—he was indeed to pay her only one visit during that summer.

In early July he dispatched the last installment of *The Princess:* the novel had again spilled over into additional chapters. With Alice away and "the interminable work" done, James was free to take a holiday. He decided however to remain in London. It was economical: in De Vere Gardens there was plenty of "high air" for the hot days, and as his rooms gradually acquired their furnishings he was pleased to enjoy the quiet and the luxury of being in his own home. By way of a holiday he paid a number of country visits, including one to Osterley Park, the home of Lord and Lady Jersey, where Lowell, who had returned to England for the summer, was a fellow-guest. The retired minister seemed to have all the social advantages of his former position and none of its responsibilities. In midsummer old Oliver Wendell Holmes arrived and struck James, who encountered him everywhere, as "rather superannuated and extinct (though he flickers up at moments)." James's summer was sufficiently strenuous. As well as visiting Stevenson in Bournemouth and Alice at Leamington, he was "supposed," he told Grace Norton,

> to be looking after Mrs. Jack Gardner, Mrs. Bronson, the Daniel Curtises and about thirty other Americans now in London, who all are holding by my coat-tails; to say nothing of polishing my periods for the purchase of my contemporaries and the admiration of posterity.

His Venetian friends had gathered in London at this moment because of an outbreak of cholera in their water-city. Mrs. Bronson installed herself in Hans Place with her big brown gondoliers and was living just as if life opposite the Salute had not been interrupted.

Henry complained to William that his two major novels of the past two years had exhausted him. But after six weeks of this kind of life— during which he read proofs of the book edition of *The Princess Casamassima*—he told his brother he felt quite refreshed. "Now I am not tired of work, but of no work, and am again taking up my pen."

A Lion in the Path

In August of 1886, when London was empty, there appeared on Henry's horizon the figure of Guy de Maupassant, "a lion in the path." James would say, in the essay he wrote on the Frenchman little more than a year later, that "those who have really taken the measure of the animal" would not make light of him. He took the personal measure of Maupassant during their few encounters that summer, in what was to be the French writer's only visit to England.

James remembered Flaubert's young disciple, present at the Sundays in the Faubourg St. Honoré: a sturdy young man of middle height, with a low forehead, bushy brown hair combed back, a big brown moustache and much talk of boating, swimming, Sundays on the Seine—and the conquest of women. Maupassant, however, was apparently not certain that James would remember him and came armed with a letter of introduction from Paul Bourget. The younger man, at the height of his fame, wanted to be shown English things; he wanted above all to meet English women.

Maupassant's letters to Count Joseph Primoli, who was his companion on this trip, suggest that the lion was a relentless woman-stalker. "On Monday we will have several agreeable ladies, it would seem—plus Henry James," he remarks in one missive. And in another, "I hope you'll be there on the 11th. I would like to present you that evening to a charming woman, at whose home you will find Bret Harte, the American writer, and also, I think, Henry James."

Primoli was a direct descendant of two of Napoleon's brothers: King Joseph Bonaparte of Spain and Lucien Bonaparte, Prince of Canino. His great-aunt was the Princess Mathilde. "An odd little member of the Bonaparte family," James called him. The woman was probably the American Blanche Roosevelt, who had been a hunter of literary lions from the days when, at seventeen, she had been told by Victor Hugo that she expressed "the beauty and genius of the new world." She had come to Europe to cultivate her voice—it was to her voice, probably, that Hugo had applied the word "genius"—and after studying with Pauline Viardot, had made her début at Covent Garden. Her vocal power was judged, however, insufficient for grand opera. She was now Blanche Roosevelt Tucker Macchetta, Marchesa d'Alligri. We find James writing to Francis Boott, during Maupassant's stay in London: "I have just escaped from the jaws of Blanche Roosevelt, who used to sing in opera—didn't she?—and who is now here married to a Milanese, trying to be literary and assaulting me (with compliments) on my productions."

Whatever Maupassant's wishes in the matter of women, James felt distinctly that the proper literary honors should be paid to a distinguished master of the short story. The French writer agreed to dine with the American novelist on 12 August. James's clubs were closed in the midsummer. He remembered however that a sufficiently good meal could be obtained at Greenwich, and this was always a charming relief in the monotony of a London August. He invited George Du Maurier and Edmund Gosse; Maupassant brought Primoli. The party assembled at 5:15 at Westminster Bridge and boarded one of the sixpenny steamers that plied the Thames. Maupassant was given a view of the great English river; once they came into sight of the Greenwich Observatory, with its two modest little brick towers, he got a sense of the general English charm of the place.

It is not recorded where they dined. But wherever it was, James in all probability concentrated on his principal guest. His verdict on the man—seen through his work—was published in the *Fortnightly Review* in 1888. The essay shows the extent to which James was fascinated by the variety of Maupassant's subjects and his extreme brevity. As for the substance of his tales, his admiration was qualified by what he deemed their excessive adherence to the senses and Maupassant's failure to take sufficient account of the reflective side of man. He was an active and independent observer of the human scene, quite unashamed of any of his faculties; but his emphasis on sex, James argued, was exaggerated. He concluded that the "carnal side of man appears the most characteristic if you look at it a great deal; and you look at it a great deal if you do not

look at the other, at the side by which he reacts against his own weaknesses, his defeats."

Discussing the "unpleasant" side of Maupassant's tales and his "pessimism," James pointed to the tendency for much of English fiction to
gloss over reality. "Does not Mr. Rider Haggard make even his African
carnage pleasant?" he remarked. The allusion belonged to the time of
Maupassant's visit. That week James had been reading Haggard's best-
selling tales with a sense of horror. He had finished *King Solomon's
Mines* and read half of *She*. He felt that "it isn't nice that anything so
vulgarly brutal should be the thing that succeeds most with the English
of today."

> Such perpetual killing and such perpetual ugliness! . . . They seem
> to me works in which our race and our age make a very vile figure—and
> they have unexpectedly depressed me.

Thus in his Maupassant essay James spoke with great clarity of both
sex and violence in fiction—not as one who wished to close his eyes to
them, but as one who felt that in the civilization in which the artist
worked it was possible to penetrate deeply into human experience without necessarily stressing the physical or carnal (as in Maupassant) or
glorifying the fantastic-violent (as in Haggard). For Maupassant, the
artist in James kept always a tender place. Again and again in his notebooks he invoked the example of the French writer, especially when he
wished to tell a tale in small compass. "Oh spirit of Maupassant, come
to my aid," he writes, or on another occasion, "*À la* Maupassant must be
my constant motto."

The Divided Self

The Princess Casamassima, which was published in book form on 22
October 1886, brings together certain of James's characteristic themes
into a subject unique in the canon of his writings—a "naturalist" subject
—the plight of the London working class and its nascent revolutionary
impulse. If his view of English poverty was largely from the "outside,"
it was none the less the view of a profoundly sentient artist. His pictures
of the miseries and affluence of London, drawn in the manner of Zola,
were the fruit of long nocturnal walks in the city's streets, and of hours
spent in pubs and probably at workers' meetings. Saturated with "high
life," thoroughly documented in his observation of the "low," James
achieved in *The Princess* what he had failed to do in *The Bostonians*—
a mastery over his materials and a dense and rich texture of "impression-
ism."

That the work should have had little appeal to its contemporary audience is understandable, although this baffled James at the time. He believed he had found an original theme, and one that was decidedly "topical." The novel conveyed, however, all too successfully, the uneasiness above and below the surface of Victorian London; it came uncomfortably close to the recent riots, the bombs, the dynamiters. The Victorians tended to look to fiction for comfort and amusement, not for the anxieties of their daily lives. In America the work fared somewhat better. Nevertheless it marked a departure from the comedies of international marriages and the adventures of American girls abroad which his readers expected of him.

Most of *The Princess* takes place on Sundays, or in the evenings, in the abbreviated hours of leisure allotted to the working classes. The settings are dark and drab save for those Sunday hours spent in parks and the streets. There is an artful chiaroscuro in the book, yet reality is never blurred. As long ago as his first year of residence in the British capital James described in one of his articles the funeral of an English radical agitator and the crowd that followed the hearse—"the London rabble, the metropolitan mob, men and women, boys and girls, the decent poor and the indecent." As he looked from a hansom cab, in which he was comfortably riding, he "seemed to be having a sort of panoramic view of the under side, the wrong side, of the London world." The "wrong" side—and also the "wronged" side: this was the world James chose to deal with in *The Princess Casamassima* and to link with the life of ease about which he had written in his earlier romantic works. Many years later, when he wished to describe the origin of this novel, he presented it in terms of his own experience of London. He had conceived of a hero, he said, "watching very much as I had watched." The little bookbinder Hyacinth Robinson possesses Henry's visual sense—it colors his whole mind. London doors had swung hospitably open for Henry James; for Hyacinth these doors—save in one instance—remain tightly closed. Hyacinth has a conflict between "the world of his work-a-day life and the world of his divination and envy." In a word he is an "outsider" and an "observant stranger"; he looks on from the slums, not from the comparative comfort of Bolton Street.

James made him a craftsman, like some of the radicals of the time, a bookbinder with an urge to be a writer. This Keats-like figure is handicapped by his origins and his poverty. Hyacinth is, in effect, another version of the artist *manqué* James had depicted ten years before in the ill-formed young sculptor Roderick Hudson. And the link with this early novel is established by the Princess Casamassima. She is the once-unfathomable—and still capricious—Christina Light, some ten years after the death of Roderick. Christina has shed her mystery; she is now a characteristic Jamesian beauty, a woman of the world bent on exercising her power over her environment and over men particularly.

Roderick had been unable to reconcile his devotion to his art and his passion for Christina. Unlike Roderick, Hyacinth is endowed with an elaborate and overpowering heredity: he is the illegitimate son of an English peer by a French seamstress, who had turned on her seducer and murdered him. "There was no peace for him between the two currents that flowed in his nature." He impulsively allies himself with revolutionary elements; he also finds himself "adopted" by the fine world of the Princess Christina, who is using revolution as a retreat from ennui. The moment comes when he joins the terrorists, receives a pistol, and is ordered to assassinate a Duke.

Between the time of his impulsive adherence to his cause and the arrival of the weapon he discovers that he has no sympathy with the revolutionaries. He has used an inheritance to visit Paris, where he experiences the *gloire* of history. Later he has an equally profound experience in Venice. In these cities of struggle and bloodshed Hyacinth the aristocrat rejects Hyacinth the revolutionary. "What was supreme in his mind today was not the idea of how the society that surrounded him should be destroyed; it was, much more, the sense of the wonderful, precious things it had produced, of the brilliant, impressive fabric it had raised."

Had Hyacinth been a hard-headed opportunist he would, when the pistol arrives, have backed away, pushed open some door of escape, perhaps gone to America. He is, however, as ruthless with himself as his revolutionary mentors are with society at large and with one another. To kill the Duke would in effect be like killing his father and re-enacting the crime of his mother. In the end he turns the pistol on himself, upon that organ which in his sensitive and romantic young body has suffered most —his heart.

Readers—and critics—coming upon *The Princess Casamassima* have assumed that James's attempt to treat a "social" subject must be factitious, or a product of libraries and "influences," and of a scant knowledge of working-class life and politics. In one respect James did follow the newspapers, which saw an "organized" conspiracy in sporadic acts of violence by malcontents and fanatics. For the rest, his achievement in this novel must be seen in his belief in the novelist's capacity to deduce the unknown from the known. He had known radicals from childhood; his father was a religious radical, who consorted with Fourierists and other Utopians; and James had known the dreams of a changed and new society peculiar to New England with its Brook Farm and its Fruitlands. Abroad he had met, in Turgenev's entourage, nihilists and emigré revolutionaries and had been an honored guest at the Nikolai Turgenevs' on the anniversary of the freeing of the serfs. And we have seen that where he had no knowledge, he sought it, as by visiting Millbank Prison.

The rest was his artist's imagination and his humanity; he felt deeply the plight of his characters, and the as yet undeveloped class struggle. He may have met Prince Kropotkin, the theorist of anarchism, at Turgenev's bedside in 1880. Kropotkin, arriving in London in 1881—the year in which the action of *The Princess Casamassima* is set—complained that the workers were torpid, unorganized, inarticulate. James's novel reflects the naïveté of the workers at that moment; it records the primitive beginnings of British Marxism, and shows the "general muddle" which then existed. The Independent Labour Party and the Fabian Society were being founded during the period of the writing of *The Princess.* And the book was appearing serially when the Haymarket bombing occurred in Chicago and the Piccadilly riots in London.

James had been "topical" indeed; more, he had been prescient. He understood better than the early Marxists the dynamics of power, the relationship between the idealism and the manipulation of people; and he characterized with complete accuracy the predicament of nineteenth-century liberalism which hated the violence of revolution though it wanted the lot of the workers changed. This was the very essence of Fabianism and the essence of Hyacinth's plight.

In the emigrés James embodied, with great affection and charm, the men he had known: their idealism, their sense of having outlived history, their chronic pain of exile. In the figure of the worker Paul Muniment, he foresaw the future union organizer and Labour politician, in his coolness, self-centeredness and capacity for opportunism. Hyacinth and Paul become bosom-friends; but the affection is really on the younger man's side. There is a touch of William James in Paul Muniment, who is concrete, practical, almost "scientific" in his working-class philosophy.

The personal statement in this novel, in the light of James's "orphaned" state on returning from America, lies near the surface. Feeling himself alone in the world after the death of his parents, clinging to art and civilization amid the unrest in British society, he seemed truly disinherited. His sense of being bereft of antecedents is emphasized by the number of fathers and mothers Henry allots to Hyacinth. There had been Hyacinth's original parents, Lord Frederick Purvis, murdered by his French mother, Florentine Vivier, whom Hyacinth had seen but once, in the Millbank infirmary. There is Mr. Vetch, the old violinist, and the dressmaker Miss Pynsent, who brought up the boy: both constitute a parental pair, advising, admonishing, helping. Miss Pynsent's savings, when she dies, enlarged by a gift from Mr. Vetch, enable Hyacinth to go to the Continent. And then he has acquired still another, a disciplined and resolute father, in the person of the anarchist Diedrich Hoffendahl, to whom the bookbinder has pledged absolute obedience. Hoffendahl in James's imagination belongs with the crippled elder Henry James—for Henry endows the anarchist with a maimed arm.

Hyacinth's parents and parent-figures demand a great deal; to obey the rule of the stern "father" Hoffendahl, he must kill the Duke and thereby re-enact his mother's deed of murder. He is divided between a ruthless though maimed father, upon whose behalf he is called to risk his own life, and the memory of a powerful Clytemnestra mother. His immediate parent-surrogates, Miss Pynsent and Mr. Vetch, want him to cut loose from his revolutionary commitment. His "parents" have put him in an impossible position. His brother—in the shape of that other revolutionary, Paul Muniment—is of no help. He has no one to turn to—and he feels betrayed.

Thus in *The Princess Casamassima,* a novel which seemed farthest removed from himself, James wrote out the melancholy experienced in the years following the death of his parents. He seems to have disposed of a primitive helplessness and outrage in *The Bostonians;* and in his novel of London and the anarchists he re-imagined his subterranean world of feeling in terms of his hero's revolt, despair and need for action. He siphoned off into his work a lugubrious state of mind, leaving himself freer and more possessed of his mature self. One solution had been his finding a new and more permanent home. And when the last chapters, written in De Vere Gardens, were done, his thoughts turned to Italy. He had been away for six years. It was time to go back.

BELLOSGUARDO

The Lonely Friends

On that February day of the riots in 1886 when Fenimore walked innocently through London's cluttered streets, she had been on her way to the Strand to purchase a trunk. She was returning to Italy. She had been living for three years in England writing her novel *East Angels,* but now she craved the south, a warm sun, Italy. In September of 1885 she had been at Leamington, working quietly and making excursions—to Stratford, Coventry, Kenilworth, Oxford. She had fallen "desperately in love" with Oxford.

In December 1885 she wrote from Leamington to John Hay. She had just heard from Henry James about the death of Clover Adams. "I should like to die without warning myself," she remarks. "But for those who are left it is very terrible." And she announces to Hay her plan to go to Italy in January.

It was March 1886 before she finally left, shortly after Henry James moved from Piccadilly to Kensington. When she reached Venice, late one evening in April, the air was as warm as July. Her gondola shot out into the Grand Canal; the moonlight gave the old houses and mouldy palaces phantasmal forms. "I think I felt compensated for all my years of toil, just in that half hour." Her destination, however, was Florence.

"I wonder, my dear Francis, whether you will do me rather a favour," Henry James wrote to his friend Boott on 25 May 1886.

My excellent friend Constance Fenimore Woolson is in Florence and I want to pay her your compliment and administer to her some social comfort. . . . She is a deaf and *méticuleuse* old maid—but she is also an excellent and sympathetic being. If Lizzie could take a look at her and attract her to the villa I should be very glad.

Boott called on Miss Woolson at her *pensione* on the Arno with some promptness, and she was made welcome at the Villa Castellani; in due course she rented rooms in one of its wings. Her grand-uncle James Fenimore Cooper had once lived on Bellosguardo, as had Hawthorne. The Castellani had figured in *Roderick Hudson* and in *The Portrait of a Lady,* so that Miss Woolson enjoyed a sense of communion with Bellosguardo's Jamesian past—and with the friends of her friend. Before she left Italy to spend the hot months in Switzerland, she had signed a year's lease for the adjoining fourteen-room Villa Brichieri-Colombi. And by the end of that summer the novelist was writing to Boott: "I have promised to go and see her after she is settled at Bellosguardo."

A great change had occurred on Bellosguardo that year, shortly before Fenimore's arrival. Lizzie Boott, after almost six years of indecision, had married Frank Duveneck. The union of this descendant of the New England Bootts and Lymans with the son of a German-American immigrant had been opposed by many of Lizzie's friends. To judge from James's comments, Francis Boott seems to have acquiesced in all his daughter's wishes. Nevertheless he was seventy-three, and for forty years he had had Lizzie's undivided company. Now a third figure had moved into the Castellani. Later, when he saw the three together, James distinctly felt that for the time at least, Boott had been "shunted," but was making the best of it. He was to recognize that in a sense Duveneck also could feel "shunted," for the ties binding father and daughter were strong.

James had followed Duveneck's career from the first with fascination: the painter seemed so ill-matched with the "admirably produced" Lizzie. When Duveneck had arrived from Munich he was like a big child suddenly transferred from the bucolic life of a farm into that of a palace. He had not been formed for the drawing-room. He had bought himself new clothes and tried his best to fit into the international "society" in which Lizzie moved. Now he had married the heiress (Boott's income was derived from certain profitable New England textile mills), and lived in a grand villa; he had to say good-bye to cherished evenings of idle drinking in *trattorie* and wine-cellars. James wrote to Lizzie urging her to make Duveneck "work—make him do himself justice." But to Henrietta Reubell he observed:

> His talent is great, though without delicacy, but I fear his indolence is greater still. Lizzie, however, will urge him forward and be an immense help to him. For him it is all gain—for her it is very brave.

Was it all gain for Duveneck? He could take a place in "society," show his works to great advantage, receive commissions for portraits. He had married not only his pupil but his patroness. The question was whether such a native talent, a figure as unbuttoned and as primitive as Duveneck, but with a distinct touch of mastery in his palette, could fit the tight clothes Lizzie wished him to wear; whether he could adapt himself to the manners of the American gentry abroad and overcome his relaxed, easygoing nature.

James saw, and was to see, a psychological situation on Bellosguardo which he would re-imagine and re-create years later in *The Golden Bowl,* although with quite different characters—that of a father and daughter so attached to one another that the husband of the daughter feels himself superfluous. He was also, in that novel, to deal with the problems encountered by the father as a consequence of his daughter's secession from their close life together. In the real-life situation James's greatest sympathy was with the elderly Boott; and during this period we find him writing to Francis more frequently, as if to console him.

After the publication of *The Princess Casamassima* James decided he would break his long stay in London by a month's trip to Italy, to keep his promise to visit Fenimore and to see Francis and the Boott-Duvenecks. He wrote to Lizzie that he looked forward to seeing her in her newly-married state, and to "many a delightful and long-deferred talk." And "our good Fenimore must also be worked in—but I shall be equal even to this. I am very glad you are nice to her, as she is a very good woman, with an immense power of devotion (to H. J.!)" Before he came away it was settled that, since Fenimore had her rooms at the Castellani until the new year, he would sublet the Brichieri-Colombi apartment from her during December. He would thus realize a very old dream of residing on Bellosguardo—and under circumstances that seemed to him very agreeable.

Alice, meanwhile, after spending the summer in Leamington had returned to London, where James found small rooms for her in Gloucester Road, round the corner from De Vere Gardens. He left on 3 December 1886, promising his sister he would return within a month. He bypassed Paris and on the 5th was in Milan, "drinking in the delicious sun"; on the 7th he was in Pisa; the next day he reached Bellosguardo. By this time he knew that he and Fenimore would be alone on their hilltop. The Duvenecks were in Florence proper. Lizzie was expecting a child.

The Two Villas

The Villa Brichieri-Colombi is a substantial rambling two-story building, the blank rear of which rises high from the wall on the winding road leading to the brow of Bellosguardo. Only the upper story is visible, so that one gets no sense of its large terrace, offering sweeping views on both sides. Two or three minutes further along the steep road is the small

piazza dominated by the yellow façade of the massive Villa Castellani,
which rises directly from the roadway. A heavy grille offers a glimpse of
its thick walls and noble quattrocento court. The Bootts lived in the north
wing. Fenimore, standing in the Boott garden and looking across a patch
of mountain terrain, could command a splendid view of the eminently
practical and solid Brichieri, with its faded yellowish walls and strong
tile roof.

James had never been in the Brichieri, though he knew its long
history. When he entered, he discovered that it gave him a view such as
he had never had from the Castellani. To the north he saw a panorama
of Florentine domes and towers, with Fiesole and the Apennines beyond;
on the Arno side, he looked upon a soft valley in its winter dress, and
across the western end the abrupt Carrara hills. When there was sun he
felt well out of London. But the season was wet and cold. Fenimore had
laid in a store of firewood and James built himself roaring fires. He
occupied a drawing-room and a bedroom on the ground floor, a section
of the villa which had been built before the discovery of America. Describing the view from his windows, he wrote to John Hay that

> they are not my windows—but those of our amiable and distinguished
> friend Miss Woolson. . . . She dwells at five minutes' distance, and I see
> her every day or two—indeed often dine with her. She has done a brave
> thing in settling herself here (for two or three years) in a somewhat
> mouldy Tuscan mansion—but I think it clear that she will get much
> enjoyment and profit from it *à la longue.* She will get quiet, sunny, spa-
> cious hours for work (a prospect, on her part, in which I take an interest,
> in view of the great merit and progress of her last book) and have Flor-
> ence in the hollow of her hand.

We know very little about the life these two writers led on their
Florentine hill-top. There are only mute witnesses. To commemorate his
tenancy James inscribed a copy of the three-volume *Bostonians* "To his
padrona Constance Fenimore Woolson, her faithful tenant and friend,
Henry James, Bellosguardo, December 1886." George Eliot's *Romola* in a
two-volume edition again has her name written out in full by James and
the copy is signed and dated "Florence January 1887." Perhaps the most
significant document is the one that was most public: an article James
consecrated to the work of Fenimore, in *Harper's Weekly* of 12 February
1887.

The occasion for the essay was the recent appearance of *East Angels,*
Fenimore's most ambitious novel. James's tribute was the expression of
a sincere admiration for the person as much as for the writer. And yet
a reader of the article today cannot but be puzzled that Henry should
have bestowed upon work as regional and as "magazineish" as hers the

discriminating literary taste which he had hitherto reserved for the leading European writers of fiction, or upon Americans such as Hawthorne
or Howells. Miss Woolson was on the whole a journeywoman of letters.
She lacked ease and the richer verbal imagination. Her work is minute
—and cluttered; she is an ardent devotee of "local color." James's essay
is graceful, yet labored. He tries very hard to say right and honorable
things, and it requires effort and ingenuity. The final impression can only
be that he is honoring Fenimore's dedication to letters less than her
devotion to himself. Again and again what he seizes upon in her novels
is her capacity for loyalty. In his discussion of *East Angels* he speaks of
her heroines as trying to "provide for the happiness of others (when they
adore them) even to their own injury."

The essay in *Harper's Weekly,* as well as dealing, one by one, with
Miss Woolson's various books, contains a biographical passage of considerable critical liveliness which James deleted when he transferred the
essay to his book *Partial Portraits.* In it he pretends to have gained his
facts from Miss Woolson's work. "It would not be hidden from a reader
of *Anne* and *East Angels* that the author is a native of New England, who
may have been transplanted to a part of the country open in some degree
to the imputation of being 'out west,' " and he goes on to tell "so far as my
knowledge goes" of her education in New York and her life in the south.
The sketch concludes with James's wondering whether she intends to
make use of her "personal familiarity with Rome, Florence, Venice and
other irrepressible cities." Has she, he asks (not without a touch of coy-
ness), "a story about Europe in reserve or does she propose to maintain
her distinguished independency?"

It is difficult, in the large scale of literary values, to read Miss Woolson's work and understand why the essay on her was included in *Partial
Portraits.* The volume contained James's major essay on Maupassant,
and the memorial to Turgenev; his celebrated essay on Emerson, two on
George Eliot, his obituary study of Trollope and papers on Daudet and
Stevenson. The title *Partial Portraits* has within it a quiet pun: the volume deals entirely with writers whom James had met and liked. The
"portraits" can be said to be "partial" because they are not complete; and
they are hardly impartial. On this ground Miss Woolson does belong in
the volume. The question can still be asked: why did James put her there
at all? He had paid no such homage to Howells. The things he chose to
say he could say sincerely enough. The article may have been largely an
act of kindness. No greater pen was to commemorate Miss Woolson's
work. Posterity would assign her a footnote in the regional fiction of
America. In the life of Henry James she occupied a larger place.

A Polyglot Society

Two weeks after James had settled beside his wood-fire in the Villa Brichieri, word was sent up from Florence that Lizzie Duveneck had given birth to a robust male child. To a household which already had a Frank Boott and a Frank Duveneck, there was now added a Frank Duveneck Jr. The baby would "apparently live and thrive—but Lizzie will plainly be much more of a wife than a mother." Duveneck would be a weight for Lizzie to carry for the rest of her life. James thought Boott's acceptance of him at every hour of the day to be "pathetic and heroic." He also remarked that the new grandfather seemed "old and shrivelled and laughs much less than in the old days."

Fenimore moved into her villa as planned at the beginning of 1887 and James descended into Florence, to the Hôtel du Sud on the Arno. Although the dusty *tramontana* and the cold were uncomfortable, he relished the winter sunshine. Florence, he told Miss Norton, had "never seemed to me, naturally and artistically, more delightful."

His winter now took an unexpected turn. Alice wrote complaining that her lodgings were too small, and James had the sudden inspiration to do for his sister what Fenimore had done for him. He offered her his flat, and his servants. Alice accepted with joy; it was like installing herself in "home" instead of lodgings. James assured her that she was conferring a favor on him; she gave his servants something to do. If all went well, he would now be able to spend the entire spring in Italy—where, he wrote to his brother, "I have been driving the pen steadily."

Whenever he drove the pen, he turned to society for relaxation. Suddenly he was dining out, paying calls, attending tea-parties. "I won't tell you their names, or more than that they were members of the queer, promiscuous, polyglot (most polyglot in the world) Florentine society." Thus to Grace Norton, in a letter in which he then devotes many pages to telling the names of all his hostesses and describing them. There was the "remarkably pleasant and sympathetic" Madame de Tchiatchev, an Englishwoman married to a Russian diplomat; there was the Marchesa Incontri, a Russian once married to Prince Galitzin, and subsequently to a Florentine, and now widowed: she went in for the arts, even wrote novels in English, under pen names, and James thought her on the whole "rather dangerous." Near Fiesole there was the Anglo-Italian Baroness Zunch, "a very kindly person." For old times' sake he called on the Countess Peruzzi, the former Edith Story, whom he had known at the Barberini. He became friendly with Dr. W. W. Baldwin, an American with a wide medical practice in Florence. In particular he liked the sculptor, Adolf Hildebrand, who lived in a former convent at the foot of Bellosguardo. Hildebrand had the "feeling of the Greeks and that of the early Tuscans too, by a strange combination." A vigorous Scotswoman, Janet Ross, the former Janet Duff-Gordon, invited him to stay at her pictur-esque villa of Castagnolo, where she played her guitar, sang Italian songs and talked a great deal. She was the original of some of Meredith's her-oines, and "a Bohemian with rules and accounts." To John Hay, Feni-more wrote: "I have never seen anyone to be so run-after as he was while in Florence."

James went often to 5 Via Garibaldi, where Vernon Lee, "the most intelligent person in the place," received daily from four to seven, and as often in the evening as people would come. He liked her clever half-brother, Eugene Lee-Hamilton, formerly attached to the British Embassy in Paris but now bedridden—or rather sofa-ridden—by paralysis. Vernon Lee attracted to the Via Garibaldi "all the world," discussed "all things in *any* language, and understands some, drives her pen, glares through her spectacles and keeps up her courage." "She has a *mind*—almost the only one in Florence," he told Gosse. It made James "a little less ashamed of the stupid English race." But Florentine society on the whole was "a vain agitation of particles." At the end of ten wintry weeks he called a halt and "escaped from the whirlpool of idiotic card-leaving of which Florentine existence is mainly composed."

Venice, where he arrived on 22 February, he found altogether strange in its dampness and cold, with watery sunshine and the gondo-liers beckoning as if it were midsummer. He had long promised Mrs. Bronson he would be her guest, in an apartment she used in a Giustiniani palace attached to the rear of Ca' Alvisi. Browning often stayed there for weeks at a time. His hostess provided a gondolier who served as a cook, and James, hugging a big plastered stove in which a fire crackled and roared, at first found the place adequate, if a bit gloomy.

But the "glutinous malodorous damp" in the *calles* and *campos* both-ered him, he developed a series of headaches, and his state of mind was not helped by a heavy snowfall in mid-March. He confined himself to the company of Mrs. Bronson, her daughter Edith, and the Daniel Curtises, whom he had met long before but whom he now saw for the first time in their splendid palace, the Barbaro, on the Canal near the Accademia. James's social life was cut short, however, by an acute attack of jaundice. He took to his bed and ran a slight temperature for sixteen days. Alice James wrote to William's wife: "He has an excellent doctor and an impas-sioned Gondolier taking care of him." Henry blamed his illness on the "insalubrious" rooms. "The apartment is not *simpatico*," he said.

Fenimore wrote offering him his rooms in the Villa Brichieri again, since she occupied only the upper apartment. Mrs. Bronson's gondolier all but wept at the Venice station when he saw James off; and his old

Roman acquaintance, Eugene Benson, the painter, whom he had seen in the Palazzo Capello on the Rio Marin (the palace which the novelist would use in "The Aspern Papers"), turned up to say good-bye. In Florence Dr. Baldwin met the Venice train and insisted on personally escorting his patient to the Brichieri. The "breezy Tuscan hilltop suits me better," the novelist wrote to his Venetian hostess. "I have the most majestic, and at the same time the most *allegro* quarters here—and the place is more beautiful than ever."

"The Aspern Papers"

Henry James's letters from his hill-top, during April and May of 1887, breathe an air of calm and release—a sense of enchantment—rarely to be found in his correspondence. After his illness and the winter mouldiness and decay of Venice he was living on Bellosguardo among devoted friends, canopied by blue sky and cradled in soft light. He could sit on the great wide terrace of the Brichieri or read and write in its pleasant rose-garden. His "vast and vaulted" rooms offered him coolness and a sense of space. Sometimes he had his meal out of doors, in the twilight, probably in the company of Fenimore. His illness was forgotten: he had privacy or sociability as he wished. He had discovered an Italian paradise.

In letter after letter he speaks of having "the most beautiful view in the world." To William he wrote, after describing his view, "I am working very well again." His pen seemed to take strength and power from the beauty around him and from his mode of life, and he entered upon one of the great productive periods of his career. In the interval between *The Princess Casamassima* and *The Tragic Muse*—what might be called his "Italian phase"—he wrote some eight or ten of his celebrated tales and a short novel.

He avoided this time the pitfalls of Florentine society, but descended into the city with curiosity to take part in one or two of the fêtes arranged that spring in celebration of the unveiling of the new façade of the Duomo. James fell sufficiently into the holiday spirit to don a crimson *lucco* and a black velvet headgear and attend the historical ball at the Palazzo Vecchio in the great Sal dei Cinquecento. "I wish you could have seen me," he wrote to Mrs. Kemble. "I was lovely."

Perhaps because Henry and Fenimore were living for the first time under the same roof, there is no allusion to her in any of his letters. He merely remarked casually to his friends that he had splendid rooms in a fine old place on Bellosguardo, with a superb view. The Boott-Duvenecks next door in the Castellani—for they had reoccupied their apartment—would see no special significance in his tenancy. To his more intimate friends James simply suggested that Fenimore was a "neigh-bour."

That was the impression of one visitor who came to the Brichieri and spent an evening with James and Fenimore. This was the novelist Rhoda Broughton, whom he had encountered in London drawing-rooms and liked, as he told Mrs. Kemble, "in spite of her roughness." She was Miss Woolson's age and possessed a fund of human wisdom and wit, and an ease and liberality in her Victorianism. It seems that she met Miss Wool-son on this occasion merely as an old and valued friend of James's who happened to be living on Bellosguardo.

Discreet as they were, we may speculate that the two saw each other frequently, even while spending their days in solitary pursuit of their individual work. Fenimore's cook Angelo served both of them. It is equally likely that even though they were under the same roof, they lived very much as they would have lived had they been housed apart. Given James's reticences and the fact that he seems to have attached at this time no particular significance to Fenimore's devotion to him (save that it called for kindness on his part); given Fenimore's personal shyness, for all her epistolary candor—the evidence would seem to point to a continu-ing "virtuous" attachment. There was not a little, in this, of James's powerful egotism: why shouldn't Fenimore like him? That this pleasant and *méticuleuse* old maid may have nourished fantasies of a closer tie does not seem to have occurred to him at this time. There was a kind of truce of affection between them. Perhaps the best evidence of this is to be found in "The Aspern Papers," the most brilliant of James's tales, which he began and all but completed at the Villa Brichieri.

The idea for the tale was in his notebook when he came to stay with Fenimore. One day in Florence he had paid a call on Vernon Lee and her half-brother and met the Countess Gamba, daughter of a Tuscan poet, who had married a nephew of Byron's last attachment, Teresa Guiccioli. She told James the Gambas had a great many Byron letters which were "shocking and unprintable," and James exclaimed to Grace Norton "she took upon herself to burn one of them up!" The Countess became angry when Lee-Hamilton told her that it was her duty to English literature to make the Byron documents public. "*Elle se fiche bien* of the English public," James wrote in his notebook.

After the Countess Gamba left, Lee-Hamilton told James an anecdote inspired by the talk of Byron. There had lived in Florence, to a ripe old age, Mary Jane Clairmont, or Claire Clairmont as she called herself, the cousin of Mary Shelley, who had been Byron's mistress and borne his daughter Allegra. For some time before her death she had a lodger, a Boston sea captain named Silsbee, whose passion was Shelley. Silsbee had long known that Claire Clairmont had in her possession certain

Shelley and Byron papers. He had made every effort to acquire these, and had finally obtained domicile in the very house in which they were kept. There were stories that he never ventured far from home lest Miss Clairmont should die while he was away. In one version of the anecdote he did, however, have to go to America and it was then—in 1879—that she died. Living with her was a Clairmont niece of about fifty, who had long nourished an admiration for the rugged Captain; when Silsbee rushed back to see whether he could obtain the papers, the niece said to him, "I will give you all the letters if you will marry me." Lee-Hamilton said that Silsbee was still running.

James wrote the bare anecdote in his notebook on 12 January 1887. What fascinated him was the thought of Claire Clairmont's having lived on into his time; he had often passed her door in the Via Romana. "Certainly there is a little subject there," James wrote in his notebook,

> the picture of the two faded, queer, poor, and discredited old English women—living on into a strange generation, in their musty corner of a foreign town—with these illustrious letters their most precious possession.

The interest would be in some price that the man would have to pay— a price the old woman, the survivor, would set upon the papers. The drama of the story would be his hesitations and his struggles, "for he really would give almost anything."

"The Aspern Papers" was an attempt by James to recapture "the visitable past"—that past which in any generation is still within the reach of its memory. His old woman lives beyond her time in a decaying Venetian palace clinging to precious letters written to her by a great American poet. The cat-and-mouse game which James devised between his Silsbee character and this lady provides the mounting tension: and in the tale James used his characteristic technique, that of making his hero his own historian—writing his story with such candor and ingenuousness that he discloses his own duplicity, his easy rationalizations and his failure to grasp the fact that, in his zeal for literary history, he is an invader of private lives. In this sense the tale is a moral fable for historians and biographers. It has dramatized, once and for all, their anomalous role: and it makes clear, as James's notes did not, on which side the novelist placed himself. He might have been shocked by the Countess Gamba's having burned a Byron letter; but in the tale all the Aspern papers are burned—sadistically we might say—"one by one." The strange tension of the story resides in its two climaxes: the first is that eerie moment when Juliana discovers the narrator trying to gain access to her desk and turns her blazing eyes upon him—those eyes which had been covered by a green shade—as she hisses out "passionately, furiously: 'Ah, you publishing scoundrel!' " This is the *coup de théâtre* of the story: the hero-worshipper, the lover of poetry, the gallant gentleman, is nothing but a common thief. But the splendid theatricality of this scene is surpassed by the third act, in which the middle-aged niece, after the death of Juliana, suggests to the narrator that the Aspern papers could be his if he became a member of the family: "If you were not a stranger . . . Anything that is mine would be yours." This is too much for the narrator. He had been ready to steal; he had even said playfully he would be willing to make love to the younger Miss Bordereau. Now all he can stammer is "Ah Miss Tita—ah Miss Tita—It wouldn't do, it wouldn't do!" He flees the palace, and as he is rowed through the canals by his gondolier, the vision of the bright decaying city fuses with his personal disaster. "I could not accept. I could not, for a bundle of tattered papers, marry a ridiculous, pathetic, provincial old woman." He may have trifled with her affections; he now understands this; yet he is not sufficiently without principle to achieve his ends at any cost.

Such was James's flight of fancy on the hill of Bellosguardo. What had begun as "a final scene of the rich dim Shelley drama played out in the very theater of our own 'modernity' " ended in a beautifully-wrought tale which was, above all, a defense of privacy and an exposure of the unfeeling egotist who exploits others' feelings for his own ends. If Venice in literature had been gilded by the poetry of Shakespeare, the satire of Jonson, the aesthetic of Ruskin, it was now immortally touched by the pen of American fiction, by Henry James. "The Aspern Papers" is a comedy raised to the level of an extraordinary time-vision, a superb play of the historic sense.

James had transferred the scene of the Silsbee anecdote from Florence to Venice; and in the writing of it he transferred—also from Florence to Venice—certain circumstances of his immediate life. On Bellosguardo he was occupying an apartment in an old Italian villa, next to a garden, even as the narrator of the tale moves into a suite of rooms in the old Venetian palace and is given the privilege of the garden. In both the actual villa and the imaginary palace there was living a middle-aged niece—a grand-niece, to be exact, in each case: of James Fenimore Cooper in the real life circumstances and of Juliana Bordereau in the fiction. Fenimore, too, reached back to a "visitable past" of American literature and to the very period in which Jeffrey Aspern flourished. James distinctly identified himself with his remote fictitious poet and expatriate, endowing him with the same qualities he possessed or wished to possess, the means "to be free and general and not at all afraid; to feel, understand and express everything"; and he said, in his late preface, that he had "*thought* New York as I projected him," thereby conferring on him the city of his own birth.

There are other such links between life and James's imagined tale. Not only is Tita actually a "grand-niece." Her name is that of a character, Tita Douglas, in Miss Woolson's most popular work, *Anne*. Much closer and more significant is the nature of the relationship between the narrator and Miss Tita. The course of this relationship in the story suggests markedly that James was—perhaps at this moment intuitively—beginning to feel uneasy about the familiar life into which he had been led with Miss Woolson. Of Fenimore's feelings James could never have been wholly in doubt; her letters written to him when he was in America had carried an implicit refrain, a demand for attention, affection, proximity. Miss Woolson would hardly suggest to James that he should pay more attention to her, and that they should find some more intimate ground of communion, or urge upon him as directly as Tita had urged the narrator, with the Aspern papers in her hands, the need for an alliance. Nevertheless she had been saying as much indirectly ever since their first Florentine meeting.

The narrator in "The Aspern Papers," fleeing the niece and the old palace, tells himself at the last that he had "unwittingly but none the less deplorably trifled." He repeats to himself, "I had not given her cause—distinctly I had not." He had been "as kind as possible, because I really liked her," and he asks himself, "since when had that become a crime where a woman of such an age and such an appearance was concerned?" This seems to have been James's logic as well. He treated Miss Woolson as a friendly and charming old maid for whom he had a feeling of kindness because she was devoted to him. And now, through the plate glass of his ego, he was beginning to feel that perhaps she nourished, on her side, more affectionate thoughts than he suspected.

In the tale the unfeeling cruelty of the narrator is softened somewhat by his dedicated artistic nature and his sense of the past. But his cruelty is manifest. His behavior has in it a kind of easy innocence and egotism that does not conceal the cad—an aesthetic cad perhaps; certainly not a sentient gentleman. In life James seems to have gained a glimmer of insight, or sensed the danger of incurring the same charge, or a charge even more serious—that of being so blinded by egotism that he might be held guilty of a total failure in awareness—he the novelist who, of all writers, could know and feel and understand.

Further, he had probably had an opportunity to see that Fenimore, with her innumerable trunks and possessions, was unable to throw anything away. And for all their promise to each other that they would destroy their correspondence, the thought may have occurred to him that somewhere among her accumulations were impulsive, scribbled pages he had dashed off to her, at various times, filled with his spontaneities of affection and irresponsibilities of feeling. "The Aspern Papers" may

have been a screen for deeper thoughts, nourished by the novelist, that
somewhere, in the Brichieri, there existed some Henry James papers that
needed burning, like the Aspern papers, one by one, to be sure that not
a scrap was left to posterity.

Palazzo Barbaro

Henry James bade farewell to Fenimore and Bellosguardo late in
May to spend ten days with the Curtises at the Barbaro in Venice. He
spoke of returning to Florence for another three weeks or a month,
"though not to Bellosguardo," but he lingered in Venice and his ten days
became a visit of five weeks, the longest private visit he had ever paid.
He was fond of the elegant palace, with its gothic windows, its marble
and frescoes, and its portraits of Doges; he particularly liked his quiet
cool rooms at the back, which looked into the shade of a court. He worked
in a room with a pompous Tiepolo ceiling (a copy: the original had been
sold) and walls of ancient pale-green damask, slightly shredded and
patched. The Curtises proved congenial hosts once James became accustomed to Daniel Curtis's puns and anecdotes, and Ariana Curtis's high
tone (she was the daughter of an English admiral) and social fastidiousness. They had left Boston in the wake of an episode of social comedy, in
which Daniel Curtis had tweaked the nose of a fellow-aristocrat and
been jailed briefly for assault and battery. They had purchased the Barbaro in 1885 and become permanent Venetian-Bostonians. With their
great ménage—servants, gondoliers, visiting friends, daily excursions to
the Lido—they provided James with access to a sociable world, from
which he could withdraw to complete privacy in his princely apartment.
Venetian society proved less strenuous than Florentine, more indigenous. One of its most remarkable members was the Countess Pisani,
partly English, whose father had been the doctor who bled Byron to death
at Missolonghi. Her mother had been a French odalisque out of the
harem of the Grand Turk. The late Count Pisani, "a descendant of all the
Doges," had married her for her beauty thirty-five years before.
Staying with the Countess Pisani was May Marcy McClellan, daughter of the Civil War general, whom James had met in Florence. She had
created a stir the previous winter in Venetian circles by writing a gossipy
letter to an American newspaper about the society which had entertained her. James was to say later that "no power on earth would induce
me to designate . . . the recording, slobbering sheet" in which Miss
McClellan's effusion appeared; it is, however, identified in his notebooks.
By modern standards the letter that was published, in all its dull prolixity
and bad English, in the New York *World* of 14 November 1886 is sufficiently mild: in its own day it must have been a scandalous repayment

of various kindnesses. Everyone the young lady met "rejoiced in some sort of a handle to his or her name." The women's jewels—and she named the women—were "something gorgeous." The Italian men were handsomer than the women and "one countess who is considered something quite lovely would not attract attention in a New York ballroom." Such had been her aimless colloquial gossip; nevertheless, the Countess Pisani "has that foolish virgin staying with her." James had described his talk with the McClellans, mother and daughter, in Florence that winter to his friend Mrs. Bronson, who as an American-Venetian had been profoundly shocked by the girl's betrayal of her well-meaning friends. Miss McClellan had spoken "with a certain resentment, as if she herself had been wronged," the novelist told Mrs. Bronson. Both mother and daughter were concerned that if they returned to Venice they might find "every back turned to them." James added: "Good heavens, what a superfluous product is the smart, forward, over-encouraged, thinking-she-can-write-and-that-her-writing-has-any-business-to-exist American girl! Basta!" He also wrote: "I should like to write a story about the business, as a pendant to 'Daisy Miller,' but I won't, to deepen the complication."

That autumn in London, however, he changed his mind. Pondering "the strange *typicality* of the whole thing," he derived from this Venetian episode *The Reverberator,* a short novel published in 1888, which dealt with another facet of the activities of "publishing scoundrels"; it became a journalistic pendant to the literary "Aspern Papers."

In mid-June Paul Bourget arrived in Venice, and during their many talks offered James still another theme. He told him of the suicide of a young friend, in Milan. The girl had discovered, he believed, that her mother had lovers, and this had weighed upon her. He also believed that she had tried to escape into a marriage—that is, she had pressed an attentive young man to declare his intentions, and when it became clear that his interest had been friendly but not marital, the girl had felt ashamed. It later developed that much of this was Bourget's fancy. James responded, however, to this new version of a woman proposing marriage to a man; he turned the material into an Anglo-American picture—a story of a puritanical young girl, horrified by her sister's immorality, who asks a young American to marry her. Before he left Venice, he was at work on this tale, to which he gave the title "A London Life."

At the beginning of July James reluctantly brought his long Italian stay to an end. He had a final dinner with Mrs. Bronson and her daughter, in their gondola, on the glassy lagoon,

> in the pink sunset, with the Chioggia boats floating by like familiar little phantom ships, red and yellow and green—the impression of that enchanting hour has never left me.

He had had his fill of Italian impressions—and Italian experience. He even thought again that he might take some little apartment in Venice, create a permanent Italian *pied-à-terre* for himself, so enamored had he become of the life of the place. However he decided not to force the issue; he would let time decide. James journeyed from Venice to Vicenza, Mantua, Cremona, Brescia, and Bergamo. Mantua was dreary and pestilential; the fleas drove him away. But he enjoyed the beefsteaks of Brescia. On 6 July he joined Mrs. Kemble at Stresa and spent several days with her. He found her an "extinct volcano," a shadow of her former self. Then he crossed into Switzerland, over the Simplon, on foot, as he had done in the days of his youth, "a rapture of wild flowers and mountain streams—but it was over in a flash." After that he went straight to London. On 22 July he was back at De Vere Gardens (Alice was again at Leamington), his Italian holiday—with the great release of creative energy it had given him—at an end.

It had given him much more: he had never had such a sense of personal freedom. Describing his visit to Mrs. Kemble, he told Grace Norton that it was rather "a melancholy mistake, in this uncertain life of ours, to have founded oneself on so many rigidities and rules—so many siftings and sortings." And then he suddenly exclaimed—as if he were addressing his correspondent, and perhaps all New England: "Let us be flexible, dear Grace; let us be flexible! And even if we don't reach the sun we shall at least have been up in a balloon."

The Compromises of Life

He had, in a manner, been up in a balloon in the immensities of the Italian sky, above the beauties of the past. He had undergone the last stages of an almost imperceptible evolution begun years before—a process which had converted this hard-working, pleasure-loving, sentient American from an old Calvinistic inheritance of codes and rigidities into a more relaxed (though still laborious) American-European. From his new altitude he had discovered new meanings in the word *flexible.* The little tragi-comedies of man engaged in his civilized round which had absorbed him seemed now less "final" than he had ever before believed. Had it been worthwhile for Roderick Hudson to tear his passion to tatters and fall over a Swiss cliff, because of an unfathomable woman? Might not his creator have offered him certain alternatives? He had pictured in his art the inflexible character of society—accurately enough—but he had also written as if everything were irreversible. He had frustrated Newman and doomed Daisy, and adhered (critically) to the *status quo,* when life seemed constantly to be built on shifting sands. In the tales written during this period, after his eight months in Italy, it seemed as if James had recognized that individuals could, on occasion, defy fate—and society—and survive. He had left London with the newspapers screaming about Lady Colin Campbell's divorce suit, in which four corespondents were named, and he had predicted to Norton that the case would "besmirch exceedingly the already very damaged prestige of the English upper classes." He returned to find that nothing had been besmirched. The perishable newspapers had had their little day, and the upper classes were as indestructible—and as unbesmirched—as ever.

James had finally abandoned his American innocence. He was aware that what he had pictured as "corrupt old Europe" represented a splendid façade of civilization, behind which existed all manner of things Americans might regard as evil—but that this façade also concealed a life of liberty; and that it offered a veil of codes and standards with which to protect "the private life." To have a private life, to be impervious to others' judgments and others' meddlings, was to have freedom: and this is what James had been discovering ever since he left Quincy Street in 1875.

The moral substance of his work now underwent a change. The evil in "The Aspern Papers" lay not in Juliana's ancient indiscretions or Jeffrey Aspern's "love-life." It lay in the invasion of privacy, the failure to enter into human feeling. In "A London Life" Henry set out to describe the sense of shock experienced by Laura, his American innocent, over her sister Selina's adulteries. He depicted a girl too rigid and meddlesome to recognize that in this world adulteries do occur, people act irresponsibly, but this is their private affair and no one else's. Moreover, the world doesn't come to an end.

Another morbid young woman appears in a tale called "Two Countries" in *Harper's,* later retitled "The Modern Warning." Agatha Grice, a thoughtful and bright American girl, marries a witty and observant Briton, Sir Rufus Chasemore. She had misgivings for he is political and critical, very critical, of the United States. Later he plans a book, a "modern warning" against the contamination of Britain by the American democracy. Agatha's brother, Macarthy Grice, on his side has a blazing hatred for all Britons, their language, manners and institutions. Henry's own divided feelings and his life between the two countries are partly traced; but he is writing also about an attachment between a brother and a sister—and his sister, Alice, reading the tale, told William, "I feel as if I were the heroine." James was constantly exposed to Alice's pro-Irish and anti-British feelings which he could not share. Agatha's divided loyalties between husband and brother, America and England, lead (as James planned in his notebook) to "depression, melancholy, remorse and shame." Like Clover Hooper, Henry Adams's wife, who was also caustic about the British, Agatha finally chooses an escape; Clover drank her photo chemicals, Agatha finds a similar poison. Alice wrote William this tale might seem *"unnatural"* to "the bourgeois." She was referring to more than the melodrama.

James seems to have had some crisis of feeling about his expatriation and the love-hate between his own and his adopted country. As he surveyed the long road he had traveled since "Daisy Miller" he found he was ceasing to believe that Americans were composed of finer moral fiber than the Europeans. He now discerned in their innocence a claustrophobic ignorance. Worse still, a need to impose it on others. He had also come to see that perhaps the faults and virtues of the Americans and the English were simply "different chapters of the same general subject." Writing a long and reflective letter to William late in 1888, when he had fully assimilated his experience of the previous year, he said that he was "deadly weary of the whole 'international' state of mind":

> I can't look at the English and American world, or feel about them, any more, save as a big Anglo-Saxon total, destined to such an amount of melting together that an insistence on their differences becomes more and more idle and pedantic.

He himself, he went on to say, aspired to write

> in such a way that it would be impossible to an outsider to say whether I am, at a given moment, an American writing about England or an Englishman writing about America . . . so far from being ashamed of such an ambiguity I should be exceedingly proud of it, for it would be highly civilized.

In the same letter, Henry alluded to his inability to do much reading, since "I produce a great deal." Energetic "producer" though he always was, James had never been as productive as during his months in Italy and immediately after in London. He had written "The Aspern Papers," "A London Life," and *The Reverberator,* all in less than a year—and in the midst of other writings as well. The tales were held back by the editors for a number of reasons, among them that the magazines were now using illustrations on a large scale, and certain of James's stories had to wait their turn on drawing-tables. They then appeared simultaneously, so that for the better part of the following year, 1888, Henry James dominated the magazines as never before: "Louisa Pallant" came out in February 1888 and "The Modern Warning" in June in *Harper's Magazine; The Reverberator* ran in *Macmillan's* from February to April, although written after "The Aspern Papers," which emerged in the *Atlantic Monthly* from March to May; "A London Life" ran in *Scribner's* from June to September and "The Lesson of the Master" appeared in two installments during the midsummer of 1888 in the *Universal Review.*

Howells likened James to a painter who had saved up many canvases and was suddenly holding an art exhibition. "One turned," he wrote in his monthly *Harper's* column, "from one masterpiece to another, making his comparisons and delighted to find that the stories helped rather than hurt one another and that their accidental massing enhanced his pleasure in them." Howells felt James had entered a new phase.

The Reverberator, his light comedy, set in Paris but based on the story of Miss McClellan's adventures in Venetian society, has all the perfection of his "Daisy Miller" period and much greater maturity. The significant figure in this little Franco-American drama is George Flack,

Paris correspondent of an American society newspaper called "The Reverberator." His conception of news is the ferreting out of society gossip
—often with the help of society. In Flack James had his vision of the
future "media"; and he saw that America would develop its own peculiar
corruptions. When the journalist writes his scandalmongering letter and
endangers Francie Dosson's marriage into French society, her Bostonian
father expresses surprise at all the fuss: "If these people had done bad
things they ought to be ashamed of themselves," he reflects, "and if they
hadn't done them there was no need of making such a rumpus about
other people knowing." James had seen the handwriting on the wall: he
forecast the evolution of a press which would, under the guise of "names
make news," create capital of people's privacy, weaken the laws of libel,
and increasingly turn themselves into journals of gossip rather than of
political and national intelligence.

In "The Lesson of the Master," which James wrote when he had
returned to De Vere Gardens, a great novelist reads a lecture to the young
would-be writer: marriage, dressing one's wife, educating one's children,
taking one's place in the world, are costly matters. The artist must
choose. He can either marry and cheapen his art—and be a success—or
take a celibate course, and produce the masterpieces which the world
will not understand and which alone justify dedication and self-denial.
Success in itself, he suggests, is a cheapening process. Re-examining his
old high standards and their relation to the facts of existence, James
pondered the extent to which an artist must be prepared to make his
compromises with the market-place; and whether life itself wasn't a
"sell." If people could sin and get away with it in society, an artist could
be a "success"—or even a humbug—and get away with it in art. The
question was now formulating itself in Henry's consciousness in some
such fashion, and it would be written out in a long novel, for which he
already had the title: *The Tragic Muse.*

The unconscious promptings, the inner messages, in this cluster of
stories from his time on Bellosguardo, with their delicate ironies and
niceties of observation, seem to arise out of James's personal entangle-
ments. He had lived very privately behind the thick walls of the Brichieri
close to Miss Woolson—and when in London had he been so regularly in
a woman's company? He seemed preoccupied in his tales with the pitfalls of too close a friendship or flirtation with the opposite sex, the
danger of being asked to commit himself further, the double-bind of his
internationalism and the invasion of privacy by gossip-mongers and
newspapers. His old and imperious defense of his privacy, his celibacy,
his distancings from women and his innocence of love-making, indeed
his substitute of manners and social formalities for passion, are clearly
present. At times the tales themselves seem to be carrying private mes-

sages to certain readers. Fenimore, at any rate, reading "The Lesson of the Master" would know exactly where this most eligible bachelor of literary London stood on the subject of marriage.

Elizabeth Duveneck

On 31 March 1888 Henry James went to pay a visit to the Cyril Flowers, at Aston Clinton in Tring Park. He came to this Easter week-end party and this luxurious house with a heavy heart. Lizzie Boott had died that week in Paris, where she had been spending the winter with her husband and child. Only a short while before she had written James a letter filled with her busy life and news of her baby: she had taken up water-colors, she said—they could be combined more easily than oils with the duties of maternity. Then suddenly she had pneumonia. On 22 March she died, at forty-two, leaving her aged father, her husband and her fifteen-month-old child.

Boott had sent the barest details. James responded, saying he was prepared to come at once to Paris if he could be of help. He had received no reply; and he turned now, writing in the midst of the chatter and laughter in the big house at Aston Clinton, to his old Parisian friend, Etta Reubell, for news: "Lizzie's sudden death was an unspeakable shock to me—and I scarcely *see* it, scarcely believe in it yet." When would Etta see Boott? Would she tell Henry what impression he made on her? What did he intend to do? What was the relation between him and Duveneck? "What a strange fate—to have lived long enough simply to tie those two men, with nothing in common, together by that miserable infant and then vanish into space, leaving them face to face!"

Lizzie Boott was the first important loss James had experienced since Minny Temple and his brother Wilky in the ranks of his own generation. He knew how deep the attachment had been and how much the Bootts and their Florentine villa had become a part of his life. "The quiet, gentle, loveable, cultivated, laborious lady!" he echoed himself, writing to Mrs. Curtis. "Poor Boott—poor Boott—is all I can say!" When he returned to De Vere Gardens from his week-end he found a letter from Francis, and replied to it with deep tenderness. Boott had apparently written that Lizzie had undertaken an effort beyond her strength. In this Henry acquiesced. "She staggered under it and was broken down by it," he wrote to Lizzie's father—"I mean," he went on, "on account of the terrible *specific gravity* of the mass she had proposed to herself to float and carry." The weight was no fault of Duveneck's—"simply the stuff he is made of."

"What *clumsy* situations does fate bring about, and with what an absence of style does the world appear to be ruled!" he exclaimed to Mrs.

Curtis. He was thinking of Boott and Duveneck at the Villa Castellani, strange companions, held together by the child. Twice in Boott's long life had such a cruel situation come about. Lizzie had been left to him when his wife died; now Lizzie was gone, leaving her child on his hands, for Duveneck, with his artistic-bohemian way of life, was hardly the one to rear the boy.

Francis Boott and Frank Duveneck brought Lizzie back to Italy. There, towards the end of April, she was committed to the Florentine earth, in the Allori Cemetery beyond the Roman gate. Fenimore was present and described the scene for Henry: Boott calm and Duveneck sobbing. Duveneck's "demeanour has won all hearts here," James's friend wrote. For a while the two remained in the villa, the old man and the young, and in time Francis Boott reversed the journey he had made almost half a century before. He took Frank Duveneck Jr. to Boston, to rear him there among Lyman relatives, and there to pass the rest of his days.

Duveneck the artist had been almost pathetically attached to his wife: she was a grand lady, whom he had had the good fortune to marry. He had painted her portrait that winter in Paris dressed for the street—wearing her hat back on her head, so that her dark parted hair is revealed; her large candid eyes look affectionately out of the canvas. He imagined her also as a Knight's Lady in death, recumbent with her hands folded on her breast, amid flowing drapery, on the tomb he designed and sculpted himself in shining bronze, which time would coat and soften into a grey-green ghostliness. Duveneck eventually returned to Cincinnati, where he taught at the Academy of Fine Arts for many years. Sargent had spoken of him as "the greatest talent of the brush of this generation"; he remained a talent, eventually in decline, as James predicted.

This was the end of the Bellosguardo chapters of James's life. More than a year after Lizzie's death, Alice James wrote in her journal: "Henry says he misses Lizzie Duveneck more and more."

In Geneva

In March 1888, James agreed to write a serial for the *Atlantic Monthly* to run through 1889. He announced that the heroine of *The Tragic Muse* would be "an actress. But there will be much more richness, and the scene will be in London, like the *Princess*—though in a very different MONDE: considerably the 'Aesthetic.' There you are. It won't be improper, strange to say, considering the elements."

By September he had dispatched the first two installments of the *Muse* to Aldrich. Early in October he crossed to the Continent, bypassed Paris and went straight to Geneva. He took rooms in the old Hôtel de l'Écu, those which had been occupied by his parents during the family's stay in Geneva in 1859–60. "I am sitting in our old family *salon* in this place," he wrote to his brother on 29 October,

> in sociable converse with family ghosts—Father and Mother and Aunt Kate and our juvenile selves. I become conscious, suddenly, . . . that I wanted very much to get away from the stale, dingy London, which I had not quitted, to speak of, for fifteen months, and notably not all summer.

Alice had assured him she could "perfectly dispense for a few weeks with my presence on English soil."

On occasion Henry—even at forty-five—felt that he had to explain his movements to William. It was not however a matter of being away from Alice. He had some need to justify his presence in Geneva at this moment for quite another reason, one that he did not mention to his brother. But his sister did, writing on 4 November, "Henry is somewhere on the Continent flirting with Constance." He was indeed keeping a scheduled rendezvous with Fenimore.

In his tale of "Louisa Pallant," written during his Italian phase, Henry had described how the elderly narrator and the love-smitten youth, on their way to Baveno in the Italian lakes to see the heroine, found it more decorous to stop at Stresa "at about a mile distance": "nothing would be easier than to go and come between the two points." The only record of the Geneva rendezvous is in a letter from James to Francis Boott. "You have been a daily theme of conversation with me for the past ten days, with Fenimore," he wrote.

> That excellent and obliging woman is plying her pen hard on the other side of the lake and I am doing the same on this one. Our hotels are a mile apart, but we meet in the evening, and when we meet she tells me, even at the risk of repetition to which I am far from objecting, the story of your last months, weeks, days, hours, etc. at Bellosguardo.

James's letters written at this time—to William, to Henrietta Reubell, to Mrs. Curtis—create the picture of a writer who has fled society and is enjoying a solitary three weeks, contemplating Mont Blanc and taking quiet walks to observe the "admirable blue gush of the Rhône," as he had done in his sixteenth year. Geneva seemed both duller and smarter than in 1859. All the old smells and tastes were present. But what his relatives and friends were not told—save Boott—was that his stay was less solitary than it seemed.

Again in a letter to Boott, three months later, 18 January 1889, James writes: "On leaving Geneva I parted with Fenimore—she went back to Bellosguardo and I went (through the Mont Cénis) to Genoa and the Riviera. I spent two or three weeks at the delicious Monte Carlo and the month of December in Paris." Miss Woolson's copy of the two-volume edition of "The Aspern Papers" is inscribed with her name "from the author, Geneva, October 16th, 1888."

In Monte Carlo James stayed at the Hôtel des Anglais; and before that was briefly at Turin as well as Genoa—"such a little whiff, or sniff, of Italy." In Paris he put up at the Grand Hotel, and on 18 December seems to have been at the salon of Madame Straus (Geneviève Halévy), thus most certainly encountering, if not the young Proust himself, some of his future characters. He saw Bourget, and Miss Reubell. And his notebook records that he visited the Théâtre Français backstage and had a chat with the *comédienne* Julia Bartet in her *loge,* an experience re-created in some detail in *The Tragic Muse.* He was back in London in time for Christmas.

The Expense of Freedom

He had captured in Italy in 1887 a new sense of freedom—that freedom which the artist in a pressing, interfering, demanding world can seldom attain. Now it seemed to him that the time had come to embody the conflict of "art and 'the world' " in a novel which he had planned as far back as the winter of 1886 when he was moving into De Vere Gardens. He had first thought of a short work, a study of the nature of an actress, her egotism, her perseverance, her image as a creature for whom reality is illusion and illusion reality. In the summer of 1887 he told Grace Norton he was beginning *The Tragic Muse,* that it would be half as long as *The Princess,* "thank God!" and that it would not be serialized. But by early 1888 the design had grown much more complicated. He had committed it to the *Atlantic;* in spite of his "thank God!" it became his longest serial, running to seventeen installments, from January 1889 to May 1890.

What had happened to enlarge the work was his desire to present an antithetical case to that of the actress enslaved by the conditions of the theater. This may very well have offered itself to him in the spectacle of the Cyril Flowers, in whose home he had been a visitor. Flower, an amateur of the arts—he had even made friends across the Atlantic with Walt Whitman—had married a Rothschild wife who cherished political rather than artistic power; and Flower found himself a Member of Parliament, and in later years was elevated to the peerage. At the Flowers' James encountered Gladstone again; his various visits to Lord Rosebery and *his* Rothschild wife also furnished him with material. And he was always meeting political figures and statesmen at his clubs.

Thus James found in his path sufficient examples to yield him a "political case" as a parallel to his "theatrical case." Of the theater he had had ample observation during his European career: he knew intimately the playhouses of England and France and to some extent of Italy. At the time that he was sketching out the *Muse* he had renewed his acquaintance with Coquelin, who came to lunch at De Vere Gardens. Henry delighted in the great actor's art and found his personality "insupportable." Struck once again by the "self-exhibitionistic" character of stage-folk, James felt he had all the materials at hand for his novel and he began it with excitement and interest.

The book is a large cheerful mural of English life and art, filled with witty talk; parts of it read as if James were writing one of his critical papers rather than a piece of fiction. It incorporates a picture of the English stage, the Parisian theater, the high bohemia of London on the very edge of the nineties. With this we are given a picture of solid English upper-class Philistinism, in the struggle of a young man to resist being pushed into Parliament by his family and by the woman he thinks he loves, when he would much rather be a painter.

James had never undertaken a work so crowded with characters and so split in theme. He was, in reality, trying to put together two novels in one and sometimes the seam shows. The four central characters in the book serve to illustrate the problem at the heart of *The Tragic Muse.*

First there is James's "theatrical case": Miriam Rooth, a half-Jewish, half-English girl who wants to be an actress, and who dedicates herself to this goal with the ferocity of her egotism and the discipline of her art. Nowhere in all his work has the novelist given us a more carefully documented picture of the evolution of a certain type of performing artist, and of an artist-nature, and of its implacable selfishness and self-assurance.

His "political case" is drawn with a less firm hand: but the ingredients are familiar to him—Nick Dormer's powerful mother, his deathbed promise to his father to keep the family name in Parliament (he is again a second son who must assume the responsibilities of the firstborn), the advantageous marriage Nick is expected to make with Julia Dallow, who aspires to Downing Street. Everyone sees Nicholas Dormer, not as he is —a quiet thoughtful artistic young man—but as they want him to be.

The opposite to Nick Dormer is Peter Sherringham, Julia Dallow's brother and a successful diplomat. His passion is the theater; it is he who "discovers" Miriam Rooth and helps her take her first steps towards the stage. He has not allowed for his falling in love with her. Nevertheless an actress will not do as an ambassadress, and when Sherringham asks Miriam to marry him and give up her career, Miriam and Nick Dormer face the same predicament. Sherringham discovers before the novel is over that there is no halfway road to art; Dormer throws over the chance to marry Julia, rejects an inheritance, and resigns his seat in Parliament. Miriam marries an actor, rather than the diplomat, and at the end of the book is well on her way to becoming a figure on the stage.

Nick Dormer's decision is more difficult than Miriam's, for it means not only throwing over wealth, public office, status, society; it means finding himself face to face with the trials and joys of his art. The actress, by the very circumstances of the interpretative art, is involved in a gregarious existence. The painter—or the writer—is alone with his canvas —or his blank sheets of paper. Nick, in his studio, closes the door as Miriam leaves and taking up his palette rubs it with a dirty cloth.

> The little room . . . looked woefully cold and gray and mean. It was lonely, and yet it peopled with unfriendly shadows (so thick he saw them gathering in winter twilights to come) the duller conditions, the longer patiences, the less immediate and less personal joys. His late beginning was there, and his wasted youth, the mistakes that would still bring forth children after their image, the sedentary solitude, the clumsy obscurity, the poor explanations, the foolishness that he foresaw in having to ask people to wait, and wait longer, and wait again, for a fruition which, to their sense at least, would be an anti-climax.

The fourth character in the sprawling and uneven novel into which James put such high skill, Gabriel Nash, is a "Gabriel" hardly angelic, but much addicted to trumpeting. And he is an aesthete whose performances tend to be those of word rather than act. James intended some of the trumpetings to sound loudly his own beliefs. Gabriel speaks with all the Jamesian warmth for sentience and high ideals: "Where there's anything to feel I try to be there." His business is "the spectacle of the world." He "talks" Henry James; and in appearance he even resembles his creator. But he is far from being the novelist. He belongs rather with those characters in James's fiction whose sole existence depends on their having an audience. We know the actual model for Nash. James kept his promise to himself of his first Venetian days in 1881 and used the image of Herbert Pratt, who had talked so well and been consistently anecdotal during James's stay in the water-city.

That such a character's portrait should start to fade, and become ghostly, after the manner of portraits in some of Hawthorne's tales, is understandable. It is the fate of most aesthetes and critics who talk but never *do.* Nick says to Nash that he wishes "very much you had more to show"—but all Nash can show are his trumpetings. He is much more the Count de Montesquiou than Oscar Wilde or Whistler—but he is also Henry James's father, who spent his life in talk.

Re-reading *The Tragic Muse* many years later, James felt that he had not succeeded with his young politician-artist Nick Dormer. The better part of him is "locked away from us." This is true. And it is strange. For it is Nick who carries the burden of what James most deeply felt: he enunciates the message of the artist and the solitary refuge of his art. But, paradoxically, James failed to identify himself with this character. He is more identified with Peter Sherringham, Nick's "double," who doesn't want to make the supreme sacrifice. James's own worldliness—his old Benvolio self—stands between him and Nick. The personal statement in this novel is that of the James who on the one hand was strongly pleasure-loving and who without his vaulting ambition and genius might have been an easy-going Herbert Pratt, an aesthetic Gabriel Nash. He had not yet reconciled himself to the loneliness of which he wrote: he wished, like Sherringham, to eat his cake and have it. Sherringham did not succeed, and James knew he couldn't, but he was still willing to try.

The plan which he was nursing, and which he publicly debated in *The Tragic Muse,* now took firm hold. There was a possible solution in this middle-aged choice which he found himself still forced to make, for he was thus constituted—a choice of quite a different order from the one of his youth, when he had turned to Europe to find freedom. What he needed now was a double freedom: that of the great place of art and that of the market-place, and these two "trumped" each other, in a kind of grim, ironic game. The paradox of success was that it cheapened everything while offering him the expensive solution. There was, however, a possible issue, he told himself, and he would seriously test it. He could descend into the market-place and try to be a playwright—an honorable and income-producing career for a man of letters—while at the same time preserving his art of fiction from all violation by the money-changers, keeping it for his sacred creative hours. James the playwright would "bail out" James the novelist. He knew, from far back, that he could launch a scene and create a drama; his artist's sense told him that in his pen there was a great ability to dramatize. In the very novel in which he discussed the stage he had boldly put together his story by scenic alternation, by not telling the reader everything but letting the scenes explain themselves, as in a play. He even pauses to explain that his method of telling the story prevents him from imparting certain facts:

> As to whether Miriam had the same bright, still sense of co-operation to a definite end, . . . that mystery would be cleared up only if it were open to us to regard this young lady through some other medium than the mind of her friends. We have chosen, as it happens, for some of the advantages it carries with it, the indirect vision.

This is the artist calling attention to his own method. On the stage James would not be able to intrude. The play would have to explain itself. James the artist would try to be impersonal. But he was not yet ready to be an anchorite of art—the happy hedonist still had the upper hand.

The Gallo-Romans

In the late Eighties and early Nineties, James was increasingly linked with a group of Gallo-Romans, as Bourget liked to characterize himself and them—various Frenchmen, in London and Paris, who represented all that the American loved in the Gallic and the Italianate spirit. In the many years of his association with France he had never found close French friends. Bourget was the sole exception. Now, however, there arrived in London a brilliant young diplomat, Jules Jusserand, Counsellor of the French Embassy; and also a young student from the French provinces who had written verses and attracted Bourget's attention, Urbain Mengin. With these two men—Jusserand, alert, swift, active, and Mengin, quiet, modest, studious and poetic—moving on different levels of London life, James had new resources of Gallic friendship. "A remarkably intelligent and pleasant little Frenchman," Henry said of the diplomat. He wrote to Grace Norton in the autumn of 1888 that Jusserand was

> a little prodigy of literary and diplomatic achievement effected at an early age. He is alive to his very small finger-tips, ambitious, capable and charming—and if he were a few inches less diminutive, I should believe that Europe would hear of him as a diplomatic personage. But he is too short!

Jusserand was to overcome his shortness, quite beyond James's prediction, and to be an important French Ambassador in Washington during the presidency of Theodore Roosevelt.

Urbain Mengin was destined to have a less spectacular but a quiet and distinguished career in education, and to become an early authority in France on Shelley and the English Romantics. He had turned up in October 1887 at De Vere Gardens with a letter of introduction from Bourget. He was twenty-three, singularly gifted and sensitive. James received him with a cordiality and warmth that Mengin remembered all his life. "I passed almost an entire Sunday with Henry James. One drinks excellent claret at his table," he wrote in a series of letters to his mother describing his meetings with the novelist. There were frequent visits and lunches in De Vere Gardens, strolls in Hyde Park "amid cantering Amazons," visits to museums and galleries and the spring show at the Royal Academy where Mengin marvelled at the way in which James was "monopolized" at every turn and the extent to which he was a celebrity. James introduced Mengin to "a really pretty young woman whose portrait was one of the highlights of the show." This was Millicent St. Clair Erskine, eldest daughter of the Earl of Rosslyn, who was about to marry the 4th Duke of Sutherland. She would remember Mengin later and for a period he was French tutor to her second son; the Duchess also received Italian lessons from him. Mengin constantly refers to Henry James's keen sensibility—at the Academy show "before a painting which provoked strong feelings in him he pressed my arm to the point of pain." He sketched James as follows:

> His entire person is distinction itself. He has a most agreeable voice and speaks with a slight hesitation, repeating the first syllable of certain words—charming proof of timidity and spontaneity at the same time ... His hair shows a bit of gray at the temples and there is a beginning of baldness which adds to the admirable extent of the forehead. He wears a finely-trimmed beard, still very dark.

James's letters to Mengin are written in a mixture of English and French. In one James urges the young Frenchman to apply himself to his study of English: "One's own language is one's mother, but the language one adopts, as a career, as a study, is one's wife, and it is with one's wife that *on se met en ménage.* English is a very faithful and well-conducted person, but she will expect you too not to commit infidelities. On these terms she will keep your house well."

A letter of a much later date shows admirably the benign yet critical eye James kept on his friend. Mengin had taken a walking-tour of Italy, scrupulously visiting all the scenes which had figured in the lives of Shelley, Byron and their circle. After telling Mengin he had read the resulting book, *L'Italie des Romantiques,* attentively and had found much entertaining matter, well presented, James went on to regret that Mengin had treated a poet of "a vertiginous lyric *essor*" like Shelley without indicating his quality and splendor:

> He is one of the great poets of the world, of the rarest, highest effulgence, the very genius and incarnation of poetry, the poet-type, as it were. But you speak only of the detail of his more or less irrelevant itinerary, and put in scarce a word for what he signifies and represents. ... He was the strangest of human beings, but he was *la poésie même,* the sense of Italy never melted into *anything* (étranger) I think, as into his "Lines in the Euganaean Hills" and *d'autres encore.* "Come where the vault of blue Italian sky ... !" is, for *me,* to *be* there *jusqu'au cou!* And *de même* for Keats, the child of the Gods! Read over again to yourself, but *aloud,* the stanzas of the *Adonais* (or I wish I could read them *to* you!) descriptive of the corner of Rome where they both lie buried, and then weep bitter tears of remorse at having sacrificed them to the terrestrial *caquetage* of A. de Musset! Forgive my emphasis.

Jusserand, Mengin, and the Anglo-French George Du Maurier, whom James often visited in company with Jusserand, offered James that elegance of spirit, delicacy of expression and fertility of mind which he sought periodically in the French capital. And he was never more aware of this than on the day in May 1889 when Jusserand arranged a little luncheon in honor of Hippolyte Taine, and invited James to meet his distinguished guest. The American had never encountered the French critic and historian, who gave James a renewed feeling "of the high superiority of French talk." He noted that Taine rated Turgenev higher in form even than he himself had done, using the very happy expression that Turgenev "so perfectly cut the umbilical cord that bound the story to himself."

The summer of 1889, when James was working at *The Tragic Muse,* had its usual interruptions. June and early July were devoted to entertaining in De Vere Gardens his old friend E. L. Godkin. James was struck by how much the Irish-American Godkin found in the Old Country that was unfavorable to the United States—in spite of Godkin's irreducible Americanism. The editor was barely gone when William arrived to attend a psychological congress and to see Alice. They had a day at Leamington together, where Henry first lunched with his sister, to prepare her for William's unheralded appearance, and then tied a handkerchief to the balcony as a signal that William might safely enter.

Later that summer he went to Whitby, where Lowell was staying. They had a ramble on the moors after a rough lunch at a stony upland inn; later they made an excursion by rail to see Rievaulx Abbey, a graceful fragment of a ruin. James missed his old friend in London when he called to say good-bye, before Lowell's return to America, and penned a hasty note wishing him "a winter of fine old wood fires and a speedy return." This was Lowell's last journey to England.

In September James went to Dover, planning to move on to Paris. He found Dover so comfortable and quiet, however, that he lingered, walked, worked, enjoyed the solitude and exercise. He dispatched further chapters of the *Muse,* and after three or four weeks went to the French capital on 24 October. He had agreed to translate Daudet's new Tartarin novel, *Port Tarascon,* and was to work on it from the printer's galleys.

Between this chore and the writing of the final chapters of the *Muse* James visited the last days of the Exhibition of 1889, spending his mornings and early afternoons in his room at the Hôtel de Hollande. He saw his job through; the last chapters of his longest serial were sent off early in December. He had an evening with Daudet, and they talked novel and theater. He saw much of Bourget and something of François Coppée. He dined twice in the company of the dramatists Meilhac and Ganderax, the drama critic Sarcey, Blowitz, the Paris correspondent of *The Times,* and

Edmond de Goncourt. He distinctly cultivated the theatrical side of the city. Early in December he returned to London.

The Private Life

Twelve days after James's return, word came that Robert Browning had died in Venice. The poet had spent a part of the late autumn with their friend Mrs. Bronson at La Mura, her summer home in Asolo. He had dedicated a book to her—his last, *Asolando.* Staying at the Palazzo Rezzonico, on the Grand Canal, the poet contracted a chill, and bronchitis followed. On 12 December, another of the great Victorians was dead.

Little more than a year before, James had been in the same carriage with Browning, at the funeral of their ancient friend Mrs. Procter. The novelist went to Westminster Abbey on the last day of 1889, a day of deep fog that seemed to make St. Margaret's bell toll even more deeply, to see Browning laid to rest—he, one of the most "modern" of poets—among the ancients in the Poets' Corner. "His funeral was charming, if I may call it so," James wrote to Mrs. Bronson, "crowded and cordial and genuine, and full of the beauty and grandeur of the magnificent old cathedral."

Years before, when he had first met Browning in London, James had been struck by his double personality—the poet incarnated in an individual as hearty and conventional and middle-class as any of the numerous privileged with whom he and Henry dined out constantly during the late Seventies. Now that Browning was gone, James allowed his imagination to play over the image of a great poet who could be deadly prosaic. An opposite case seemed to him to exist in the President of the Royal Academy, Sir Frederic Leighton, a painter who had all the gifts and all the versatilities of his art; he could make graceful after-dinner speeches— was, so to speak, the poet of diners-out—and James imagined that he evaporated into thin air the moment he had no audience.

James's little tale, "The Private Life," is his picture of a playwright staying at a Swiss inn who has promised an actress a play, but who seems quite incapable of writing it. The narrator discovers, however, that the playwright has a double, who stays in his room and does his writing for him. The "playwright's opinions were sound and second-rate, and of his perceptions it was too mystifying to think. I envied him his magnificent health," the narrator observed. On the other hand Lord Mellifont, also staying at the inn, is a man whose personality pervades English life. "He *was* a style." He puts more art into everything than is required.

The tale is Henry's picture of Robert Browning as he had known him. The world had seen always the commonplace Browning. The genius was in his books. Browning had been all "private life" and had no life in public, save the usual and the expected. Lord Leighton had been all

public, and had no corresponding private life. James remembered that
when he had heard Browning read, it had been almost as if he were
reading the work of another.

Henry's little fantasy about the poet was also a fantasy about himself;
it reflected the dichotomy which he envisaged in his own life: his dedication to art and to privacy; his eagerness at this moment to set this aside,
and seek the worldliness and publicity of the stage.

PART FIVE

The Dramatic Years

1890–1895

A success was as prosaic
as a good dinner: there was
nothing more to be said about
it than that you had had it.

HENRY JAMES

1

THEATRICALS

A Chastening Necessity

Henry James's beloved Aunt Kate—Catherine Walsh—who had been a second mother to the James children and almost a second wife to the elder Henry James, died early in 1889. She left a substantial estate, but mainly to the women of the Walsh family and only token gifts to the James children. Henry James had no expectations of inheritance; but at this time he was seriously re-examining his professional and financial position. He felt that he could not keep up the pace of the previous five years during which he had run three large serials through the magazines, while producing articles and reviews at the same time. The work gave him a sufficient income; but when the serials appeared in book form they did not sell. He usually received an advance of around $1,200 for the book version of a novel, but his royalties often did not cover this sum. When *The Tragic Muse* had run its course in the *Atlantic,* the Macmillans told him they doubted whether the book would sell and this time offered him only £70 in advance instead of the usual £250. "In spite of what you tell me of the poor success of my recent books," James wrote to Frederick Macmillan, "I still do desire to get a larger sum, and have determined to take what steps I can in this direction." He knew that these steps might carry him away from the Macmillans, but, he went on,

> I would rather not be published at all than be published and not pay— other people at least. . . . Unless I can put the matter on a more remunerative footing all round I shall give up my English "market"—heaven save the market—and confine myself to my American.

For the first time in his career he turned to a literary agent, the well-known firm of A. P. Watt. They negotiated a contract by which James surrendered all his rights in *The Tragic Muse* for five years to

Macmillan in return for the £250 he wanted. James was mollified; but he had had his warning. He announced this would be his last long fiction: from now on he would write only short stories and articles; and this would leave him time for a sustained "assault" on the stage.

James might have been more cautious had he not at this moment received overtures from the theater. Edward Compton, a young actor-manager who had been playing classical comedies in the provinces for a decade, asked James to turn his 1877 novel, *The American,* into a play. He saw in the role of Christopher Newman a vivid part for himself, and in Claire de Cintré a suitable role for his wife, the American actress Virginia Bateman. In his notebooks James reflected: "The theatre has sought me out—in the person of the good, the yet unseen, Compton." And then, settling down to a review of the story of *The American,* Henry wrote: "Oh, how it [the play] must not be too good and how very bad it must be!" There was never, from the first, any doubt in his mind that the theater would be for him a kind of artistic slumming expedition: it would offer its amusement but also financial rewards; it would be a compromise —an exciting gamble.

Confessing to Stevenson that he had begun experimenting with plays, he wrote: "Don't be hard on me—simplifying and chastening necessity has laid its brutal hand on me and I have had to try to make somehow or other the money I don't make by literature. My books don't sell, and it looks as if my plays might. Therefore I am going with a brazen front to write half a dozen."

James had perhaps intuitively realized that it would be better to begin his theatrical experiment with a modest company, and discover in the provinces some of the secrets of this "most unholy trade." Edward Compton wanted to establish himself in a theater in London. He gave James a £250 advance to dramatize *The American,* and early in 1890 the novelist set himself to his task. "My zeal in the affair is only matched by my indifference," he writes to Stevenson. He was certainly far from indifferent. In the same letter he could write: "I find the *form* opens out before me as if it were a kingdom to conquer."

The American took shape rapidly. By 6 February 1890 James had sent the second act to Compton; at this moment he was calling the play *The Californian.* "I have written a big (and awfully good) four-act play, by which I hope to make my fortune," he confided to Henrietta Reubell. And he told his sister he had met "exactly the immediate, actual, intense British conditions, both subjective and objective." The play would run two and three-quarter hours. He was to receive a ten per cent royalty on gross receipts. And he dreamed of £80 a week during the provincial run and £350 a month when the play came to London.

These castles in the air were encouraged by a lively young man, a

friend of Howells, who had come to London from America as agent for
a New York publishing house. Wolcott Balestier was twenty-nine. Recognizing that the impending international copyright agreement would end
years of piracy in America, he set out to make arrangements with English writers for legal publication of their works. He established an office
at No. 2 Dean's Yard, overlooked by the towers of the Abbey and overlooking a portion of Westminster School. Here amid the chiming of Abbey
bells this young American combined the picturesque with the commercial. Within a few months he had made friends with most of the established English writers, and with the new "infant prodigy"—for so James
called him—Rudyard Kipling. Balestier had no sense of difficulty and no
awe of greatness. James consulted him in all his theatrical affairs.

Fenimore, lonely on her Florentine hill-top after the death of Lizzie and
the departure of Boott and Duveneck, was also planning a change. Much
as she liked the Italian climate, and the city to which Henry James had
introduced her almost ten years before, she felt that she had to find a new
home. Her thought was that she would go back to England.

Leaving the Villa Brichieri was difficult. She had become embedded
in the place, almost morbidly, one might say, for in a tale she wrote about
Bellosguardo her widowed heroine prefers death to leaving her villa and
wastes away for no other visible reason than her grief and her memories.
Fenimore was of stronger fiber. She went through the ordeal of getting
her belongings together, and in the autumn of 1889 spent a month at
Richmond. She was joined by her sister, and the two left for a winter's
tour of the Mediterranean, to Corfu and the Holy Land. Early the following spring, however, she returned to England and fixed upon Cheltenham as her new abode. She preferred it to London, for she had started
work on another novel. But she would again be near to James.

He, however, once his play was in Compton's hands, decided to leave
for Italy. That he should have gone abroad that summer while awaiting
production of his play was not altogether strange: but it may have seemed
so to Fenimore. He was not in the habit of journeying directly into the
Italian heat. Nevertheless in the middle of May we find him at Milan,
whence he writes to William about Howells's new novel, *A Hazard of
New Fortunes,* finding in it much "life and truth of observation and
feeling."

James went to Genoa, Pisa, Lucca, then hurried to Florence for emergency dental care. Dr. Baldwin insisted on his coming to stay with him
in the Via Palestro. He paid two sad visits to Bellosguardo, and in early
June proceeded to Venice, to the Barbaro. The palace was "cool, melancholy, empty, delicious." The Curtises persuaded James to accompany
them to Oberammergau to see the 1890 Passion Play. The play struck him

as "primitive" and he disliked the way in which it was commercialized. Returning from this excursion he made a little tour of small Tuscan towns with Dr. Baldwin in the suffocating summer heat. He was staying at Vallombrosa, near the Countess Peruzzi (Edith Story), enjoying the mountain coolness, when an urgent telegram came from Alice at Leamington and he left promptly for London.

The sudden summons meant a new breakdown; and James decided that Alice had been immured too long in the provinces. With Miss Loring's help he had her moved to London, to the South Kensington Hotel. In due course he found rooms for her in Argyle Road, Campden Hill, about ten minutes from De Vere Gardens. Dr. Baldwin was staying with him at the time. "Can she die?" James and Miss Loring asked the doctor (whom Alice apparently refused to see). "They sometimes do," Baldwin answered. There came a moment when another doctor had to be summoned, and he found a tumor of the breast. Some months later Alice allowed Baldwin to examine her when he was again in England. He diagnosed cancer, and predicted to James the form it would take. Miss Loring from now on remained with Alice. A silent and as yet remote death-watch had begun.

James now began to discover how difficult the writing of a play could be —even for one as experienced with dialogue as he was. When *The American* went into rehearsal that autumn, he found himself doing a great deal of play-carpentry. A scene did not sound right. Actors objected to certain lines. Speeches needed to be made more colloquial. There was constant revision. Most important of all was the task of teaching the tall and handsome Edward Compton how to talk "American."

Southport, near Liverpool, was selected for the out-of-town opening. There was a large winter population and a comfortable theater, the Winter Garden. Here on New Year's Day 1891 James arrived in a state of feverish excitement. Balestier joined him. Also to Southport came William Archer, the drama critic, whose arrival indicated that at least one important notice of the production would be written. James had urged him to wait for a more finished play—to see it after its try-outs. But Archer refused to be put off.

The first night took place on 3 January 1891 and James spent a nervous day writing letters to all his friends, asking them to pray for him. The hour finally came. James, watching the play from the wings, found the audience appreciative and enjoyed its laughter. He enjoyed also, for the first time in his life, being dragged in front of an applauding house, and giving himself up, as he said, to a series of simpering bows, while from the "gas-flaring indistinguishable dimness" came the pleasant sounds of acclaim. Compton pressed his hand. So far as Southport was concerned, "the stake was won."

Next day James journeyed from Birmingham to Cheltenham, to spend the day and rehearse his minor provincial triumph to Miss Woolson. A month later he wrote to his brother: "You can form no idea of how a provincial success is confined to the provinces."

A London Début

Henry James had been given a lively taste of what it meant to be a strolling player. His sallies into the provinces, his continuing rehearsals and his constant amendment of scenes, provided him with a liberal education in theatricals. "The authorship in any sense worthy of the name of a play," he now explained to William, "only *begins* when it is written, and I see that one's creation of it doesn't terminate till one has gone with it every inch of the way to the rise of the curtain." The evening at Southport had been in reality a larger rehearsal: the curtain would rise only after *The American* was brought to London.

While waiting for his London first night James began to write a second play, and presently a third. His second was a comedy then called *Mrs. Vibert* (later the title was changed to *Tenants*), based on a tale he had long ago read in the *Revue des Deux Mondes.* He transferred the setting of the little melodrama—about a general and his mistress, a ward, and two sons who are really half-brothers—to England, substituting fisticuffs for the duel the brothers fight. John Hare, an enterprising actor-manager, asked James to submit a play and was offered *Mrs. Vibert.* As possible interpreters, the novelist fixed his attention on Geneviève Ward, who had had a career on the operatic stage in New York and later in the theater, and W. H. Vernon, who had frequently been her leading man. There were letters and telegrams, tea-hour readings. Mrs. Ward decided against the part and James turned to the celebrated tragedienne, Helena Modjeska. She told him she could only see Geneviève Ward in the role. Hare speedily lost interest in the comedy and James set it aside.

That winter he wrote still another comedy, during six weeks spent in Paris. This was based on his tale "The Solution," set in Rome, about a diplomat who is persuaded that he has compromised a young woman by taking her on an unchaperoned walk. James transferred the scene once more to England. He thought of the play as suitable for Ada Rehan, the Irish-American actress who had made a great hit on the London stage under the management of the veteran Augustin Daly. Daly took an option on the play on the strength of James's literary reputation. He was building a theater in London, and *Mrs. Jasper,* as the play was then called, was scheduled to be one of the "attractions" of the new house.

During one of his calls on Geneviève Ward—on 12 January 1891—James had encountered a young woman with extraordinarily large clear blue eyes, and more "personality" than he had found among most of the actresses in London. Her name was Elizabeth Robins. Kentucky-born, she was twenty-seven, and had been on the stage for almost a decade. She had played small parts in New York and Boston, had toured up and down the United States in minor Shakespearian roles, and had then gone abroad. During a visit to Norway she had heard the name of Ibsen. Now, in London, she was appearing in *A Doll's House* before scandalized Victorian audiences.

Miss Robins's diary leaves no doubt of the impression James made on her that day:

> I like this man better I think than any *male* American I have met abroad. He is delightfully *grave* and without the Yankee traveller's thin pretence of cosmopolitanism. This meeting is a ray of sunshine in a dark day.

On 27 January, at a matinée of *A Doll's House* which he attended with Geneviève Ward, James watched Miss Robins in the first Ibsen play he had ever seen. Later that spring he saw her in *Hedda Gabler;* it was "the talk of the town," he wrote to Miss Reubell, "with the most interesting English-speaking actress (or rather the *only* one) that I have seen for many a day."

James took Compton to see Miss Robins perform and it was settled that they would invite her to play Claire de Cintré in *The American.* Mrs. Compton was relinquishing the role in London because she was pregnant. Several other changes were made in the cast. Kate Bateman, Mrs. Compton's older sister, came out of retirement to play the Marquise, and a young and vivacious French actress, Adrienne Dairolles, was given the part of Noémie.

In the spring of 1891, when he had all but completed recasting *The American,* James had a bout of influenza. It left him weak and dispirited. He had always wanted to pay a longer visit to Ireland than his brief stay in Cork in 1882 and this seemed an opportune time. He went at the end of June to Kingstown, six miles from Dublin, and settled in the Royal Marine Hotel. Here he wrote "The Private Life," and his little tale of "The Chaperon," another of his stories of how a lady can breach the laws of society and then, with society's own amused consent, be re-accepted. The dramatist Arthur Pinero, on reading this tale, pointed out that it had all the elements of an amusing stage play. The novelist promptly made notes to that end, though only a fragment of a scenario survives.

In Ireland he found "peace and obscurity and leisure" and he recovered rapidly from his illness. In mid-July he wrote a gossipy letter to Francis Boott, mentioning among other things that Fenimore was moving from Cheltenham to Oxford "for a year, a very right and good place for her. She believes she is then—after a year again—going to Italy to spend the rest of her life. But *chi lo sa?*"

On 20 July James wrote to Lowell, a letter filled with the warmth of an old and sympathetic friendship. He described the Irish coast, the blueness of sea and greenness of shore, the graceful Wicklow mountains and hills of Howth and Killeny. "The very waves have a brogue as they break—and they broke Bray Head, the fine southernmost limit of the bay, long ago." Lowell probably received this letter and read it a few days before he died, on 12 August 1891. "It is a loss, and a pain, and a dear friend the less," James wrote to Du Maurier a few days after he had the news (he was now back in De Vere Gardens). Before the year was out he was to compose his long memorial essay, published in the *Atlantic,* in which he reviewed Lowell's career and his own fond memories of him.

Six days before the opening night of *The American* William James suddenly appeared in London after a rapid autumn crossing. He had come to say good-bye to Alice. He spent as many hours as he could with his sister; and he was at Henry's first night, and the intimate supper Henry gave afterwards, at which the guests were the Comptons, Miss Robins, William Heinemann the publisher, and Wolcott Balestier.

The first night on 26 September 1891, in the refurbished Opera Comique Theatre in the Strand, was a dubious success, but distinctly a social one. Robert Lincoln, the American Minister, was in a box, and the stage journals spoke of the presence of various American "millionaires." Grace Norton was in London, and so—with William—Cambridge, Massachusetts, was thoroughly represented. And Fenimore, by this time settled in Oxford, came to London for the occasion and met William for the first and only time. It is possible to see the opening through her eyes:

> The house was packed to the top, and the applause was great. When the performance was ended, and the actors had been called out, there arose loud cries of "Author, author!" After some delays, Henry James appeared before the curtain and acknowledged the applause. He looked very well —quiet and dignified, yet pleasant; he only stayed a moment. The critics have since then written acres about the play. It has been warmly praised; attacked; abused; highly commended etc.

To read the critics today is to see quite clearly what was wrong with *The American.* Even men like William Archer, who were eager to see novelists working on the stage, had to admit that James had sacrificed too much of the originality of his novel for mere melodrama. Miss Robins's Claire tended to be frantic and nervous. She had great difficulty with the role; one critic said she imported into the play "the hysterical manners of Ibsen's morbid heroines." The comedy figure of Christopher Newman was not altogether liked. There was a strong element of travesty in Compton's appearance. His long chocolate-colored coat with sky-blue trimmings and buttons "as large as cheese-plates" was the subject of much satiric reference; the critics knew that American millionaires dress in much better taste. It was probably A. B. Walkley, one of the most literate of drama critics, who twitted James in an anonymous review for his "stage American, with the local colour laid on with a trowel." Compton definitely had the accent, and for the rest "a great deal of ugly overcoat."

The production was lagging when the Prince of Wales decided that he wanted to see it. Compton asked James to "dress up" a couple of boxes with "smart people." The visit of royalty had its desired effect; the play's run was prolonged. James and Compton decided to give it a further "lift" and invited the critics to a "second edition" on the fiftieth night—James having taken a number of the critical suggestions and revised certain of the scenes. The critics were flattered and found the play improved. *The American* eked out seventy nights. The run had now been "honorable," Henry felt. The revenue had been negligible.

Ten days after the closing James was summoned to Dresden, hurriedly crossing the Channel to stand in a dreary little suburban cemetery at the grave of Wolcott Balestier. Somewhere Balestier had taken a drink of contaminated water; and now he was dead, in a strange city, his dream of rivalling (in partnership with Heinemann) the great Baron Tauchnitz abruptly ended. James had willingly accompanied Heinemann to Dresden to bring solace to the youth's mother and sisters. In a later time James wrote annually to Wolcott's mother on the anniversary of Dresden, mourning the young man almost as if he had lost a son.

Alice James too mourned him: "The young Balestier, the effective and the indispensable, is dead! swept away like a cobweb, of which gossamer substance he seems to have been himself compounded, simply spirit and energy, with the slightest of fleshly wrapping." This was her comment in her journal in 1891—a tribute of the dying to the dead.

A Divine Cessation

Alice James announced her impending death by cable to William James. She dictated it to Henry on 5 March 1892: "Tenderest love to all. Farewell. Am going soon. Alice." She had then but a few hours to live. During those hours she also dictated to Katharine Loring the ultimate passage in her journal:

I feel sure that it can't be possible but what the bewildered little hammer that keeps me going will very shortly see the decency of ending his distracted career. However this may be, physical pain, however great, ends in itself and falls away like dry husks from the mind, whilst moral discords and nervous horrors sear the soul.

That sentence bothered her; during her last night Alice tried to improve it. "Oh, the wonderful moment when I felt myself floated for the first time, into the deep sea of divine *cessation*," she dictated, "and saw all the dear old mysteries and miracles vanish into vapour." She was alluding to the fact that she had fainted away the previous evening, and felt as if she were dying. She came to just as Henry was being sent for.

The climax of her long years of invalidism had come suddenly. She had been weaker at the end of February and had been given doses of morphine to assuage her pain. At William's suggestion Dr. Lloyd Tuckey, an eminent psychiatrist, had been called in and used hypnotism as a further aid. At the beginning of March Alice contracted a cold; James, coming to see her on 5 March, was struck by the supreme deathlike emaciation that had come over her within forty-eight hours. It was on this day, a Saturday, that Alice dictated her farewell cable. Henry himself sent the final word the next day. The "divine cessation" had come.

On the last page of Alice's journal, in Katharine Loring's hand, is a postscript: "The dictation of March 4th was rushing about in her brain all day, and although she was very weak and it tired her much to dictate, she could not get her head quiet until she had it written; then she was relieved and I finished Miss Woolson's story of 'Dorothy' to her"—Fenimore's Bellosguardo story, of the lingering death of a woman who does not want to live.

This was the first time that Henry James watched someone through the hours of death—and someone close to him. It was both as brother and as novelist that he set down the final scene of his sister's undramatic life for their Cambridge brother. "Alice died at exactly four o'clock on Sunday afternoon (about the same hour of the same day as mother), and it is now Tuesday morning," he began, and then followed a painful step-by-step account. On Saturday, when Alice had taken on the look of death, the pain diminished, and "left her consciously and oh longingly, close to the end." James wanted to stay the night on Campden Hill, but Miss Loring thought this was pointless. There was nothing he could do. Alice said a few barely audible things to him, then sank into a gentle sleep. "From that sleep she never woke—but after an hour or two it changed its character and became a loud, deep breathing—almost stertorous." This was her condition when James reached the house again on Sunday morning at nine. From that hour until four he, Katharine and the nurse sat beside Alice's bed.

An hour before the end there came a "blessed change." Alice began to breathe without effort, gently, peacefully and naturally, like a child. After an hour her breathing seemed to become intermittent, "her face then seemed in a strange, dim, touching way to become clearer." James went to the window to let in a little more of the afternoon light. "It was a bright, kind, soundless Sunday." When he came back she had drawn, he told William, "the last breath." Then the novelist, to be more precise, crossed out the word "last" and made the sentence read "she had drawn the breath that was not succeeded by another."

Alice's body lay in her room, on the bed in which she died, from that Sunday evening until Wednesday. During that time Henry spent many hours beside her. She had asked to be cremated with the simplest possible ceremony. At 11:45 on Wednesday morning, 9 March 1892, Henry, Katharine Loring, the nurse, and an old Cambridge friend who lived in England, Annie Ashburner Richards, took the train to Woking, where there was a brief service. Henry and his companions waited in a room next to the chapel till the cremation was completed. The ashes, by Alice's wish, were to be sent to Cambridge and interred beside the graves of her parents. On his way back from Waterloo Station the novelist stopped at the Reform Club and wrote half a dozen sentences to William, describing the scene. "It is the last, the last forever. I shall feel very lonely in England at first. But enough."

Alice James left an estate valued at $80,000. This she divided largely among her three brothers and Katharine Loring. Henry, William and Katharine received $20,000 each. Robertson was left a smaller amount, because, she had reasoned, his wife and children had large expectations, whereas William and Henry had none. Robertson James protested at this discrimination, and Henry announced that he was willing to transfer $5,000 from his inheritance, since he felt Katharine Loring could hardly be asked to do so, and that William, with four children, should not be asked to part with any share of what he was receiving.

Alice's journal remained in Miss Loring's possession. Some time later, by agreement with William, four copies were printed, for the three brothers and herself. When Henry received his copy he expressed great alarm. The journal was "heroic," as he wrote to William, "in its individuality, its independence—its face-to-face with the universe for-and-by herself—and the beauty and eloquence with which she often expresses this." But it was filled with much minor gossip retailed by him to Alice to entertain her, and he feared that, if disseminated, it would have the

effect of his fictitious *Reverberator*. At Henry's insistence the diary was
not published during his lifetime.

In Dante William had found a passage which he and Henry agreed
could fittingly be inscribed upon the marble urn that was carved in Italy,
later in 1892, to hold Alice's ashes: *ed essa da martiro e da essilio venne
a questa pace.*

The Wheel of Time

William James, on seeing Henry in De Vere Gardens in 1889 after
their long separation, had written home to his wife:

> Harry is as nice and simple and amiable as he can be. He has covered
> himself, like some marine crustacean, with all sorts of material growths,
> rich sea-weeds, and rigid barnacles and things, and lives hidden in the
> midst of his strange heavy alien manners and customs; but these are all
> but "protective resemblances," under which the same dear old, good,
> innocent and at bottom very powerless-feeling Harry remains, caring for
> little but his writing, and full of dutifulness and affection for all gentle
> things.

William's picture of his "dear old, good, innocent" Harry is essentially that of the "angel" of long ago. Henry was "powerless-feeling," to
be sure, whenever he was in William's presence; but he had never been
more ambitious, and indeed never more powerful, than at this moment.
Between the time of William's description and the death of Alice—between 1889 and 1892—he had brought out a long novel and a volume of
tales and had written many articles. During the year of Alice's death he
published ten tales and four articles. And in the year following Alice's
death—1893—he surpassed all his previous records of publication by
bringing out five books: three volumes of tales and two of essays. In
addition, there now lay on his desk the scripts of four comedies and that
of *The American.*

Henry James had a full sense of the power he wielded in literary
circles. But he also had a sense of an encroaching loneliness as familiar
figures in his life continued to drop away: Mrs. Procter and Browning, the
young Balestier, the beloved Lowell. Late in 1892 he learned that his loyal
friend Theodore Child, whom he had known ever since the summer of
1876 at Étretat, was gone, "prematurely and lamentedly." He had died in
Persia, near Ispahan, and been buried in a lonely grave at Tulfa.

There were not only deaths but unexpected breaks with the past. For
old times' sake James had kept up a correspondence with his Newport
friend, Thomas Sergeant Perry, and had regularly sent him his books.

But some impulse, some sense of his own failure in the American literary world, had prompted Perry to send Henry a "most offensive and impertinent" letter in which he expressed disapproval of James's expatriation. "It was too idiotic to notice," Henry told William, and he decided to have nothing further to do with this "singular helpless mediocrity." A large gap now occurred in their otherwise voluminous correspondence.

Old figures were disappearing; new ones were on James's horizon— a generation of attractive young men only too willing to be acolytes and call him "Master." Balestier had been one of the first—eager, earnest, enterprising, with a certain abrasive charm which troubled Edmund Gosse but which James found endearing. He had died early, after making himself indispensable to James. There now appeared others, also in their twenties (James was by now fifty), bringing to the novelist their young worlds and intimate gossip of the metropolis. Singularly attaching was a journalist from Connecticut who at twenty-five had won a position on the London *Times.* This was William Morton Fullerton, a dashing well-tailored man with large Victorian moustaches and languid eyes, a bright flower in his button-hole and the style of a "masher." He had considerable sexual versatility. And he had great respect for the Master, probably confiding only cautiously some of his milder amatory exploits. James would have liked to see more of him, but Fullerton was soon dispatched to the Paris bureau of the *Times* where he covered major stories and carried on many heterosexual affairs—indulging also in a covert Victorian homosexual life. He knew Oscar Wilde and he had an affair with the sculptor, Lord Ronald Gower. James had intimations of a different affair, that between Fullerton and the elegant Margaret Brooke, Ranee of Sarawak. The novelist's letters to Fullerton of this period are affectionate and filled with regret that he was never in London. When in Paris, they sat in cafés, went to theaters; Fullerton quoted much poetry and made himself agreeable in a tender romantic way with his teasing and mysterious intimations of his wider life.

Then there was Jonathan Sturges, of an old New York family. Born in Paris, and educated in Princeton, Sturges had been crippled by polio when young. From the waist up, he gave the effect of a handsome sultry man, with dark intense eyes, broad shoulders and a sharp quick manner. He liked to ride in hansoms, which concealed his wizened legs. James from the first took a fatherly interest in him; and in later years Sturges would stay for weeks on end in the novelist's country house, where he was, according to Percy Lubbock, "a pleasing fount of scandal, stimulating with its dash of vitriol." Ford Madox Ford remembered Sturges as "a queer tiny being who lay as if crumpled" on James's stately sofa. In London, Sturges was liked by hostesses and moved in literary circles; he wrote short stories and translated Maupassant (with a preface by James).

He was also a friend of Whistler's. Strange, troubled, often depressed, he nevertheless diminished James's loneliness, and was given loving attention by the novelist. As his health declined he became increasingly alcoholic, and he finally withdrew to an isolated Sussex cottage, where he refused to see his friends and was tended by a guardian nurse.

Another new friend was a New Yorker named Henry Harland, who had written novels about immigrant life under the name of Sydney Luska and later wrote English best sellers. He became the editor of the *Yellow Book* to which James contributed tales and essays. A more interesting though passing figure was Henry Bennett Brewster, another American, who attracted James by his achieved cosmopolitanism. Handsome, bearded, with clear sharp eyes, Brewster had grown up in Europe with a mastery of several tongues and several literatures and a penchant for meditative writing. His book *L'Âme Païenne* had many admirers. James and Brewster dined whenever they met, in London or abroad; and the novelist cherished the memory, after his death at a comparatively early age, of this "strange handsome questioning cosmopolite ghost." Brewster had a prolonged love affair with the composer Ethel Smyth.

They came, these younger ardent men, into James's life, and some survived to create the legends of the Master. We catch their reflection in tales of the literary life such as "The Death of the Lion" or "The Figure in the Carpet," where there is always a young acolyte, a youthful spirit touched by the art of the great writer. One of the first of these tales was written during James's fiftieth year. "The Middle Years" was the one new tale he published during 1893—as a kind of half-century manifesto. In this story a middle-aged writer has had a serious illness and fears he may die before he has his "second chance," his opportunity for a "later manner." He meets a young doctor who is prepared to abandon everything to take care of him, so powerfully has he been affected by the novelist's books. And Dencombe, dying, realizes that perhaps the most important thing is not whether there is to be another chance, a second existence: the important thing was to have created works which could arouse a response. "The thing is to have made somebody care."

These new young men surrounding James cared. The world might ignore him; but James knew that so long as certain readers experienced his work as profoundly as they did, his personal *gloire* was assured. He was beginning to feel that the greatest art is not that which creates a sensation or a success. By some strange process of human relation, true art inspired in others an interest, an attachment, a sense of "transference."

Another revealing tale, written a year earlier—in 1892 (when James was forty-nine)—is called "The Wheel of Time." In it he spins a variation on a story he had written when he was thirty-six, and which he had then called "The Diary of a Man of Fifty." At thirty-six one could imagine oneself fifty without too much pain; at forty-nine he made his character —forty-nine! The hero of "The Diary of a Man of Fifty" tries to persuade a young man to do as he has done—turn his back on the daughter of the woman about whom he himself has been unsure; the young man does not heed his advice and marries happily. In "The Wheel of Time" Maurice Glanvil, in his twenties, has turned his back on the plain but charming Fanny Knocker, to contract a bohemian marriage. His wife dies, leaving him a daughter who grows up to be very plain. Then at forty-nine he meets Fanny Knocker, now the widowed Mrs. Tregent, again. In middle age her early charm has blossomed into beauty. Moreover she has a handsome son—who repeats the history of the hero, by turning his back on Glanvil's plain daughter.

There is, however, a deeper discovery made by Maurice: that he has been the one passion in the life of Fanny Knocker Tregent—and this passage gives us pause. For the date on which the tale was set down in the notebook, 18 May 1892—a month after Henry James became forty-nine —was also the day on which he had paid a visit to Constance Fenimore Woolson at Oxford. Maurice, in the tale, discussing the past with Mrs. Tregent at one point provokes her to tears; later he meditates:

> She had striven, she had accepted, she had conformed; but she had thought of him every day of her life. She had taken up duties and per- formed them, she had banished every weakness and practised every virtue; but the still hidden flame had never been quenched. . . . Women were capable of these mysteries of sentiment, these intensities of fidelity, and there were moments in which Maurice Glanvil's heart beat strangely before a vision really so sublime. He seemed to understand now by what miracle Fanny Knocker had been beautified—the miracle of heroic docilities and accepted pangs and vanquished egotisms. It had never come in a night, but it had come by living for others. She was living for others still; it was impossible for him to see anything else at last than that she was living for him. The time of passion was over, but the time of service was long.

The "intensities of fidelity," the remark about "living for others": James was to say this of his mother in his autobiographies. But it was as if at this moment he seemed to be speaking of Constance Fenimore Woolson, as in his essay describing her long-suffering heroines.

Had Henry James reached some crisis in his long relation with Feni- more? We know that he went to see her in Oxford eight days after Alice's funeral, on 17 March, and was there the entire day. He went again on 18 May 1892. That Alice's death brought about some kind of change in Feni- more's attitude seems possible. In the novel she was writing at this time,

Horace Chase, the heroine has an invalid sister who plays a dominating role in her life. Alice had played such a role in Henry's life; and we may speculate that the question which now arose between them was whether Henry—now that Alice was gone—should not be more attentive to Fenimore.

The speculation might be gratuitous, were it not for a solitary paragraph which spilled out of Fenimore's pen a few months after James published "The Wheel of Time." In a letter to her nephew, Samuel Mather, Miss Woolson discussed her plan to return to Italy. "You will see in all this," she wrote, "I am giving up being near my kind friend Mr. James." She went on:

> I don't know what made me tell you and Will that last message of his sister to me, that touched me so much. But I suppose it was simply the relief of having some of my own family to talk to, after being so long alone. I felt that I could say anything to you, without having to think whether it was safe or not, wise or not, prudent or not.—But Mr. James will come to Italy every year. And perhaps we can write that play after all.

What Alice's message was, we do not know. It might have been praise for Fenimore's Bellosguardo story, read to her during her last hours; it might have been something more significant, some comment on the relationship between Henry and Fenimore, perhaps a sisterly wish that they would marry. As for the talk of collaboration on a play, it can only leave us wondering. James was, in all his writing years, an arch-solitary of literature. He would have regarded collaboration as an abandoning of sovereign ground, the most sacred ground of his life. Within the medium of the stage, however, he might have been willing. One must also consider that since James could not "collaborate" with Fenimore in the one way in which she would have liked him to, that is in the realm of the affections, he may have proposed a union in their art. Was the play begun? It is doubtful whether we shall ever know. It may never have gone beyond the stage of conversation.

This is the only point in James's long career when the question of collaboration comes up—save that at this very time it becomes the title of the tale "Collaboration," one of James's trifling and artful anecdotes. A young French poet and a young German composer fall in love with each other's work and set out to write an opera together. In doing this the Frenchman rejects his French fiancée, whose father fell in the Franco-Prussian war and whose mother can tolerate no alliance with a member of the race that invaded France. The brother of the German musician, who has been supporting him, also cannot tolerate collaboration with a former enemy. The two artists are left alone. They take up life together —and the fiancée is spurned, as the woman was spurned in "The Diary of a Man of Fifty," or as Fanny Knocker was spurned, or Maurice's ugly daughter. If the spurning was a mistake—as these various personages wonder or believe—James could not conceive of it otherwise. Things would have to go on pretty much as before. Whatever his affections might be, his career, his complicated relations with the older generation of his friends and the new young friends, were his way of life. He had never been ready to sacrifice any part of this for Fenimore. And he was probably only too glad to make Italy more than ever into a place of annual pilgrimage.

The Two Queens

In the spring of 1892, when Henry James had accustomed himself to the absence of Alice, he set out for Italy; with the Season about to begin, this was an ideal time for flight. Paul Bourget had married during the previous year, and gone to Italy on a prolonged honeymoon. He was now at Siena and the newlyweds beckoned to James.

He reached Siena on 5 June, and put up at the Grand Hôtel de Sienne, where the Bourgets were staying. He was charmed by Bourget's wife, the former Minnie David. She was slim, petite, fragile, "a beautiful child," ministering to Bourget "like a little quivering pathetic priestess on a bas-relief." Towards noon the writers would have their déjeuner together; then they would retire to their rooms. Bourget was finishing a novel; James was working at a series of tales. At six they would sally forth, dine, walk in the Lizza, eat ices, hang over the Castello and enjoy the medievalism of the ancient Tuscan town. James knew it well but he had never paid so enjoyable a visit to it and never at this time of the year. On balmy moonlit evenings he found the place a "revel of history vivified." It was a pleasure, moreover, to look at things in the company of the fragile and charming Minnie, "to study the beautiful in her society."

As for Bourget, James thought him as always one of the most civilized of conversationalists—and despised his novels. Moreover he sooner or later told him what he thought of them. Bourget possessed a certain delicacy of perception and an admirable prose instrument; his fiction was narrow, deterministic, mechanistic; it was Zola's naturalism with a little superficial psychology added. "I absolutely don't like this work," James had written to Bourget some years earlier, on reading his *Mensonges*:

> I speak with no false delicacy or hypocrisy; but your out-and-out eroticism displeases me as well as this exposition of dirty linens and dirty towels. In a word, all this is far from being life as I feel it, as I see it, as I know it, as I wish to know it.

In this letter of 23 February 1888 (written in French), James attacked
Bourget for trying to describe the physical-erotic too minutely—"the
number of embraces, their quality, the exact place they occur, the manner in which they occur and a thousand other particularities more intensely personal and less producible in broad daylight than anything else
in the world." And he added, "it would never occur to me to want to know
what goes on in their bedroom, in their bed, between a man and a
woman." Such candor was possible only between friends; and if Bourget
demurred it was because he, on his side, could see life only in his sado-
masochistic way.

Differences vanished when the two authors were together. One day
in June they drove to San Gimignano, "a long, lovely day of the teeming
Tuscan land, a garden of beauty and romance." On 3 July they saw the
Palio from a balcony of the Marchese Chigi's palace. Each day had its
adventures; and in the middle of their stay there arrived another Gallo-
Roman, Count Primoli, who had been in the party in 1886 when James
had taken Maupassant to dine at Greenwich.

Early in July, when the heat became intense, the Bourgets left for the
mountains, and Henry turned towards Venice and the summoning Mrs.
Gardner. It was that lady's pleasure, for the second summer in succession, to occupy the Palazzo Barbaro, which she had rented from the
Curtises, and to create within it the "court" with which she liked to
surround herself. When James arrived, he found the Palazzo filled with
guests. To his delight his hostess placed a bed in the library, where, like
his heroine Milly Theale much later, he awoke every day to find himself
staring at the medallions and arabesques of the ceiling. A scorching
sirocco was blowing; inside the palace, however, he was cool. The novelist reveled in the grandeur and the loveliness of the city—and Queen
Isabella's game of modern life carried on within the frame of the past.
People were always coming and going. There was much music and much
floating in gondolas. "It is the essence of midsummer, but I buy five-franc
alpaca jackets and feel so Venetian that you might almost own me," he
wrote to Mrs. Curtis.

The more permanent and more reticent American Queen of the
Grand Canal, she of Ca' Alvisi, was at Asolo. Even as Isabella Stewart
spoke of her descent from the Stuart kings, so Katharine De Kay Bronson
had come to identify herself with Caterina Cornaro, who had been Queen
of Cyprus, Jerusalem and Armenia, and who in 1489 had taken possession
of Asolo, in the mountains behind Venice, and held court there in her
ancient stone house, La Mura. Discreet and of a mild temperament,
Queen Kate of Asolo felt no threat to her sovereignty in the Boston
Queen's temporary *villeggiatura* on the Canal. Instead there was a noble
exchange of salutations, a fine respect for each other's domains and
queenship.

The two Queens corresponded, as Queens might. "I am glad to hear that our dear friend Henry James is with you," came the word from the tower-house in Asolo. "Tell him I wrote to him at Siena the other day and have just despatched a card to the director of the hotel to forward that valuable missive to the Barbaro. I hope he will be able to come here, and that you will find it agreeable to be here at the same time."

Fond as James was of Mrs. Bronson, he was not fond of Asolo. Its conditions of life were too primitive. La Mura had originally been a part of the rampart of Asolo; highly romantic and picturesque, and inspiring to Robert Browning, it did not correspond to James's ideal of Venetian splendor. The expedition, however, was a success. Donna Isabella accompanied her famous courtier on a journey which she remembered as "so romantic, so Italian," and James wrote to Mrs. Bronson that his return with Mrs. Gardner, "in the fragrant Italian eve, is one of the most poetical impressions of my life."

That summer of 1892, William James, on sabbatical leave, brought his family abroad for the first time—four children, two of them infants, and his wife. They had gone straight to Switzerland, and now William was at Lausanne. From Venice James, with his sense of family loyalty, announced he would join them. But when the time came he would gladly have remained in the amusing entourage of Mrs. Gardner. The pleasures of a palatial existence had not yet palled.

Early in August he took a train for Lausanne. He put up at the Hôtel Richemont, expecting to join an intimate family group and to enjoy, for the first time, the full extent of his unclehood. William, however, had not kept Henry informed of his plans and two days after the novelist arrived, he departed on a walking tour in the Engadine. The novelist discovered his young nephews had been parceled out in *pensions* with Swiss pastors, and Alice with the two younger children was staying in a Vaudois *pension.* Henry felt let down and superfluous. He had quit the shining softness of Venice for the Swiss mountains out of a sense of duty, and found a scattered family that took casual heed of him, as if they had not been separated for years. It reminded him with sudden sharpness of his own itinerant childhood days in Europe.

He remained for ten days. During this time he did what he could in his avuncular role. Billy, the second son, who grew up to be a portrait painter and Henry's favorite nephew, was to remember the extreme gravity and politeness of the massive uncle.

From Lausanne, in mid-August, the novelist-uncle journeyed to Paris. At the end of the month he was back in De Vere Gardens.

Mrs. Kemble

"The year's end is a terrible time," wrote Henry James to Miss Reubell, on 1 January 1893, "and the year's beginning is a worse." In a bare three and a half months he would be fifty: and how "terrible" a time it was he found out shortly after he had clinked hot punch with London friends to see the year in. His plan was to return in mid-January to Italy, where his brother and his family were wintering in Florence. But he did not get away as he had planned. First he caught a cold; and when this seemed at an end he had his first attack of gout. "It is an atrocious complaint," he told Miss Reubell in mid-January. "I am still very lame and it will be several more days before I can put on a Christian shoe."

On the evening of the day he wrote this, Mrs. Kemble, while being helped to bed by her maid, gave a little sigh and fell dead. On 20 January, still hobbling, and with a shoe slit so that he could put it on, James made his way to Kensal Green to say farewell to one of the oldest and most cherished of his London friends. The day of the funeral was soft, and, as he said, "kind." The number of mourners was limited. At eighty-four Mrs. Kemble had long outlived her contemporaries. She was laid in the same earth as her father, under a mountain of flowers. Returning to De Vere Gardens, James wrote one of his elegiac letters to Mrs. Wister, in far-off Philadelphia, to bring home to Mrs. Kemble's daughter the scene he had just witnessed. Mrs. Kemble had wanted to go, he said, and "she went when she could, at last, without a pang. She was very touching in her infirmity all these last months—and yet with her wonderful air of smouldering embers under ashes, she leaves a great image—a great memory."

On the day of the funeral George Bentley, who had published Mrs. Kemble's various books, asked James to write a tribute in the magazine *Temple Bar*. The article, which was published almost immediately, is one of the most vivid of his series of memorials. In it James sought to sketch "the grand line and mass" of Mrs. Kemble's personality, to bring her back to a new generation. "A prouder nature never affronted the long humiliation of life," he wrote, and he also said that the death of the actress seemed like the end of some reign, the fall of some empire.

In his own life this was decidedly true. Mrs. Kemble was the last and the most important of the three old dowagers of his London life. She had reigned for many years, giving him love and tenderness and the support of her grand and assertive manner. From Mrs. Kemble had come more *données* for novels and tales than from anyone else, as James's notebooks testify. She exemplified for him the various—and the copious—in life. Her traveling clock, which she left him, ticked away the hours on his table and her photograph, an aged and wrinkled, worldly-wise female, hung ever after in his study.

Tale of a Tiger-Cat

While he was still recovering from his gout, James received a letter from Morton Fullerton inquiring about a tale by Vernon Lee which was supposed to have satirized the novelist. James answered he had heard that "the said Vernon has done something to me." He did not know what she had done and was determined not to find out, so that he wouldn't have to bother—"I don't *care* to care," he said.

James had indeed been satirized and quite pointedly by his Florentine friend. What seemed to have rankled had been his interest during her writing of *Miss Brown* nine years before, and the coldness with which he had received the book. In her tale "Lady Tal" she depicted an American writer named Jervase Marion, a "psychological" novelist, "an inmate of the world of Henry James and a kind of Henry James." Marion encounters in Venice the striking Lady Tal, who is writing a novel; he interests himself in her work so that he may find out more about her. There were many remarks in the tale which James (if he had read it) would have found cruel and unkind, not least the statement that he was "not at home" in England, and had "condemned himself to live in a world of acquaintances."

James had originally urged William to call on Vernon Lee in Florence. Now he wrote warning him that he should "draw it mild with her on the question of friendship. She's a tiger-cat!" He told William he had not read her story and knew of it only by hearsay. Nevertheless he considered that she had indulged in a piece of "treachery to private relations."

His warning came too late. William had already dined in the Via Garibaldi. Far from following Henry's advice, William wrote to Vernon Lee that he had read the story, found the portrait "clever enough" and not exactly malicious. However, to use a friend for "copy" implied on her part "such a strangely *objective* way of taking human beings, and such a detachment from the sympathetic considerations which usually govern human intercourse, that you will not be surprised to learn that seeing the book has quite quenched my desire to pay you another visit."

Vernon Lee was penitent. William wrote to her a week later: "Your note wipes away the affront as far as I am concerned, only you must never, *never,* NEVER, do such a thing again in any future book! It is too serious a matter." When Henry learned of William's *démarches* on his behalf, he expressed himself as "partly amused and partly disconcerted." He would have preferred indifference. Henry was convinced that what she had done was "absolutely deliberate."

From then on Henry James "cut" Vernon Lee. An attempt by a mutual friend to bring the two together in 1900 proved unsuccessful. Vernon Lee had committed, as far as Henry was concerned, an unpardonable sin: she had taken a portrait from life, but had transformed it by mockery and spite and had not exposed it to the process of art. She had invaded James's privacy. There could be no forgiving.

In the Market-Place

At the beginning of 1893 James's situation in the theater was as follows: *The American* had been revised and turned into a comedy; Valentin de Bellegarde was made to recover instead of die after the duel. Claire, instead of going into a convent, married Newman. The play continued to be given in this form in the provinces. *Tenants,* offered to John Hare, was for the moment on the shelf. *Mrs. Jasper,* Daly's play, was scheduled for production at the end of the year. James had sketched out a second play for Ada Rehan, which would later become the tale "Covering End." And he had three other scenarios either on paper or in his head.

He lingered in De Vere Gardens after writing his memorial essay on Mrs. Kemble, and went to Paris towards the end of March. He had planned to go on to Florence, to be with William and his family; it now looked, however, as if William was coming north, so Henry settled in the Hôtel Westminster, to work at another play, and enjoy the Parisian spring. He visited Daudet and found him more of an invalid than ever; they dined together twice, and on one of these occasions Henry encountered in his home Maurice Barrès, whom he had met in Florence.

A further attack of gout limited James's activities for a few days, and Morton Fullerton came with some regularity to see him at his hotel. When he recovered he dined and went to art exhibitions with Miss Reubell, had lunch with Jusserand, and encountered some of the "babyish decadents." On one occasion he went to tea with the Whistlers, installed now "in their queer little garden-house of the rue du Bac," which he was to use in *The Ambassadors.* One afternoon James spent talking with Henry Harland at a café in the Champs Élysées.

On 4 May he went to Lucerne and put up at the Hôtel National, to be near his brother, whose sabbatical year was running to its end. The family was about five miles away, on the lakeside. Henry's stay at Lucerne was not prolonged. Theatrical affairs were summoning him to London—the opening of Daly's new theater, and a production at the St. James's of *The Second Mrs. Tanqueray,* in which Elizabeth Robins had yielded the main role to the then almost unknown Mrs. Patrick Campbell.

He was back in time to see Mrs. Pat's great triumph as Paula Tanqueray on opening night. On the following morning he wrote to Arthur

Pinero: "I was held, as in a strong hand, by your play." What was more, the production convinced him that George Alexander was a manager for whom a serious drama might be written. James sought a meeting with him and told him he was prepared to outline three subjects. This he did on 2 July in a letter written from Ramsgate.

His first proposal was for a romantic costume play, originally offered to Compton, about a young man destined for the priesthood. This Alexander liked; the actor had a fine pair of legs and was always partial to costume. James settled down at Ramsgate to the writing of his drama, later called *Guy Domville.* Thus was formed a curious partnership in the theater—that of the fifty-year-old James, exasperated by his unsuccessful efforts to get himself produced on the London stage, and the actor-manager of the St. James's, who at thirty-five was the talk of London because of *Mrs. Tanqueray.*

From the first James had no doubt that he was dealing with a cool businessman. This was clear from Alexander's terms. Like Daly, he offered to pay £5 a night; however he placed a ceiling of £3,000 on royalties, with the full rights in the play to go to him after the ceiling was reached. "I should be obliged to you if you can put the case to me more dazzlingly, another way," Henry James replied. The novelist finally settled for £7 a night for London and America and £5 elsewhere, and ceded rights for a ten-year period. He brought Alexander the completed play that autumn, knowing that it would have to wait until *Mrs. Tanqueray* had run its full course, and that Alexander had at least one other commitment—to a play by Henry Arthur Jones.

Meanwhile James's play for Ada Rehan was approaching production. Augustin Daly had long been a manager in New York. He had been a drama reviewer in his youth, and later an adapter of plays from French or German. He had now built his theater in London, and while his reputation rested largely on his staging of comedies of manners, in which Miss Rehan brilliantly played, he had welcomed the opportunity to do a new play by an American novelist of James's eminence.

The original script of *Mrs. Jasper* had seemed to him weak, and earlier in the year James had made many revisions at his suggestion. What Daly wanted above all was a strong part for Miss Rehan. James, aware of this, had yielded ground on almost every proposal. The script, however, must have been rather carelessly read by Daly, and even by Miss Rehan. For when they finally took it in hand it became clear to them that they had an amateurish unactable play. Entrances and exits were handled with an awkwardness that could have created laughter in the theater. The characters had occasional funny lines; yet they never came to life even as caricatures. The play was mechanical and contrived.

Daly had publicly announced the work when he opened his new theater, and James had gone over the models of the stage sets. Daly's season, however, ran into difficulties. The London audiences were attached to certain playhouses and had not yet accustomed themselves to the existence of his new establishment. James believed that with the losses Daly had suffered, his play would be a distinct asset for the new season.

Late in October Daly re-read the play, with more misgivings than ever, and asked for further cuts and revisions. "I will go over the copy," James replied, "and be as heroic as I can." Six days later James reported "utter failure." He assured Daly, however, that he would leave himself quite "open to impressions" during the rehearsals. In November Daly announced the production of the play for January and promised rehearsals early in December. The manager was unhappy over the new title, *Disengaged.* He wanted to get Miss Rehan's role into it. James bombarded him with more titles, and *Mrs. Jasper's Way* was finally selected.

In the production of *The American* James had been a participant from the first; now, however, he had to wait for signals from the managerial office. One or two readings of the play seem to have taken place privately in Daly's office, and the first James heard of these was in a letter from the manager on 3 December informing him that the comedy still lacked "story." Since James had conceded this point long ago, it seemed to him late in the day to have it brought up again. "I am very sorry, not a little alarmed," he wrote to Daly; and it was agreed that they would hold their first rehearsal on 6 December.

For what happened at that rehearsal, we must depend on Henry James's rather colored version. He arrived expecting to be allowed to read the play to the actors and to explain its fine points to them, as dramatists did in France. "I was not given a single second's opportunity of having the least contact or word with any member of the company," he complained afterwards. It was all "a ghastly and disgraceful farce." The actors read their parts "stammeringly" and vanished at the end of the third act. James described Miss Rehan as looking "white, haggard, ill, almost in anguish." He could not bring himself to speak to her.

The next morning James wrote to Daly withdrawing the comedy. He said that his play might not contain "the elements of success," but that at "my stage of relationship to the theatre I am much too nervous a subject not to accept as *determining,* in regard to my own action, any sound of alarm, or of essential scepticism, however abrupt, on the part of a manager." Daly replied that he was as disappointed as Henry "at the unexpected results" of the several readings. The rehearsals, however, had convinced him that "the lack of situation and dramatic climax could not be overcome by the smartest wit however much it might be accentuated by expression or enforced by the actor's art."

The correspondence between the manager and James does not substantiate the novelist's charge that Daly deliberately provoked withdrawal of *Mrs. Jasper's Way.* The play, and the possibility of being produced by Daly, loomed much larger in Henry's life than in that of the manager. Faced with an experienced manager and a highly competent company, James had offered a trivial and inadequate piece of work. He had counted passively on the actors. On a deeper level it might be said that James worked in the theater "against the grain." His own resistances could not be overcome. The text of the play bears witness against him.

2

THE
ALTAR OF
THE DEAD

༓

A Venetian Christmas

"Mr. James will come to Italy every year. And perhaps we can write that play after all." Fenimore packed her trunks at 15 Beaumont Street in Oxford. She sent the heavy ones and a heavy box of books by sea to Venice. She had finished the serial of *Horace Chase* and planned that summer to revise it for book publication. It was June when she was ready to leave. In London she paused for some visits to the dentist, and then was ill with influenza for some days. When she finally left for the Continent she felt weak; and she was deeply depressed.

She had no thought of returning to Florence, much as she loved that city. There had been too much heartache in leaving Bellosguardo. But she longed for Venice. Arriving in late June, gliding through the canals, it seemed as if she could recover some of her old happiness. She found rooms in the Casa Biondetti, not far from the Salute. She had five windows on the Canal and spent hours looking at the water traffic. She had a drawing-room, a small dining-room, two bedrooms and a one-room penthouse, where there was always the sea-breeze and a splendid view.

Fenimore, however, wanted a furnished apartment rather than mere lodgings, and began an active search almost immediately. It was part of her Venetian adventure, to travel by gondola to various palaces and smaller houses, in search of a place she could make into a home. In October James wrote to Francis Boott, announcing he would go to Italy —to Tuscany—in the spring, and

> I shall take Venetia by the way and pay a visit to our excellent friend Fenimore. She has taken, for the winter, General de Horsey's Casa Semitecolo, near the Palazzo Dario, and I believe is materially comfortable; especially as she loves Venice, for which small blame to her! But I

figure her as extremely exhausted (as she always is at such times), with her writing and re-writing of her last novel. . . . She is to have, I trust, a winter of bookless peace.

General de Horsey, who never stayed in Venice in the winter, was delighted to have Miss Woolson as his tenant. He leased her two floors on an eight-months' lease at $40 a month; Fenimore had two drawing-rooms, a winter bedroom on the side opposite the Canal looking down into a little *calle,* a summer bedroom on the Canal, a dining-room, kitchen and three servants' rooms. The furniture was excellent.

By early winter she was installed in the Semitecolo. There, with her Pomeranian, Otello, called affectionately Tello, she gave herself over to the lonely life she had always led. She spent much of the day in her gondola, compiling for Mrs. Bronson a list of islands in the lagoon which during the centuries had been swallowed up by the sea. She often visited San Niccolò di Lido, where there was a fort and a cemetery with English and German graves. She took copious notes on many islands, visited patiently, day after day, during December. She seemed to be content with a cataloging of these scraps of land and the play of light and the fishing-boats in the background. She told herself she would begin a new novel with the new year. In the spring Henry James would pay his promised visit.

Towards Christmas she seems to have made up her mind that she might take root in the place, for she began to look at unfurnished apartments. One, a magnificent apartment in the Palazzo Pesaro, on the Grand Canal below the Rialto—ten or twelve superb high-ceilinged rooms with great balconies on the Canal, all in perfect order, owned by the Duchess of Bevilacqua, was available for $400 a year. But how did one heat such a place in winter?—especially with those high ceilings? And where would she find enough furniture?

On Christmas Eve it was so warm that Fenimore had no use for her fur cloak. She went to the Lido in her gondola and walked for two hours on the Adriatic beach. For a while she sat on the grassy embankment of Fort San Niccolò. The sea and sky were blue, and the long line of the Alps was visible with more distinctness than she had ever noticed before. She remarked that the large tree at San Niccolò was a sycamore; and she wrote down the inscription on one of the graves in the cemetery:

. . . *dopo 45 anni vita laboriosa ed onesta, affranto dalle sventure, per troppo delicate sentire, finiva di vivere, agosto 1887* . . .

And then she wrote, on a note of melancholy: "I should like to turn into a peak when I die; to be a beautiful purple mountain, which would please the tired, sad eyes of thousands of human beings for ages."

That same day she wrote to an old friend:

> I have taught myself to be calm and philosophic, and I feel perfectly sure
> that the next existence will make clear all the mysteries and riddles of
> this. In the meantime, one can do one's duty or try to do it. But if at any
> time you should hear that I have gone, I want you to know beforehand
> that my end was peace, and even joy at the release . . . Now I am going
> out again for another walk through the beautiful Piazza.

In London, in De Vere Gardens, Henry James spent a lonely Christmas,
rejoicing in his solitude. A few evenings earlier, calling on Elizabeth
Robins, he stayed past midnight, and apparently talked at length of his
difficulties in the theater. The episode with Daly had shaken him
severely; he persevered, however, in the hope that he would fare better
with Alexander. Just before Christmas he made certain new cuts and
revisions in the *Guy Domville* script.

On the day after Christmas, sitting by his fire, he began to sketch a
new play. Calm though London was, in the season of peace, James's mind
seemed to be filled with violence. He drew up an outline for a drama of
Ibsen-like intensity in which he devised a climax more terrible than any
he had ever set down before. There would be a dying woman, who would
exact a pledge from her husband that he should never remarry so long
as their child was alive; and this would be an open invitation to another
woman to do away with this human obstacle. The wife dies. The "Bad
Heroine," who is "fearfully in love with my Hero," was to drown the child
—a denouement unusual in a man whose novels record little violence.

After Christmas, and until the new year, James attacked a large mass
of correspondence. He wrote a long letter to William describing the Daly
episode, which had been "a horrid experience." However, he was not
giving up the theater.

> I mean to wage this war ferociously for one year more—1894—and
> then (unless the victory and the spoils have not by that become more
> proportionate than hitherto to the humiliations and vulgarities and dis-
> gusts, all the dishonour and chronic insult incurred) to "chuck" the
> whole intolerable experiment and return to more elevated and more
> independent courses.

"I have come," he told William, "to *hate* the whole theatrical subject."

On the last day of 1893 he wrote a letter to Venice, to Mrs. Bronson.
As in his other letters, he described the Christmas quiet that had descended on London, and the peaceful days he had spent. Elsewhere in
this letter he asked: "Do you see anything of my old friend Miss Woolson?
I am very fond of her and should be glad if there was any way in which
you could be kind to her."

Miss Woolson

In the early morning hours of 24 January 1894—a little after one o'clock—two men walking in the *calle* beside the Casa Semitecolo noticed, in the dark, a white mass on the cobbles. One of the men thrust at it with his stick and evoked a startling unearthly moan. The frightened men began to shout. Lights appeared, and servants: a nurse came running out of the building. Miss Woolson was carried back into the Casa. She had been ill with a new bout of influenza and had had a high fever. A few minutes before the men came upon her, she had sent her nurse to get something from one of the drawing-rooms. While the nurse was gone, she had apparently opened the second-story window of her bedroom and thrown herself—or, as her relatives claimed, fallen—into the little street.

The grand-niece of James Fenimore Cooper was placed on her bed. She lay peacefully, with no sign of pain and little sign of life. The doctor was summoned. She was, however, beyond recall. By the time the wintry dawn broke over the little canals and the lagoons, and over the Alps she had so recently contemplated, the solitary, shut-in life of Constance Fenimore Woolson had come to an end.

The American consul was promptly informed and cables were dispatched to Miss Woolson's sister, Clara Benedict, in New York. A cousin, Grace Carter, who was in Munich, was summoned. Miss Woolson had died on a Wednesday; on Thursday the 25th the cousin arrived and took charge. From the nurse she gathered that Fenimore had spoken of wanting to be buried in Rome. The servants were dismissed and the Casa locked up under consular seal to await the arrival of the sister. Miss Carter accompanied the body to Rome, where John Hay, friend of Fenimore, happened to be on a holiday. He took charge of the final arrangements.

Henry James received the tidings of Miss Woolson's death from Mrs. Benedict in a cable from New York. She asked him whether he might find it possible to leave for Venice. Shocked and mystified, he assumed that Miss Woolson, like Lizzie Boott, had died of natural causes; an exchange of telegrams with Dr. Baldwin in Florence and word from John Hay gave him the facts about the funeral in Rome, which had been set for Wednesday the 31st, but no other details. He accordingly went, on the Saturday afternoon, to Cook's and made his travel plans. On returning to De Vere Gardens, he found a note from Constance Fletcher, who lived in Venice, and who was at that moment in London. She enclosed a clipping from a Venetian newspaper which gave a circumstantial account of the manner in which Miss Woolson had met her end.

It was now that James experienced the full shock of her strange death. By the next day, Sunday, he had made up his mind that he could not face the ordeal of her funeral. Before the "horror and pity" of the news, he wrote to John Hay, "I have utterly collapsed. I have let everything go, and last night I wired to Miss Carter that my dismal journey was impossible to me." He went on to say that

> Miss Woolson was so valued and close a friend of mine and had been for so many years that I feel an intense nearness of participation in every circumstance of her tragic end and in every detail of the sequel. But it is just this nearness of emotion that has made—since yesterday—the immediate horrified rush to personally *meet* these things impossible to me.

It is clear that James had been quite resigned to going to Rome when he had thought Fenimore had died of natural causes. From the moment that he learned she had taken her own life—as *The Times* finally reported the next day—he had been sickened and overwhelmed, not only by grief and, as he said, horror and pity, but also by a feeling that in some way he too had some responsibility for her last act.

His decision not to go to Rome was apparently an instinctive act of self-protection: he could have faced the dead Fenimore if she had died as his sister had died. It was the brutality, the violence, the stark horror, the mystery, the seeming madness of Fenimore's last act which lacerated him. In doing violence to herself, she had, so to speak, done violence to him and he sought now some shield behind which he could withdraw and take care of his deep wound and his guilt.

Writing on the day after his decision not to go to Rome, to Margaret Brooke, the Ranee of Sarawak, who was in Italy, he spoke of Fenimore as "a close and valued friend of mine—a friend of many years with whom I was extremely intimate and to whom I was greatly attached." He had never quite expressed it in this way—"with whom I was extremely intimate." Fenimore had always been his "admirable" friend, his "distinguished friend." But the Ranee had not known Miss Woolson, and he could speak to her, perhaps, more freely.

On the day of the funeral James wrote to Francis Boott: "I feel how, like myself, you must be sitting horror-stricken at the last tragic act of poor C.F.W." Seeking explanations, reasons, motivations, James suggested to Boott that the event demanded

> the hypothesis of sudden *dementia* and to admit none other. Pitiful victim of chronic melancholy as she was (so that half one's friendship for her was always anxiety), nothing is more possible than that, in illness,

this obsession should abruptly have deepened into suicidal mania. There was nothing whatever, that I know of, in her immediate circumstances, to explain it—save indeed the sadness of her lonely Venetian winter.

Fenimore was buried in a corner of the Protestant Cemetery in Rome, near the point where the pagan pyramid of Caius Cestius thrusts its sharp diagonal beside the Christian ground. She lies under the tall cypresses, not far from the graves of Shelley and Trelawny, and a short distance from the graves where Keats and his friend Severn are placed side by side. A modern visitor among these clustered tombstones cannot but be struck by the fact that she also was buried—fate so arranged it— almost in the very spot where Henry James had tenderly laid to rest one of his most famous heroines. Here Daisy Miller had been interred on an April morning, "in an angle of the wall of Imperial Rome, beneath the cypresses and the thick spring-flowers." It was still winter when the earth covered Miss Woolson's coffin. John Hay caused the plot to be planted with violets, and in due course a wide marble coping was placed round the flower-bed, and a Celtic cross of stone laid within it. On the coping there is simply the name Constance Fenimore Woolson, and the year of her death, 1894.

Casa Biondetti

"There is much that is tragically obscure in that horror of last week —and I feel as if I were living in the shadow of it," James wrote to Edmund Gosse, who read the paragraph in *The Times* and questioned him about his dead friend. To Mrs. Bronson he spoke of "the strange obscurity of so much of the matter" and said that it had the "impenetrability of madness." James was unable to penetrate the obscurity; he could only offer himself consoling thoughts. He learned that Miss Woolson had been delirious, he was aware of the deep depression that often accompanies influenza; he reminded himself again of the circumstances of solitude and melancholy. "My own belief," he wrote to William, "is that she had been on the very verge of suicide years ago, and that it had only been stood off by the practical interposition of two or three friendships which operated (to their own sense) with a constant vague anxiety." Again and again, to his inquiring friends, he repeated the sentence that "half one's friendship for her was always anxiety," and he thereby discerned in his relationship with Fenimore those elements that had made for disquiet and uneasiness in himself. There had been, from the first, the obstacle of her deafness. Communication with her had never been easy; and doubtless it had been at its best in their correspondence. Had they really understood one another? Had her act been a partial consequence of frustration—of frustrated love for James? The promise of an annual visit was thin support for an elderly devoted spinster living in a comparatively soundless world. It is clear that in time James took comfort in the thought that Fenimore had been seriously ill, and that she had not been altogether responsible for her actions.

There was another question, of a practical kind, which may have been a source of anxiety to the novelist. This was his correspondence with Fenimore. The author of "The Aspern Papers" was all too aware of how many trunks Fenimore possessed; he had seen her constitutional difficulty in extricating herself from the clutter of her days. He could imagine—he who was intensely private and secretive—what piles of paper, notebooks, possibly even diaries, there might be lying at this moment in the rooms of the temporarily sealed apartment in the Casa Semitecolo. Fenimore had spoken of a will, shortly before her death; none was found. She had even—he heard later—told Francis Boott that her last testament would contain a "surprise." In the absence of a will, Clara Woolson Benedict, Fenimore's sister in New York, fell heir to all her possessions. And James, in his correspondence with Mrs. Benedict, suggested that he would meet her when she came abroad, escort her to Venice and give her all the assistance she might need in taking charge of Fenimore's belongings. His good offices would be of great help to the bereaved woman, particularly since she spoke no Italian. At the same time he would be in Venice when the Casa was opened up, and at hand to cope with whatever privacies might require safeguarding among the dead woman's papers.

Without divulging why he was coming to Venice, he asked Mrs. Bronson to find him some rooms—if possible the rooms Miss Woolson had occupied in the Casa Biondetti before moving into the Semitecolo. "A combination of circumstances, some of which I would have wished other, but which I must accept, makes it absolutely necessary I should be in Venice from the first of April," he explained. Mrs. Bronson sent him a cable very promptly to say that the apartment had been secured.

He reached Genoa five days before Mrs. Benedict, and was on the pier on 29 March 1894 when the *Kaiser Wilhelm II* docked. Mrs. Benedict, who was accompanied by her daughter Clare, went first to Rome, to visit the grave. James went directly to Venice, to await their coming. "I found this pleasant little apartment quite ready for me and appreciably full of the happy presence of your aunt," he wrote from the Casa Biondetti to Clare Benedict in Rome. It was probably while he was waiting for the Benedicts that James visited, by himself, the little street behind the Casa Semitecolo and looked at the window from which Fenimore had jumped. "The sight of the *scene* of her horrible act is, for that matter, sufficient to establish utter madness at the time," he wrote to Francis Boott. "A place more mad for *her* couldn't be imagined."

The Benedicts arrived within a matter of days. Henry, Grace Carter, and Fenimore's two gondoliers leading her dog Tello, met them. On the morning after their arrival the seals were removed and the silent rooms were entered—"a heartbreaking day, followed by many weeks of a task beyond words hard," Mrs. Benedict wrote in her diary. To a friend she wrote that "Henry James met us at Genoa, and never never left us until all her precious things were packed and boxed and sent to America." Mrs. Benedict distributed mementoes to Fenimore's friends. James recovered such of his letters as were found and was invited to take such books of Fenimore's as he wished. Among those he took were eleven volumes of her Turgenev in French, bound in half-morocco ("You are now our Turgenev," she had once written to Henry); and her personal volume of *Rodman the Keeper,* containing the place and date of each sketch, inserted in her own hand.

As Henry had suspected, the literary remains were voluminous. There were the notes she had been taking on the lagoons and islands of Venice. There was a commonplace book filled with comments on her reading. There were notebooks containing her reflections on art, music and literature, most of them of a distressing banality. Occasionally, however, an interesting thought crept in, such as: " 'He is interested in indexes,' said H. with profound stupefaction."

There were jottings of remarks she had heard; comments in drawing-rooms; ideas for stories. There was one note above all which James may have seen and which could have been the source for an entry in his own notebooks. Fenimore wrote:

> To imagine a man spending his life looking for and waiting for his "splendid moment." "Is this my moment?" "Will this state of things bring it to me?" But the moment never comes. When he is old and infirm it comes to a neighbour who has never thought of it or cared for it. The comment of the first upon this.

James's note, written seven years later, ran:

> A man haunted by the fear, more and more throughout life, that *something will happen to him;* he doesn't quite know what . . .

This was the germ from which he would write "The Beast in the Jungle."

Early in May twenty-seven boxes containing the effects accumulated during Miss Woolson's literary life abroad were dispatched to America. James, Mrs. Benedict recorded in her diary, "came every day to see and help us—we could not have gone through it without him." Apparently, once he had satisfied himself about Fenimore's literary remains, he reverted to his usual working hours, spending his forenoons and early

afternoons at the Casa Biondetti. On most evenings he dined with the
Benedicts. He wrote to William James of "the great hole bored in my time
and my nerves by the copious aid and comfort I couldn't help giving to
poor Mrs. Benedict"—though in fact the novelist's direct aid to Mrs. Benedict seems to have ended with his first fortnight in Venice. A notebook
entry of 17 April 1894 suggests the term of his principal funereal duties,
but suggests also the inner outrage he had suffered.

> Here I sit, at last, after many interruptions, distractions, and defeats,
> with some little prospect of getting a clear time to settle down to work
> again. The last six weeks . . . have been a period of terrific sacrifice to the
> ravenous Moloch of one's endless personal social relations—one's eternal
> exposures, accidents, disasters. *Basta.*

Exposures, accidents, disasters. There had been danger of exposure;
there had been accident; there was the disastrous inroad on his working
time: there was the greater disaster of his personal hurt. We may guess
that when he made this note—that is, two weeks after the work at the
Casa Semitecolo began—James had settled all the practical questions
that concerned him in Fenimore's death, and he could relax. The most
difficult part was over. The mystery of her life and death remained. As
for the rest—*basta!*

Early in May the Benedicts left for further travels in Europe. Few of
James's friends were in Venice. He could settle down to work that had
been delayed. He had promised Henry Harland a long tale for the *Yellow
Book.* The first issue, earlier that year, had contained his sardonic tale
of "The Death of the Lion," written just after Fenimore's death. Its picture of an elderly, neglected man of letters, who becomes a "lion" because
a newspaper finally takes notice of him, was one of the bitterest—and
most amusing—of the "tales of the literary life" which James now began
to write.

The tale which James set down in Venice was "The Coxon Fund,"
built around his recent reading of a life of Coleridge by James Dykes
Campbell. His story of the gifted Saltram, who has magic in his talk, and
lives his life unconcerned by the philistines around him, is perhaps the
first in which James's "later manner" begins to emerge: in it he struggled
to express, in a bolder way than ever before, his belief in the supremacy
of the artist, whose vagaries and idiosyncrasies society must learn to
tolerate. The artist, he is saying, must be given full freedom; but it must
be recognized that if he is too well endowed, he might cease to struggle
altogether. When finally an American fund is established for the gifted
Saltram, he lapses into benign indifference. "The very day he found
himself able to publish, he wholly ceased to produce." His wife says he

has simply become "like everyone else." "The Coxon Fund" was like James's other "tales of the literary life," which emerged, he was to say, from "the designer's own mind" and were fathered "on his own intimate experience." They expressed James's disappointment in the market-place as well as in the world of letters. He felt that his work was misread —when it was read—and more often discussed without having been read at all. James was at last beginning to say that he did not care; that he would go his own way, publicly and privately, and—*que diable!*—take from life what he could get from it. In the Casa Biondetti that gruesome summer, he began to find the light for his later years.

This did not mean that the old ingrained puritanism in him found-ered at this moment. The obverse of "The Coxon Fund" was still an individual carrying his bundle of guilt on his shoulders. And in the Casa Biondetti he set down the idea for a tale he would write many years later: that of a young man with some unspecified burden—"a secret, a worry, a misery, a burden, an oppression"—who seeks someone to listen to him, that he may find release. The tale, "A Round of Visits," was not written until 1910, by which time it underwent many modifications. But the note for it in Venice, at the time of the writing of "The Coxon Fund," is relevant to the anxieties of that time.

While he worked in the Casa Biondetti, the hot weather came and with it the Grand Canal was transformed into Marlborough Street and Back Bay. Venice became, "if I may be allowed the expression, the mere *vomitorium* of Boston." He had never seen such an Americanized Ven-ice, all mixed up with the Germans and other European tourists in the Piazza. Late in May he decided to make the pilgrimage he had promised himself. He would pay his visit to Fenimore; he would keep his solemn promise to her—and to himself.

When James left Venice, crowded with his countrymen, he felt like "Apollo fleeing the furies." Rome seemed empty by comparison, and it happened to be cool. The city spoke to him "with its old most-loved voice as if a thousand vulgarities perpetrated during the last fifteen years had never been." He went to the Barberini and called on William Wetmore Story. He found the old sculptor now "very silent and vague and gentle" and "the ghost of his old clownship."

Count Primoli invited James to luncheon in his picturesque palace near the Tiber, and here he found himself sitting next to the "she-Zola" of Italy, Matilde Serao, "a wonderful little burly Balzac in petticoats." Here Madame Serao told James the astonishing news that Paul Bourget had just been elected to the Academy—had arrived comparatively young among France's "immortals."

When he stood before Miss Woolson's grave for the first time it had already received its marble coping. It was purple with Roman violets; veins of newly-planted ivy crept round its base. James had always been deeply moved by the Protestant Cemetery ever since the time of "Daisy Miller." He described the grave to Boott as "beautiful—in a beautiful spot —close to Shelley's. It was her intense desire to lie there." Thirteen years later, on his last visit to Rome, he made the pilgrimage again, for he wrote then to the Benedicts:

> The most beautiful thing in Italy, almost, seemed to me . . . that very particular spot below the great grey wall, the cypresses and the time-silvered pyramid. It is tremendously, inexhaustibly touching—its effect never fails to overwhelm.

We may believe that he was overwhelmed when he saw the grave in its violet-sprinkled newness in 1894. "I echo your judgment of her life and fate—they are unmitigatedly tragic," he wrote to Boott.

The Desecrated Altars

The remainder of James's stay in Italy that summer of 1894 was a scramble and a continual heartache. He spent a few days in Naples; he returned to Rome; he went to Florence and stayed with Dr. Baldwin. He went to Bologna, where it was quiet, and he had a few peaceful days. He didn't want to go back to Venice. He wondered whether he would ever return. Finally, at the end of June, he journeyed there just long enough to pick up some luggage, and even then he withdrew to visit Mrs. Bronson at Asolo, at the uncomfortable La Mura. There were tourists everywhere. To this had his great American-European legend come. He, who had been its veritable historian, was now the spectator of a great invasion. One Mrs. Jack Gardner, bestriding Europe, could be a source of amusement; a thousand Mrs. Jacks was a catastrophe. He was to write in his notebook a year later of "the Americans looming up—dim, vast, portentous—in their millions—like gathering waves—the barbarians of the Roman Empire."

Early in July he went to the Splügen: he found the little river that girdled the hotel at Chur thin and brown, "and the voice of the compatriot rings over it almost as loudly as over the Grand Canal." His great temple had been desecrated; his altars ravished. The long quiet of his personal "Europe" was shattered. He had planned to stay away from London until August. He was back in De Vere Gardens on 12 July. He had left the Continent, almost, for life. He would cross the Channel but three times during his remaining years, and at very long intervals.

There were importunate Americans in London as well; Mrs. Gardner was on the horizon, and James left to pay rural visits. He spent some days

at Torquay with W. E. Norris, a minor novelist of the time whom he had
come to know, and whom he liked. In mid-August he went to St. Ives, in
Cornwall, to stay near the Leslie Stephens. He put up at the Tregenna
Castle Hotel; and every day he went for long walks with his former
Cornhill editor, "the silent Stephen, the almost speechless Leslie," paying occasional visits to Talland House, the Stephen summer home. For
a fortnight James moved in the future landscape of *To the Lighthouse*
and among its people; and went striding over the moors with the future
Mr. Ramsay. Although he had known Stephen since 1869 they still met
and walked in great intervals of silence. James found this kind of English
"dumbness" a relief after the chattering tourists of the Continent. And
the vigorous walks on moor and seacoast gave him the physical exercise
and relief he had hoped to get in Switzerland.

At the end of the summer, quite without design, but by circumstances
not altogether coincidental, he found himself housed once more with the
ghost of Fenimore. The Bourgets had come to England to spend a brief
holiday while their new apartment was being prepared for them in Paris.
They went to Oxford and put up at the Randolph, where James joined
them. To be in Oxford was to be in the very spot—as it happened, the very
street—where Fenimore had spent her last months in England and
where, on occasion, he had visited her. "Disturbing as it was to enter the
house," James nevertheless walked the few steps from his hotel to No. 15
Beaumont Street to call on Fenimore's former landlady, Mrs. Phillips.

He did not spare himself this re-encounter with a recent past; he not
only invited it, but ended by taking lodgings in the same house, as he had
done in Venice. He seemed to cling to Fenimore—to her memory. His
letters during most of September 1894 and several entries in his notebook
are dated 15 Beaumont Street, Oxford. He saw much of the Bourgets. He
and his confrère would spend the day at their work and meet in the late
afternoon for long strolls through college gardens and cloisters in the
waning light. Bourget, for all his success, was deeply depressed; his election to the Academy, which would have gratified most writers, seemed to
him one burden the more. The image comes to us of James and Bourget,
both rather short and stout, walking solemnly through the ancient town
and its historic colleges, haunted by private phantoms, yet turning them
into brilliant talk. This was the background for the theme James entered
in his notebook one day in Beaumont Street, after the Bourgets had left.
He wanted to write a tale called "The Altar of the Dead." It would be the
story of an individual who cherishes for "the silent, for the patient, the
unreproaching dead" a tenderness which finally takes the form of some
shrine—some great altar in which a candle is lit for each person who is
gone. James emphasized that the altar was "an altar in his mind, in his
soul." Later in working out the tale he gave it material form: his hero,

Stransom, actually arranges to establish the altar in a church.

"The Altar of the Dead," completed very rapidly in De Vere Gardens, is an eerie tale, flimsy in its materials, yet written in great prose organ-tones, and evocative in its symbolism: for it embraces the universal relation between the living and the dead. Stransom, lighting candles for all his dead, cannot bring himself to light one for Acton Hague, the friend who had once wronged him. He has forgiven Hague, but he will not include him in his particular shrine. Presently Stransom discovers that a woman is also worshipping at his altar, and that for her the entire altar is but as a single candle, lit for the very man he has excluded. Acton Hague had wronged her also. She had forgiven and she worships his memory. Stransom, who had expected that the last missing candle would be lit for himself, finds her insisting that it be lit for Hague.

In effect the woman in this tale takes from the man his "altar of the mind"; she will have it only on her terms. Presently Stransom recognizes that "she was really the priestess of his altar." In these circumstances he loses all taste for his creation. There is little left for him to do. One day he dies before his ravished altar. She is contrite at the last moment; but the triumph is hers.

Decidedly Fenimore's act had stirred up in Henry James a sense of personal betrayal, a desecration of his private life, his altar of the mind. What we may read in "The Altar of the Dead" is that there had been between him and Fenimore a strange matching of personalities, and strange distortions in their mutual vision of one another. In Fenimore he had found a disinterested devotion—as distant as was consonant with his own sense of freedom and sovereignty. Then apparently, in some way, Fenimore had made him feel that she made claims on him—claims he had not been prepared to meet. The final "arrangement" that he would visit her once a year in Italy had been apparently an ultimate compromise. Yet in the end she had performed an act of horror. His altar was spattered with her blood. And the mystery of her grave was intolerable to someone like James, who sought total vision and total insight. Had she died a normal death James would have taken possession of her and been able to light a candle for her within the altar of his soul where candles were lit for his near ones of Quincy Street; for Minny, long ago; for Lizzie; for his great literary comrades; for Turgenev; for the young dead of his recent years. How light a candle for Fenimore, when he could not possess her? She had possessed herself: she had arbitrarily cut herself off from him. Fenimore had asked for too much: and her legacy was an eternal secret.

The old and long-buried equations of James's life had been acted out in Fenimore's death. In the struggle between man and woman, in many of his tales, one or the other had to die. It was impossible for two persons to survive a passion—and in this case had it been a passion? Certainly not on his side. But on hers apparently it had. These were the mysteries which now began to haunt James, and were to haunt him for years, until he would find a partial answer—a decade later—in the tale of "The Beast in the Jungle." But other experiences would intervene to offer illumination for that tale.

For the moment all he had was the silence of the grave in Rome, and the malaise that something had happened in his life: a great barrier, thrown across its roadway. In the past he had always "taken possession." In his tales of artists it is always someone else who makes the sacrifice for the great man, just as, twenty-five years before, he had felt, when his young cousin Minny Temple died, that she had surrendered her life to give him the strength to live.

Minny Temple had died at the end of James's twenty-seventh year, when he stood on the threshold of his literary life. Constance Fenimore Woolson had destroyed herself when he was in his fifty-first year, and a famous man. And now, before the long-burning candle of Minny, and the unlit candle of Fenimore, James found himself dreaming of a novel in which a young woman, with all life before her, an heiress of the ages, is stricken and must die. In the year of Fenimore's death he returned to his memories of Minny. Early in November 1894, shortly after writing "The Altar of the Dead," he made his first notes for the large fiction that would become, almost a decade later, *The Wings of the Dove.*

He named his heroine Milly Theale, thereby echoing Minny's name; however, when he set down his first notes for the novel the figure of Fenimore also stood beside him. We can glimpse her in his search for a place where he would assemble his characters. "I seem to see Nice or Mentone—or Cairo—or Corfu—designated as the scene of the action." James had never been in Cairo or Corfu; but Fenimore had. Her account of her eastern tour with Mrs. Benedict now appeared posthumously as a book, *Mentone, Cairo, and Corfu.* In the end James chose none of these places. Fenimore's death in Venice, that for the time had changed the aspect of his days, became the death in Venice of *The Wings of the Dove.*

The novel belongs to the later time, to the same period as "The Beast in the Jungle." And at its end the image of the dead girl dominates the living, and changes the course of their lives. In *The Wings of the Dove* James incorporated the two women whose deaths he had faced at the beginning and at the end of the middle span of his life—Minny, the dancing flame, who had yielded everything and asked for nothing and whom he possessed eternally; and Fenimore, the deep and quiet and strong-willed, who had given devotion "and intensities of fidelity" but had yielded nothing and had disturbed the innermost altar of his being.

The struggle for that altar was ended. In his altar-tale the hero died. In life James endured. Standing on the edge of winter late in 1894, James turned from his contemplation of the dead to the immediate problems of his life. George Alexander shook him out of his Oxford reverie by announcing rehearsals for *Guy Domville.* James had written to his brother that he would wage his theatrical "siege" for "one year more." The year was running to its term. Early in 1895 the play would be produced on the stage of one of London's best theaters, and by one of London's best companies. Perhaps the novelist would have his *revanche,* retrieve lost ground, find again a reasonable show of fame, perhaps even a modest show of fortune.

The period of his mourning was over. The recently-installed electric lights of the St. James's Theatre burned like some twinkling mundane altar, lit in the London market-place, where his newest work would find its public. Perhaps *Guy Domville* would be the better chance he had talked of in his tale "The Middle Years." At Christmas of 1894, when one of the most tragic years of his life approached its end, he waited for the rising of the curtain on his new play—and on his future.

The Scenic Idea

On the clock-stroke of fifty—in 1893—Henry James had had his first attack of gout. In quick succession, he had had three further attacks, one while he was staying in the Hôtel Westminster in Paris. The years were catching up with him—but not with his fertility. In a burst of alliteration he told Edmund Gosse he was "moody, misanthropic, melancholy, morbid, morose." The malaise was however more than gout. He had set it down in his notebooks. "Youth," he wrote, "the most beautiful word in the language." People grew old; institutions grew old; the very century had grown old. Everyone talked of *fin de siècle*. The Victorian Age was coming to an end and James had called his new volume *Terminations*. Three of the tales were about writers, dying or moribund, ignored by the work-a-day world. The volume that followed was called *Embarrassments*.

Moody, misanthropic, melancholy, morbid, morose—embarrassment seemed a mild enough word for such states of feeling. But James had been trying to become a playwright since 1890 and his life in the theater had not gone well; there had been endless delays; and his financial resources dwindled. His days were filled with personal relations not of his choosing. He was paying a heavy price for quitting his tower of fiction. He had told himself there would always be a line of retreat to the peace of his writing desk. "Among the delays, the disappointments, the *déboires* of the horrid theatric trade nothing is so soothing as to remember that literature sits patient at my door . . ."

Literature sat patiently at his door—and he kept it waiting. He might complain of "the vulgarities and pains" of stage production, yet he continued to suffer them. Perhaps he felt there could be no turning back; a kind of pride of endeavor possessed him. If he spoke of his contempt for the stage and for thespians, he was less willing to recognize that there was a kind of contempt of himself too for having truck with the perpetual self-exhibition around him. He rationalized his persistence in a little autobiographical story called "Nona Vincent" in which a young playwright sees a play through its production.

> The scenic idea was magnificent when once you had embraced it— the dramatic form had a purity which made some others look ingloriously rough. . . . There was a fearful amount of concession in it, but what you kept had a rare intensity. You were perpetually throwing over the cargo to save the ship, but what a motion you gave her when you made her ride the waves—a motion as rhythmic as the dance of a goddess!

In spite of his experience of "concession," he got a rude shock when he had first offered the scenario for *Guy Domville,* written in 1893 amid twinges of the gout, to Edward Compton and his wife for their provincial repertory. James proposed a drama of a young man destined for the priesthood who has to abandon his vocation because he is the last of his line. He owes it to his family name to marry and produce children. The scenario provided a touching love affair; and at the end James planned to have the novice reject the world—and the woman—for the monastery. The Comptons promptly expressed alarm that there would be no happy ending. James replied that renunciation of love was "the only ending I have ever dreamed of giving the play," indeed, he said, "it *is* the play." Would it not be "ugly and displeasing" to the audience to marry off someone who has one foot in a monastery? The Comptons argued it would please English audiences very much. James answered stiffly, "my subject is my subject to take or to leave." The Comptons did not take it.

James had been in the same predicament long ago when *The American* was serialized in the *Atlantic Monthly.* Howells had wanted the hero to marry the aristocratic lady and James had replied, with similar *hauteur,* "They would have been an impossible couple." He repeated to the Comptons that "to make a Catholic priest, or a youth who is next door to one, *marry,* really, when it comes to the point, *at all,* is to do to spectators a disagreeable and uncomfortable thing." What the Comptons could not convey to James was that the artistic discomfort was his own: it would not be the audience's. He could not conceive of the coarse. Nor did he recognize that an audience was entitled to a happy ending in a romantic work—that this was the tradition of popular "romance." His confusion between the romantic play he was writing and his sense of reality was strong. It was difficult for him, as a bachelor, to bestow a bride on his hero. Moreover, *The Second Mrs. Tanqueray* demonstrated to James that a certain kind of English audience would accept an unhappy ending. He had taken *Guy Domville* to George Alexander with the feeling that the actor-manager had a larger view than the provincial-touring Comptons.

In reality George Alexander had accepted *Guy Domville* for reasons that had nothing to do with its ending. A costume play which allowed him to be romantic in the first act, disillusioned in the second act, visionary in the third, would fill his matinees with sighing ladies; any play he produced was assured of a month's run. Most audiences at the St. James's wouldn't know who Henry James was; but they knew their George Alexander of the handsome profile and the trim legs. And when Alexander at last sat down to a critical reading of *Guy Domville,* late in 1894, he asked that scenes be cut and speeches abridged. James swallowed his pride and threw himself into the revisions, feeling as if the stage were exacting flesh from him every time he altered a scene. He told Elizabeth Robins that his play had been "abbreviated and simplified out of all *close* resemblance to my intention."

By 1894 James had admitted to himself that four of his comedies, which he had passed around the London theaters for two years, stood little chance of production. He accordingly published them as *Theatricals* in two volumes with rueful Addisonian prefaces, acknowledging that it was "an humiliating confession of defeat" to have to print unproduced plays. This was the first time during his dramatic years that he spoke of "defeat."

William James read his brother's plays when they came out and found them "unsympathetic." He offered a pointed criticism. He had noticed that the comedies depended wholly on verbal play and on characters not understanding what they said to one another, so that they were constantly explaining themselves. To such criticisms James's answer was—he put it into one of the prefaces—that the stage demanded of him "an anxious excess of simplicity." The word *anxious* catches our eye.

The Northern Henry

Henry James had first heard of Henrik Ibsen—"the northern Henry" as he later referred to him—from Edmund Gosse, who was fluent in the northern languages. "You must tell me more," he had written as far back as 1889. Gosse obliged his friend; and in 1890 we find James writing to him: "How provincial all these poor Dear Norsefolk, including the Colossus himself." By 1891, when he attended his first performance of Ibsen— *A Doll's House* with Elizabeth Robins—he had read excerpts from *Brand* and *Peer Gynt* in translation. In April 1891 James was still protesting. He found *Rosmersholm* dreary; *Ghosts* shocked him. *"Must* I think these things works of skill?" he queried Gosse. They seemed to him of a "grey mediocrity."

A few days after this he had gone to see Elizabeth Robins in her own production of *Hedda Gabler.* The play had "muddled and mystified" him when he read it; now he was fascinated. He sat through three performances and then had promptly written an article, "On the Occasion of *Hedda Gabler,*" which placed him on the side of the Ibsenites against the old-school Victorians. He could not, however, overcome his sense of Ibsen's "bare provinciality." Indeed he always found uncomplimentary adjectives to season his praise of Ibsen. He was "ugly, common, hard, prosaic, bottomlessly bourgeois"—and yet "of his art he's a master." But James recognized two things. The first was that Ibsen would be the "adored" dramatist of the acting profession; he made it possible for actors "to do the deep and delicate thing." The second—and this touched James personally—was Ibsen's extraordinary skill in projecting a situation, in choosing a crucial hour in the lives of a group, and within that hour making the audience aware of "the whole tissue of relations" among his people. In this sense Ibsen's influence on the later novels of Henry James was profound.

James did not discern at first Ibsen's symbolic power. He had complained of "the absence of style, both in the usual and larger sense of the word." This might have made Ibsen "vulgar," for he was "massively common and 'middle-class,' but neither his spirit," wrote James, "nor his manner is small." These remarks prompted William Archer, most dedicated of drama critics and one of Ibsen's translators, to a rejoinder. In a long letter he assured James that, in the original, Ibsen was a master of style—if style, on the stage, meant giving to every word a vital function. Ibsen, he maintained, had "a gigantic imagination," for he could seize a few fragments of experience and endow them with the depth and complexity of life. "Remember," Archer told James, "it is not as a realist, but rather as a symbolist, that I chiefly admire Ibsen." James was to remember this, for in a complementary piece, "On the Occasion of *The Master Builder,*" two years later, he spoke of "the mingled reality and symbolism of it all" that "gives us an Ibsen within an Ibsen."

The Master Builder arrived act by act in London. James, receiving the translation piecemeal, was driven "from bewilderment to madness." He looked for a leading part for Miss Robins, but saw only the Master Builder's role. When he later witnessed Miss Robins's great triumph as the heroine in the play he recognized the triumph of Ibsen as well, and he wrote of "the hard compulsion of his strangely inscrutable art."

Although the deeper influence of Ibsen on James's fiction belonged to the future, a direct influence could be seen in two plays projected in 1893, the year of his piecemeal reading of *The Master Builder.* Decidedly Ibsen, still a playwright for a small coterie in London, was hardly a model for a novelist who wished to find a large audience. Miss Robins obtained her hearings for Ibsen through subscription evenings, special performances, subsidized management. Nevertheless James had Ibsen in mind when, in planning *Guy Domville,* he shaped the play for a handful of characters and chose a critical moment in the hero's history; and when, late that year, he first sketched the scenario for what ultimately became *The Other House,* he planned a "bourgeois" drama and "provincial" characters in the manner of Ibsen—with a tense and violent "Bad Heroine" who seemed ideally suited for the special talents of the actress who had played Hedda in England.

"Saint Elizabeth"

The battle for Ibsen brought James close to Elizabeth Robins and their friend Mrs. Hugh Bell. We can glimpse these interesting ladies in James's theatrical tale of "Nona Vincent," written immediately after his experiences with *The American* in 1891. Miss Robins is embodied in the ambiguous, faltering actress with the two-toned name of Violet Grey—for she had her grey side as well as her violet. And Mrs. Bell, who was a wise and worldly English cosmopolite, is the quiet Mrs. Alsager—very sage and purposeful—who helps the young dramatist find a producer. The friendship between Miss Robins and James, begun during the days of *The American,* was one of backstage camaraderie and common dedication. The novelist, in his playwriting phase, nourished a dream of writing a great part for her. Miss Robins could be all fire and passion—and perversity—as Hedda or Hilda; but she could do little with other parts and other plays. She knew this and became an Ibsen specialist, although James repeatedly warned that she was narrowing her career.

Elizabeth Robins had a way of disarming those who talked with her —and she talked mainly to the great. She was all attention, her lustrous blue eyes creating an effect of hearing and understanding everything. She had managed with extraordinary skill, within a week after landing in London, to involve a dozen leading stage figures (among them Beerbohm Tree and Oscar Wilde) in her personal affairs. Only Bernard Shaw cut through her pose and for a long time Elizabeth Robins feared and detested him. He dubbed her "Saint Elizabeth." He understood her way of making herself the center of her environment. He had interviewed her when he was still a round-the-town journalist, and before they had ended their talk Miss Robins "swore she would shoot me if I said anything she didn't approve of."

Elizabeth Robins, with her large liquid eyes and her inner toughness, regarded men as creatures to be manipulated. She could love women; men were to be conquered and "used," and her secret love affair with the critic William Archer was a kind of collaboration in the theater as much as a passion. She remained secretive all her life. "What the world wants from her is not noble conduct but acting," Shaw told a friend. Miss Robins preferred noble conduct. And Shaw discerned one thing more—that Elizabeth Robins was a great actress only when she was acting her own life. He recognized that the emotion, so powerfully infused into Ibsen, was "really yourself and not your acting." In this the dramatist put his finger on her greatest secret. In later years Henry James also came to understand this.

In America Miss Robins had married an actor named George R. Parkes, when they were both players in the Boston Museum company. He offered her much attention and gallantry; he was ready to be her flunkey, and Miss Robins, who had resisted a number of wooers, finally—after much conflict and secrecy—married him almost as if it were a business arrangement. Between them they earned a comfortable income; they lived at good hotels; but Miss Robins always got better parts and more notice. She spent much of her day sewing her costumes, dressing her hair, studying her roles; she also studied German and French at night and read serious philosophical books. Her husband was baffled and frustrated. Miss Robins seems to have considered sex superfluous in her marriage. Parkes, a man of little resource, tried to domesticate Elizabeth. He urged her to give up the stage and become a home-keeping wife. The ending of this domestic strife was like one of Ibsen's stark tragedies.

Parkes had always kept a suit of stage armor in his hotel room. One day the suit was missing—and so was Parkes. In the letter he wrote and mailed to his wife he said he could not continue a loveless marriage: and gave Elizabeth the exact time at which he would be drowning himself, weighed down by the armor, in the Charles River. When she received the letter it was past the fatal hour. For ten days the actress lived in the glare of newspaper headlines and a police search. The body was finally recovered in Boston harbor.

The widow's weeds which Elizabeth wore when she arrived in London in 1888 were a symbol of her shock and sense of guilt. In her marriage she had lived out *A Doll's House* and *Hedda*—several years before she heard the name of Henrik Ibsen. And when Hilda Wangel knocked on the door and sounded the fate of the Master Builder, Miss Robins was playing the "Saint Elizabeth" who expected men to serve her as her husband had done, by total abdication of the self. As he read the installments of the Ibsen play, Henry James little dreamed with what magic and witchery Miss Robins would render Hilda Wangel: nor would he ever know that all of herself was in the part.

Elizabeth Robins was intelligent and intuitive. She knew exactly on what plane to pitch her friendship with Henry James. She gave him a feeling of mystery; but she aroused no anxieties. Understandably, it was her Isabel Archer side which appealed to James even though she

came closer to possessing the historic self-absorption and self-centeredness of his actress Miriam Rooth in *The Tragic Muse.* He befriended
her as a compatriot and as a woman of temperament. What he never
discovered was that Miss Robins had a Henrietta Stackpole side to her
as well. From her earliest days she had regarded all her experience as
potential "copy." When there were no more Ibsen parts for her to play,
she abandoned the stage and under the name of C. E. Raimond wrote a
series of sensational best-selling novels based on "questions of the day"
—euthanasia, votes for women, white slavery. Dressed in a Salvation
Army costume she gathered material at first hand from the prostitutes
in Piccadilly. She had clung to a mass of papers, minute diaries recording dates and meetings. But she began too late to write her memoirs;
the one volume she published barely covers her pre-Ibsen experiences
in England. Had James known that Miss Robins dreamed of turning all
that happened to her into copy, he probably would have kept a greater
distance.

Mrs. Alsager in the tale of "Nona Vincent" has a large comfortable house
in London. She is married to an indulgent wealthy husband and she
throws "her liberty and leisure into the things of the soul." The attributes
of Mrs. Alsager would fit a number of James's literary lady friends; but
they fit best of all Florence Bell, wife of the colliery-owner and iron-
master Hugh Bell. She had grown up in France and from childhood had
often sat in a box at the Comédie Française. She had a flair for comic
dialogue and could write witty comedies. One of them had been performed at the Théâtre Français by Coquelin. A lady of delicate perceptions, she was warm, attentive, generous. When she was in London,
James found her house at 95 Sloane Street a welcome place to spend a late
afternoon, and Mrs. Bell was an eager listener. They had met in the
mid-1880s and had the habit of going to theaters and discussing plays
when Elizabeth Robins came into their lives. Their interest in the actress
was almost that of watchful parents trying to cope with an opinionated
daughter. They agreed about Miss Robins's "unworldly careering." Reporting after seeing Elizabeth in *A Doll's House,* James said: "She ought
to take more what she can get—to do whenever she can, *any*thing she can
—be it Norwegian or not."

   A great opportunity did come her way in the spring of 1893, when she
was offered the part of Paula Tanqueray in Pinero's play which Alexander had in production. Alexander had offered the part earlier to Mrs.
Patrick Campbell, slightly younger than Miss Robins and less known, but
she was under contract elsewhere. Later Mrs. Pat was released from her
contract, and with a show of renunciation worthy of a Jamesian heroine,
Miss Robins surrendered the prize part to her. It was a handsome and

gallant—indeed a Saint Elizabeth—gesture; Miss Robins had made of the incident one of her Ibsenite moments.

Henry James, in Paris at the time, seems to have gained the impression that the loss of the part was simply a bit of bad luck. He felt Miss Robins had behaved "admirably well." But Mrs. Pat, who was to be forever grateful, though not always loyal, recognized that the bluestocking in Miss Robins was in conflict with the actress. "The peculiar quality of Elizabeth Robins's dramatic gift," she said, "was the swiftness with which she succeeded in sending *thought* across the footlights; emotion took a second place, personality a third."

Oscar

Although James had confided to friends at the time of their first meeting—in Washington in 1882—that he thought Wilde "an unclean beast," there was no ill-will or animosity between them. Oscar simply irritated James; and the novelist regarded with curiosity and a certain condescension the public antics and public wit of the younger man. The American writer was eleven years older than Wilde; he worked hard and was highly productive. Wilde had a lazy facility that James found "cheap"—the cheapness of the actor who knows how to provoke applause. Whether James read *The Picture of Dorian Gray* when it came out in 1891 we do not know. What we do know is that Wilde turned to the theater at the same time as James; and from this moment on, they were —from James's point of view—rivals, or fellow-contenders in the same arena.

In 1892 Henry James attended the opening of *Lady Windermere's Fan*. "Oscar's play," he wrote to Mrs. Bell, "strikes me as a mixture that will run, though infantine to my sense, both in subject and in form." It contained things one had always seen in plays, and from this point of view there was nothing to analyze or discuss. There was a perpetual attempt at epigram, and many of these fell flat, "but those that hit are very good indeed. This will make, I think, a success—possibly a really long run." There was no characterization; all the personages talked "equally strained Oscar" and the central situation "one has seen from the cradle." As for Oscar's curtain speech, which the newspapers had criticized for its levity, it may have been impudent but it was "simple inevitable mechanical Oscar," that is, said James, the usual trick "of saying the unusual—complimenting himself and his play."

"Ce monsieur," James wrote to Miss Reubell, "gives at last on one's nerves." One suspects however it was not only Wilde who made James nervous. It was his recognition that Wilde had an infallible sense of his audience.

During James's gouty winter of 1893 in Paris, word reached him that Wilde's second play, *A Woman of No Importance,* was about to be produced. When he heard of its subject he became worried; the play sounded singularly like his own unproduced comedy, *Tenants,* which dealt with a woman "unimportant" in the same sense as Wilde's, and her illegitimate son. James wrote promptly to Miss Robins begging her to "tell me three words about Oscar W's piece—when it is produced; and if in particular the *subject* seems to discount my poor three-year-older that Hare will neither produce nor part with." Miss Robins, busy arranging an Ibsen season, did not reply, and James turned to Mrs. Bell for "any stray crust or two about Oscar's play."

He was satisfied only after his return to London. He found Wilde's play "a piece of helpless puerility." Yet his own *Tenants,* in which he had assembled all the Victorian stage clichés, could be similarly described. He had written the play before seeing any of Wilde's comedies, but he was attempting a similar though more serious kind of comedy. James's comedies were full of unexpected situations and drolleries, and his wit was often superior to Wilde's; but he lacked Wilde's common touch, the sense of what would amuse. James was not only too subtle, but also too earnest; and when he tried to be less subtle, he became banal.

We have the spectacle of two gifted writers each attempting in his own way to put intellectual comedy on the stage. Wilde accomplished his by being off-hand and casual, as if he were shrugging his shoulders. James anxiously cared; indeed he cared to excess. Returning from Paris, James went to see Eleanora Duse with her "exquisite delicacy and truth and naturalness." He also had some evenings at the Comédie Française, then visiting London, seeing Sarah Bernhardt. Duse had neither the temperament—nor the vulgarity—of Sarah, "but a pathos, a finish, an absence of the tricks of the trade that are strangely touching and fascinating." In a sense one might have said that Sarah resembled Wilde. The qualities of Duse were in James himself.

The Young Bard

After the ceremony at which Henry James had stood, in 1891, at the graveside in Dresden of his young American friend Wolcott Balestier, James came away with Balestier's sister, Caroline. She had whispered she wanted to talk with him. What Caroline Balestier, a trim young woman with tiny features and tiny hands and feet, had to say to the novelist in the black-and-silver funeral coach we can only surmise. What we know is that a month later (on 18 January 1892), Henry James, playing his paternal role with becoming gravity, gave Caroline Balestier in marriage to the young poet and story-teller, the great success of London,

Rudyard Kipling. It was a quiet, almost a secret wedding—the family in mourning, the mother and Wolcott's other sister confined to their beds with influenza. The marriage of the poet of Empire, from India, to this daughter of the New World, mainly illustrated for James "the ubiquity of the American girl." To "give away" Caroline Balestier to Rudyard Kipling was "a queer office for *me* to perform—but it's done—and an odd little marriage," James wrote to Morton Fullerton.

It would seem always to James an odd little marriage, but he was to count the Kiplings as friends from first to last. The novelist and the young genius had met in 1890. "I liked Rudyard," James told Rhoda Broughton, calling him "the young Bard." Later he called him "the star of the hour," "the infant monster." "That little black demon of a Kipling," he wrote to Robert Louis Stevenson, "will have perhaps leaped upon your silver strand by the time this reaches you—he publicly left England to embrace you, many weeks ago—carrying literary genius out of the country with him in his pocket."

In the first flush of his admiration for Kipling, James had praised his precocity by writing an introduction to the American edition of *Mine Own People.* He had done this as a favor to Balestier. The introduction was hedged with precautions: he spoke of this "strangely clever youth who has stolen the formidable mask of maturity," and prophetically remarked that if invention should ever fail Kipling "he would still have the lyric string and the patriotic chord, on which he plays admirably."

Disillusion set in quickly. James began to have doubts when he read *The Light That Failed*—"there," he wrote, "the talent has sometimes failed," even if that talent was enormous. By 1893 Kipling was living in America near Brattleboro and writing James of the winter cold, the rude conditions. James confided to a friend he believed the writer well-satisfied—"he needs nothing of the civilized order." And he went on, "He charged himself with all he could take of India when he was very young, and gave it out with great effect; but I doubt if he has anything more of anything to give." A year later, when he read *The Jungle Book,* James exclaimed *"how* it closes his door and sets his limit! . . . The *violence* of it all, the almost exclusive preoccupation with fighting and killing is also singularly characteristic." He repeated that he expected nothing from Kipling "save some beast stories."

The novelist and poet of civilization had looked carefully upon the poet of the jungle and the barrack-room and by the turn of the century he delivered his final judgment to Grace Norton:

> My view of his prose future has much shrunken in the light of one's increasingly observing how little of life he can make use of. Almost nothing civilized save steam and patriotism—and the latter only in verse,

where I *hate* it so, especially mixed up with God and goodness, that that half spoils my enjoyment of his great talent.

James had been alienated from Kipling

in proportion as he has come steadily from the less simple in subject to the more simple—from the Anglo-Indians to the natives, from the natives to the Tommies, from the Tommies to the quadrupeds, from the quadrupeds to the fish and from the fish to the engines and screws. But he is a prodigious little success and an unqualified little happiness and a dear little chap.

He also remarked, "and *such* an uninteresting mind."

The "Wanton" of the Pacific

The recipient of Henry James's confidences—his ambitions and misgivings in the theater—was his old friend Robert Louis Stevenson. To far-away Samoa Henry James dispatched from time to time a record of his hopes and his doubts as a struggling playwright. He loved Stevenson with a tenderness of memory unique among his friends; he rejoiced in Stevenson's new-found vigor in the South Seas, yet he could no longer invest him with reality—"you are too far away, you are too absent—too invisible, inaudible, inconceivable." He told him his friends brandished laurel over his absent head; he called him a "buccaneering Pompadour of the Deep" and "a wandering wanton of the Pacific." The visual-minded James wanted always to see—and Stevenson's adventures in Polynesia seemed to belong to fairy tales. Snapshots only whetted his appetite. When John Hay sent him certain of Henry Adams's letters from the Pacific, including an account of his visit to Stevenson, James complained that Adams had not given him "the *look* of things."

He soon had a chance to learn more of Tusitala—Stevenson's adopted native name—and his manorial house on the Samoan hilltop. From beyond the seas there appeared in London late in 1891 another ghostly figure, that of Henry Adams himself, together with the distant ghost of James's Newport youth, John La Farge. James had not seen Adams since before the suicide of his wife, in 1885. In his *Education,* Adams uses the word "extinct" repeatedly as he describes his emotions of this time. Life, he wrote, "had been cut in halves" for him. He brought his countenance of despair to Henry James in De Vere Gardens.

James tried to cheer him up. On one occasion Adams found him excited by Kipling's marriage which he had witnessed six days before; the two friends gossiped about the poet and his American bride. But to Elizabeth Cameron, his Washington confidante, Adams wrote, "I feel even deader than I did in the South Seas, but here I feel that all the others are as dead as I." He called James "a figure in the same old wall-paper." James on his side wrote to his Scottish friend, Sir John Clark, that he liked Adams, "but suffer from his monotonous, disappointed pessimism." Each thus seems to have believed he was comforting the other; in reality they made each other uncomfortable.

When Stevenson told James that he had been visited by Adams and La Farge, the novelist replied: "Henry Adams is as conversible as an Adams is permitted by the scheme of nature to be; but what is wonderful to me is that they have both taken to the buccaneering life when already 'on the return'—La Farge many times a *père de famille.*"

Stevenson had gone on horseback to visit the western wanderers, swimming his horse through a river to get to them. He and his wife had not yet managed to arrange their food supplies at Vailima, and Adams and La Farge, returning the visit, sent food ahead. They arrived after a long weary tramp and spent several hours. At the end, the frail and sickly Stevenson seemed greatly refreshed, while Adams was completely exhausted. Stevenson's fragility, Adams observed, "passes description, but his endurance passes his fragility." The eye of Quincy and of Lafayette Square never understood the carefree ways of the bohemian. Adams considered the Stevensons' mode of existence "far less human than that of the natives"; he decided that Stevenson's ability to live in this "squalor" was due to his education. "His early associates were all second-rate; he never seems by any chance to have come in contact with first-rate people, either men, women, or artists." How he reconciled Stevenson's knowing the first-rate Henry James we do not know. Adams moreover felt uncomfortable in a belief that Stevenson, with his gregarious nature, had contempt "for my Bostonianism." Stevenson however had written to James, "we have had enlightened society; a great privilege—would it might endure."

To Sir John Clark again, Henry James voiced his wonder "how Adams and La Farge could, either of them, have failed to murder the other." La Farge, passing through London briefly on his way back to America, felt that James did not understand Adams. Probably there had been peace in Polynesia between the two only because La Farge was too busy absorbing the painter's visual world and the South Sea colors, and Adams had tried to keep pace with him. James wondered afresh at "La Farge's combination of social and artistic endowments." He was delighted to find that neither his charm nor his talk had changed; for a brief moment they were back in Newport. "I was all young again," La Farge wrote to Adams.

It was probably with a sense of relief that Henry James saw Adams off to America in February of 1892. The latter had hardly emerged from his cabin to take the sea air, "when I fell into the arms of Rudyard Kipling and his new wife, and wife's sister, and wife's mother." "Fate was kind on that voyage," he remembered in the *Education.* "Rudyard Kipling, on his wedding trip to America, thanks to the mediation of Henry James, dashed over the passenger his exuberant fountain of gaiety and wit—as though playing a garden hose on a thirsty and faded begonia."

That voyage had been almost two years before and now in the midst of the rehearsals of *Guy Domville,* on 17 December 1894, James read in the newspapers that Stevenson was dead. The news had traveled slowly from Vailima where Tusitala had been buried on his hilltop. "This ghastly extinction of the beloved R.L.S.," James wrote to Gosse that evening, "it makes me cold and sick—and with the absolute, almost alarmed sense, of the visible material quenching of an indispensable light."

To his surprise, James found himself named one of Stevenson's executors. He had not been consulted, and had no relish for the task. "It would be a dreadful disaster to his heirs," he said, asking to be excused. In the long letter he wrote to Mrs. Stevenson, the note from the first is that of a requiem: "What can I say to you that will not seem cruelly irrelevant and vain? We have been sitting in darkness for nearly a fortnight, but what is *our* darkness to the extinction of your magnificent light?" And the image is taken up again a few sentences further on—"he lighted up a whole side of the globe, and was himself a whole province of one's imagination."

From the eloquence of this tribute James returned to the rehearsals of his play. They seemed "tawdry and heartless." Stevenson's ghost "waves its great dusky wings between me and all occupations," he told Edmund Gosse.

Preparations

He had looked forward to the first rehearsal of *Guy Domville,* when he would read the play aloud and expound it to the actors. However, on the morning of the first reading, at the beginning of December 1894, he awoke with acute laryngitis, and he had the chagrin of sitting in the dark empty theater while Alexander read the play for him. Then, day after day, for four weeks, he came in the wet and cold to the West End to participate in "the poverty and patchiness of rehearsal." It involved him in a great deal of anxiety; and also amusement. Alexander had assembled a highly professional cast, a group of polite, hard-working actors. Ellen Terry's gifted sister, Marion, had the lead opposite Alexander; the second male part was entrusted to Herbert Waring, who had recently

played Solness with Miss Robins in *The Master Builder.* Another part
was played by H. V. Esmond, whom James judged to be the one "true"
actor in the piece. The villain, however, Lord Devenish, was played by
W. G. Elliott, who grimaced too much; James thought he was "stagey."

James alternated between approval of Alexander and doubt; the
manager did have a distinct flair; yet he was all profile and posture, with
an almost metallic suavity. As regards material things, he spared no
expense. The white parlor of the third act impressed by its sense of
having been lived in (and was to do service in a number of Alexander's
later productions). The costumes were meticulously faithful to the late
eighteenth century.

James was euphoric one day and in the depths of despair the next.
"I am *too* preoccupied, too terrified, too fundamentally distracted, to be
fit for human intercourse," he told a hostess who invited him to dinner
during the Yuletide of 1894. "I would be a death's head at the feast."

On the day of the opening—5 January 1895, a Saturday—James found
his nervousness unbearable. He went for a long walk through London
parks and streets. The weather was cold and dreary. In the late afternoon
he returned to 34 De Vere Gardens in a state of panic. He scribbled a
hasty, almost illegible, note to his brother. Alluding to William's interest
in spiritualism he counted on "psychical intervention from you—this is
really the time to show your stuff." Alexander had told him there had
been a large advance sale of seats, "but my hand shakes and I can only
write that I am your plucky, but all the same lonely and terrified Henry."
He added after the signature the date and the hour. It was 5:45 P.M. James
decided it would help speed the dragging clock to go and see Oscar
Wilde's new play, *An Ideal Husband,* which had opened two days before
at the Haymarket.

The Three Critics

Mr. Bernard Shaw, the drama critic of the *Saturday Review,* who
had attended the first night of Oscar's play that week, was preparing to
review *Guy Domville.* He was new in his job: he had assumed his duties
five days before. Shaw was thirty-eight and had been a music critic for
some years, signing himself Corno di Bassetto. He had also recently produced a play, *Widowers' Houses;* it had attracted little attention. A second
play, about prostitution, *Mrs. Warren's Profession,* had been refused a
license by the Lord Chamberlain. The lanky Irishman was known in
socialist circles as an indefatigable pamphleteer and a speech-maker to
working-men's clubs on a variety of subjects: Marx and Wagner, wages,
common sense, food, the importance of Henrik Ibsen. A vegetarian, he
attacked the barbarism of meat-eating. He had learned to face audiences

and to amuse them by paradox and persiflage. Paradoxes came to his lips as naturally as epigrams did to his compatriot Oscar.

He had arrived in London from Ireland at twenty, in 1876—that is, in the same year that Henry James had come from Paris to settle in Bolton Street. During the 1880s, when James wrote *The Princess Casamassima,* Shaw was helping found the Fabian Society and in the parks and on the Embankment had begun his socio-economic discourses.

Shaw railed at ugliness and poverty and wanted to change the world. James was troubled by the crudities of existence and hoped to exorcise them by devotion to beauty. Shaw tried to make the world his classroom. Yet he knew the nature of art. "You cannot be an artist until you have contracted yourself within the limits of your art," he wrote to a friend shortly after the production of *Guy Domville.* At the same time James was writing "Art should be as hard as nails." Shaw was journalist and preacher; James was a finder and maker.

What was happening, however, in the waning years of the century, was that James was attempting to woo the world in a manner closer to Shaw's nature than to his own. When someone in 1892 booed *Widowers' Houses,* the dramatist subdued the audience with a three-minute speech and changed the boos into applause. In the theater the two men were at this moment equal failures. The difference was that James had a reputation at stake, and Shaw had a reputation to make. The would-be playwright, Bernard Shaw, was a critic of other men's plays. On this Saturday in January the Irish critic donned his corduroy jacket and made his way to St. James's through the cold and wet to see the American novelist's long-awaited play.

The critic of the *Pall Mall Gazette,* also new at his job, was a thin, undernourished, wispy man named H. G. Wells. He had been offered the post on the newspaper a few days before, and on 3 January had reviewed Wilde's play at the Haymarket. He had actually only been to a theater twice, and when he told his editor this, the reply had been "Exactly what I want. You won't be in the gang. You'll make a break." Apparently his first review, written late into the night, had satisfied the editor. Wells went to James's play, in the dress suit he had had made in twenty-four hours, in time for the Haymarket opening, with greater assurance.

Son of a housemaid and a gardener who later became a shopkeeper, Wells had served an apprenticeship in a draper's shop before he obtained a scholarship to a grammar school. At the University of London he studied under T. H. Huxley and embarked on a career in science; he discovered now he had a flair for journalism. Magazines accepted his pieces and paid him decently; and he had just written a novel called *The Time Machine* which promised to be successful. His job on the *Pall Mall Ga-*

zette would be short-lived, and the only regular job (save for the early apprenticeship) he ever held.

Like Shaw, Wells was interested in working-class movements. They were both atheists and socialists. Thus in the theater that night "the new men" of James's time were sitting in judgment on his play. Wells felt, however, that he was the newest of the new: that science put him in the forefront, and that in their devotion to art, Shaw and James lagged behind. In that formally dressed audience on this first night, however, it was Shaw who broke the ranks of the boiled shirts and the black and white ties in the stalls with his modest brown jacket suit. Wells, more rebellious and *gamin* than Shaw, had conformed to job and society by dressing the part assigned to him. The two men, future "prophets" of their generation, met for the first time at the James play.

Still another "new man" sat in the audience at the St. James's that evening as critic of *Guy Domville.* Enoch Arnold Bennett, assistant editor of a magazine called *Woman,* like Shaw and Wells had come to London from the provinces. Bennett was simple, shy, insecure, ambitious. He had a marked stammer. He wore a boiled shirt, and probably would not have dreamed of wearing anything else. His father, a potter in the Midlands, had succeeded in making himself into a lawyer, and Bennett had worked first as a shorthand clerk in his father's office. Arriving in London in 1889 determined to make himself into a man of the world, he borrowed £300 to buy himself a share in the magazine *Woman,* thereby becoming assistant editor. Later he was its editor, and like Wells a giver of opinion to the average man through the medium of the press. But where Wells was brilliant and erratic, Bennett spoke with a kind of plodding honesty, a supreme matter-of-factness. Like Wells and like Shaw, Bennett was liberal and sceptical; but he, more than the other two, felt himself in James's camp. He had an ideal of art, a desire to be a storyteller; he saw the world brighter than it was. He wanted success and all the glitter of success; unlike Shaw and Wells, he believed in the fairy tale of achievement.

James, product of an American aristocracy of the mind, would have held it an irony that in this theater, where his future as a playwright was to be decided, the plebeians were sitting in judgment on him: the Edwardian world-to-come was already present to review a play of the Victorian world. The names of Shaw, Wells and Bennett were to be linked constantly in the next three decades and would be—with certain others —among the supreme literary names of the new time.

The Last Domville

There were in reality two audiences at the first night of *Guy Domville*. Literary and artistic London came to see an Alexander production of a James play: many members of that audience were friends of the novelist. The world of art was represented by such figures as Leighton, Burne-Jones, Du Maurier, Sargent; letters were represented by Edmund Gosse, Mrs. Humphry Ward, and other late-Victorian luminaries; there were several well-known actresses in the audience, not least Miss Robins; there were representatives of the English aristocracy, who had always admired James. This first audience came prepared to applaud and to praise. The second audience, in the gallery, had never heard of James; it had come to be entertained by Alexander. "Alex" could be relied upon for a good show.

By the time the little curtain-raiser had been acted, and the orchestra had fussed through an overture, the distinguished and well-dressed were in their places. The curtain rose on a set visually pleasing, the garden of a wealthy young widow, Mrs. Peverel, near Richmond in 1780. In this setting James developed with great simplicity the dilemma of young Guy Domville, on the eve of his departure for France, strong in his determination to become a Benedictine monk. He has been tutor to Mrs. Peverel's son; he loves Mrs. Peverel; his love for the Church however has not permitted him to recognize his deeper feelings. Mrs. Peverel has resigned herself to losing him to Mother Church. Guy is also fond of a neighboring squire, Frank Humber, who pays court to Mrs. Peverel, and is prepared to plead his friend's cause.

All this James set forth with considerable charm; it won both audiences: the gallery, knowing Alexander as a romantic hero, lived in hope that he would throw over the Church and marry Mrs. Peverel. The more sophisticated members of the audience experienced, after seasons of tawdry and violent drama, the delicacy of James's dialogue. Into the quiet of this garden, however, there enters Lord Devenish, the Mephistopheles of the drama, bringing the news that Guy's kinsman has just fallen from a horse and been killed. Guy, as the last of his line, must renounce religion, take over the encumbered estates, make an advantageous marriage. The Domvilles must not be allowed to die out. In a sudden shift of feeling, Guy, who to his friends had "such an air of the cold college—almost of the cold cloister," makes a grand exit shouting "long, long live the Domvilles."

In the second act, at the villa of the dowager Mrs. Domville, Guy has shed churchly black for the breeches, lace and wig of a man-about-town. He has learned very quickly to play cards and to drink; he is ready to marry his cousin, the dowager's daughter. The cousin turns out to be the illegitimate daughter of Lord Devenish and Mrs. Domville; she in turn is in love with a naval lieutenant. When Guy learns the truth, he aids in their elopement, after a mock drinking scene in which he and the lieutenant pour glass after glass of port into the flower pots while pretending to make each other drunk. At the end of the act, having found nothing but deceit around him, Guy again reverses himself. He must, after all, go into the Church.

The third act, even though it brings back the sympathetic Mrs. Peverel and her suitor, could not repair the damage. Lord Devenish rushes to Mrs. Peverel, hoping still to save Guy for worldly things, and his own devices, by marrying him to Mrs. Peverel. Guy returns, and in another scene of great delicacy shows a glimmer of awareness of Mrs. Peverel's love. But Lord Devenish has left his gloves in the room; and the sight of these freezes the novice into a sense of the world's treacheries. All hesitation is gone; he will say good-bye to everything:

> GUY: [*Gathering himself slowly from a deep, stupefied commotion.*] The Church *takes* me! [*To* MRS. PEVEREL.] Be kind to him. [*To* FRANK.] Be good to her. [*At the door.*] Be good to her.
> FRANK: Mrs. Peverel—I shall *hope!*
> MRS. PEVEREL: Wait!

This was the play on which James had placed all his hopes and it had much in it that was literary and fine. But while the novelist was sitting at the Haymarket Theatre, fidgeting uneasily as Wilde's epigrams burst from the stage like well-timed firecrackers, curious things were occurring on the stage of the St. James's. W. G. Elliott played Lord Devenish with a villainy so obvious as to wither (Shaw said) "all sense and music out of James's lines." Wells remarked that "he might have come out of Hogarth, but he has certainly no business to come into this play." Mrs. Edward Saker, in the role of the dowager Mrs. Domville, appeared in what Shaw described as "a Falstaffian make-up." With her elaborate hoop-skirted gown she wore an enormous hat, made of velvet and shaped like a muff; it towered on her head under nodding plumes. When she made her entrance in this extravagant headgear the gallery, in which there had been a great deal of coughing and shuffling of feet, began to titter. Mrs. Saker, struggling with her huge skirt, was unnerved. Her costume filled a large area of the stage and her plumes waved with every motion she made. Illusion was gone. Alexander was unaccustomed to signs of discontent in his audience. He played the drinking scene which followed, Shaw said, "with the sobriety of desperation."

The third act did little to save the situation. The unintended comedy had thoroughly demoralized the gallery, and the last lines with their subtlety of phrasing and calculated repetitions irritated the audience. There would be no romantic ending. Moreover, the audience's sympathies were no longer with Guy or the actor who embodied him. When Alexander delivered himself of what, in other circumstances, might have been a touching and deeply felt speech, "I'm the *last,* my lord, of the Domvilles!" there floated out of the darkness a strident voice from somewhere in the gallery: "It's a bloody good thing y'are."

Henry James remained to the end of the Oscar Wilde play. He left the Haymarket Theatre with the applause ringing in his ears. It was late evening. He walked down the short street leading into St. James's Square, and entered the St. James's Theatre by the stage door. On stage Alexander was backing away towards the exit, saying to Mrs. Peverel with some awkwardness, in measured accents, "Be kind to him," and to Humber, "be good to her."

Backstage in these nervous moments no one said anything to James about the evening's accidents. The curtain came down and the panic-stricken author faced the angry manager. Outside there was a great roar of applause. Alexander took the curtain calls. He received the ovation to which he was accustomed. Then James's friends in the orchestra began to call "Author, author." The press reports of the evening agreed that a manager who knew the temper of the audience would have left well enough alone. But Alexander was unnerved. He brought James on, leading him by the hand. The novelist, having heard applause, came forward shyly, hesitantly; and at that moment the gallery exploded. Jeers, hisses, catcalls were followed by great waves of applause from that part of the audience which esteemed James and recognized the better qualities of the play. The two audiences declared war. "All the forces of civilization in the house," Henry later wrote to his brother, "waged a battle of the most gallant, prolonged and sustained applause with the hoots and jeers and catcalls of the roughs, whose roars (like those of a cage of beasts at some infernal zoo) were only exacerbated by the conflict."

James faced this pandemonium; his dark beard accentuated the pallor of his face and his high bald dome. He showed, some of the witnesses said, a "scornful coolness"; others described it as a display of "quiet gallantry." Alexander shifted nervously from one position to the other and followed with quick paces as the novelist fled.

The brawl in the audience continued. Alexander, feeling that the situation was getting out of hand, reappeared in front of the curtain. He held up his arm. English courtesy and discipline reasserted itself. He said slowly and with emotion that in his short career as actor-manager he had met with many favors at the hands of his audiences and "these discordant notes tonight have hurt me very much. I can only say that we have done our very best." He added that if he and his company had failed "we can only try to deserve your kindness" by doing better in the future.

A voice from the gallery said: "T'aint your fault, guv'nor, it's a rotten play."

The house lights came on. The well-dressed poured into the small lobby to wait for their carriages; the gallery emptied itself into the cold streets. James escaped as soon as he could. He had his answer. He had said he would "chuck" the theater if *Guy Domville* did not succeed. The theater had "chucked" him.

PART SIX

The Treacherous Years

1895–1900

Never say you know the last word
about any human heart.

HENRY JAMES

1

THE
BLACK
ABYSS

Postscripts

Henry James walked home in the cold damp from St. James's to
Kensington after he left the theater on the night of 5 January 1895. He
later said that he felt weary, bruised, disgusted, sickened. The audience
—that is, the gallery—had behaved, he said, like a set of savages pounc-
ing on a gold watch. To him *Guy Domville* had been like a tightly built
gleaming piece of machinery. The play had had every advantage of
production. And yet it had failed.

From all that he wrote later it was clear that James returned to De
Vere Gardens in a deeper state of shock than he knew. He had made
mental allowance for possible failure; that could happen to the best of
dramatists. He had not allowed however for a display of violence against
himself. He had been hooted by a brutal mob as if he were some old-time
criminal, led through the streets for execution. These had been, he said,
"the most horrible hours of my life."

Edmund Gosse called the next day, having been invited to lunch with
other guests, among them W. E. Norris, who had come to London from
Devon to see James's play. James received his guests with melancholy
politeness. "You would have been proud of your friend," he later told
Margaret Brooke. He was far from being "perfectly calm," as Gosse
would later claim; he was in a state of nervous exhaustion. But he put on
a bold face. He confessed a day or two later to Norris that he had become
aware, sitting at the table, how great was his weariness after five weeks
of intensive rehearsal and the rude climax of the previous evening.

James felt much better the following day—sufficiently well to return
to the theater and sit in quiet anonymity in the gallery where the rumpus
had occurred. The audience was well-behaved; nothing occurred to disturb the players. At the end there was warm applause for the cast. In this

way James satisfied himself that the events of the first night were not altogether induced by what he had written. The press carried reports that there had been an anti-Alexander "cabal" at the first night; various witnesses testified that the roughs had a leader and "refreshed themselves copiously between the acts."

James's play had a good reception from the establishment critics, in particular William Archer and Clement Scott. Among the other notices, Bernard Shaw's was one of the most cordial. Of "the handful of rowdies" who had brawled at James, Shaw said, "It is the business of the dramatic critic to educate these dunces, not to echo them." He likened the music in James's lines to an evening of Mozart after Verdi. *Guy Domville* was a story and not a mere situation—a story of fine sentiment and delicate manners. H. G. Wells's review was written in the tone of the scientist. It was a question, he said, of a prognosis—and the prognosis was bad. The play was beautifully written but too delicate for acting. The diagnosis pointed to "an early deathbed." Arnold Bennett, writing in *Woman* as "Cécile," offered a conscientious and platitudinous notice, tailored for his feminine readers. The future author of *The Old Wives' Tale* found "fitful beauty" in James's work and certain "exquisite scenes." The melodrama of the later acts was hardly in keeping with the "unrivalled work which Mr. James has produced in fiction."

Thus the "new men" of the 1890s rallied to the side of art—and indeed of courtesy. The older reviewers were staunchly with James. A. B. Walkley brilliantly contrasted Wilde's new play with *Guy Domville*. Wilde's, he wrote, would not move the English drama forward an inch, nor would it add to his reputation. James's play was "a defeat out of which it is possible for many victories to spring." James himself took no such heroic view of what he had done. *Guy Domville* ran through its allotted month, and even a few days longer to include some profitable matinées at Brighton. The play had yielded James £275 in royalties, token of the prosperity that would have awaited him had he succeeded. Then, in a crowning bit of irony, Alexander rushed into rehearsal a play by the very dramatist whose work was being compared with James's: *The Importance of Being Earnest* settled in promptly at the St. James's for a promising run.

Embarrassments

James went, five days after the *Guy Domville* opening, to pay a promised visit to the Archbishop of Canterbury, Edward White Benson, who had at various times expressed admiration for James's work and even quoted him in a sermon. At the archiepiscopal residence, Addington, outside London, James found two of the Archbishop's sons, Arthur Christopher, then a master at Eton, and E. F. Benson. Both remembered

James's talk and recorded it. He said he had been, during his play-writing, in a dim "subaqueous" world. Now, he said, he felt he had got his head, "such as it was," above the surface. This picture of himself as a drowning man suggests the depth of his melancholy; and equally suggestive was James's fascination, as he sat and conversed over a cup of tea, with a little anecdote which the ecclesiastic told him. They had been talking about ghost stories. The Archbishop spoke of an incident he had heard long ago, of a couple of small children in some out-of-the-way place to whom the spirits of certain "bad" servants were believed to have appeared; they had seemed to beckon, invite, solicit across dangerous places, so that the children might destroy themselves. The Archbishop was vague—but the ghostliness, the mystery, the terror in the anecdote touched a raw nerve at this moment in the life of the novelist.

He had talked of his struggle in a dim water-world, as if he were drowning; he had suddenly been hurt by violent and uncontrollable forces. Henry James could indeed muse on a tale of horrible threats to children, the baleful influence of the extra-human that lies in wait for man in the very midst of serenity. Returning to De Vere Gardens he scribbled in his notebook: "Note here the ghost-story told me at Addington (evening of Thursday the 10th) by the Archbishop . . . the mere vague undetailed faint sketch of it." Three years elapsed before he was ready to write "The Turn of the Screw."

He had pronounced the detestable incident closed; but he could not stop the pain as easily as he could lower the curtain on his play. The behavior of the audience at the St. James's had struck at the very heart of his self-esteem, his pride and sovereignty as artist. The theater doubtless had been one kind of hell, and he was now out of it. He lived on however in his other, his private hell—wounded, sore, depressed. His personal letters after *Guy Domville* were a cry of outrage and defiance. Later there came the nursing of private grief, the search for balm, the rationalization and self-consolation that might ease his spirit. The explanation to which he adhered above all, and which was the fundamental truth, was that his was too refined and subtle a talent to reach the "common man." The truth had been before him during all his "dramatic years" and he could not say that the Comptons had not warned him. Yet it had required a rebuff of the most violent kind to bring it home, so deep had been his ambition and determination to achieve stage glory—and the royalties that went with success.

When he looked at his curious experience through the light of his intellect he could see it with wry and sardonic humor, charged with irony and paradox; and he wrote this into a series of stories about writers who are applauded, although their works are unread, or who try to "take the measure of the huge, flat foot of the public" but who succeed only in writing another distinguished failure. He was to see, a few months later, the massive Victorian funeral offered the votary of classicism in painting, Lord Leighton, and to muse on the elaborate mourning and the way in which Leighton's artistic relics were ignored; buried, the painter was quickly forgotten. "So much beauty and so little passion," James mused. The public could recognize neither the presence of the one, nor the absence of the other.

In his notebooks, he now returned to the idea for a story recorded a year earlier.

> I was turning over the drama, the tragedy, the general situation of disappointed ambition—and more particularly that of the artist, the man of letters: I mean of the ambition, the pride, the passion, the idea of greatness, that has been smothered and defeated by circumstances, by the opposition of life, of fate, of character, of weakness, of folly, of misfortune; and the drama that resides in—that may be bound up with—such a situation. I thought of the tragic consciousness, the living death, the helpless pity, the deep humiliation . . .

And then—"the idea of *death* both checked and caught me." He went on to think of this man whose passional and sentient life is dead, as finding renewed life in some woman. *"She is his Dead Self,"* he wrote, underlining the words, *"he is alive in her and dead in himself."* Having written out the note he finally abandoned the idea; he feared "there isn't much in it: it would take a deuce of a deal of following up." It would require more than this: the fortitude to deal with his own failure.

Outside his notebooks, his letters reflect his soreness of heart. "My youth is gone," he writes to his old friend, Sarah Wister. "Life's nothing —unless heroic and sacrificial," he tells the Archbishop's son, Arthur Benson. He is weary of London; he feels as if he were homeless. His comfortable De Vere Gardens flat no longer seems to suffice. He talks of finding "a much needed bath of silence and solitude" in some rented house in the English countryside. His preoccupation with houses and children fills his writings at this moment—children, unwanted, displaced, seeking an anchorage and love.

He spoke of himself as unwanted a fortnight after the collapse of his play in a letter to his old friend Howells who, with a certain prescience, had written before *Guy Domville,* to remind James that whatever the outcome of his theatrical ventures, he was still primarily a novelist, possessed of a public that waited to read everything he wrote. "You put your finger sympathetically on the place," James wrote in reply, and spoke of what I wanted you to speak of. I *have* felt, for a long time past, that I have fallen upon evil days—every sign or symbol of one's being in the least *wanted,* anywhere or by any one, having so utterly failed. . . . The sense of being utterly out of it weighed me down, and I asked myself what the future would be. All these melancholies were qualified indeed by one redeeming reflection—the sense of how little, for a good while past (for reasons very logical, but accidental and temporary) I had been producing. I did say to myself "Produce again—produce; produce better than ever, and all will yet be well."

The communion with his old-time editor had a tranquilizing effect. On the morning after writing the letter James roused himself and set down, with an air of finality, the following words in his notebook:

I take up my *own* old pen again—the pen of all my old unforgettable efforts and sacred struggles. To myself—today—I need say no more. Large and full and high the future still opens. It is now indeed that I may do the work of my life. And I will.

The Young Heroes

During the first phase of his work in the theater, in 1891 and 1892, Henry James had written two tales whose pages are filled with personal history. One was a story of an itinerant family on the Continent and the fate of their gifted son—Americans as footloose as his own family had been long ago. The other was a story of a rigid military family, whose tradition was to supply gallant soldiers for England's army. In the first story, "The Pupil," the sensitive boy is ashamed of his down-at-heels parents who lead a hand-to-mouth existence. In the second, called "Owen Wingrave," the young Owen, a few years older than the pupil, is determined to study the art of literature rather than the arts of war. Both heroes have in common their perception of the false values by which their families live; and both die as a consequence of their self-assertion. The stories are markedly different: the life-myth they embody is the same.

James got his hint for "The Pupil" from his Florentine friend and doctor, William Wilberforce Baldwin, who had attended a generation of wayfaring Americans as they passed through Italy. During James's 1890 visit to Florence, Dr. Baldwin had proposed to him that they tour small out-of-the-way Etruscan towns, using rail and carriage as available, and walking to less accessible spots. Accompanied by an obese Falstaffian friend and language-tutor of Baldwin's, named Taccini, they visited Volterra, Montepulciano and Torrita, and certain villages in between. The little trip proved too hot and fatiguing to James, but he came away from it with one of his finest tales. In their "very hot Italian railway-carriage, which stopped and dawdled everywhere, favouring conversation," Baldwin happened to speak of a "wonderful American family" to which, briefly, he had been doctor. It was an itinerant family; it jumped its hotel bills; its members were an "odd, adventurous, extravagant band of high but rather unauthenticated pretensions." They had a small boy, who was precocious, but who had a weak heart. The boy saw the prowling and precarious life of his parents and siblings, "and measured and judged them." Here, James wrote in his preface, was "more than enough for a summer's day even in old Italy—here was a thumping windfall."

James wrote "The Pupil" at the end of that summer of 1890 when he was back in London. He too had been a precocious boy on the Continent; his father had dragged his family about from place to place; Henry and his brothers had been "hotel children"; they had known the loneliness of strange places and been confided to tutors and governesses. He had memories of anxieties provoked by money shortages during the American depression of 1856–7 which caused his parents to beat a hurried retreat from Paris to Boulogne-sur-Mer. Out of this personal past and Dr. Baldwin's anecdote, James wove his tale of a sensitive boy and his attachment to his tutor, the first of a series of the 1890s in which children suffer from parental neglect and indifference, and little boys die asserting their claim to live.

"The Pupil," written with the technical virtuosity of these years, is told through a double vision: the boy's "troubled vision" of his family "as reflected in the vision," James explained, "also troubled enough, of his devoted friend" the tutor. Like the James family, the Moreens are a country unto themselves, and "ultramoreen" is a key word in their private vocabulary. Little Morgan knows from the first that his tutor, Pemberton, will never be paid for his services; he attaches himself to him with the tenderness of a loved and neglected child who feels also guilty and ashamed at his family's improvidence and dishonesty. The tutor, on his side, becomes attached to his charge; he stays on, unpaid, in conflict between his personal needs and his feelings for Morgan—but not a little also because there is something irresponsible and shiftless in his own character. Quick of mind, Morgan is thoroughly aware of his mother's shameless use of Pemberton's love for him; she even borrows money from him. The parental decision to take advantage of the attachment and "unload" Morgan on the tutor leads to a swift and complex ending. Pemberton had had a fantasy, into which Morgan had entered, that the two might some day go off to lead a life together. But when they are left alone Morgan, expecting to find Pemberton enthusiastic, sees him wavering— and his life becomes a void. Betrayed by his parents, frightened by the glimpse of vacillation in the beloved tutor, not old enough to tolerate disillusion, he feels himself suddenly alone. The panic is too much for his weak heart.

The second tale, "Owen Wingrave" (Owen, a Scottish name, means "the young soldier": the title accordingly meant "The Young Soldier Wins His Grave"), was written early in 1892, just after the death of Alice James. The idea for it occurred during a reading of the memoirs of Napoleon's General Marbot—a work popular in England throughout the 1890s. James's notebook entry begins:

> The idea of the *soldier*—produced a little by the fascinated perusal of Marbot's magnificent memoirs. The image, the type, the vision, the character, as a transmitted, hereditary, mystical, almost supernatural force, challenge, incentive, almost haunting, apparitional presence, in the life and consciousness of a descendant—a descendant of totally different temperament and range of qualities, yet subjected to a superstitious awe in relation to carrying out the tradition of absolutely *military* valour—personal bravery and honour.

James's idea was to create a hero who was a soldier in every fiber, but who had a horror of "the blood, the carnage, the suffering." He would make his hero perform a brave soldierly act even while defying militarism.

Marbot was one of Napoleon's most articulate generals; he was the second son of a soldier, and James was always interested in second sons. The three volumes of his memoirs which James read disclose in their marked pages—the description of a cavalry charge; the battles of Austerlitz and Aspern; Napoleon's "magic personality" and its effect on the troops; the great cold at Vilna—that James was reading the passages of violence and glory with a deep identification and absorption but with confused feelings. Napoleon had cast a long shadow; and Henry James, who had seen the pageantry of the Second Empire and lived in a Paris in which the memories of Napoleon remained vivid, was clearly attracted to him more as a man of action and a symbol of glory than as a soldier. He abhorred violence, he respected courage. He was impressed, as his notebook shows, with the sense of military tradition. The Marbots had all been soldiers, and the sons of soldiers.

James's notebook entry seems, at first glance, unrelated to the death of his sister; but "Owen Wingrave," in its picture of the dead weight of "family" and personal past as brought to bear upon the living, reached very far back into the novelist's experience. It stemmed from the days of the Civil War when public opinion had told him he must himself become a soldier while his own terror of violence and fratricidal murder, his own will to peace and to poetry, held him back. The story reminds us also of the way in which Henry was under pressure as a young man to leave art alone, urged by his father, his practical mother and his elder brother to take a steady job when he wanted simply to be "literary." He had resisted the family pressure, had refused to study science, had thrown away his law books. He had quietly and determinedly locked himself in his room and written his tales and read novels while his brothers banged and shouted. So young Owen Wingrave goes into the park carrying the poems of Goethe when he should be reading the hard prose of Clausewitz.

Owen is a second son like Henry; the older brother has been locked away, a mental case; and upon the second son falls the burden of upholding the family name. The name has a single historical virtue: that of the soldier. Owen's father died of an Afghan sabre-cut. His grandfather, Sir Philip, has survived to eighty, "a merciless old warrior." At Paramore, seat of the Wingraves, there is a haunted room; here a military ancestor killed a son as rebellious as Owen. To Paramore come Owen's "crammer" Spencer Coyle, who is preparing him for military college; his best friend, also destined for the army, and his intended, Kate. All assail young Wingrave. Sir Philip will cut him off without a penny. His friend and his coach believe in more subtle modes of coercion; to the sweetheart he is simply a "coward." Owen resists this terrible pressure. When his friend questions whether he has "the military temperament" of his ancestors, Owen's rejoinder is "Damn the military temperament!"

We do not hear his quarrel with his sweetheart; but we know their voices are raised, and that he locks himself into the haunted room. There he is found in the eerie dawn, after strange noises have been heard during the night. Owen lies on the floor, dressed as he had last been seen: "He looked like a young soldier on the battlefield." The young pacifist has won a victory for his own beliefs. But the victory has in reality been won by tradition, by family. Owen could not escape his fate.

The two tales—those of the unhappy pupil and the young pacifist— were recollections of adolescence. They were of a piece with the experience of *Guy Domville.* It was as if James had to return constantly to a dream of second sons, forced to take up family burdens: Owen Wingrave, young Domville; Nick Dormer in *The Tragic Muse.* The young heroes are subjected not only to family pressure, but to a kind of inexorable weight of history. And resistance is punishable by defeat—or death. The ivory tower, the religious cell—there one could live with the eternal, and avoid the passions and the demands of flesh and family. But for those who did not withdraw, the young, the self-asserting, the verdict in James was death. Life had, indeed, stepped in to prove to James the truth of his fictions. He, a second son, had asserted himself by writing plays in defiance of his long-established reticences. He had left his ivory tower. His punishment had been inevitable. The world he strenuously wooed had

told him he was not wanted. He had suffered a kind of spiritual death like
the young Owen, killed by irreversible forces, by the fates; or like Morgan
Moreen for whom "family" was more than an historical weight. It was
a pressing humiliation, an eternal shame.

Discoveries

By the middle of February 1895, little more than a month after *Guy
Domville,* James had begun to dissociate the disaster from himself—"It
is rapidly growing to seem to have belonged to the history of someone
else." This transference of the unbearable burden to mythical shoulders
made it possible for him to try to work again. His intellect was as powerful and as active as ever; indeed it now began to discover all kinds of
solutions—artistic solutions. His emotions were blocked, defended, confused, full of past and recent hurt. His best, his "safest" identity was the
intellect of art; there he was in full command. In this way James arrived
by stages at the idea of moving the architectonics of the theater into his
De Vere Gardens study.

Howells had reminded him that he was in reality a novelist not a
playwright; the entry in James's notebook of 14 February 1895 shows him
becoming aware that he might think now of these roles as reversed; he
could be a playwright turning back to the novel. On this day James begins
by looking at his old notes for the story that will become *The Wings of
the Dove.* He goes on to read a note that represents a first sketch for *The
Golden Bowl.* The note troubles him, for it contains too much of "the
adulterine element." *Harper's* had asked for a light tale, and this
wouldn't do. "But may it not be simply a question of *handling* that? For
God's sake let me try: I want to plunge into it: I *languish* so to get at an
immediate creation. . . . *Voyons, voyons;* may I not instantly sit down to
a little close, clear, full scenario of it?" The word *scenario* is "charged
with memories and pains." Yet it touches a new chord of association.

> Has a *part* of all this wasted passion and squandered time (of the last five
> years) been simply the precious lesson, taught me in that roundabout and
> devious, that cruelly expensive, way, of *the singular value for a narrative
> plan too* of the (I don't know *what* adequately to call it) divine principle
> of the Scenario?

If this was so, he was ready, he told himself, to bless the pangs and pains
and miseries of his tragic experience; if what he called "the divine principle" was "a key that, working in the same *general* way fits the complicated chambers of *both* the dramatic and the narrative lock," then his
"infinite little loss" might be converted into "an almost infinite little
gain."

The image of the key and the lock was apt: and it applied to his life as well. He was closing a door behind him. He was opening a door on his future. He would never again write the kind of novel he had written during his earlier years, before he began playwriting. The stage had given him new technical skills; these he would now use in his fiction. A story could be told as if it were a play; characters could be developed as they develop on the stage; a novel could be given the skeletal structure of drama. Beginning with *The Spoils of Poynton,* written during the ensuing months, there emerged a new and complex Jamesian novel. He did not achieve at once a full-blown dramatic method for his fiction. He proceeded by trial and error, experimenting with systematic scenic alternation; with telling a story wholly in dialogue; with devices by which he left out certain scenes and supplied material through retrospective action. Above all he grew watchful, as if he were a lens, over "point of view." He had begun long ago by thinking of storytelling as a form of painting; he now merged the idea of painting with drama. In his earlier novels James had emulated the richness of Balzac by creating a large background and describing an entire environment. Now only relevant stage "properties" are described. No chair is mentioned if a character is not to sit on it; a mirror is on the wall only because we see the heroine looking in it. He was to be endlessly delighted with "the charm of the scenic consistency," and with those "scenic conditions which are as near an approach to the dramatic as the novel may permit itself."

He had been unable to meet the conditions of the stage. Now he imported the stage into his novels. He had no need of managers, actors, scenery. He had abandoned all hope of box-office earnings; but he had gained an artist's grasp of what narrative fiction might be if he had a plan, a design, a method. He could at last create the "organic" novel of which he had long ago spoken, so that everything in his story was related to everything else, as the organs are in the human body. He learned that he need be neither a "realist" nor a "naturalist"; if what he created was real to him it could be real to others. His final novels were a synthesis of all that he had learned about his art, and he wove into this the complex civilization of his mind and his vision of essences.

The years devoted to the writing of plays were to become for James, after a long period, "the strange sacred time"—strange because of the suffering, the pain and mastery of technical resource in the teeth of failure; sacred, because there resided in this the mystery and passion of his imagination, which enabled him to triumph again and again over "the sacred mystery of structure." But in another part of his being, in that part which masked a continuing despair, these "sacred years" might also have been called the "treacherous years"; they had harbored within them false prospects, false hopes, cruel deceptions, private demons.

In Ireland

Early in March of 1895—five weeks after the closing of his play—
Henry James went to Ireland. He had little heart for visits, but he had
promised his old friends, the Wolseleys, that he would spend a few days
with them in Dublin, where Lord Wolseley—once Sir Garnet—was Com-
mander-in-Chief of the English forces. And then in his *Guy Domville*
mail had come a friendly note from the second Lord Houghton—son of
the "bird of paradox" who had befriended James long ago—now Lord
Lieutenant of Ireland, inviting him to spend a week at the viceregal
court. James appears to have felt that it would be graceless to decline. He
crossed to Dublin on 9 March.

James had visited Ireland twice before, in 1882 and again in 1891, but
the country was best known to him in the continuing Home Rule struggle
in Parliament, in the recent drama of Parnell, which he and his sister
had followed with deep feeling, and in fairy-tale memories out of his
childhood. The senior Henry James had made much in old bedtime stories of his visit as a young man to the County Cavan village from which
the first William James had emigrated to America. With a strong sense
of the "Irishism" of his family, the younger Henry James now set foot on
the ancestral soil, but with less exuberance than his father and with a
sceptical eye.

He went first to stay with Lord Houghton's private secretary, Herbert
Jekyll—"the kind and clever Jekyll"—in his lodge in the Phoenix Park.
Then his brief taste of viceregal life at the Castle began. Here he had a
feeling of shock—"the sense of the lavish extravagance of the castle, with
the beggary and squalor of Ireland at the very gates." The viceregal court
was boycotted by the Irish aristocracy, the gentry and the landlords, since
Lord Houghton was the appointee of a Home Rule government. In his
isolation, Houghton sought to enliven his court by inviting large parties
from England. A widower with three daughters, he had lately inherited
great estates from his uncle Lord Crewe (and was indeed to become
himself the Marquess of Crewe), and passed his uncomfortable time in
Ireland bestowing luxurious hospitality. James squirmed at this "grandeur in a void." He developed lumbago and found it a weariness to have
to stand all evening "on one's hind legs" during the four balls given by
the viceroy in the six days of his stay. To some friends he was even more
candid: the visit had been "an unmitigated hell." He was deeply moved
by "the tragic shabbiness of this sinister country." It was too much for the
grandson of the County Cavan William James. With great relief he bade
farewell to the well-meaning viceroy, and drove to another part of the
city for his stay with the Wolseleys.

After the hollow viceregal splendor the military alertness of the Wolseley establishment at the Royal Hospital was a welcome change. Lady Wolseley gave James the run of the Sèvres room in the mornings; the inkpot on the desk was the largest he had ever used, overflowing "like the Wolseley welcome and their winecups." He liked being in "an intensely military little world of aides-de-camp, dragoons and hussars." He was full of admiration for the place, built by Charles II, and in particular the great rococo hall, where Lady Wolseley staged a costume ball at which the women dressed like ladies in the paintings of Sir Joshua Reynolds, Gainsborough and Romney. James spent ten delightful days in these surroundings, watching the sentinel-mounting and a great deal of military ritual.

For a "man of peace" (as he constantly reminded Wolseley) he was happier among soldiers than among courtiers. But then he had known the Wolseleys since his first dinings-out in London, when he had been made welcome at their great house in Portman Square. Lady Wolseley, the former Louisa Erskine, was attractive in her younger years, dark-haired and dark-eyed, and from the first James became, as he said, "quite thick" with her.

As for her husband, he was one of Victoria's bravest and most renowned soldiers. James liked his eye of steel—the one that remained, for he had lost the other in the Crimea—and admired his record in all the colonial wars of the era. Badly wounded in the Crimean war, Wolseley had fought in Burma, had been at Lucknow and in China; he had gone to the relief of Gordon in Khartoum. Stationed at Ottawa, he had handled the Red River rebellion in Manitoba and had crossed into the United States to cast an expert British eye on the Civil War. His exploits in the Ashantee campaign were legendary, and on his return to civilian life, he had been a great leader in the War Office for reform of the British Army. A decade later, when he had been named Field-Marshal and Viscount, Wolseley wrote his *Story of a Soldier's Life.* James read these stout volumes with the same fascination as the memoirs of General Marbot, and again marked salient passages, such as, "a nation without glory is like a man without courage, a woman without virtue ... glory to a nation is what sunlight is to all human beings."

It was the masculinity of heroism and glory rather than the masculinity of the barracks and the smoking-room, that James cherished. He had no stomach for the violence of Kipling, but he had a deep admiration for the probity of a soldier such as Wolseley. Thus he could write, at the end of his stay in Dublin—of that part of it passed at the Royal Hospital —that "the military *milieu* and type were very amusing and suggestive to me."

For the rest, he was completely clear about his stay at the Castle. "I

was not made for viceregal 'courts,' especially in countries distraught
with social hatreds."

A Squalid Tragedy

The Oscar Wilde case burst upon London, a few days after James's
return from Ireland, with a kind of moral violence that fascinated and
disturbed the novelist. From the first he characterized it as "a very
squalid tragedy, but still a tragedy." The brilliant maker of epigrams, the
wit of London society, the playwright, was convicted of homosexual
offenses and sent off to serve two years at hard labor.

Two days after Wilde was committed for trial, James wrote to Gosse
that he found the affair "hideously, atrociously dramatic and really interesting" but added that its interest was qualified by "a sickening horribil-
ity." Wilde, he wrote, "was never in the smallest of degree interesting to
me—but this hideous human history has made him so—in a manner."
James had sealed this letter when he had a further thought. He scrawled
across the back of the envelope, *"Quel dommage—mais quel bonheur—
que J.A.S. ne soit plus de ce monde."* ["What a pity—and a joy—that J.A.S.
is no longer in this world."]

The allusion to John Addington Symonds would have been lost upon
most Victorians. It had a particular meaning for Gosse. Both he and
James had known for some years that Symonds had been a crusading
homosexual, eager but unable to proclaim from the housetops the ecstasy
he felt in love between men. Wilde, in an impulsive and self-destructive
way, brought his tragedy on himself by denying the truth and suing for
libel when he was called a sodomite. Symonds, erratic, disturbed, tuber-
cular, wavering between caution and the need to protect his wife and
daughters, carried on a subterranean campaign on behalf of inversion,
using the Greeks, and the example of the *Symposium,* to discuss the
subject most intimate to him.

James met Symonds at lunch early in 1877 with Andrew Lang. He
reported to his brother that he found him "a mild, cultured man, with the
Oxford perfume, who invited me to visit him at Clifton." James never
accepted the invitation; and shortly thereafter Symonds went to live in
Switzerland. Some time after James's essay on Venice appeared in the
Century, in 1882, the novelist sent a copy to Symonds

> because it was a constructive way of expressing the good-will I felt for
> you in consequence of what you have written about the land of Italy
> ... your pages always seemed to say to me that you were one of a small
> number of people who love it as much as I do—in addition to your know-
> ing it immeasurably better.

James added that "it seemed to me that the victim of a common passion should sometimes exchange a look." But Symonds was concerned with a different level of "common passion"; and James never knew how critical Symonds was of what he called "the laborious beetle-flight of Henry James."

Early in their friendship Gosse, who had been in Symonds's confidence since the mid-1870s, told James the history of Symonds's unhappy marriage, without apparently divulging that Symonds had sought a wife in an attempt to escape from his homosexuality. James's notebook entry of 26 March 1884, a month after he had corresponded with Symonds, substantially foreshadows his tale of "The Author of Beltraffio" as he set it down shortly afterwards—"the opposition between the narrow, cold, Calvinistic wife, a rigid moralist, and the husband impregnated—even to morbidness—with the spirit of Italy, the love of Beauty, of art, the aesthetic view of life." Gosse told James, in praising the delicately-told yet lurid little tale (culminating in a violent Medea-like action), that he had shown great insight into the secret of Symonds's character; the novelist promptly asked to be told what this secret was. James said he was "devoured with curiosity as to this revelation. Even a postcard (in covert words) would relieve the suspense of the perhaps-already-too-indiscreet H.J." We know James ultimately was made a party to Gosse's intimate knowledge and while the Oscar Wilde trial was in progress, shown some of Symonds's letters. When the latter's privately-printed pamphlet on homosexuality, *A Problem in Modern Ethics,* appeared in 1891, Gosse showed it to James, who thanked him for "bringing me those marvellous outpourings," adding:

> J.A.S. is truly, I gather, a candid and consistent creature, and the exhibition is infinitely remarkable. It's, on the whole, I think, a queer place to plant the standard of duty, but he does it with extraordinary gallantry.

Symonds died in 1893, and when Gosse wrote to give James the news the novelist responded warmly in tribute to the "poor much-living, much-doing, passionately out-giving man." When Horatio Brown's biography of Symonds appeared early in 1895, James read the two volumes promptly, and marked a few passages in them—one in which Brown describes how Symonds abandoned speculation, inquiry and analysis in a metaphysical sense and concentrated "on man, on human life."

Just before leaving for Ireland, James had been urged by his Venetian friend, Mrs. Curtis, to write an appreciation of Symonds. James replied he was too busy; moreover "the job would be quite too difficult." There was, he wrote, an entire side of Symonds's life which was "strangely morbid and hysterical." To write of him without dealing with it would be "an affectation; and yet to deal with it either ironically or explicitly would be a Problem—a problem beyond me." James thus injected Symonds's own term for homosexuality.

His attitude towards Symonds suggests that James passed no moral judgment on his homosexuality or his passionate private crusade. What seems to have bothered James was Symonds's desire for public display in matters the novelist deemed wholly private. Both in his friendships, up to this time, and in his correspondence, James seemed to maintain the "distance" he had always kept from questions of sex. A kind of cool formality intervened—and almost a touch of condescension towards his more "involved" friends.

This "distance" from people and from passion enabled James to be both cool and compassionate to Wilde as well. On 26 April 1895 he wrote to his brother,

> you ask of Oscar Wilde. His fall is hideously tragic—and the squalid violence of it gives him an interest (of misery) that he never had for me —in any degree—before. Strange to say I think he may have a "future" —of a sort—by reaction—when he comes out of prison—if he survives the horrible sentence of hard labour that he will probably get.

To Paul Bourget he wrote, once the sentence had been pronounced, that he considered it "cruel." Solitary confinement, he said, rather than hard labor, would have been more humane. Later that year James was approached to sign a petition drawn up by the American poet Stuart Merrill, and circulated on behalf of Wilde among French and English writers. The overture was made through James's young friend Jonathan Sturges, who reported to Merrill:

> James says that the petition would not have the slightest effect on the *authorities* here who have the matter in charge and in whose nostrils the very name of Zola and even of Bourget is a stench and that the document would only exist as a manifesto of personal loyalty to Oscar by his friends, of which he was never one.

James did discuss the Wilde case with a Member of Parliament (probably R. B. Haldane) who sat on the commission for penal reform and visited Wilde in jail. On 10 November 1895 James wrote to Alphonse Daudet that he had had news from this man that Wilde was *"dans un état d'abattement complet, physique et moral"* ["in a complete state of moral and physical prostration"]; and that some easing of conditions for him might occur. He said also his political friend had discerned in Wilde no will to resistance, no faculty for recuperation. If he had this faculty, James added, "what masterpiece might he yet produce!"

The Two Romancers

In June 1893, when he had been actively corresponding with Robert Louis Stevenson, Henry James had written of his recent trip to the Continent.

> I saw Daudet who appears to be returning from the jaws of slow death—getting over creeping paralysis. Meredith I saw three months ago —with his charming *accueil,* his impenetrable shining scales, and the (to me) general mystery of his perversity.

When James coupled Alphonse Daudet and George Meredith in his little budget of news for the South Seas, he little dreamed that two years later he would be present at a memorable meeting of the two romancers. Indeed James was instrumental in bringing together the Provençal Gaul and the English "Gaul," both crippled by similar forms of paralysis, in a touching little comedy that played itself out that spring.

Of the generation of French writers whose members he had met when he had first settled in Europe, James had come closest to Alphonse Daudet. This had gone back to their common attachment to Turgenev. A greater part resided in Daudet's meridional expansiveness and his vivid and pictorial style. "He cannot put three words together, that I don't more or less adore them," James wrote. Daudet, on his side, receiving a letter in French from James, told Theodore Child, "if he can handle English the way he handles French, he's some guy!" [*"S'il se tire de sa langue comme de la notre, c'est un rude lapin."*]

On his visits to the rue de Bellechasse, in the Faubourg, James had been struck by the French writer's courage in face of his creeping paralysis, the fruit of indiscretions in his bohemian days. The last thing he expected, however, was that Daudet, with all his infirmities, would want to travel. In the midst of the Oscar Wilde excitement came a letter from Paris—the French novelist wanted to pay a spring visit to London, bringing his wife, his sons, Léon and Lucien, his young daughter Edmée. There would also be Victor Hugo's grandson and his wife. Would James find some comfortable rooms for all seven of them? "I will probably inflict a thousand annoyances on you," Daudet had written—and Henry remarked to his brother, "he will doubtless be as good as his word." But if there was annoyance, there was also amusement. James arranged an intimate dinner in Daudet's honor at the Reform Club, took rooms for him at Brown's Hotel, sent off letters of advice and guidance, and arranged to bring Daudet to visit George Meredith at Box Hill near Dorking.

For Meredith, James had an affection much more profound and intimate than for Daudet. He had met him long ago (in 1878), and admired the man rather than the novelist. He liked his wit, his paradox, his brilliant intelligence, his faculty for piling fantasy upon fantasy to some ultimate absurdity, until it all collapsed amid his own hearty laughter. He would have liked to see more of him. But as it was, he went periodically to Dorking to spend long hours with his distinguished contemporary. "He is much the wittiest Englishman, and the most famed for conversation, that I have ever known," James wrote in 1888. In 1892 we find him speaking of "the great once-dazzling George Meredith, whom I like, and whom, today, one can't but be tender to in his physical eclipse— overtaken by slow (very gradual) paralysis."

On 6 May 1895, James met the Daudet party at Victoria Station and conducted them to Brown's. As a sightseer, Daudet was insatiable; when he could not stagger into places on his own legs, he arranged to be wheeled in a bath chair. By this means, he visited Westminster Abbey and was given tea in the Deanery. James enjoyed talking to the sons, although he strongly disliked the twenty-seven-year-old Léon Daudet, a notorious royalist and anti-Semite, who was to lead a turbulent life. For the younger son, Lucien, then seventeen, James had much sympathy. The "rotund and romantic" Madame Daudet he found worldly and amusing; he enjoyed her comments on the way Englishwomen dressed—or rather failed to dress. On one day of the British spring, which that year was rainless and mild, James took his French celebrities to Oxford; on another to Windsor. *"Ah, si vous saviez comme ces petits coins d'Angleterre m'amusent,"* said Daudet. ["You can't imagine how entertaining I find these little corners of England."]

The dinner at the Reform Club was staged with James's customary care and seems to have gone well. James mustered a dozen French-speaking notables in London—among them John Morley, George Du Maurier, Arthur Balfour, Lawrence Alma-Tadema, Sir Edward Burne-Jones, Meredith's friend Admiral Maxse, the old dilettante Hamilton Aïdé, and Gosse. The latter seems to have been referring to this occasion when he described how the French novelist struggled up a short flight of stairs and once seated at table "a sort of youth reblossomed in him." Daudet was silent at first, almost motionless, and then head, arms, chest "would vibrate with electrical movements, the long white fingers would twitch in his beard, and then from the lips a tide of speech would spout —a flood of coloured words."

Léon Daudet was to record that "every day Henry James came to fetch us for a walk, a tea, a lunch, a dinner at the Club." He seemed to the younger Daudet like a doctor or a judge who "inspired serenity and confidence." James himself wrote, in a letter to Lady Wolseley after the Daudets were gone: "They clung to me like a litter of pups to an experienced mamma. They were very amiable, very uninformed, very bewildered, very observant and perceptive, on the whole, and very overwhelming."

The meeting of Daudet and Meredith occurred on 16 May, when Daudet and his son Léon made the trip by train from Charing Cross to Dorking, accompanied by James. With great effort Daudet climbed from the train and almost fell into the arms of the tall, white-bearded, white-haired Meredith. Henry described to his brother William how "strangely and grotesquely pathetic" was the meeting of the "two romancers" on the railway platform:

> each staggering and stumbling, with the same uncontrollable paralysis into the arms of the other so that they almost rolled over together on the line beneath the wheels of the train.

The little party slowly got into the carriage and drove to Flint Cottage where Meredith was giving dinner to his guests.

Meredith told Daudet that he had set aside some bottles of Côtes-Roties '54 in the hope of such an occasion. "His old Southern God is in that wine," said Meredith to James. The English poet-novelist read aloud Mistral's *Poème du Rhône;* certain of the passages in the Provençal, Meredith could not decipher. "I live here in the midst of Scythians, you understand, don't you, Daudet," Meredith said. And later he remarked to his guest, "How lively you are," and as if to explain his appreciation of this liveliness he added, "You know, I'm not really English; I'm a Gaul." When the name of Wilde came up, Meredith said, "a mixture of Apollo and a monster." A few days after the visit to Box Hill, Meredith came to London to dine with Daudet; and he returned again, in spite of his infirmities, to go to Victoria Station to say good-bye to the visitors. The two invalids clasped hands through the window as the train began to move —and with their muscular infirmities disengaged them with difficulty.

Daudet was expansive to the last. Within a day of his return to Paris he wrote James that he had had great admiration for the subtleties of his talent and the profundity of his spirit; but that now after spending three weeks near to him "during which I looked at you closely, I want to give you all my friendship and I demand all yours. Let's have not another word on the subject."

"That is charming," Henry commented to William, "and genuine, I think, and I am sincerely touched, but it is a rather formidable order to meet. However, he inspired great kindness." The Daudets had made James promise he would some day visit them at Champrosay; but James did not go abroad for several years, and in 1897 Daudet died. He had been "as warm as the south wall of a garden or as the flushed fruit that grows there," and of all finished artists he had been, said James, the most "natural." And James also said, "The sun in his blood had never burnt out."

The Figure in the Carpet

After the Daudets left, Henry James had a violent attack of gout—his foot was "like the Dome of St. Paul's." To Dr. Baldwin he wrote of his "fruitless six months, with gout, sore throats, a futile month's visit to Ireland, interruptions innumerable, and just lately, to finish, the whole Alphonse Daudet family." He would not be going to Italy this year, he told Baldwin, and referring to a recent earthquake there he added, "Our earthquake, here, has been social—human—sexual (if that be the word when it's all one sex). You probably followed in some degree the Oscar Wilde horrors."

There had been also his personal earthquake. The passage of six months since *Guy Domville* had not diminished his indecision or his melancholy. He was face to face with a long summer and did not know where to turn. He had never felt so much at loose ends. He talked much of abandoning London for the English countryside but shrank from doing so. Instead he involved himself with passing Americans. "There is a compatriot for every day in the week," he said. John La Farge appeared, reviving old memories, but seemed "Americanly innocent." Then Mrs. Jack Gardner came and for a few days James played out his usual comedy of pretending he was her most abject courtier; but her queenliness no longer amused him. Life, he told her, was too "complicated and conflicting." With characteristic irony he added, "you are a great simplifier —I wish you would simplify *me!*"

He lingered until late July amid the visiting "barbarians" and then suddenly bolted to Torquay in Devonshire where he had spent a few days the previous year. He obtained a fine suite in the Osborne Hotel, with a large sitting-room and a balcony. He took bicycle lessons and boasted of his black and yellow bruises. He paid calls on W. E. Norris, who lived with an only daughter in a large villa on a nearby hilltop—"exactly," James wrote to Francis Boott, "as you used to do at Bellosguardo." Norris had shown James much sympathy at the time of *Guy Domville.* They ran out of conversational subjects during the first quarter of an hour every time they met. This did not trouble James. Norris, "the gentlest and sweetest of men," was "accepting"—and he needed this now more than anything else.

"Peace wraps me round," he wrote to Miss Reubell. He liked the view; the sea had a lovely Italian blueness. And the tranquillity—"not a cat in the house!" What he did not reveal to his friends was that, in spite of his

vows and his denunciations of the stage, he was at work on a new play
—a one-acter for no less an actress than Ellen Terry. A woman of quick
sympathies and openness of feeling, she had asked him, after *Guy Domville,* to give her an original play for her forthcoming American tour. It
had taken James some weeks to accept the idea. Now in Torquay the
comedy of *Summersoft,* with its gentle American heroine, Mrs. Gracedew, came with comparative ease. The moment he completed it, he
rushed up to London to see Miss Terry, but she could give him only a few
minutes—time enough to pay him £100 for her option. She told him she
had a sure-fire vehicle for America in *Madame Sans-Gêne,* but promised
a British production of his play on her return. Once again the theater was
proving fickle—but James pocketed the money and wrote to Miss Terry,
"it will seem a long year—but art *is* long, ah me!"

If the actress was the principal reason for James's dash to London
there was also another which few of his friends knew. An entry in the
journals of Clara Benedict, Miss Woolson's sister, notes that "Mr. James
said he would come up from Torquay and be with us the week before we
sailed." After a twelve-month, he still seemed to feel some sense of duty
or obligation, some need for common kindness to Fenimore's relatives.
He took the Benedicts to dinner at the Indian exhibition to which all
London was flocking. They dined also in Mayfair and he saw them off to
America.

After they sailed, James was free to return to Torquay. Instead he
remained entangled with visitors and London society. He saw the Kiplings, on the eve of their return to America. He spent a Sunday in the
country with the Humphry Wards. Count Primoli, the Bonaparte dilettante, turned up from Rome, and in his company was the young Prince
Karageorgevitch of Montenegro, whom James described as "only a well-
directed little faintly-perfumed spray of fluid, of distilled amenity." Still
complaining of being "confined to the torrid town," he went off to spend
a week-end with George Du Maurier at Folkestone. *Trilby* was breaking
records as a best-seller, and would be a roaring success as a play. Yet he
found Du Maurier depressed "in spite of the chink—what say I, the
'chink'—the deafening roar—of sordid gold flowing in to him." James
wrote to Gosse: "I came back feeling an even worse failure than
usual."

It was now early September. James made arrangements for the installation of electric light in his De Vere Gardens flat. As painters, paper-
hangers and electricians took over, he left once more for Torquay. His
Devonshire retreat promised to be sociable. The Paul Bourgets, passing
through London, had once again decided to join him for a month. They
were much less demanding than the Daudets. The pair clung to James;
he in turn clung to them and to Norris. "Bourget's mind is, in the real

solitude in which I live, beneath what has been so much social chatter, a flowering oasis in conversational sands."

James had promised Heinemann two novels during the coming year; and he was supposed to write three tales for the *Atlantic Monthly.* He felt a certain pressure not only to fulfill these agreements, but to begin earning money again. But he was caught now in the complexities of his troubled imagination as well as his desire for experiment. By telling his stories in short dramatic scenes, he required more words than had been necessary in his *laisser-aller* days. His goal was 8,000 to 10,000 words; and now he nearly always ended with 18,000 or 20,000. He had begun a story for the *Atlantic* about a squabble between a mother and son over some antiques. At 25,000 it was not yet complete. He set it aside and began what seemed to him another small tale which he called "The Awkward Age." When it reached 15,000 he wrote to the editor, "I must try again for you on a tinier subject—though I thought this *was* tiny." He attempted a new story inspired by having seen, riding on top of a London bus, an attractive woman's face disfigured by a pair of abnormally large spectacles. It took him almost a month to write "Glasses," and then he ruefully informed the *Atlantic* it had exceeded 15,000. Apologetically he asked the editor, Horace Scudder, to print it in two installments. But Scudder liked the tale and ran it in a single issue. James was elated. "Ask *anything* of me then —I won't refuse it!" Scudder offered to take the overblown story about the squabble over a houseful of antiques as a three- or four-installment novel of about 35,000 words. James bargained for 5,000 words more; by the time he finished, it had become a 75,000-word novel, published in seven installments as *The Old Things.* In book form it would be *The Spoils of Poynton.*

What had happened to the author who could, with his turning hand, produce tale after tale, sometimes one or two a week? We may surmise that at this stage, given his mood and his despair, he resisted writing altogether. The substance of his tales—the four he would complete in 1895—showed a state that he himself called "embarrassment." One feels that at this moment James wanted simply to be left alone; to have the consoling company of Norris; to ride his bicycle, and brood on his problems or dawdle on the Torquay Crescent. Instead he had to keep at his work, to refill his empty purse. A fantasy he set down in his notebook begins by his recalling that old Mrs. Procter long ago described how pleasant it was simply to sit by her fire and read a book. He began to plan a tale about an "old party" who finds delight in modest elderly pastimes —"a quiet walk, a quiet read, the civil visit of a friend, or the luxury of some quite ordinary *relation.*"

He did not write this tale of the "old party." Instead he wrote another, about an author and an unfathomable secret, that was perhaps prompted by his re-exposure to the Benedicts in London and the reawakened Bellosguardo recollections at Torquay. Miss Woolson had, long before, written a story called "Miss Grief," about a woman writer like herself, who takes a piece of work to a successful literary man. Dissatisfied with one of the characters, he tries to edit it, only to discover that it contains an "especial figure in a carpet," which unravels when he tampers with the copy. Whether James remembered that image, or found it elsewhere, he now planned a tale called "The Figure in the Carpet" and wrote it shortly after his return to De Vere Gardens.

It is one of his artificial conceits about authorship. A young critic has reviewed the latest novel of Hugh Vereker and he hears Vereker call his review "the usual twaddle." Later Vereker discovers the identity of the critic, and is contrite; he explains to the young man that no one has understood his work nor discerned its secret—its "figure in the carpet." Pressed further by the critic, the novelist says that what nobody had ever mentioned in his writings was "the organ of life." In the context of his entire work, and his pronouncements, often reiterated, that it was art that *made* life, we may say that for James the "organ of life" is art. The order, the form, the texture of a work constituted the art with which it was written.

The young critic repeats Vereker's words to a fellow-critic, George Corvick, who begins a systematic search for the author's secret. He and his fiancée, Gwendolen Erme, who has written a youthful novel James whimsically called "Deep Down," find common ground in their shared pursuit of Vereker's "exquisite scheme." Corvick finally makes his discovery; he journeys halfway across the world to consult Vereker, who confirms it. Gwendolen marries him, but Corvick dies in an accident during his honeymoon. Later Vereker dies; and after him his wife. Only Corvick's widow now knows the secret and the curious little critic, the narrator, asks her bluntly for it. She is just as blunt: "I mean to keep it to myself," and with this knowledge she writes a better novel, called "Overmastered." The critic wonders whether he shouldn't try to marry her—the figure in the carpet seems traceable and describable "only for husbands and wives." However, she marries another critic; and when, after a time, she dies, the narrator discovers that she had never told this husband Vereker's secret. "I was shut up in my obsession forever—my gaolers had gone off with the key."

We have a convergence in this tale of the two themes that constituted James's "embarrassment." The first, the more obvious one, was his sense of being a misunderstood author; criticism was blind; it cared not one bit about the clever secrets of his art—his own figure in his Persian carpet. The *Guy Domville* audience had behaved like a bunch of savages with a gold watch. The second theme was the burden of Miss Woolson. Had her death been a secret of human relations, a defect in his own "system" of friendship? He was left shut up with this mystery—for ever! "The Way It Came" (later renamed "The Friends of the Friends"), which immediately followed the story of Hugh Vereker, is a tale of a man who will never know whether he talked to a woman just before or after her death. As his fiancée, also left in eternal doubt, kneels by the bedside of the dead woman, her thought is that "Death had made her, had kept her beautiful; but I felt above all, that it had made her, had kept her, silent." Again James's image is that of a key—"it had turned the key on something I was concerned to know." And there was no way of knowing.

James remained at Torquay for two months while his London apartment was renovated. During the last days of his stay, Jonathan Sturges came to stay with him. He was depressed, and unwell. One evening, Sturges told James of an incident that had occurred months before in Paris. He had met Howells one day in Whistler's garden in the rue du Bac. Howells had just arrived, but had been recalled to America because his father was dying. He said to Sturges: "Oh, you are young, you are young—be glad of it: be glad of it and *live*. Live all you can: it's a mistake not to. It doesn't so much matter what you do—but live." Howells had added, "I'm old. It's too late." James listened to the story as if the message were for him. He felt old. His best years had fled. He was aware of his unlived life rising within—and yet it seemed "too late." He could do no more, in his own black abyss, than set down Howells's words in his notebook. Five years later they would speak to him again.

2

THE

TURN OF

THE SCREW

♀

A Quiet Hermitage

Henry James returned to London at the beginning of November 1895. He would have lingered in Devonshire but for the increasing illness of Jonathan Sturges. Rather than risk having a seriously sick friend on his hands, he got him to London and into hospital.

James rejoiced in the fresh paint in De Vere Gardens and the brightness of his new electric lamps. He wrote two tales and resumed work on his serial for the *Atlantic.* To Mrs. Wister he said he cared more than ever for his work. With the "necessary isolation the years bring with them (quantities of *acquaintances*—oh yes!)" his fiction was "almost the only thing I do care for."

Before the Yule season, James visited George Meredith who was about to bring out *The Amazing Marriage;* and he wrote to Daudet about Du Maurier's *Trilby,* which in its play form seemed destined to run for at least two or three years. "See what it is to take the measure of the foot —as we say—of the gross Anglo-Saxon public. The rare Meredith is not that kind of shoemaker—nor," added Henry, "the poor James."

On 18 December 1895, the London newspapers brought the novelist a horrible war scare. There had been for some years a boundary dispute between Venezuela and British Guiana. Suddenly President Cleveland reasserted the 70-year-old Monroe Doctrine. He denounced British "aggression" against Venezuela and declared that the United States had a serious interest in the determination of the boundary.

James had for so long taken for granted the continuing friendship of the English-speaking peoples—which his own career symbolized—that it came to him as a violent shock to discover how deep transatlantic animosities could run. Feelings between the two nations had been on the whole friendly since their differences during the Civil War. Now Cleveland's belligerence, and a huge outcry against England in the American press, shook the foundations of James's security. His letters during the early weeks of 1896 show how profound his anxiety was. If there were a war he would have to make a choice, for his allegiance was double; his sympathies lay in London, in Europe, in the cosmopolite world.

"One must hope that sanity and civilization, in both countries, will prevail," he wrote to his brother. The British put on their coolest diplomatic manner; and as the days passed, belligerent words were succeeded by cautionary moves. To Howells James confessed that the war scare had brought home to him the length of his absence from America. "Those were weeks of black darkness for me."

James agreed that winter to do a serial for an unusual medium—for him —the *Illustrated London News.* His friend Mrs. W. K. Clifford had hinted to the editor, Clement Shorter, that James might be willing to strike a "popular" note and he was very positive about this. "I should be very glad to write you a story energetically designed to meet your requirements of a 'love-story,' " he wrote. With the final chapters of *The Old Things* still to be written for the *Atlantic,* James decided to quit London early and get his books done in some quiet corner of England. If he could find a house near London, he could be in and out of the city as necessary. He began to lay plans in February 1896.

The house was found for him by an architect friend, Edward Warren. It was called Point Hill, located at Playden in Sussex. The novelist got a three-months occupancy, from May to August 1896. "The cottage was, in its kind, perfection," James would remember,

> mainly by reason of a small paved terrace which, curving forward from the cliff-edge like the prow of a ship, overhung a view as level, as pure, as full of rich change as the expanse of a sea; a small red-roofed town, of great antiquity, perched on its sea-rock, clustered within the picture off to the right.

The town at which James looked was one of England's ancient Cinque Ports—Rye in Sussex, whose red-brick houses, many of them extremely old, huddled about the town's church, set on the highest point of the rock —a church part Norman, with a square tower.

Rye had an ancient tower, built in the twelfth century as a Channel watch-tower; on the London side was a landgate, also a remnant of the Middle Ages. The waters had long withdrawn from the base of the rock and the marshes had been drained, so that Romney Marsh, once covered by the sea, now had hundreds of sheep peacefully grazing. The High Street was lined with old shops; at night when they were lit by candle or smelly oil-lamp it seemed to James as if he were back in the eighteenth century. Cobbled Mermaid Street, with its Elizabethan houses, went back much farther. During his rambles James was particularly struck by a stout red-brick Georgian house, at a curve in the steep street leading to the church; next to it was a curious little hall of which he had seen a watercolor in the London home of Edward Warren, who had lately sketched it. James was told that the house had for generations been in the hands of the Lambs, one of Rye's prominent families.

His Sussex retreat was quiet, quaint, simple and salubrious, and "the bliss of the rural solitude and peace and beauty are a balm to my spirit," James wrote to William after a month at Point Hill. "This little corner of the land endears itself to me." The weather was exceptionally fine, and every evening in the thickening twilight he would dine at eight on his terrace, as if he were living in a Florentine villa. When he was not walking the hilly streets of Rye, he took to the circling sea roads on his bicycle, going to nearby Winchelsea, where Ellen Terry had her cottage, and to a host of little towns with soft quaint names—Brookland, Old Romney, Ivychurch, Dymchurch, Lydd.

Long before the first of August when he was supposed to surrender Point Hill to its returning owners, James had decided he did not want to leave. A systematic hunt yielded him a haven for the rest of the summer. This was the town's Old Vicarage, as it was formally called, situated in Rye itself. The "musty, bourgeois parsonage" gave him no view, and brought him down to the cobbles of Rye itself; but he was able to work well within it. He liked its "very ancient and purple brick-walled garden, where the pears grow yellow in the September sun," and he clung to the house until it was time to give it up at the beginning of October. The little red-roofed and clustered old-world town, James told Grace Norton, was "in a manner a small and homely *family.*"

For the Henry James who ever since *Guy Domville* had felt "homeless," the parochial domesticity of this one of the guardian ports of England offered a kind of solitude and intimate friendliness which he could not find in London. Before leaving he mentioned, in chatting with the local ironmonger, that he was interested in finding a year-round house in Rye. The ironmonger would remember.

Houses and Old Things

The Spoils of Poynton—a story of an old house and "old things"—marked a turning point in James's fiction, although the novelist, struggling with his work on his terrace overlooking Rye, seems hardly to have been aware of this. Re-reading *The Spoils* today one is struck by the dramatic quality of its slight but strong theme—the struggle between a mother and son for possession of a houseful of antiques; the scenic deployment of its four principal characters; the shrewd study of personal relations. The precious furniture is moved from one house to another—very much as furniture was moved by stage-hands in the novelist's recent play. *The Spoils* becomes in James's hands an unconscious allegory of his five years of failure in the theater. But it is also—within its technical virtuosity—an amused commentary on the collecting spirit, "the fierce appetite for the upholsterer's and joiner's and brazier's work, the chairs and tables, the cabinets and presses, the material odds and ends, of the more labouring ages." These are the objects which the dedicated owner of Poynton, on the death of her husband, seeks to prevent her son from inheriting—unless he can marry a wife capable of caring for them as she has done.

The original idea for *The Spoils* had been jotted down in James's notebook two years earlier; during one of his London dinners, the woman next to him had spoken of "a small ugly matter" in which a widowed Scottish lady was suing her son over the rare furnishings he had inherited and which she refused to yield. In the notebooks we can see that James began by wanting to be sorry for the displaced and deposed mother, sent away to a dower house. But as he got into his story, what emerged was Mrs. Gereth's destructive rage and her determined effort to marry her son Owen off to the helpless Fleda Vetch. She is a young artistic girl whom Mrs. Gereth places in the impossible position of having to pursue her light-hearted son, who is himself pursued by the philistine Mona Brigstock. James thus constructs a chain of personal pressures; Mona will marry Owen only if he obtains Poynton. Fleda wants to marry Owen, but holds back out of moral scruples, indecision, and an inability to assert herself—until finally, holding all the trump cards in her hands, she throws them away.

Fleda's reasons for her renunciation of Owen are noble; yet they have no relation to the realities James incorporated into his story. He seems to have fixed his mind on the ultimate destruction of Poynton; in the end no one is to have anything—as he had been left with nothing when his own artistic work went up in smoke at the St. James's. And having begun with the idea for one kind of novel, that of the dispossessed mother, he ends with another. He removes Mrs. Gereth from the center of the stage and puts Fleda in her place. But the Fleda James described in his late preface, the "superior" girl with the "demonic" mind and "free spirit," is not in the book. In the book she is as confused and filled with tergiversation as James had been in the theater.

His imagery in the novel went further back than the recent *Guy Domville* disaster. In describing Mrs. Gereth's departure from Poynton and her loss of her antiques, *her* personal work of art, James wrote, "the amputation had been performed. Her leg had come off—she had now begun to stump along with the lovely wooden substitute; she would stump for life, and what her young friend was to come and admire was the beauty of her movement and the noise which she made about the house." James does not confine himself to this lugubrious metaphor which evokes his father's early amputation and, in a way, his own old back injury in a Newport stable fire. In the very last pages of the novel his father's ghost seems to greet Fleda Vetch as her train arrives at Poynton—the railway carriage door is opened by "an old lame porter of the station" she remembers from an earlier time. This crippled figure brings her the intimation of the disaster. Poynton and its treasures have gone up in flames.

Amputation and fire. These powerful symbols and memories out of the past forced themselves into the story James was telling. Poynton and its "spoils" had to be destroyed as *Guy Domville* was destroyed in a moment of melodrama. And Henry James felt himself crippled by this event, as his father had been for life, after the old stable fire in Albany. James's five-year struggle to sacrifice art to the Moloch-materialism of the stage was retold in *The Spoils of Poynton* in the form of an irrational issue of a rational conflict—but in terms of irrational behavior. The violence of the *Guy Domville* audience had revived the violences and dramas of childhood—and James would embody portraits of himself as a little boy and a little girl in the succeeding novels from *What Maisie Knew* to *The Awkward Age*—and above all in "The Turn of the Screw."

The Spoils of Poynton represented James's first attempt to use his scenic method and his play-writing techniques. *The Other House,* which he wrote immediately afterwards, was a direct adaptation into the novel form of the play scenario he had sketched early in 1894. The punctuality with which he dispatched his installments from Point Hill, and later from the Old Vicarage, suggests that the scenario must have been in effect a first draft of the play. The work is almost entirely dialogue, save for settings and occasional brief narrative passages.

There are two houses in this novel: Eastmead and Bounds, separated by a garden and a nearby stream, the homes of the two partners in the banking firm of Beever and Bream. Mrs. Beever, who inherited her husband's share in the bank, lives at Eastmead and to her, Bounds is "the other house." Eastmead is "a great, clean, square, solitude," and Mrs. Beever's own life is equally ordered. She intends to marry off her son to a girl of her choice: a "slim, fair girl," whom James in his notes has designated as his "Good Heroine." The "Bad Heroine" is installed in "the other house," Bounds, handsomely and expensively renovated by the younger partner in the bank, Anthony Bream. Bream's wife has just given birth to a daughter. Certain she will not survive childbirth, and having a morbid fear of stepmothers (her own had been too demanding), the wife exacts a promise from Tony Bream that if she dies, he will not remarry so long as her child lives. She does indeed die, and the Ibsenite drama can now act itself out, between the house of quiet and the house of passion, between the Good Heroine, Jean Martle, and the Bad Heroine, Rose Armiger.

Rose, an old companion of Mrs. Bream's, had loved Tony without hope so long as her friend lived; and she is now prevented from marrying him so long as the child, Effie, lives. Tony on his side is much more interested in the Good Heroine, Jean Martle, than in his wife's friend. The other girl is frightening. When Tony looks into Rose Armiger's eyes, he sees a kind of "measureless white ray of light steadily revolving"; it was "always somewhere; and now it covered him with a great cold lustre that made everything for the moment look hard and ugly." It *is* hard and ugly; for the frustrated passionate Rose drowns little Effie and tries to fix the guilt on the Good Heroine. The hero is left undefended.

This is the melodrama James devised for the readers of the *Illustrated London News. The Other House* is an unpleasant novel: a piece of subtle mechanical play-tinkering with powerful stuff of the emotions which James does not seem to understand or to command: an outburst of primitive rage that seems irrational however much it is dramatically "motivated"; and with a crime which defies the tradition of murder stories by going unpunished. Perhaps James felt that his Bad Heroine's future would in itself be sufficient punishment. But the reader puts down the work feeling that for once in his career as artist James has seriously faltered. Some instinct told him that he had; for he published the novel amid the pictorial sensationalism of a journal he disliked.

Thus the two novels which James wrote at the outset of this new period of creativity contain within them the violence that had come into his own life. The sudden burning of Poynton was the metaphor for the sudden destruction of his play; the passion of Rose Armiger and its destruction of the little girl meant the murder of innocence—as if some remote little being within James himself had been "exterminated" by the audience during that crucial night a year and a half earlier, and left him open to the indifference of the world. In the midst of the sun and sea and summer of Rye, the change from urban life to quiet English ruralism, James continued to live within his deepest self in a struggling world of nightmare and melancholy. What saved him from total despair was his work: it was his refuge during the period of his "black abyss."

Paradox of Success

Soon after he returned that autumn to London, James went to stand in Hampstead churchyard, amid the elite of England, beside the grave of a man he had seen often during his London life, and whom he had dearly loved. His old and cherished friend, George Du Maurier, died early in October. James had loved his cartoons in *Punch* long before he had met him; he had always admired the comedy and craft of this supreme gentle satirist—Du Maurier's ability to capture people's postures while they wait for dinner, while they are thinking what to say, pretending to listen to music, making speeches they don't mean. And then in his first years in London Du Maurier had become his friend. James liked the mixture of French seriousness and English drollery in Du Maurier; Du Maurier liked James's American observation and his French wit.

The artist was blind in one eye, but when he and James walked together on Sundays on Hampstead Heath his other eye had an extraordinary optical reach. "I always thought I valued the use of my eyes and that I noticed and observed," James wrote, "but the manner in which, when out with him, I mainly exercised my faculty was by remarking how constantly and how easily his own surpassed it." He saw mystery, reality, irony, in everything.

Du Maurier was a marvelous spinner of tales. One night he told James a fantastic story of a pair of lovers changed into albatrosses. They were shot and wounded; one resumed human shape and waited and watched in vain for the other. The germ of *Peter Ibbetson* seemed to be in this tale. And then there was the famous evening, of 25 March 1889, when, walking with James through the streets of Bayswater, Du Maurier offered him "an idea of his which he thought very good—and I do too— for a short story." The story James then recorded dealt with a girl with a wonderful voice but no genius for music, who is mesmerized and made to sing by a little foreign Jew "who has mesmeric power, infinite feeling, and no organ." *Trilby* thus acquired existence first as a note in James's scribbler. James decided he could not write it: "the want of musical knowledge would hinder *me* somewhat." He then urged Du Maurier to tell it himself. Du Maurier tried, but instead wrote *Peter Ibbetson*, about a hero whose dreams become his only reality. Six years after their evening walk *Trilby* was published—with the results the world knows.

For James there was a striking—and mocking—psychological drama in the final events of his friend's life. Du Maurier had for years lived his private Hampstead life, with his wife and children and dog, his drawing-board and his notations of London comedy and London society. Then he had written *Trilby* as a piece of natural and intimate story-telling, and it had taken the public by storm. The amateur, writing his tale as it were on the edge of his drawing-board, had achieved what James with all his consummate art of story-telling could never do. He was not jealous of his friend, but he was amazed by the paradox of "success." In the end, *Trilby* seemed to have murdered her creator. The old witty intimate Du Maurier disappeared; in his place there remained a melancholy successful man. What did it mean, this showering of adulation on a man who loved privacy and quiet? The long article in *Harper's* which James dedicated to his friend takes up this question but finds no answer. Why was Du Maurier so "overtaken and overwhelmed"? Why had the public pounced on his gentle writings with such eagerness, such greed?

> The whole phenomenon grew and grew till it became, at any rate for this particular victim, a fountain of gloom and a portent of woe; it darkened all his sky with a hugeness of vulgarity.

Du Maurier had wanted to simplify, but "the clock of his new period kept striking a different hour from the clock of his old spirit."

One more door had closed on James's old "London life," and its closing illustrated the ironies of "success," the strangeness of "reputation." If one part of his memorial to Du Maurier dealt with a deeply personal friendship, the other part was a kind of memorial for his own dream of theatrical fame, an attempt to tell himself that this fame would have been in reality worthless, perhaps fatal.

A Fierce Legibility

Between 1895 and 1898 the twentieth century began to knock loudly at Henry James's door. He had installed electric light in De Vere Gardens in 1895; in 1896 he had begun to use the bicycle whenever he was in the country; in 1897 he purchased a typewriter and engaged a part-time typist. The telephone and motoring were to come.

In the 1880s, when the use of the typewriter had become general, James had begun to send his manuscripts to a public stenographer. In earlier years he had simply dispatched his pages, written in his rapid hand, directly to editor and publisher. Early in 1896 he had become aware of increasing pain in his right wrist; it was probably the familiar writer's cramp, understandable enough in a man who for years had worked six to eight hours a day at his desk. His brother had acquired stenographic help at Harvard, and Henry agreed he might come to this—for his correspondence. During the autumn and winter of 1896–97, when he was working on *What Maisie Knew,* his wrist condition became chronic. He accordingly engaged a part-time stenographer, William MacAlpine, a silent Scot who worked regularly as a shorthand reporter, and began by letting him take letters in shorthand, but disliked the delay involved in transcription from shorthand to text. By the end of the first month, James was dictating directly to the typewriter; this was a useful short cut. "I can address you only through an embroidered veil of sound," he dictated to his Parisian friend, Morton Fullerton. "The sound is that of the admirable and expensive machine that I have just purchased for the purpose of bridging our silences." James became so accustomed to the sound of his machine that he was unable to dictate one day when it broke down and an alien typewriter temporarily replaced it. The repose enabled his wrist to do a certain amount of letter-writing in the old way, so that part of his correspondence was relegated to evenings, and remained private. A certain number of letters continued to be typewritten, with elaborate apologies for their "fierce legibility"; but the machine in the end was reserved for his art.

Very early, Morton Fullerton raised the question: what would the typewriter do to James's style? "I can be trusted, artless youth," James answered, "not to be simplified by any shortcut or falsified by any facility." But Henry James writing, and Henry James dictating, were different persons. Some of his friends claimed they could put their finger on the exact chapter in *Maisie* where manual effort ceased and dictation began. After several years of consistent dictating, the "later manner" of Henry James emerged. Some part of it would have been there without benefit of the Remington. Certain indirections and qualifications had always existed. But the spoken voice was to be heard henceforth in James's prose, not only in the rhythm and ultimate perfection of his verbal music, but in his use of colloquialisms, and in a greater indulgence in metaphor. And doubtless having a companion always in his work-room had its effect: the actor in him could not resist exhibitory flourishes.

The typewriter was, in those days, a large and not easily transported object. It never occurred to James—and doubtless he would have been very clumsy at it—to learn to typewrite. Acquisition of his machine meant not only that he lost his mobility, but that he was dependent upon help to get his daily work done. He could not travel with his machine, as he explained to a friend in June 1897:

> The voice of Venice, all this time, has called very loud. But it has been drowned a good deal in the click of the typewriter to which I dictate and which, some months ago, crept into my existence through the crevice of a lame hand and now occupies in it a place too big to be left vacant for long periods of hotel and railway life.

In the spring of 1897 London readied itself for Queen Victoria's Diamond Jubilee. James was impatient with the scaffold-carpentry, the defacing of the capital, the bidding for seats; this was a drab commercializing of national sentiment. He looked for another house in the country, but found none to his liking. So he remained in town, promising himself he would go away just before the "Victorian Saturnalia." He told William he "saw not the tip of the tail of any part of the show." The young George Vanderbilt offered him a place on his large balcony overlooking Pall Mall. James declined, and left for Bournemouth. His typist was free and he took him along to the seaside, leaving the "Babylonian barricades" to the hordes. He engaged rooms at the château-like Royal Bath Hotel and in a Bournemouth utterly deserted spent the show-day by a hot blue sea.

James passed most of July 1897 in Bournemouth, enjoying the emptiness of the place. He cycled and purchased a bicycle for MacAlpine, thus providing company for his rides. The Bourgets visited him, as had become their custom, but stayed only four days. Bourget went to Oxford to lecture on Flaubert, and James, who could not resist the singular honor done to his craft and his two friends—the dead Flaubert and the living Bourget—journeyed through encumbered London to attend. The rest of the month was spent in daily dictation and seaside relaxation. MacAlpine was an excellent typist but a dull companion.

James did have to return to London at the end of July, summoned unexpectedly to jury duty. The case, a divorce hearing, lasted only two days at the Court of Queen's Bench, and Henry's remark to William, "Doing British Juryman threw lights—and glooms!" suggests that the novelist was not bored. He had described a divorce in the opening installment of *What Maisie Knew*—but by the time he went to the court he was at work on the final pages of the short novel.

What Maisie Knew, serialized in 1897 in *The Chap-Book* in Chicago and in England in the *New Review,* is a work of intellectual wit. It reflects James's awareness of a child's world as a piecemeal world, containing quantities of literal observation but lacking clues to wider connections. Many serious things are said in the presence of Maisie, and many bawdy things; but she, like a kitten, keeps her eye on the piece of string, or the direction in which a hand is moving. Handed over, in a custody suit, to periodic visits with each of her parents, she becomes the carrier from one to the other of hatred and rage. Presently she is moving in the world of their adulteries and those of her surrogate parents, but with her innocence intact; we never know how much it has been damaged. With great skill and subtlety, James keeps the reader constantly within the eyevision of the little girl. The story is written scenically, like *The Spoils,* and shows in its form and tightness that James was not as yet yielding to the prolixity of dictation.

Like other works of this period, *Maisie* illustrates to an extraordinary degree the way in which the adult mind and professional skill can create a work in the face of inner bewilderment. Maisie's bewilderment and isolation is James's—it is the bewilderment he had felt since the collapse of his world in *Guy Domville:* but the world's cruelty and hostility are refashioned into a comic vision of benign childish curiosity. In the depths of this novel—which on the surface is very much like a bedroom farce—we can discern James's own confusion before the collapsing Victorian moral façade. The worldly bachelor of Kensington and Mayfair still possessed a fund of innocence and wonder. Maisie's "small demonic foresight," as James was to describe it a decade later in his preface, harbored his own. The little girl observes "the rich little spectacle of objects embalmed in her wonder" and "she wonders to the end, to the death—the death of her childhood." It is Maisie's sense of wonder that makes the sordid elements of her life appear phantasmagoric, like a child's fairy tale, or the images projected by a magic lantern. The reader sees both the wonder and the nightmare.

A Question of Speech

On 3 July 1897, at Bournemouth, while reading the letters of the Suffolk genius, Edward FitzGerald, whose rendering of *Omar Khayyám* had brought a breath of hedonism to Victorian England, James came on the name of Saxmundham, which had for him a certain "strangeness and handsomeness." That same afternoon, during a walk, he encountered a rugged boatman from Suffolk—from Saxmundham—whose brother had been FitzGerald's boatman. On returning from the walk, he found a letter from Saxmundham, from an American cousin, sister of the long dead Minny Temple, who was staying in the FitzGerald country, at Dunwich on the Suffolk coast, with her three daughters. She urged James to join her. The coincidence of a thrice-encountered mouth-filling topographical name and his feeling that he should get to know his American cousins better, combined to make James promptly agree. Moreover, he was at a loose end. He wrote to his cousin Ellen Hunter (who had been Ellen James Temple in his Newport days), that he would come for most of August. He hoped a room could be found also for his typist.

Elly Temple had married one of the New York Emmets; her sister had married another, so that there was a proliferation of Temple Emmets, whom James called "the Emmetry." The widowed Elly was now remarried to an Englishman. Her three Emmet daughters were Rosina, then twenty-four, who had sent Cousin Henry some of her writings and had been warned by him against introducing too much low life and slang into fiction; Ellen Gertrude, called "Bay," twenty-two, who had been studying art in Paris; and Edith Leslie, just turned twenty. The four of them, and another Emmet cousin named Jane, seem to have awaited the coming of the novelist as if he were a royal personage. A bedroom and sitting-room were found for him in one of the local houses, but as there was neither butcher, baker nor grocer in Dunwich, a decayed little seaport for centuries eroded by the sea, Cousin Ellen was forced to organize the food services "Bonapartistically," James was later to say.

From Jane Emmet in Dunwich, Saxmundham, Suffolk, to her sister Lydia Emmet, 6 August 1897:

> Well, at last Henry James arrived, and he is the nicest thing, but what a mental epicure. . . . Poor thing, he must miss so much, being so horrified by accent. He can't get past it. He must miss so much real refinement and cleverness and niceness. We do nothing but thank our stars that we are not Henry James. I am afraid our voices and sentences hurt his eardrums.

From Henry James in Dunwich, Saxmundham, Suffolk, 1 September 1897, to William James in Cambridge, Mass.:

> The resources of Dunwich are not infinite, and I should, without the cousins, have made a briefer dip of it. It was of course for them that I came and for them I am staying on a little. The girls . . . would be thoroughly "sympathetic" if they only had a language to be it in! Their speech, absolutely unaffected as yet, so far as I can see, by a year of Europe . . . remains really their only fault. But it is a grave one. I attack it, however, boldly, and as much as I can. It will be hopeless, I fear, ever —or at least for a long time—to interfuse Bay and Leslie with a few consonants, or to make any of them sound the letter "i" in any of the connections in which it occurs. . . . However, they *want* to improve, and are full of life and humour and sentiment and intelligence.

In later years Rosina would tell how on one of their walks Henry James, with much affection, and yet a kind of merciless regularity, kept her attention fixed on the sound of her own voice. Hoping to engage him in conversation, she had commented on how charming she found the jewel in his tie-pin.

"Jew-*el,* not *jool,*" her Distinguished Cousin rejoined, ignoring the compliment.

"I'm afraid American girls don't speak their vowels distinctly," Rosina ventured.

"Vow-*el,* not *vowl,* Rosina."

Tears came, "Oh Cousin Henry, you are so cruel."

"Cru-*el,* not *crool,* Rosina."

That James enjoyed himself enormously at Dunwich, in spite of the absence of luxuries and the bad roads and the girls' bad enunciation, is clear from an article he wrote for *Harper's Weekly,* one of his last fugitive travel pieces. There was enough to fascinate in Suffolk—the wide pebbly beaches, the towns that had disappeared in the great wash of the sea during the centuries. He delighted in the appeal of "desolate exquisite Dunwich," surveying with his professional eye the ruins of the great church and its tall tower, the crumbled ivy wall of the Priory, the low heathery bareness of the countryside, the rare purple and gold that ran to the edge of the sea. In the afternoons he would go on long bicycle runs, wearing his old baggy trousers and his rough-textured Norfolk jacket, jaunty bow-tie and golf cap. There is one snapshot of James standing with a large grin beside a lifeguard on the stony beach; and another of him leaning on a cane as if he were Neptune. Best of all he liked his talks with the seafaring folk. "I had often dreamed that the ideal refuge for a man of letters was a cottage so placed on the coast as to be circled, as it were, by the protecting arm of the Admiralty."

Before leaving in September, he wrote a long letter to his brother in which he spoke of his sense of being a nomad. He was "tired of oscillating between bad lodgings and expensive hotels," but this would continue to be his lot, he said, "until I can put my hand on the lowly refuge of my own, for which, from year to year, I thirst." And he added, "On the day I do get it—for the day must come—I shall feel my fortune is made." The day was only a fortnight away.

Lamb House

Henry James's quest for what he called a "lowly refuge" suddenly acquired a momentum of its own. He remembered the pleasant little watercolor he had seen in the home of Edward Warren, his architect friend, of an annex to a house—Lamb House—with Roman-arched bow windows rising above the street, a peaked roof, an old-fashioned lantern set in the wall and ivy climbing up one side. Warren, who was staying near Dunwich, went cycling with James on the last day of his stay. As they bumped along on their bicycles they talked of Rye and of Lamb House in particular. Returning to De Vere Gardens, James found a letter from Milson, the Rye ironmonger whom he had alerted about his house-hunting, informing him that the owner of Lamb House had died; his son was off to the Klondike gold rush, and the house was available on a long lease. To James this seemed like magic. He scribbled to Warren, "to be fairly confronted with the possibility and so brought to the point is a little like a blow in the stomach." He rushed down to Rye and obtained first refusal of the lease; a few days later Warren pronounced favorably on the house after a close professional inspection. All his inclination, James said, had been to take it: it had "a teetotal charm" and he added, "I feel in fact *doomed* to do so."

Lamb House stands at the top of cobbled West Street which climbs the hilltop of Rye out of the High Street. It is located at the turn, where West Street curves towards St. Mary's Church. The three-story house looks towards the ancient church, and the detached garden room down the hilly street up which James had come. The garden room was called the "banqueting room"; doubtless the Lamb family (its members had been mayors of Rye for over a century) had used it for civic purposes. Lamb House, built in 1723, had provided shelter for the first King George when his tempest-tossed ship, homeward bound from Hanover, put in at the port. In its "King's Room," later, George II and his son, the Duke of Cumberland, also slept during visits to the town. The house was of red brick that had turned russet; the garden room, built somewhat later, was of brick that had faded to a tawny color.

James entered Lamb House by its high-canopied Georgian doorway; the brass knocker had to be turned sharply to the right to unlatch the door. A well-proportioned balustraded staircase of oak faced the entrance. To the right was a small paneled room, a kind of waiting room. On the left was an oak-paneled parlor from which a door opened into a comfortable stretch of garden—a little less than an acre. Next to this room was a squarish dining room, with another French door giving on the garden. Opposite, under the stair, the novelist passed into a high and spacious kitchen. Upstairs the King's Room, wainscoted from floor to ceiling, looked towards the church; across the hallway on the right was a small square paneled room looking towards Winchelsea and onto the Lamb House garden. There were two more bedrooms, also a dressing-room and a bathroom. On the floor above were four rooms that could be servants' quarters. At the top of the stairs, on the first floor, was a pleasant sitting room called the Green Room: it would serve as a study.

James passed through the ground-floor parlor into the garden; to the left was a short flight of curved stone steps leading into the garden room. This was spacious and would make an ideal work room; its bow window commanded a fine expanse of the changeable Sussex sky. The garden itself was charming. There was a big mulberry tree offering generous shade, a kitchen garden and a row of greenhouses. There were peaches —a memory of Albany. There was also an annex to the property, a studio, with a pillared entrance in adjacent Watchbell Street which James would be able to use or to let.

The house was in good condition. Some improvements in the sanitary arrangements were needed; the place required redecorating. The renovation could be done during the coming winter; the house would be ready by spring. Alfred Parsons, the landscape painter, inspected the garden for James and pronounced in an equally favorable manner. The back windows of houses facing the church threatened the privacy of the garden but could be screened by planting Lombardy poplars.

Before the end of September 1897 James had signed a twenty-one-year lease for £70 a year; the large parchment committed him, among other things, to horticultural pastimes; he undertook to keep the garden, the hothouse and greenhouses "well and properly stocked, cropped and manured." He agreed to repaint the woodwork of the house with three coats of "good oil colour" at the end of the seventh and fourteenth years of his lease; and at the end of these years he had the option to surrender the lease if he wished. To A. C. Benson he wrote that his house was "really good enough to be a kind of little becoming, high door'd, brass knockered *façade* to one's life." This indeed was what Lamb House became.

In the midst of his elation, James felt uneasy. There was the problem of his flat in De Vere Gardens. There was the question of his servants, the Smith couple he had had for some years. Would they be ready for country life? He had agreed to take over the gardener at Lamb House and might need a maid. Looking ahead to the time when he might dispose of his flat he put himself on the lengthy Reform Club list for a bedroom with a view of Carlton Gardens. He was not yet ready to cut all his ties with the metropolis. And there was the question of furnishing Lamb House—he referred amusedly to some Chippendale and Sheraton, a little faded tapestry, "a handful of feeble relics."

The lease for the house was well within his means. He had a comfortable margin in his bank. Yet he now acted as if he were in a kind of financial panic—as in the days when he had totaled up his assets for his mother during his European travels. With sudden eagerness he decided —after several years of hesitation—to yield to the pressure of William Wetmore Story's children and write a life of the sculptor. The contract provided an advance of £250—and he stipulated there was to be no immediate deadline. The London *Times* was founding a book review then called *Literature* and James accepted their offer of £40 a month for a regular article on American publications. Thanks to Howells he opened negotiations with *Harper's Weekly* for a serial: his price was $3000. Then, quite unexpectedly, he had a windfall: *Collier's,* the illustrated New York weekly, wanted a ten-part ghost story by the end of the year. This meant a popular audience, wider than any he commanded in the literary journals. He felt financially safe; he had weathered his immediate money insecurities: his earnings for the coming year would far exceed those of recent years.

Three months after signing the lease, when he felt sure of all the details, he finally informed Cambridge of his good fortune. Writing to Alice James, he described how the southern exposure of the russet garden wall of Lamb House was covered with pears, apricots, plums and figs. His letter was cheerful and filled with a sense of possession. He added a bit of literary intelligence (in late December 1897): "I *have,* at last,

finished my little book—that is *a* little book." This was the *Collier's* ghost
story, "The Turn of the Screw."

The Little Boys

Henry James's decision to take Lamb House on a long lease sounded
eminently sensible—and practical—as he described it to his sister-in-
law. He was forsaking London. He was providing for his old age. He had
chosen the kind of house that suited the taste and sensitivities of an artist.
True, it was a reversal of all that he had done in the past. He had been
from the first a foot-loose American in Europe; the lodging house, the
foreign *pension,* the hotel, had been his way of life for the greater part
of a quarter of a century—or at least until he had committed himself to
De Vere Gardens. And then he was accustomed to the sounds of towns
and cities, the feeling of working in a dense human medium. His deeper
anxieties seem to have been that Lamb House would make him an anchorite, a lonely prisoner beyond London's suburbs. He experienced
"psychic" feelings: the possibilities of Lamb House were a "blow in the
stomach"—a remark he would use soon in "The Turn of the Screw" when
the housekeeper, seeing the ghost of Miss Jessel, takes the vision "as she
might have taken a blow in the stomach." In his letters about Lamb
House, James had written that he "felt coerced by some supernatural
power that relieves me of all the botheration of a decision or an alternative. I feel absolutely foredoomed to take a lease." He was walking old
familiar family paths; he feared to assert himself in business matters—
although he could readily do so in dealing with publishers. It had been
more than a "botheration" to answer his mother's questions about money
matters long ago.

Between September and December 1897, James rapidly dictated to
his phlegmatic Scots typist, MacAlpine, the strange ghostly history of an
untried young woman, from a Hampshire vicarage, sent by her Harley
Street employer to a remote house to care for his nephew aged ten and
niece aged eight. It is her first job; and the unnamed employer gives her,
in spite of her inexperience, all responsibility. James named his fictional
house Bly, placing it in Essex, at the moment when he was about to settle
into Rye in Sussex. The governess is the sole teller of the tale; she too is
nameless. She begins her narrative in June, during the long English
twilights, and ends it in the darkness of November, when the trees are
stark and bare and Bly is blighted. During these months, the governess
encounters her predecessor, Miss Jessel, and Peter Quint, the master's
valet, only to learn that both are dead. The daughter of the vicarage,
arrayed against the devil, decides promptly that the ghosts have come to
possess the children. The children, however, do not see the phantoms and

their actions suggest complete bewilderment at the governess's behavior towards them.

As the summer advances, the children grow restless under the governess's protective and suspicious eyes. She watches them constantly and sees in their every innocent act confirmation of her hypothesis. One Sunday, in the country churchyard, Miles asks why he can't go back to school. Actually he has been expelled, but the governess has not investigated the reasons for his expulsion, and expects him to volunteer the information. He complains instead of being cloistered with a baby sister and a female governess—"I want my own sort," he says. "I'm a fellow, don't you see?" The governess considers this an affront. She asks devious questions and quite naturally receives vague answers. There is a parallel scene with the little girl. Flora rows across a pond pursued by the governess, who accuses her of seeking an encounter with the wraith of Miss Jessel. Flora replies with the concreteness of an eight-year-old: "I don't know what you mean. I see nobody. I see nothing. I never have. I think you're cruel. I don't like you." The governess throws herself on the ground in a fit of hysteria and the housekeeper rescues the child from this horrible scene.

In the tense final moments of the story, the governess finally asks Miles why he was expelled and tries to get him to speak of Peter Quint. The boy answers directly that he "said things," and the reader must surmise that he either cursed and swore or used blasphemy. James does not explain. We then have another vivid hysterical scene in which the governess screams at the ghost of Peter Quint outside the window to which Miles's back is turned. The boy is frightened and bewildered; she clutches him but "his heart, dispossessed, had stopped." As with Morgan Moreen or Owen Wingrave, the young male is doomed—and invariably a woman is responsible.

"The imagination," Henry James would write to Bernard Shaw, "leads a life of its own." If we cannot trace that mysterious process we can at least determine some of its ingredients in the case of a tale as ambiguous and vague as "The Turn of the Screw." There was originally the shadowy anecdote of the Archbishop of Canterbury; there were the traditions of the ghost story, as in the works of Mrs. Radcliffe and the Brontës (to whom James alludes in his tale)—the use of the remote country house, the mentally curious governess; and there were James's own insecurities and anxieties of this time. We must reckon however with another element, the kind of journal for which James wrote his story. *Collier's* represented for Henry James not only a wider public, but its illustrated form reminded him of his Manhattan childhood, when, sprawling before a warm fire on the rug of the red-curtained front parlor, he studied the pages of *Punch* and other popular journals and, as he said, "lived in the imagination, no small part of the time."

The widely read Victorian predecessor of *Collier's* was *Frank Leslie's New York Journal* "of Romance, General Literature, Science and Art," with its impressive masthead representing the muses of the pen, the lyre, the stage and accessory palettes, scrolls and piles of heavy bound books. Indeed there was one story in *Frank Leslie's* called *Temptation,* serialized between January and June 1855, which readily identifies itself as the supreme and distinctly imitated source of "The Turn of the Screw." Its central theme involves a struggle for possession of an inheritance: and after the fashion of Victorian cliffhangers it uses a series of subplots about strolling players, valets, housekeepers, governesses, and above all children who are victims of "horrors"—with a prime villain whose name is Peter Quin. James needed but a single letter of the alphabet to make him his own; Quint may be read as a gallicized version of the original Irish Quin. Peter Quin's henchman is a ruffian named Miles "who had been trained in the school of Peter Quin" even as little Miles in James's story is presumed to have gone to "school" to the valet of the man in Harley Street. The *Frank Leslie's* tale uses a splendid house set in Harley Street. James, it is apparent, didn't take the trouble to choose another suitable street—this one had been fixed in his mind for almost half a century. Among the children in the melodrama we find a brother and sister, Felix and Fanny, whom we may discern as the originals of Miles and Flora, and it is Felix who dies, like other little boys in James, victims of family and adult coercions and cruelties. We may speculate that Peter Quint had to be dead when James's story begins, because he had been hanged by his henchman Miles, in the New York journal's serial forty years before—a scene vividly illustrated, showing Quin suspended from the ceiling of his room.

Temptation was published anonymously, but it is possible to deduce who the author was—none other than Tom Taylor, a former editor of *Punch,* a prolific writer of penny dreadfuls, best known for his melodramatic plays, some of which little Henry James had seen on the New York stage. We can imagine the excitement of the little boy during 1855 as the crisp print-smelling weekly arrived and was perused at the tea hour. What James seems to have carried over into his later years, more than the memory of the names he borrowed, was the sense of portentous evil in Tom Taylor's story, the insidious power of Peter Quin and the stories of the child victims. A sentence in the serial sums this up—"when will those on whom the holy duties of paternity devolve, comprehend that the key to the heart of youth is affection, not severity."

Above all we may imagine that the lurid illustrations were remembered by Henry James, whose own story was in the hands of *Collier's* illustrators. Later, when a leader of British psychical research, F. W. H. Myers, a friend of William James's, wrote Henry about the story, the novelist dismissed it as "an inferior, a merely pictorial subject." He was telling the truth. He had chosen an old cliffhanger, and its pictorial nature resided in the dark and awesome illustrations that accompanied every installment in *Frank Leslie's*—scenes in churchyards with strange angular figures leaning or sitting on tombstones (James incorporated the cemetery scene into his story); horses in frenetic gallop during the abduction of a young girl, tall gaunt Englishmen wrapped in thick Victorian garments, night scenes with tapers and torches, all in considerable chiaroscuro which only accented the evil for the enthralled juvenile reader.

We can now understand why for James, "The Turn of the Screw" was "a piece of ingenuity pure and simple" or as he said, an "irresponsible little fiction," a work of "cold artistic calculation." He also called it "shameless" since he regarded it as a hack job to fit *Collier's* specifications, and described it as "a down-on-all-fours potboiler." His main goal seems to have been to recapture the emotions of his twelve-year-old self, to make the reader feel "the depths of the sinister" and to have his story "reek with the air of Evil." As readers questioned the tale's ambiguities and vaguenesses, and James's failure to offer specifications, he was quite clear about his general plan—without revealing anything else. His governess had been a young woman who kept a clear record of all the "anomalies and obscurities . . . by which I don't mean her explanation of them, a different matter." By not producing the usual stock-in-trade of ghost stories, his goal had been to make the reader "*think* the evil, make him think it for himself and you are released from weak specifications." And he had worked for "an excited horror, a promoted pity, a created expertness."

This then was the inner calculation of this master of daylight ghosts, who understood that "the terror of the usual" runs deeper than rattling chains or trapdoors and dungeons: and he tried to thrill the readers of *Collier's* as he had been thrilled by another Manhattan journal half a century earlier. In borrowing the stock-in-trade of Taylor's cliffhanger, James worked for "a blest golden haze." He endowed its artlessness with his art, turned "a sow's ear into a silk purse" as he had said of his plays. His imitations of Tom Taylor or of the *Frank Leslie's* published tale extended to his asking for a masthead for "The Turn of the Screw." *Collier's* responded handsomely and got no less an artist than James's old friend John La Farge to draw it—a picture of a distraught governess and a frightened little Miles.

"The Turn of the Screw" was serialized in *Collier's* from January to April 1898. Later that year it appeared—with "Covering End," a story version of the Ellen Terry play—in a volume to which James gave the title *The Two Magics.* Not since "Daisy Miller" had James written a tale that so caught the public fancy. As inquiries from mystified and fascinated readers poured in, he was careful not to give away his secret. He was to tease both readers and critics later by saying the story was "a trap for the unwary," and he quite regularly reminded questioners that he regarded the tale as a piece of hack-work. When one psychologist, interested in the unconscious, queried James about his intentions he replied that he blushed "to see real substance" read into his "wanton little tale."

James said in private exactly what he said in public about "The Turn of the Screw," as we know from a comment made more than a decade later in his physician's consulting-room, recorded in a learned study on *Angina Pectoris* by the great Edwardian heart specialist Sir James Mackenzie. Before James came to see him, the doctor had read one of his stories, he said,

> in which an account was given of an extraordinary occurrence that happened to two children. Several scenes were recounted in which these children seemed to hold converse with invisible people, after which they were greatly upset. After one occasion one of them turned and fled, screaming with terror, and died in the arms of the narrator of the story.

"You did not explain the nature of the mysterious interviews," Mackenzie said to his distinguished patient. The novelist then set forth the principles on which to create a mystery: "So long as the events are veiled the imagination will run riot and depict all sorts of horrors, but as soon as the veil is lifted, all mystery disappears and with it the sense of terror." In a word, terror exists for us anywhere, and at any moment that we imagine it.

James wrote "The Turn of the Screw" accordingly on a theory of unexplained extra-human terror, that terror within himself that had not revealed to him why he felt a sinking of the heart at the simple daylight act of providing himself with an anchorage for the rest of his days.

3
THE
GREAT GOOD
PLACE

♎

A Russet Arcadia

Henry James slept for the first time in Lamb House towards the end of June 1898, probably on the 28th. The furniture acquired during the winter months was moved on 9 June; presently carpets were laid and curtains hung. James supervised every detail; he remained in flurried consultation with his architect; he acted with a sense of well-being and happy accomplishment. His uneasiness, at the time of the signing of the lease, had long been banished. "The Turn of the Screw" had taken care of the ghosts.

He had planned his move from London with the greatest care. Workmen had peeled off the paper and disclosed the handsome paneling in certain rooms; fresh paint had been applied; tile fireplaces had been repaired. "Getting into" Lamb House, the novelist wrote to his brother, "is the biggest job of the sort I have ever tackled and the end is not yet." He had bought, aided by Lady Wolseley, discreet pieces of Georgian mahogany. His possessions showed discrimination and taste. The Green Room would lodge many of his books; and presently certain pictures were hung—a Burne-Jones, an inscribed photograph from Daudet, a small portrait of Flaubert, some illustrations from an edition of "Daisy Miller," a Whistler etching. In the hall there were selected reproductions from Piranesi's *Vidute di Roma*. Elsewhere he would place family portraits, and prominently, a picture of Constance Fenimore Woolson. The garden room was also furnished for work. James installed here many of the inscribed volumes received from author-friends, as well as works of reference. There were books in the entrance hall, in massive bookcases. It would be some time however before his library would be weeded out and fully transferred from De Vere Gardens, where he had at this moment more books than Lamb House could accommodate.

At first James's staff consisted of MacAlpine, his amanuensis, the Smiths from De Vere Gardens, and a part-time gardener, George Gammon. Later there would be a housemaid; and early in his life at Rye he took in an "apprentice," a diminutive local lad named Burgess Noakes. Burgess was fourteen and still lived at home when he became James's house-boy. His master treated him as he would a son, corrected his English, taught him manners, made him conform to personal ritual. Ultimately he was James's valet.

His new life began with a visit from his nineteen-year-old nephew and namesake, the eldest son of William. "I have but just scrambled in here by the skin of my teeth," he wrote to the young Harry James who was arriving on a cattle-boat at Liverpool, "and am all ready—nay yearningly impatient for you. (I have slept here two nights—tonight the third, and shall feel an old inhabitant.) Your room awaits you—right royally— and the garden grins in anticipation." His first visitor to his new domain was, appropriately enough, "family" and the "right royally" indicated he was installing his nephew in the "King's Room."

At the time of his visit to his uncle, Harry James was a solemn, rather conceited youth. His diary entry for 14 July 1898 begins:

> I came down here a week ago last Wednesday and was met at the station by Uncle H. who brought me up the hill to the house, showed me over part of it, holding me by the arm and keeping up a perpetual vocal search for words even when he wasn't saying anything. He left me in my oak panelled room to dress, with the injunction that I must "come down" bursting with news. In the evening he walked me about the town, to the old tower with its little terrace, to the "land-gate", down round the back past the bit of shipping. It is all extremely pretty, pleasant, charming, or picturesque, but owing to my self-consciousness and slowness to expression I was much bothered by the duty of seeming properly appreciative.

The novelist's first two months in Lamb House were a cavalcade of visitors. In letter after letter James reported "the bump of luggage has been too frequent on my stair." This also meant anxious conferences with his cook. It was one thing to entertain at luncheon or dinner in De Vere Gardens; it was another to have friends and relatives descend at the little Rye station to spend twenty-four hours or more. James invariably met the train, escorted by his servant, who brought a little hand-cart or wheelbarrow for the luggage. If guests were elderly, he sometimes had a carriage; more often he would saunter with them up the cobbled hill, pointing out the delights of his rural existence. In fast succession that first summer came his old friends, the future Justice Holmes, Mrs. J. T. Fields, the Bourgets, the Curtises, the Edward Warrens, the Gosses—"a good many irrepressible sojourners"—and James complained that he did not achieve at first "all the concentration I settled myself in this sup-posedly sequestered spot in search of."

However, he himself issued the invitations. And the visit of the Bos-tonian Mrs. Fields, bringing with her the delicate and gifted writer Sarah Orne Jewett, was a particular pleasure, a revival of memories of youth. In James's apprentice years, when her husband had published him in the *Atlantic*, Mrs. Fields had welcomed him as a precocious young man of letters to her salon in Charles Street. James remembered her as a singu-larly graceful young wife, with a beautiful head and hair, smile and voice, and as a singularly winning hostess. As he put it a few days later, writing to Mrs. Humphry Ward, "Mrs. Fields took me back to my far-away youth and *hers*—when she was so pretty and I was so aspiring." She wore, for her visit to Lamb House, a black lace mantilla, allowing it to descend from the head, as George Eliot had done; it gave Mrs. Fields, with the traces of her earlier beauty, "a general fine benignity." In Miss Jew-ett, whose tales James had admired, and whom he now met for the first time, he found "a sort of elegance of humility or fine flame of modesty." Her work was minor; it combined the sober and the tender note. In Mrs. Field's diary of that day at Rye, we hear the novelist telling Miss Jewett that her famous sketches were done with "elegance and exactness," they were "absolutely true—not a word overdone." He had invited Mrs. Fields and her companion to spend the night, but they preferred to come to luncheon and leave by a late afternoon train, after being taken by car-riage to see the ancient village of Winchelsea. Mrs. Fields noted in her diary "dear Mr. James's pleasure in having a home of his own to which he might ask us."

In spite of his joy in showing visitors the place, James felt abruptly cut off from London. He was reduced now to communication with Lon-don by letter and telegram; indeed, the telegram began to play a new role in his life. "Are you utterly absent or can you dine with me Friday at seven to go afterwards with three others to the theatre," was a typical message dispatched that summer when he planned a foray into town. The sense of isolation from his clubs and the murmur of London society contributed probably to his tale—the first written in Lamb House—of a young girl handling telegrams in a branch post office in Mayfair. As with the story "The Great Good Place," which he wrote just before he moved, James created "In the Cage" out of immediate emotion. And however much he might complain, as guests descended from the Ashford local, and the luggage bumped on his eighteenth-century stairs, he actually felt himself protected by visitors against the solitude of country life with which he would now have to make his terms.

Bit by bit, however, the sense of the place asserted itself. Rye proved a constant delight, a "russet Arcadia." He liked the brown tints in the town and the glimpse of the Channel; the quiet at night seemed almost audible; he could hear with great comfort in every room the friendly tick of the clock in his hallway.

Aside from his hospitality, much of the novelist's time was given over to long leisurely spins on his bicycle. From Winchelsea, the decayed sister-port, he would study the view of Rye in the distance—the crowned hill, of which he now had such complete possession. James's thoughts ran on the Robert Louis Stevenson aspect of the place—the contraband running from the Continent and the yards where once the King's ships had been built out of solid Sussex oak. The shipyard had declined, as had the town itself, from its ancient commerce. But there were always three or four fishing boats on the ways and some ship in the shrunken harbor. James liked to go to pubs and talk with the sailors; to wander on his bicycle to every nook and cranny.

So began a famous tenancy that would link Henry James permanently to this corner of Sussex. The morning click of the typewriter in the Garden Room became known to Rye—and the distant sound of a grave and measured voice weaving sentences. By midsummer Henry James was offered (and declined) the vice-presidency of the local cricket club. Later he would join the Golf Club, not to play golf, but to partake of tea in the clubhouse. He had indeed found a great good place; and late that year he could proclaim to Francis Boott, now living in Cambridge, Massachusetts, "Lamb House is my Bellosguardo." He had never dreamed, in the old Italian days, that he too would have something resembling a villa, in—of all places—an isolated rural corner of England.

A Summer Embassy

Henry James's installation in Lamb House was accompanied by the alarums of the Spanish-American War. The *Maine* blew up in Havana harbor in February 1898; and the press headlines, the dispatches from the United States, and finally the outbreak of hostilities in April, were a heavy burden to the novelist, for whom any conflict evoked memories of the Civil War. To his brother he wrote, "I see nothing but the madness, the passions, the hideous clumsiness of rage." The new hostilities, largely naval, touched his ingrained pacifism; and from the outset he feared that America's seaward cities might come under Spanish shells. He was "mainly glad Harvard College isn't—nor Irving Street—the thing nearest Boston Bay." On the day after the United States issued its call for volunteers, James wrote to Frances Morse in Boston that he felt "in a vile unrest . . . wretchedly nervous and overdarkened."

James was to be extremely well-briefed during this war that, in a matter of weeks, turned the United States into a world power. The defeat of the Spanish navy at Manila, the blockade and destruction of the Spanish ships, the surrender of the Philippines, the ultimate cession of Puerto Rico, the freeing of Cuba, the annexation of Hawaii—all this James learned not only through the newspapers but from his friends at the American Embassy in London—the Ambassador himself, John Hay, and the First Secretary, Henry White.

Shortly after James had installed himself in Lamb House, he heard that the Hays, Henry Adams, Senator Don Cameron and his wife Elizabeth—to whom Adams had been closely attached in recent years—had taken the large Elizabethan manor house of Surrenden Dering, in Kent, a dozen miles from Ashford, within easy distance of Rye. Surrenden Dering, set in its large park, and described ironically by Adams as "about the size of Versailles," became the "summer embassy." James could find, at any time, authoritative reports and the diplomatic background for the American history being written overseas. He could not visit frequently; his own house was filled; but he did go for a short stay a couple of times.

He found the summer establishment interesting in many ways, not least for the human relations being carried on in the large house. "Everyone is doing—to my vision—all over the place—such extraordinary things that one's faculty of wonder and envy begins at last rather to cease to vibrate," he wrote to a friend in Boston. There were signs that his faculty of wonder, and his novelist's curiosity, were vibrating as strongly as those of his narrator in *The Sacred Fount,* whom he would place two years later on as peopled an estate as Surrenden Dering. Concerning Adams and Mrs. Cameron he remarked that he envied Adams "as much as was permitted by my feeling that the affair was only what I should *once* have found maddeningly romantic." He had met Mrs. Cameron on other occasions; she was, he found, "hard"—considering her "prettiness, grace and cleverness." The word "clever" in James's lexicon was not always a compliment. Mrs. Cameron was indeed a skillful managerial woman—a Mrs. Touchett or a Mrs. Gereth—able to be a Senator's wife, keep tight control of a busy home and social life in Washington, and at the same time be available as a social resource and comfort to the widowed Adams. James was to say, in a letter to Henrietta Reubell two or three years later, that Mrs. Cameron had "sucked the lifeblood of poor Henry Adams and made him more 'snappish' than nature intended." He added that "it's one of the longest and oddest American *liaisons* I've ever known. Women have been hanged for less—and yet men have been too, I judge, rewarded with more."

It was at Surrenden Dering that John Hay that August received the cable from President McKinley summoning him to Washington to be Secretary of State. James had come to know the diplomat and writer well in the 1880s when Hay and Clarence King, the geologist, were in Paris staying at the Grand Hotel. Hay, King and Henry Adams were a kind of private Washington triumvirate: Hay was the party office-holder and man of political action that the ironical and worldly-wise Adams could not allow himself to be; Clarence King, a man of the out-of-doors, who could accept the irrational and primitive forces within himself, represented that part of Adams which was most submerged in his New England rigidity. Hay was simply "the good Hay" in James's letters; but Clarence King he watched with the eyes of a storyteller and a lover of character. "The most delightful man in the world, Clarence King!" he said, yet he was also "slippery and elusive, and as unmanageable as he is delightful."

A conversationalist of great spontaneity, King quite eclipsed in interest the meticulous and politic Hay. Hay had in him something of the distance of a politician and statesman; James had his kind of "distance" as well, although he had developed considerable tenderness for the statesman at the moment of Miss Woolson's death when Hay, in Rome, had performed the offices of friendship for James at her funeral. Otherwise, a kind of top-hatted ceremoniousness prevailed between them.

James came to Surrenden to salute his honored friend before his departure for Washington. He was to remember the way in which Hay "paused before the plunge, on the great high Surrenden terrace"; and he had wondered often if Hay remembered that moment—the soft September day, the baronial quiet of the place, the general air of enchantment —as well as the "lovely women and distinguished men just respectfully hanging on to your coat-tails."

Surrenden Dering was a minor incident in the crowded life of Henry James that summer, although it evoked old memories and kept him in touch with America and Americans. The war had been "a deep embarrassment of thought—of imagination. I have hated, I have almost loathed it." For some friends there was no qualification. "I detest the war," he said. When it was over, and America's frontiers were extended to the south-east, and westward, far into the Pacific, James shrank from the thought of "remote colonies run by bosses." At the same time—perhaps as a consequence of the rationalizations of diplomacy heard at Surrenden Dering—he began to take a more benign view of the matter. The extension of American power was perhaps a New World version of Britain's *imperium;* the British he felt had been good colonizers, and the cause of civilization had, on the whole, been advanced. He wanted, however, he said, "to curl up more closely in this little old-world corner, where I can successfully beg such questions. They become a spectacle merely." His probing intelligence nevertheless tugged at them continually; and much as he hated the newspapers he read them with critical curiosity.

Brother Jonathan

In London, that spring, before he had moved to Lamb House, Henry James reached a moment of intense weariness. The war was a burden to him; every morning there was the same little mountain of newspapers, the casual bundles of proof, journals, books: the tide of the world's words sweeping into De Vere Gardens and overwhelming him. What could any creature want of so much print? He was to ask the question in a fantasy called "The Great Good Place" which was a prevision of Lamb House. "The Turn of the Screw" had recorded old lingering fears of childhood when the occupancy of Lamb House was in prospect; but once the terror had been siphoned off, James could dream peacefully, and pleasantly. In his story the good and great place is more than a private retreat. A mixture of monastery, hotel, club, country house, it is an ideal cushioned silent refuge, accessible to the Protestant as a "retreat," yet not of the religious sort: a place of material simplification.

The interest of the story, on its biographical side, is not only in its obvious wish for respite from worldly pressure, but in James's desire for an exclusive man's world, a monastic Order, a sheltering Brotherhood. The admiring acolyte who comes to the great writer, George Dane, puts a hand on his knee, and gives him at once a "feeling of delicious ease." At the mysterious "place" the "dream-sweetness" experienced by the harried writer resides in the absence of all demands upon him and in the discreet quiet. Above all there is the blessing of anonymity. Dane is freed from being a *persona* in the world; the inner life can wake up again. He can re-possess his soul.

This was a very old fantasy of Henry James's. In *Roderick Hudson* of 1875 he had depicted a similar place, near Fiesole, where Rowland Mallet finds peace within a cool cloister. In a monastery the world's burdens drop away; this had been the theme of the ill-fated *Guy Domville;* and we may note that the names George Dane and Guy Domville have the same initials. The craving for a great good place and the touch of a Brother's hand had existed in James for years. George Dane, however, identifies himself with his young acolyte: the great good place is also the place of youth. James's fantasy expresses the wish to be young again, to be the younger Brother that he had once been. And finally the great good place is "the great want met"—and the want is not so much "the putting off of one's self " as in a religious retreat; it is "the getting it back—if one has a self worth sixpence."

He was getting it back at Lamb House. The autumn that year was dry and warm and Rye seemed even more beautiful—more *nuancé,* as he said—than in the summer. The war, now that it was over, seemed merely to have flashed by; he felt, more than ever, that he could stay close to his little plot of land and cultivate his little garden. He watched his gardener plant bulbs and seedlings, with the promise they held for the spring. He relished the mellow fruit of autumn on his south wall. The novelist decided to linger in Rye until Christmas. De Vere Gardens—London—could wait.

The summer's end had brought an end to the rush of visitors; now, undisturbed, he worked steadily at the *Harper's* serial, *The Awkward Age.* Jonathan Sturges came to stay with him for a few days in the middle of October and remained for two months. In his crippled state he was accustomed to quiet and he was excellent company at other hours of the day. "Little Brother Jonathan has his share of the national genius," James had written to Edmund Gosse, and this quality, plus his bright eyes, his mordant wit, his fund of gossip, made the American always a delightful companion. Like Alice James, the invalid Sturges had a sharp tongue, which was why James called him "the little demon." "Do you remember young Jonathan Sturges?" he asked Henrietta Reubell.

> He is full of talk and intelligence, and of the absence of prejudice, and is saturated with London, and with all sorts of contrasted elements of it, to which he has given himself up. Handicapped, crippled, invalidical, he has yet made his way there in a wondrous fashion, and knows nine thousand people, of most of whom *I've* never heard.

Having forsaken London, James had a small incarnation of London beside him. There was something more, however, than the amusing asperities and touching physical helplessness of the younger man (Sturges was thirty-four). He was literary, he was sentient; he observed; he was a civilized presence. James admired the crippled young man's stoicism—"he is only a little body-blighted intelligence—a little frustrate universal curiosity—and a little pathetic Jack-the-Giant-Killer's soul." In "The Great Good Place" he had dreamed of being cared for in a company of Brothers. In Lamb House he cared for Brother Jonathan; and it was as if he were being cared for himself. For he had reached that time of life when he was turning to younger men to capture an image of his own youth.

The story called "In the Cage" which James published as a volume-size tale in the autumn of 1898 is of a piece with his immediate feeling of being cut off from London. His sense at times of being confined and "out of things" seems to have contributed to his imagining a young girl

confined daily to a little cage in a branch post office at the back of a
Mayfair grocery store handling the brief and cryptic telegrams of the
outer world, counting the words and reckoning the fees. She is sufficiently alert to take in the meanings of the messages; they tell her of
certain scandalous goings-on in society. James gives the girl no name. We
know her only as a troubled observer, using her inductive and deductive
capacities to satisfy an insatiable curiosity about her environment. The
cage-girl and the governess in "The Turn of the Screw" both feel shut out
—or shut in—as James in Rye now felt shut out from the great world. But
where the governess remains locked in her own imaginings, the cage-girl
constantly returns to reality—she is always aware of her poverty, her
station in life, and the contrast between this and the world's splendors
about which she is so touchingly curious.

By many delicate and subtle touches, "In the Cage" keeps us within
the girl's limited range of vision as she practices, in a modest and simplified form, the deductive methods celebrated in Sherlock Holmes. She
is a detective of her own confined soul; she must make the best of her
world. "In the Cage" shows James going about the business of seeing
what he can do with his own alienation from Mayfair. Like the girl, after
her encounter with the dashing Captain Everard, he feels abandoned—
almost as if London had left him rather than he London—and like Captain Everard without so much as a "thank you." If he no longer had his
London, he at any rate had his little plot of ground in Rye, as the tele-
graphist, once she leaves her cage, will have her modest home with her
young man, Mr. Mudge, and be the humble wife of a tradesman. James
had had, after all, his "position in society," had it for a quarter of a
century; indeed he still had it. But society had turned out to be full of
pitfalls and deceptions. *The Awkward Age,* which James now wrote, was
to be his strongest indictment of that corrupt society. In a certain sense
this novel seems to have been James's way of telling himself that he was
well out of London.

"The Awkward Age"

With the writing of *The Awkward Age,* between September and December 1898, James was on the verge of becoming his own self again. He
seemed ready to shed the protective disguises of girlhood and to take his
own shape in his fiction—that of the elderly and fastidious observer of his
world. His elderly character is named as if he were invoking the rejected
metropolis—Mr. Longdon. He gave him his own age, fifty-five, the age at
which he was writing the novel. Mr. Longdon has lived for a very long
time in the country, in Suffolk. His house is square and red-roofed and
be-gardened and russet-walled, like Lamb House in Sussex.

At the beginning of *The Awkward Age,* Mr. Longdon accompanies a younger man, Gustavus Vanderbank, to his rooms during a night of downpour. There they discuss at great length the drawing-room they have just quitted. Mr. Longdon cross-examines Vanderbank closely about the life of the Brookenhams in their expensive Buckingham Crescent flat. "We're cold and sarcastic and cynical," says Vanderbank, a heavy fashion-plate, "without the soft human spot." The novel becomes the story of the elderly man's attempt to discover a "human spot" for the young Nanda (Fernanda) Brookenham, a charming adolescent who mingles knowingly with her elders and hears outrageous things in her mother's social set.

Decidedly Henry James was writing as if he felt "out of it"—of the London scene. And "what's London life?" Vanderbank asks point-blank. He provides the answer: "It's tit for tat!" Everything has its price. "Ah, but what becomes of friendship?" Mr. Longdon inquires "earnestly and pleadingly"—we might say almost ruefully. It was as if James, after his long inner struggle with the demons of "success" and neglect, of feeling himself "unwanted" and cast aside, had to start all over again. Having once conquered London, and learned it intimately, he must now re-explore it from a new distance. Had he really learned to know "society"? —the British aristocracy? Had he really grasped from his novelist-cage what went on in the gilded salons? Behind the façade of bright and brittle talk he could now discern intricate human relations, meetings, partings. One couldn't be quite certain who was sleeping with whom. In the old days one didn't ask such questions.

James knew well that somewhere, in some extra-human zone of being, there was evil. He had never been as innocent as Emerson in that respect. But he had lived in a kind of luminous, sexless and unphysical world—at least until his descent into the theater. That had been the beginning of change. He had become aware by degrees that women in life as well as in fiction were not immaculate; they were organisms, possessors of temperament and passion who like Miss Robins could serve cocoa in her rooms amid a smell of powder and perfume and greasepaint, and talk about the men who fell in love with her. In the wings of the theater, in the dowdy dressing-rooms, in the costly defeat he had suffered, a process of re-education had been going on. Mr. Longdon, or the unnamed narrator of *The Sacred Fount,* or the curious New England "ambassador" Lambert Strether, would re-embody a new, still slightly bewildered, novelist who had once chided Maupassant for looking too much at the monkeys in the monkey-cage. Perhaps Henry James had looked too much at the reflective side of man—and looked too far away from the monkeys? He had dramatized, always, the loss of American innocence in its encounter with a corrupt and decadent Europe. In his citadel of art he had remained one of the pure of mind. Now, by the process of living, feeling, suffering, he seemed on the verge of losing his own safeguarded—almost unbelievable—innocence.

The Awkward Age is about two *jeunes filles,* one English and one Italian, products of two distinct methods in education. Nanda, the English girl, has been treated, as we now say, "permissively," and has been exposed to her mother's "fast" set. Aggie, the Anglo-Italian girl, brought up in the continental manner, has been treated like "a little ivory princess." The subject seems almost "quaint" in our time; what makes James's treatment of it highly contemporaneous is his grasp of the dilemmas of adolescence. Published in 1899, *The Awkward Age* would qualify as an outmoded Victorian novel were it not for the novelist's vision of the essence of his dual subject—and the formidable technique he used to give it a frame. The novel is constructed almost entirely out of drawing-room "talk," and set scenes. Little is told about the characters, save as they tell it themselves. The reader is asked to supply voices, inflections, gestures, the very things which actors give to a script. The story is dramatized, as James himself later put it, in a series of "presented episodes." Each episode is a piece of the building—and it is we who build as we read. In this way James demonstrated, after his own miserable failure in the theater, that a fine dramatic comedy could be placed within the novel form.

In this masterly frame, Mr. Longdon has a special function. He asks the right questions; he insists on the right answers; he bridges gaps created for the reader by James's strict dialogue-method. He has however much more than a mere structural function. Mr. Longdon and Nanda reveal two kinds of innocence, those of age and of youth; and both are engaged in voyages of discovery. Mr. Longdon re-discovers the London from which he has been long absent; he knew it in its Victorian prime, when society was fearfully respectable on the surface and all its corruptions were carefully concealed. Now the corruptions are in the open. Nanda's voyage of discovery is more painful. *The Awkward Age* is the story of her growing up. James may seem, at first, to approve of the continental way of rearing young girls; yet he returns at the end to the truths of the Garden of Eden. Knowledge need not be dangerous, he seems to say to us, if men and women learn to face it with eyes unsealed, in full awareness of what is real and what is factitious in the world about them.

Indeed, *The Awkward Age* contains a kind of "theory of education" for the female young. James had been offering such theories or opinions in his works since "Daisy Miller" or *The Portrait of a Lady.* If he protested against America's permissiveness, he also admired the spirit, candor and innocence of its children. What he now seems to be saying is that a corrupt society corrupts its young: that sentience and "awareness," carefully cultivated, constitute a greater safeguard than ignorance. Mrs. Brookenham's salon contains a queer assortment of characters: the complacent, the newly-rich, the divorced—idle women, scheming mothers, questionable "affairs." Mrs. Brookenham herself, in the end, is in competition with her daughter for Vanderbank: disillusioned, ambiguous, arbitrary, she is beset by all the troubles of her world—her vapid, ineffectual husband, her daughter who loves her lover, her light-fingered son; and her cherished salon is foundering in the crisis between mother and daughter. Mrs. Brookenham must place her daughter in life; and Nanda's exposure to the corrupt morals of the salon makes her unplaceable. Her virginity has been "de-emphasized." She will have difficulty finding a husband. Moreover she loves Vanderbank.

Like all of James's late heroes and heroines, Nanda has to arrive at self-awareness through a vision of the cold determining world with which she must make her peace. In the process of muddling through, she recognizes that her most important discovery has been herself. Nanda *knows.* And she learns that one pays a price for knowledge. If she cannot have the younger man, Vanderbank, she will accept the protection of the elderly Mr. Longdon. He will minister to her mind and endow her with eternal richnesses of the heart rather than the ephemeral exaltations and torments of passion.

It seems in *The Awkward Age* that in removing Nanda from her mother's drawing-room Mr. Longdon achieved what Henry James had done all his life—harbor within his house, the house of the novelist's inner world, the spirit of a young adult female, worldly-wise and curious, possessing a treasure of unassailable virginity and innocence and able to yield to the masculine active world-searching side of James an ever-fresh and exquisite vision of feminine youth and innocence. For this was the androgynous nature of the creator and the drama of his novels: innocence and worldliness, the paradisial America and the cruel and corrupt Europe—or in other variations, youthful ignorant America and wise and civilized Europe.

The Awkward Age records a great disenchantment. James tells himself that he is well out of London, well out of its lies and camouflage. He had, he says, in a letter written at this moment to Paul Bourget, "an inalienable mistrust of the great ones of the earth and a thorough disbelief in any security with people who have no imagination. They are the objects, not the subjects, of imagination and it is not in their compass to *conceive* of anything whatever. They can only live their hard functional lives."

A compromise with functional living was however possible. James was beginning to say that civilization and society, forms and manners

which ennoble man and make rich his life, would founder without illusions, or artistic lies, the old "suspension of disbelief." In a word, society
must have faith in its illusions and yet paradoxically remember they are
illusions. This would be the philosophy of his last and greatest works.

The Little Girls

The Awkward Age was James's last novel in a remarkable sequence
dealing with female children, juveniles and adolescents, written between 1895 and 1900. His precocious little females grow a little older in
each book, as if they were a single child whose life experience is being
traced from the cradle to coming-of-age—as if indeed these books were
the single book of little Harry James of Washington Square and 14th
Street, of Paris, Geneva, Boulogne and Newport. Taking them in their
sequence as he wrote them, we begin in the cradle with Effie, who is
murdered at four (*The Other House,* 1896); she is resurrected at five
(*What Maisie Knew,* 1897) and we leave her at seven or eight, or perhaps
a bit older. Flora is eight ("The Turn of the Screw," 1898) and the sole boy
in the series, Miles, is ten. (And here we also have a young adult, the
governess.) Then we arrive at adolescence: the adolescence of an unnamed girl in a branch post office ("In the Cage," 1898). Little Aggie, the
Anglo-Italian girl in the next novel, is sixteen, and Nanda Brookenham,
eighteen when the story begins (*The Awkward Age,* 1899).

It is sufficiently clear from James's notes and prefaces that he did not
deliberately set out to create a sequence. And yet the sequence is there—
in his imagination he moved from infancy to childhood, from childhood
to adolescence and then to young adulthood. Moreover we can discern
within the total record an extensive personal allegory of the growing-up
of Henry James. Beyond the conscious intellectual exploration of states
of childhood, James was intuitively questioning his own unconscious
experience, reliving the long ago "education" of his emotions. The murder of little Effie in *The Other House,* which inaugurates the series, can
be read as the age at which the little Henry, within the mature artist, felt
himself annihilated by the brutality of the audience at *Guy Domville.*
His selective imagination chose for Effie the form of death he himself
had described at the Archbishop's when he had spoken of having been
under water—"subaqueous"—at the time of his *débâcle. Maisie* is a careful presentation of the Henry James of the late autobiography *A Small
Boy and Others:* she possesses his curiosity, she is engaged in a systematic study of her elders, she searches determinedly for her identity amid
her absent and estranged parents and governesses. Her "vivacity of intelligence" and her "small vibrations" are those of a storyteller in the mak-

ing. She might have been "rather coarsened, blurred, sterilized, by ignorance and pain." Art saves her and protects her innocence, as it had saved
Henry. In his late preface he describes the "exquisite interest" he found
in his study of this little girl, for in reality she is a study of himself;
unwittingly he has treated her as a kind of psychological "case history."

After Maisie we arrive at the latency period, represented by little
Miles, his boy in the series. The consequence of Miles's self-assertion was
death, as we have seen; after that James reverted in his stories to the
disguise of female adolescence. His remembrance of himself as an observant little outsider, in his autobiography, seems to parallel the adolescent girl who, from her cage, tissues together the society around her.
Then, in Nanda and little Aggie of *The Awkward Age,* we may see a
projection of the Henry of late adolescence—that part of him which was
continentalized and ranged freely in the forbidden fruit of French novels, and the other side of him, the serious young literary novice who had
to make what he could out of the New England environment to which he
was brought—the life of Newport—when he was Nanda's age.

Some such history of the psychical "growing-up" of Henry James is
traced in the depths of these stories. It was more than an intricate reflection of the biography of James's psyche. In resuming, after the trauma
of *Guy Domville,* the disguise of a female child, the protective disguise
of his early years, James performed unconscious self-therapy. As his old
feelings and imaginings had defended him long ago against the brutal
world, they now served as aid against the new brutalities.

The little girls had thus emerged out of a personal healing process
during the years 1895–1900. The period of the post-dramatic nightmare
had been short-circuited by the writing out of the nightmare; the period
of bewilderment over his buffeting by the theatrical world and its audience had been discharged in his study of the bewilderment of female
adolescence. Each tale had eased some of his emotional suffering, so that
from story to story he had dispossessed himself of certain intensities of
pain. Meanwhile the novelist's outward self moved in the world in full
command of its intellectual powers. The mature Henry leased houses,
visited friends, dined in clubs, wrote and discussed his art, grew in authority and dedication to his craft; struggled against failure and commanded the attention of editors and publishers. Below or beyond the
adult self, the hurt self was finding its healing substance. The subject, the
essence, of these works was that of the growth and development of the
human, the artistic, imagination. What else are these children doing if
not trying to balance magic-lantern phantasmagoria against reality? The
particular sequence of stories James created reveals the benign workings
of the imagination—in this instance in chronological fashion—that

moved from direct confrontation of disaster through the death of the spirit and to its re-emergence and growth in the familiar shapes of the past.

The language of his notebooks during these and later years, in his eloquent and mystical prayers to his Muse and his Genius, reflects James's strong feeling that his art was the very source of his life. He speaks of his "workings-out" of his stories as "the dear old blessed healing, consoling way." "Oh, sacred beneficence of *doing!*" he suddenly exclaims. And again, "Oh, celestial, soothing, sanctifying process!" *Healing, consoling, soothing, sanctifying:* art was for James an anodyne, a balm, a religion, a sacred fount. In the service of art he renewed himself. What he came to call in the end the "religion of doing" steadied him and sustained him.

His long-deferred trip to Italy, including his promised visit to the Bourgets in France, suddenly became possible early in 1899 with the letting of De Vere Gardens on a six-months' lease. To make arrangements for this he had to go to London after his prolonged residence in Rye, and he had the sensation of his Mr. Longdon, that of returning to the city as from another country. He felt himself an outsider; and he fled back to Lamb House.

James had to read large bundles of proof of *The Awkward Age* before leaving. January and February were mild, however, save for winter gales, and he settled down beside great fires in his hearths; he spoke with pleasure of the "indoor winter cosiness." "This is a grey, gusty, lonely Sunday at Rye, the tail of a great, of an almost, in fact, *perpetual* winter gale," he wrote in his notebooks, "and I feel the old reviving ache of desire to get back to work. Yes, I yearn for that—the divine unrest again touches me." For the first time in many months he prayed to his muse, as of old—

> Ah, once more, to let myself go! The very thought of it soothes and sustains, lays a divine hand on my nerves, and lights, so beneficently, my uncertainties and obscurities. *Begin* it—and it will grow. Put in now some strong short novel, and come back from the continent, with it all figured out. I must have a long *tête à tête* with myself, a long ciphering bout, on it, before I really start. *Basta.*

But he could not think of big novels on the eve of his journey. He read his galleys; suffered a longish influenza; made arrangements to have Jonathan Sturges live in Lamb House while he was away. Late in February he sat up till the early hours clearing his desk before his departure. "I go to Italy after more than five years' interlude," he wrote to a friend. At this moment he became aware that his room was filled with a smoky haze; and then he saw smoke squeezing through the planks of his floor. He roused his servants, and Smith hacked, sawed and pried up a couple of planks nearest the fireplace. Thick smoke poured out: a charred beam was smouldering under the hearthstone. It was a matter of minutes to douse it with water, and for safety's sake pack it with soaked sponges. The Smiths returned to bed, and James resumed his letter. He thanked his friend for being an agent in his discovering the fire, and signed himself with a "Good-night—it's 2:45 and all's well. I *must* turn in."

All was not well. There was flame now beneath his floor. He shouted anew for the servants. Firemen and police were summoned. To reach the burning beam they had to pickaxe their way through the wall and ceiling of the dining-room below. But the firemen were "cool as well as prompt"; moreover, they used water sparingly. His epistolary passion in the small hours of the morning had saved his house, perhaps his life. After a sleepless night, James despatched a long telegram to his architect which ended "now helpless in face of reconstructions of injured portions and will bless you mightily if you come departure of course put off Henry James."

4

THE

SACRED FOUNT

L'Affaire

In the *New York Times* of 7 January 1895, below a large headline, is the account of the public humiliation of a Jewish officer two days before on the parade-ground of the École Militaire in Paris. Found guilty of selling military secrets to Germany, the officer had been marched before 5,000 soldiers, had his epaulettes torn from his uniform, his sword broken —while beyond the stiff ranks a mob hissed and jeered. Below this story of the disgrace of Captain Alfred Dreyfus, a small headline describes the jeering of Henry James in London on the first night of *Guy Domville*. The two episodes reported on the same day were related only in that they speak of humiliation, outrage, hurt—and a howling mob. The military humiliation in France was sinister, tragic, world-shaking; the literary humiliation was minor, limited, private.

James's response to the Dreyfus "affair," in the ensuing years, may have had in it an unconscious element of recognition. He had from the first been fascinated by the public drama. Three years after the officer's incarceration on charges of high treason, Zola had published his letter to the President of the French Republic known as *J'Accuse*. "Truth is on the march and nothing will halt it." In February 1898 he had been put on trial for libel. James thought *J'Accuse* "one of the most courageous things ever done and an immense honor to our too-puling corporation!" On the day that Zola was found guilty, James said he "worked off" some of his emotions by writing a letter of support and encouragement to his old friend of the Flaubert *cénacle*. The letter may not have reached him, for Zola fled to England, to a retreat in Surrey, on the advice of his lawyers and friends. Whether the two novelists met during Zola's exile is doubtful. "I sit in the garden and read *l'Affaire Dreyfus*," James wrote to Mrs. Humphry Ward in September 1898. "What a bottomless and sinister *affaire* and in what a strange mill it is grinding. The poor

French." He took the same attitude in a letter to Bourget, who had written him in great detail, and with much hatred of the Jews, about what James called "these unfortunate things" in France. "I don't understand," James wrote:

> I am too distant both from the experience of them and the way in which you feel them. Nothing here corresponds to them—neither the good relations which we maintain with the Jews, and, in sum, with one another, nor the supreme importance we attach to civil justice, nor the "short work" which we would make of the military if they attempted to substitute their justice for it. I can well sympathize however—to the point of tears—with your stricken country.

The Dreyfus affair was much in James's mind as he journeyed to Paris on 8 March 1899, and later to the Riviera, at the end of the month, to visit the Bourgets. He knew that his French friends believed in Dreyfus's guilt; and he was aware of Bourget's pronounced anti-Semitism. James was stoutly convinced of Dreyfus's innocence, and there was no touch of bigotry in his make-up. At the moment of his journey all France was split by *l'affaire;* and as a consequence of Zola's action and the clamor of the "League for the Rights of Man," a court-martial was scheduled to review the case. James had committed himself long ago to visit the Bourgets, but "The odious affair is rather in the air between me and that [Riviera] retreat," he told Mrs. Gardner. "I don't feel about it as I gather our friends there do." He added, "one must duck one's head and pass quickly."

He ducked his head at first by lingering in Paris. He remained at the Hôtel Meurice, reading page-proofs of his novel and receiving regular dispatches from Edward Warren about the repairs to Lamb House. "Reparation, amended and scientific reconstruction is already under way," he reported to the Curtises in Venice. The early spring sun in the French capital was comforting; and he saw much of his young cousins, Rosina and Leslie Emmet. Ever avuncular, he "breakfasted, dined, theatr'd, museumed, walked and talked them," he told William—without counting constant teas and little cakes of which he was a large consumer. He paid his usual homage to the salon of Henrietta Reubell, and the apartment of Morton Fullerton. "This extraordinary Paris," he wrote to Edward Warren, was

> the biggest temple ever built to material joys and the lust of the eyes. . . . It is a strange great phenomenon—with a deal of beauty still in its great expansive symmetries and perspectives—and *such* a beauty of light.

The beauty would prevail over the poisonous items in the newspapers. The large impression he received of the capital during this visit would emerge in the novel he began to write within the year about an American returning to France in middle age.

After hanging back for a fortnight, James went to the Riviera in one straight jump; he spent a night at Marseilles and reached the Bourget villa, Le Plantier, at Costebelle near Hyères the next day. The twenty-five-acre estate in one of the most beautiful spots on the Riviera spoke for the French writer's literary prosperity. The large house, and the guest-pavilion in which James was placed, were on a terraced mountain slope; the walled park of pine and cedar afforded views both inland and to the sea. "It's classic—Claude—Virgil," James wrote to his brother. Before these splendors "poor dear little Lamb House veils its face with humility and misery." That James was not altogether at his ease with the Bourgets is suggested by his managing very promptly to set fire to the curtains in the guest-house. The carelessness was not in character, especially after his own brief ordeal by fire in Lamb House.

His fellow guests were the Vicomte Eugène Melchior de Vogüé, who in recent years had introduced the great Russian writers to France, and Urbain Mengin, the sensitive young Frenchman James had befriended ten years earlier when he was a student in London. James was bored by the Vicomte and overwhelmed by the bigotry of Bourget. Minnie Bourget was a convert from her Jewish faith, and Mengin described later how on one occasion a young priest paid a call at Le Plantier. Minnie's face "expressed ecstasy and Bourget showed eagerness. The three fell to talking as if James and I shared their dogmas, rites and practices, and with the same rigidity. This continued when they shifted to politics—Dreyfus's guilt seemed to them a revealed certitude and beyond discussion. James led me outside. We walked briefly in silence. Then he seized my arm in that iron grip of his which expressed high emotion and he suddenly burst out, 'Suffocating, suffocating, I suffocate in that atmosphere. Poor Bourget—and such a talent, such an intelligence. He's lost, he's beyond saving . . . unless his fame suffers reverse; maybe that would make him look inward and acquire a noble disgust for the flattering pharisees surrounding him.'" James defined Bourget's Catholicism as "acquired, conceived and constructed like a private house, a social position. I can't believe he's sincere. This isn't faith."

His week at Le Plantier passed quickly enough. "I treat the *Affaire*," he wrote William, "as none of my business (as it isn't), but its power to make one homesick in France and the French air is not small. It is a country *en décadence.*" There were sundry sociabilities. On one occasion Lady Randolph Churchill, who was editing a journal called *The Anglo-Saxon Review,* paid a call on the Bourgets and made James promise to do a story for her. There were walks and talks—wide-ranging talks about current literature and the literary situation in France. The essay James published in the *North American Review,* six months after his visit to the Bourgets, on "The Present Literary Situation in France," contained his one public allusion to the Dreyfus case. In discussing Jules Lemaître as critic, he regretted that when Lemaître finally developed a conviction, it had turned out to be one of the "ugliest"—"his voice was loud, throughout the 'Affair' in the anti-revisionist and anti-Semitic interest." Bourget was mentioned only in passing in the article, in which James did not conceal his feelings that men of the second rank now held sway in the Republic. "The great historians are dead—the last of them went with Renan; the great critics are dead—the last of them went with Taine; the great dramatists are dead—the last of them went with Dumas; and of the novelists of the striking group originally fathered by the Second Empire, Émile Zola is the only one still happily erect."

"I've been here a week and depart tomorrow or next day. It has been rather a tension," James wrote early in April from Le Plantier to his brother. A day or two later he journeyed to St. Raphael and by easy stages to Genoa. If Hyères had induced tension, he now felt relief, for he wrote a lively and affectionate letter to Minnie Bourget. "I am full," he told her, "of grateful memories and blessed pictures. The beauty and harmony and nobleness of your eternal medium—that nothing can injure, diminish or disturb—has added a great stretch to my experience."

The clatter and chatter of Genoa came up into his hotel room as he wrote to Madame Bourget. He rejoiced in the sunny warmth of the Italian air and the shuffle below of Italian feet. He was recovering again "the little old throbs and thrills" of his old Italian journeys.

The Brooding Tourist

He had fallen in love with Italy as a young man, thirty years before, never again—as he put it—to fall out. Now, in his middle age, the "dishevelled nymph" seemed to have grown stout and orderly and become a votary of "progress." He was aware of "the tone of time," he hated the desecrations and erasures. Yet there were new sensations and new pictures as well. He was not one to allow nostalgia to efface immediate reality. Still, there was a change in his manner of looking. He had called himself of old "the sentimental traveller"; in England he had been "the observant stranger." Now in Italy he was "the brooding tourist."

He did not linger long in Genoa. A couple of days—visits to friends on the Ligurian coast—and he was off to Venice where he had promised to stay with the Daniel Curtises at the Palazzo Barbaro. In that high historic house there was (as he wrote in a travel sketch of this time) "such a quantity of recorded past twinkling in the multitudinous candles that one grasped at the idea of something waning and displaced, and might even fondly and secretly nurse the conceit that what one was having was just the very last." There was no future for such manners and customs and the comprehensive urbanity of his host and hostess; but he would not bother with the future; it was better to stay with the picture into which Venice resolved itself. During this visit the Palazzo Barbaro placed itself more vividly than ever in James's imagination, superimposed itself on memories of earlier years. He did not, as legend has it, write *The Wings of the Dove* while he stayed there. But he did work at the Barbaro on this occasion: to fulfill his promise to Lady Randolph Churchill, he wrote for her *Anglo-Saxon Review* his tale "The Great Condition." A variant on his old stories about women with a "past," it was based on an idea furnished by one of his conversations with Meredith.

If he gave this task as his primary excuse for delay in going to Rome, there were other reasons as well. One was the presence of a charming older woman, a fellow-guest, Jessie Allen. Miss Allen was of a distinguished family and full of good talk and lively gossip; she was a delightful companion in the alleyways and tiny curiosity shops of Venice. They wandered in the twists and turns of the passages, dipped into cool chapels when the heat became insufferable, evaded the parent-like vigilance of the Curtis servant Angelo, went for long rides in a gondola. Miss Allen, James reported later to Ariana Curtis, wrote thirty-page letters, "very agreeable ones," and seemed to lead "a labyrinthine life." For the next fifteen years, in her flat at 74 Eaton Terrace, she would pour tea for Henry James whenever he was in London.

To visit Venice was to pay homage to his oldest friend in that city— Mrs. Arthur Bronson, whose Casa Alvisi on the Grand Canal he had celebrated in an essay of the early 1890s as "the very friendliest house in all the wide world." He found his friend now at La Mura, her country place at nearby Asolo, a sadly aged and limited figure—she who had once ruled over the Canal. In the little house, which he had always found uncomfortable, he got a painful picture of the waning of a life once filled with ease, power and relaxed and open-handed generosity. Mrs. Bronson had become "the strangest mixture of folly of purchase and of discomfort about necessaries." There wasn't an easy chair in La Mura for her to be ill in, or for him to sit in comfortably. They had an immense quantity of talk, however, and much reminiscence. But Mrs. Bronson was helpless and demoralized, "a great deal of rheumatism, an enormous appetite, not a scrap of possible action," with two nurses, a flock of servants and queues of shopkeepers trying to sell her antiques. Asolo still had its old charm, but Mrs. Bronson could no longer undertake excursions and explorations. She was "of this world that she so much loved," but it would not be for long. This was to be James's last vision of her before her death in 1901.

He was overdue in Rome, where the Waldo Storys awaited him at the Barberini, in the old many-roomed apartment of William Wetmore Story whose life he was to write. James had no desire to stay with them; he preferred to be near the Spanish Steps and he put up at the Hôtel de l'Europe, where he had a sitting room that looked on the Piazza Mignanelli. To Bourget he wrote, "Rome is always Rome—at this moment generally empty and quiet but more and more 'modern' as I grow more and more antique." He half-heartedly examined the large Story archive —letters from the Brownings, his old friend Lowell, Charles Sumner, the accolades of the world bestowed upon this amateur sculptor of strained awkward statues. It was clear to James that he could write Story's life with ease; but not perhaps with much pleasure. "There will be all the Rome I can put into so small a compass, and as little Story as I can keep out," he said to Grace Norton.

For the rest, he paid calls as always and continued to tour—and to brood. He went to Castel Gandolfo to visit the Humphry Wards and promised to return for a stay; and he called with pleasure and some regularity at the studio of John Elliott and his wife, the former Maud Howe, daughter of Julia Ward Howe. He liked Elliott's work and he liked their charming place near St. Peter's—a flowered terrace on the roof of the Palazzo Accoramboni, looking down into the square of St. Peter's and beyond to the Campagna and the Alban and Sabine hills. And he met again, after long years, the indomitable Louise Von Räbe, whom he had once found so formidable (when she was Annie Crawford) and who was now elderly and widowed. Maud Elliott gave a dinner for her on the terrace under the pergola at which James was toasted in Orvieto and said with great solemnity—as a brooding tourist might—"this is the time when one lights the candle, goes through the house and takes stock."

On another day at the Elliotts' James was introduced to a young American sculptor from Boston, of Norwegian birth. His name was Hendrik Andersen—it sounded very like the name James had given to the sculptor he had created long ago, Roderick Hudson. Andersen was of "magnificent stature," Henry wrote. He was much taken by his sincerity, his seriousness—and his handsome blond countenance. The sculptor invited him to his studio in the Via Margutta. Back in the 1870s, James had talked art and smoked cigarettes with the assorted American artists in this very street. Andersen had his grand dreams. He wanted, like Roderick Hudson, to do large statues, big conceptions. The novelist took him to lunch. They talked until it was time to have dinner. They continued to talk. In Hendrik's studio, James took a fancy to a small terracotta bust

Andersen had done of the young Conte Alberto Bevilacqua. To encourage the sculptor, he took the unusual step of purchasing the bust. The price was $250, the sum he usually got for a short story. Andersen said he would pack it carefully and ship it to Lamb House. He promised too that he would come to England to visit James.

Three Villas

Mrs. Humphry Ward in a Roman villa, writing one of her novels—with an Italian background! The thought fascinated Henry James. He was due in Florence to talk to William Wetmore Story's daughter, the Countess Peruzzi; but he could not resist the invitation from the "irrepressible" Mrs. Ward to return to the Villa Barberini. He had liked its high position at Castel Gandolfo, the great slope of the Campagna seaward, the ruins of one of Domitian's villas far below. At the end of May when he began to find the heat of Rome uncomfortable he arrived for a stay of a couple of nights. He remained a week.

Mrs. Humphry Ward—Mary Augusta Arnold—was granddaughter of the great Arnold of Rugby and niece of Matthew Arnold, whom James had long ago met in Story's apartment in the Barberini Palace. The bee-emblem of that noble house was much in evidence in this seventeenth-century villa, massive but carelessly built. "We perch over the blue Alban lake by one set of windows—vast campagna by other sets," James wrote. "Mrs. Ward reads and writes hard." Something about her —perhaps her Arnold blood, certainly her high seriousness, her tremendous moral tone, her appeal to James's artistic wisdom—found him always ready to be kind to her. She for her part took his assiduous criticism of her novels in good spirit, knowing it was well-intentioned; she seemed however unaware of some of its ironies. "One fears a little sometimes," James had written to her of *Robert Elsmere,* "that he [Elsmere] may suffer a sunstroke, damaging if not fatal, from the high oblique light of your admiration for him." Perhaps James experienced a little the same oblique light. Mrs. Ward had had enormous success with *Robert Elsmere,* the kind of success James envied. He had satirized her kind of literary aspirations in "The Next Time," in the person of Mrs. Highmore, the woman who wished she could have an artistic rather than popular success. He, on his side, would have liked to win her kind of readers, but he knew he could not write her kind of novel. Yet patiently, consistently, he lectured her on the art of fiction—*his* art—in all the years of their friendship. "She is incorrigibly wise and good, and has a moral nature as Patti has a voice," James wrote to Edmund Gosse, "but somehow I don't, especially when talking art and letters, *communicate* with her worth a damn. All the same she's a dear."

Mrs. Ward went about her novel writing with great thoroughness. When she decided to write a novel about Italy on the Elsmere formula —one in which she would show "progress" as prevailing over Papal inertia—she felt a need to live herself into an actual background. She had arrived at the Villa Barberini in March, while Henry James was making his slow journey along the Riviera. There was snow on the Campagna; a wind was moaning in the Alban hills. The villa was rudely furnished and without heat; the kitchen was fifty-two steps below the dining-room; the Neapolitan cook was formidable. Mrs. Ward's husband predicted she would end up in a heated hotel in Rome. Even Humphry Ward did not reckon with the blood of Dr. Arnold. Stoves were brought in; books were unpacked, the meager furnishings repositioned, and Mrs. Ward's daughters and servants were mobilized against the elements.

Mrs. Ward looked at James during this visit with new eyes. In England she had known the social James. Now she discovered the Italianate James—with his thorough knowledge of antiquity and the Roman countryside; and when, in London or at her country home, Stocks, had she heard him speak Italian? She watched him in fluent conversation with a brown-frocked barefoot monk, from the monastery of Palazzuola, drawing the man out, questioning him, looking into his face with searching eyes, and "getting something real and vital in the ruder simpler mind." What struck Mrs. Ward—and she seemed surprised—was that James too could be erudite. She found that he conveyed his knowledge of things Roman and Italian by indirect hints, a grave way of being politely certain that his listeners themselves knew all that he knew; then he walked "round and round the subject, turning it inside out, playing with it, making mock of it, and catching it again with a sudden grip, or a momentary flash of eloquence." James made the fullest use of the resources of speech.

One afternoon James, his hostess and her daughters went on an excursion to the blue lake of Nemi visible on their horizon. They passed on their way over the great viaduct at Aricia, where Diana had been barbarously worshipped. In the late soft hours of the afternoon the landscape was bathed in golden light. Everywhere there were ruins and fragments. As they crossed the high ridge above the deep-sunk lake, the excursionists perceived the niched wall and the platform of the temple; they speculated that the historic spring—the spring of Egeria, who had instructed Numa Pompilius in modes of worship—must be in an embrasure in the wall. The spring had been a "sacred fount." James's next novel would bear this title.

During this excursion they encountered among the strawberry-beds, in the vicinity of the temple of Diana Nemorensis then being excavated, a dark-eyed youth. The boy talked of fragments and artifacts lying in the furrows of the freshly ploughed field. James walked beside him, unable to take his eyes from his face. He asked him his name and repeated it, Aristodemo, a noble Greek name. He was "straight and lithe and handsome as a young Bacchus," said Mrs. Ward. Henry James murmured the name: his voice, said Mrs. Ward, caressed it—Aristodemo—a kind of caress of the boy himself. The youth, aware that he had the center of the stage, described to James a marble head he had found—yes, he!—complete, even the nose preserved. The sun sank, the enchantment lingered. "For me," James wrote to his hostess later, "the Nemi lake, and the walk down and up (the latter perhaps most), and the strawberries and Aristodemo were the cream"—and he added for emphasis, "I am clear about that."

Mrs. Ward's excuse for sending James proofs of *Eleanor,* her novel of Italy, some months later was that she had introduced an American girl into her story, a very churchy young Puritan, named Lucy Foster, who becomes the rival in love of the heroine Eleanor, an Egeria figure. Lucy and the man who falls in love with her are proponents of differing philosophies. She is anti-Catholic and all for a democratic Italy. He defends the past, the Pope, the Jesuits. The novel was a successful serial in *Harper's* and its American edition at one time was selling 1,000 copies a day—more copies in one day than an entire edition of some of James's works.

James's letters to Mrs. Ward about *Eleanor,* whose impending success he could foresee, are solid little essays on the art of the novel as he practiced it. He thought Lucy Foster insufficiently American. Her religious stiffness seemed to him untypical. The American reader would say "Why this isn't us—it's English dissent." Nor did he think an obscure American girl would be shocked by Rome, the Pope, St. Peter's, kneeling, or anything of that sort. He told Mrs. Ward she was throwing her story too obviously at the reader; no suspense, no "crooked corridor," no attempt to keep readers guessing. Since Eleanor, the Egeria, was the focus, she should keep her at the "centre," make her consciousness "full, rich, universally prehensile and *stick* to it—don't shift—and don't shift *arbitrarily*—how, otherwise, do you get your unity of subject or keep up your reader's sense of it?" The story must get its unity not from the personality of the author—as apparently Mrs. Ward had argued—but from the nature of the subject.

What James was defending so ardently was not only his kind of novel —which Mrs. Ward could never write—but the method of limited "point of view." He anticipated the criticism that this might restrict the freedom of his storytelling. When *Eleanor* was published a year later he offered Mrs. Ward extravagant praise, calling it "a large and noble performance," although confessing that in reading it he had "recomposed and reconstructed Eleanor from head to foot."

There was one page in the novel which James read with a certain humor and irony of his own. Mrs. Ward included a man of letters, a poet, who visits Eleanor's villa. Mr. Bellasis figures as a "walk-on" character. "So you have read my book?" is his first question and he wants to know whether Eleanor has *re*-read it: "my friends tell me in Rome that the book cannot really be appreciated except at a second or third reading." The physical Bellasis does not resemble James; but something in the way Mrs. Ward made him talk caused James to write to her, when she sent him her first installment: "I've read every word, and many two or three times, as Mr. Bellasis would say—and is Mr. Bellasis, by the way, naturally—as it were—H.J.???!!!"

A few days after his visit to the Villa Barberini, Henry James stood on the deck of the little steamer that took pilgrims—and brooding tourists—from Sorrento to Capri. Far aloft, on the great rock, was pitched "the amazing creation of the friend" who was offering him hospitality—the San Michele of Dr. Axel Munthe. His visit to Munthe was to be an affair of twenty-four hours, a side-trip from another he was paying in Naples. He had met the famous society doctor on the train to Rome, almost a month before, and had received several pressing invitations to Capri. At the same time no less pressing invitations came from the popular Italianate-American novelist F. Marion Crawford—son of the sculptor Thomas Crawford and nephew of Julia Ward Howe—to visit his elaborate villa at Sant'Agnello di Sorrento.

James had scarcely known Marion Crawford when he used to visit the novelist's mother and stepfather, the Luther Terrys, in the Palazzo Odescalchi in Rome in the 1870s. Now the occupant of modest Lamb House was finding the later generation living in villas that spoke for great affluence; in the case of F. Marion Crawford a best-selling prosperity not unlike Mrs. Ward's. To his intimates James wrote that Crawford was "a prodigy of talent—and of wealth! It is humiliating." The novelist had planned a brief visit to Sorrento. However, Crawford announced a grand *festa* to celebrate his wife's birthday, and James had promised to return after his excursion to Munthe's.

The Munthe weekend was a continuous *divertissement.* There was first the fantastic villa itself with its loggias and its statued pergolas hanging dizzily over splendid views. The white arcades and the cool chambers offered at every step some fragment of the past, a rounded porphyry pillar supporting a bust, a shaft of pale alabaster upholding a trellis, some mutilated marble image, some bronze that had roughly resisted the ages. "Our host," James wrote, "had the secret; but he could only express it in grand practical ways." James however also had a feeling of discomfort; the villa of black Tiberius had overhung the immensity of Capri and this evoked "the cruel, the fatal historic sense . . . to make so much distinction, how much history had been needed!" Munthe attributed to James the statement that San Michele was "the most beautiful place in the world." But a letter to Venetian friends gives us James's direct impression—"a creation of the most fantastic beauty, poetry, and inutility that I have ever seen clustered together." Munthe also had, James remarked, an "unnatural simplicity." The novelist seems to have enjoyed however the local feast-day of St. Anthony, when Munthe held open house. Huge straw-bellied flasks of purple wine were tilted for the thirsty—and the general thirst was great. "It was antiquity in solution," wrote James, "with every brown mild figure, every note of the old speech, every tilt of the great flask, every shadow cast by every classic fragment."

After Munthe and Capri, the novelist had a few more days with the Crawfords, days of a continually festive kind. But the summer heat was over the land and James did not linger. While in Florence, James's hotel room was rattled and shaken early one morning by an earth-shock. "Praise be to earthquakes of small calibre," he remarked; a little more would not have been at all amusing. Early in June he was in Paris: crossing the Channel he went straight to Folkestone and to Rye. He had been away nearly four months. Lamb House, with its refurbished fireplaces and reduced fire hazards, seemed to him a haven of coolness and greenness. "Oh, it is a joy to be once more in this refreshed and renovated refuge!" he wrote to Edward Warren. He had had enough of villas built or rented with the proceeds of best-selling novels. Almost a decade would elapse before he would travel again to the Continent.

A Young Sculptor

A fortnight after James's return from Italy there arrived at Lamb House the small terracotta bust of the Conte Bevilacqua which James had purchased from Hendrik Andersen in the Via Margutta. The novelist set it in the niche of the newly remodeled chimney-piece in his dining-room where it would face him for years during lonely repasts—the neat amateurish head and shoulders of adolescence, somehow weighted and lifeless, for Andersen did not care for such trivial things as busts: and his touch was heavy. His dream was of great equestrian statues gleaming in the sun, of huge American cities displaying form-filled fountains—sculpted by Hendrik Christian Andersen. But it was a new experience for him to receive a letter from a famous novelist telling him, "I've struck up a tremendous intimacy with dear little Conte Alberto.... He is the first object my eyes greet in the morning and the last at night." It would be a life attachment, James said—"Brave little Bevilacqua, and braver still big Maestro Andersen."

The bravos rang loudly in the ears of the hopeful artist. He had been working in comparative obscurity, making such friends as he could among Roman-Americans and dreaming his dreams. James's letter seemed an augury of friendship, intimacy, patronage. And when the novelist wrote that the bust would "make many friends here," Andersen immediately assumed James had written an article about him and his work. The novelist was quick to correct this impression. He had simply meant that the bust would be visible in its niche to his many friends who came to Lamb House.

Andersen had planned to leave for New York that summer. In the light of James's praise, and his invitation, it seemed to him practical to go to America by way of Rye. James was delighted. His trip to Italy had made him feel old; and in Rye he was lonely. To have a splendid eager youth come rushing to his side at this moment made him feel that someone still cared, that he was not cut off from the world. Sensing that Andersen had dreams of grandeur, James warned him that Lamb House was hardly a *palazzo* or even a villa. "I feel you to be formidable, fresh from your St. Peterses, Vaticans and Trattorie Fiorentine—formidable to my small red British cottage and small plain British *cuisine*—but you will be very welcome."

The relationship between the two had its complexities from the first. James looked at Andersen with an inward vision of his own youth, his distant Roman days. Andersen, on his side, saw a kind, benignant, fatherly figure, who might aid him in the hard climb to fame and fortune. He made himself agreeable, with a show of modesty on the one hand and of ambition on the other. It is doubtful whether James saw, at the beginning of their friendship, much beyond the chiseled countenance, the flaxen hair, the big frame, the vitality of the young sculptor. Andersen knew he was admired, and responded warmly; but he seems to have thought mainly of how "useful" James could be to him.

Coincidence indeed added a few charming touches. Henry and Hendrik—they bore the same name. And then James's birthday and the sculptor's fell in the same month. They were second sons. They had talented brothers: Hendrik's elder brother, Andreas, was a skillful painter. From the first James treated Andersen as if he were his *alter ego*. The old Henry and the young—it was as if Andersen had been fashioned out of James's old memories and old passions. A warm nostalgia filled their hours together during the sculptor's first visit to Lamb House. James bestowed on Andersen his own taste, his own high standards, his own feeling for beauty. He looked into the mirror and saw smiling and healthy youth instead of his obese and aging self. The image charmed— one might say it enchanted.

They talked, on this first visit, of art, work, career, success, how to confront and woo the world; they spoke of intimate things, family, friends, affections. So Roderick and Rowland had talked long ago. The novelist could offer the wisdom of his decades and Hendrik listened with tender deference. They sat under the big mulberry tree in the Lamb House garden at the summer's richest hour. Andersen was all sincerity and respect—and James was unexpectedly happy. Forgotten for the moment was the pride of reputation, the envy of the best-sellers, the weight of the world. He lived for a small, a cherished idyll, of happy summer months.

With his curiosity and questioning, James learned more intimately the facts of his new-found friend's life. The sculptor had been born in Bergen, Norway, and brought to America as a child by his immigrant parents. The family had lived in genteel poverty at Newport, where however the Howes, the La Farges, and others had taken an interest in the talented Andersen children. There were three sons, all artistic. With some help from well-wishers, Hendrik had gone to art school in Boston; then he had lived in the Latin Quarter in Paris and attended the École des Beaux Arts. He showed much skill in drawing, but he decided that he did not want to follow in the footsteps of his elder brother, the painter. He took up sculpture and presently, in Rome, joined the art life in and around the Piazza del Popolo. At the dawn of the new century all was still hope and hard work—a familiar story of zeal, dedication and the dream of Arcadia.

A great tenderness seems to have welled up in James as he listened. To the Elliotts in Rome, in whose apartment he had met Andersen, he wrote, "That most lovable youth, as he strikes me, Hans Christian Andersen, turned up in due course nearly a fortnight ago—came down, that is, spent two days and was as nice as could be; then whirled himself off into space after making me grow quite fond enough of him to miss him."

In the letters James began to write now to the young sculptor trying his fortune in New York, he hovered a great deal over him; he had advice and encouragement and an abundance of love: "I have *missed* you," he wrote, "out of all proportion to the three meagre little days (for it seems strange they were only *that*) that we had together." Thinking "ever so tenderly of our charming spin homeward in the twilight" after they had cycled to Winchelsea, "and feeling again the strange perversity it made of that sort of thing being over so soon," he promised the young man: "Never mind—we *shall* have more, lots more, of that sort of thing!" He hoped he could put him into his Watchbell Street studio "and we shall be good for each other; and the studio good for both of us." And James added, "I feel in you a *confidence,* dear boy—which to show is a joy to me."

James felt "confidence" in Andersen, but he was to discover, as the months passed, that the "lovable youth" would have to be loved at a distance. They were to have in all only half a dozen meetings and at long-spaced intervals. Andersen came again to Lamb House two years later, after abandoning New York, and only after much pleading on James's part; and finally some months afterwards. They met in America in 1905; they met in Rome in 1907. Each meeting brought a renewal of affection, renewed and often intense outpourings from James, who wrote to Andersen with a freedom not to be found in any of his other letters.

The novelist's correspondence with Andersen—the saddest and strangest perhaps in his entire *epistolarium*—is notable for the quantity of physical, tactile language employed: James repeatedly offers his *abbraccio*—puts out his arms to embrace the younger man, pats him tenderly on the back—in words. While these speak for a certain physical intimacy in their meetings, they can be seen also as forms of endearment in one who was overtly affectionate in public. James in his late years was wont to embrace friends at his club or at a railway station in the Latin fashion, with much patting on the back. Nevertheless there is a quality of passion and possession in the reiterated "I hold you close," "I feel, my dear boy, my arms around you," or "I meanwhile pat you affectionately on the back, across the Alps and Apennines, I draw you close, I hold you long." In letters written to Andersen in 1902 on the death of the sculptor's elder brother, James enjoins him, as from Olympus, to "lean on me as on a brother and a lover."

A second element in the correspondence is James's reiterated cry for the absent one. The pain of separation is strong. "I even," James is writing in 1901, "go so far as to ask myself whether visits so damnably short haven't more in them to groan, than to thank, for." In 1903: "Don't 'chuck' me this year, dearest boy, if you can possibly help it." In 1904 he signs himself "your poor helpless far-off but all devoted H.J. who seems condemned almost and never to be near you, yet who, if he were, would lay upon you a pair of hands soothing, sustaining, positively *healing* in the quality of their pressure." In 1905: "We must hold on in one way or another till we meet. It is miserable how little, as the months and years go on, we *do*." In 1911, when James is sixty-eight and Hendrik thirty-nine, there is a final clinging to a hopeless wish, the tired words of an old man:

> It's a sad business, this passage of all the months and years without our meeting again. . . . I want to see you—and I so hold out my arms to you. Somehow it may still come—but it seems far off.

And in 1913, when James is seventy, he still hopes that perhaps they "will meet (and still embracingly) over the abyss of our difference in years and conditions."

The embraces were postponed; the abyss remained. But there lingered this particular love, which flickered up whenever he heard from

Andersen, even when it was smothered by the sculptor's failures in perception or his indifferences. The question may be asked whether the use of the term "lover" and the verbal passion of the letters was "acted out." We simply do not know. Most Victorians kept the doors of their bedrooms shut: certainly Henry James did. Some might judge the question irrelevant in the life of a writer who had defended himself for so many years against sex, and had exalted the intellectual and emotional rather than the physical in human relations. In any case, it would be presuming too much to insist on the inevitability of a physical relationship, particularly in the absence of Andersen's letters to James. We know that James had hitherto tended to look at the world as through plate glass. It is possible that the touch of those strong fingers of the sculptor's hand gave him a sense of physical closeness and warmth which he had never allowed himself to feel in earlier years; and it is this which we read in his letters. We may speculate endlessly without discovering the answers. One thing is clear. The "heavy" Andersen, whose brightness would fade so quickly, inspired feelings in Henry James akin to love—to a love such as Fenimore had had for him. She had written of her loneliness and complained of the years that passed between their meetings as James now wrote to Andersen. She had known what it was to have the object of her love fail her, fail to recognize the depth of her feeling. This James would in due course discover.

The Third Person

Henry James had returned from Italy vaguely depressed. Just before leaving Rome, he had received word that his brother William was coming abroad for his health. William had always seemed to Henry the embodiment of restless energy, a mind and body constantly questioning and active: now he was on his way to take the cure at Bad Nauheim, like so many elderly invalids.

Henry soon learned the essential facts. Dr. Baldwin of Florence happened to be at Nauheim, also taking a cure. He examined William and reported to the novelist that his brother had developed a serious heart condition—a valvular lesion. Henry wrote to the doctor that what he learned made him "rather sick and sore and sad." Physiological details always terrified him. He too began to worry about his heart. "I am coddling my organ at such a rate that I no longer bicycle up anything less level than a billiard table," he wrote to Dr. Baldwin. Fortunately he had a billiard table of some twenty miles in the area of Rye. To William he wrote that he was deeply moved by Baldwin's "inscrutable physiological definiteness"; and he added, "oh, how I want you convalescent and domesticated here!"

A few days after his return from Italy, James learned that his landlord had died and that Lamb House was for sale. The price was £2,000.
This was substantial for the time, yet reasonable given the excellent
condition of the house and the increasing value of real estate in Rye.
James had lived himself sufficiently into the dwelling to know that he
wanted to own it. However he had very little ready money, and not much
practical knowledge about financing such a purchase. He wrote to his
brother in Germany. William had for a long time handled Henry's
finances in America; Henry now gave him the arguments for and against
his making what would be the largest investment of his lifetime. He
seemed once again to be the younger brother asking for guidance—even
while announcing he had made up his mind. William, in the midst of
debilitating baths and general fatigue, took Henry at his word. He had
not yet seen the house; but Dr. Baldwin had. Lamb House had struck him
as a kind of rural *pied-à-terre* for the London-identified novelist. He
judged $10,000 to be "a very extravagant price." William passed the word
along to Henry.

The effect of this on the younger brother was registered in a long
letter of anger and frustration. Forgetting that he had asked for his
brother's opinion, Henry exclaimed, "I do, strange as it may appear to
you, in this matter, know more or less what I'm about . . . I am not yet
wholly senile." Brushing aside the question of cost, he told William his
fondness for Lamb House was reason enough for acquiring it. Baldwin,
who had spent only one night in the house, had "scarcely appeared to
me to appreciate the place at all." He wasn't qualified to judge. Edward
Warren, the architect, considered the house not only worth the price,
but also an excellent investment. Moreover, Henry had learned that he
needed only $4,000—£800—since the rest represented a mortgage he
could take over at four per cent. He wouldn't have to borrow any
money.

The obsessed pleading of the reply and the self-justification revealed
memories of Quincy Street and his parents' watchfulness over his
money; revealed also how vulnerable Henry was to anything critical
William might say. His anxieties were transferred to more recent history
as he wrote:

> My whole being cries out loud for something that I can call my own—and
> when I look round me at the splendour of so many of the "literary" fry,
> my confrères (M. Crawford's, P. Bourget's, Humphry Ward's, Hodgson
> Burnett's, W. D. Howellses etc.) and I feel that I may strike the world as
> still, at fifty-six, with my long labour and my genius, reckless, presump-
> tuous and unwarranted in curling up (for more assured peaceful produc-
> tion) in a poor little $10,000 shelter—once for all and for all time—*then*

I do feel the bitterness of humiliation, the iron enters into my soul, and (I blush to confess it,) I *weep!* But enough, enough, enough!

Enough, enough, enough! His sense of outrage abated. He apologized to William. He had felt, he said, "the impulse to *fraternize*—put it that way—with you, over the pleasure of my purchase, and to see you glow with pride in *my* pride of possession." This was the heart of the matter. As a boy Henry would have done anything for a loving glance, a pat on the back. William had once again—this time in the most innocent way imaginable—hit an exposed nerve.

William James, his wife, Alice, and young daughter, Peggy, arrived at Lamb House early in October of 1899. The elder brother felt tolerably well after his Nauheim cure. He responded with his old painter's sense to the greenish-yellow autumn light in which Rye was bathed. He found the town, with its miniature brick walls, houses, nooks, coves and gardens, alternately suggestive of English, Dutch and Japanese effects. Lamb House itself seemed to him like a toy compared with his own large New England house in Cambridge; he wondered "how *families* ever could have been reared in most of the houses," they were so small. He characterized his brother's house as a "most exquisite collection of quaint little stage properties," and his brother as still interested above all "in the operations of his fancy." He recognized that life in this out-of-the-way town must be lonely, yet he felt his brother was in equilibrium with his loneliness. As usual in William's presence, Henry was reticent, closed-in, on his guard, full of awe and respect.

At first William took everything in his old stride, save that he tired easily after his walks. But within a fortnight he began to complain of being unwell again, and quite suddenly one day he had a return of the terrible chest pains he had experienced in America. Alarmed, Henry and Alice took him at once to London and installed him in De Vere Gardens, where they called in an eminent heart specialist, Bezly Thorne. He ordered the unwilling William to bed, put him on a strict no-starch diet. This time the philosopher obeyed. Watching him, the novelist became aware that he was "a graver and more precarious case than I had dreamed of."

After three weeks of this regimen the patient improved. Thorne then dispatched him—it was December by now—to Malvern for hydropathic treatment. Here the bitter cold and the rigors of the baths quickly made William ill again, and he came back with Alice to London. Henry in the interval had let his flat for the coming year. He met the two on their arrival and the next day brought them back to Rye. There, once again, William showed improvement.

In the waning days of the year, in wintry Rye, the brothers and the sister-in-law awaited the coming of 1900: "this dreadful gruesome New Year, so monstrously numbered," as Henry wrote on 1 January to Rhoda Broughton. The advent of a new era had been announced that autumn by the guns in South Africa. The brothers had been together as young men in the other war, the War between the States—and Henry wrote early in the new year remembering "the general sense, the suspense and anxiety, stricken bereavement, woe and uncertainty" of that long-ago time. Now, as the coastal storms raged and he built great fires in his reconditioned fireplaces, Henry had a different source of anxiety. He later spoke of how he had been "worried, depressed, tormented in a high degree" about his brother. "My spirits were in my boots about him and my time all went in trying to create for him here an atmosphere of optimism and an illusion of ease." In these moments William's wife Alice became for him a counterpart of his own mother. "I bless the high heaven hourly for her." He spoke of the renewed sight she gave him "of what a woman can do for a man. Her devotion, her courage, her cheer, her ability and indefatigability, her ingenuity and resource in his service, are pure magnificence. She is *always* in the breach."

Peggy James spent Christmas at Lamb House with her parents and uncle. As William grew stronger it was decided that he would go to the Riviera, to escape the hardest part of the English winter. A wealthy French admirer had made available to him a fine little château at Costebelle, not far from the Bourgets. In mid-January Henry escorted his brother and sister-in-law to Dover and saw them aboard the Channel steamer.

In the tales which tumbled from Henry James's desk that autumn of 1899, one finds a complex network of old themes, re-awakened by the anger he felt at William's seeming hostility to his acquisition of a home—anger which he could not discharge more directly, since his brother was seriously ill. The new stories contain a fund of the feline, and strange notes of cruelty. The old theme of revenge is stated in new and shrill terms. Mrs. Grantham in "The Two Faces" is a woman scorned. When his lordship, after jilting her, turns round and asks her to help introduce his inexperienced child-bride into society, Mrs. Grantham complies—her young victim is "overloaded like a monkey in a show," while she herself is attired with *éclat.* In "The Beldonald Holbein," the beautiful and proud Lady Beldonald uses her plain companion to enhance her own beauty; the companion, whose plain face triumphs, is seen as a perfect Holbein. In "The Special Type" there is a sacrificial lady who helps the male egotist marry the woman he wants, but takes her own quiet revenge. The theme will be used in "The Tone of Time," in which a woman painter is asked by a lady to supply her with the "portrait" of an imaginary husband. The lady painter puts on canvas the countenance of the man who long ago jilted her, only to discover that this man figured in the life of the very woman for whom she is painting the "portrait." She is jealous enough to refuse his image to the other woman. In these stories, in which Henry is casting himself as the woman, we recover elements of the little three-cornered ballets of his old novel *Confidence,* written when William married Alice, which had reflected his jealousy of his sister-in-law. The emotions the stories incarnate—old love, old jealousy, old anger—are those of the little Henry who loved William and yearned with intensity for acceptance by his brother. The legend of childhood took still another form in a tale Henry wrote just before William's arrival from Germany—before he began to feel the old envy again. In "Broken Wings" a writer-lady and a painter-man had been in love years before, but each had believed the other to be too successful for them to have a life together. Then they discover each has had his fame without the financial reward that goes with it. Now, their wings "broken," they can face the future together. It is a wishful parable in which Henry equates his own recent failures with William's broken health. Perhaps now, he seems to be saying, he and William are on the same footing—in the same boat.

Nothing had changed in Henry's inner world; what had changed was his adult power of fantasy. His tales are richer and more jewel-encrusted; but they show him still trying to resolve old problems, as in the themes of murdered little boys and surviving little girls. In "Maud-Evelyn," a stiff young man gives up the living woman he is courting to love a young woman whom he has never known—and who is dead, though her parents pretend their daughter lives. This venture into morbidity—to a feeling of the deadness of his past and his inability to love women—had its counterpart in a good-humored ghost story to which James gave the significant title of "The Third Person." It was written while William and Alice were with him that cold December of 1899. Two elderly ladies in the ancient south-coast town of Marr have inherited a fine old brick house in which 200 years of the "little melancholy, middling, disinherited" town have "squared themselves in the brown, panelled parlour, creaked patiently on the wide staircase and bloomed herbaciously in the red-walled garden." We are in Rye, we are in Lamb House. Presently the two spinster cousins become aware of the presence of a man, who carries his head always distinctly to one side. He haunts one and then the other until, with the aid of the local clergyman, the third person is established as an ancestor who had been hanged for smuggling—that is why his head is so mournfully tilted. For a while the cousins enjoy having a man about the house—even if he is a ghost. But they have also tense jealous moments.

In the end they decide the troubled spirit must be returned to its rest. The tale peters out in a joke, but in Henry James's creative consciousness that winter, William, laid low by his heart trouble, was as shorn of his power as the hanged smuggler. The two women competing for him might be Henry and Alice; or they belonged to the perpetual triangles of the Jamesian childhood and youth, with himself or William cast as "third person" —depending on the situation. Ghosts might be conquered in tales: but they had a way of returning in life. They still could be recalled at a given signal, by anything that touched an ancient hurt.

The Visitable Past

One day that autumn Henry James took the Brighton train from London and went to Rottingdean to have lunch with the Kiplings, back from America. The "great little Rudyard," inspired by the Boer War, which had just broken out, had been spouting chauvinistic verses and publishing them in the press. James couldn't swallow these "loud brazen patriotic" mouthings. It was like exploiting the name of one's mother or one's wife.

F. N. Doubleday, Kipling's American publisher and friend, had talked to James about his doing another volume of ghost stories like "The Turn of the Screw." Thinking of this, he seemed to see, as the return train sped him back to London in the thickening dusk, "the picture of three or four 'scared' and slightly modern American figures," against European backgrounds. His travelers were "in search of, in flight from, something or other." James did not apply these words to himself when he recorded them some days later in his notebook; yet the statement contained his essential life experience in eerie form. He had been the archetypal American in flight from home; he had gone in search of "something or other" in the great House of Europe, with its centuries of bloodshed and *bric-à-brac.* And now his brother William had made him aware again of the things from which he had taken early flight—the whole daylight world of Quincy Street, Boston, New York, that confined him to the invisible barriers of his childhood and youth.

James did not then attempt the story: all he could do was record the emotion and the sense of terror. Instead, he set down a scenario for a tale of a young American who walks into a house just inherited in London— to find himself in the past. Part of James's Brighton-to-London fantasy was incorporated into this scenario. He had a title for his story almost from the first: he would call it *The Sense of the Past.*

James wrote the opening chapters in the early days of 1900, at a time when, with the new year and the new century, he was unusually conscious of the clock and the calendar. The idea, fascinating in its possibilities, proved extremely difficult. He could get his young man back into the old house and into the past of 1820: that was easy enough. But how arrange for his return to the twentieth century where he belonged? The year 1820 was James's "visitable past," the period of his father's boyhood. It was a past he could call up in his memories of his grandmother in Albany, in her old-time clothes, reading books with the candle set between her eyes and the printed page; the kind of past to which Fanny Kemble used to transport him during winter evenings by her fireside. In invoking a "visitable past," James suggested his ambivalence towards old things, towards Europe itself. His horseback rides long ago in the Campagna had given him an uncomfortable feeling of the insolence of power, the primordial cruelty and brutality of man. The unreachable past partook of nightmare; it held within it man's accumulated evil, the terror of the ages.

Out of such ambivalent feelings, James wrote his fragment of *The Sense of the Past,* seeking to recapture a "Turn of the Screw" horror in it by having his twentieth-century man blunder cheerfully into history —and into the terrible discovery that he can become its prisoner. The young historian in the story, pausing in the doorway of the house that will admit him to the world of 1820, has the thought that "it was for the old ghosts to take him for one of themselves." This was interesting as a thought—but also frightening. One hardly wants to believe oneself a ghost. It may account for Henry James's ultimate failure to finish this book.

In the story James planned, his American historian, Ralph Pendrel, possesses a sense both of art and of history, but he has never been abroad. A young New York matron he wants to marry, Aurora Coyne, will have him only if he will promise to keep his national virginity and stay away from Europe. Pendrel's dilemma is that he not only wants to go to Europe, but has a particular incentive to do so. Like his author, he has just acquired—indeed inherited—an old house, the house of the English Pendrels, in Mansfield Square in London. He has, so to speak, been made custodian of the Pendrel family past. Aurora knows she cannot persuade him to stay in America. But she may agree to marry him if, after his adventure, he returns—and then promises never to go again.

The ensuing two or three chapters, all James wrote at the time, take Pendrel to London. His visit to the house in Mansfield Square reminds us of James's own close stock-taking in Lamb House; and in his nightly wanderings he studies an old family portrait of a young man painted in unusual pose. His back is turned, looking, one gathers, to the past rather than the future (as James had turned his back on America). Lighting his candle late one night, Pendrel perceives himself in one of the mirrors holding his candle aloft to light his way. But he now has a shock: it is not

a reflection in a mirror. It is himself, descended from the picture, his
alter ego out of the past, who wants to visit the present. It is Pendrel who
must now turn his back, take the pose in the picture: and the man in the
picture will replace him.

Leaving the house with the certitude that on his return he will
change places with his ghostly double, his dead ancestor, Pendrel has a
long talk with the American Ambassador to London, whom James set
down in the image of James Russell Lowell. When he tries in the dawn
of the twentieth century to explain that he is about to go back to the
nineteenth—to 1820—the Ambassador thinks him harmlessly mad. He
takes Pendrel to the entrance of the house in Mansfield Square: from the
pavement he watches the young man take hold of the knocker, hears the
rat-tat-tat, and sees his supreme pause "before the closing of the door
again placed him on the right side and the whole world as he had known
it on the wrong."

In January 1900 James here abandoned his story at this exciting
moment. Later that summer he picked it up again, but could not go on
with it. He would not return to this manuscript until 1914 made him want
to escape from a terrible present into a remote past. At that point several
further chapters were written, and part of a scenario, in which the history of the Pendrels becomes an almost commonplace tale of the kind
James had written during the Civil War. The vivid past of the novelist,
rather than of the remoter 1820s, is to be felt in these late pages. That
James should come to this at the outbreak of a new war suggests that he
was reliving crucial moments at the time of the story's genesis: the Boer
War, William's presence in Lamb House, the purchase of that historic
house—the uneasy feeling that in acquiring it he was re-enacting the
adventure of his long-ago "passionate pilgrim"—and above all his malaise at the thought he was trapped in the past, *his* past. It was a story too
large for him to write, a plot that would remain unresolved. *The Sense
of the Past* remains a fragment of what might have been an extraordinary ghost-novel, James's ultimate discovery—had that been possible—
of how to complete his journey into himself and his personal past.

There was still another meeting of recent and old experience in *The
Sense of the Past.* In Ralph Pendrel, contemplating himself as a figure
seemingly reflected in a mirror, we may see the visage of the three-day
visitor of the past summer, Hendrik Andersen. During the fleeting hours
spent with the young sculptor, James had felt his own past stirring: he
had *seen* his *alter ego,* "the young man revealed, responsible, conscious,
quite shining out of the darkness." To return to the past was to meet
oneself. The story was hardly a myth of Narcissus. It was the attempt of
an aging man to accept the hard fact of his aging, and to tell himself that

he could be both old and young at the same time. He could possess his past; he need not be swallowed up by it.

The Sense of the Past was Henry James's way of bringing together the essential elements of what he himself called "the Americano-European legend"—*his* legend, the legend of the world he had peopled. The great adventure of his life had been his embrace of Europe—of a past that had set him free—but not without exacting its touch of nightmare. He would borrow from the unfinished novel seven years later for his tale of "The Jolly Corner." For the moment the vision of Hendrik, "shining out of the darkness," remained with him—Hendrik who now had taken a studio in New York and was attempting to make his way in America, the land of the future, while James watched from the land of the past.

A Rage of Wonderment

During that crowded autumn of 1899 and well into the new year James worked—in spite of distractions, anxieties, interruptions—as if pursued by the furies. He wanted to pay for Lamb House and he turned out tale after tale, a series of articles, and then scenarios for two novels which his agent circulated among the publishers. After long hesitation, he had enrolled himself in the "stable" of the literary agent James B. Pinker, who in a very short time made himself indispensable to James. An experienced former magazine editor, Pinker was wise, shrewd, tactful, friendly. He reviewed James's confused copyrights; found new publishers; reopened old relations. James spoke of "the germs of a new career" as Pinker began to place his work.

From the record of that winter of 1899–1900 it seems that for a while James was producing a story a week—and most were sold at Pinker's standard price of £50 per story. "Paste" was sent by James late in the summer; then on 8 September, "The Beldonald Holbein"; 17 September, "Broken Wings"; 24 September, "The Special Type"; 3 October, "another short tale," not named; 11 October, "The Faces" (later called "The Two Faces"); in December, "Miss Gunton of Poughkeepsie" and "The Third Person." The scenario for *The Sense of the Past* was dispatched and an early scenario of *The Ambassadors.* In the thick of winter three more tales were produced, "The Tone of Time," "Flickerbridge" and "The Story in It." When William Heinemann, who had published James's work from *The Spoils of Poynton* to *The Awkward Age,* balked at dealing with an agent, Pinker established new relations for the novelist with Methuen and Constable. The tales of that autumn and winter were rapidly assembled into the volume *The Soft Side* for which Pinker obtained a £100 advance.

In the spring James began another short story, planned at 8,000 to

10,000 words. This one, however, ran away with him. By June it had become a short novel, *The Sacred Fount,* which Pinker sold to Methuen in England, and in America to Scribner, who had long wanted to publish James. The money for the initial payment on Lamb House had been speedily earned. Self-confidence was restored; and James had margin in his bank.

The novel James dispatched to Pinker at the beginning of the summer of 1900 was "fanciful, fantastic," he wrote, "—but very close and sustained, and calculated to minister to curiosity." Read critically, it seems to express, in its elliptical formulations, the discovery by a too discreet and innocent observer, that life is less innocent and less puritanical than the old virtues suggest: that men and women are physical as well as moral beings, that love and passion exact very high prices behind Victorian reticence and avoidance. The narrator wonders in his mental sleuthing just how much men and women gain or lose in their intimate relations. How costly is the sacrifice—if it is a sacrifice? In this brief novel, James seems to have been extending his idea of "what Maisie knew" into his own adult knowing. How much did a novelist like himself, who had always looked away from sex, really know about its ubiquitous presence, its insistent claims?

The Sacred Fount is the last of the experimental series from *The Spoils of Poynton* through the tales of the little girls and the record of their "range of wonderment": James uses the word "range," although one wonders whether he might not have written "rage." In the novel the unnamed narrator is turned loose among the weekenders at Newmarch. We are confined to his observations and theories. Meeting some of the other guests, he is struck by the fact that Mrs. Brissenden, who had married a man much younger than herself, has grown remarkably young. Later he will see that her husband, "poor Briss," has grown appreciably older. Out of this he evolves his hypothesis: people are capable, vampire-like, of draining one another. Another guest, Gilbert Long, hitherto possessed of a banal mind, has become alert, intelligent and witty. The logical narrator decides that someone is being drained by Long of wit and intelligence. His weekend quest is to discover this particular "sacred fount," the one that has ministered to Long. He judges those around him as if they were suspects in a detective story. For one of the guests he does have, however, a marked sympathy. She is his prime "suspect"; once beautiful and intelligent, she now seems drained of life. Her name is May Server. "I saw as I had never seen before what consuming passion can make of the marked mortal on whom, with fixed beak and claws, it has settled as on a prey. . . . Voided and scraped of everything, her shell was merely crushable."

Of all writers, James was the novelist perhaps most in tune with what people said behind the masks they put on. The aggressive emotion that masquerades as a cutting witticism; the euphoria that disguises depression; the sudden slip of the tongue that reveals the opposite of what is intended—James had learned long ago to read "psychologic signs. . . . What's ignoble is the detective and the keyhole." But in *The Sacred Fount* there seems to be a distinct uneasiness: "Have I been right? How can I be sure?" A little voice whispers that omniscient novelists can be wrong as well as right. "People have such a notion of what you embroider on things," Mrs. Brissenden tells the narrator. "You see too much . . . You talk too much . . . You build up houses of cards . . . You overestimate the penetration of others." In the long talk she has late at night with the speculating mental detective, her parting shot is, "I think you're crazy." The effect of this final dialogue is to echo how reality can come barging in and destroy the fine fruits of speculation. "You're costing me a perfect palace of thought," the narrator pleads with Mrs. Brissenden.

In *The Sacred Fount,* the last of his series of tales of curiosity and wonder, James is inquiring into the extent to which man lives not by bare realities but by the embroidery of these realities within his mind. The world of the imagination, he seems to tell us, arrives at its own truths; but it can hold within it the terror of the unreal, the delicate uneasy balance between what is and what might be. "Light or darkness," says the narrator in this novel, "my imagination rides me." The question of "reality" is resolved into a little scene in front of a glass-covered pastel of a young man without eyebrows, like a circus clown, and a pale and livid face. He holds an object, some work of art, that appears on closer examination to be "the representation of a human face, modelled and coloured, in wax, in enamelled metal . . . a complete mask, such as might have been fantastically fitted and worn." One of the spectators calls the picture "the mask of death." The narrator argues that the face in the pastel is more dead than the mask. He would call it "the mask of life." May Server adds a further touch—perhaps out of her own depleted life—by discerning a grimace on the mask: in the cliché of opera, the clown's mask of laughter conceals a breaking heart. But the mask is art—the face is life. And the art which is a grimace and a mask can express—James implies—more life than life itself.

The scene reminds us that the obsessed narrator is trying, in his compulsive way, to arrive at the meaning and unity of his abundant impressions. If the same picture can yield opposite meanings, how real —or how phantasmagoric—are his own "discoveries"? How much does he really see?—how much does he read into what he thinks he has seen? In this novel James inquires into "the high application of the intelligence" involved in modern psychology. The themes of *The Sacred Fount* disengage themselves: the aging process, the invulnerability of art, indeed the "madness of art," which insists on seeing more than the immediate "real"; and the vulnerability of love. One of the most touching figures in the novel is the unhappy May Server, whose children have died; for whom love has died; who flits pathetically from man to man, "the absolute wreck of her storm," yet remains a person to whom "the pale ghost of a special sensibility still clung." She seems almost to be a parable-figure for the other side of her creator, not the intellectual-imaginative side, but that side of James whose children—his fiction, his tales, his plays—seemed to die when launched in the world while he still tried to face society as the "personality" he had been. He had had his good years; he had had his fame. And now he was vulnerable—as vulnerable as the fragile May Server, flitting in her loneliness about the grounds at Newmarch. Strange, beautiful, alienated from the impersonal and the gross, the social falsity, she craves affection, and seeks someone: she needs love. At last James, the egotist and "man of the world," a singular intellectual and artistic phenomenon, was allowing himself to feel not only the beauty of art, into which ugly life constantly intruded, but to recognize that his exquisite "palace of thought" was not enough. One had not "lived" if one had not loved.

James's work had never dealt with love, save as a force destructive of—or in competition with—power and aesthetic beauty. Now, at the very last of the century, when in his loneliness in Lamb House he reached out to his younger friends and mourned the absence of the bright young sculptor, when he saw in the mirror the grey streaks in his once glossy brown-black beard, he attained a new awareness, a new insight. *The Sacred Fount,* this trivial, yet often beautiful tale, embodied the final stage of his "self-therapy." He could now write his last books. The way was clear. He could stop looking at the past, and its entrapments; he could ask himself what uses the past may have for the present. The words that formed on his lips now, that he whispered to himself—or wrote into his notebook—were "too late." Was it "too late"? Out of this old remark of Howells to Jonathan Sturges, in the garden in the rue du Bac, would grow —in the cleared vision of James's sensibility, in his renewed power as artist—the history of the middle-aged American returning to Paris, starting over again the same voyage Henry James had made a quarter of a century before. He had settled then in the French capital, and written a novel about an American in Paris—a romantic tale of an American's quest for the refinement and beauty and nobility of the Old World. Christopher Newman was about to become Lambert Strether.

The Great Relation

Too late? Too late? Turning the pages of one of Turgenev's novels at this time, in the English translation—he had read it long before in French—James drew a pencil line beside the words, "Youth, youth, little dost thou care for anything!" The novel was *First Love*. He was discovering the insolence of youth; he knew himself young in thought and even in strength, and yet it was an anguish to contemplate the ravage of time. "I like growing old: fifty-six!," he had written to Henrietta Reubell, "—but I don't like growing *older*. I quite love my present age and the compensations, simplifications, freedom, independences, memories, advantages of it. But I don't keep it long enough—it passes too quickly."

Shortly after Hendrik's visit, James had begun to reach out to younger friends, offering them the hospitality of his home, the rural distractions of Rye, an anxious avuncular affection. A. C. Benson, second son of the Archbishop of Canterbury, came to spend a night in Lamb House at the beginning of the new century, after receiving a warm invitation, and recorded in his diary a picture of the house and its master. James met him at the station as was his custom, but "looking somewhat cold, tired and old." He was affectionate in his greeting; he patted the younger man on the shoulder, and was "really welcoming, with abundance of *petits soins.*" They dined simply at 7:30 with many apologies about the fare. "He was full of talk, though he looked weary, often passing his hand over his eyes; but he refined and defined, was intricate, magniloquent, rhetorical, humorous, not so much like a talker, but like a writer repeating his technical processes aloud—like a savant working out a problem."

The next morning, Benson wrote,

> He establishes me in a little high-walled white parlour, very comfortable, but is full of fear that I am unhappy. He comes in, pokes the fire, presses a cigarette on me, puts his hand on my shoulder, looks inquiringly at me, and hurries away. His eyes are *piercing.* To see him, when I came down to breakfast this morning, in a kind of Holbein square cap of velvet and black velvet coat, scattering bread on the frozen lawn to the birds was delightful ... We lunched together with his secretary, a young Scot. H.J. ate little, rolled his eyes, waited on us, walked about, talked— finally hurried me off for a stroll before my train. All his instincts are of a kind that makes me feel vulgar—his consideration, his hospitality, care of arrangements, thoughtfulness ...

Another younger man, Morton Fullerton in Paris, had in the novelist's letters been "my dear Fullerton" from the beginning. Now he is addressed as "dearest boy," and the letters are warm—and importunate. Had Fullerton been working too hard? He surely needed a rest what with the Dreyfus case and the vagaries of French politics—of course at Lamb House! "You shall be surrounded here with every circumstance of tranquillity and comfort, of rest and consecration. You talk of the *real thing*. But that is the real thing. *I* am the real thing." Fullerton was ready to concede this: but he was embedded in his Gallic way of life. He sent James the latest French books. He responded to his affectionate letters. But he seldom left Paris.

To Fullerton, late in 1900, James wrote one of his grandiose letters, a confessional document couched in the majesty of the late style. Fullerton, having written that once again he was prevented from visiting Lamb House, had then asked James one of his thoughtful questions—what had been the "port" from which the novelist believed he had taken sail, as it were, the *point de départ* of his life? James first expressed his regret that Fullerton could not visit him. Was there some "obscurity of trouble" in his young friend's tone? James wondered whether he mightn't be of help: "Hold me then *you* with any squeeze; grip me with any grip; press me with any pressure; trust me with any trust." He then rose to the larger question.

> The port from which I set out was, I think, that of *the essential loneliness of my life*—and it seems to be the port also, in sooth, to which my course again finally directs itself! This loneliness (since I mention it)—what is it still but the deepest thing about one? Deeper, about *me,* at any rate, than anything else; deeper than my "genius," deeper than my "discipline", deeper than my pride, deeper, above all, than the deep counterminings of art.

Within this awareness of his "essential loneliness," the loneliness of being which was both his art and his alienation as artist, James now moved towards a greater and deeper understanding of human experience. In such fantasies as *The Sacred Fount* we see him still in bewilderment before the exigencies, depredations and vulnerabilities of what he spoke of as "the great relation" between man and woman—in a word, love; his mind could grasp what his feelings were still probing. Two essays on Italian writers, corallary to *The Sacred Fount,* express what lay closest to his thought. Life was not a matter of who slept with whom, or of tearing passions to tatters, as he put it in his essay on Matilde Serao, the Neapolitan novelist; one could not get to know people simply by their sexual "convulsions and spasms." It was not "the passion of hero and heroine that gives, that can ever give interest to the heroine and the hero, but it is they themselves, with the ground they stand on and the objects enclosing them, who give interest to their passion." And if, as in Serao's novels of "passion," the writer begins to treat physical sex in a close and intimate way, a strange thing occurs:

> the effect . . . of the undertaking to give *passione* its whole place is that by the operation of a singular law no place speedily appears to be left for anything else; and the effect of that in turn is greatly to modify, first, the truth of things, and second, with small delay, what may be left of their beauty.

In an essay on D'Annunzio, written in the autumn of 1903, James analyzed the dangers of an art which blows aesthetic gold-dust over life's uglinesses, and masks with serious beauty the empty passions of persons possessed of nothing but their senses. Love in D'Annunzio is a simple physical act; it has no relation to human values. Faced with the erotic in two Italian novelists of the time, James now speaks of the wholeness and totality of love that will find expression ultimately in his symbolism of *The Golden Bowl.* He does not espouse the aesthetic view, which would seek beauty in order to look away from ugliness. His requirement is for both ugliness and beauty, the lies and deceptions as well as the truths of life; for only by knowing the lies is it possible to know the truth.

At the end of the essay he uses a striking image to characterize the emptiness of novels that isolate the physical from the act of loving:

> Shut out from the rest of life, shut out from all fruition and assimilation, it has no more dignity than—to use a homely image—the boots and shoes that we see in the corridors of promiscuous hotels, standing, often in double pairs, at the doors of rooms.

Max Beerbohm, in one of his celebrated cartoons of Henry James, would portray the bewildered novelist, heavy-jowled, kneeling in a hotel corridor before two pairs of shoes, a man's and a woman's, placed beside the shut door. The state of bewilderment too literally portrayed in the witty cartoon belonged in reality to the mental detective narrator of *The Sacred Fount,* not to the Henry James of the new century. James was pleading that the novel use the fullness of life, and attempt new divinations and discoveries. D'Annunzio illustrated for James how much a novelist could overlook: he had seen "neither duration, nor propagation, nor common kindness, nor common consistency, with other relations, common congruity with the rest of life." With these views James expressed his faith in the beauty and elasticity of the fictional form. For novels fulfilled one of man's deepest needs. "Till the world is an unpeopled void," he would say in another essay, taking Stendhal's metaphor, "there will be an image in the mirror."

In these essays, James was giving intellectual utterance to feelings adumbrated in his stories—and in this meeting of sentience and idea, his

intellectual power and his new openness to feeling, he showed his readi-
ness for a *vita nuova.* In his "deep well of unconscious cerebration" he
had moved slowly from inner sickness to health. Step by step James's
imagination had found, had wrought, the healing substance of his art—
the strange, bewildering and ambiguous novels in which somehow he
had recovered his identity so that he might be again a strong and func-
tioning artist. In this process he had opened himself up—life aiding—to
feeling and to love. He was teaching himself to accept old age, and to face
loneliness, and turned again and again for solace to the discipline and
difficulty of his craft. In his indirect soothing of his soul, the frigid wall
of his egotism had been breached to an enlarged vision of the world, and
a larger feeling of the world's human warmth. It emerges in his correspondence from this time on: he is less distant, looser, less formal. He
writes with more emotional freedom.

During the century's first summer, when James picked up again *The
Sense of the Past,* a short struggle showed him this was not what he
wanted to write. He wanted to write the story, long buried in his notebook,
about the middle-aged American who arrives in Paris wondering
whether he is rediscovering human experience and life's values "too
late." With his message of "live all you can"—his *cri de coeur* that was
now Henry James's as well—his protagonist would express James's new
will to live and create. He was no longer willing to write his international
ghost story; he no longer felt trapped by his past. And one day that spring,
confronting himself again in the mirror, he had a sudden impulse—he
would shave off his beard. It had hidden his face since the days of the
Civil War. He was prepared now to shed an old identity, to divorce himself from his youth, his past, to be a new man—and in a new century.

On 12 May 1900 he wrote to his brother William that he had been
unable to bear any longer his increased hoariness, "it had suddenly
begun these three months since, to come out quite white and made me
feel, as well as look, so old." Now he felt *"forty* and clean and light." He
had made his face correspond to a kind of physical youth he could feel
again. A new face for the new century! Now the massive forehead, the
great dome, the smooth cheeks, the strong line of the nose, the full sensuous lips, and the deep blue penetrating eyes showed to the world another,
a stronger visage—that of the Henry James whom the younger men coming up around him would address as *cher maître, maestro*—master. And
daily now, in the brightening summer that heralded the twentieth century, *The Ambassadors* took its shape in the Garden Room of Lamb
House.

PART SEVEN The Illusion of Freedom

1900–1905

> Live all you can; it's a mistake
> not to. It doesn't so much matter
> what you do in particular, so long as
> you have your life. If you haven't
> had that, what *have* you had?
>
> HENRY JAMES

NOTES

ON

NOVELISTS

Vie de Province

On afternoons in the late autumn and early winter, when the roads were sufficiently dry, the clean-shaven master of Lamb House would descend from his hilltop into the High Street, wrapped in a heavy coat. Sometimes he wore a small peaked cap; sometimes a felt hat. There was invariably a touch of color—in his knotted cravat, or, if he unbuttoned his coat, in a show of orange or blue waistcoat. He walked massively, carrying one of his many sticks. Behind him, waddling slowly, was one of his dogs—say Maximilian, his dachshund, successor to the long-lived Tosca of the De Vere Gardens time. When James walked alone, he was unsmiling and grave, greeting old and young alike with deliberate courtesy. Sometimes his typist walked with him; sometimes he was accompanied by a guest. On occasion James walked to Playden, where he had lived briefly in 1896; or along the sea by Camber, past the golf course and the grazing sheep; or he would take the road to picturesque and desolate Winchelsea. He still bicycled; on some days, dressed in knickerbockers and a jacket of black and white stripes, he would sweep off to more distant towns or along the salt flats of the Cinque Ports.

In the better season of the year he found other occupation out of doors. Early in his life at Lamb House he had set about improving his garden; with his purchase of the house he felt even more strongly that he wanted as much vernal beauty as possible in the private acre outside his French doors. But he felt himself "densely ignorant." He barely knew a dahlia from a mignonette. To Miss Muir Mackenzie, whom he had met once at Winchelsea, he turned for expert advice. Presently she was suggesting that certain kinds of tobacco leaves might be decorative; and then some crocuses at strategic spots in the lawn. James found himself ordering bulbs and roses, and his gardener George Gammon industriously carried out his and Miss Mackenzie's designs. The time would come when Lamb House flowers would win prizes in the local flower show.

Within his first year and a half—that is from mid-1898 to 1900—James had lived himself into the provincial life of Rye. He quickly became a local "fixture." The shopkeepers knew him; the local gentry dined him; with characteristic English respect for privacy, he was registered by many of the townsfolk simply as an odd literary gentleman of great courtliness, who often met his guests at the station himself. Neither James nor his guests aroused curiosity; the town was more interested in golf than in literature. But when in June 1900 Lord and Lady Wolseley came over from their nearby country home at Glynde to visit their novelist friend, the word got round quickly that the great soldier, victor of the Ashantee, was in Rye; his afternoon's visit coincided with the news of the occupation of Pretoria, and a wave of patriotic emotion seized the town. An informal delegation of officials and leading citizens knocked at the canopied door and asked permission to pay their respects. "Rye rather lacked history," Henry wrote to Lady Wolseley, "now she *has* it. You didn't leave me where you found me. I am inches and inches higher."

Except on this occasion, when national grandeur touched modest Lamb House, the establishment and its tenant blended into the town. James was on good terms with local organizations and generous to local charities. And when the local clergy asked him for favors, he was only too willing to help. During the summer of 1900 he billeted a young curate when the Bishop of Chichester came to Rye for certain ordinations. To Lady Wolseley James wrote that the priest fasted "on fish, eggs, vegetables, tarts, claret, cigarettes, coffee and liqueurs," which the generous Lamb House larder and cellar provided. He was happy to be hospitable. But finding himself "face to face with him, at meals," was trying. He would on the whole, he remarked, have been happier to billet a soldier.

These small moments of involvement in rural life were sufficiently limited. "The days depart and pass, laden somehow like processional camels—across the desert of one's solitude." He felt severed from his old life—"the blessed Kensington fields" for which, as he confessed in his New Year letter of 1900 to Rhoda Broughton, he now felt "so homesick." He had originally planned to live in Rye only half the year; but he had sublet his De Vere Gardens flat (and later, in the summer of 1902, disposed of the lease), so that he would have had to use clubs and hotels in the city. During his second winter in the country, he found himself pining for London lamplight and the sound of its buses. To Edmund Gosse he spoke of going up to London late in 1900 for a real go at town life—"I shall have been confined to this hamlet for two and a half years on end —save for three or four months abroad. You *must,* all, take me to Madame Tussaud's." To Mrs. W. K. Clifford, one of his oldest and most cherished London friends, he wrote in May 1900 of his domestic comforts in Rye, but then: "it would be so infinitely nicer to be sitting by your fire and tasting your charity—and your Benedictine."

James had always known how to be alone; he had sought and invited solitude. But he also had always known how to avoid—urban dweller that he was—a feeling of loneliness. The cities, and London in particular, provided people, theaters, tea-talk, the pleasant privacy or gregariousness of his clubs, as he wished. Now in Rye he suffered "for want of social, domestic, intellectual air." And yet he was tied to Lamb House even in the winter: his typewriter was not easily movable. A trip to London meant divorce from his work, and his writing was as necessary to him as the social, domestic, intellectual air of which he spoke; indeed it was more than necessary, for he was trying to work off his book contracts and pay for his house. These were the conflicts of his new "exile," an intermittent debate between the loneliness of Rye and the life of London.

To an outsider it might have seemed that Rye had been for so urban a man a grave mistake; its simplified life could not meet the needs of so complex a being. On the other hand, the world owes to the long periods of his solitary encaged state some of his finest writings. The dictation in the morning; the recuperative walk in the afternoon when possible; the re-reading and revision of what had been dictated; the preparation for the next morning's work; the planning of new stories; the writing of scenarios; the long evenings of thought and toil before he was ready to meet his typist once more for renewed endeavor: out of the hours of Rye's loneliness, there took shape and were written within four years the three last novels, the summit of his creation.

In the end, after long trial and much work, Rye would cease to be possible as a continuous abode, and James again established an apartment in London. But at the threshold of the decade he obtained his metropolitan perch which served him well and gave him a place for temporary work. In the autumn of 1900 a room at the Reform Club conveniently fell vacant, and he had "a town-cradle" for his declining years. He refurbished the room, installed his own bed, new blinds, new curtains. He kept enough things there so that he could come up from Rye with minimal luggage. The room, high up over Carlton House Terrace, looked at embassies and lordly houses. "Nothing could be more *chic,*" he proclaimed. It made him feel less of an outsider. Nevertheless, once in London, he was divorced from the continuity of his work; even though at the Reform he also installed a typewriter and was able to dictate according to habit, he tended to loiter and ramble and seek mild sociabilities. The general effect of going up to town at first was to make him want his work desk in Rye; and the effect of Rye was to make him pine for London. The city was no longer wholly possible. But neither was the country.

An Innocent Abroad

In March of 1900, James had descended on London for a brief holiday. He was surprised to be greeted by friends and acquaintances "almost as if I had returned from African or Asian exile." He liked to feel the pavement under foot again; he window-shopped; he wandered into back streets; he browsed in the book shops; he dined out every night. He went to see Sargent's new painting of the Wyndham sisters, "vast and dazzling"; it reminded James of the feeling he had had at a fair when a woman was shot out of the mouth of a cannon—its force made him feel "weak and foolish." With Sargent he went to call on Edwin Austin Abbey, working on one of his large Shakespearian paintings, "diabolically clever and effective." "I came away biting my thumb, of course, and with my ears burning with the sense of how it's not the age of my dim trade."

His trade was almost at a standstill. Publishers shook their heads sadly and thinned their lists; the effects of the Boer War were being felt everywhere. London was filled with mourners. One day his thirteen-year-old niece Peggy, with three of her playmates, came to the city from Harrow, where she was living, and James took a box at the Biograph to show them the primitive newsreels of the war. The pictures, it was later learned, were faked. The mobile camera was yet to come. Peggy, true to her father's anti-imperialism, was pro-Boer. She seemed surprised that her uncle wasn't. His identification with England had been long; he was, however, sufficiently American to decry "the fetish-worship of the Queen."

The novelty of London wore off quickly, and at the end of seventeen days James was back in "little restful, red-roofed uncomplicated Rye." But having broken his spell of absence, he made a second descent on London in mid-May. In the interval between visits he had removed his beard. Writing about his changed appearance he remarked to a correspondent, "still, it will be always I." Nevertheless it seemed a new "I" that descended from the train at Charing Cross and now brought his clean-shaven countenance into the familiar drawing-rooms of Mayfair.

One afternoon James went to call on a friend of his Newport youth, Helena De Kay, the wife of Richard Watson Gilder, editor of the *Century*. Mrs. Gilder had a special claim on James's affections: she was a sister of his old Venetian friend Mrs. Bronson, and she had been a close friend of Minny Temple. Before her tea-hour fire James encountered the grizzled, white-maned, white-clad Samuel Langhorne Clemens, most famous—as Mark Twain—of America's "innocents" abroad. Their paths had crossed before, but they faced each other now as changed men. Both were in late middle life, both had passed through long battles with private demons. The nineties had been as hard on the world-seeking prosperous Mark Twain as on the privacy-seeking Henry James. The latter's clean-shaven face was symbolic of his recovery and awareness of the approaching century. Mark Twain was announcing that "the twentieth century is a stranger to me."

Twenty years before, in 1879, during the days of James's constant dining out, he had met Mark Twain a number of times in various London mansions, "a most excellent pleasant fellow, what they call here very 'quaint.' " James and Twain had been then at the height of their first fame. They met again in 1897, when James was teaching himself to dictate directly to the typewriter. Mark Twain wrote to Howells, their mutual friend, "I was amused when I was in London last fall, to have James tell me that he had taken to dictating all his fiction, because he had heard that I always dictated. He makes it go, but if there could be anything worse for me than a typewriter, it would be a human typewriter." Twain loved the "damned human race" or he would not have had so much fault to find with it; and Henry could not talk to a machine that did not have a human being beside it.

Mark Twain and Henry James were not by nature destined ever to be intimate. Twain was outgoing, expansive, capable of great exuberance. James was inward-turned, ruminative, secretive. No two American geniuses were more dissimilar: in their sense of humor, James was highly condensed, epigrammatic, and private; Mark Twain was broad, visceral, and public. Both were lovers of the truth; both critical of their fellow-Americans. Mark Twain had gratified his countrymen by criticizing Europe in *Innocents Abroad.* James had shocked them by making himself a critical analyst of American innocence. The two writers had great respect for each other, even though Mark Twain had once said he would rather "be damned to John Bunyan's heaven" than read *The Bostonians.* James, reading Mark Twain's *Life on the Mississippi,* had found in it the presence of "sublimity."

When the two men met in London in 1900 Mark Twain had been living abroad—Switzerland, France, Austria, Sweden, England, with brief trips to the United States. To Henry James he seems to have talked largely of his symptoms, probably coming to them through Henry's telling him that his brother William had returned to Bad Nauheim for another "cure." Twain, who was at this phase all for osteopathy, had recently been to Henrick Kellgren's health establishment in Sweden. Kellgren could cure anything, Twain said. He told Henry he had been in correspondence with William, whom he had met in Florence in 1892, and had offered him medical advice. He also discoursed on "albumen." The talk was rather confused. When Twain spoke of Kellgren, Henry thought he was referring to Lord Kelvin ("Why Sweden?" he asked of William's wife), and told Alice that Twain had given him "a muddled and confused glimpse of Lord Kelvin, Albumen, Sweden and half a dozen other things on which I was prevented from afterwards bringing him to book."

Mark Twain was eight years older than Henry; and his best work was done. James's greatest work was about to be written. In the future they would be archetypal figures in the history of American innocence. In the novel on which James was now embarked—a novel that would confront America and Europe, provincialism and cosmopolitanism, innocence and experience—Lambert Strether would hardly be a Mark Twain. He would be much closer to Howells, and even to Henry himself—the Henry who listened confusedly to Twain's hypochondriacal babble. But a little touch of this babble would be imported into *The Ambassadors* in the "sacred rage" of the dyspeptic Waymarsh. In James's original plan for the novel, we discover that the character was first named Waymark.

A Natural Peculiarity

Ford Madox Hueffer, son of a German musicologist and grandson, on the English side, of the Pre-Raphaelite painter Ford Madox Brown, had called on Henry James during the summer of 1896 when the novelist first discovered Rye. James had just moved into the rented Vicarage and Hueffer—who would later be known as Ford Madox Ford—came to lunch one September day with an introduction from Mrs. W. K. Clifford. James received the tall, lean, blond young man, then twenty-three, with his customary civility. He chatted with him about his relatives and interrogated him about his literary ambitions. By Hueffer's testimony, Smith, the red-nosed butler, served an efficient meal while markedly tipsy. James sent the young man away with perhaps less than his usual avuncular tenderness for aspirants to literature. And there was no immediate invitation to return.

Hueffer himself only vaguely remembered the Old Vicarage. In his vast recollections a quarter of a century later he recorded a first meeting with the clean-shaven James in Rye, where he had gone with Joseph Conrad—but that was in the era of the motor-car. Later he recalled the bearded James of 1896. His memories of this and other meetings are scrambled. Hueffer readily confessed to "a large carelessness" of recall, insisting, however, that he was not reporting literal fact. He was, he explained, "an impressionist." His impressions, however, were a strange amalgam of half-truths, vague recollections, anecdotes garnered from reading, and other persons' memories. Thus he remembered the color of Lamb House as gray, and said it was built of stone, forgetting that its characteristic russet was derived from weathered brick.

Hueffer's tendency to change his own name was symptomatic of a lifelong quest for an identity. Baptized Ford Hermann Hueffer, he later adopted his mother's name of Madox. During another phase, he claimed he was Baron Hueffer von Aschendorf. The final shift to Ford Madox Ford occurred after the First World War when he wanted to forget his German antecedents. Under this name, the writings of Henry James aiding, he made his long friendship with "the Master" the very center of his myth through four volumes of self-inflating but genial inventions and half-truths.

Whether the American novelist recognized that he had invented Hueffer long before he met him, it would be hard to say. In the early 1880s James wrote an artful tale simply titled "The Liar," about a Colonel Capadose, who "lies about the time of day, about the name of his hatter." It is quite disinterested. He is not in the least a scoundrel, "there's no harm in him and no bad intention. . . . He simply can't give you a straight answer." Like James's Capadose, Hueffer was inclined to a mixture of the correct and the extravagant; he had good manners and yet could tell stories in bad taste. Also like Colonel Capadose, he inspired affection. His "natural peculiarity" was forgiven by many devoted friends because it testified to an overflow of life and genial spirits. Hueffer would be kind and generous to many young writers; and from James and Conrad, with whom he collaborated, he borrowed a high seriousness about the art of fiction.

A slender thread of fact informs some of Hueffer's Jamesian gossip; other details were culled from his reading of *Partial Portraits* or *Notes on Novelists,* and became a kind of free rewrite of James's own cautious reminiscence of some of the French novelists he had known. In his late essay on the French master, which is wholly complimentary, James tells us that Flaubert wore "up to any hour of the afternoon that long, collo-quial dressing-gown, with trousers to match, which one has always as-sociated with literature in France—the uniform really of freedom of talk." He was thinking of the way in which French writers are often described as *en pantoufles.* In the repertoire of Hueffer, it emerges that James hated Flaubert because the French writer had had the indecency to welcome him in a bath-robe. Reading of James's correspondence with Mrs. Humphry Ward about how novels should be written, Hueffer said James always corrected that lady's manuscripts. He pictured James in Rye as practicing black magic—or so he said the townsfolk believed. He told how a murderer once confessed his crime to James. He also made James out to have been a financial supporter of the *Yellow Book;* and said *Guy Domville* was booed because the audience did not like to pay for its programs. One of his most charming myths was that James telegraphed

Wanamaker's in Philadelphia to have apple butter and pumpkin pie sent to England to the dying Stephen Crane.

In this way James was given legendary form by Hueffer's shaky ego. There was a certain pathos in Hueffer's need to stand in the good graces of the Master, and in his strange swagger and boast of later years. If it is true that James described him to Conrad as *"votre ami, le jeune homme modest,"* the Master's remark may have had a certain character- istic irony. Modesty was not one of Hueffer's outstanding qualities. He claimed, for instance, to have been the "original" of Merton Densher in *The Wings of the Dove*—a claim based largely, it seems, on Densher's being "longish, leanish, fairish."

Hueffer described James as "the most masterful man I have ever met," and this probably was true. To which he added, with equal truth, that "I do not think that, till the end of his days, he regarded me as a serious writer." James did offer qualified praise for *Poems for Pictures* which Hueffer had sent him. Thanking him for his "so curious and interesting book of verses," James said he found some of them "terribly natural and true and 'right,' drawn from the real wretchedness of things." He ended this letter, one of his less impersonal missives to Hueffer, by asking him to stop by, if he happened to pass his way.

In one of his essays Hueffer remarked of James, "I think I will, after reflection, lay claim to a very considerable degree of intimacy." He did make this claim; and it remains highly at variance with the available testimony. James's secretary recorded that James once made her jump a ditch in order to avoid an encounter with Hueffer on the Winchelsea road; on another occasion he quickly pulled her behind a tree, till Hueffer had walked by. There is also the testimony of a Rye neighbor, a writer, Archibald Marshall. In his memoirs he relates "how very coldly Hueffer's name was received." There had been some question of an invi- tation that would "bring that young man down upon me again" and James exclaimed to Marshall, "I said to myself, No! and again No!"

Flowing into Hueffer's mythology was Conrad's admiration of James, and the worship of him by Hueffer's wife Elsie and her Garnett friends, especially Olivia Rayne Garnett, who had a curious "fixation" on the American novelist. Two years before she ever set eyes on James, Olivia Garnett recorded in her diary: "I had a dream this morning: Henry James looked up at me from writing and said smiling: 'You know, life isn't ONLY reality, it's a small part of a great whole.' I believed him and awoke." Later we find her working on a story "of what it would be like to love and be loved by Henry James." Finally, in an entry of November 1901, Miss Garnett relates how, when visiting the Hueffers at Winchelsea, she was summoned with Mrs. Hueffer to tea at Lamb House. Elsie

Hueffer describes to James how Conrad and Hueffer are collaborating on *The Inheritors.* James looks at Olivia Garnett. He speaks of the dissimilar traditions of Hueffer and Conrad, and how "inconceivable" such collaboration was. "To me," said James (and Miss Garnett later records it), "this is like a bad dream which one relates at breakfast."

The diarist meekly added, "we all munched bread and butter and no more was said on the subject."

A Master Mariner

Ford Madox Hueffer moved to Winchelsea early in 1901, and during the next two years Joseph Conrad visited him frequently, for they were collaborating on *Romance.* It was during this period that Conrad "haunted" Winchelsea and, as James said, Winchelsea "in discretion" haunted Rye. The novelist continued to marvel at Hueffer's collaboration; he had a certain sense of the unsounded depths of Conrad; he could not reconcile them with the shallows of Hueffer. On occasion, Conrad alone, or sometimes with Hueffer, knocked at the canopied portal of Lamb House for a tea-time talk or an afternoon's walk with the Master. James would take Conrad's arm and start off with him along the road, leaving Hueffer and James's nephew Billy to bring up the rear. "Hueffer babbled," the frustrated nephew recalled, "and I didn't listen. I wanted to hear what the great men were saying up ahead, but there I was stuck with Hueffer. Occasionally a word or two would drift back and what I always heard was—French!" The two novelists, the American and the Pole, discussed the form and future of the English novel in the language of art and diplomacy—and with appropriate gestures. So it would always be between them—a mask of politeness, a kind of guarded "distance," a mixture of languages and of friendliness and anxiety.

Hueffer insisted that James actively disliked Conrad; but it would be more accurate to say that he was simply troubled by him—by his nervousness, his "temperament" and the signals James picked up of a deep morbidity. The Pole and the American exchanged compliments and books. James praised Conrad's early works. On his side, Conrad always saluted James as *cher maître* and in the end as "very dear Master." James responded by disclosing to him a few of the secrets of his writing desk, something he seldom did. James honored Conrad the craftsman but was uneasy about the man. He spoke of him as "curious" and "interesting," or as "the interesting and remarkable Conrad." On a later occasion he spoke of Conrad as "that poor queer man." This was not condescension. James was saying—he who prided himself on his insights—that he couldn't quite fathom the gifted Pole.

They met when Conrad was thirty-nine and James fifty-three. Both were occupied at that moment with a world that seemed to them "illusion." James had been in the depths of despair after his failure in the theater; Conrad was trying to understand his two decades of seafaring and to find an outlet for his inner nightmares of violence in the writing of fiction. Józef Teodor Konrad Nalecz Korzeniowski had left Poland in 1874 "as a man gets into a dream." He had been living that dream ever since, attempting to understand and describe, as he would later say to James, "the poignant reality of illusion." James had also come to wonder about the phantasmagoria of being, but it led him always back to immediate realities—the "real, the tideless deep" of man.

The first gesture had been made by Conrad as early as 1896. He debated whether to send James his second book, *An Outcast of the Islands,* fearing he might be thought "impudent." He finally dispatched the volume, writing on the flyleaf the equivalent of a letter. "I address you across a vast space," he wrote to James. He had read his novels while sailing many seas. James's characters, "Exquisite Shades, with live hearts and clothed in the wonderful garment of your prose," had stood "consoling by my side under many skies. They have lived with me, faithful and serene—with the bright serenity of Immortals. And to you thanks are due for such glorious companionship." The inscription was flowery; yet it seemed deeply felt. James liked it. He also liked the book. He waited for a few weeks, and when *The Spoils of Poynton* was published, he dispatched one of the first copies to Conrad in February 1897, inscribing it "Joseph Conrad, in dreadfully delayed but very grateful acknowledgment of an offering singularly generous and beautiful." Conrad had not expected such spontaneous acceptance. The American did not let the matter rest with this exchange of books. He was curious about the mariner novelist and he sent a lively note suggesting Conrad come to lunch.

They lunched on 25 February 1897 in De Vere Gardens and the master mariner got a sense of the established power of James's literary life. We can imagine the two face to face. Both were short stocky men. James was all repose and assurance. Conrad, with his head tucked between his shoulders, looked at James with eyes which somehow, for all their penetration, sought the very "heart of darkness." The man who would write a tale of such a search faced the man who would write "The Beast in the Jungle." The two stories speak for the two temperaments. Conrad, making the descent into the irrational jungle of himself, James fearing the irrationality, anxiously on guard against the beasts that might leap—yet knowing that the beasts were those of his own mind.

If we do not know the precise nature of their talk we know that James would speak of the "independent nobleness" in Conrad's work and the "moral radiance" that he apparently did not find in the man. He got from Conrad a vivid sense of long lonely vigils on ships in distant waters, of landfall in the dark, of adventures such as he had learned of only in books or from men of action. "I read you," James would write to Conrad, "as I listen to rare music—with the deepest depths of surrender." This would not always be so. Conrad on his side liked the nobility of James's world and the way in which he created characters with "fine consciences." Above all, James's people rode always to moral victory: "His mankind is delightful," Conrad would write. "It is delightful in its tenacity; it refuses to own itself beaten."

Conrad's admiration was not lost on James. Writing to the Royal Literary Fund in 1902 in support of a grant to Conrad, he said that *"The Nigger of the Narcissus* is in my opinion the very finest and strongest picture of the sea and sea-life that our language possesses—the masterpiece in a whole great class; and *Lord Jim* runs it very close." And he wrote:

> When I think that such completeness, such intensity of expression has been arrived at by a man not born to our speech, but who took it up, with singular courage, from necessity and sympathy, and has laboured at it heroically and devotedly, I am equally impressed with the fine persistence and the intrinsic success.

The Fund in due course bestowed the sum Conrad needed, £300.

When in 1906 Conrad dispatched *The Mirror of the Sea,* his book of reminiscences, to James, he once more filled the end-paper with an epistolary inscription in French, saying, "Your friendly eye will know how to distinguish in these pages that piety of memory which has guided the groping phrase and the ever-rebel pen." James responded that whatever Conrad might say of his difficult medium and his "rebel pen," he knocked about "in the wide waters of expression like the raciest and boldest of privateers":

> You stir me to amazement and you touch me to tears, and I thank the powers who so mysteriously let you loose with such sensibilities, into such an undiscovered country—*for* sensibility . . .

He concluded with "I pat you, my dear Conrad, very affectionately and complacently on the back, and am yours very constantly Henry James." *Complacently,* we must assume, for being so admirable a disciple, so admirably a fellow-artist.

Dissimilar as the two writers were, and distinctive as Conrad's genius was, James played a much greater role in Conrad's craftsmanship than has perhaps been allowed. "The Turn of the Screw" and "Heart of Darkness" appeared within a year of each other; and both tales begin in the same way—the quiet circle, the atmosphere of mystery and gloom, with the hint of terrible evil, the reflective narrator, the retrospective method, the recall of crucial episodes. And perhaps from the "Mr. Quint is dead" of the ghostly tale there sounds in Conrad a powerful echo, "Mistah Kurtz—he dead." The stories are as different as their authors, but they suggest that Conrad went to school to the works of Henry James —and notably learned James's devices for obtaining distance from his materials. A decade later, James would criticize Conrad's excesses in indirect narration; perhaps the Master felt that his lesson had been too well learned. In his 1914 article, "The Younger Generation," James paid Conrad the compliment of taking him seriously; for Conrad alone, in the array of writers he dealt with, he reserved the title of "genius." But when it came to matters of technique, Conrad was also "absolutely alone as the votary of the way to do a thing that shall make it undergo most doing." Analyzing the Polish writer's modes of narration in *Chance,* James complained about the "prolonged hovering flight of the subjective over the outstretched ground of the case exposed." Taking his image from the recently developed machines of flight—for he had seen, one day at Rye, Blériot's plane over the Channel—he likened Conrad's narration within narration (an extension of James's own devices) to a series of airplane shadows which create an eclipse upon "the intrinsic colour and form and whatever, upon the passive expanse."

In forgetting that Conrad (by then fifty-one) was hardly of the "younger" generation of which he was speaking, and in failing to mention other works which had pleased him more than *Chance,* James understandably hurt Conrad. "I may say with scrupulous truth," wrote the latter, "that this was the *only time* a criticism affected me painfully." Long afterwards, when James was dead, Conrad found himself describing to John Quinn, the Irish-American patron of the arts, how he had felt about the American novelist. He could not bring himself to say positively that James had liked him; perhaps the memory of his hurt over *Chance* made him cautious. "I had a profound affection for him," he told Quinn, adding that James "accepted it as if it were something worth having. At any rate that is the impression I have." Then, almost as if he were ruminating aloud, he said James "wasn't a man who would pretend" to like someone. What need had he?—even if he had been capable of the pretense?

A Ghostly Rental

Henry James met H. G. Wells and Stephen Crane during 1898 and within months both became his neighbors—Wells at Sandgate on the Kentish coast, across Romney Marsh from Rye, and Crane at Brede, in Sussex, an eight-mile bicycle run from Lamb House. Legend has it that Crane and James met at a bohemian party in London, at which a Madame Zipango poured champagne into James's top hat. James protested this affront to the symbol of his dignity. Crane is said to have spirited the offender away from the party and addressed himself tactfully to salvaging the hat and soothing the Master. They had been discussing literary style. Crane may have been alluding to this incident a few days later when he spoke of seeing James "make a holy show of himself in a situation that—on my honor—would have been simple to an ordinary man." He added, "it seems impossible to dislike him. He is so kind to everybody."

Crane's friend Harold Frederic, a fellow-American and London correspondent of the *New York Times,* took a less generous view of the rituals of the Master. A rough-and-ready newspaperman who had written a best-selling novel, *The Damnation of Theron Ware,* he characterized James as "an effeminate old donkey who lives with a herd of other donkeys around him and insists on being treated as if he were the Pope." He spoke too of James's "usual lack of a sense of generosity." Both Crane and Frederic lived "hard" and died young—Frederic of a stroke that very year. He had maintained two households and left illegitimate as well as legitimate children, and would have been astonished to learn that the man he described as lacking generosity was among the first to sign an appeal for money for the illegitimate children. James wrote to Cora Crane, Stephen's common-law wife, "deeper than I can say is my commiseration of these beautiful children." If he passed judgment on this group of American journalist-novelists, it was not that they led bohemian lives but that they made their bohemianism an excuse for poor art. When Cora Crane sent him Frederic's posthumous work, *The Market Place,* he read it "with a lively sense of what Harold Frederic might have done if he had lived—and above all lived (and therefore worked) differently."

James's meeting with Wells had in it less of the bohemian and more of the dignity of letters. The younger writer had been enjoying increasing prosperity with his tales about man in time and space. In the summer of 1898, on a bicycle trip with his wife along the Kentish coast, he had collapsed at New Romney with a high fever. An old kidney ailment had declared itself, and he spent a number of weeks under medical care. In August there appeared at his cottage two important-looking middle-aged gentlemen, wheeling their bicycles. Wells recognized Henry James. He had seen him on the night of *Guy Domville.* The other visitor was Edmund Gosse. They had cycled over from Lamb House to inquire about his health. Wells was then thirty-two; James fifty-five. The younger writer was touched—and flattered—to have two outstanding members of the literary establishment show such a kindly interest in his welfare. Some years later Wells put two and two together and realized that James and Gosse had been quietly ascertaining, on behalf of the Royal Literary

Fund, whether the younger writer was in financial need.

From this time, and through the Edwardian years, Wells and James were excellent friends. James sent Wells "The Turn of the Screw" which was published that year, and Wells sent James *The Time Machine.* From then on he bestowed all his books on the Master, who invariably offered a full-dress critique. He liked the utopias for their abundance of ideas and originality; but he candidly complained that Wells was not concerned sufficiently with art in his fiction. Wells, in an anonymous review, before he met James, had spoken of the American's "ground-glass style," but admitted that James's characters were "'living men and women." James's main criticism of Wells was that he failed to create such men and women.

In the summer of their meeting, Wells decided to stay on in Kent. He occupied Beach Cottage at Sandgate, and later built himself a solid brick house, Spade House, symbol of his growing prosperity. Both Wells and James, during the early months of their friendship, would be spectators of the passage at nearby Brede House of Stephen Crane and his honey-haired Cora.

James had known about Crane some time before he met him. He knew that Howells had praised *Maggie: A Girl of the Streets* and he had read *The Red Badge of Courage,* seeing in it qualities he associated with Zola. James quickly appreciated Crane's intensity, his industry, his dedication. He belonged to a new breed of literary journalists who ministered to what James called "our growing world-hunger" by going to scenes of war and violence. When James met him Crane had returned from the Greco-Turkish War, and was on his way to the Spanish-American War. It was after his brief and violent experiences in the Cuban war, and the Puerto Rico campaign—heedless where his personal safety was concerned—that he returned to England.

Crane and the twice-married Cora Taylor (as she was then known) had been living together ever since the Greco-Turkish War. They had met at her high-class bawdy house, "Hotel de Dream," in Jacksonville, and she had followed him to Greece as a war correspondent. Some of her dispatches, filed under the *nom de plume* of Imogen Carter, were published. Cora's second husband, Captain Donald Stewart, son of a baronet, would not give her a divorce, and she did not relish trying to live with Crane as his common-law wife in the United States, where he was by now a celebrity. The English, by contrast, were more "accepting." And then Cora had large social aspirations. Even before Stephen Crane returned from Cuba, she had arranged to rent Brede House from Moreton Frewen (an uncle of young Winston Churchill) for £40 a year. A massive manor house begun in the fourteenth century, Brede had a large hall, a chapel, great fireplaces; but it was in disrepair, and cold and damp. Its sanitary arrangements were minimal. Nevertheless the place ministered to Cora's dreams of social glory.

She showed Brede House to Crane in January of 1899; in February they moved in and she wrote promptly to Henry James to announce their arrival. James was then on the verge of leaving for Italy. By the time he returned, the Cranes were well established. They had no money; they lived from hand to mouth on the charity of their friends and the credit of the neighborhood. The place was meagerly furnished but they strewed rushes on the floor and kept mastiffs in the Elizabethan style. Whole trees were burned in the capacious fireplaces. In the grounds romped "the young barbarians," as James called them, Harold Frederic's illegitimate orphans. Crane had a wagonette and also rode on horseback, wearing riding breeches and a flannel shirt. Shortly after James returned from Italy, in July 1899, he cycled to Brede and left his card on which he scrawled in pencil, "Mr. and Mrs. Crane: Very sorry to miss you—had a dark foreboding it was you I passed a quarter of an hour ago in a populous wagonette. Will try you soon again."

So far as we know the Cranes came to Lamb House for tea on two, perhaps three, occasions during the rest of that summer; and James in turn visited them at Brede perhaps the same number of times. James had little opportunity that year to be neighborly. He was preoccupied with his new friendship with Hendrik Andersen, who visited him that August; then his brother William came abroad after his heart attack. Finally Lamb House at this moment was put up for sale, and James was in a fever of writing, to earn the sum needed for the initial payment.

At Brede, Crane too sat daily in the tower, trying to write tales in order to provide money for the improvident Cora. James was fascinated —and pained—by the spectacle of the Cranes. They were living out his tales—about old English houses in need of repair let to Americans; about ambitious American women with a "past"; about talented writers struggling to do the successful thing in order to dress their wives and pay for food and rent. The situation at Brede had also a touch of the eerie, as in James's ghostly tales. There was a legend that Brede had had an ogre, a consumer of children; he had ultimately been done to death with a wooden saw. There were said to be underground passages which served generations of smugglers. But aside from its ghosts, its drafts, its creaking boards, its tree-consuming fireplaces, Brede was clearly the last place in the world for a malaria-ridden consumptive to spend a cold damp English winter. Wells remembered Crane as "profoundly weary and ill." Cora Crane did not notice—what everyone else saw—that he was destined to be very soon one of the ghostliest of Brede's ghosts.

Late in August 1899 James attended a party at the Brede Rectory organized by Cora. Of this occasion two significant snapshots survive:

one of James in his trimmed spade-like beard standing beside Cora and another with his mouth wide open—he was snapped in the act of eating a doughnut. When he received "the strange images" James wrote to Cora protesting that "no surely, it can't be any doughnut of yours that is making me make such a gruesome grimace. I look as if I had swallowed a wasp or a penny toy." His scribbled social notes to Cora are cordial and friendly. At the end of September there is a telegram accepting an invitation to tea. After that there are no communications for a full six months, during the period William James was in England, but the activities of the Cranes are abundantly documented.

H. G. Wells has told the story of the great Christmas-week party Cora organized to welcome the year 1900. The guests were asked to bring their own bedding. There were few furnished bedrooms in Brede House and Cora created a dormitory for the ladies and another for the men. There was an acute shortage of toilets. Crane tried to organize American-style poker games which his English guests did not take seriously. On Christmas Eve a play was given in the local school house written in part by Crane, who asked James, Conrad, Wells, Gissing, and others to add a few words to the script, making it the most "authored" play of the century. It was about the Brede ghost—the child-eating ogre who was sawed in half. James's contribution to the script was part of the name of one character—who was called Peter Quint Prodmore Moreau—Peter Quint from "The Turn of the Screw" and Prodmore the sharp businessman from "Covering End." The Moreau belonged to H. G. Wells. The party had a painful finale at just about the hour when Henry James, in nearby Lamb House, was invoking the "gruesome" year of 1900 in his letter to Rhoda Broughton. Eight miles away Cora was waking up Wells. Crane had just had a lung hemorrhage. Wells's final memory of the party was a ride into the drizzle at dawn on a bicycle in search of a doctor.

During the first months of the new year, when Crane was ill most of the time, Henry James wrote *The Sacred Fount*. It may have derived some of its poignancy from his vision of Crane visibly dying in the damp old house while Cora thrived unaware. Late in May, she finally grasped the truth, and rushed Crane off to the Continent, borrowing money on all sides, arranging for a special train, taking the local doctor, Ernest Skinner, along. They paused at Dover and James and Wells planned to drive over to see Crane off. James was detained and Wells went alone for a last glimpse of the American lying wrapped in blankets before an open window at the Dover hotel, "too weak for more than a remembered jest and a greeting and good wishes."

Cora got Crane to the Black Forest. James received the news of Crane's impending end from the Moreton Frewens, who had returned to Brede House, and in early June 1900 wrote his longest letter to Cora. He had heard how ill Crane was; he was sorry not to have seen him at Dover; he enclosed a cheque for £50, asking her to "dedicate it to whatever service it may best render my stricken young friend. It meagrely represents my tender benediction to him." He had barely posted this letter when he read of Crane's death. He wrote again to Cora, and a few days later told Wells: "You will have felt, as I have done, the miserable sadness of poor Crane's so precipitated and, somehow, so unnecessary extinction. I was at Brede Place this afternoon—and it looked conscious and cruel."

That autumn James wrote to the Royal Literary Fund at Cora's request, but he doubted whether this British fund could allocate money to Americans or to widows. She wrote to James and asked for more money —but he told his agent, "I can do very little more." He added, "my heart, I fear, is generally hard to her." He was particularly incensed that Cora had made no effort to pay Dr. Skinner. Nevertheless, when she sent him Crane's posthumous *Wounds in the Rain,* James answered her that "if Crane could have lived—success and he would evidently have been constantly, no strangers. The greater the tragedy!"

At a later time, when she had remarried, Cora Crane tried to call on James. He announced himself unavailable. James had been too close a spectator of the tragi-comedy played out in the old manor house: Crane had been a Jamesian hero, but unlike the young aspirant who tries to learn "the lesson of the master"—the lesson that a writer must choose between art and worldliness—Crane had not made a choice. He had been caught passively between the two. "His short, so troubled, yet also so peaceful passage" at Brede, James wrote, was "a strange, pathetic, memorable chapter."

"The Ambassadors"

During the last summer of the old century, when Henry James was writing *The Ambassadors*—an uncommonly hot summer for England— he sat for his portrait to the gifted member of the "Emmetry," his cousin Ellen Emmet, known as "Bay." He wanted to aid his cousin in her career, and, in all probability, to put on canvas his newly-shaven countenance. The finished portrait is a close-up. James looks directly out of the frame: his eyes are veiled; half the face is in deep shadow. The wear and tear of the years is erased and the artist has given the face an effect of greater length than it possessed.

Many years later, when it was being cleaned and repaired, the restorer found beneath the portrait, on a separate canvas, a sketch Bay Emmet had abandoned. She had posed James differently, at an angle, and had applied a great deal of red to the uncompleted face: the suggestion is of great ruddiness, a figure as of a country squire; a haunter of pubs. There is a great deal of life in the sketch, and the eyes are large, clear, alert, much more than in the "set" and inanimate finished portrait.

The novelist varnished the finished painting himself, found an old frame for it, placed it above the sideboard in his dining-room. There it hung for the remainder of his life. Though he never considered it a good likeness, it reminded him, as he wrote to his young cousin a couple of years later, of "our so genial, roasting romantic summer-before-last here together, when we took grassy walks at eventide, and in the sunset, after each afternoon's repainting."

The Ambassadors was written as "the picture of a certain momentous and interesting period, of some six months or so, in the history of a man no longer in the prime of life." James himself had had such a six months, from the time in 1899 when he had met Hendrik Andersen, purchased Lamb House, written *The Sacred Fount* and suddenly found himself— after removing his beard—wanting to write things of "the altogether human order." At fifty-seven he seemed to be starting a new career: this was suggested by his return, after almost two decades, to the "international" subject by which he had first established his fame. He came back to it with unconcealed pleasure; James felt, as he dictated his work in the Garden Room, as if all his data were "installed on my premises like a monotony of fine weather." He finished the book in about eight months. Its twelve parts, one for each month of a year of serialization, were shaped in pictures and scenes, using the techniques he had perfected since his play-writing.

Its story was simple, almost conventional; it told of a young man from New England who lingers too long in Paris; and of a middle-aged "ambassador" sent out by the young man's mother to bring him home. James named the principal envoy Lewis Lambert Strether after Balzac's hero in the novel *Louis Lambert*. Balzac's *roman philosophique* is the inflated story of the education of a young man, a near genius, who writes a portentous *Treatise on the Will* and dies young, after a painful love affair. James's novel tells us that life is willed to us, that each person must make the best of his or her existence. He must have felt that he too was writing a "philosophical" novel—a novel of a certain kind of "education," in which Strether, strapped tight by his New England "conditioning," unwinds in the Parisian circle of Chad Newsome's friends, discovering that the flexible cosmopolites "live" by being open to experience, while the New Englanders keep themselves closed.

Lambert Strether refuses to accept the preconceptions of Woollett, Mass. The Newsomes, mother and daughter, have made up their minds that Chad, the son and heir, remains abroad because some woman has taken hold of him. Strether has known Chad as a rough, spoiled small-town boy. Now he finds a smooth egotistical young man obviously improved by his life abroad. He has cosmopolite friends—a young artist named John Little Bilham, and above all Madame de Vionnet, an aristocratic French lady who has a grown daughter. She embodies French elegance, tradition, discretion and privacy; Strether assumes it is she who has given the young man his high continental polish. He believes at first that she is trying to marry her daughter to Chad.

Mrs. Newsome's ambassador is in no hurry about his mission. Chad is old enough not to be accountable to his mother; and Strether has no relish in making inquiries about his Parisian way of life. He gives himself over to enjoying the city, with the aid of a sophisticated American lady he has met in England, Maria Gostrey; very quickly she becomes his confidante. He has told her the details of his mission; she gives him useful advice and helps constantly to correct his active, romantic imagination. Strether finally musters the courage to ask Little Bilham about Chad and Madame de Vionnet. Little Bilham, being a gentleman, answers that theirs is a "virtuous attachment." Strether has reached the conclusion that Chad should stay abroad. He feels Madame de Vionnet is good for him. The result is that in the exact middle of the book, Strether is relieved of his high office. New ambassadors are dispatched from Woollett—Chad's sister Sarah and her husband, Jim Pocock. On arrival Sarah proclaims to Strether that Madame de Vionnet is "not even an apology for a decent woman." Pocock goes off to the Folies.

The novel has two brilliant climactic scenes, set with classic symmetry in the fifth and eleventh parts of the book. The first is the scene in Gloriani's garden, which had been the original "germ" for the story. Long before, James had learned, Howells had murmured to Jonathan Sturges in Whistler's garden in Paris that, really, one should "live all one can." James knew Whistler's garden—he had visited Whistler there; but he had also seen it years before, during 1875–76, when he called on occasion in the house overlooking the garden, and talked with old Madame Julius Mohl, the former Mary Clarke, Fanny Kemble's friend. There may be a touch of Whistler in James's image of the artist Gloriani, resuscitated from *Roderick Hudson,* his Roman novel of 1875. Now the fictional character, like Whistler, has matured. Gloriani has acquired greatness. It has come to him by his having the courage to live the passion of his art.

In this garden Strether delivers himself of one of the most poignant soliloquies in all of James's fiction. He begins his quiet speech to the artist-expatriate, Little Bilham, by wondering whether it is too late for someone like himself to "live." "Live all you can; it's a mistake not to. It doesn't so much matter what you do in particular," he tells Bilham, "so long as you have your life." He adds, "If you haven't had that what *have* you had?" After this Strether speaks the words that give the novel its "deterministic" post-Darwinian philosophy. We are all moulds, "either fluted and embossed, with ornamental excrescences, or else smooth and dreadfully plain, into which a helpless jelly, one's consciousness, is poured." You are what you are, James seems to say, and you must make the most of it. Still, Strether observes, "one has the illusion of freedom; therefore don't be, like me, without the memory of that illusion."

The second crucial scene, late in *The Ambassadors,* is that of Lambert Strether's relaxed day in the country. The Strether of the early part of the novel is always looking at his watch, always patting his pocket to make sure his wallet is in its place. The later Strether sets off casually in search of a certain metallic green in the French landscape that he had encountered once in a painting by Lambinet. To find this he takes a train to a station indiscriminately chosen—the exact terminus isn't needed. He has discovered a kind of freedom which can escape rigidities and a life conducted like a railway timetable. He can avoid even the names of places—can find "a river of which he didn't know, and didn't want to know, the name." Strether escapes Woollett during these carefree hours; he cultivates his "illusion of freedom." He waits for his dinner at the inn, on the bank of the river. He sees a boat, as in a Manet painting. The boat contains Chad and Madame de Vionnet. In the rustic twilight, Strether suddenly experiences the anguish of his disillusion. Woollett had been right after all. Or had it? At any rate, he feels "sold." The grand lady is indeed Chad's mistress: their informality, their casual clothes reveal to Strether that they must be staying at a nearby inn.

No bald sketch of *The Ambassadors* can convey the brilliance and the wit of its comedy, the ironic delicacy of its scenes and conversation, the ways in which James, with the ease and skill of his maturity, dissects America and Europe and re-imagines his international myth. America is Mrs. Newsome, an implacable, immobile force: she is there, in Woollett, or a hundred cities where values are unambiguous, and where everyone pays a price—the price of muffled feeling, the conventional, the prescribed. One doesn't "live all you can." The only solution—the one James had sought—is casually mentioned in the book: "you've got morally and intellectually to get rid of her." The ex-ambassador learns how to relax his moral and intellectual bondage. He will return to Woollett with a recognition that if Europe is amoral (by Woollett standards) it offers him beautiful illusions of freedom. He can live by his illusions—if he remains open to experience and doesn't require life to measure up to the Woollett yardstick.

The Ambassadors was told by James in a complex indirect style he had never attempted before and it revealed that he had at last reconciled himself to diminished omniscience. One could never know everything.

Rather than accept the old tradition of the novel which told everything, James allowed his readers to know only as much as one learns in life. And he developed for the first time mobile angles of vision. In terms of old-fashioned storytelling this resulted in a novel without action. The excitement was intellectual, the pleasure resided in the unfolding of minute detail. It has often been said that in *The Ambassadors* the story remains wholly in the "point of view" of Strether. But we discover soon enough that James brings in clouds of witnesses, first person intruders, spectators, individuals with "adjusted" vision; he asks us to use our imagination and to enjoy the personal relations he is showing us at the very heart of his story.

Beyond "technique" and its resourceful experiments, beyond its neat symmetrical design, the care with which it is "composed," the novel spoke for the central myth of Henry James's life. James had long before made up his mind that his choice of Europe was wise, that Woollett and Mrs. Newsome—that is, the U.S.A.—could not offer him the sense of freedom he had won for himself abroad. Woollett was all constraint—it was Puritan. James seems to be struggling still with authority figures of his past. There is first America itself, the mother, sitting, waiting, in Woollett (or Cambridge), asking the son to perform in the great world into which he has ventured—but at the end of a silver cord. He struggles to free himself, to pursue his own life abroad. Madame de Vionnet is "Europe" and passion; she is also the temptress-mother, a mysterious fount of anxiety. Miss Gostrey is intelligence and common sense and *savoire faire*. In the symbolism of the book the two motherlands of James's life take primary place—beneficent Europe, exigent America.

We can see in *The Ambassadors* James's prolonged struggle to cut the silver cord that bound him to Quincy Street, to Boston and New York. He could, at the end of his novel, send Strether back to Woollett—for he was quite prepared to re-visit America himself. Circumstances had provided him with transatlantic roots, but he is no longer sure that native rootedness would not have been better. In effect he is saying that had he stayed at home, life would have been, for him, less ambiguous. Yet this had made possible his life of art and involved him in a constant balancing of the good and the bad of America and Europe. It had enabled him to be Henry James, now "the Master"—to write *The Ambassadors,* and to live "all you can."

A Poor Ancient Lady

William James and his wife Alice had been abroad ever since the autumn of 1899. In the spring of 1900 William was in Rome, trying to recover strength and well-being. His young daughter Peggy had been living with an English family, the Joseph Thatcher Clarkes, friends of William, attending an English school at Harrow. Uprooted from the familiar American environment at adolescence, confined to English rural life, homesick, lonely, Peggy vigorously protested. Life was difficult for her at the Clarkes', where the exuberant Clarke boys visited various petty indignities on her. The Clarke family were good-natured, prosaic, middle-class. Peggy wrote homesick letters to her parents on the Continent and received from her uncle gentle letters of encouragement—"your poor old lonely uncle misses you very much," he wrote, "and takes the greatest interest in your new form of life and feeling greatly."

James had large sympathies for her; he remembered out of his early years what it meant to be cast adrift as a child in Europe. He had urged William to send Peggy to a school in England; now he pleaded with her mother to worry a little less about inculcating "moral and spiritual" ideas in the child. What Peggy could use, he said, was something more worldly. "With her so definite Puritan heritage, Peggy could afford to be raised on almost solely *cultivated* 'social' and aesthetic lines." He recommended that his niece be entrusted to the well-known Marie Souvestre, whose school for girls at Wimbledon had, he reported, "formed the daughters of many of the very good English *advanced* Liberal political and professional connection . . . (all Joe Chamberlain's daughters were there and they adore her)." Henry's only objection to Mlle Souvestre's establishment was that it was definitely "middle-class"—but then, he added, *"all"* schools here are that." But the William Jameses opposed such a school for their only daughter. They wanted her to live in a family environment, which was one of the reasons they chose the Clarkes.

The lonely uncle had asked his lonely niece to come and stay with him at Lamb House that Christmas of 1900. England was in mourning for its dead and dying in Africa; and the old Queen's life was running to its end. Henry was uncomfortable—a troublesome eczema had bothered him ever since the middle of the year and would continue throughout the writing of *The Ambassadors.* In the midst of the general depression, and his own discomfort, James acted with his quick empathy for the female young. He plied Peggy with sweets and good food, and planted her in his oak parlor with the novels of Sir Walter Scott. A serious, solemn, articulate, slightly depressed girl, Peggy was a good reader. She made her way, during the wet and windy days at Lamb House, through *Redgauntlet, Old Mortality, The Pirate, The Antiquary.* When weather permitted, novelist and niece went forth for walks with the little wire-haired fox terrier Nick, one of the Master's most beloved dogs. "It was very nice," wrote Peggy to her parents. "Nothing much happened." James retreated to London on 31 December, taking his niece with him to restore her to Harrow.

The old Queen was dying; England at war and in mourning prepared itself for deeper mourning still. Profoundly American though he was, James experienced to the full the public emotion. Victoria was too much a part of his own life for him not to feel stirred; he wrote of her as "a poor and ancient lady," a tired creature of pomp who had patiently labored and lasted. Victoria had been an immovable presence when he reached London in 1855, a boy of Peggy's age. He had seen her riding in her carriage when the Prince Consort still lived, then in her widowhood, and at the last in her final dropsical old age, "throwing her good fat weight into the scales of general decency."

The tiny figure on the canopied bed in Osborne House took its last breath on the evening of 22 January 1901. The novelist, coming out of the Reform Club, saw the headline, "Death of the Queen." The streets of London seemed to him "strange and indescribable," the people hushed as if helpless—almost, he wrote, as if scared. He had not thought that he himself would experience grief, for it had been "a simple running down of the old used-up watch." When he found himself at the Reform Club writing letters on the club's black-bordered stationery, his unexpected emotions were only partly for Victoria; she had embodied his lifetime experience of governing women. "It has really been, the Event, most moving, interesting and picturesque. I have felt *more* moved, than I should have expected (such is the *community* of sentiment), and one has realized all sorts of things about the brave old woman's beneficent duration and holding-together virtue." Dining at his club amid various Privy

Councillors and the leaders of England, James caught the wave of sympathy which always flows towards the new monarch—"an arch-vulgarian," he had called him—as he heard John Morley say that Edward "made a good impression" at his first Council. But, James whispered in a letter to William, *"speriamo."*

He arranged for Peggy James to watch from a window in the home of friends the slow procession, built around the tiny coffin—it seemed almost a child's coffin—in which Victoria was borne through the streets of the capital she had graced so long, to Paddington Station, to last obsequies at Windsor. Peggy's uncle had fully briefed her; and he had insisted she wear a little black mourning hat which he purchased for her. James himself was seeing the procession from other windows, at Buckingham Gate, where the visual-minded novelist was not altogether happy. The ladies wore high plumes and bows and as a "lone and modest man" (he explained to his niece), "I had the back seat, as it were, of all. However I saw a good deal." The formidably large gun carriage on which the coffin was placed "just grazed the ridiculous" yet he found it all "interesting and moving and picturesque." The new King looked well on horseback. There were, he remarked, "no anarchist bomb, no ugliness, nor infelicity of any sort. But strange is the feeling that the door is closed on the past sixty years." He mourned "the safe and motherly old middle-class queen, who held the nation warm under the fold of her big, hideous Scotch-plaid shawl and whose duration had been so extraordinarily convenient and beneficent," he wrote a few days later to Wendell Holmes. Victoria had been for him "a sustaining symbol."

Miss Weld

James had lost the habit of London, but he came back to the metropolis during the winter of 1901 with all his old energies, and this in spite of the fact that his skin irritation continued to trouble him. He described it to his brother as "visible *gout"*—in spite of "extreme sobriety and abstinence," the smallest drop of wine or spirits "sets my face on fire." It did not prevent him from dining out strenuously, as of old; and he worked strenuously too. He was able to have MacAlpine in his newly furnished room at the Reform Club from mid-mornings until almost two o'clock to receive dictation of *The Ambassadors.* He worked with a certain desperation, for he had decided some weeks before to part with the Scottish typist, "not in anger or as a catastrophe" but simply because "he's too damned *expensive. . . .* I can get a highly competent little woman for half." He had found a new position for MacAlpine, which the latter would assume after Easter. In the interval he sought to get as much of his novel as possible completed before reorganizing "this branch of my establishment."

His mornings were consistently given over to work; after a late lunch he was ready for his renewed town life. The occasions were muted, because of the universal mourning. He noticed, in some of the great houses, how much more the diamonds gleamed against the black of the ladies' dresses; and the servants, in ubiquitous black, looked "as if they were of more exalted station." He dined with the Humphry Wards, Jonathan Sturges, A. C. Benson, Gosse. He did not lose sight of his niece. When he could not go out to Harrow on a Sunday to visit her, he made arrangements for her to come into town. He took her to a performance of *Twelfth Night;* he marched her through museums; to the Clarkes he spoke of his search for "some innocent place of entertainment—say the Hippodrome or the Alhambra."

In the cold days of March, after little more than eight weeks of London life, he felt "a yearning for cabless days and dinnerless nights." The William Jameses were coming north again after Easter. The series of lectures William had been preparing on "the varieties of religious experience"—the Gifford Lectures—was to be delivered that spring at Edinburgh. Recognizing that there would be interruptions of his work, Henry addressed himself to a secretarial bureau. He wanted a young woman, he explained, willing to live out in Rye, capable of learning to take dictation directly to the machine. He could promise few distractions for a young person save those of rural charm and the bicycle.

The William Jameses arrived at Lamb House at the end of the first week in April, Peggy coming with them. Just after their reinstallation, Mary Weld, young, clear-eyed, round-faced, came to Rye to discuss working for Mr. James. She had first-class references. She had attended a college for young ladies, and then had gone to secretarial school. She seemed modest, willing, and delighted at the prospect of Rye and the bicycle. They discussed what she would do during the long pauses that sometimes occurred during dictation. MacAlpine had smoked; it was settled that she might crochet. At lunch, where she met the William Jameses, there was a discussion as to what an amanuensis should wear for such duties. Mrs. William agreed that a "suit"—that is, a coat and skirt—would be appropriate. That same afternoon Miss Weld went hunting for a room in Rye.

Her diary records that there was snow in the town on 15 April, when she arrived to start work; and the next morning she began. Miss Weld would say later that typing for Henry James was like accompanying a singer on the piano. James's dictation was "remarkably fluent. The hesitation and searching for the right word . . . was simply nervousness and

vanished once he knew you well." Sometimes in the afternoon he bicycled with her. Sometimes she accompanied him on his walks. She also
recalled that a certain woman in Rye came to Lamb House to make sure
that everything was "respectable"—since so young a lady was working
for an elderly bachelor. In little more than a month Henry James was
writing that "Miss Weld proves decidedly a *bijou.*" MacAlpine's "lady
successor is an improvement on him! and an economy!" he wrote. And
again: "Miss Weld continues dressy and refined and devoted."

He was delighted when she took up bookbinding with the help of a
friend. He saw that this employment would relieve the monotony for so
young a person. He made available to her the adjacent studio in Watchbell Street, which he had offered repeatedly to Hendrik Andersen, and
allowed her to bind certain of his French books. "Poor binding," he told
her, "is an abject thing, good a divine. Go in for the latter."

It fell to Miss Weld to receive dictation of the latter part of *The
Ambassadors, The Wings of the Dove,* and *The Golden Bowl.* Her typewriter also took down masses of correspondence, the biography of W. W.
Story, some of James's finest late essays, and some of his most remarkable
tales. Her punctuality, efficiency, and good nature contributed markedly
to the environment he needed for this sustained period of his labors, the
summit of his career.

From Peggy James, fourteen, 26 April 1901, at Lamb House in Rye, to her
older brother Bill, nineteen, in Cambridge, Mass.:

> Dear old Billy—We are down here at Rye again and it is mighty nice. In
> the morning I moon around and take pictures. . . . Uncle Henry, Mama
> and I used always to go for a long walk in the afternoon, that is to say
> when Nick allowed us to go, by not chasing sheep or chickens, and having
> to be brought home again. It is too funny for words sometimes when this
> happens and it nearly drives Uncle Henry to distraction and he yells in
> a terribly loud voice "Oh! oh! oh! oh! oh! you little brute! you little brute!
> you beast! oh! oh! oh!" Then he hurries home with the unfortunate wretch
> and leaves Mama and me to follow on at our own sweet pace. Lately
> however Papa has felt better and we have all gone to drive . . .

William James, looking at his brother after a winter's absence, wrote
to Dr. Baldwin that "he works steadily, and seems less well than he did
—possibly the result of a London winter." The London winter had, as a
matter of fact, done Henry much good; and what William saw, but could
not recognize, was Henry's usual worried state whenever his brother was
on the scene. In a letter to Miss Robins, the novelist spoke of "anxiety-
breeding relations in my house." The family party was joined by Harry,
the elder son, who came to attend his father's Edinburgh lectures. With

four more mouths to feed in Lamb House, James was in constant consultation with his cook.

In May, when his relatives left for the Continent, the novelist found himself finally free to get on with *The Ambassadors.* On 9 May 1901 he dispatched the first nine parts of his novel to his agent in a form destined for serialization. The remaining parts were transmitted shortly afterwards.

James enjoyed the early days of summer at Lamb House. Miss Weld arranged flowers in strategic places. "She does so charmingly—has a real gift," he told his niece Peggy, who stayed with him while the William Jameses were abroad. Lamb House was filled with other guests as well. On a day in June, H. G. Wells brought George Gissing and the two spent the night at Lamb House. James was fascinated by Gissing, disapproved of his "amazing" relations with women—"why will he do these things?" —but approved of *New Grub Street.* However, he deplored its style.

On another day James received the Kent contingent, "Joseph Conrad, wife, baby and trap and pony," who came to tea and stayed all afternoon. The previous day he had had the Winchelsea contingent, the Hueffers, "for hours." Various Bostonians turned up, including Wendell Holmes; and English intimates such as Edmund Gosse, and Hamilton Aïdé, whom James characterized as "the Diane de Poitiers of our time." As between Holmes, Aïdé, and Peggy, he was happiest with his niece. Peggy imposed no strain; she showed off her continental frocks to her uncle and he approved of her speech and manners. "She is a most soothing and satisfactory maid, attached and attaching to her (poor old) Uncle."

By the middle of July, Henry James announced the title of his next novel, *The Wings of the Dove,* and said it would be a love story. He had made a start on the book in 1900 but had dropped it to write *The Ambassadors.* Before returning to it, he wrote the last of his theatrical articles— on the French neo-romantic, Edmond Rostand. James had seen Sarah Bernhardt in *L'Aiglon* and *La Princesse Lointaine,* and Coquelin in *Cyrano de Bergerac.* He considered Rostand a journalistic Victor Hugo; he liked his theatricality, his swagger, his combination of whimsicality and nationalism, the sentimental with the sublime. He equated the French dramatist's success with that of Kipling, finding in both writers "the patriotic note, the note of the militant and triumphant race." Rostand's themes were close to James's own—Cyrano's love and renunciation; the frustration of the faraway princess and the pilgrim; the play about Napoleon II, an "eaglet" unable to soar. James was writing a novel about a dove, which also could not soar. The poetry, the melancholy, the gloom in Rostand's plays touched James; although we gather not as deeply as the plays of Maurice Maeterlinck, which he saw at this time, and to which there are explicit references in *The Wings of the Dove.*

The William Jameses sailed for America at the end of August. Henry gave them a sad send-off at Euston Station. With all the anxieties William induced in him, Henry's deep love for his brother remained. And his attachment to the young "Peggotina" was now profound. "I feel very lonely and bereft," he wrote his brother, "more than ever eager to borrow a child from you, if you only had the right one." He returned to Rye having caught a cold, and feeling seedy. Lamb House remained, as he ruefully testified, "an hotel." Young Percy Lubbock "of long limbs and candid countenance" visited Henry James that summer for the first time; most important of all, Hendrik Andersen was due in Paris and promised to dash over for a few days. James was expecting various other visitors, and warned Andersen they would have very little time alone; however, he added, "I shall, at the station, take very personal possession of you." Andersen's visit, so long and so eagerly awaited, with all its overtones of affection and love, occurred in the midst of a series of unscheduled events. "A below-stairs crisis that has been maturing fast for some time, reaches visibly its acute stage," James wrote to a friend on 19 September 1901. Three words in Miss Weld's diary, the next day, "the Smith tragedy," tell us that the crisis had—after many years—been reached.

A Domestic Upheaval

For some sixteen years—ever since he had settled in De Vere Gardens in 1886—James had had as servants an English couple, the Smiths. They had kept house for him with great efficiency, the husband as butler, the wife as cook. The two, with the addition of a parlormaid, and his house-boy Burgess, constituted his total staff in the country. James had been a generous employer, once (in 1892) even permitting Mrs. Smith's sister to convalesce at De Vere Gardens after a cancer operation. He paid the couple well. They did not work hard. They had more work, however, at Lamb House than in London, especially with so many visitors during the summers. And they had never wholly accommodated themselves to their absence from the metropolis. Rural life encouraged an alcoholism to which they had become prone in earlier periods of idleness when James was abroad. Only ten days before Andersen's arrival, James had written to his brother, "I am living from hand to mouth with the Smiths, who remain exactly the same queer mixture of alcohol and perfection." The "perfection" had to give way.

The collapse of the Smiths was sudden, however expected. On 19 September, a Thursday, Lily Norton, daughter of his old Cambridge friend, came to spend the night at Lamb House. The next day she and James were joined at lunch by another Boston lady, Ida Agassiz Higginson, and in the afternoon T. Bailey Saunders, a writer friend, arrived from Eastbourne to spend the weekend. Smith seems to have managed the lunch; but he was out cold shortly thereafter. James got the ladies off to London without their suspecting a domestic crisis. "Smith," Henry wrote to Mrs. William James, "was *accumulatedly* so drunk that I got him out of the house—i.e. all Friday and Saturday and Sunday." Andersen arrived on Saturday. James got the local doctor, Skinner, to treat the man; in the meantime Mrs. Smith anesthetized herself. James summoned Mrs. Smith's sister, who helped to pack their belongings (they were still too drunk to help themselves), and on the Monday they left, "simply two saturated and demoralized victims, with not a word to say for themselves and going in silence to their doom." It was clear at the end that most of their wages had gone into liquor. James gave the Smiths two months' wages each, "till they can turn round." He added, to Alice James:

> They will never turn round; they are lost utterly; but I would have promised *anything* in my desire to get them out of the house before some still more hideous helplessness made it impossible.

He paid their liquor bill in the town and settled down to makeshift living with only Burgess and the housemaid, Fanny, taking some of his meals at the Mermaid Inn, while he sent out appeals to his London lady friends for help.

In retrospect James wrote good-humoredly to Andersen of "my little squalid botheration." The long-awaited reunion of the old Master and the young sculptor had however lost some of its intimacy. James was too upset. Andersen prolonged his stay into the middle of the week and the two recaptured at the end a few hours of privacy. The sculptor had had a difficult time in America. One of his statues had been turned down because of the nudity. James was consoling. "What a dismal doom for a sculptor to work for a great vulgar stupid community that revels in every hideous vulgarity and only quakes at the clean and blessed nude—the last refuge of Honour!" But when it came to a statue of Lincoln, of which Andersen sent James a photograph, the novelist was direct and uncompromising. He liked the head but thought it "rather too smooth, ironed-out, simplified as to ruggedness, ugliness, mouth, etc." His principal complaint, however, was that Andersen had not conveyed the sense of a *physical* Lincoln, "especially the presence of shoulders, big arms and big hands." He had made " a *softer,* smaller giant than we used to see." Also the figure was too "placid." The image of history and James's own memory was "benevolent, but deeply troubled, and altogether tragic: that's how one thinks of him."

The young sculptor took these criticisms with good grace. They were gently given "for the love of your glory and your gain." Moreover, Andersen's self-assurance was impervious to subtleties. When they were together it was his own stature, his shoulders, his arms and hands, the solid physical presence that counted. James escorted him as far as the junction point of Ashford and wrote to him promptly, "I miss you—keep on doing so—out of all proportion to the too few hours you were here." When he got word of the sculptor's safe return to his studio in Rome he imaged him as a young priest returned to his altar—but a pagan priest, for he saw him with "your idols, bless their brave limbs and blank eyes, ranged roundabout."

With Andersen gone James addressed himself to restoring his household. "Peace now reigns—I am happy to say—though a peace a little sharply distinguished from Plenty," he wrote to his other recent guest, Bailey Saunders. A charwoman was recruited as emergency cook. To Peggy, with whom he now began a fairly regular correspondence, he described his staff and household as reduced to "picknicking lines." He was glad the catastrophe had been stayed until after the William Jameses had left. "I see now," he told Peggy, "how heavily for years, the accumulated (the thousands of gallons of) whisky of the Smiths has weighed on my spirits, how odiously uneasy I had chronically been."

Of the London ladies to whom James appealed for help the one who entered most into his domestic crisis was Mrs. W. K. Clifford. The former Lucy Lane, in her youth a golden-haired, red-cheeked art student, had married the great mathematician W. K. Clifford, who died at thirty-four. Finding herself a widow—she was then twenty-four—with two young daughters to support, Lucy turned to writing—journalism, fiction, and later, plays. James met her in 1880; he was the same age as her husband but she treated him as if he were one of her young literary protégés. In the 1890s, she had induced the editor of the *Illustrated London News* to publish his serial *The Other House.* Formidable in her ability to get things done, she had helped launch Rudyard Kipling in literary London after reading some of his work published in India. Her own novel *Mrs. Keith's Crime* proved a great success, as did *Aunt Anne.* Because of the latter, James often addressed her in his letters as "Dearest Aunt Lucy." She responded by calling him her "nevvy." She was brisk, original, loyal, self-assertive, and full of warm feelings. Late in life James would speak of "that admirable Lucy Clifford—as a character, a nature, a soul of generosity, and devotion."

Mrs. Clifford had just returned from Vienna when James wrote her of his domestic débâcle. She immediately got into touch with a housemaid and canvassed others for interviews. James reassured her. He was not "in extreme discomfort; therefore don't pity me or think of me too much." He would be in town early in the new year and probably could make do until then. And he told Mrs. Clifford that other friends had recommended a certain lady named Paddington, with a record of having held only two posts, nineteen years in one and ten in another. "Bear with the lonely celibate," he wrote to loyal Lucy, "who has, as it were to boil his own pot. . . . " Lucy continued to send him telegrams; and James came to confer with her when he arrived in town for his interview with the matronly Mrs. Paddington.

The matron had impeccable references. She seemed to like the idea of a bachelor establishment. She was ready to come for £3 a month: such was the wage-scale of the time for a good housekeeper-cook. She would not, however, be free until mid-November. Writing then to his garden-lady Miss Muir Mackenzie, James said, "I go down at last, only tomorrow (to the station) to meet the lady of the Gorringe's costume, on whose convenience I have been waiting all this time. She is my Fate! may she not be my Doom."

Olivia Rayne Garnett, she who had dreams of Henry James saying profound things to her, stepped off the train at Rye station the next morning on her way to visit the Hueffers, and beheld James approaching a matronly lady. "I have come to meet my doom," she heard him say. Thus began the long régime in Lamb House of Mrs. Paddington, a woman who was severe and autocratic with her fellow-servants, but who knew her business thoroughly. Three weeks after her arrival, James was writing of the "peace" she promised his household—

> a *real,* trained, all-round excellent cook, up to the wildest want, or flight . . . a *supreme* economist, manager, mistress of thrift, foresight (my tradesmen's books going steadily down and down); and an equally excellent, genial, sensible, good-tempered, friendly woman . . .*The* blessing in Mrs. P. is that she clearly likes my service, as much as I cling to *her.*

"The Wings of the Dove"

Henry James began dictating *The Wings of the Dove* on 9 July 1901; he worked on the book intermittently during August when Peggy was with him; and he continued through the domestic interruptions in October and on into the new year. Jonathan Sturges paid one of his long visits to Lamb House through Christmas and the year's end, with the consequence that James stayed on in Rye until the end of January before going up to London where he planned to remain during the worst part of the winter. So confident was he of completing his novel that he sent off 500 pages of the manuscript to Constable and was reading proofs of his book even while writing the final sections—the pages devoted to the rage of the elements in Venice as Milly, his heiress, dies in her rented palazzo. In the Venetian chapter James relived old memories, not only the long-ago death of Minny Temple, but the wasting illness of his sister, and the violent end—in Venice—of Miss Woolson. He went to London on 27 January—the anniversary week of Miss Woolson's death in 1894—and had no sooner settled into the Reform Club than he became "painfully" ill with what he described as an "inflammation of the bowels." In mid-February he dashed back to Rye; even in mid-winter Lamb House, with its servants, was preferable to his lonely club room in time of illness.

During ensuing weeks he had "botherations, aberrations, damnations of the mind and body." The subject or central dilemma of his novel, the death in Venice, was a heavy charge on his emotions. Within the year his memories of Miss Woolson's suicide had been stirred by a visit to Rye of Grace Carter, Fenimore's cousin, who had seen Miss Woolson in death, had arranged for her burial in Rome; from that troubled time they had been friends. Then he learned from the Benedicts that Miss Woolson's dog, Otello, had died. The dog, James reminded them, stood "for a particular terrible passage" in their lives. The passage had been terrible in his life as well; and he was in a sense reliving it for he had decided to have his heroine die, as Miss Woolson had done, in an old Venetian palace.

To Mrs. Curtis, whose guest he had been in "the divine Barbaro, noblest of human habitations," he wrote that "Venice . . . seems such a museum of distressed *ends.*" They were discussing the disappearance from the scene of many familiar figures, among them his beloved Mrs. Bronson, who had presided queen-like over the Grand Canal in her charming Ca' Alvisi. Her death with the onset of the new century had made James feel "older and sadder," he wrote to her daughter, the Contessa Rucellai. "It is the end of so many things—so many delightful memories, histories, associations—some of the happiest elements of one's past." By a coincidence, the news of Miss Woolson's dog was followed by the sudden death of his own beloved wire-haired terrier. Everything seemed to contribute to the encroachment on mind and memory of the crowded recent past. James's illness delayed the novel; the final pages were written late in May. In June he had a return of his winter's illness, but he recovered rapidly. After that Lamb House began to receive its summer quota of visitors. His novel was published on 21 August 1902 in New York and nine days later in England.

The idea for the novel about a doomed young woman had been with him ever since the death of Minny Temple in 1870. The death of one or the other partner in love had been his theme in tales as early as "De Grey: A Romance" or "Longstaff's Marriage." In later years, reworked, it had become the macabre story of "Maud-Evelyn" in which a young man imagines himself the widower of a dead girl he has never known. In "Georgina's Reasons," in which two sisters bear names that would be used in *The Wings of the Dove,* Kate and Mildred Theory, the doomed Mildred is "as beautiful as a saint, and as delicate and refined as an angel"; in short, she too is a "dove." Minny Temple—Mildred Theory— Milly Theale—the three belonged to a single line of fantasy. In its essence it was that of the Henry James who could not bring himself to love and marry. He could worship a younger woman in a utopia of the mind. But in life he required the friendship of protective and sheltering females, to whom he could be kind and attentive, but who gave him everything and seemed satisfied that he simply be "kind" in return. Constance Fenimore Woolson had been the most important of his "protective" ladies in the twelve years he had known her; only after her death had it occurred to him that she might have loved him more than he knew.

We can read in these repeated fantasies of James's inner passional life a reflection of the old situation in the James family. The real-life sisters, Mary and Kate Walsh, the omnipresent older female figures of Henry's childhood, may be regarded as the figures behind the Milly and Kate of fiction, the idealized mother and the down-to-earth aunt—Kate Theory and Mildred, Kate Croy and Milly—the strong and the weak, the good and bad heroines of the various stories, representatives of spirit and flesh. They represented the everlasting vision of a mother who seemed compliant and sacrificial and an aunt who was assertive and perhaps manipulative. James's myth of women had been translated early in life into the apotheosis of Minny Temple as the "heroine of the scene." Later, with Miss Woolson, the old triangle of his father's life, and his own, was redrawn. Minny Temple remained a "luminary of the mind." Fenimore was a fellow-writer, with womanly demands. The myths of the ethereal and the fleshly, of spirit and body, in James's equations were converted into art and passion—and in his existence the two could not be reconciled. One renounced love, or was deprived of it. Accepted, it represented ruin.

In returning to these themes now, James was making a supreme attempt to understand and resolve a life-dilemma in which he had feared the love of woman and learned to keep himself emotionally distant from all human relations lest he commit himself to unforeseen catastrophes. With *The Ambassadors,* he had begun a kind of rewriting of his past. That novel had been a return to *The American.* Now he was re-telling *The Portrait of a Lady,* which had been his attempt to construct a story for Minny Temple as if she had gone on living. "Live all you can" had been the theme of *The Ambassadors;* but the question now was, "What if one can't really live?" The answer would be, in part at least, "One can still love—and love can endure from beyond the grave." However, renunciation and sacrifice were now directly coupled with thoughts of fleshly love. In his sixtieth year James found himself writing about a love affair

—and on a large scale. As in *The Portrait of a Lady,* there would be scheming and treachery: Kate Croy, discovering that Milly the heiress is doomed, will deny to the heiress that she loves Merton Densher. Milly will be free to love him; and Kate will instruct Merton to be "kind" to the dying girl, in the hope that the heiress will "endow" Merton—and so endow their marriage.

As with *The Ambassadors,* James brought all the resources of his art to bear on this melodrama, which he had begun by seeing as "ugly and vulgar." He would gild the ugliness and the vulgarity with his prose. To do so he summoned the full orchestra of his symbolic imagination. James had never paid attention in his critical writings to the symbolist movement in France. His early reading of Hawthorne to be sure had shown him the uses of allegorical symbolism; but he had enrolled himself instead under the banner of Balzac. He discovered symbolism in the theater, in Ibsen, and even then it had had to be called to his attention by William Archer. Once he had grasped the uses of the symbol, however, he possessed the power and poetry to assimilate it promptly into his art.

Now for the first time he finds a symbolic title—*The Wings of the Dove*—as he will find *The Golden Bowl.* Psalm 55 has the words, "Oh that I had wings like a dove, for then would I fly away, and be at rest"; and Psalm 67, "yet shall ye be as the wings of a dove covered with silver, and her feathers with yellow gold." Milly the dove who wants ultimately to fly away and be at rest has gold-covered wings; with her fragility she possesses the gilded power of an heiress. *The Wings of the Dove* borrows the symbolism of Judaism and Christianity to clothe the sordid drama it has to tell, to convert the gold-weighted Milly into a seraph and a dove and the predatory Kate into a creature motivated by her poverty to seek a better life for herself. In the novel's imagery, Kate is a panther and she is named Croy—the crow, a blackbird, of which the name in French is *merle* (and Madame Merle in *The Portrait of a Lady* had played a similar role). The bird imagery is sustained in the name Theale—the silver-and-gold dove is also thus a little duck. The realist of the novel, turned poet, seemed to be trying to reconcile the divine and the earthly, to bring about, as in Milton and Blake, the marriage of heaven and hell.

In *The Portrait of a Lady* a physician who is given a brief walk-on part is named Sir Matthew Hope. In *The Wings* he is at the center of the action and his name is that of the healer, Luke—Sir Luke Strett. There is also Lord Mark, who journeys to the city of St. Mark as the *deus ex machina* of Milly's drama, and brings a new pair of wings into the novel, those of the winged lion, emblem of Mark, and of Venice. *The Wings of the Dove* seems a riot of symbols, not least that of the ascending dove of the title, whose wings shelter those left behind. Since they are wings of gold, the gold weighs down Merton Densher at the end, and he turns away from Kate Croy. Their cruel gambit has succeeded; but they can no longer be as they were. The solution of *The Wings of the Dove* still finds James rewriting an old equation. The dead interfere with the living; the worship of woman as goddess is a prohibition to human love.

For all his disguises as active and even coercive lover, Merton Densher is in reality the classical passive, renunciatory Jamesian hero. He drifts in his passivity into a solution comfortable to himself. He sits back and allows women to be kind, devoted, sacrificial. Kate serves him, and plots for him; Milly is a fine rare creature who loves him; he "takes the comfort of it." But in drifting, and accepting, he becomes irritated by his "so extremely manipulated state." He threatens to spoil Kate's plans; and exacts as his price for continued passivity that the woman he loves come to his rooms, and sleep with him. It is in this sudden show of active (but also aggressive) male force that Densher finally differs from all his predecessors. The effect of this change in the old Jamesian equation, however, is simply to offer a new justification for old conclusions. Densher's physical love of Kate frees him for his spiritual love of Milly. The hand reaching from beyond the grave, offering him continued sustenance, fills him with remorse. In the final scene Densher has withdrawn into greater passivity than ever. Kate now believes that Densher is in love with Milly's memory. Yet it has been clear throughout that Densher does not love the sick girl. If Milly's wings cover him from beyond life, his freedom has been diminished; he chooses to live with a ghost rather than with the strong and living woman, like the young man in "Maud-Evelyn." The renunciation is as complex as all of James's renunciations; nevertheless it is touched by the exquisite delicacy with which James describes the final meeting of the lovers.

In this book, for the first time in all his fiction, James writes believably of sexual passion. Nowhere in his novels is there a stronger sense of the physical than in the account of Densher left alone in his rooms after Kate's visit. The entire place is changed. Eros has touched everything. James had come face to face at last with "the great relation." But he had not been able to banish his other ghost—the ghost of doubt, of guilt, the double-love of the heroine of the spirit and the heroine of the flesh; they were still the "good" and the "bad" heroines of all his stories. The resolution would have to be attempted once again.

James would speak later of his quest for a "compositional key" to the structure of *The Wings of the Dove*. "The way grew straight," he wrote, "from the moment one recognized that the poet essentially can't be concerned with the act of dying." To depict the stages of Milly Theale's illness, as in the doleful last act of some opera, was merely to create a novel of the "graveyard" school or a modern "soap opera." His solution was to omit the tearful scenes, the very scenes which the sentimental novelists put in so as to wring every possible emotion out of the audience. The reader is kept out of certain rooms; he may not be present at certain encounters. We remain with the living—their greed, their guilt, their anguish. The *expected* moments do not materialize. We accompany Densher in the gondola, as he goes for his "last interview" with Milly. We expect to see her on her couch, to hear her words, to listen to Densher's explanations. He is received at the palace. The doors close in our face. When we turn the page we are no longer in Venice. We will never know what passed between the hero and the heroine, although Densher will have brief moments of memory. It would fall to a later generation of dramatizers and opera librettists, attracted to the book, to insert the very scenes James purposely left out, making it into the "tear-jerker" it was not supposed to be.

If James resorted to omission and indirection, thereby further disposing of the omniscient author, as he had done in *The Ambassadors,* he gives full play to those scenes in which we are allowed to see Milly resisting her fate. The novel is never more in command of itself, nor of its existential materials, than in the quiet give-and-take of Sir Luke Strett, the physician, and his doomed patient. Once again James is careful not to specify. The only medical word he uses in these scenes is "auscultation." There is never a hint of the nature of Milly's illness. We are present rather at a comparatively modern therapeutic session. Sir Luke is "supportive"; he emphasizes the immediate, the real. Milly is still in possession of her faculties and her strength; the physician is determined not to allow her to be sorry for herself, nor to convert self-pity into pity for him. He dismisses the past—her past of dead parents, dead relatives, her being alone in the world. "Don't try to bear more things than you need . . . You've a right to be happy. You must make up your mind to it. You must attempt any form in which happiness must come." Milly feels as if she has been to confession and been absolved. She faces the world with renewed hope. She rents a palace in Venice and invites her friends to join her.

In Venice life and art are deeply mingled for James. He embodies in these beautiful chapters memories of his visits at the Palazzo Barbaro, here described, with its *piano nobile* and the shuttered light playing across its floors. There is a recall of Mrs. Gardner and her famous string of pearls in the scene in which Kate studies Milly's pearls, ". . . the long priceless chain, wound twice round the neck, hung, heavy and pure, down the front of the wearer's breast," and recognizes that the weak dove has the strength of her wealth. Densher, listening, knows that for Kate Milly's wealth was "a power, a great power," and was "dove-like only so far as one remembered that doves have wings and wondrous flights, have them as well as tender tints and soft sounds."

The center of emotion in this novel is fixed in Merton Densher, a figure not unlike James's Parisianized friend Morton Fullerton, who lived a life similar to James's hero's. Fullerton's personality, and the use of the name Merton, permit us to speculate that it may have been he whom James had in mind. Certainly it was not Ford Madox Hueffer. We must recognize, however, that there is much of James's own moral feeling in Densher, his own reticences, his own fear of women. In writing this novel he touched the mystery of Fenimore and the painful weeks of questioning and mourning when he had lived in her Venetian apartment —above all the great riddle of death. This may explain James's uneasiness and uncertainties—and troubled health—during these months. If he could not find an answer to the riddle of death he would try to answer the riddle of life.

Billy

From Billy James, 7 October 1902, in Lamb House, to his parents in Cambridge, Mass.:

> I arrived here last night and am drunk—with Rye, and Lamb House, and Uncle Henry. By Jove! Isn't it great? Uncle Henry's welcome to me, and his treatment of me in general, is kinder than that of a mother, if such a thing can be, and as for the place, I could rest right here for the rest of my days and be perfectly happy. The length of my stay will only be a question of my boring Uncle Henry, Dad, the thing will never work the other way as far as I am concerned.

When William James's second son had been told in his boyhood that his uncle was a famous writer, he remarked a trifle enviously, "I suppose there's nothing that Uncle Henry can't spell." Now twenty, an enthusiastic oarsman and a fine tennis player, he was being sent abroad to spend a year on the Continent. A tall slender youth, well turned out by his tailor, he had an elegant upright carriage, a certain hesitancy of speech, and an intensity and sincerity that endeared him promptly to James. "I congratulate you all on him," the uncle wrote to Billy's elder brother, "so beautiful he is, and so attaching; so formed to charm and interest and, as it were, repay."

Billy always remembered the days of his first stay at Lamb House, spent on the bicycle, with long walks in between, and the arrival of his Emmet cousins, Bay and Leslie, whom he found "devastatingly" beautiful. He remembered, too, how the age of the motor-car came to Lamb House—the Rudyard Kiplings driving up in their new £2,000 machine, an object of curiosity and wonder. There had been a lively lunch at which

Kipling was talkative, anecdotal, poetic. Then, when they got into the car to return to Burwash, twenty miles away, the vehicle "in the manner of its kind" wouldn't start. Rudyard had baptized it Amelia. It behaved as he believed all women behaved. The Kiplings had to take a train.

Billy left for the Continent, but he was not a letter-writer, and his uncle became worried. He had visions of the innocent nephew "swindled or bamboozled in Paris," or even "robbed and murdered in your night train in Geneva." He sent an uneasy wire to Geneva. All was well, though the doting uncle wondered "when you *did* mean to write!" Billy stayed briefly in Geneva and then spent the winter at Marburg, where he attended classes at the university. In emulation of his father he returned to study medicine in Cambridge, after another stay at Lamb House. Ultimately he was to abandon medical studies and return to Europe to study art. One day his uncle gave Billy advice that remained fixed in the young man's memory for the rest of his life. After standing behind him silently watching as he struggled with a canvas, slowly and with characteristic deliberation James spoke: "Bill, remember that no captain ever makes port with all the cargo with which he set sail." A long pause. "And Bill —remember—there is always another voyage."

In the Workshop

Life in Lamb House had a certain military regularity. At eight every morning Burgess mounted the stairs to the Master's bedroom, bringing him hot water for shaving. There followed the hot bath, the meditated choice of what to wear and finally the descent of the sartorially neat and bright-cravatted novelist, wearing an equally colorful waistcoat, into the dining-room. Breakfast was always served at 9 A.M. and while James slowly ate this repast he issued his instructions to the housekeeper. At 10 A.M. Miss Weld arrived and work began, usually in the upstairs Green Room during the winters, and in the detached Garden Room as soon as warm weather permitted. Visitors knew they could never see the Master before lunch. The voice dictated rhythmically—with long pauses—until 1:45. They could hear James pacing constantly with the quality of a restless animal, and in rhythm with the familiar response of the typewriter.

When friends suggested (as Morton Fullerton had done years before) that dictation affected his style—which to a degree it did—he insisted that "The value of that process for me is in its help to do over and over, for which it is extremely adapted, and which is the only way I can do at all." In the old days James had not been able to "do over and over." His novels of the middle period had all been written in longhand. There had been revision in proof, and from magazine to book. Now, with the typewriter in his own study, he revised constantly; and while revising, new metaphors, large similes, were inserted into the text. Miss Weld retyped the manuscript repeatedly—James could as it were read proof on his work continually, from day to day. The late style is a "revised" style, a building of the prose page by a process of accretion.

Dictation also enabled James, as never before, to work at several things at once. He had tended, when he wrote in longhand, to push ahead with a given piece of work. The record kept by Miss Weld of her work-days shows us how James would start a story one day, drop it for other work the next, go on with still another story, return to the first, start still another: there were always several hares running at once. An illustration of such simultaneity of work occurs immediately after his completion of *The Wings of the Dove* during the summer of 1902. While James is read-ing the final proofs he is already assembling a collection of tales to make up a book called *The Better Sort.* Two or three more stories are needed. On 1 July 1902 he begins a story titled provisionally "John Marcher," the tale destined to be known as "The Beast in the Jungle." There is then no further reference to it for three months, until 12 October. In the interval James has been working on three other stories: the one first called "Maud Blandy," later the very long tale of "The Papers"; the story called "The Birthplace"; and a tale known in Miss Weld's record only as "The Beauti-ful Child," never completed. Miss Weld's entries say very clearly when each tale was completed—"The Birthplace" on 10 October, "The Beast in the Jungle" on 16 October, "The Papers" on 13 November. The record suggests that the tale of John Marcher, a remarkably unified tonal pic-ture and perhaps James's finest story, was written in three sessions, due allowance made for manual revisions. There were days when Miss Weld was allowed to idle: an entry of 8 August 1902 tells us "no work, Mr. James revising." There were other days when the typist was pressed into over-time: in 1903, to meet a deadline for an article, Miss Weld worked "nine hours with Mr. James on D'Annunzio to finish." In 1902, in between work on the tales, James was sorting out the papers of William Wetmore Story and Miss Weld typed such letters as he would use in the long-postponed memoir. An entry of 22 September records that she had finished copying the letters "so really begin W. W. Story."

In his workshop James found himself studying closely the working methods, the large creative designs, of his predecessors. During the open-ing years of the new century, circumstances aiding, he was led to write a series of papers on George Sand, and large explanatory essays on Bal-zac, Flaubert, Zola. He had dealt with them in the past, often in piece-meal fashion; now he found himself looking at their total achievement. Criticism had always been, for Henry James, an extension of his own creative act: one always felt, in what he wrote of other novelists, a surfac-ing of a buried question, "Is there anything I can learn for the work I have to do?" His essay of 1902 on Balzac begins with his asking himself what he had learned from the French master. Re-reading him on the threshold of his old age, he recognized that Balzac had passed long ago into the very texture of his life. "Endless are the uses of great persons and great things," he told himself, and what he discerned, in each of these large "cases," was the manner in which his ultimate literary monument had been erected.

At sixty James could well ask himself—looking back at all the books he had written, and in the very midst of this period of extraordinary fertility—where he stood in the history of the novel. He had sought always to win success, and had always remained an ambiguous figure in the market-place. What future did he have? What would be the fate of his "reputation"? Thus he embraced opportunities to preface a Balzac novel and a new edition of *Madame Bovary* for a series Gosse was editing. In his essay on Balzac we find James writing of that novelist's "mass and weight," his "scheme and scope." From this he is led to "the question of what makes the artist on a great scale." This was what interested Henry James above everything: what had made James an artist—perhaps on the grand scale? Balzac's imagination had encompassed all his experience. He had created with enormous fertility. Flaubert was the opposite of Balzac. He was not on the "monumental" scale. But then one could hardly have wanted, James implied, more books of the type of *Madame Bovary* or *Salammbô*. George Sand, James wrote, had had great abundance, but she had produced much less *literature* than Flaubert. The omniscient Balzac had created a world. Flaubert had created a single classic. Zola, in his particular and grosser way, had established a "massive identity." And George Sand, in her fluency, her liquid qualities, had been "a supreme case of the successful practice of life itself."

James's essay on Zola, written a few months later for the *Atlantic Monthly,* was a final tribute to the author of *Les Rougon-Macquart* and the courageous defender of Dreyfus. James had begun by being fascinated by Zola, but had deprecated the Frenchman's tendency to deal with "dirty" subjects, his pronounced physicality. But he had always liked the determination and persistence, the dogged seriousness of the man. James recalled also in this essay how in his talk with Zola in the 1890s the French writer appeared to him to have lived only for the writing of his great series of novels. It was almost "as if *Les Rougon-Macquart* had written him as he stood and sat, as he looked and spoke, as the long, concentrated, merciless effort had made and stamped and left him." But then something fundamental had happened. *J'Accuse* had happened— and in his defense of Dreyfus Zola had finally found his commitment to life as well as to art.

Thus in his exploration of what made the artist "on a great scale" the

Master was led to the question of biography. What distinctions were to be made between the man and the artist? He was about to write a biographical memoir, the only one he had ever undertaken; and in his stories there had for a long time been an increasing interrogation of the question of the private life of art and the public life of the work issuing from that art. At this time, however, on the evidence of his stories, a more fundamental question seemed to trouble James. What if he had lived all his life for his great moment, for that *gloire* in which he believed—and what if the moment never came? Out of this troubled emotion, the "ferocious ambition" to which he had early testified, he now fashioned two tales, "The Beast in the Jungle" and "The Birthplace," one tragic and mysterious, and the other comic and ironic. Both were parables of the artist and the acts of life.

The Impenetrable Sphinx

"The Beast in the Jungle," as we have seen, was begun in July of 1902 but seems to have been written largely in two sessions that autumn, during the first days of Billy James's stay in Lamb House. Miss Weld's diary tells us, "October 12, return to John Marcher or The Beast in the Jungle." The next day she notes that Kipling lunched at Lamb House. Three days later, "Finish the Beast in the Jungle. Back to The Papers."

Presence of the author of *The Jungle Book* in Lamb House at the moment of the writing of "The Beast in the Jungle" was a coincidence. However, James had mentioned Kipling when he was writing, earlier, about Rostand, as a figure who, like the French dramatist, had had a phenomenal public success. James himself had had, in the English-speaking world, what might be termed a private success, a *succès d'estime.* In "The Beast in the Jungle" a man believes himself reserved for a special destiny, whether public or private, only to discover that his name is writ in water. Moreover, this man is so absorbed in his ultimate destiny that he fails to live the life given him; and fails to discover the meaning of love. In all James's work there is no tale written with greater investment of personal emotion. The unlived life of so many of his heroes is embodied in John Marcher, the great Anonymous Man, who in thinking of his fate blinds himself to his anonymity.

"The Beast in the Jungle" is a tale of melancholy and loneliness. The passage of an entire lifetime is told in six neatly balanced sections. John Marcher feels "lost in the crowd" at the start of the tale; and he finds this anonymity unbearable. In a house called Weatherend, he encounters a woman named May Bartram. They have met before—ten years earlier, and one day at Sorrento, he had confided to her his secret: he believed himself reserved for an unusual experience. What it is to be, whether beautiful or horrible, he does not know. The occurrence is imaged as a beast tracking him in the jungle, waiting for its moment to spring.

Marcher and May are thirty-five and thirty when they renew their acquaintance at Weatherend. Believing in Marcher's haunted vision, she is ready to participate in his life's vigil. In the next two sections of the story Marcher and May keep company—and the years pass. He is devoted to her as Henry James had been to Miss Woolson in the first days of their friendship, when in Florence in the early 1880s they had sought each other out almost daily. A crucial episode in the story is set in April. Half a lifetime has passed; Marcher now is aware that May is ill; and for the first time he recognizes that they have both grown old waiting for the beast to spring. May stands before a fireless hearth. She wears a green scarf, but like her life it is faded. Marcher looks once more into her eyes and finds them "as beautiful as they had been in youth, only beautiful with a strange cold light." At this moment Marcher images her as "a serene and exquisite but impenetrable sphinx, whose head, or indeed all whose person, might have been powdered with silver." We are face to face with the supreme keeper of the Riddle, the possessor of "the figure in the carpet."

May Bartram keeps the riddle of John Marcher's life. She tells him that the beast has sprung, that his fate—or doom—has already occurred. "You were to suffer your fate," she says. "That was not necessarily to know it." It is an agony for Marcher. At this moment, he joins another image to that of the Sphinx. He sees May, in her whiteness of age, as a lily under a bell of glass, the green of her scarf forming the leaves. Thus John Marcher's dream of woman mingles with the eternal dream of Henry James; she is sphinx, matron, virgin, beast, all in one—artificial and safely preserved under glass, an artifact, as the novelist had long ago imaged the virginal Minny Temple, shut within the "crystal walls of the past."

"You've had your experience," Marcher desolately says to May—"you leave me to my fate." May can do nothing else. If James had avoided the last confrontation between Milly and Densher in his just-completed novel, he gives us the final interview between Marcher and May. And May's last words come to him as "the true voice of the law; so on her lips would the law itself sound." The Sphinx has spoken. He never sees her again. She has left him with the unsolved riddle, which he must live with for the rest of his life, as James lived with the unsolved riddle of Fenimore's death. As the grave closes over her he stands looking at the gravestone, "beating his forehead against the fact of the secret" kept by the name and date. "He kneeled on the stones, however, in vain; they kept what they concealed."

In "The Figure in the Carpet" everyone who knew the secret died and the secret remained untold; in "The Friends of the Friends" death turns the key on something the jealous narrator is concerned to know. The time had come when James could no longer stand such frustration; and his imagination gives John Marcher a final scene, one of the most painful in any of his tales. It occurs at the cemetery. In the interval between his visits to this cemetery Marcher has traveled to the East, to Asia, India, to Egypt—to the land of the Sphinx. But the riddles of history offer him nothing that doesn't seem "common" compared with the dream he has nourished of being one of the elect.

Turning from the great temples and sepulchres he comes back to his private altar of the dead. Face to face with May Bartram's grave, Marcher happens to notice a mourner at another grave. He suddenly allows himself to see not his own grief, but the grief of the other, an "image of scarred passion." Insight comes at last. He realizes what May had wanted him to see on that April day beside her cold hearth, when he had turned her into an artificial flower and put her under glass. "No passion had ever touched him, for this was what passion meant . . . He had seen *outside* of his life, not learned it within." The expected climax in Marcher's life is an anti-climax. He had been singled out—such might be his consolation—as someone to whom "nothing on earth was to have happened." He had not allowed himself to "live" or to love. Circling perpetually in his little private jungle—a hunter hunted—he had not recognized love when it had been offered to him. In the final sentences of the story the passion and tension James was setting down seemed to carry the deepest message of his own egotism:

> He saw the Jungle of his life and saw the lurking Beast; then, while he looked, perceived it, as by a stir of the air, rise, huge and hideous, for the leap that was to settle him. His eyes darkened—it was close; and turning, in his hallucination, to avoid it, he flung himself, face down, on the tomb.

In a moment of perception James was, it would seem, revisiting the grave in the Protestant Cemetery in Rome where Constance Fenimore Woolson's name and her dates were simply carved on the stone embedded in violets. Long ago James had imaged the frosty Winterbourne, a predecessor of John Marcher, standing on this spot unable to answer the riddle of Daisy Miller. Marcher has deciphered his riddle. What he had lost would have made him mortal; to be mortal—that is, to live one's life and to love—that is the real escape from anonymity.

The Real Right Thing

"The Beast in the Jungle" had provided a catharsis for Henry James: it was a moment of insight such as his brother William described in *The*

Varieties of Religious Experience—a book that we know the novelist was reading when he wrote the tale. He was recognizing anew—and more intensely than ever—the ways in which people "use" one another. Miss Woolson had killed herself in Venice for reasons of her own. Her death had been *her* fate and *her* mystery; and it would remain a mystery. In "The Beast in the Jungle" James seems to have reached a moment when he could say to himself that he must occupy himself with his own mysteries, light up the gloom in his own soul. He was searching out the riddle of his "impenetrable sphinx." The answers always seemed simple—yet he had had to wait until he was ready to understand them. Strether's "live all you can," in *The Ambassadors,* had been answered by Milly's fate in *The Wings of the Dove:* one really hadn't lived until one had learned to love. The story of Marcher and May implied that one could love only when one ceased to love oneself. James had treated Miss Woolson as if she had been his Aunt Kate. And he had expended his love for years on ethereal heroines of the mind. Now, on the edge of sixty, he had had this profound revelation which freed him for the things he had to do.

First was the great sustaining question of his life's work. Scattered in the magazines, arrayed on the bookshelves, were the novels and tales he had written in his early chamber in Cambridge, in dim lodgings in Bolton Street, in half a hundred hotels on the Continent, amid the affluence of De Vere Gardens—his whole life, all the adventures of his soul, were in these works. The time had come for him to take stock—to pay attention to his own legend. A writer on the grand scale had to shore up all that was worth preserving out of his years of endeavor. No one else could do it for him. The spinning years had brought him to the moment when he could reflect on the lessons of literature—the example of Balzac, the mystery of Shakespeare—and make the decisions that would lengthen his own shadow beyond the grave. One such decision would result in the "definitive edition" he had planned for years of a great part of his *oeuvre.* Then too, he had always said that an artist should not leave his personal papers to accident. In the coming time he would act on this, burning his manuscripts and hundreds, thousands, of letters he had received. And two years before his death he would issue instructions to his literary executor, his nephew Harry, for a provision in his will, "a curse no less explicit than Shakespeare's own on any such as try to move my bones," declaring his "utter and absolute abhorrence" of any attempted biography or any "giving to the world" of any of his private correspondence.

The Shakespearian curse recalled in this letter of 1914 was implicit in the Shakespearian story, "The Birthplace," which James wrote, together with "The Beast in the Jungle" and the story called "The Papers," during the autumn of 1902. The novelist at that moment was embarking on his biography of William Wetmore Story. In the story "The Real Right Thing," published in December 1899, a young biographer working in his subject's study receives ghostly warnings to leave the dead man's privacy intact. In the end the biographer tells the widow—who wants to do "the real right thing"—that the right thing is to leave the dead alone. As if to drive the lesson home, the biographer (to whom James gave the symbolic name of Withermore) one day finds the ghost of his subject standing on the threshold of the chamber.

It was as if James, about to join the ranks of biographers, wondered whether this was the real right thing for a novelist to be doing. George Sand, subject of a brilliant essay of 1899, offered the "special case." She had always lived in public, but the revelation, long after she died, of the endless train of men she had taken as lovers seemed to make of her a "rueful denuded figure" on the highway of life. Modesty caused one to avert one's eyes, James supposed, but after all, "we have *seen* . . . and mystery has fled with a shriek." The artist ceased to be the transcendent figure of the imagination; the unearthly voice of divine inspiration became an ordinary human voice. Reading at this time the life of Robert Louis Stevenson by Graham Balfour, James found that his beloved friend had become merely a picturesque figure in literary history. Stevenson's books, he wrote Balfour, were now "jealous and a certain supremacy and mystery" had gone from them. The biographer had made Stevenson too *"personally* celebrated."

In writing of George Sand, James suggested that perhaps the artist, the subject, should organize the game of biography on his own terms, rather than leave it to the biographer. The thing was to burn papers, keep secrets, challenge the biographer to dig harder for facts, demand a genuine effort of inquiry and research. It was all too easy to leave a massive archive. "Then," wrote James,

> the pale forewarned victim, with every track covered, every paper burnt and every letter unanswered, will, in the tower of art, the invulnerable granite, stand, without a sally, the siege of all the years.

Shakespeare had withstood the siege of the years; he had survived as invulnerable granite: even generations of actors, raving and ranting, could not spoil him. Shakespeare seemed immune—immune as no other artist in literary history. James had always mocked the legends of Stratford-on-Avon. He argued that the facts of Stratford spoke for a commonplace man; the plays for the greatest genius the world had ever known. This was "the most attaching of literary mysteries." James refused to accept the Baconian theory, or the parochial *bêtise,* as he called it, of the Ciphers.

All of Henry James's work shows that he had been saturated with Shakespeare from his earliest days. He had known him as a boy in Lamb's re-telling of the plays; he had seen him acted in many forms— not only the Shakespeare of old New York theaters, but the Shakespeare of Dickensian London, and the Shakespeare of the Lyceum, the heavily costumed creations of Henry Irving. He had made his pilgrimage long ago to Warwickshire, to the Shakespeare country. He had revisited Stratford five years later, in 1877, on the eve of "Daisy Miller." Even then, at Stratford, he found a "torment" in Shakespeare's "unguessed riddle." If it was "the richest corner of England," it was also the most mysterious. Visiting Sir George Otto Trevelyan, the historian, at Welcombe, near Stratford, we find him writing "it's lovely here—and awfully Shakespearian—every step seems somehow, on William's grave and every word a quotation." He knew the grave well; he admired the spire and chancel of the church in which the Bard was buried; and he knew by heart the cryptic doggerel bespeaking the curse on anyone who would disturb Shakespeare's bones. Long ago, when he had spent a Christmas with Fanny Kemble at Stratford, they had gone to service in this church —the actress whose talk was so saturated with the language of the plays that she made the Bard "the air she lived in."

In a little-known preface to *The Tempest*, written in 1907 for Sir Sidney Lee's edition of Shakespeare, James maintained that he could under no circumstances swallow the legend that Shakespeare wrote *The Tempest* and then gave up writing. This was not the way of a genius with so much abundance in him. "By what inscrutable process was the extinguisher applied and, when once applied, kept in its place to the end?" Recorded circumstances, of course dim and sparse, indicated at any rate, James wryly remarked, "that our hero may have died—since he did so soon—of his unnatural effort." Shakespeare, the man, he went on, did not exist. What existed was simply the Artist—"the monster and magician of a thousand masks . . . so frankly amused with himself, that is with his art, with his power, with his theme, that it is as if he came to meet us more than his usual halfway," gave us the illusion of "meeting and touching the man." But the man was "locked up and imprisoned in the artist."

Artists, James believed, live in the ways in which they express themselves. Shakespeare was not a sensitive harp set once for all in a window to catch the air: he had descended into the street in quest of every possible experience and adventure. James was prepared to accept the art of biography only if it became "a quest of imaginative experience." In such circumstances it could be "one of the greatest observed adventures of mankind."

James's tale of "The Birthplace" does not mention Shakespeare; nor does it mention Stratford. But the birthplace is "the Mecca of the English-speaking race." Morris Gedge, the newly appointed keeper, realizes soon enough that this birthplace is a lot of humbug. He would have liked to stick to hard facts, but the visitors impose upon him their desire for homely detail. Then, when he realizes that he may lose his job, he starts to embroider the legend; he becomes a creator himself, improvising as he stands in the Birth-room:

> Across that threshold He habitually passed; . . . over the boards of this floor—that is over *some* of them, for we mustn't be carried away!—his little feet often pattered, and the beams of this ceiling (we must really in some places take care of *our* heads!) he endeavoured, in boyish strife, to jump up and touch.

Gedge is now a success. The directors vote to double his pay. The creative imagination triumphs over the mundane. The keeper of the shrine pays his tribute to art by being imaginative himself.

3

THE

BETTER SORT

ရွာ

Goody Two Shoes

The crowded years had fled; but the new years, the approach of old age, had their own crowdedness, and the traveler to the Continent—the tourist in France, the voyager in Italy—now had his beaten path from Rye to London. Henry James might pose amusedly as a rural aristocrat, a member of the landed gentry; he had his eye nevertheless on the metropolis that had sheltered him through most of his expatriation. It was his little joke that he lived a dutiful life among his "peasantry" in "the solitudinous and silent nature of Lamb House." Was this kind of life good for him? He asked the question of Grace Norton and answered it promptly: yes, it was beautiful—for three quarters of the year! For the remaining quarter he needed the spaciousness of the capital.

In London one path always led to Lucy Clifford's—that was the road to the literary salon, a hearth where he talked of old friends and met the children of the New Novel and the New Poetry over whom Aunt Lucy fussed devoted and hen-like. The other path led to Eaton Terrace, to Jessie Allen's, and the echoes of the grand world offered by his newer friend, two years younger than himself, whom he had met in Venice in 1899. He had begun by going to her small corner house at No. 74 by invitation, but increasingly was allowed to turn up at the tea-hour, uninvited.

James found Elizabeth Jessie Jane Allen lively and amusing from the first. One of the Allens of Cresselly, she was a great-granddaughter of the Earl of Jersey; various of her relatives in various generations had married Wedgwoods and Darwins. She was always on the move, to Wales, to the castles of the Scottish border, to great English homes. In Eaton Square, with her two loyal maids, her cat, her delicate Victorian watercolors, her choice miniatures and her fine antiques, she served tea or dinner to Henry James, usually in her upstairs drawing-room. She might have been in earlier years a Madame Merle, though less calculating. Now she was more like Maria Gostrey. Indeed James compared her to that lady of *The Ambassadors* when he told her that he had been writing "some stuff in which a woman who has in certain circumstances rather launched a man, has occasion to say to him afterwards: 'Ah, I did it all, but now you can toddle alone!' "

The two toddled charmingly for the last seventeen years of James's life. Miss Allen affected a cape and bonnet when she went to the theater with James. She attached a great importance to her little glass of port at lunch. Her voice was deep and low. She was above all an old-fashioned Lady Bountiful. James had begun by saying that her letters brought him "something of the rattle and the fragrance—as of a thousand expensive essences—of the great world" and exclaiming "how much good you must do and how many people you make happy!" But soon he found himself included in Miss Allen's largesse.

On the first Christmas of their friendship, in 1899, Jessie sent her new friend a Venetian *cinquecento* taper. James thanked her with full euphemism: it would be "the flower of my collection, and the pride of my house." The following Christmas, Miss Jessie's gift consisted of two fine brass Venetian candlesticks. James told her he bowed his head very low in gratitude; but he also had an uneasy feeling, he said, that "the positive frenzy of your altruism" required close watching. The Christmas after that, still keeping up the Venetian memory, it was a fine casket, doubtless like one of Portia's. In the fourth Christmas, and perhaps because it was a winter of blizzard at Rye, what descended on Lamb House were two large bearskin rugs.

James had addressed her as "Dearest and unspeakable Miss Allen" for her earlier gifts. Now he wrote to "Dearest and worst Miss Allen." He told her he would have to bring the rugs back to Eaton Square. They were "impossible, unspeakable, unforgivable." He refused to regard them as his. What was more, he said, he wouldn't even "growl" his "thank you" for the bearskins. To such ungraciousness was he reduced by her perversity.

A day or two later, James went up to London. There was a confrontation in Eaton Square between the Great Novelist and the Altruistic Lady. Whether he carried the bearskins with him we do not know. But he seems to have faced utter defeat. In a letter of 15 December 1902 he agrees to keep the gift. "I promise," he wrote, "to wear the bearskins in bed in the blizzard that I feel to be now again preparing; but all on one condition." The great condition was that from this time on he would address Miss Allen as "Goody Two Shoes," as in the eighteenth-century moral tale attributed to Oliver Goldsmith. And so the descendant of the Allens of

Cresselly became, in the Jamesian mythos, for all her future "dear generous Goody" or "my dear Goody—best of goodies," and their abundant
correspondence a constant play of elegant, ironic persiflage between the
latter-day Goody Two Shoes and her Novelist, humblest, yet most Napoleonic of her friends.

A Queer Job

Henry James called his book about William Wetmore Story "a queer
job." It was a mixture of biography, documents, reminiscence. The tone
of reminiscence dominated the book. The two thick volumes published
late in 1903 were distinctly autobiographical. The novelist had found that
he had to eke out the scant history of his subject with "my own little
personal memories, inferences, evocations, and imagination." James
was not in reality a biographer; he had no intention of becoming one.
Moreover, he had never liked Story. Faced with bundles of letters and
certain diary notes he had neither the time nor the inclination to do the
required "research" which would have provided him with a full background. His own creative and organizing imagination played around the
impersonal and inanimate documents and sought constantly to "novel-
ize" them. Story himself, a consistent amateur—he sculpted, wrote
verses, plays, essays, staged theatricals—James had considered a case of
"prosperous pretension." The world had been more than kind to him. Set
against his time and his generation, the Bostonian-Roman sculptor was
an archetypal Jamesian subject—the American expatriate with a penchant for the artist life. Originally a lawyer and a professor of law, Story
had never learned the law of the artist.

With delicate tact which enabled him to speak the truth—a felici-
tously varnished truth—James described Story's amateurism, and turned
to the other question that must have originally interested him—Story's
expatriation. Had Story paid in his art for having chosen to live abroad
—and in a seductive country that beguiled, tempted, distracted the artist?
Robert Browning, Story's friend, had lived in the same country and produced some of his finest work. "Italy, obviously, was never too much," for
the author of *Men and Women.* But Browning was "devoted to no other
art." Story had been divided and dispersed; he was more social than
artistic, and much too worldly.

James disposed of his "queer job" in about two months, dictating
eloquent commentaries around a series of letters to Story from the
Brownings, from Norton, Lowell, and others. He gave the book a careful
title: *William Wetmore Story and His Friends: From Letters, Diaries and
Recollections.* The key word was "recollections." Speaking always in the
first person he created a series of exquisite pictures of the old Roman

time. To start remembering was to run away from his material. The digressions were numerous. Small wonder certain of James's critics in the United States described the life of Story as the "sacrifice" of a fine subject to Henry James's egotism. Yet the Story volumes now stand as a separate work of art, filled with lessons for the modern biographer— hints from a powerful creative intelligence on how to use significant detail, how to employ the organizing imagination, the transfiguring touch. Not only do the volumes show the struggle of the free imagination within the documentary prison; they illustrate how a work of art can be created about a subject the biographer dislikes.

The Story life is not a "debunking" biography. James addresses himself instead to extracting such richness as he can. The writing had proved "a damnedly difficult job—to make an at all lively and shapely and artful little book—which should not give poor dear W.W.S. simply clean away." The two volumes represent still another instance of the power of the artist to illuminate whatever crosses his path. Story's sculptures rest most often in basements of the art museums and few pause to look at his public statues. But in the pages of Henry James he is enshrined in the grandeur of a style—decidedly not his own.

Henry James's old friend Henry Adams read the Story volumes during a stay in Paris in the autumn of 1903. Adams was moved by the book and, with his asperity and melancholy, saw a deeper message in it. In a remarkable, and very personal, letter, Adams told James he had chronicled in Story's life the history of a generation. "Harvard College and Unitarianism kept us all shallow," wrote Adams. "We knew nothing—no! but really nothing! of the world." One could not exaggerate, he said,

> the profundity of ignorance of Story in becoming a sculptor, or Sumner in becoming a statesman, or Emerson in becoming a philosopher. Story and Sumner, Emerson and Alcott, Lowell and Longfellow, Hillard, Winthrop, Motley, Prescott and all the rest, were the same mind—and so, poor worm—was I!

In the long historical perspective Adams had touched an important truth. The Bostonians, products of a puritan tradition, Story, Sumner, Emerson, Lowell, and the others, had all been intellectuals, to a degree writers of disguised sermons; they had lacked the larger imagination. It had been New York that supplied the largest imaginations in American literature—in Melville, in Whitman, and in Henry James, who went to Europe as Melville had gone to the Pacific, in quest of himself and of freedom.

James's reply was mild and quietly reproving, for he could not join Adams in his pessimism. He had wanted, he said, to invest old Boston out of which William Wetmore Story came with a mellow and a golden glow and he had succeeded only in making it bleak for Henry Adams.

The Master at Sixty

Henry James was sixty; but this birthday, which placed him distinctly in the autumn of life, came and went on 15 April 1903 in a heedless London. Moreover James himself would have liked to forget it. He wrote to Grace Norton, "Any age is in itself good enough—even the latest." The devil of it was that its identity was so brief; it passed so quickly. Landmarks of time there were, on all sides. Grace Norton's brother, Charles Eliot Norton, loomed one day on James's horizon, at Lamb House, but he belonged, James felt, to "some alien epoch of my youth"; even Norton's critical terminology, filled with echoes of the days of Carlyle and Ruskin, seemed quaint. Another Cambridge friend of the old days had just crowned his career by being named to the Supreme Court. Wendell Holmes visited James in Rye during the summer of 1903, and the novelist continued to marvel at the associate justice's "faculty for uncritical enjoyment and seeing and imagining." Wendell moved through life "like a full glass carried without spilling a drop."

Norton, and Holmes—and then, there was Howells, "the dear man." He too belonged to James's old Cambridge. Miss Norton told Henry James that Howells, in an intimate moment, had confided to her his feeling that he had lived his life under the dominion of fear. James, commenting on this, said he had always felt the depression in Howells, but believed he was able to disconnect it from his *operative* self." It had never been, said James, "the least paralysing, or interfering, or practically depressing." On the contrary, Howells had arrived at compensations "very stimulating to endeavour."

If we see James at sixty glancing at the aging countenances of some of his contemporaries, his own life had wide room for the newer generation. Late in 1903 we find him in the presence of Virginia and Vanessa Stephen, now grown, daughters of his old friend, Sir Leslie Stephen. Sir Leslie was slowly dying. To Anne Thackeray Ritchie, sister of Stephen's first wife, James wrote of one of his last visits to Stephen in the house at Hyde Park Gate. His approaching end seemed to James "very handsome, noble, gentle" and "surrounded with such beauty in present and past— beautiful ghosts, beautiful living images (how beautiful Vanessa!), beautiful inspired and communicated benevolence and consideration on the part of everyone." James found Stephen lying on his couch reading; and told him of some new French books that might interest him.

James lived now on a new plane; after the long desolation of the 1890s he had greeted the new century with an outburst of writing. Since 1900 he had published three novels, two volumes of tales, a series of articles. The life of Story was in the press. He might complain during the winter stretches in Rye of solitude, but no writer of his age was more productive, and no American author had ever, so late in life, written with such power and such serene command of craft. Among the young Edwardians now emerging, his presence was a living force—still providing new works, and works strange in style and "difficult," a figure mysterious to the literary world beside the ubiquitous Gosse, or those who wrote for the newspapers. His private life unknown, his rare public appearances always portentous, he was pointed to in clubs and sought after by hostesses; he remained aloof and oracular. When he spoke he delivered himself with a kind of dramatic wit, in sedate, austere phrases that amplified, described, touched, retouched. His short frame had become heavy. He was always clothed elegantly but sometimes with a certain extravagance of color. Henry Dwight Sedgwick, glimpsing him in 1901 in the New Forest, saw him as a figure of vaudeville—tight check trousers, waistcoat of a violent pattern, coat with short tails like a cock sparrow, and none matching; and this topped by a cravat in a large, flowery bow.

Gosse was reminded of a canon he had seen preaching in the Cathedral of Toulouse—in the unction, gravity, yet vehemence of his speech. James had about him the suggestion of an actor; there was a theatrical look in the extravagant costume, and the skin of his face seemed blue, from his close shave, as Clive Bell remembered. An English journalist, Ella Hepworth Dixon, described his eyes as "not only age-old and world-weary, as are those of cultured Jews, but they had vision—and one did not like to think of what they saw." Lady Ottoline Morrell in her memoirs said "they were unlike any other eyes I have ever seen," and Hueffer quoted his servants as saying, "It always gives me a turn to open the door for Mr. James. His eyes seem to look you through to the very backbone."

In the volumes of Victorian and Edwardian reminiscence, images invoked for James are usually images of power—he recalls Caesar or Napoleon, or a Rothschild, or the Catholic "Lacordaire in the intolerable scrutiny of the eyes." And he could be "as ceremonial as an Oriental." The dramatist Alfred Sutro recalled, "One had to wait a long time for the thought to be expressed; . . . but when it came one felt that it had been tremendously worth waiting for." There was in this behavior, without doubt, a form of aggression—this coercing of the listener's attention. One is led to the conclusion that James was a bore to the bores; but when he found his intellectual peers he could relax; the sentences became shorter, the give and take easier.

The image of James at sixty is that of a man who, if he seemed at moments idiosyncratic, eccentric, even comical, exuded aggressive strength. He was assertive and uncompromising, a formed figure, shaped by two continents and many journeys, a tireless observer with an ability to see behind the frail and doubting, the conflicted and ambiguous façade of humanity. Gloriani's eyes in *The Ambassadors* are James's—and we remember how Strether is "held" by them. He thinks of them as "the source of the deepest intellectual sounding to which he had ever been exposed."

In the midst of his work in London James had to rush back to Rye for "a tiresome little episode, one of the sorrows of a proprietor." He found himself having to purchase at what was then a high price—£200—a large piece of garden next to his own; it had been acquired by a local tradesman who could have built on the lot and ruined James's view. A little while later another townsman threatened to tear down two "little old-world whitey-grey cottages" at the end of James's garden wall, in the direction of the church. New negotiations ensued, and the destruction was averted, at what cost we do not know.

As always in such matters, James moved quickly to rectify depletion of his bank account. He received from Blackwood £250, the balance of his advance on the Story biography; but he also signed a contract for a new book—over and above contracts he had already signed to produce two novels during the ensuing year. Macmillan had for some time wanted the novelist to write a book about London, for a series they were publishing. James told them he would need space to turn around in, at least 150,000 words. He agreed to a royalty of 20 percent and an advance of £1,000 to be paid on publication. The book would never be written; too many other things intervened, not least a journey to America. But with the Blackwood money, and assurance of the Macmillan advance, James had a renewed sense of margin.

He returned to Rye in the early summer of 1903, with his productions of the past two years in the press. He returned also with the most famous of his dogs, Max, "a very precious red Dachshund pup . . . with a pedigree as long as a Remington ribbon." Thus to Miss Weld. A few days later the typewriter ticked again in the Garden Room. James had begun a new novel. It was called *The Golden Bowl.*

The Reverberator

Fifteen years earlier, in his witty comedy of manners, *The Reverberator,* James had had a snooping American gossip writer named George Flack declare:

The society news of every quarter of the globe, furnished by the prominent members themselves (oh, *they* can be fixed—you'll see!) from day

to day and from hour to hour and served up at every breakfast-table in
the United States—that's what the American people want and that's what
the American people are going to have.

There came a moment when James himself, lover of privacy, student of
private lives, was served up on the American breakfast-table as a "lover"
(at sixty) of a young scandal-creating beauty, mistress of a tycoon, who
barged into British society like one of James's early heroines. That spring
of 1903 in London, at a tea party, a young woman, dressed in white, fresh
and radiant, detached herself from those present and confronted the
author of *The Wings of the Dove.* She was small, plump, alert, and had
beautiful red hair. "Oh, Mr. James," she fluttered, "everyone says I look
like Milly Theale. Do *you* think I look like Milly Theale?" The anecdotes
do not record Henry James's reply. The fictional Miss Theale and the
real-life Miss Grigsby had two things in common; both possessed red hair
and a great deal of wealth. It little mattered to Miss Grigsby that she was
meeting James almost a year after publication of the novel. With a fine
disregard for chronology, she would always give herself out as the "original" of James's heroine.

Emilie Busbey Grigsby was the daughter of a Confederate officer and
a certain Sue Grigsby of Kentucky. Emilie was said to be convent-bred;
but all her history is a tissue of rumor and publicity. Her wealth came
from her elderly "protector," the Chicago traction magnate Charles T.
Yerkes, who had installed her in a five-story mansion at 660 Park Avenue
in New York. James met her when she was twenty-three. He knew of her
from his friends the Henry Harlands, and from Meredith's daughter.
Miss Grigsby would claim in due course that Meredith, seeing her, had
said he had at last met the heroine of *The Ordeal of Richard Feverel.* In
her pursuit of literature as well as "society" she resembled an earlier
American adventuress, Blanche Roosevelt, who had made friends with
Victor Hugo and Maupassant, but had not conquered Henry James. Emilie Grigsby, later annals would record, dined Yeats; and one legend said
that Rupert Brooke "spent his last night in England at Old Meadows"
where Miss Grigsby lived. But then she also turned up in Westminster
Abbey for the coronation of George V, and claimed an acquaintance with
Princess Mary, later Queen.

By James's account he saw her only four or five times. She invited
him to various parties. He declined. Then feeling that he at least should
be civil, he paid a formal call on her at the Savoy, and spent ten minutes
chatting with her. This was all—except for a story that she dispatched
to the Master at Christmas, not bearskins, but a fine ham, cooked in
champagne.

Miss Grigsby's meeting with Henry James would be a matter for scant attention had not her subsequent history proved so lurid. Two years after that London springtime, Charles Yerkes, the very prototype of an American tycoon, died at the Waldorf and Miss Grigsby was with him. The indomitable Emilie was projected onto the front pages of all the scandal sheets of America. And some time after this another story about her reached the Hearst press: "Heroine in Master's Novel; Grigsby in Language of Love." The New York *Evening Journal,* which ran this headline on 4 January 1906, printed a caricature of a long-faced lecherous-looking bald-headed Henry James seated at his writing desk looking at a bust on a pedestal and at a portrait on his wall of Miss Emilie Grigsby. A subheading pushed harder: "Famous Author, some say, has Romantic Attachment for Girl he idealized as Mildred Theale."

"It may or may not be true," the accompanying story said,

> that Henry James was . . . at one time deeply in love with Emilie Grigsby —that at sixty-five he sneered at conventionalities and in full knowledge of her past laid his great fame at her young feet and asked her to marry him. Men who came to him warning him that there was in the girl's career and antecedents that which would turn his romance over to the sneers of the world, are said to have been sent away from him with crackling words of anger and scorn.

"Friends of Miss Grigsby," the report went on, "while not denying that Henry James honored her with his admiration, declare as fiction itself the tale of his love for her and his proposal of marriage to her. James himself is simply silent on the subject."

But James had not been totally silent. In a letter of 6 May 1904 to his brother William, who had inquired whether it was true (as rumor then already had it) that he had proposed marriage to Miss Grigsby, Henry wrote:

> Dearest William. Your "Grigsby" letter, which has just come in, would be worthy of the world-laughter of the Homeric Gods, if it didn't rather much depress me. . . . My engagement to *anyone* is—as a "rumour" —exactly as fantastic and gratuitous a folly as would be the "ringing" report that Peggy, say, is engaged to Booker Washington, *ouf!* or that Aleck is engaged to Grace Norton. There *is* a Miss Grigsby whom I barely know to speak of, who has been in London two or three June or Julys.

He had seen Miss Grigsby, he said, half a dozen times in all.

> *She* must have put about the "rumour" which, though I thought her silly, I didn't suppose her silly *enough* for. But who—of her sex and species— isn't silly enough for *anything,* in this nightmare-world of insane *bavardage* . . . When you "deny," deny not simply by my authority please, but with my explicit derision and disgust.

He signed himself as "always your hopelessly celibate even though sex-agenarian Henry."

An Exquisite Relation

During the spring of 1903, when the sexagenarian bachelor was still in London, he received a letter from Mrs. Frances Sitwell, who had been the "muse" of Robert Louis Stevenson's early days. She told Henry James that she and Sidney Colvin would marry that summer, and invited him to the wedding. Colvin, Keeper of Prints and Drawings at the British Museum, was fifty-eight—almost a sexagenarian; and the bride was six years older. James had known the two since the days when he saw Stevenson regularly at Skerryvore, near Bournemouth. Theirs had been a romance of forty years' standing, but only now were they free to marry. "Besides being good, your intention is beautiful," James replied to Mrs. Sitwell, "which good intentions always aren't. It has a noble poetic justice." He little dreamed that the wedding, a quiet, almost a secret one, would prove an extraordinary occasion in his own life.

Only four guests were invited to the ceremony in Marylebone Church, on 7 July 1903. James went in the company of Lucy Clifford. The formalities were soon over and the party went on foot to the Great Central Hotel a quarter of a mile away, where, as Mrs. Clifford reported, "a quiet little luncheon party had been arranged." The Colvins were full of happy embarrassment, the guests were afraid to laugh, and "when the waiter was out of sight and hearing we drank to the bride and bridegroom with little nods and whispers."

The party was joined at the hotel by a friend of the former Mrs. Sitwell's, a handsome, elegant man who looked younger than his years: he was actually thirty. Dudley Jocelyn Persse was a Persse of Galway, a nephew of Lady Gregory. He carried himself with ease; he was gentle, self-assured, yet with a touch of shyness. He laughed a great deal. James found him attractive from the first. A week later he wrote to Mrs. Colvin of the presence in Lamb House "of your delightful young Irish friend Jocelyn Persse. I feel as if I ought to thank you for him."

Two days after the wedding Persse had called on the Master at the Reform Club. That same week-end he journeyed to Rye, where the two spent three days together, not unlike the long week-end four years earlier when Henry James had discovered how much he loved the young sculptor, Hendrik Andersen. He loved Persse, one judges, quite as much—if not more. The first letter from James to Persse, nine days after their meeting, is addressed from the Athenaeum Club to "my dear, dear, Jocelyn." James was, he said, lunching, tea-ing and dining out, "but finding it all less good, by a long shot, for soul and sense, than the least moment of that golden westward walk and talk of ours on Monday afternoon. A blessing rested on that, still rests, will ever rest." James added that it would "rest better still if you will remember that you promised to send a photograph to yours always and ever" and he signed his name with his customary grand flourish. When four days later James returned to Lamb House, Jocelyn's photograph "welcomed me home to my empty halls and made them seem for the moment less lonely." The novelist enjoined his new friend to remember—"and never doubt of it"—that "no small sign of your remembrance will ever fail even of its most meagre message to yours, my dear Jocelyn, always Henry James."

This was the note, the consistent tender note, of a friendship that would grow in warmth and feeling and remain devoted and loyal to the end—into the time when James grew old and ill and Jocelyn's golden hair turned white. James would speak of "this exquisite relation of ours." Even more than Andersen, Jocelyn Persse became for him a kind of image in a mirror of his younger days. He made James feel as if he were still thirty. Andersen had helped break the plate-glass front of James's life and Persse and the novelist were able to approach one another with an ease and directness James had not allowed himself in his earlier and more reticent years.

Jocelyn wasn't the least bit "literary." He was a finely-turned-out specimen of the Anglo-Irish gentry—addicted to good manners, food and drink, fine cigars and brandy, hunting, flirtation, romance, the "fun" of living. Very early in their friendship James wrote to Jocelyn: "I seem to see you roll, triumphant, from one scene of amiable hospitality and pro-miscuous social exercise to another." The novelist envied, he said, "the magnificent *ease* with which you circulate and revolve—spinning round like a brightly-painted top that emits, as it goes, only the most musical hum. You don't *creak.*" Or again: "I rejoice greatly in your breezy, heath-ery, grousy—and housey, I suppose—adventures, and envy you, as always, your exquisite possession of the Art of Life which beats any Art of mine hollow."

Others—Hugh Walpole for instance—who observed James's friend-ship with Persse wondered what the two talked about, how this young man whose spelling wasn't up to scratch and whose talk was social and gossipy could hold the formidable Master. Walpole mentioned this once to James (for he was jealous of Jocelyn) and asked what "subjects in common" they found to talk about. He got a clear answer. "One gets on with him in a way without them, and says to one's self, I think, that if *he* doesn't mind, well, why should one either?" Jocelyn's simplicity, his charm, his good looks, these mattered for James much more than any high intellectual talk. He had had enough of that sort of thing in the *grand monde* of literature.

What existed between him and Jocelyn was one of those friendships in which neither friend makes large demands on the other. Persse wandered in "society," visited, traveled—and eventually came to Lamb House. When the younger man was in London, at his flat in Park Place, James periodically issued one of his elaborate invitations to Jocelyn to join him for dinner and the theater in town. "Can you miraculously dine with me either tonight or tomorrow *here*—at 8:15—and perhaps 'go' somewhere; or at any rate *talk?*—when I will tell you many things—most of all how indeed I remember last year." James was writing on the first anniversary of their first weekend together at Lamb House. When Jocelyn considerately wondered whether he wasn't keeping James from work and from doing important things instead of simply gossiping with him, James replied, "Don't, my dear boy, afflict me again by talking of my 'sacrifices.' There is, for me, something admirable and absolute between us which waves away all that." James sent Persse *The Ambassadors* when it was published—"if you are able successfully to struggle with it try to like the poor old hero, in whom you will perhaps find a vague resemblance (though not facial!) to yours always Henry James." He knew that Jocelyn probably wouldn't read the book. But this mattered not at all to James. What mattered was the air of charm and enchantment they seemed to weave for one another. "Why he liked me so much I cannot say," Persse would write many years later. He said also James was "the dearest human being I have ever known."

James continued to write intense letters to Hendrik Andersen—although letters increasingly critical—even while he enjoyed his periodic meetings with Jocelyn. The letters to Persse do not contain the quantity of verbal embracings that we find in those addressed to Andersen. Perhaps the intimacy with the young Irishman did not need so much verbalizing. We may speculate that James's involvement with Andersen had in it a part of his passion as artist. The sculptor had a strong touch of megalomania that James, with his own Napoleonic drive, would recognize: and when Andersen did not measure up to James's high standards and codes of art, there was strong and poignant disillusion. With Jocelyn no such tensions seem to have existed.

The exact nature of James's friendship with Jocelyn Persse, as that with Andersen, is difficult to describe. We have so little beyond the affectionate language of his letters. Whether the homo-erotic feeling between Persse and James was "acted out" is perhaps less important than the fact that an intimate affection existed between them. We must remind ourselves that James was old, stout, Johnsonian. He probably loved Persse in some ways as Johnson had loved his Boswell. But Boswell was a "publishing" individual who consumed his life in his diaries—and planned to write the life of Johnson. Persse simply lived his life; and his memories of James remained unrecorded; they were absorbed into one great memory—that of an abiding affection. We are left with the impression that James's love meant more to Persse than James's greatness. They both possessed a fund of hedonism. It was the love of an aging man for his lost youth, and the evocation of it in a figure of masculine beauty, as with Hendrik Andersen. James found in his relationship with Persse what he did not find with Andersen, the serenity that enabled him to make *The Golden Bowl* a work unique among his novels, in that things come out right for the characters—the marriage survives, there is progeny, and the hero has a unique strength and masculinity. In his relation with Persse, James finally freed himself from the prolonged innocence of his earlier years. And while he tried to write more novels after *The Golden Bowl,* he no longer needed to do so: he had finally resolved the questions, curious and passionate, that had kept him at his desk in his enquiry into the process of living.

Lessons of the Master

He had become a presence, an oracle, a legend. Not only the increasingly conferred title of "master," but the awe he seemed to inspire in the drawing-rooms, the adulation of the young men, the fact that he was now imitated, parodied, caricatured—all this spoke for the imprint of a style and a personality. He had a particular and even painful instance of the effect of his personality and his literary power in the autumn of 1903 when Howard Overing Sturgis brought him the galleys of a long-planned novel. Howard Sturgis—not to be confused with James's other friend, the crippled "little demon," Jonathan Sturges—was the youngest son of the banker Russell Sturgis, whom James had known since the 1870s. James remembered the youthful Howard, but he had not really got to know him until the young man completed his education at Eton and Cambridge, and came into his inheritance. Howard visited Lamb House rarely, but James stayed quite often in the American's comfortable oversize Georgian villa, Queen's Acre—called by everyone "Qu'Acre"—on the edge of Windsor Great Park. Here at various times during the coming years James would be at the center of Sturgis's entourage: A. C. Benson, Percy Lubbock, the young American historian Gaillard Lapsley, Rhoda Broughton, and a bit later Edith Wharton, who had known Sturgis at Newport.

Howard had settled promptly into Victorian domesticity. His most characteristic eccentricity was his addiction to embroidery and knitting. He would sit with his thick golden hair beautifully brushed, his small feet daintily crossed, in the middle of a square carpet on the lawn, or by his fireside, with his basket and his dogs about him, working on some large golden-threaded design. He lived with a friend, a younger man, William Haynes Smith, known to the Qu'Acre circle as "The Babe." In spite of his eccentricities, "Howdie" had a very successful career at school; he had embodied his Eton experience in a sentimental novel called *Tim.* He was witty, poetic, sociable, gentle, and not at all intellectual: a passive nature lodged in the sturdy frame of a moustachioed and vigorous male. His villa had a quiet domestic air, with its white-paneled walls hung with watercolors, its furniture of faded slippery chintz, its French windows opening on an old-fashioned large American-style verandah. Qu'Acre provided a warm hearth for Howdie's intimates— dandies, distinguished dames, the *literati*—who weren't bothered by his feminine traits. The atmosphere was a mixture of the maternal, the paternal and the matriarchal. Perhaps this was why James once told Howard he could find it possible to live with him—an unusually affectionate declaration from a novelist who lived so proudly alone. It would have been for James a little like living with his mother.

Sturgis had long before told James of the novel he was writing, and had received strong encouragement. Now he had completed his long work, *Belchamber.* It was about a young English marquis, of an extremely passive nature, who marries a pushing young woman more out of chivalry than affection: the marriage is never consummated. She takes lovers and in due course presents him with an heir. The young nobleman remains passive. Howard thus provided himself in his novel with a babe, without having to sleep with any woman. The best part of the novel is the affection Sainty—Howdie's hero—bestows on the infant.

"Bring your book and read it aloud!" James told Sturgis, inviting him to Lamb House in October 1903. Howard seems not to have read his novel aloud, but he left behind a batch of galleys. In a matter of days he received the first report. The novel was going "very solidly and smoothly," James wrote. Having delivered a series of compliments, James settled down to the essentials. After all he was "a battered producer and 'technician'" himself, and could read only critically, constructively and "*re*-constructively." The one detail over which he paused was Howdie's choosing as his main character a member of the English nobility and of such high rank, a marquis. "When a man is an English Marquis, even a lame one," he said, there were "whole masses of Marquisate things and items . . . which it isn't open to the painter *de gaité de coeur* not to make some picture of." James was sure however other readers wouldn't notice this. And he applauded the way in which Howdie had stayed with the inner world of Sainty.

What James perhaps overlooked initially was that Howdie had recorded, with great accuracy, the natural history of a passive male. In his second letter, after he had read a further batch of galleys, he came to the question of the passivity. It wasn't only Sainty's aristocratic "point of view," said James, it was that he was *"all* passive and nullity." Where was the *positive* side? Sturgis gave Sainty *"no state of his own* as the field and stage of the vision and drama." The novel didn't seem to happen to Sainty, but *around* him. When Sturgis replied that after Sainty's marriage "nothing happens to him," James replied as from Olympus:

> Why, my dear Howard, it is the part in which *most* happens! His marriage itself, his wife *herself,* happen to him at every hour of the 24—and he is the only person to whom anything does . . .

James's unveiling of the work's central weakness overwhelmed Howard Sturgis. He announced to the Master he was withdrawing his novel from publication. James, clearly upset, wrote in haste:

> If you *think* of anything so insane you will break my heart and bring my grey hairs, the few left me, in sorrow and shame to the grave. Why should you have an inspiration so perverse and criminal? If it springs from anything I have said to you I must have expressed myself with strange and deplorable clumsiness.

If Howdie loved him, said James, "let your adventure take care of itself to the end."

A. C. Benson, in his diary, records a conversation with James in April 1904. *Belchamber* had just been published—for Howdie had allowed himself to be mollified. James had read it and "Good Heavens, I said to myself, he has made nothing of it! . . . Good God, why this chronicle, if it is a mere passage, a mere ante-chamber, and leads to nothing." He had tried, he said, "with a thousand subterfuges and doublings such as one uses with the work of a friend" to indicate the fault. Thus the doctrinaire lessons of the Master: much kindness, much truth, great integrity—yet often the weighty foot stepping on tender toes. Even with the "subterfuges and doublings" James's criticisms had come through to his friend with distinct clarity, and Howdie felt the disapproval all the more profoundly because he loved the Master.

Edith Wharton said that Sturgis—his "native indolence and genuine humility aiding"—accepted James's verdict and "relapsed into knitting and embroidery." But in the privacy of his study Sturgis wrote out his painful feelings in a tale called "The China Pot"—about a great writer who demolishes the work of a younger man. The younger man takes this so to heart that he commits suicide; and in a scene at the cemetery, the Great Author and another friend discuss why the young man has taken his life; the Great Author finds his death "amazing, mysterious and inexplicable." But the other man "could see that he knew as well as I did, and that he knew that I knew." This was an ending worthy of James himself, and one that would have given the deepest pain to the Master, which is perhaps why Howdie never published the story.

An Agreeable Woman

For some years the Master had been quietly pursued by another American writer, more professional in her work than Howard Sturgis, more determined, more ambitious. Edith Wharton came out of James's "old New York," although born two decades later. His locale had been essentially Washington Square (before the city had moved uptown); hers was the higher reach of the then residential Fifth Avenue. Edith Newbold Jones came to maturity in a small and wealthy Manhattan society that was now threatened by the new industrialism, the *arrivistes* James had only tentatively sketched in his fiction. She knew to the core this small world, with its old decencies, its stratified codes, its tradition of elegance, and the daily life within its brownstone mansions already fenced in by tall buildings.

She had been reared in a masculine family circle. Her two brothers were grown men when she was still a child, and she was deeply attached to her father. Edith Jones would have more men friends than women and they were always men high in the life of the country. It was said of her that she brought a man's strength to the sympathy and solicitude of a woman, and a man's organizing power to a woman's interest in dress and the decoration of houses. She was, in James's life, one of the "queenly" women he had studied closely in earlier years; but Mrs. Wharton did not have to assert her queenliness in the eccentric ways of Mrs. Jack. It was instinctive, inbred—and what endeared her to James was that she possessed also a civilized mind and an artist's style.

She would later recall that she had crossed James's path twice in the 1880s and the early 1890s: but she was then too shy and in awe of the Master to speak to him, and he paid no attention to her. At the home of the Edward Boits in Paris, Mrs. Wharton had sported an example of the *haute couture* in the hope that she might catch the attention of the pensive bearded novelist. She failed. She tried again one day in Venice in the Curtis entourage, where she made a point of wearing a particularly fetching hat. To this too he seems to have been impervious: or perhaps to Edith's assertion of personality through dress. She had not, then, published anything and was living with her socially prominent husband, Edward Robbins Wharton, largely at Newport, and paying extended visits to Europe. In the closing years of the century, the Bourgets began to speak to James of their valued American friend, Madame Wharton. He heard of her also from Mary Cadwalader Jones, the divorced wife of Edith's older brother, whom he had known for some years. Through the Bourgets, Mrs. Wharton sent James a message of goodwill at the moment of *Guy Domville.* And in 1899 she sent him her first book of tales, *The Greater Inclination.* Towards the end of that year he wrote Bourget he had read Mrs. Wharton's stories. What was best in them was "her amiable self." What was "not best was quite another person." He had recognized himself, his style.

Almost a year elapsed before he acknowledged the tales. What prompted him finally to write was a story in *Lippincott's,* called "The Line of Least Resistance." He found Mrs. Wharton's tale "brilliant." It possessed "an admirable sharpness and neatness and infinite wit and point." And in his most charming law-giving vein he continued, in his first letter to her, dated 26 October 1900:

> I applaud, I mean I value, I egg you on in your study of the American life that surrounds you. Let yourself go in it and *at* it—it's an untouched field, really . . . And use to the full your remarkable ironic and valeric gifts; they form a most valuable (I hold), and beneficent engine.

Still her irony and her "valeric" quality needed moderating. The *Lippincott's* tale was "a little hard, a little purely derisive." James ended by urging Edith Wharton to send him what she wrote. "I'll do the same by you!" he promised. He asked her also to come to see him some day.

She had finally made a distinct impression. But they had not yet met when in 1902 she sent James her two-volume historical fiction, *The Valley of Decision,* which she dedicated to Bourget. Mrs. Cadwalader Jones sent him as well her new collection of tales, *Crucial Instances,* and her short novel *The Touchstone.* James acknowledged the historical novel and told Mrs. Wharton he had read it with sympathy, "high criticism, high consideration"; then he returned to the charge of his earlier letter. He wanted "crudely" but "earnestly, tenderly, intelligently," to admonish her in favor of "the *American Subject.* There it is round you. Don't pass it by." Pausing to apologize for his "impertinent importunities" he still returned to the charge with "All the same DO NEW YORK! The first-hand account is precious." The Master saw, with great clarity, where Mrs. Wharton's talent and subject lay. A few days later he sent to Mrs. Cadwalader Jones his famous statement that Edith "must be tethered in native pastures, even if it reduce her to a backyard in New York."

The two writers did not actually meet until December 1903, when James had passed his sixtieth birthday and Mrs. Wharton her fortieth. She came abroad that year, and when she arrived in London, James called on her, one day just before Christmas. He saw a woman of about his own height, dressed with taste and distinction; she spoke in the civilized manner of her tales, with a range of literary knowledge and quotation. She was cosmopolitan like himself, yet she was grounded in New

York; and she was concrete and observant. On her side, she saw a different James from the bearded "Penseroso" of Mrs. Boit's Parisian drawing-room, or the light-jacketed James of Venice. For the first time she looked upon his shaven countenance, "the noble Roman mask" of his face and "the big dramatic mouth," and she noticed well-tailored clothes which loosely enveloped the now considerable embonpoint. James was massive and masterly. He seemed to her "in good spirits" and she said he talked "more lucidly than he writes," for she did not like his later manner. She no longer stood in awe of the Master. But he remained, and would remain, a figure of magnetic charm and force. Their sense of irony and humor was tuned to the same key, and on this ground Mrs. Wharton said that "Henry James was perhaps the most intimate friend I ever had though in many ways we were so different." James would not have used the word "intimate." Mrs. Wharton was always for him the *grande dame;* but he admired her intellectual and literary qualities and her style. His affection was genuine; his reservations were strong.

The following spring, at Whitsuntide, Edith Wharton and her genial and totally non-intellectual husband, familiarly called Teddy, hired a motor—they did not then own one—and were chauffeured to Rye where they spent twenty-four hours with the Master. By that time Henry James had no doubt of Mrs. Wharton's role in her marriage. "The Edith Whartons," he told Howells, had been with him "in force." James had long before expressed his suspicion of "the great ones" of the earth; he had complained that they lacked imagination. This can be discerned in the things Mrs. Wharton noticed in Lamb House and we have her description —in her later reminiscences, written long after James was dead—of Jamesian hospitality. The Garden Room with its Palladian windows pleased her; but she alone of all James's guests would speak of his "anxious frugality," would comment on the "dreary pudding or pie of which a quarter or a half had been consumed at dinner" and its reappearing on the table the next day "with its ravages unrepaired." From her point of view James—whose servants called him a martinet and "an old toff"—did not know how to give them orders. When James visited Edith Wharton she clearly took command; and before a commanding woman—as with his older brother—James withered and passively surrendered. She made him feel powerless—he who otherwise exuded power.

Mrs. Wharton's remark that James "lived in terror of being thought rich, worldly or luxurious" must be understood as stemming from his continued ironies about his inability to live up to *her* style. James's visitors usually testified to the solid bourgeois comfort of his house and the quality of his table; his claret had been praised and the efficiencies of his small household staff. What Mrs. Wharton did not grasp—she could be very literal in such matters—was that James amusedly posed as a country squire and treated her with great flourishes as a visiting lady of high estate. In fact, especially during these years, the novelist was decently well off; he had a modest £2,000 a year (about $10,000) as against Mrs. Wharton's $50,000. Moreover, James liked to mock forceful ladies.

He was writing of Mrs. Wharton's world in the novel he was finishing when she and Teddy came for their first visit to Lamb House. The Whartons were on their way back to the United States and he promised Edith he would visit her later that year—for by this time it was settled that the native would return after his twenty-year absence. To Mrs. John La Farge, the former Margaret Perry, he wrote that he had seen more of the Whartons, "—of her—than ever before, and greatly liked her, though finding her a little dry." He added these significant words: "she is too pampered and provided and facilitated for one to be able really to judge of the woman herself, or for *her* even, I think, to be able to get really *at* things." The judgment would be muted in later years, but when James wrote of Prince Amerigo in *The Golden Bowl* that "below a certain social plane, he never *saw*" he was describing in effect Edith Wharton's failures in perception.

"The Golden Bowl"

During the Christmas season of 1902, in that busy year in which he had published *The Wings of the Dove* and written the life of Story, Henry James had an opportunity to view, in a vault at the local bank, an *objet d'art* which belonged to the descendants of the Lambs, whose house he now owned. It was a golden bowl, presented by George I when, during his stay in Lamb House, he attended the christening of a recently born baby in the family. To one of the Lamb descendants, James wrote that "this admirable and venerable object" had "a beautiful colour—the tone of old gold—as well as a grand style and capacity." He added that he was eager for "every ascertainable fact" about Lamb House, the "charming, graceful, sturdy little habitation" in which he hoped "in time (D.V.) to end my days." King George's bowl was more than an "ascertainable fact" about Lamb House. It gave him the title for his last novel.

The idea for *The Golden Bowl* had been in his notebooks for more than ten years. On 28 November 1892 he sketched there the plot for what he thought would be a short story, about a father and daughter who both become engaged, the father, a widower, still youngish, to a girl of the same age as his daughter. "Say he has done it to console himself in his abandonment—to make up for the loss of the daughter, to whom he has been devoted." The marriages would take place "with this characteristic consequence," that father and daughter would continue to see one another and in fact maintain their old interest, while the husband of the one and the young wife of the other would be thrown together—with the father's second wife becoming "much more attractive to the young husband of the girl than the girl herself has remained." The subject for James resided in "the pathetic simplicity and good faith of the father and daughter in their abandonment. They feel abandoned, yet they feel consoled with *each other.*" A necessary basis "must have been an intense and exceptional degree of attachment between the father and daughter —he peculiarly paternal, she passionately *filial!*"

From the days of *Washington Square,* James had written stories of "dutiful" daughters in various stages of revolt, or of daughters so "fixated" on their fathers that they ruin the paternal chances of remarrying, as in his tale "The Marriages." His own sister Alice had been a dutiful and invalid daughter, who had kept house for her father after their mother's death. Even more, there remained with him the image of Lizzie Boott and her father, leading their self-sufficient life in the Villa Castellani, on Bellosguardo; that life had gone on as before even after Lizzie married: Frank Duveneck had seemed to James very much of a third party. Finally in the close-knit family constellation James created in *The Golden Bowl* he was dealing with the deepest part of his own inner world—his father's having had in the house not only his wife Mary, but her sister Catherine, the loyal Aunt Kate. There had always been triangles in James's life. In this ultimate work, they culminated in two joined triangles: father, daughter, and daughter's husband; and the husband's mistress, who then marries the father and so becomes the stepmother of the heroine, and mother-in-law of her lover. Everyone begins by having his cake and eating it. The daughter marries but remains close to her father. The father acquires a bride, but still possesses his daughter. The Prince acquires his Princess, but doesn't have to give up his mistress. The mistress makes the marriage she had waited for, a marriage of wealth and position, but keeps her lover. In Elizabethan tragedy such "incestuous" situations could lead to a sanguinary end. In *The Golden Bowl* the energies of the characters, and of the work, have as their goal an extraordinary attempt to maintain a balance—without rocking the boat.

There is little doubt that, in addition to the memory of King George's offering to the Lambs, James had in mind Ecclesiastes 12:6–7—"Or ever the silver cord be loosed, or the golden bowl be broken, or the pitcher be broken at the fountain, or the wheel broken at the cistern, Then shall the dust return to the earth as it was: and the spirit shall return unto God who gave it." He may also have remembered Blake's lines, "Can wisdom be kept in a silver rod, or love in a golden bowl?" The golden bowl is seen originally by Charlotte Stant and the Prince in a London curiosity shop; she wants to offer it as a marriage gift, but the Prince, whom James called Amerigo, is deeply superstitious; he discerns a flaw in the bowl: it is not made of gold, but is gilded crystal; and it contains a crack—emblematic not only of the marriage of the Prince and Maggie Verver (he too is a discoverer of America) but of the entire civilization in which this marriage has been consummated. The Prince, Maggie, and her father, Adam Verver, belong to a world also imaged for us in the metaphor of the pagoda with which the second half of the novel begins, "a structure plated with hard, bright porcelain, coloured and figured and adorned, at the overhanging eaves, with silver bells that tinkled, ever so charmingly, when stirred by chance airs." Its great surface remains "impenetrable and inscrutable" to Maggie. She has never really sought admission. She has remained outside, living in proximity to this artificial, hard-surfaced, beautiful but lifeless object. And it is the plebeians who will break the artificial world: the dealer in antiques will reveal inadvertently the liaison between the Prince and Charlotte to Maggie; she will come into possession of the flawed golden bowl; and another plebeian, Fanny Assingham, will perform the single act of violence in the novel, when she deliberately drops the bowl on the polished floor and it splits neatly into three pieces.

Nothing in Maggie's life has prepared her for her discovery that the princely husband she has acquired as if he were still another artifact is treacherous and unfaithful; and that he is being unfaithful with her friend, Charlotte, whom she had induced her father to marry in order to "console" him for the loss of herself. Maggie's loss of innocence is violent, a complete collapse of her pagoda-life. But James was writing a story of the education of a princess, an American princess. What Maggie possesses is the knowledge of her power. She comes to recognize that the Prince, having married wealth, will hardly wish to renounce it; that Charlotte in turn has gained the position of comfort and ease she has wanted. With the coolness of an heiress of the ages, Maggie brings about a "palace" revolution that gives her full command. Accepting that if she is to remain a wife she must cease to be a daughter, she dispatches her father to America to lead his own life. Charlotte, the adulteress, is thereby banished from Europe. And the Prince, who has wanted a wife instead of an immature father-attached girl, finds that he now has one. They have a child, a boy, and for the first and only time in all of James's fiction the offspring is allowed to live.

In *The Golden Bowl* James was finally able to bring into the open the deeply buried scenes of his childhood, that of the curious little boy who has to contend with triangular enigmas of father, mother, aunt, and has to make choices, not always knowing to whom exactly he belongs—like his Maggie, who belongs to her father and to her husband, and yet must surrender one, if she is to have the other. In doing so he had finally found the combination that could unlock the secrets of his life. He had written nineteen novels and in many of them he had affirmed that no marriage was possible between the Old World and the New—that America and Europe were irreconcilable. Now in his twentieth he brings the marriage off. Prince Amerigo, descendant of explorers, can as it were "marry" the continent of their journeyings; and Maggie—and America—can with the proper will respond not in ignorance but in awareness.

In terms of another of his favorite symbols—that of the cage—Henry James in this novel is able at last to set free the young female adolescent imprisoned within his spirit and his imagination. She had grown from childhood with his growth; she had revolved in the glass cage of *The Sacred Fount.* Now she emerges from the pagoda-cage. She has ceased to observe actively while remaining physically passive; she at last refuses to "renounce." She can act—with strength, with resolution, even when necessary with hardness and cruelty. The fable is finally complete.

As he wrote his novel, Henry James believed (so he told his agent and his publisher) that he was "producing the best book I have ever done." He had written *The Ambassadors* and *The Wings of the Dove* each in less than a year; but he spent more than a twelvemonth over *The Golden Bowl.* Rewriting almost every page, as he had done long ago with *The Portrait of a Lady,* he had produced 200,000 words "with the rarest perfection." To Scribner's, who were to publish the book in America in the autumn of 1904, he wrote, as he was reading proof, "it is distinctly, in my view, the most *done* of my productions—the most composed and constructed and completed"; he would shamelessly repeat, and his publisher could quote him, that "I hold the thing the solidest, as yet, of all my fictions."

Some of his readers would say it was too solid, too compact, too filled with suggestions and associations, too crowded and imaged. Reviewers would call it "detached," "cold," "cruel," and "a psychological dime-novel." They would find it over-intellectual and overloaded. But few denied its greatness in 1904. Read with the kind of leisure that went into its writing, *The Golden Bowl* on every page shows clarity of intention and consummation. The prose is dense, yet fluid, and the surfeit of architectural and museum-world imagery, the gathering of social and artistic materials to suggest the fabric of civilization, combined the art of realism James had learned long ago from Balzac with the old art of the fable.

The first half of the book belongs to the Prince, and James makes us see him and the civilization that has produced him in architectural terms, the spaciousness of old palaces and formal gardens, the thousands of years of human endeavor that molded him into a certain kind of heir of the ages. Grandeur and history lead to the ironic marriage that unites this descendant of one kind of Imperium with the daughter of the still newer Empire created out of original exploration and voyage, which even bears the name that originally belonged to the family of the Prince. The imagery changes when we come to the second half of the novel, in which Maggie must face the crack in her life and her phantoms—"the horror of finding evil seated, all at its ease, where she had only dreamed of good." For the first time the insulated American innocent learns that life has its treacheries and that the pagoda, with its pleasant bright surfaces and the gentle sound of its tinkling bells, can conceal the ominous and sinister. Animal imagery, the prowl of predatory creatures, is felt in the gradual unveiling of Maggie's inner world; she must live through her jealousy, her sense of the collapse of her world, her re-education, and do it with calm duplicity. James makes us feel the power of her subdued passion—the power of the "really agitated lamb." Lions are as nothing compared to them, for lions "are blasé, are brought up from the first to prowling and mauling," as the cynical Fanny Assingham remarks to her husband.

James treats Adam Verver, the enigmatic, poker-faced, check-suited American tycoon, as a mystery figure, a kind of "Uncle Sam" whose thoughts are never known, but who represents American indulgence where his daughter is concerned, and American shrewdness in the gathering in of Europe's creations. If he is Adam, the first man, he seems often in this novel to be still living in the Garden, "in a state of childlike innocence," as the Prince observes. But father and daughter throughout the book "protect" one another. In silence, and with calm, they work out their problem with the calculations of a game of chess. And the imagery of the Princess with her pagoda-claustrophobia gives way in the final confrontation between the "bad" heroine and the "good," when Maggie, waiting and wondering whether she and Charlotte will meet, feels herself to be like Io, in the old legend, goaded by the gadfly, or Ariadne, who having helped Theseus find his way out of the labyrinth, is left "roaming the lone sea-strand."

The symbolic statement of *The Golden Bowl* is most personal and autobiographical not in the artifact of the bowl but in the crack in the artifact. In the earlier work of the novelist society was accepted as a *status quo* and James was interested in personal relations within that society. In this novel, having put together the strange pagoda of Maggie Verver's life, the novelist is able to face the truth reflected by the image. The pagoda's bells tinkle when brushed by "chance airs"; but they give off a remote sound. The golden bowl contains a crack; moreover it is only a *gilded* bowl. The flaws must be discovered, the correct values re-established. In his questioning of society James re-expresses what he had once asserted as an epigram: that life could get by sufficiently without art; but that "art without life is a poor affair." One can possess a pagoda, and it can be exquisite, yet in the end it is no substitute for living; it remains an ornament of life. The golden bowl may have great beauty of form, but in reality it is a fake. The crack in the bowl stood thus for the cracks in James's life: as in the life of the Ververs. He had for too long cast his life exclusively with art; he had not allowed himself to experience the force of life itself. In *The Golden Bowl* Prince Amerigo wants the genuine, not the fake.

In creating a hero who no longer rationalizes away the claims of love, of physical love, James reflected the presence in his life, at the moment that he began to write this book, of Jocelyn Persse, whom he adored. Having found love James had come to see at last that art could not be art, and not life, without love. In the larger experience, he saw the crack in civilization, which has to contend with human force and human frailty and the grandeurs and terrors of the human heart. The "sinful" relations of Chad and Madame de Vionnet, Densher and Kate, the Prince and Charlotte, were no longer the essence of the matter; each had had to make the most of the process of living and the vulnerability of love—and of life itself. To be sure, Maggie had to lose her father to keep her husband; the Prince had to lose his mistress to keep his wife. Henry James had had to give up America in order to have Europe. But in all such decisions, civilization alone assured equilibrium and a rule of law. Many lies are told to save the marriage of Maggie and the Prince, but they have been, as in *The Wings of the Dove* and *The Ambassadors,* "constructive lies"—the lies or myths by which civilization holds together. The whole truth, James suggests, could destroy civilization, for everything, as the Prince is made to say, is "terrible in the heart of man." All the more reason, this novel seems to imply, that the terrors of the heart should not be translated into life.

So, in the last of the three pragmatic novels with which he ended his career as a novelist, James places himself on the side of the "illusions" by which man lives. *The Golden Bowl* is the summit of that career.

4

THE

AMERICAN

SCENE

A Passion of Nostalgia

One day in November of 1903, James went down to Tilbury to see Mrs. John La Farge and her daughter off to America. By his own account, he went because his friends were "rather helpless and alone." He boarded their ship, the *Minnehaha,* went "almost into their very bunks in the electric-lighted dark of the day." And he said to himself: "Now or never is my chance; stay and sail—borrow clothes, borrow a toothbrush, borrow a bunk, borrow $100; you will never be so near to it again." If he had only had a thicker overcoat and the ladies had had an extra bunk, "I would have turned in *with* them and taken my chance." As it was, he experienced a sudden acute wish to be in America again. Resisting it, he "turned and fled, bounding along Tilbury docks in the grimy fog and never stopping till I clutched at something that was going back to London."

Behind the humor and exaggerations of this little episode lay a profound emotion. James had become aware of it during the writing of *The Ambassadors;* it had made him urge Edith Wharton to stay with her American subject. He found himself remembering the leaves he had kicked in the autumn along the lower reaches of Fifth Avenue; but perhaps there were "no leaves and no trees now in Fifth Avenue—nothing but patriotic arches, Astor Hotels and Vanderbilt Palaces." He had in his younger years known only the eastern seaboard and had made a single foray as far as Wisconsin in 1883. Now the land of his birth extended to California. It was time to return. "I must go before I'm too old, and, above all, before I mind being older," he wrote to William James. To Howells he said, "I *want* to come, quite pathetically and tragically—it is a passion of nostalgia." The long letter he wrote to his brother on the eve of his sixtieth birthday describes his inner debate between desire for the journey and practical obstacles—the letting of his house, the unaccustomed voyage, the proper itinerary, the financing of the trip. He should look after his long-neglected literary interests, he said, and examine what opportunities there might be to "quicken and improve them." But the process would be so "damnedly expensive." He could finance the trip by writing a book of "impressions"—it would have to be "for much money."

William's reply was characteristic. He listed the things in America that displeased him and he thought would displease Henry—the sight of Americans having boiled eggs for breakfast with butter on them and the *vocalization* "of our countrymen." On the other hand, there was the American out-of-doors. If Henry would travel to the South, to Colorado, across Canada, possibly to Hawaii, he might find the journey rewarding. William advised him to come in spring and to stay till October. He invited Henry to spend the hot months with his family at Chocorua, their summer home in New Hampshire. The letter was friendly and helpful, but it had a certain diffidence in it and the younger brother had his usual emotional reaction. William had been very "dissuasive—even more than I expected." It was all very well for him to speak in this way: he had moved around America at his ease. If Henry couldn't bring off his American trip he would have to settle down to his shuttle between Rye and London, with nothing left for him "in the way of (the poetry of) motion." The trip to America would represent "the one big taste of travel not supremely missed." As to the boiled eggs and the "vocalization" and "the Shocks in general"—the ways in which Americans ate their eggs were just the sort of thing that interested him as a novelist. "I want to see them, I want to see everything." He preferred to avoid the summer in America; arriving in August, he would have the American autumn, which he had always loved, and he could go to the warmer areas in the winter months. The plan for his journey was complete in his mind. There remained only the practical details to be settled.

What astonished Henry was that friends and relatives seemed to have a picture of him as likely to get lost in America and to hate everything he would see. Grace Norton wrote that she talked with Mrs. William James of Henry's "dislike" of his native land. He admonished her in his reply: "Never, never, my dear Grace: you must have misunderstood Alice—or she herself—as to the fabled growth of my still more fabled 'dislike.'" On the contrary, "The idea of *seeing* American life again and tasting the American air, that is a vision, a possibility, an impossibility, positively romantic." To another friend he wrote, "I think with a great appetite . . . of the chance, once more, *to lie on the ground,* on an American hillside, on the edge of the woods, in the manner of my youth." If he did achieve a few months in the country at large, he told Miss Norton, "the thing will have been the most private and personal act of my very private and personal life."

By the autumn of 1903, the nostalgia had become a challenge. It would be "ignobly weak" not to find solutions to his problems. Presently all his friends seemed involved. James had been dreading the voyage, having crossed the sea in the days when the potential rage of the ocean was a constant anxiety, but the peripatetic Benedicts, Miss Woolson's relatives, wrote as if a crossing in one of the new "liners" were as routine as a bus trip in London. He could sail with them, when they returned in August from their annual visit abroad. In January of 1904, with the end of *The Golden Bowl* in sight, James paid his deposit on an upper promenade deck cabin on the North German Lloyd liner *Kaiser Wilhelm II,* sailing from Southampton on 24 August. In spite of the long inner debate there had never been any real doubt of his going.

Overtures from America began to come the moment word of his visit got round. Colonel George Harvey, head of Harper and Brothers, agreed to serialize James's American impressions in the *North American Review* and make a book of them afterwards. One of the Harper editors, an energetic young woman named Elizabeth Jordan, was asked to canvass lecture possibilities. James had never lectured and had said he would not do so in America. But he became interested from the moment he learned that he could command substantial fees; Colonel Harvey spoke of as much as $500 a lecture. James intimated that he was prepared to lecture but not "if the personal exposure is out of proportion to the tip."

More pressing than the American arrangements was the problem of Lamb House. The irrepressible Goody Allen had come up with possible tenants, the Miss Horstmanns, one of whom was in England to marry John Boit of Boston. Lamb House would be a "honeymoon" house. James asked for a rental of £5 a week that would include "the servants, the forks and spoons, and house linen and books, and in short everything that is in the house except my scant supply of clothing." A bare four weeks before sailing, he was able to telegraph Miss Allen, "Little Friends accept for six months hooray and glory to immortal Goody." James's letter to his prospective tenants, outlining his domestic arrangements, ended with a plea. "Lastly," he wrote,

> I take the liberty of confiding to your charity and humanity the precious little person of my Dachshund Max, who is the best and gentlest and most reasonable and well-mannered as well as most beautiful, small animal of his kind to be easily come across.

James bought a new steamer trunk. He visited his London tailor. He made last-minute calls. On 19 August he said good-bye to his servants, buried his nose in Max's little gold-colored back, "wetting it with my tears." As he made his way to the boat-train at Waterloo Station he was conscious of "a pandemonium of uncertainties and mysteries." He sailed on the 24th, having said his farewell to Jocelyn Persse a few days before, and written also a long letter to Hendrik Andersen. In it he began to express misgiving about Andersen's enormous statues, of which he had received photographs. None the less he patted Hendrik "lovingly, tenderly, tenderly," and sailed with the sense of further "dreary and deadly postponements" of their meetings.

Pacing the deck of the *Kaiser Wilhelm II* as it left Southampton, James felt himself acting out a significant part of his destiny. He had said that he felt the romance and curiosity of his journey—the return to the landscapes of his childhood and youth—as if it were a new voyage of discovery. The vision was expressed by Mrs. Assingham towards the end of *The Golden Bowl.* "I see the long miles of ocean and the dreadful great country, State after State—which have never seemed to me so big or so terrible."

Just before leaving, James instructed his agent to inform Charles Scribner that the time had come for the long-planned definitive edition of his works. "Mr. James's idea," Pinker wrote, "is to write for each volume a preface of a rather intimate character, and there is no doubt that such a preface would add greatly to the interest of the books." What would contribute to the intimacy of the prefaces would be the seeing again of scenes and places in which his great adventure—in art, in life —had begun.

The Jersey Shore

On 30 August 1904 a reporter covering the waterfront found Henry James on the pier at Hoboken among the passengers from the *Kaiser Wilhelm II,* guarding his luggage while waiting for a customs inspector. His nephew Harry had met him, and a representative of Harper and Brothers. James seemed unruffled and relaxed amid the confusion. The reporter noted his "regular and sharp" features; for a celebrity, he appeared "remote," inconspicuous. But then the author of *The Reverberator* seldom talked to reporters. After the baggage was cleared, James came out into the sunshine. As he turned and surveyed the New York skyline, he paused and, said the reporter, "almost gasped for breath." He might have been Rip Van Winkle awakening out of a twenty-year sleep.

Henry James had skipped two decades of his country's life. And yet certain things were unchanged. Crossing to Lower Manhattan he saw from the ferry the new buildings, called skyscrapers, stuck in here, there and everywhere like extravagant pins in an extravagant pincushion. There were recognizable smells. As the ferry approached the terminal he noted all the ugly old items—loose cobbles, unregulated traffic, big drays pulled by struggling long-necked sharp-ribbed horses. There were huddled houses from the older time, off balance amid an assortment of newer buildings.

James rode uptown, discovering familiar things among the unfamiliar. At Washington Square he noted the truncated arch; it was wholly without suggestion of grandeur or "glory." At Gramercy Park he paused in the home of a friend. He had planned to leave that evening for Boston with Harry, to join William James at Chocorua. However, Colonel Harvey of Harpers had sent a pressing invitation—almost a summons. James was expected at his country place on the Jersey shore. The novelist felt that he was falling into some kind of a social "trap"; nevertheless he yielded. His nephew took most of his baggage on to New England; James piled into another four-wheeler and returned to the docks.

Presently, having crossed on another ferry, he was being driven along a straight road, following a blue band of sea, between the sandy New Jersey shore and a chain of big villas. Colonel Harvey's cottage near the sea, at Deal Beach, was spacious and substantial. The tall sociable host and a plump Mrs. Harvey greeted the distinguished visitor. He discovered a fellow guest awaiting him—the grizzled, white-suited, cigar-smoking "natural" Samuel Langhorne Clemens; Colonel Harvey had gathered in his two literary lions. "Poor dear old Mark Twain beguiles the session on the deep piazza," Henry James scrawled in a hasty penciled note to his brother. The remark sounded condescending, but it was in reality sympathetic. Clemens had lost his wife a few months earlier, and was now at loose ends; behind his volubility and wit he was more depressed than ever.

Colonel George Harvey was a symbol of the new America, as Mark Twain represented the old. A native of Vermont, he had been a "boy-wonder" in journalism: later he had amassed a fortune in Wall Street and purchased the *North American Review*. When at the century's turn Harper and Brothers went into receivership, J. P. Morgan had Harvey appointed administrator. Howells remained the firm's principal literary adviser, Mark Twain its lucrative author, and Henry James its principal ornament.

The repatriated novelist enjoyed his brief interlude in New Jersey although he stayed only 36 hours. The weather was good and he took pleasure in the air, and the play of light over the coast. James was driven to various places during the following day and on the roads saw "the chariots, the buggies, the motors, the pedestrians—which last number, indeed, was remarkably small." On his arrival in New Hampshire his thank-you note to Harvey spoke of having "a bushel of Impressions already gathered." The note of affluence and advertising, of impermanence, of a civilization created wholly for commerce, had been struck for him.

A New England Autumn

He had a strange feeling the evening he stepped out of the South Station in Boston, a sense of "confused and surprised recognition" as he rode through the warm September night to Cambridge. The town was still faithful to its type—but the rustle of the trees had a larger tone and there was more lamplight. New and strange architecture loomed through the dark. James spent the night at 95 Irving Street, the large shingled house William James had built ten years before. The next day he took the train into the White Mountains, to Chocorua, where he found —so he wrote Edith Wharton—"the Domestic circle blooming for the poor celibate exile."

William James's summer home, a low rambling two-story bungalow on the edge of a forest-fringed slope, looked out on a great sweep of country, a chain of small lakes, and off to the right the grey head of Chocorua mountain. The family installed Henry in a suite of rooms at one end of the L-shaped house, where he had a sense of total privacy. Later he spoke of the "Arcadian elegance and amiability" of this part of New England. He liked the hush of the landscape; he found elegance in common objects, the silver-grey rock showing through thinly grassed acres, the boulders in the woods, "the scattered wild apples . . . like figures in the carpet." He found everything "funny and lovely."

The loveliness resided in nature. The "funny" element was represented by the people, their incongruities and manners—and absence of form. He was troubled by the "sallow, saturnine" people driving teams, carts and conveyances, their slovenliness of dress and careless articulation; there was a kind of general "human neglect" surrounding farmhouses and towns. In *The American Scene* James would write of the villages, their lack of civic pride, their absence of standards. He wondered at the high wages paid unskilled "hired" men and servants, not because he grudged them their earnings but because there was no matching of skill with remuneration. He disliked the attitude of the employed. They seemed to feel that everything was "owed *to* them, not to be rendered, but to be received."

Henry James thought too many roads were being built in New England. He wasn't happy being driven in buggies or wagons behind ostrich-necked horses at breakneck speed. However, he enjoyed the domestic life in William James's house; he had an enormous appetite for the country butter, cream, eggs, chickens, and the delectable home-baked loaf, such as he had not eaten in years. Shortly before leaving England he had decided to try the new fad of "Fletcherism." An American, Horace Fletcher, was teaching the virtues of slow and lengthy chewing of food. James's deliberate mastication seemed to go hand in hand with his slow ruminative conversation.

The novelist appears to have been restless at Chocorua. He liked to move about; and he made three trips within a matter of days after his arrival. He went first to Jackson, New Hampshire, to spend a day with the seventy-four-year-old Katherine Prescott Wormeley, who had devoted her life to translating and writing about Balzac. She was a sister of Ariana Curtis, his hostess in Venice. He arrived at nightfall, high in the White Mountains, and stayed at the inn next to the Wildcat River. The next morning he climbed to Miss Wormeley's house where he found five verandahs for the view, and "images of furnished peace, within, as could but illustrate a rare personal history."

His second journey was to Howard Sturgis, temporarily translated from Qu'Acre to Cape Cod. James went, by the slow jogging train from Boston, to West Barnstable and thence to Cotuit by horse and buggy. The drive was long and he enjoyed "the little white houses, the feathery elms, the band of ocean blue, the strip of sandy yellow, the tufted pines in angular silhouette, the cranberry swamps, stringed across, for the picking, like the ruled pages of ledgers." The place looked for him like a pictured Japanese screen. He had three pleasant days with Sturgis.

His third trip was farther away, a sally into Connecticut to visit his Emmet cousins, who were now living on a farm near Salisbury—the mother, Mrs. Hunter, and Rosina, Leslie, and Bay. Going there James suddenly realized that every trip in America involved distance, compared with the easy little journeys in and out of London he had been making for years. He found Connecticut "a ravishing land," and he was pleased particularly by the fine houses, the elms, the general aspect of Farmington. In one house he was shown an array of impressionist paintings, "wondrous examples of Manet, of Degas, of Claude Monet, of Whistler." It made him realize, he said, that he had been starved of such things in his early weeks in America. Everywhere he had discovered a desire among people for "sameness" rather than difference.

That autumn, as the colors of the trees continued to change and the leaves began to fall, James explored the no-longer-familiar contours of Cambridge, the mysteries of expanded Boston. In William James's spacious house in Irving Street, there were memories of his father and mother, including the striking sketch, in oils, for the paternal portrait by Duveneck, and his father's old large work-table which William now used. The novelist had his isolated quarters in the upper reaches of the house and worked in the mornings as usual, but without a typist. Accustomed always to talking and observing, he strolled in the afternoons, read, took notes. Just across the way from William's home lived the aging Grace Norton, his confidante of many years. He still felt an old affection for her, in her spinsterish aloofness; but she was "intellectually inaccessible" and this fact destroyed his old desire to write to her, once he was abroad again.

He visited another friend from the past, the indomitable "Mrs. Jack" Gardner at Green Hill in Brookline, and saw the all-but-completed and already inaugurated Venetian *palazzo* she had built in the Fenway, admiring her gift in shoring up the fragments of her far-flung purchases abroad. What he had once spoken of as "the age of Mrs. Jack" had now composed itself into a set form, a museum mold. Mrs. Gardner's *palais-musée* was, as he wrote to Paul Bourget,

> a really great creation. Her acquisitions during the last ten years have been magnificent; her arrangement and administration of them are admirable, and her spirit soars higher still. . . . She has become really a great little personage.

James's inspection of Cambridge began, as might be expected, with Harvard, where he found himself musing anew at the shape of the Yard and the fact that it was still not sufficiently enclosed. He remembered the high grills and palings at Oxford, and the sense of mystery these created for him. His nephew Harry, so lately a graduate, guided him to the various buildings; and the novelist, thinking back on the small Harvard of his own youth, looked at each item of the new "pampered state" of the students—"multiplied resources, faculties, museums, undergraduate and postgraduate habitations . . . pompous little club-houses." He went into the Law Library and saw in the distance John Gray, whom he had known in his youth when they had both admired his cousin Minny Temple—but "to go to him I should have had to cross the bridge that spans the gulf of time." He kept his distance.

James's concern in all he saw that autumn was most often with the relation of the past—his personal past—to the America of 1904. One of his first pilgrimages in Boston was to Ashburton Place, in quest of the house in which he had lived during the last two years of the Civil War—the house of his early "initiations." He found it isolated behind the State House in an area already much cleared out; some of the little old crooked streets had disappeared. Here had come the news of the death of Lincoln, the end of the war; here he had counted the first greenbacks earned by his book reviews. The place held old secrets, old stories, "a saturation of life as closed together and preserved in it as the scent lingering in a folded pocket handkerchief." Yet when he returned a month later, for another look, the old house was gone—every brick of it—"the brutal effacement, at a stroke, of every related object, of the whole precious past." It gave him a vivid impression of the impermanence of American life.

Beacon Hill was full of memories. There was Mount Vernon Street where his father had died and where he had stayed, in the house of death, through the spring of 1883 with his sister Alice. In Charles Street he passed the house which had been the center of culture in his day—the home of J. T. Fields and his beautiful wife, where Dickens and Thackeray and the Brahmins had been entertained, even himself as a young aspirant. Behind the effaced anonymous door he could remember the long drawing-room looking over the water towards the sunset. In the same locality he passed the spot where Dr. Oliver Wendell Holmes had lived and remembered the August emptiness, the closed houses, and how he had in his youth come to ask for news of Wendell Holmes, "then on his first flushed and charming visit to England," and had *"vibrated* so with the wonder and romance and curiosity and dim weak tender (oh, tender!) envy of it."

In Back Bay he revisited Marlborough Street, comparing it to Wimpole and Harley Streets; he studied the individual house-fronts, finding too many bow windows, and suddenly recalled a phrase from Tennyson, "long, unlovely street." He looked closely at the Florentine palace that was the new Public Library in Copley Square. He inspected its murals by Abbey and Puvis de Chavannes and noted the comings and goings of readers, and yet found—it was his common complaint—that the majesty of such a place was diminished by the absence of "penetralia." One failed to get the feeling in these American buildings that there was an innermost shrine, some sacred center. Even a work of art like Saint-Gaudens' noble monument on Boston Common to Robert Gould Shaw and the Fifty-fourth Massachusetts, the regiment in which James's brother Wilky had served, seemed placed with a casualness that was a disrespect both to art and memory. There was an absence of majesty. America could scatter emblems of things far and wide; it seemed to pay no attention to their meaning.

Much of James's progress through America during these intensely-felt weeks is recorded, with swelling phrase and large metaphor, in his book. In Newport, scene of his younger self, he experienced the bittersweet of finding little corners full of old recall amidst the work of the real estate operators and the American wealth and pretension that had superseded old views and old values. He viewed the villas and palaces "into which the cottages have all turned" as if he were living in the ancient story of King Midas. The place seemed heaped with gold "to an amount so oddly out of proportion to the scale of nature and of space."

At Concord he found less change. He remembered Emerson in his orchards; he saw anew the Old Manse. He hung over the Concord River, setting its pace and taking its twists "like some large obese benevolent person." His youngest brother, Robertson James, was living in Concord. He had aged much; but he talked as brilliantly as ever. Henry could remember when Bob, and their long-dead brother Wilky, had gone to school in Concord; yet what prevailed above personal memories was the sense of the two geniuses of the place, Hawthorne and Emerson. James went in quest of Hawthorne also in Salem; he found the birthplace, set in an area taken over by industry; he looked at, but did not venture into, what was said to be the House of the Seven Gables. He had a horror of "reconstituted antiquity." For the same reason he paused before the Salem Witch House with a kind of "sacred terror" and a "sacred tenderness." The wooden houses of the place, he said, "look brief and provisional at the best—look, above all, incorrigibly and witlessly innocent."

The Lady of Lenox

As might be expected of a woman who had collaborated on a book *The Decoration of Houses,* Edith Wharton had built her new home at Lenox, Massachusetts, in the Berkshires, with a sense of style and comfort. The Mount was spacious; it was dignified. It overlooked the wooded shores of Laurel Lake. In the French style, its drawing-room, dining-room and library opened on a terrace beyond which was a stretch of formal garden. Henry James sank into the house as into a bed of luxury. The Mount was "an exquisite and marvellous place," he wrote to Howard Sturgis, "a delicate French Château mirrored in a Massachusetts pond" and a monument to "the almost too impeccable taste of its so accomplished mistress."

From Lenox, Mrs. Wharton motored constantly, with her handsome heavily mustached husband, a Pekinese, and the increasingly absorbed and fascinated distinguished visitor. Henry James was won over to this form of travel in spite of bad roads, and they visited every accessible part of Massachusetts and crossed into New York to large Hudson vistas. To find himself in the heart of New England and of New York State was to make him feel as if a great deal of freshness was breaking through old staleness, "when the staleness, so agreeably favored with hospitality, and indeed with new ingredients, was a felt element at all." Mrs. Wharton must have provided an active commentary on the mores of the villages through whose streets they passed; it had been put to him, James would write, that "the great facts of life are in high fermentation on the other side of the ground glass that never for a moment flushes, to the casual eye, with the hint of a lurid light." This was James's way of alluding to what Eugene O'Neill would call "desire under the elms"—the hidden life of sex—adultery, incest, passion and puritanical concealment, in the villages and on the lonely farms; as he looked at them from the moving motor they "became positively richer objects under the smutch of imputation." Edith Wharton would write of these subjects in *Ethan Frome* and *Summer.*

The days at The Mount, both that autumn and the following summer when James revisited it, had a great calm, a luxurious ease. Hostess and guest spent their mornings writing; Teddy Wharton smoked his cigars and came and went. Lunch was late; they motored in the afternoons and spent evenings by the fire, in talk and in jest. When Howard Sturgis was there they might as well have been at Qu'Acre or Lamb House. Some of the talk was inevitably literary. Mrs. Wharton's admiration for James was profound—he was becoming one of the largest figures in her life. And her account of his various remarks to her about her work conveys complete acceptance, on her part, of their barbed quality. On one occasion Teddy Wharton made some remark about "Edith's new story" just published in *Scribner's,* and the Master's answer was prompt: "Oh yes, my dear Edward, I've read the little work—of course I've read it. Admirable, admirable; a masterly little achievement." And turning towards her, he went on (as she recorded):

> "Of course so accomplished a mistress of the art would not, without deliberate intention, have given the tale so curiously conventional a treatment. Though indeed, in the given case, no treatment *but* the conventional was possible; which might conceivably, my dear lady, on further consideration, have led you to reject your subject as—er—in itself a totally unsuitable one."

Mrs. Wharton recognized in this the characteristic tendency of James to begin with praise and then find himself "over-mastered by the need to speak the truth." So, on a much later occasion, after praising *The Custom of the Country,* he burst forth to her: "But of course you know—as how should you, with your infernal keenness of perception, *not* know?—that in doing your tale you had under your hand a magnificent subject, which ought to have been your main theme, and that you used it as mere incident and then passed it by."

Small wonder Mrs. Wharton found such comments "withering," even though she joined in the laughter and spoke good-naturedly of "our literary rough-and-tumble." The sharpness of James's remarks, as she recorded them—so stark when compared with the tone of similar strictures made in letters to Mrs. Humphry Ward, or some of the young writers—seems to suggest that there existed between the Master and the lady novelist a directness, an openness and freedom—and truth—that gave to their friendship a rare quality of mutual "ease." At the same time we may imagine that James's tone of voice could have softened the harsh-ness of his Johnsonian dicta.

Edith Wharton appreciated a good story and could tell her own sto-ries well; and she had a love of poetry even though her published verses are indifferently stiff and solemn. She would remember James's reading poetry by her fireplace in Lenox, his taking up Emily Brontë's poems and in his rich flexible voice chanting the sonnet that begins, "Cold in the earth—and the deep snow piled above thee." His reading she felt was "an emanation of his inmost self, unaffected by fashion or elocutionary ar-tifice." On another evening, they began to quote Whitman. In his young manhood James had been sharply critical of old Walt; he had published an uncompromising review of *Drum Taps,* attacking his "flashy imita-tion of ideas." Since then he had made his peace with him. Perhaps it was a result of his renewed vision of America, the touching of old emotions; or Whitman's homo-eroticism. At any rate "his voice filled the hushed room like an organ adagio" as he read from "Song of Myself" and "When lilacs last" and "Out of the cradle" which he "crooned rather than read." They "talked long that night of *Leaves of Grass,*" Mrs. Wharton remem-bered, "tossing back and forth to each other treasure after treasure." At the end, the Master flung his hands upward, a characteristic gesture, and with eyes twinkling said: "Oh yes, a great genius; undoubtedly a very great genius! Only one cannot help deploring his too-extensive acquaint-ance with the foreign languages."

At Lenox, James met Walter Berry, whom he would see intermit-tently during the ensuing years. Berry was to be a peripheral friend of Proust as well as James; he was already one of the closest of Edith Whar-ton's friends. James found him very much a man of the world and a familiar cosmopolite figure—one of the characters he had invented. A product of old New York—his full name was Walter Van Rensselaer Berry—he was in his forties when the novelist met him. Born in Paris, educated at Harvard, he practiced as an international lawyer, and would be president of the American Chamber of Commerce in Paris. He was handsome, tall, a bit stiff, a bit dry—so some saw him. In James's letters to Mrs. Wharton he is "the brave Berry" and James speaks of him as having "greatly endeared himself to me" with his mixture of his "gifts and his unhappinesses," his alertness, and his melancholy.

Edith Wharton wrote to Minnie Bourget in France of James's visit to Lenox. "Nobody," responded Minnie in Gallic-tinged English,

> who has not actually lived with him will ever completely appreciate this *great artist,* the wonderful companion, the charm of whom resides in that perfect simplicity and adaptation of everyday life with the ever-springing source of comprehension and keen sensitiveness.

Minnie also spoke of Mrs. Wharton's having discovered "the compatriot" in James—"he loves his country, perhaps even when he does not know himself to what extent."

The Medusa Face

One Sunday in Cambridge James went in search of the Fresh Pond of his youth, where, when Howells was also young and learning to edit the *Atlantic,* the two used to walk and speak of the novels they wanted to write and what a novel should be. He found the muses of the place had fled, "the little nestling lake had ceased to nestle." A charming country club now stood on the grounds towards Watertown, all verandahs and golf-links, "all tea and ices and self-consciousness." And there was a great deal of highway across the rural scenery. The old haunt, "desecrated and destroyed," could no longer be a place for "shared literary secrets."

He reserved one other stroll in Cambridge for some "favouring hour," when he was in the mood to face his long-dead personal past. One evening in November, sometime after his return from Lenox, he set out on foot from Irving Street. He walked past Longfellow's house, admiring its ample style and its symmetry, thinking of it before it had become a tourist-haunted spot. He passed high, square, sad and silent Elmwood, remembering his best-loved Cambridge friend, James Russell Lowell, "the very genius of the spot." Lowell had had a perhaps humorous thesis that "Cambridge, Mass., was, taken altogether, the most inwardly civilized, most intimately humane, among the haunts of men." James's friends had committed themselves to cultivating the *genius loci.*

His lonely walk was carefully planned. Presently he was making his way among the graves in the Cambridge cemetery, slowly and deliberately, until he came to the James family plot, on its little ridge—an "unspeakable group of graves": those of his mother, his father and his sister Alice, and nearby that of one of William's children who had died young. It seemed to James as if he had returned to America precisely for this vision and for this moment. As he scribbled in a notebook some weeks later, when he was in California, "I seemed then to know why I had *come* —and to feel how not to have come would have been miserably, horribly, to miss it." James carefully took in the scene, noting the quality of the air, the stillness, the waning light. The place "bristled with merciless memories." Turning back to look at the graves, he read through his tears the words from Dante which William had had carved on the little marble urn of his sister's ashes: *ed essa da martiro e da essilio venne a questa pace.* The line "took me so at the throat by its penetrating *rightness."*

James stood there a long time; he looked again across the Charles. It was the old Cambridge—and he had moved past ghosts of friendship to reach ghosts of family. This was "the cold Medusa-face of life." He remembered "the old thinner New England air and more meagre New England scheme." "But why do I write of the all unutterable and the all abysmal?" he asked himself as he sat with these autumn memories beside the Pacific. "Why does my pen not drop from my hand on approaching the infinite pity and tragedy of all the past?"

The Shepherd and His Flock

Between the time of his visit to Lenox and his travels at the beginning of 1905, Henry James went through "an interminable and abysmal siege of American dentistry," lasting through the greater part of November and December. He slipped away to New York, however, in November to keep a promise to Colonel Harvey: the long-planned public dinner in his honor, held at the Metropolitan Club, was a modest one. Mark Twain, Booth Tarkington, G. W. Smalley, Hamlin Garland, and the journalist Arthur Brisbane, were among the thirty guests. James's dental difficulties deprived him of full enjoyment of the food.

After Christmas, when the Boston dentist released him, he returned to New York, staying first with Mrs. Cadwalader Jones, at 21 East Eleventh Street, in that part of the city most crowded with boyhood memories. He moved uptown after the new year to visit Mrs. Wharton's flat, at 884 Park Avenue—"a bonbonnière of the last daintiness naturally," he told Howard Sturgis—but after eight days he returned with relief to Mrs. Jones's. From this time on he made East Eleventh Street his headquarters, in his comings and goings in Manhattan. Minnie Jones provided privacy and quiet, and her daughter Beatrix showered attention on him. He felt himself "half-killed with kindness." Mrs. Jones had a pet name for James, Célimare, out of a French farce by Labiche—perhaps because the central character, *"le bien aimé,"* inspires universal affection. The novelist seems to have been the center at Mrs. Jones's of an adoring circle.

En route to Washington, to stay with Henry Adams, James stopped in Philadelphia to see his old friend Mrs. Wister, and to deliver the first of what proved to be a series of lectures—or, as one critic who watched him closely described them, "oral essays." He had finally decided to ask $250 as his fee for speaking to a ladies' group in Boston; the honorarium was designed to discourage them, and did. But the Contemporary Club of Philadelphia had the money for such occasions. James read his lecture on "The Lesson of Balzac" to an audience of more than a hundred elegantly dressed ladies and gentlemen—the most distinguished representatives, said the press, of letters, art, the learned professions, and public life in Philadelphia. The novelist read without emphasis, and without a trace of embarrassment, holding the loose sheets in one hand and keeping the other in his pocket "save," said the newspaper, "where two or three times there came an involuntary gesture." The essayist Agnes Repplier, cultural leader of Philadelphia, presided with style and charm, and Sargent's friend, the eminent surgeon Dr. J. William White, supported James before the ordeal and gave him a triumphant supper afterwards. James, who had suffered stage fright, was elated. "A dazzling success," he reported to his New York circle: "a huge concourse, five or six hundred folk, a vast hall, and perfect brazen assurance and audibility on Célimare's part. *Il s'est révélé conférencier.*" Carey Thomas, president of Bryn Mawr, had also invited James to lecture, offering him the standard fee of $50. James replied he did not have anything suitable for young girls but then, having tasted triumph, he added, "to be lucid, the honorarium you offer is not sufficient." He reduced his fee, however, to $200 and agreed to double back from Washington to speak at the college before proceeding south.

"The Lesson of Balzac," which James was to read to assorted audiences across the American continent, was decidedly not the lecture of a man who doubted his own powers; and apparently James's delivery of it was an admirable piece of conversational reading. The writer Edna Kenton remembered him as massive and clear-eyed on a Chicago platform, speaking with a total absence of oratorical effect, in a voice filled with subtle tones. Van Wyck Brooks, who heard James that spring at Harvard, recalled his voice rolling "like an organ through a hall that could scarcely contain the aura of his presence." One listener who heard the novelist in Brooklyn wrote that if James's sentences were long they were perfectly clear and "the average high school boy of today would have been able to grasp all that he said." James's reading was always deliberate; when his witticisms were appreciated and the audience laughed, he nodded and smiled. Otherwise he was solemn. There was never a lapse into insistence. Everything was low keyed and "evenly modulated."

In the content of the lecture there was no compromise with popular standards. James was his Jamesian self. The opening sentences suggest his strategy of formal informality:

> I have found it necessary, at the eleventh hour, to sacrifice to the terrible question of time a very beautiful and majestic approach that I had prepared to the subject on which I have the honour of addressing you. I recognize it as impossible to ask you to linger with me on that pillared portico—paved with marble, I beg you to believe, and overtwined with charming flowers. I must invite you to pass straight into the house and

bear with me there as if I had already succeeded in beginning to interest you.

No audience in America, we might speculate, had ever been so ingratiatingly approached; the tone was confidential; the suave assumption was that the listeners were the speaker's peers, and they all had deep and intimate matters to deal with. James went on to deplore the absence of a genuine criticism, resorting to his favorite pastoral imagery. American readers were the biggest flock straying without shepherds and "without a sound of the sheepdog's bark." Worse still, "the shepherds have diminished as the flock has increased." From this it was a direct step to Balzac as a novelist who offers example and invites criticism. "I speak of him," said James,

> and can only speak, as a man of his own craft, an emulous fellow-worker, who has learned from him more of the lessons of the engaging mystery of fiction than from anyone else, who is conscious of so large a debt to repay that it has had positively to be discharged in instalments, as if one could never have at once all the required cash in hand.

The lecture repaid that debt. With many subtle strokes James sketched Balzac's qualities but with constant reference to novelists more familiar to his audiences, as in one beautiful passage beginning:

> Why is it that the life that overflows in Dickens seems to me always to go on in the morning, or in the very earliest hours of the afternoon at most, and in a vast apartment that appears to have windows, large, uncurtained, and rather unwashed windows, on all sides at once?

Such passages provoked charmed murmurs from certain members of his audience and brief stirrings of applause. A great part of the lecture was devoted to a close analysis of Balzac's way of painting the conditions and environment of his characters, his possession always of all the elements of his picture; "It is the art of the brush," said James, "as opposed to the art of the slate pencil." Only at the end did the lecturer artfully take notice that he was speaking "as if we all, as if you all, without exception were novelists, haunting the back shop, the laboratory, or, more nobly expressed, the inner shrine of the temple." Balzac was in the sacred grove, he said, the idol, "gilded thick with so much gold—plated and burnished and bright, in the manner of towering idols." And his final sentence—"it is for the lighter and looser and poorer among us to be gilded thin!"

City of Conversation

Washington was a pleasant surprise. James remembered it from his visit in 1882 as still a rather nude capital, with the dome and the shaft presiding over much parochialism, and the President visiting in various houses as if he were a local—rather than a national—celebrity. This time everything was on a much grander scale. He stayed with Henry Adams in his big house on Lafayette Square; the friend of his youth, John La Farge, was a fellow guest. Old circles, old familiarities were briefly re-established. As in 1882, Adams's house was a hotbed of Washington gossip; but James missed Clover Adams, who had been such a lively companion. Adams seldom spoke of her; and James hesitated to ask him about her tomb for which Augustus Saint-Gaudens had carved a much-talked-of mourning figure. At lunch at Adams's one day James whispered to Mrs. Winthrop Chanler that the one thing in Washington he wanted to see was this statue in Rock Creek Cemetery; Mrs. Chanler took him there in her brougham immediately after lunch. James stood uncovered for a long time before the bronze symbolic figure, with draperies shrouding its head. Mrs. Chanler remembered that on their return to Lafayette Square James talked of Clover's career as a Washington hostess; there had always been good talk at her table—indeed James had ever after that first visit spoken of Washington as a "city of conversation."

In 1882, James had received no official recognition during his Washington visit, nor had he expected it. In January of 1905, thanks to his friend John Hay, the Secretary of State, and the artistic entourage at Adams's, James was welcomed as a literary Master, so that even President Theodore Roosevelt—who disliked and had even denounced the novelist as "effete" and "a miserable little snob"—opened the White House to him. James had quite as low an opinion of Roosevelt, considering him "a dangerous and ominous jingo." But at their meeting the amenities were observed to the last letter of the alphabet, and the novelist was flattered. To William James he wrote that the President "did me the honour to cause me to be placed"—the monarchical "cause" could not have been lost on William—"at his table (of eight) and on the right of the lady at *his* right . . . It was very curious and interesting . . . The President is distinctly tending—or trying—to make a 'court.' "

Secretary Hay gave an impressive dinner for James; so did his old friend the French Ambassador, Jules Jusserand. He lunched with Senator Henry Cabot Lodge. And at the invitation of Charles McKim, he went with La Farge and Saint-Gaudens to a dinner of the American Institute of Architects at which official and artistic Washington was present in force. He was enjoying his role of literary lion, but was bewildered when

Admiral Dewey, hero of Manila, left his card. A call from a naval personality seemed the last thing he expected; perhaps it was a case simply of one celebrity paying respects to another.

If James was amused by the glitter of Roosevelt's Washington it left him with no illusions. "To *live* here," he wrote to Mrs. William James, "would be death and madness—" and doubtless, he added, one would pay calls forever "in one's delirium." He returned after eight days to his civilized friends in Philadelphia, and enjoyed his night at Bryn Mawr. The audience of young women was enchanted by James's charm and delicacy, and he promised to return as Commencement speaker in the spring.

He spent several days in Philadelphia, visiting with the Whites and Mrs. Wister, and seeing something of Dr. J. Weir Mitchell, the medical novelist, a friend of Mrs. Wharton who was credited with having started her on her career as a writer (prescribing it as a kind of "occupational therapy"). A distinguished Canadian, Dr. George Robert Parkin, organizing secretary of the Rhodes Scholarships, happened to be visiting Weir Mitchell in Walnut Street during that week. Taken by his host on a round of visits, Parkin in one residence found himself introduced to a "Mr. James." Mr. James, not realizing Parkin's involvement, listened as the idea for the Rhodes Scholarships was explained and promptly denounced it as "deplorable." What, the Master asked in his loftiest manner, "does Oxford want of men from Nebraska and Canada?" And anyway, he inquired, "Why should we all be asked to fall down and glorify Rhodes?" Dr. Parkin defended his mission against his unknown interlocutor. And later, when their respective identities had been made known, James seems quite to have charmed away the Canadian's ruffled feelings. "We got on capitally," Parkin wrote.

James found Philadelphia to be, after Washington, a city of culture and refinement; "of all goodly villages," it was "the very goodliest, probably in the world." His less official view was that Philadelphia was "kind, plenitudinous, promiscuous." But in the midst of his sociabilities, he lost an upper front tooth. "I look like a 'fright' but I am cynical, indifferent, desperate," he told William. Then, when he would have sought local dental help, snow came, more than a foot; deep drifts were under his window at Mrs. Wister's. "The trolleys don't run, I can't get to the station; high drifts and a polar hurricane bar the way." Philadelphia, that goodly village, now seemed a "fearsome ordeal." He took a train for Richmond —"the southern sun, for which I fairly sicken, will re-create me." A night in the Pullman shook his faith still more. There was snow at Richmond and "the ugliness appals." He put up at the Jefferson Hotel, discovered that he had run out of linen and shirts, and had to wait for his laundry to be done before going on to visit the George Vanderbilts in North Carolina. In a moment of sociability and curiosity he had accepted an invitation to stop en route to the South at Biltmore, the palatial Vanderbilt home. On 3 February, he set out once more. There was a new, driving snowstorm; but he was confident that he would be expensively sheltered from it.

The Blighted Invalid

He was sitting in front of a large picture window—"a hideous plate-glass window like the door of an ice-house." It had no curtains, no shutters, no blinds; north light shone cold and intense, reflected from a vastness of snow. His room was icy. He had gout in his left foot. When he rang the bell for a servant none came. He found himself hobbling and hopping down long corridors to a remote bathroom to fetch hot water. The fantastic Biltmore—"the château of Biltmore" he called it—built by George Vanderbilt, culture-seeking youngest son of the railroader, was "impractically spacious." James's room was "a glacial phantasy." He estimated it to be half a mile from the "mile-long library."

The first thing that had happened after his arrival at the dream castle in the North Carolina mountains was this sudden flare-up of his gout. He needed bran footbaths; he was taking pills. He was minus a front tooth. He hopped about, alternating between anger and despair, furious at the circumstance that had brought him into deeper cold than any he had fled. His gout had brought him to a standstill, trapped in a château set 2,500 feet in the air—magnificent, imposing "and utterly unaddressed to any possible arrangement of life, or state of society." After the first pain subsided, and his foot was reduced to manageable proportions, James took in his surroundings with less violence of feeling, but with continuing bewilderment. He would later ironically call Biltmore "a castle of enchantment." He put in the better part of a week there, where "the climate stalks about in the marble halls in default of guests." His stay was lonely. There were only two other guests. He had come at the wrong season. When he was able to put a normal shoe on his gouty foot, he made the night-long journey to Charleston, to begin in earnest his brief visit to the South.

Four decades had elapsed since the Civil War: but the old muffled ache, the anguish of fratricidal struggle remained. James looked upon the South with time-wearied eyes—also with eyes that had seen the ravages of history in Europe. The hurts and wounds, the stirred feelings of defeats and victories, had shrunk now to paper mementoes, hollow-eyed statues and renovated ruins. In Charleston, visiting an old cemetery, he seems to have walked with memories of Miss Woolson. An allusion, in the midst of his description of the place, to its lagoon as a "possible site of some Venice that had never mustered the luxury . . . of shrub and plant and blossom that the pale North can but distantly envy," suggests that he was remembering Fenimore's *Rodman the Keeper;* and then she had talked to him of these very places—for she had lived in the post-bellum South and had been its modest fictional historian.

He looked at Fort Sumter, and the other forts at Charleston, remembering the far-off historical moment; his guide, the novelist Owen Wister, standing beside him, remarked, "I never look out to the old betrayed forts without feeling my heart harden again to steel." Even though he lived in the South and felt its sadness and sorrow, Wister wrote about the West and had had a boyhood abroad. His grandfather, however, had been a famous slave-owner and his grandmother, James's old friend Fanny Kemble, had written an anti-slavery book, describing her life on a Georgia plantation. In the Richmond Confederate museum, James found another kind of witness. He got into conversation with a young Southern farmer who had come to the city for the day, and was reliving the War Between the States. As James followed him about he pointed out certain relics preserved also in his family, and related some of his father's exploits in the war. When James complimented him on "his exact knowledge of these old, unhappy, far-off things," the young farmer remarked, "Oh, I should be ready to do them all over again myself." Then with a smile, he added, "That's the kind of Southerner *I* am." The young man's consciousness, James felt, "would have been poor and unfurnished without this cool platonic passion." He reflected too that though the farmer wouldn't have hurt a Northern fly, there were things—for they had talked of the blacks—that "all fair, engaging, smiling, as he stood there, he would have done to a Southern Negro." The novelist wondered at the way in which the Confederate world had pinned everything on the institution of slavery. Deprived of this, a great vacuity remained. At the end he imaged the South as "a figure somehow blighted or stricken, discomfortable, impossible, seated in an invalid-chair, and yet fixing one with strange eyes that were half a defiance and half a deprecation of one's noticing and much more of one's referring to, any abnormal sign."

Part of his small "historic whiff" of the South he got by looking out of "the Pullmans that are like rushing hotels and the hotels that are like stationary Pullmans." After a glance at Jacksonville, he went on to Palm Beach, where he put up at the Breakers, enjoying the hotel luxuries and concluding that one might live in the soft climate "as in a void furnished at the most with velvet air." He enjoyed the sea and the air; but he shrank from the human picture—"decent, gregarious, and moneyed, but overwhelmingly monotonous and on the whole pretty ugly." In St. Augustine, where he went to see his brother Robertson's wife and their daughter Mary, later Mrs. Vaux, he stayed at the Hotel Ponce de Leon. He wrote to his brother William of his pleasure in meeting his niece, "very matured and very agreeable," and "highly susceptible, I think, of culture." They went sightseeing together to look at the little Spanish fort and the old Spanish cathedral, "these poor little scraps of Florida's antiquity so meagre and vague." But his true impression of Florida was conveyed to Mrs. Cadwalader Jones. It was, he said,

> a fearful fraud—a ton of dreary jungle and swamp and misery of flat forest monotony to an ounce or two of little coast perching-place—a few feet wide between the jungle and the sea. Nine-tenths of this meagre margin are the areas of the hotels—the remaining tenth is the beauties of nature and the little walk of the bamboozled tourist.

A Western Journey

On 4 March 1905 James left Boston again and traveled for forty hours across great tracts of snow to the banks of the Mississippi. Word of his Philadelphia performance had spread and he now knew he could pay his way with "The Lesson of Balzac." He was due in St. Louis, Chicago, South Bend, Indianapolis, San Francisco. Other places beckoned. Indianapolis, thanks to Booth Tarkington, had arranged a double audience of two cultural organizations, with the result that he was offered $400 and could have had $500. With a grand gesture he accepted the lower sum, murmuring "bloated Indianapolis!"

He had covered a thousand miles—"a single boundless empty platitude"—when he reached St. Louis, "a vast grey, smoky, extraordinary *bourgeois* place." A soft gentle rain fell most of the time he was there. He read "The Lesson of Balzac" before the Contemporary Club of St. Louis on 7 March. He had a feeling as he read that the lecture was "too special, too literary, too critical." But the audience was enthusiastic; and he also experienced a sense of embarrassment when, *coram publico,* the chairman handed him the check in payment—almost before he had said the last word. Business was strictly business in America. At a reception held in his honor at the University Club of St. Louis, he found himself seated at a large table with some forty club members around him, relaxed and eager for literary gossip. A minute of the occasion, written afterwards by a lawyer, records that James was asked whether Mrs. Humphry Ward could be compared with George Eliot. He carefully replied, "George Eliot was a great woman. I have the profoundest respect for the cleverness of Mrs. Humphry Ward." Oscar Wilde he called "one of those Irish adventurers who had something of the Roman character —able but false." He said that Wilde had returned to "the abominable life he had been leading" as soon as he got out of prison and his death was

"miserable." When *Ben-Hur,* written by Indiana's Lew Wallace, was
mentioned, James said he could not account for its success "except that
there are multitudes of people who have little taste; or upon the ground
that religious sentiment is more prevalent here than elsewhere."

James had done his fellow-Americans the honor of lecturing to them
on Balzac as if they were novelists like himself, even though America
was then addicted to "molasses fiction." *The Little Shepherd of Kingdom
Come, Mrs. Wiggs of the Cabbage Patch, Rebecca of Sunnybrook Farm*
were the current best-sellers. James had no illusions as to why men and
women—and especially women—came in such numbers to hear him. He
was aware that they wanted to see the lecturer rather than hear the
lecture. Everywhere people still remembered "Daisy Miller," even after
a quarter of a century. A waggish Chicago reporter with more literary
sense than most wrote his account of the novelist's arrival as if James
were Lambert Strether giving himself up to

> the little dreary pictures of Chicago life, which framed themselves on
> either hand in the square of cab door glass. It came home to him in the
> orthodox Jamesian manner that all he had heard of Chicago was stock-
> yards and boards of trade and dirt and coarse fearful exploits in the
> getting of money.

It was flattering to be reported in one's own style. Other midwestern
newspapers, however, spoke of James as "a novelist of the aristocracy,"
a condescending expatriate who talked of "the advance of civilization"
in America as if he were still in the world of Fenimore Cooper. An
Indiana editor angrily rejoined that if there was an "advance" it surely
could not have been stimulated by reading Mr. James's "inane" fictions.

In Chicago James stayed with Higginson cousins at Winnetka, and
later at the University Club. One day he returned from a luncheon engagement on the far South Side in the company of Robert Herrick, the
Chicago novelist, who recorded a glimpse of him as they rode through
"the smudged purlieus of the untidy city into the black gloom of the
Loop": James sits huddled on the dingy bench of the suburban car,
draped in the loose folds of his mackintosh, his hands clasped about his
"baggy" umbrella, "his face haggard under the shuttling blows of the
Chicago panorama." "What monstrous ugliness!" he murmurs in a tone
of pure physical anguish.

In Chicago James visited the studio of the sculptor Lorado Taft, and
dined at the studio of Hamlin Garland, novelist of the "middle border"
and friend of Howells, to meet some of the local literary and artistic folk.
When Garland went to the University Club to pick up James, he noted
how "worn and haggard" he looked. "His derby was too large for him, his
vest being a little awry and his collar was a trifle wilted." The novelist

met the people at the studio "with entire friendliness but with only an abstract interest so far as most of them were concerned." One gets the impression that James was depressed and dissociated. "He had forgotten many of his books and spoke of them rather vaguely. . . . He has lost his enthusiasm but still has his intellectual interests. He is going on now out of sheer momentum." What Garland's diary notes tell us is that James was exhausted—and bored.

From Chicago James swung over to Notre Dame, where he spoke to two Catholic groups in one day; then he went to Indianapolis, where he spoke before the massed culture groups. He also made a side trip to Milwaukee for a brief visit with the wife and children of his long-dead brother Garth Wilkinson. Then, with $1,350 in his pocket and complaining of "the fatigue of the good kind but too boresome people," he boarded a Pullman in Chicago for the west coast. "I am just escaping with my life," he wrote to his sister-in-law in Cambridge. "The visual ugliness of it all . . . the place a desolation of dreariness."

He went straight to Los Angeles: three days and three nights, "through unspeakable alkali deserts," across Kansas, Arizona, and New Mexico. He almost broke down, he said, from tension, sickness, and weariness; he would never again, he said, attempt a journey "of that confined and cooped up continuity." The train arrived many hours late, and the old backache of his youth threatened to return. "This country is too *huge* simply, for any human convenience," he wrote to Jocelyn Persse, "and so unutterably empty that I defy any civilization, any mere money-grabbing democracy, to make on it any impression worthy of the name."

The great green Pacific, the golden orange groves, the huge flowers, and Southern California "manners and human forms" gave promise of interest. Nevertheless, he told Persse, he was "well-nigh *rotten* with the languishment of homesickness." He was to lecture to a ladies' "culture club" in Los Angeles, and decided to give himself a holiday in the interval. He moved into the Hotel del Coronado at Coronado Beach, near San Diego, in a room hanging over the Pacific, to work at his American travel essays. The days were of "heavenly beauty." He was reminded of Italy. After the strain and tension of the winter he felt his heart "uplifted"; and he dreamed of the time when in Lamb House he would plunge "my hand, my arm *in,* deep and far," into "the heavy bag of remembrance" he would draw on for *The American Scene.*

Some 800 ladies came to his Los Angeles lecture; one, aged ninety-five, spoke to him familiarly of his mother and father whom she had known in New York, and of her memories of Margaret Fuller. After this James spent a few days at Monterey and journeyed to San Francisco. He wandered up and down its primitive hills, enjoyed being fêted by the

Bohemian Club, and met the tenor Enrico Caruso. He talked of Polynesia
with his old friend, Mrs. Robert Louis Stevenson, in her house in Hyde
Street; they had not seen each other since she and Louis had sailed on
their romantic journey, in the 1880s. "Poor lady, poor barbarous and
merely instinctive lady," he would murmur later to a cultivated San
Francisco bachelor named Bruce Porter, a man of artistic taste with a
flair for architecture and landscape gardening, whom he met during this
visit. James little dreamed—and would never know—that this man was
destined to become the husband of his beloved niece, Peggy. James was
critical of San Francisco; he found in it "a poverty of aspect and quality."
But he experienced a touch of western openness when the owner of St.
Dunstan's, the hotel where he stayed, refused to render him a bill—it had
been a privilege to have so distinguished a guest.

James took a train for Seattle, passing through the beflowered valleys
of Oregon and spending a night in Portland. In Seattle he visited his
brother Robertson's eldest son, Edward Holton James. The eccentric Ned
James would later be cut out of his uncle's will because he espoused
attacks against George V, who he alleged had made a morganatic marriage. But this occasion was genial; Ned James wrote years later:

> I sat by the hour, with wide open mouth, drinking in his wonderful exotic
> conversation. He was bored by the west, by the "slobber of noises," which
> we call our language, by the stream of vacant stupid faces on the streets
> and everywhere the "big ogre of business."

By now James was in a hurry to return to the East. His nephew got
him a comfortable Pullman bedroom. He broke the journey at St. Paul,
and at Chicago his Higginson cousin guided him onto the night train to
New York. The next morning, when he reached Albany, scene of so much
of his childhood, he had "the absurdest sense of meeting again a ripe old
civilization and travelling through a country that showed the mark of
established manners." There was "thicker detail"; and then there was
the familiar Hudson River whose shore the train followed into New York.
Once again in Manhattan he relapsed into the safety and comfort of
Minnie Jones's house in Eleventh Street, and wrote of his bliss in "having
(approximately) done with Barbarism."

The Terrible Town

Henry James left to the last his exploration of New York, his home-
city, and during May and June he inspected what he called, half-lovingly,
half-seriously, "the terrible town." He had had a panoramic vision of it
when, arriving from Washington, bound for Boston, his Pullman car was
taken by barge around the tip of Manhattan and on up to Harlem. Look-

ing from his Pullman window at New York's "pin-cushion profile," he pondered the "depressingly furnished and prosaically peopled" shore. New York had made no use of its surrounding natural beauty, the bay, the little islands, the farther shores. The tall buildings were "impudently new—and still more impudently novel." They had this in common "with so many other terrible things in America"—they were "triumphant payers of dividends." But they did not have, for him, "the authority of things of permanence or even of long duration." Skyscrapers, he wrote, "are the last word of economic ingenuity only till another word be written."

This would be the theme of his poetic pictures of Manhattan as he viewed the city during the spring of 1905—the new city spreading itself into the modernity of the new century. It was created on a foundation of impermanence. America seemed to build—only to re-build. Remembering the beauty of Giotto's tower in Florence, James looked at Trinity Church in downtown New York, which he had known when its simplified Gothic spire towered over Wall Street. Now it was submerged, surrounded, smothered, caged, dishonored. The skyscrapers looming over it created an effect of a mountain wall; one expected an avalanche to drop from such a wall on village and village spire at its foot.

In search of personal memories, in the lower Fifth Avenue neighborhood, James studied an old house on Waverly Place that had survived and the "lamentable little Arch of Triumph" built into Washington Square. The author of "The Birthplace" walked over to Washington Place, to that part of the street leading from the Square to Broadway, where his father's house had stood at No. 21 and where he had been born sixty-two years before. The house was gone. In its place had been built a high, square, impersonal structure, proclaiming its lack of interest in the past with a crudity all its own. James felt "amputated of half my history." Yet the sense of personal affront was perhaps not so powerful as the thought that the city lacked self-confidence; it didn't really believe in itself. Otherwise it would not tear itself down so often.

The pages of *The American Scene* that record James's energetic exploration of Manhattan that spring are filled with nostalgia and shock, surprise and resignation. He cared for "the terrible town," cared for it deeply, as one born in it; and it hurt him that man could create so blindly and so crudely the foundations of inevitable "blight." As he wandered in the Italian and Jewish neighborhoods, he was struck by the alienation of the immigrant Italians when compared with Italians in Italy; here they seemed remote and melancholy. On the other hand he found the Jewish ghetto, on the lower East Side, animated and bewildering. He saw Jews swarming over the fire-escapes attached to the tenements, listened to the babel of children in great numbers, and noted the old, with marked distinctive faces, occupying doorstep and pavement, curbstone and gut-ter. He commented on "the unsurpassed strength of the race" which had withstood the forces of history. With their reverence for intellect, he would have toasted the Jews as "an intellectual people," but America seemed to do its work and he saw the "hard glitter of Israel." Pondering the abundance of the ghetto shops, James wondered whether the United States wasn't inventing "a new style of poverty." He had seen enough of the sordid and squalid in New York to feel that "there is such a thing, in the United States, as freedom to grow up to be blighted." And he reflected that this "may be the only freedom in store for the smaller fry of future generations."

At the Café Royal, on the lower East Side, where Jewish literati and café-philosophers mingled, James listened to the accents of Europe as they fractured the English language. Language for the novelist was sacred; in these warm-lighted cafés he felt himself in "the torture rooms of the living idiom." He was happier in an upper East Side bowling alley and billiard room, a German beer-hall which however served no beer. In this dingy place James found a conception "of decency and dignity"—a few tables and chairs, a few coffee cups and boxes of dominoes. The host had omitted learning "the current American." He spoke but a dozen words—and since he talked little, James felt the stillness to be friendly.

He inspected Riverside Drive, pausing at Grant's tomb; he liked its direct democratic accessibility to spectators—who didn't remove their hats in the shrine! He wandered in Central Park and found it filled with "eruptive and agitated effect" and afraid "to be just vague and frank and quiet." In the Metropolitan Museum he winced "at the expense which, like so much of the expense of New York, doesn't educate." He wandered in upper Fifth Avenue, seeing the palatial houses of the rich as a "record, in the last analysis, of individual loneliness." They never became seats of family; they were as discontinuous as much else of American life, reduced to "the present, pure and simple."

The Brothers

Henry James's incursion into the orbit of his elder brother, after a three-decade absence, revived the long-buried power struggle that had existed between the two—ever since their nursery days in Washington Square. In their youth they had been like Jacob and Esau. In the language of that myth Henry James now spoke of his return as "taking up again my birthright." Mutual guilt had made them feel as if each were encroaching upon the other's birthright. Henry had felt most free in his young days when William was away. William had felt free only when he could escape from his family—to Brazil, to Germany. Both relapsed into petty illnesses when they had to be together for too long a time. But between 1875 and 1905 each had carved out his own empire. Henry James had made himself the culture bearer of America in Europe. William had made himself the hero of American pragmatism.

The differences between the brothers were never more marked than in 1904-05 when Henry, all power and drive, came as a "restless analyst" to study William's America, and suddenly caught the public eye in a country where the philosopher's public image was large. At Chocorua in the autumn of 1904 there were walks and talks and the old communion of their youth. But Henry did not spend much time with his brother. He was in New York; he was in Lenox; he went south; and then that spring when Henry arrived in the middle west and the press began to pay increasing attention to him, William quite suddenly, on an impulse, set sail for the isles of Greece. He had never been in Athens or for that matter southern Italy. His reason for going at this moment was that he wanted to escape the "influenza season" in Cambridge; he was apparently escaping something else, and perhaps in part, his brother.

Although William always attacked Europe, at least to Henry, he was, during his trip to Greece, in a somewhat different mood. The end of middle age, his heart attacks, his years of work, seemed to make him conscious of missed opportunities. "I have come here too late in life," he wrote, "when the picturesque has lost its serious reality. Time was when hunger for it haunted me like a passion." Was it the sense of "too late?" —the theme his brother had written into *The Ambassadors* and "The Beast in the Jungle"—that made William, in defiance of his heart condition, journey through rugged Greece and stand before the Parthenon, as so many romantics had done before, with tears in his eyes? *J'ai vu la beauté parfaite,* he wrote, lapsing into the language he criticized his brother for using so often. Turning to Rome, he attended a philosophical congress, and with great spontaneity read a paper in French on "consciousness." He was quite the hero of the meeting. He returned in May to Cambridge, strengthened, refreshed, to find his brother Henry in Irving Street full of impressions of old New York. They saw each other briefly. Henry went off to stay with Mrs. Wharton at Lenox before sailing; William left for Chicago to deliver a series of lectures. The brothers did not meet again during Henry's American trip. William sent Henry a cheerful letter of good-bye. Henry waved back one of his regular epistolary flourishes.

What Henry did not know—and would never know—was that William had just made one of the most unusual epistolary flourishes of his life—with Henry as object if not subject. The brothers were both members of the National Institute of Arts and Letters, having been elected in 1898 when the Institute was founded. During 1905 the Institute began procedures for establishing an Academy of Arts and Letters of limited membership, like the French Academy; its members—ultimately there would be fifty—were to be chosen on successive ballots by an inner core of seven Academicians from the ranks of the Institute. Henry James was among those elected during the second ballot in February 1905; he received word of his election in Richmond on his way to the South. William was elected during the fourth ballot in May and found the notification of election awaiting him on his return that month from Europe. In a letter dated 17 June 1905 he informed the Academy secretary, Robert Underwood Johnson, that he could not accept the honor. He never accepted honors in academic bodies which did not have some work cut out for them, he said, and this Academy seemed to him purely honorific; moreover it would be contrary to his preachings of a lifetime "against the world and its vanities." But he gave a third reason for declining:

> I am the more encouraged to this course by the fact that my younger and shallower and vainer brother is already in the Academy and that if I were there too, the other families represented might think the James influence too rank and strong.

The gesture was private, and Johnson revealed it only years later in his memoirs, without however quoting the letter.

William had not considered there was a redundancy of Jameses in the Institute when he and Henry had been elected to it in 1898; in his letter he rectified this inconsistency by resigning from the Institute forthwith. And despite his "pretensions to austerity and righteousness" he had accepted honorary membership in the Institut de France, as well as a number of honorary degrees. But the Academy had elected Henry James—younger, shallower, vainer—ahead of the older brother; and while admitting that his act was "sour" and "ungenial," William's letter seemed to imply once again that it was impossible for Jacob and Esau to live under the same roof, to occupy seats side by side in the same room—or Academy.

In the ensuing months William James would express the fraternal differences in the most consistent barrage he had ever laid down against his brother's work. He launched a measured critique of *The Golden Bowl* which he had not read earlier, saying it had put him, "as most of your recenter long stories have put me, in a very puzzled state of mind." The method of elaboration went "agin the grain" of all his own impulses in writing. And the philosopher added:

> Why don't you, just to please Brother, sit down and write a new book, with no twilight or mustiness in the plot, with great vigour and decisiveness in the action, no fencing in the dialogue, or psychological commentaries, and absolute straightness in style. Publish it in my name, I will acknowl-

edge it, and give you half the proceeds. Seriously, I wish you *would,* for you *can;* and I should think it would tempt you, to embark on a "fourth manner."

Henry James's answer was sufficiently direct, and he fell in with William's barbed aggression. He would write, he said,

some uncanny form of thing, in fiction, that will gratify you, as Brother —but let me say, dear William, that I shall greatly be humiliated if you *do* like it, and thereby lump it in your affection with things of the current age, that I have heard you express admiration for and that I would sooner descend to a dishonoured grave than have written.

William wanted him, he suggested, quoting from his lecture on Balzac, to take up the art of the slate pencil instead of the art of the brush.

I'm always sorry when I hear of your reading anything of mine, and always hope you won't—you seem to me so constitutionally unable to "enjoy" it . . . I see nowhere about me done or dreamed of the things that alone for me constitute the *interest* of the doing of the novel—and yet it is in a sacrifice of them on their very own ground that the thing you suggest to me evidently consists.

Always the younger brother, Henry softened his firm response by assuring William he was reading him "with rapture."

William was to return to the charge in 1907, when *The American Scene* was published. He accused Henry of having become a "curiosity of literature." "For gleams and innuendos and felicitous verbal insinuations you are unapproachable, but the *core* of literature is solid. Give it to us *once* again! The bare perfume of things will not support existence, and the effect of solidity you reach is but perfume and simulacrum." He enjoined Henry not to answer "these absurd remarks." Henry obliged. He told William he found his critical letter "rich and luminous." The younger brother went his own way as he had always done, simply inscribing the English edition: "To William James, his incoherent, admiring, affectionate Brother, Henry James, Lamb House, August 21st 1907."

In attacking his brother's style William James was adding a private fraternal voice to hostile voices raised in public throughout Henry's visit to the United States. Jokes circulated about the lady who knew "several languages—French, New Thought, and Henry James," or the lady who boasted she could read Henry James "in the original." The Commencement address James delivered at Bryn Mawr in the spring of 1905 on "The Question of Our Speech" was his fullest statement to the effect that language was sacred; speech was sacred. He reminded his young audience that "the human side of vocal sound" was being corrupted by slovenly speech and kept "as little distinct as possible from the grunting, the squealing, the barking or the roaring of animals." His many examples testified to his conscious ear, and to his belief that language—one's own —was to be learned and cultivated and cherished and not allowed to disintegrate. The press paid scant attention to the fact that James's remarks were addressed to the slipshod ways in which American girls spoke. It assumed James was attacking the American language itself, and Dr. Woodrow Wilson, the president of Princeton, defended newspaper English against the "laborious" style of the novelist.

James's "morality" seems to have offended even more than his style. Not a Sunday passed without an indignant letter to the *New York Times* about his books. *The Ambassadors* was described by one correspondent as a "notably warped situation." Did not Lambert Strether advise the nice clean American youth to cleave unto the questionable married woman in Paris? and to harden his heart to the tender claims of his mother and sister in far, humdrum, inartistic Massachusetts? A letter-writer, signing "Optimist," asked "is not the world worse for the decadence shown on the pages of Henry James?" A Brooklyn correspondent reported that in a reading club of 1,000 only three out of every hundred read Henry James. The popular novelist Alice Duer Miller, who was reaching a large audience, said that James, in *The Golden Bowl,* indulged in "a situation only scandalmongers are supposed to discuss."

As the day of James's departure approached, there were more caricatures and editorials in the press. He had never been a public figure on this scale, recognized even in the street and in shops. Robert Cortes Holliday, then a salesman in Scribner's bookshop, watched James browse in the store. "He ran his nose over the tables, and inch by inch along the walls, stood on tiptoe and pulled down volumes from high places, rummaged in dark corners." Not knowing he was recognized, James explained, "I live in England myself and am curious to know this," and he asked what percentage of the novels on the fiction table was the product of English writers. He barely glanced at a high pile of *Golden Bowl*s.

At the end of his time in America James found himself involved in a series of visits. Hendrik Andersen turned up in Boston and the two went briefly to Newport. He journeyed to Kittery Point in Maine to say farewell to Howells. Mrs. Wharton beckoned emphatically from Lenox, and James replied, "Be indulgent and don't shoot. I am doing my best." He managed to squeeze in a few days with her. She had a "big, commodious new motor" and they swept through the countryside. It was a fine way to rope in "a huge netful of impressions at once." During the last days J. B. Pinker arrived from London and in a series of conferences with Scribner's worked out the initial plans for the definitive edition of

James's novels and tales. Things were sociable to the last. Walter Berry, Europe-bound, booked a cabin on James's ship, the *Ivernia;* so did Elizabeth Robins, who had been revisiting her homeland. On 5 July James bade farewell to America. Tired, stimulated, his expenses covered by his lectures, he would now try to sort out his impressions.

The voyage was lively. James sat on deck revising *Roderick Hudson* for the Scribner edition. Berry and Miss Robins played a game called "hunt the adjective"—trying to see how many adjectives could be eradicated from whatever they were reading—while James hunted superfluous commas in his own past writings. Miss Robins remembered James "sending that melancholy look of his out over the Atlantic waste" and protesting against light-minded flittering of Americans back and forth across the sea. The *Ivernia* docked at Liverpool after a nine-day voyage. Restored to his London club, James briefly saw Jocelyn Persse. Then he was in Lamb House facing a vast accumulation of books, papers, magazines, letters—and a staff in revolt. Unhappy with the tenants, his housekeeper had threatened to leave. She was comforted by an increase in wages and the prompt discharge of two superfluous maids. Young Burgess was promoted from houseboy to valet. "The situation is clearing —Rye and my four-square little garden better and sweeter than they ever were," James reported to Mrs. William in far-away Cambridge. The Master was home again.

PART EIGHT   The Master

1905–1916

Art *makes* life, makes interest, makes importance.

HENRY JAMES

1

ESTIMATES

AND

REVISIONS

The Supreme Relation

In his earlier years Henry James had longed for Europe when in America, but had felt himself a claimant to kingdoms not his own in Europe. Now, in the fullness of time, he had re-possessed America. In some way his visit had answered an old riddle, resolved a double exile. He had thought of America as having rejected him: now he found that even when it laughed at him it loved him. He recognized, as he said in his book of impressions, that "one's supreme relation, as one had always put it, was one's relation to one's country."

During the night of 3–4 August 1906, James found himself kept awake by an idea for a story—a story about a repatriated American who goes in search of himself in a house in New York—himself *as he might have been* had he stayed at home. He called the story at first "The Second House"; presently it was renamed "The Jolly Corner." James seems to have written it during the next few days. His unfinished novel *The Sense of the Past* dealt with an American who inherits a house in London, and finds himself, on entering it, within the past of his English ancestors. The reverse of this idea was the tale of Spencer Brydon, who returns from years of living abroad to rebuild a Manhattan house for rental purposes; the house, on a corner in lower Fifth Avenue, is that of his birth and childhood. As he wanders through its rooms night after night, carrying a sputtering candle, he is haunted by the thought of what he might have been had he not gone to live in Europe. He has discussed this with his friend Alice Staverton, who has remained a spinster in her old house in Irving Place. It becomes an obsession with him—"how he might have led his life, and 'turned out,' if he had not so, at the outset, given it up." He feels he had, in his early American years, "some strange *alter ego* deep down somewhere within" him which, transferred to a strange climate, didn't have a chance to grow.

His nights of curiosity and meditation in "the jolly corner" become a quest for this *alter ego*—the self that might have been. The tale is a kind of active "Beast in the Jungle"; Brydon unlike John Marcher goes in pursuit of the "beast" instead of waiting for it to spring. On one occasion he notices with a *frisson* that a door in the house, hitherto closed, is open; someone must have opened it. Descending the staircase to the vestibule he sees dark shadows taking material form. A figure rises before him rigid, conscious, spectral, yet human—a man of his own substance and stature. The apparition stands there with its hands over its face, "splendid covering hands, strong and completely spread!" But two fingers are missing from the right hand, as if they had been "accidentally shot away." Then the hands move and the answer Brydon has sought is revealed. He sees a face of horror. Falling back, he feels "the whole vision turn to darkness and his very feet give way." Alice Staverton arrives to rescue him from his fainting spell. She has seen the same figure, with the two missing fingers, in a dream. But she doesn't agree with Brydon that the figure is a "horror." "I had accepted him," she says.

Personal myths seem bound together in this strange tale by which James announced to himself that had he stayed at home the hand that held the pen might have been crippled, but that he might also have been a titan of finance, a remodeler of old houses—even as this enterprising side of himself was about to remodel his writings in the New York Edition. Spencer Brydon and Alice Staverton—to whom James had given his sister's and his sister-in-law's name—agree that if Brydon had remained at home he would by now be a millionaire. "The Jolly Corner" embodied James's recurrent dream of pursuing a ghost or other self—a haunting creature—and defying and conquering it. He was always more powerful in his night-dreams than in his waking thoughts. Always these dreams begin with a sense of foreboding and terror; an anxiety that seeks relief. Threatened, he then turns the tables; it is *he* who suddenly frightens the *alter ego*. James would never forget this—the idea that a haunted person's fright can also frighten others. In "The Jolly Corner" Spencer Brydon is frightened by his own creation—the self he has materialized, the thought of what his life might have been. The resolution of the story is that he had had to fulfill his destiny; that he must accept himself even as America accepted him.

The elements of this low-keyed, tense little tale seemed to compose themselves in some magical way out of unconscious depths where they had lain hidden for years. The thrill for James was that it settled the whole question of his American journey. The next four years would be years of great fertility in spite of his advancing age; and they would be

Henry James's "American years," more American even than the years of
his lost youth. In the decade that remained to the Master, all that he did
was to be intimately related to his recaptured American self.

The American Scene was written with all the passion of a patriot and all
the critical zeal of an intellectual who could not countenance national
complacency and indifference. Civilization meant order, composition,
restraint, moderation, beauty, duration. Using this standard of measure-
ment, James found America terribly wanting. The country was founded
on violence, plunder, loot, commerce; its monuments were built neither
for beauty nor for glory, but for obsolescence. And then James hated the
continental "bigness" of America. Homogeneity, rootedness, manners—
modes of life—these were his materials and everywhere he looked he
found there had been an erosion of the standards and forms necessary
to a novelist, necessary also to civilization. The self-indulgence and advertisement of the plunderers were carried over to the indulging of their
young. Americans had interpreted freedom as a license to plunder. This
was the burden of the impressions James set down, in the days when they
were still vivid, and in the light of his native, his early emotion.

"I would take my stand," he wrote, "on my gathered impressions."
Then, perhaps remembering how he had been pilloried in America for
his little study of Hawthorne, he added he was prepared to "go to the
stake" for what he had written. The American critics had no violent
reaction. They spoke of James's "antipathy" and they complained about
his style. At the same time the usual compliments were paid to his "fas-
tidiously probing mind."

James could not resist an opportunity offered him shortly after his
book was done to discuss further the ways in which American women
sacrificed the tone and the form of their inherited speech. Asked by
Elizabeth Jordan to write three articles for *Harper's Bazaar* he ended by
doing eight, four on American speech and four on American manners.
Bad speech bred bad manners. He blamed American men for cultivating
and fostering a state of "queenship" in the women; and he blamed the
women for their failure to meet the responsibilities of sustaining and
molding the young. The essays were written in haste and with great
looseness; James had spent his best efforts on *The American Scene.* Yet
these chips from the workshop reflect the same critical spirit, the same
indignation; and the same energy. "We have, as a people, no sense of
manners at all," said James, and by manners he meant the totality of the
forms of human relations. His conclusion was that the sacrifice of manners had always "in the long run to be made up, just as the breakages and
dilapidations have to be paid for at the end of the tenancy of a house
carelessly occupied."

He had planned a second volume of American impressions. He wanted to write a paper on the middle west; another on "California and the Pacific Coast"; there was to be one on the universities and the colleges, for he had lectured at almost a dozen from Bryn Mawr to Harvard, from Notre Dame to Berkeley. But by the time he had completed *The American Scene* and the articles on speech and manners he found his impressions fading; he felt also he had sufficiently exploited his trip. And then more important work needed to be done. The western journey was never written.

The Better Chance

The four years between 1905 and 1909 were spent by Henry James preparing the collective edition of his novels and tales. "I should particularly like to call it the New York Edition if that may pass for a general title of sufficient dignity and distinctness," he wrote to Scribner's, adding that it "refers the whole enterprise explicitly to my native city—to which I have had no great opportunity of rendering that sort of homage." The months of unrelieved toil James expended in the preparation of his works (their full title was *The Novels and Tales of Henry James,* New York Edition) show beyond question that he regarded this as his literary monument. With a courage and zeal few writers had shown, he rewrote his early works to bring them up to the level of his maturity. And he was ruthless in his omissions. As his publisher announced, the New York Edition contained "all of the author's fiction that he desires perpetuated."

From the very beginning James had decided the set should consist of twenty-three volumes. Scribner's were ready to print James's total work; the "complete" novels and tales would have come to thirty-five volumes. The idea of making the edition *selective* was entirely James's, and the choice of twenty-three was not arbitrary. In James's first essay on Balzac in 1875, inspired by the issue of the collected edition of that novelist, we find him saying, "Balzac's complete works occupy twenty-three huge octavo volumes, in the stately but inconvenient *édition définitive* lately published." Thus the Master paid homage not only to New York in his Edition; he bowed respectfully to the *Comédie Humaine.* His edition would be the *"comédie humaine"* of Henry James.

As Balzac had grouped his scenes of provincial, Parisian, political and private life, so James arranged his works, not chronologically but according to themes and subjects. But the limitation to twenty-three volumes meant that the novelist did not have room to turn around in. Six of his novels were of such length that they required two volumes. With the addition of three single-volumed novels, he used up fifteen of his twenty-three volumes at the very start. He then had to fit his shorter novels, and a selection of his tales, into the remaining eight volumes, and had to juggle with stories according to their length as well as their subject or theme. In the end part of his scheme collapsed. His volumes of tales proved too long, and spilled over into a twenty-fourth volume. We can read his deep irritation and disappointment in a long letter James wrote to Scribner's. The arcane plan was spoiled. "My groupings had been, of course, affinities much observed, so that each volume should offer, as to content, a certain harmonious physiognomy; and now that felicity is perforce—I abundantly recognize—disturbed." Nevertheless the architectural form of the monument was preserved; it constitutes, in the totality of Henry James's work, a work of art in itself.

Balzac had "read the universe, as hard and as loud as he could, *into* the France of his time," James had said. He set himself a comparable task: he read America and Americans into the world—the European world—read them back into the civilization from which they had seceded. The first three novels in the Edition deal with three pilgrims abroad—Roderick Hudson, the artist, Christopher Newman, the man of business, Isabel Archer, the archetypal American woman. The next volumes contain James's English novels. There follow the short novels and the long tales which are arranged thematically, and then the volumes of short stories: those of the artist's life, the supernatural, the international scene. James omitted his "Scenes of American Life"—*The Bostonians, Washington Square, The Europeans,* and nearly all of his American short stories. They would have required too much revision especially in the light of his recent travels in America. Also set aside was the early potboiler, *Confidence.* James wrote to Howells in particular of the "tolerably full and good *Bostonians*" which had never, he said, "even to my much-disciplined patience, received any sort of justice." But it would take "a great deal of artful redoing" and "I haven't now had the courage or time for anything so formidable as touching and retouching it."

In James's tale "The Middle Years," an elderly writer dreams of "a better chance" in which to do the supreme writing of his life. He is "a passionate corrector, a fingerer of style." In creating the New York Edition James got his better chance. Not only could he alter his old texts, but he could apply the varnish of his late style. Revision for James was not a matter of choice but of "immediate and perfect necessity." Even much-revised older work found itself revised again. *Roderick Hudson* had been retouched in its progress from magazine to book in 1875. Preparing the English edition four years later James had made "a large number of verbal alterations." In 1905 he rewrote portions of it once more. *The Portrait of a Lady* was wholly renovated. His emendations strengthen his characters and eliminate ambiguities. Isabel Archer is so altered as to be almost a different personage. In this "fingering" of his text, James introduced no new scenes or new incidents. His method was to use reinforcing imagery to overcome earlier failures in explicitness. If erotic feeling was absent in the earlier work, the Master now made amends. In the first edition of *The Portrait* James described Caspar Goodwood's kiss in the closing paragraphs in a single sentence: "His kiss was like a flash of lightning; when it was dark again she was free." In the New York Edition this becomes a paragraph:

> His kiss was like white lightning, a flash that spread, and spread again, and stayed; and it was extraordinarily as if, while she took it, she felt each thing in his hard manhood that had least pleased her, each aggressive fact of his face, his figure, his presence, justified of its intense identity and made one with this act of possession. So had she heard of those wrecked and under water following a train of images before they sink. But when darkness returned she was free.

The earlier Isabel was incapable of this kind of feeling. Her fear of passion is now made explicit—and in the language of Eros.

The American, which James revised after the *Portrait,* is the most rewritten of all the novels. James made a certain number of significant substantive changes. He altered the time-scheme of the entire novel by adding five years to Christopher Newman's age—making him forty rather than thirty-five. The general effect of most of the revisions is in the direction of verbal precision, clarification of motive and a strengthening of the fiber of the work. James simplified conversation, substituted more direct language for pompous words and introduced fresh colloquial utterance. Occasionally his revisions went in the opposite direction. In the first edition of *The American* James described Newman—"his eye was of a clear, cold grey, and save for a rather abundant moustache, he was clean shaved." In the New York Edition this became: "His eye was of a clear, cold grey, and save for the abundant droop of his moustache he spoke, as to cheek and chin, of the joy of the matutinal steel." James himself had been experiencing this joy ever since he had shaved off his beard. Such comic details aside, the net effect of James's revisions, and particularly in the *Portrait,* is to enhance the text, and in that instance, the rewriting has been so subtle and skillful as to create almost a new novel.

The prefaces—eighteen in number—which James created for the Edition enabled him to say what he had hoped all his life critics would say for him. The novel in English had long been taken for granted as simple storytelling. James, arriving on the English scene late in the century, had taken the novel-machine apart in a very American way, given it a tech-

nology it had not possessed, and practiced his craft strenuously and pro-
fessionally. In his prefaces, to list but a few of the subjects, James discussed the extent to which the sense of place has to be created; the way
in which a novelist must make his reader feel the passage of time; the
need, as he felt it, for placing the novel's vision in a "central intelligence." In perhaps the finest of the prefaces, affixed to *The Portrait of a
Lady,* James discussed the way in which a novel must be considered an
"organic" structure—quite like the human body—in which everything is
related to everything else. He talked of form, and the way in which it is
substance; he talked of indirection in storytelling, and how to arouse
terror in the reader by artful ambiguity; he dealt with the plasticity of the
novelist's medium and the use in alternation of "picture" and "scene"; he
described his way of turning narrative into drama—and how he used to
say to himself "dramatize! dramatize!"

Playing through the prefaces is the human light by which James
worked—the situations he chose to develop and explore. In his preface
to "The Aspern Papers" there is an eloquent excursion on the uses of the
past, that "visitable" past, in which the artist can still recover the human
fact and the human dilemma, instead of the broken artifacts of the early
centuries. A great sense of poetry is infused into the prefaces; and then
they are touched by a gentle mood of reminiscence. James recalls the
occasions on which an idea first came to him: a dinner-table conversation, a sudden flash of inspiration while riding in a horse-car in Boston,
an anecdote told by a lady in Rome. Or he recalls the places in which his
stories had been written: how the chattering waterside life had floated in
through his hotel window in Venice as he composed certain pages of *The
Portrait of a Lady;* or how he had written parts of *The American* in
elaborate rooms in Paris. He spoke of the fog-filtered Kensington mornings when he had worked in De Vere Gardens in that comfortable bourgeois flat with its sky windows; or his hotel bedroom during the centenary
exhibition in Paris in 1889. Less than a treatise, these prefaces, in their
colloquial ease and flow, dictated at intervals between 1906 and 1908,
show the embodied truths of the art of fiction as James had practiced it.
The prefaces were James's supreme gift to criticism: and at the same
time they elucidated what criticism in its chronic blindness had failed
to perceive in his work.

From the first, James had taken it for granted that each volume of his
definitive edition would have a frontispiece. Twenty or more such frontispieces, "of thoroughly fine quality," were needed—each of "some
scene, object or locality" associated with one or other of the tales in the
volume. Scribner's underwrote the cost.

In the United States early in 1905 Henry James had been approached by a photographer named Alvin Langdon Coburn, an artistic young man of twenty-three who photographed him for a New York magazine. James had seen Coburn's work; not only his portraits but his pictures of London, his landscapes, photographs of docks at Liverpool and arches in Rome, all attempting, in the fashion of the time, to give a painter-like texture to photographic surface. The novelist had the idea of trying him out on some of the scenes needed for the edition. During a visit in 1906 to Rye, Coburn was given his preliminary instructions. His illustrations would be "optical" symbols. They would be photographs of general scenes, material objects. They would enhance, but in no way intrude irrelevant images upon, James's own literary images.

James dispatched Coburn to the Continent, to the cities of his fictions, and promised that he would himself guide him in London. In a series of letters he gave Coburn his instructions—as if he were an envoy on a delicate mission. First James wanted a portal of an aristocratic hotel in the Faubourg St. Germain—a *porte-cochère,* "a grand specimen of the type for *The American."* After driving in a cab through every street in the Faubourg, Coburn was urged to "go back and walk and stare at your ease." He was asked to look out in the Place de la Concorde "for some combination of objects that won't be hackneyed and commonplace and panoramic" to serve for *The Ambassadors.* James wanted a photograph of the Théâtre Français; also "something right" from the "sad Luxembourg Gardens."

Early in December 1906 Coburn went to Venice. James sent the photographer to his old friend Constance Fletcher, the American writer who lived in the Palazzo Capello on the Rio Marin, diagonally opposite the railway station. It had that rare thing in Venice, a garden, and was the Palazzino James had had in mind in 1887 for "The Aspern Papers." The other Venetian picture was a photograph of the Palazzo Barbaro. James referred to "the beautiful range of old *upper* Gothic windows" and it was these Coburn photographed for *The Wings of the Dove.*

London subjects were searched out together—the front of the old antique shop for *The Golden Bowl,* the front of the grocery shop for "In the Cage," a house in St. John's Wood where James's memories went back to his boyhood. On another occasion they went to Hampstead Heath to find and photograph, for the "tales of the literary life," the bench on which James had sat, long ago, with George Du Maurier, during their rambles on the Heath. For the second volume of *The Golden Bowl* Coburn took a memorable picture of a slightly blurred Portland Place—the rear view of a hansom in the broad thoroughfare, the distance fading into a haze.

In his preface to *The Golden Bowl* the novelist paid tribute to Coburn's art, but he was precise about the threat of the visual to the verbal.

The quest for the small antiquarian shop was in reality a quest for "a shop of the mind"; for this reason nothing would induce James to say where they had found their picture.

The volumes of the New York Edition began to be issued in December 1907 and continued into 1909. Long before he had finished his work on the Edition, James was exhausted and even bored with it. To his nephew Harry, he wrote that his

> terror of not keeping sufficiently ahead in doing my part of it . . . has so paralysed me—as panic fear—that I have let other decencies go to the wall. The printers and publishers tread on my heels, and I feel their hot breath behind me.

There were in reality only certain moments when this pressure was intense. The issuing of the novels—that is, the first fifteen volumes— proceeded with great regularity, though later the overflow of the Edition into twenty-four volumes meant dismembering some of the prefaces already written to suit the new story arrangements. Long afterwards—in the last year of his life—James would describe the Edition as "really a monument (like Ozymandias) which has never had the least intelligent critical justice done to it—or any sort of critical attention at all paid to it." He added that "the artistic problem involved in my scheme was a deep and exquisite one, and moreover, was, as I held, very effectively solved."

The House of Mirth

By the spring of 1907, after almost two years of unremitting labor, Henry James began to feel restless. *The American Scene* was in the press. He had given himself a long head start on the New York Edition and was revising *The Princess Casamassima,* the fifth and sixth volumes. He had written "The Jolly Corner" and several fugitive pieces. He longed to be out of his Rye-cage. For some weeks the "Angel of Devastation," as he called her, had been beckoning. Mrs. Wharton had leased an apartment in Paris at 58 rue de Varenne. Would Henry come and stay? Would he go on a motor trip to the South of France? The Master spoke in hyperbole of the Whartonian "eagle pounce and eagle flight." He squirmed at the pounce; he loved the flight. Mrs. Wharton's energy was "devouring and desolating, ravaging, burning, and destroying." She destroyed by taking him away from his work. But he wanted to be taken away. Early in March of 1907 he crossed the Channel; in the rue de Varenne, he announced himself in "gilded captivity." He remained in Paris a fortnight and then they went for the tour Mrs. Wharton celebrated in *A Motor-Flight*

Through France; after that there was a further stay at No. 58, which James called "the house of mirth"—an allusion to Mrs. Wharton's novel. James felt this might be his last visit to the Continent and he prolonged it. It was the longest visit he ever paid to a private home.

James had never penetrated the life of the Faubourg St. Germain and now he found himself agreeably ensconced in it, not far from the Invalides. Mrs. Wharton respected James's working hours; she had hers as well. The two novelists remained in their rooms until lunch, sometimes into the afternoon. For the rest of the day, Mrs. Wharton, the American aristocrat, moved with ease and elegance among the newer French aristocracy. "Our friend is a great and graceful lioness," James told Howard Sturgis. There were charming small dinner parties in the rue de Varenne at which, as Mrs. Winthrop Chanler remembered, "the guests were carefully chosen for their absolute compatibility." When the parties were over and the guests were gone, James would draw his chair to the fire, invite his American friends to approach and opening his eyes wide would murmur: "Now let us say what we really think."

Mrs. Wharton was to speak of James's "schoolboy's zest" on these occasions. Her friends told her they had never met an Anglo-Saxon who spoke such admirable French. He was not only correct and fluent; he translated the Jamesian style into it. He reported he had had "an indigestion of Chères Madames"—he who had always wanted to meet French society. But "It has really been lovely," he wrote to Sturgis on the eve of his motor tour with the Whartons to the south of France.

They left on a bland March morning, the first day of spring, in the Whartons' new Panhard, with the Yankee chauffeur Charles Cook at the wheel, and various servants dispatched ahead with the luggage as for a royal progress. They visited Rambouillet, they paused in Chartres, they looked at châteaux, they lingered in churches. It was leisurely; it was princely. They went to Blois, to Poitiers, to Bordeaux, and thence to the Pyrenees. "The motor is a magical marvel," James wrote, and "this large, smooth old France is wonderful." At Pau, Teddy Wharton was ill for several days, and Henry and Mrs. Wharton made a series of neighborhood excursions. Then they went to Carcassonne and Toulouse; remounting the valley of the Rhône they paused at Nîmes, Arles, and Orange.

They stopped at Nohant to visit the old country mansion that had been the home of George Sand. James surveyed the plain house which had harbored so much ancient passion. Edith heard him muse, "And in which of those rooms, I wonder, did George herself sleep?" He looked at her with a twinkling eye. "Though in which, indeed, in which indeed, my dear, did she *not?*"

The Master and Mrs. Wharton had a great community of interest: it was Teddy Wharton who was the "third person" in this party. And it is clear that when the Panhard turned again into the Parisian traffic, after three weeks, the Master and the lady novelist felt they had had a charming adventure together, a little tour of high intelligence and perception and for James a great deal of luxurious living. He had always stayed at first-class hotels but had never cultivated the *hôtel de luxe:* and he discovered that this kind of travel drained his modest purse. He was living, as he put it in a letter to Goody Allen, "an expensive fairy-tale," proof again of the old saying that it was "one's rich friends who cost one!" But, "Ah, the lovely rivers," he said, "and the inveterately glorious grub."

He was in no hurry to return to his "poor frowsy tea-and-toasty Lamb House." Waiting in the rue de Varenne were piles of Scribner proof. He settled down to the galleys, as the life of the Faubourg continued. "We *déjeunons* out, and we dine, and we visit countesses in between." James was writing to Gaillard Lapsley. "The Teddies are divinely good—and their inflamed Academician lunches here Sunday." James continued to be shocked by the changes in Bourget; he spoke of his "almost *insane* bad manners, snobbishness, and folly," a talent spoiled by social pampering and worldliness. James's old Newport friend Thomas Sergeant Perry turned up. They had drifted apart, but met now almost as if there had been no gap; they took long walks, and went to a concert. James spent agreeable hours with his nephew Billy, who was painting at Julien's when he wasn't playing tennis or rowing. A little in the tone of Lambert Strether talking about Chad Newsome, Henry urged his brother to allow Billy to remain longer in Paris: "He ought absolutely to stay another year and not *retomber* to the art-desert of home, before, like a camel, he has filled his stomach-pouch with water to see him through."

James himself remained in Paris for three more weeks, well into May, "steeped up to my chin in the human and social imbroglio." His weeks with the Whartons had marked a difference "from one's promiscuous boulevardian quarters of the past." To Jocelyn Persse he wrote: "I have had a very interesting agreeable time—one of the most agreeable I have ever had in Paris." He had "come in for a great many social impressions of a sort I hadn't had for a long time—some of them of a more or less intimate French sort that I had *never* had." In the past, it had often been James who pleaded with Persse to bring him news of the great world. Now he had "plenty to tell you on some blest Sunday, after my return, when you come down and stroll with me in the alentour of poor dear russet Lamb House."

But that return was again postponed. Italy called. Howard Sturgis was in Rome; Hendrik Andersen beckoned. James traveled in a sleeper to Turin, pausing to revise certain pages of *The Princess Casamassima;* it was a way of ministering to his constitutional need for a few—even if very few—days "of *recueillement* and solitude."

James kept speaking of this as the "last continental episode of my aged life," which it was not. A year later he would visit Mrs. Wharton in Paris once more. Yet he felt quite correctly that he would never see Italy again. He spent seventeen days in Rome. Here he found Alice Mason, with whom he had once gone riding in the Campagna, now a "silvery ghost" of the strong and passionate woman he remembered. He had some hours with Howard Sturgis, and he spent much time with Hendrik Andersen, who did a bust of the Master, making him look like a Roman senator. One gets a feeling that James's original ardor had cooled; yet a certain tenderness remained. There were sessions at a restaurant, visits to a foundry where some of Andersen's work was being cast, and a long last evening on a terrace. One day James went to the Protestant Cemetery to see once more the violet-covered grave of Miss Woolson. James communed silently there—feeling this to be his last farewell.

Rome no longer had its old charm. "The abatements and changes and modernisms and vulgarities, the crowd and the struggle and the frustration (of real communion with what one wanted) are quite dreadful," he wrote to his nephew Billy. "I quite revel in the thought that I shall never come to Italy *at all* again." He dined one evening with his old cosmopolitan-American friend Henry Brewster; this was the last time he saw him, for Brewster died shortly afterwards. "I had an impression of great goodness and kindness, almost tenderness," Brewster wrote, of "something delicate and strong morally." But he also noted that "the spring, the flash of steel has gone."

James was to have the novelty of motoring in Italy with the Italian explorer and traveler Filippo de Filippi and his American wife. These excursions, with the explorer himself driving, included a two-day jaunt to Naples, going down by the mountains, to Monte Cassino, and returning by Gaeta, Terracina, the Pontine Marshes, and the Castelli—"quite an ineffable experience," James wrote to Mrs. Wharton later. It had brought home to him "how incomparably the old *coquine* of an Italy is the most beautiful country in the world—of a beauty (and an interest and complexity of beauty) so far beyond any other that none other is worth talking about." The "dishevelled nymph" of his youth, however, was now an "old hussy."

The Naples journey was memorialized, with other occasions from this last visit, in certain pages James added to his earlier writings about Italy when he assembled *Italian Hours*—that book in 1910 was his way of saying farewell to the Italy of all his years. As always in his pictorial travel sketches, James brought to these added pages hints of the personal —his exploration of "sordidly papal streets" in the heterogeneous city "in the company of a sculptor friend." And he ended the pages of memory with an allusion to the last dinner with Andersen on an old loggia that overhung, not just "the great obelisked Square" and the Tiber, but also, "as it were, the whole awkward past, the mild confused romance of the Rome one had lived and of which one was exactly taking leave."

He had long ago said farewell to Florence. On this final visit, he spent four days with Howard Sturgis and "the Babe" who were staying at the Edward Boits', at Cernitoio, over against Vallombrosa, "a dream of Tuscan loveliness." Then he went on to Venice to the familiar Palazzo Barbaro and the Curtises.

Venice was his old Venice, unique, exquisite, beloved of all his years —this in spite of a sirocco that blew during part of the time. But he found the Curtises restrictive, formal, rigid, bound up by their prejudices and with "such a terror of the vulgar"—perhaps this was because he himself had so considerably "loosened up." They too had grown older, and made James feel "they discriminated so invidiously against anyone I might weakly wish to see, of my little other promiscuous acquaintance in Venice, that I felt I could never again face the irritations and the inconvenience of it." So it was farewell to Venice, too. Yet it was the most difficult farewell of all. "I don't care, frankly, if I never see the vulgarized Rome or Florence again," James wrote that summer to Edith Wharton—"but Venice never seemed to me more lovable."

Late in June he turned north again. He spent three days at Lausanne, and on 4 July was in Paris, where he stayed at the Hôtel du Palais d'Orsay, Mrs. Wharton being no longer in the rue de Varenne. A few days later he was back at Lamb House, writing to Hendrik Andersen in his "little deep-green garden, where the roses are almost as good as the Roman, and the lawn is almost as smooth beneath the feet as your floors of No. 3— I try to forget what I've lost."

His farewell to Italy had been unmistakable. His farewell to Paris was more tentative. In the spring of 1908, after a busy autumn and winter, James repeated his visit of the year before. The Olympian world still fascinated and Mrs. Wharton—now in a rented apartment at 3 Place des États-Unis—was possessive. But this time James came with the understanding that his stay would be brief. The great lady had arranged for the Master to have his portrait painted by the *littérateur*-painter Jacques-Émile Blanche, who had an enormous facility and was a great social lion. He posed James full face. When the portrait was finished it turned out to be in profile. James characterized Blanche as a "do-you-any-way-you-like sort of painter." When he saw the painting in London he could not recognize it. It was a *chic'd* thing, but had "a certain dignity of intention."

Paris was "wonderful" but a "fatal and prostrating vortex." "I am kept here in gilded chains, in gorgeous bondage, in breathless attendance and luxurious *asservissement,*" he wrote to Henry Adams. The visit was soon over and James rushed back to his Edition. By this time he had had a larger vision of Mrs. Wharton. She was "the wonderful, the unique Edith Wharton" and also the devastation "of one's time and domestic economy." He imaged himself as a "poor old croaking barnyard fowl" pitted against "a golden eagle." If we discount the euphemisms and playful ironies, we may still accept one designation as carrying the essence of his feeling about her—she was, he remarked, "almost too insistently Olympian."

Miss Bosanquet

When Miss Theodora Bosanquet went that summer's day in 1907 to Miss Petheridge's secretarial office and employment agency, she had no notion that this would be one of the most eventful days of her life. For some time she had been proofreading in that office an index to the Report of the Royal Commission on Coast Erosion. A young, slim woman in her early twenties, with bright blue eyes and a shy manner, she was wearing that day her usual office outfit, a white blouse and green skirt, a belt and a tie—a "business-like and, I hoped, becoming costume." At about noon she learned that Mr. Henry James was in the office. She had expected an interview but had not known on which day. She fidgeted nervously; she felt cold.

It is doubtful whether James ever learned that Miss Bosanquet had trained herself especially to be his amanuensis. Earlier that summer she had heard chapters from *The Ambassadors* being dictated in the office. On inquiry she had learned James needed a typist. Miss Bosanquet promptly set herself to learn typing. She had gone to Cheltenham Ladies' College and then to University College where she had taken a degree. She had, thus, much more education than Miss Weld, who had married while the novelist was in America and left his employ. But Miss Bosanquet had no intention of parading her education, or her "literary" interests before James. Her diary of that August day gives us a picture of a figure "like Coleridge"—"very expansive."

> He wore green trousers and a blue waistcoat with a yellow sort of check on it and a black coat—that was rather a shock. I'd imagined him as always very correctly dressed in London. He is bald—except for tufts of not very grey hair at the sides. His eyes, grey I think, are exactly what I should expect—but the rest of his face is too fat. He talks slowly but continuously—I found it hard to get in any words of my own.

James was interested in two or three essential things. Rye was remote; would she find it too lonely? He informed her he was slow at dictating; she would have to amuse herself while he was evolving a sentence. "He was careful," Miss Bosanquet noted, "to impress on me the danger of boredom." They could start in the autumn.

Miss Bosanquet arrived in Rye on 10 October 1907 and James met her at the station. He walked her to her rooms, "the talk being slightly constrained," and left his new employee in the care of her landlady. She felt "horribly desolate." Her rooms were nice but she missed her London flat.

Sharp at 10:15 the next morning Miss Bosanquet mounted the cobbled street to Lamb House. James let her in. He led her to the Green Room upstairs. Dictation began. James was working on a preface to *The Tragic Muse* "in a tone of personal reminiscence." Her diary records,

> he dictates considerately—slowly and very clearly—giving all the punctuation and often the spelling. I was abominably slow and clumsy—but he was very kind—even complimentary though he admitted that he hoped I should soon go a little faster. He sat in a chair at first—then paced about, smoking—finishing soon after half past one.

Miss Bosanquet ended her diary of that first day, "Mr. James assumes complete ignorance of any literary knowledge on the part of his amanuensis. He told me that *The Newcomes* was in one word and that it was by Thackeray!"

Things were easier on the second day. She was less nervous and typed more rapidly. In a very short time James knew that he had an accomplished amanuensis. A week after she had begun work for him he was writing William James that the "young boyish Miss Bosanquet" was "worth all the other (females) that I have had put together." James did not keep his feelings from Miss Bosanquet. Nine days after her arrival, "at the close of the morning, Mr. James looked out of the window and said 'Ah—it's coming better today—I don't mean the dictation—though as to that I have great pleasure in saying that I'm extremely satisfied, Miss Bosanquet. You seem to have picked things up so quickly and so intelligently.' " Miss Bosanquet replied that the work was so interesting it was natural she should do her best. James replied, "Among the faults of my previous amanuenses—not by any means the *only* fault—was their apparent lack of comprehension of what I was driving at." So, added the new amanuensis, "we parted quite pleased with each other."

From this time on, with certain gaps, James is mirrored almost daily in the lucid prose of his typist. Miss Bosanquet was always discreet, always tactful, always efficient. There were certain gallantries between them. On a day when Miss Bosanquet was indisposed, he would usually turn up at her lodgings with a bouquet of roses; if he kept her overtime and she grew hungry he would strip the silver foil off a bar of chocolate and place it beside her typewriter. At Christmas he had her to dinner to

Lamb House and gave her a glove-box as a gift. After a while she stopped recording details of her routine, but made a point of setting down any incidental remarks made by the novelist, her diary thus offering us many little touches, a kind of "work-table-talk" of the Master that could not otherwise have been preserved. What James did not know was that Miss Bosanquet was writing as well. She tried her hand at verse, an occasional essay, and even a bit of fiction. After James's death she was able to enter on her own career, publishing a book on Paul Valéry as well as an admirable pamphlet describing James's working methods. An early feminist, she would be associated with *Time and Tide* as its literary editor.

Miss Bosanquet's diary records during the summer of 1908 what James meant when he said to a friend, "I am deep in family." The William Jameses came abroad in the spring of that year. William was to give the Hibbert Lectures at Oxford; these became *A Pluralistic Universe.* Henry James was on the fifteenth volume of his Edition and writing the preface for his tales of the supernatural. He worked every morning. But thereafter he was with his brother and Alice. Three of William's children also came to Lamb House at various times. Miss Bosanquet liked William James, "a delightful man—small and thin—he looks about ten years older than Mr. Henry James but it's only one more, I believe." One day she found him using the typewriter and enjoyed having him dictate part of a page to her. Peggy James, now twenty-two, often sought Miss Bosanquet's company and they went on walks together. "Miss James hasn't much sense of humour, which makes her just a bit heavy in hand." She found Mrs. William James "most pleasant"—"a fine strong face framed with white hair. Her daughter is just like her."

On 27 July 1908 Miss Bosanquet recorded: "In the course of the morning Mr. James made me go and peep through the curtain to see 'the unspeakable Chesterton' pass by—a sort of elephant with a crimson face and oily curls." James thought it "very tragic that his mind should be imprisoned in such a body." Chesterton's presence in Rye produced the incident remembered by H. G. Wells, when William James climbed the gardener's ladder to peep over the wall at Chesterton. Henry apparently found it proper to look out of his window at Chesterton as passer-by, but felt that it was wrong to invade privacy by peeping over a wall. They quarreled about this, and when Wells arrived he found "Henry had instructed the gardener to put away that ladder and William was looking thoroughly naughty about it." Wells carried William off in his car, and they passed Chesterton, so the pragmatist met him after all.

Harry James, now twenty-nine, visited briefly at Lamb House that summer. A successful executive, he had taken the Syracuse properties of the Jameses in hand and improved their yield. Harry had the dignity and the distinction of the Jameses and the same "heavyness" that Miss Bosanquet noted in Peggy. During this summer William's youngest son, Alex, aged seventeen, came to Lamb House also and Henry found him shy, silent, but "a dear young presence and worthy of the rest of the brood."

William wrote their younger brother Robertson that he found Henry stolid and grave, the natural result of the years; Henry on his side was impressed by William's vitality. In spite of several heart attacks, William took long walks, insisted on vaulting over gates and stiles and was "in general better, I think, than I have of late years *ever* seen him."

Theatricals: Second Series

In the midst of his work on the New York Edition, Henry James received fresh overtures from the stage he had abandoned twelve years earlier. In 1895 he had written the one-act play for Ellen Terry, *Summersoft,* which she had never produced. Three years later, needing a tale to go with "The Turn of the Screw," he turned the Terry play into a short story called "Covering End." As soon as it was published, George Alexander told him the story would make a good play. James shrugged his shoulders, and declined. Eight years later Johnston Forbes-Robertson also found the tale dramatically appealing, an ideal vehicle for himself and his American wife, Gertrude Elliott, sister of the famous Maxine. James was more receptive to him; he found himself "re-aching and re-brooding and re-itching for the theatre." With his work on the Edition going smoothly, it seemed to him he could try once again—it was after all simply a matter of re-writing "Covering End" into its original form. Moreover, Forbes-Robertson had asked him to expand the one act into three; the thought of enlarging rather than cutting a play appealed to James. To Lucy Clifford he wrote, "I assented, for the lust of a little possible gold." To which he added, as of old, that it was a deep secret: "I breathe the weird tale into your ear alone."

The language of his dramatic years was again on his lips—he would do it for gold; it had to be kept a secret. To Edith Wharton he wrote: "I loathe the Theatre, but the Drama tormentingly speaks to me." It spoke sufficiently for James to write *The High Bid* (as "Covering End" was now renamed) in twenty days; and then to go on to a scenario of one of his old short stories, "The Chaperon," which Pinero had once told him would make a fine comedy, and then to a play based on his tale "Owen Wingrave." After that he began revising *The Other House,* which he also had converted to fiction, and now returned to its original form. Miss Bosanquet found herself typing scripts and James began attending rehearsals. "Whatever happens," he wrote to Lucy Clifford, *The High Bid* was "a very *safe* and neat and pleasing (orthodox-pleasing) little invention—which no monstrous doom can overtake." This was his way of saying that he did not fear a repetition of *Guy Domville.*

The try-out took place in Edinburgh in March 1908. James was so confident that he invited Lucy Clifford to the first night and when Jocelyn Persse, then traveling in Algeria, expressed an interest, he invited him also, and Jocelyn made the long journey back. The production was well received. James cautiously disappeared at the curtain calls. He liked the way in which Gertrude Elliott played Mrs. Gracedew, an American widow who arrives as a tourist in an English country house and pleads with its owner, Captain Yule, for the house's preservation on grounds of tradition, history, art. James's central irony was that the American woman should turn out to be more English than the English. It was the sort of thing that might have been expected from him before *The American Scene,* but hardly after. Indeed, the play would have been fine in the 1890s; in the Edwardian period it was out of date. Audiences had had a great deal of Bernard Shaw; they were "socially-minded." To the embarrassment of Gertrude Elliott they responded to the "radical" speeches of her husband, playing the socialist-tinged M.P., Captain Yule, rather than her own romantic-historic flights. When Captain Yule replied to her emotional appeal with "There are thousands of people in England who can show no houses at *all,*" the audience burst into applause. Gertrude Elliott asked James to do something about this. It was after all *her* "vehicle." The Master could do nothing, short of scrapping the entire play.

Forbes-Robertson sensed that the play was far too delicate for the theater audiences. His actor's instincts told him that a script he had received from Jerome K. Jerome titled *The Passing of the Third Floor Back*—about a stranger in a lodging house, who seemed to be a reincarnation of Christ—might have greater success. James was derisive and angry. He predicted to Lucy Clifford instant failure or at least an "imperfect success." The Jerome play ran for four years; it made Forbes-Robertson's fortune. The best the actor and his wife could do, to keep their commitment to James, was to perform *The High Bid* for five London matinees. These attracted a Jamesian type of audience and got him excellent notices from ardent followers like Max Beerbohm and A. B. Walkley. Max's review described Forbes-Robertson making his exit at one moment as the Christ-figure in *The Passing of the Third Floor Back* and then, it seemed, re-entering the next in his street clothes as the radical Member of Parliament saying, "What are you exactly?" to an old family butler—"I mean, to whom do you beautifully *belong?*" The sound of those words, wrote Max,

> sent innumerable little vibrations through the heart of every good Jacobite in the audience . . . The words could not have been more perfectly

uttered than they were by Mr. Forbes-Robertson. He realized at once to
whom *he* beautifully belongs. It is to Mr. Henry James . . . In his eyes, as
he surveyed the old butler, and in his smile, and in the groping hesitancy
before the adverb was found, and in the sinking of the tone at the verb,
there was a whole world of good feeling, good manners, and humour. It
was love seeing the fun of the thing. It was irony kneeling in awe. It was
an authentic part of the soul of Mr. James.

To which Max added, from the authority of his critical position and out
of his adoration, "little though Mr. James can on the stage give us of his
great art, even that little has a quality which no other man can give us;
an inalienable magic."

James's renewed confidence in the theater, in spite of the limited production of *The High Bid,* sprang in part from the evolution of the English
stage since the 1890s. The battle for Ibsen had been won. Arthur Pinero
and Henry Arthur Jones had demonstrated, in strong social dramas, that
British audiences did not need to be fed trivialities. The plays of Bernard
Shaw, aided by the directorial art of Harley Granville-Barker, taught
audiences to accept a discussion of ideas if properly seasoned with a
certain amount of clowning and a measure of Irish wit. James had seen
the Shaw plays, usually with Jocelyn Persse—*Man and Superman, Major
Barbara, The Doctor's Dilemma;* he had gone to Granville-Barker's
Voysey Inheritance. He met Barrie and Galsworthy and joined them in
their attack on the censorship of British plays, writing a letter almost
Miltonic in its phraseology which was read into the proceedings of a
Royal Commission.

Early in 1909 he found himself engaged in an unexpected debate with
the wittiest and most didactic of the new men. The Master had converted
"Owen Wingrave," his old ghost story about a young pacifist in a military
family, into a one-act play, *The Saloon,* in the hope that the Forbes-
Robertsons would use it as curtain-raiser to *The High Bid.* Another play
was used and James was induced to submit *The Saloon* to the Incorporated Stage Society which gave subscription performances of non-com-
mercial plays. The script was read by the board members and rejected.
The board minutes of 12 January 1909 record that "Mr. Bernard Shaw
undertook to write to Henry James with reference to *The Saloon.*" Five
days later Shaw carried out his undertaking.

He had read *The Saloon,* he wrote, and it had been "sticking in my
gizzard ever since." That play needed another act—by James's father, an
allusion by Shaw to the elder Henry's general optimism. "What do you
want to break men's spirits for?" he queried. James had tried to establish
the irony that the military "conditioning" Owen had received enabled

him to fight and die for his pacifism like a young soldier. To Shaw, arguing as a socialist, this kind of determinism was anathema. He knew "the enormous power of the environment as a dead destiny," but "we can change it: we must change it: there is absolutely no other sense in life than the work of changing it." In effect Shaw argued that the play should be rewritten—Owen Wingrave should kill the ghost, not the ghost Owen. He ended his letter:

> No man who doesn't believe in ghosts ever sees one. Families like these are smashed every day and their members delivered from bondage, not by heroic young men, but by one girl who goes out and earns her living or takes a degree somewhere. Why do you preach cowardice to an army which has victory always and easily within its reach?

People needed, Shaw said, "encouragement," and he repeated that word five times and signed his name.

James pondered the letter for a week. Shaw had a wit and an Irish irrationality akin to James's father's. To answer him was a little like trying to answer Quincy Street. Shaw had asked him why he did such things and James's reply was:

> I do such things because I happen to be a man of imagination and taste, extremely interested in life, and because the imagination . . . absolutely enjoys and insists on and incurably leads a life of its own. . . . Half the beautiful things that the benefactors of the human species have produced would surely be wiped out if you don't allow this adventurous and speculative imagination its rights.

As for people wanting not works of art but "encouragement," James could only reply that works of art were "capable of saying more things to man about himself than any other 'works' whatever are capable of doing."

Shaw answered briefly and militantly. James was trying to evade him.

> The question of whether the man is to get the better of the ghost or the ghost of the man is not an artistic question. . . . And your interest in life is just the very reverse of a good reason for condemning your hero to death. You have given victory to death and obsolescence: I want you to give it to life and regeneration.

James's second rejoinder pointed out to Shaw that he was quarreling with the subject itself and that every artist had to be allowed his subject. There was no competition between man and ghost in the play. Owen Wingrave actually wins the victory, James argued, even if he pays for it with his life. What sort of play would it be if there were no danger and no resistance?

James's first debate with one of the new men foreshadowed the entire question of didactic art in the twentieth century—art in the service of a theory or a state. In reality it was also a debate between a writer concerned with psychological truths and one whose art rested on satire and intellectual humor. Implicit in the exchange was James's taking the world as he found it, and seeking to demonstrate its realities and existential absurdities; he was saying to Shaw there was the question of "human nature." Shaw was brushing this aside and saying "let's change the system."

In this second series of theatricals—a mere skirmish compared with the old struggle—James had in effect two failures. *The High Bid,* written ostensibly for revenue, had its five matinees and was on the shelf; *The Saloon* yielded only a pleasant exchange on "the purposes of art." James was, however, not discouraged. He rewrote *The Other House,* which he had first sketched in 1894 as an "Ibsen-type" play. In June of 1909 Herbert Trench, the Anglo-Irish poet-scholar, who was planning a repertory at the Haymarket, paid James £100 for an option on this play. It was not produced.

This was the time of the rise of "repertory" in England and early that year Charles Frohman, the successful American producer, urged on by James M. Barrie and Harley Granville-Barker, announced a season of repertory in the Duke of York's Theatre, offering substantial advances for new plays. Bernard Shaw wrote *Misalliance;* Galsworthy *Justice;* Granville-Barker *The Madras House.* A young Abbey Theatre actor, Allan Wade, who felt strongly the drama in England was losing a fine talent in not being more hospitable to Henry James, urged Granville-Barker to obtain a play from the novelist for Frohman's season. James offered the unproduced *The Other House,* and one morning read it to Granville-Barker at the Reform Club. The latter felt that a fresh play was needed, "not an adapted novel." James agreed and wrote *The Outcry,* receiving an advance from Frohman.

The new play was long and required cutting. Granville-Barker remembered "he had to be induced to part with first one bit; then after a while another. But it was really necessary." The play was "topical," a comedy about connoisseurship and the moral question involved in selling British works of art to Americans. In its quiet way it satirized Bernard Berenson and the question of art expertise. A young amateur art historian recognizes in a great house a classic work of art. The owner decides to sell it to Breckenridge Bender, an art dealer from America, a man with a "really *big* Yankee cheque." The young art scholar and his fiancée, daughter of the owner of the picture, decide to raise an "outcry." The picture must be kept in England. Then the Berensonian experts are called in.

James had not then met Berenson, but he had heard about the young Harvard precocity from Grace Norton, and from Mrs. Jack Gardner, as early as 1903. Berenson would later say he didn't get along well with James because James didn't like Jews. But the evidence seems to be that James was not interested in art experts, and found "writing upon art," as he told Miss Norton, "the most boring and *insupportable* identity a man can have." At any rate his comedy on the subject seemed thoroughly manageable in the hands of another kind of expert, Granville-Barker, who defended it from attacks on its "inhumanly literary" dialogue— Shaw's phrase. The real problem with the play was finding a cast capable of speaking James's lines. As Granville-Barker put it, the dialogue was "artificial—very; but that is legitimate." He added that he thought "most of it could be made very effective once the right method had been found." When the last volume of James's New York Edition came off the press, late in 1909, Granville-Barker was seeking a cast for *The Outcry.*

The Tone of Time

During the four years James had been at work on the New York Edition he had given continuous proof of his undiminished creativity: he had written plays, and lived his social life—to be sure at a reduced pitch, yet with a liveliness of spirit that showed him to be mentally and spiritually younger than his aging body. He commented on this in one of his New Year letters to W. E. Norris:

> I am engaged in a perpetual adventure, the most thrilling and in every way the greatest of my life, and which consists of having for more than four years entered into a state of health so altogether better than any I had ever known, that my whole consciousness is transformed by the intense alleviation of it and I lose much time in pinching myself to see if this be not, really, "none of I."

His sense of well-being had been evident ever since publication of *The Golden Bowl.* That novel represented some kind of resolution of old unconscious stress; and his subsequent trip to America smoothed the sharper edges of his years-long quarrel with his homeland, as well as the buried sensitivities of his relation with his brother.

The Master, however, had the normal revolt of a powerful individual who feels his powers shrinking. To Mrs. Clifford he spoke with philosophical resignation of having left behind the period of "the Passions."

And he had not accustomed himself to the dropping away of old friends. It was always a wrench. His devoted admirer Henry Harland died in 1905, comparatively young, of tuberculosis. James had considered him a supreme case not of the expatriate—*that* case was himself—but of the *dis*-patriate. Harland had genuinely detached himself from America. Next to go was old Hamilton Aïdé, whom he had met in endless drawing-rooms of late Victorian London. In London for the requiem service, James looked about for certain common friends; then it occurred to him that they weren't there "simply because they were dead." Aïdé's death made him feel, he wrote, as if the room "of the dusky p.m. of our common existence" had become greyer and poorer. One of its pink lampshades was gone. Soon after, in 1908, he lost one of his oldest friends, Charles Eliot Norton, that votary of culture in America, who had published James's first book reviews, taught him to look at early Italian art, introduced him to Ruskin, Darwin, William Morris.

His country life, with all its limitations, offered much solace at this time to the novelist. "I have lived *into* my little old house and garden so thoroughly that they have become a kind of domiciliary skin, that can't be peeled off without pain." There were perpetual teas and motors pulling into the cobbled street with unexpected visitors. He lost his dachshund Max and buried him sorrowfully in the small row of dog-graves at one end of his garden. He decided he would have no more pets. One hot summer an exquisite little temporary pet turned up on his lawn: a chameleon that blushed and flushed black and brown and blanched to pinkish grey ten times a minute. And one night in a rage against a too-audible feline, he killed the creature on the lawn with a blow of his stick—and promptly was sick at the stomach.

Between 1905 and 1910 James found in Rye a new circle of friends whose firesides offered him tea and conversation at the end of his long walks. He had an excellent walking companion in Sydney Waterlow, a contemporary at Cambridge of Strachey, Woolf, Keynes, and others who would be part of "Bloomsbury." Waterlow was in the Foreign Office and married then to Alice Pollock, daughter of the eminent jurist, whom James had known since her childhood. To Waterlow, who had the precision of his diplomatic training and kept a lively diary, we owe a vivid account of James's characteristic talk—about current affairs, his immediate reading, his literary friends, his old memories—during the long walks they took in and around Rye. At a cottage called The Steps, James could stop for tea with an "elfin" lady named Alice Dew-Smith, who believed in psychical phenomena; one of her books was called *Soul Shapes.* James's characterization of Mrs. Dew-Smith's dog as "a positive emetic" was long remembered in Rye. Above all James found a new and lively woman companion in the "Irishly amiable" Fanny Prothero, wife of George Prothero, editor of the *Quarterly Review*. They lived in Dial Cottage. Small, bird-like, direct, Fanny Prothero had easy access to Lamb House; she gave James advice unceremoniously about household matters, and used to go below stairs, put her feet up on a chair and chat with his servants. It was her way of keeping an eye on them. Fanny—later Lady—Prothero understood the novelist very well. "Henry James," she once said, "is very fond of people when they are here, but I don't believe he cares a bit when they aren't." She added: "It's the artist in him." It was also the Henry James who preferred to be alone rather than be bored. Fanny was never boring.

If a new circle of friends replaced the dead—friendships formed all in the new century, among Edwardians—James still kept in touch with certain old American friends. In his later years Howells crossed the Atlantic more frequently than before; and on each occasion, in London and in Paris, James saw him and revived in their talk many memories. James had also kept up a friendship out of his very old 1874-75 New York days with the Manton Marbles—a very Jamesian name—and used to disappear for weekends to their home near Brighton. Edith Wharton and her friends had a theory James "luxuriated" in the Manton Marble bathroom, rumored to be one of the best-appointed in England. Marble, a famous bi-metallist, had been an editor of the *World*. His interests were only peripherally literary; he and James wrote doggerel to one another.

There remained also his old attachment to the crippled Jonathan Sturges, who was increasingly ill. "Sturges, poor unspeakable little demon," spent the summer of 1908 in a hotel at Eastbourne "with a nurse (and more or less without a bottle!)." James went over to see him, and at Christmas made the journey again, when he found Jonathan "at the best, more and more, but the ghost of his former self." It was "pure tragedy—unrelieved."

A less chronicled friendship was with Antonio de Navarro and his actress wife Mary Anderson. She had retired from the stage on her marriage in 1890 and lived at Broadway, where James had often visited in the past. They had friends in common, particularly Sturges. Navarro was the son of an engineer who had created a steamship line to Cuba. On one occasion, when he had written candidly to James about himself and his idleness, the novelist replied with forthright tenderness:

> From the bottom of my heart I pity you for being without some practicable door for getting out of yourself. We all need one, and if I didn't have mine I shouldn't—well, I shouldn't be writing you this now. It takes at the best, I think, a great deal of courage and patience to live—but one must do everything to invent, to force open, that door of exit from mere immersion in one's own states.

Max Beerbohm belonged to an older generation of James worshippers. He was of the 1890s and he had caricatured James first as a bearded Victorian and later as the clean-shaven ecclesiastical-looking Edwardian. His later parodies of James's style had in them a great affection for the Master, a veneration for his use of words. Max was also slightly afraid of the massive overpowering personality—he having remained the eternal mischievous small boy who mocked his elders. James was equally of two minds about Max. He liked his praise and his wit; at the same time he experienced the hostility implicit in caricature and parody even when it also contains affection. Sydney Waterlow recorded that during one of their walks James said that he had just read "The Mote in the Middle Distance," and was "delighted with Max's parody of himself, only it affected him in a curious way: whatever he wrote now, he felt that he was parodying himself." James went on to say there was "something unpleasant about a talent which turned altogether to exposing the weaknesses of others. It was indelicate." And, said the Master, "the older I get, the more I hate indelicacy."

The Younger Generation

After forty-five years of "the literary life" Henry James's reach could now go far beyond the memory of the young. He was that strange "relic" —unique and larger than life because he had become legendary—an Anglo-American Victorian. Now he was meeting the young of the unpredictable future, and "Bloomsbury" in particular. The gifted men and women dedicated to the overthrow of the Master's world—who sought the New at the very moment he cherished the Old—yet looked at James with a mixture of affection and awe. When Lytton Strachey, in full revolt against the Victorians, scanned the windows of Lamb House and there saw, as large as life, Henry James, looking into the street, the New faced the Old for one brief minute. Strachey wrote to his friend Virginia Stephen that the face he saw through the glass seemed like "an admirable tradesman trying to give his best satisfaction, infinitely solemn and polite." The next day James walked into the Mermaid Inn, in Rye, where Strachey was staying, to show the antique fireplace to one of his guests. "I long to know him," Strachey wrote to Virginia. They never met.

E. M. Forster had tea with the Master once in 1908 in Lamb House. James mistook him for G. E. Moore, the Cambridge philosopher whom he had met with Sydney Waterlow. Forster's diary records, "H.J. very kind. Laid his hand on my shoulder and said: 'Your name's Moore.'" Forster also noted, "Head rather fat, but fine, and effectively bald. Admired the Queen's letters." Discussing A. C. Benson's edition of Victoria's letters, James remarked, "She's more of a man than I expected." Forster's diary note concludes, "He was very anxious one should eat and drink. First great man I've ever seen—not alarming but that isn't my road." He would always be affectionately critical of the Master.

When Desmond MacCarthy met James in 1901, the Master left a profound impression on the sensitive and critical young man, who was a novelist *manqué*. MacCarthy remembered the unhurried quality of James's talk. It was to him that James made his much quoted remark, as they stood together in an exceptionally gilded drawing-room: "I can stand a great deal of gold." James also said to him, "my books make no more sound or ripple now than if I dropped them one after the other into mud." MacCarthy assured the Master that in Cambridge he had been religiously read. James was sceptical. "I doubt if he believed," said the younger man, "that anybody thoroughly understood what, as an artist, he was after." MacCarthy once expressed to James a thought about his own problems as a writer. Writing made him feel "absolutely alone." James's answer was, "Yes, it is solitude. If it runs after you and catches you, well and good. But for heaven's sake don't run after *it*. It is absolute solitude."

Through Lady Ritchie, Henry James occasionally had news of her step-nieces, the Stephen girls, Virginia and Vanessa. He had known them as children. James had mourned the passing of their mother, the beautiful Julia Duckworth; and more recently of their father, whom he had esteemed most among the Victorians. In 1906 he was touched by still another death in that much-bereaved family, that of the girls' brother Thoby. To Lady Ritchie he wrote:

> I haven't really borne to *think* of the bereavement of those brave and handsome young Stephen things . . . and have taken refuge in throwing myself hard on the comparative cheer of Vanessa's engagement.

But when he met Vanessa's fiancé, the young Clive Bell, James actively disliked him. To Lucy Clifford he wrote in 1907 of going to see Vanessa on the eve of her marriage

> to the quite dreadful-looking little stoop-shouldered, long-haired, third-rate Clive Bell—described as an "intimate" friend of poor, dear, clear, tall, shy superior Thoby—even as a little sore-eyed poodle might be an intimate friend of a big mild mastiff.

He presumed Vanessa knew what she was doing. She seemed very happy and eager and "almost boisterously in love (in that house of all the Deaths, ah me!)." The Clive Bells spent the month of September in the year of their marriage at Playden, in that part of Rye where James had lived some ten years before. His further view did not reconcile the Master to Bell—as late as 1912 he told Sydney Waterlow he could not cultivate the

Stephens, because of the presence of "that little image."

Leonard Woolf would wryly comment on James's dislike of Clive Bell and Saxon Sydney-Turner, two who "understood and admired him" far more profoundly than Sydney Waterlow and Hugh Walpole. There was no accounting for antipathies. Woolf did not see that young Bell was bumptious and Sydney-Turner a bore, while Waterlow was a good listener and Hugh was "lovable." Nor did Woolf know how much there was of admiration for "the crushed strawberry glow of Vanessa's beauty and credibility and the promise of Virginia's printed wit." That wit was more than a promise. Virginia Stephen went to tea with the oracle during that summer of 1907, and left a caricature of one of James's sentences:

> My dear Virginia, they tell me, they tell me, they tell me, that you—as indeed being your father's daughter, nay your grandfather's grandchild, the descendant, descendant of a century—of a century—of quill pen and ink, ink, in, pots, yes, yes, yes, they tell me ahmmm, that you, that you, that you write in short.

Meanwhile to his friend Sara Norton James recorded his glimpse that year of these fair visitors to Rye:

> ... as I write the handsome (and most lovable) Vanessa Clive-Bell sits on my lawn (unheeded by me) along with her little incongruous and disconcerting but apparently very devoted newly acquired *sposo.* And Virginia, on a near hilltop, writes reviews for *The Times*—and the gentle Adrian interminably long and dumb and "admitted to the bar" marches beside her like a giraffe beside an ostrich—save that Virginia is facially most fair.

Some sense of his lost youth, his distant days with the parents of these girls, the feeling of the "generation gap," seems to have touched him deeply at this moment. With a flourish of the pen, he added: "And the hungry generations tread me down!"

The future Bloomsbury males were of the generation of the turn of the century at Cambridge. Almost a decade later a new generation there was reading James and worshipping him. On New Year's eve in 1907 Geoffrey Keynes, then at Pembroke, Charles Sayle, under-librarian at the University Library, and Theodore Bartholomew, an assistant librarian, sent a card of greeting to the Master. To their surprise he replied: "I am extremely touched and very grateful and all responsively yours, Henry James." Emboldened, they invited James, without success, to visit them at Cambridge. They tried again on the eve of 1909, and this time the answer was, "Yes, I really will come this year."

To his American friend Gaillard Lapsley, who was a don at Trinity, James wrote: "I literally go to Cambridge to stay for forty-eight hours, at 8 Trumpington Street with my bevy of 'admirers' . . . (none of whom I have ever seen). I feel rather like an unnatural intellectual Pasha visiting his Circassian Hareem!" The minutely-planned occasion began on 12 June 1909. His hosts had arranged a strenuous program. James was given dinner on arrival, taken to a concert at which he did not conceal his boredom. Back in Trumpington Street, they talked until late. One subject was Walt Whitman: James maintained that it was impossible for any woman to write a good criticism of Whitman or get near his point of view. The next morning, James was escorted to King's Chapel and the University Library. At Pembroke, Keynes gave them lunch and the guests included Sydney Cockerell, director of the Fitzwilliam Museum, and Rupert Brooke. There was no question that the future war poet "made" the occasion. James visited the Fitzwilliam and met Francis Cornford and John Maynard Keynes. Desmond MacCarthy, arriving at some point, remembered James "surrounded by a respectful circle of silent, smoking, observant undergraduates." MacCarthy claimed that James cross-examined him about Rupert Brooke. The youth wrote poetry, MacCarthy said, which was no good. James was relieved, "for with *that* appearance if he had also talent it would be too unfair." James advised Brooke "not to be afraid of being happy." This was Lambert Strether talking to Little Bilham.

The best-remembered episode of the visit was James reclining in a punt on velvet cushions—the image of the Pasha had come true—"gazing up through prominent half-closed eyes at Brooke's handsome figure clad in white shirt and white flannel trousers." To Sayle in his formal thank-you letter James recalled he had been made to "loll not only figuratively but literally on velvet surfaces exactly adapted to my figure." He sent thanks to all "with a definite stretch towards the Rupert—with whose name I take this liberty because I don't know whether one loves one's love with a (surname terminal) *e* or not."

Hugh

Leonard Woolf had wondered what James saw in Hugh Walpole when he could have admired the intelligence and perceptions of Clive Bell. James hardly admired Walpole as an intelligence. Something else drew him to this young man who descended on London and the literary establishment in 1909. Hugh was ingenuous, good-looking and a bit pathetic in his reaching-out to people. He had had a fragmented childhood. Born in New Zealand, he was uprooted when his clerical father moved to New York, and was sent to school in England at a tender age. Deprived of parental love, his school days were a nightmare of pain and loneliness. Things were better at Cambridge; he went through exultations, agonies, a religious crisis. Now he faced the world, with a forward-thrusting chin and a boundless need for love.

Hugh was unashamedly "on the make" as he settled into his small rooms in Chelsea. He got work as a reviewer; he clipped and sent his reviews to authors he wanted to meet. To Henry James he wrote late in 1908 invoking A. C. Benson's name. James responded with a characteristic mixture of kindness and caution. He warned Walpole on the dangers of "the deep sea of journalism" and concluded, "let me believe that at some propitious [hour] I may have the pleasure of seeing you." Meanwhile he encouraged the young aspirant to

> keep as tight hold as you can of the temper and faith of your almost unbearably enviable youth. I am a hundred years old—it's my one merit —but the breath of your enviability (that name says all for it) quickens again, after all, yours with every good wish Henry James.

They faced each other for the first time in February 1909 when James came up to London to attend a matinee of *The High Bid.* Walpole's diary records: "Dined with Henry James alone at the Reform Club. He was perfectly wonderful. By far the greatest man I have ever met—and yet amazingly humble and affectionate—absolutely delightful. He talked about himself and his books a good deal and said some interesting things. It was a wonderful evening." Never one to be shy, young Hugh also talked a great deal about himself.

The invitation to Lamb House followed. "Can you come some day— some Saturday—in April? I mean after Easter. Bethink yourself." The aspirant came to Rye towards the end of April 1909. "I shall be here, at your carriage door with open arms (and with my handy man for your bag). Bring a love-scene or something, and read it to yours immensely Henry James." The love-scene Hugh brought was his own responsive affection and his bright habit of demanding total commitment from those who showed any inclination to give it. His diary offers its testimony —"a wonderful week-end with Henry James. Much more wonderful than I had expected. I am very lucky in my friends." Walpole would later record in *Fortitude,* one of the most successful of his early novels, the lessons of the Master; still later we can find the emotion of their meeting in a tale called "Mr. Oddy." James would always seem odd to Hugh, who felt overpowered by him. He named his fictitious novelist, in both novel and tale, Henry Galleon; James, in his obesity, with his large Johnsonian body set on his short legs, must have seemed like some great old ship— and like those ships he was also, to Hugh, a great prize or catch. In *Fortitude,* Galleon talks to the young aspirant in simplified Walpolian sentences, but we catch the reverberation of the great style in the invocation to "the sacredness of your calling," the discourse on the treacheries of the market-place. "Fortitude," says Galleon,

> is the artist's only weapon of defence . . . the Artist's life is the harshest that God can give to man.

In his diary Hugh noted that James said to him: "I've had one great passion in my life—the intellectual passion . . . Make it your rule to encourage the impersonal interest as against the personal—but remember also that they are interdependent." "It is a wonderful thing for me and will of course alter my whole life," the ebullient Hugh informed his mother. "He is, I think, really a great man."

To Benson, James wrote that he felt for "the delightful and interesting young Hugh Walpole . . . the tenderest sympathy and an absolute affection." This was in June 1909. A month later he told Benson, "We have become fast friends; I am infinitely touched by his sympathy and charmed by his gifts."

It must be recorded that in matters of craft very few of the Master's lessons rubbed off on young Hugh. James was talking from the high places of art and from his ardent existence. Walpole possessed neither James's sense of craft, nor his dedication; he was always active, always spontaneous. He was a born storyteller. His novels flowed with the same steadiness as they had flowed from his model, Sir Walter Scott. Success came to him easily. Hugh would find love—the love of men, for he feared women, though he was attractive to them—and wealth, and be knighted, and lecture in America and have an honorable career and a loyal public. Of his relation with James he would write, a dozen years after the novelist's death, "I loved him, was frightened of him, was bored by him, was staggered by his wisdom and stupefied by his intricacies . . ." He also said,

> When he told me gently that I was an idiot and that my novels were worthless, I believed that, from his point of view, it must be so, and that if the world had been peopled with Henry Jameses I should certainly never publish a line. The world was not.

The letter James wrote to Hugh after his first visit to Rye suggests a kind of pact of affection between them. To "my dear, dear, Hugh," James writes that his

> confidence and trust and affection are infinitely touching and precious to me, and I all responsibly accept them and give you all my own in return. . . . See therefore how we're at one, and believe in the comfort I take in you. It goes very deep—deep, deep, deep: so infinitely do you touch and move me, dear Hugh.

Hugh had asked James how he might address him and the novelist replied that "for the present" he might call him *très cher maître* or "my very dear Master." Hugh complied. The Master on his side was less solemn. He wrote "belovedest little Hugh," "beloved boy"; on one occasion "dearest darlingest little Hugh" which in the same letter he laughingly abbreviated to "d.d.l.h." A strong possessiveness is to be found in these letters as well. James pictures himself on occasion as an "old ponderous Elephant" reaching out to grasp Hugh with an embracing trunk. On another occasion the Elephant "paws you oh so benevolently"; still another assures him that the Master is "a steady old beast."

James might smother Hugh with affection; yet he gave him no quarter as a writer. In that respect he was the law-giving Master. His love was earthly; his philosophy of craft Olympian. They had been friends but a few months when Walpole sent James his second novel, *Maradick at Forty.* James's answer was to say he had "in a manner" read it. As always he complimented the young man on his love of life. However he found the book "nearly as irreflectively juvenile as the Trojans"—an allusion to Hugh's first novel, *The Wooden Horse.* The "whole thing," he said, was

> a monument to the abuse of voluminous dialogue, the absence of a plan of composition, alternation, distribution, structure . . . so that the *line* (the only thing *I* value in a fiction, etc.) is replaced by a vast formless feather-bediness—billows in which one sinks and is lost. And yet it's so loveable —though not so *written.* It isn't written *at all,* darling Hugh.

Then James was contrite. "Can you forgive all this to your fondest old reaching-out-his-arms-to-you H.J.?" Hugh did not betray the hurt. This he buried very deeply, and it did not surface until long after James's death when he wrote out a primordial fantasy in which a slayer becomes the man he slays—and dedicated the book to the memory of the author of (as he put it) "The Turning of the Screw."

James's letters, even the most critical, breathe a cheerful affection, that of a man who enjoys Hugh's company enormously—whenever he can have it—loves his easy enthusiasms and his prattle and wants to do everything he can for him. He sent presents; he inscribed books; he insisted that Hugh pocket a £5 note during the first Christmas of their acquaintance. On one occasion at Rye, when Hugh kept asking the Master the time (he had a train to catch), James took his watch from his pocket and gave it to him. He always dined him in London. The letters to Walpole are among the finest James ever wrote in their playfulness, their mixture of affection and literary doctrine, their shrewdness, their breadth of feeling. At times these feelings become intense, although there is never quite the same "tactile" quality, the laying on of hands, which is to be found in the letters to Hendrik Andersen. With James and

Hugh the correspondence is of writer to writer. The verbalization of love was important to both.

James had loved Hendrik Andersen when he himself was in his fifties. He had reached his mid-sixties when he met Hugh, in 1909, and for various reasons they saw little of each other until late in 1911. By that time Hugh was in the first great whirl of success; and the best part of their friendship, and James's finest letters, belong to the time when the Master was turning seventy. Still James could write to Hugh in the autumn of their first year of "our admirable, our incomparable relation."

What that relation was must remain—beyond the evidence of the letters and the testimony of Hugh's diaries—a matter for conjecture. "I think I don't regret a single 'excess' of my responsive youth," James wrote on one occasion to Hugh, "I only regret in my chilled age, certain occasions and possibilities I *didn't* embrace." According to Hugh there was one occasion which James did not embrace: in later years Walpole told the young Stephen Spender that he had offered himself to the Master and James had said, "I can't, I can't." (Somerset Maugham, Walpole's old enemy, used to tell a more highly colored version of this story.)

In his most important reminiscence of James, Walpole wrote:

> He was curious about everything, he *knew* everything, but his Puritan *taste* would shiver with apprehension. There was no crudity of which he was unaware but he did not wish that crudity to be named. . . . I was, alas, too crude myself to present anything without naming it, and I learnt to dread that shy look of distress that would veil his eyes as he apprehended my clumsy intrepidities.

A striking incident throws doubt on this. In Edinburgh, where his father was Bishop, Hugh met the Catholic priest John Gray, whom Oscar Wilde had admired, and the wealthy European-Russian André Raffalovich, said to have wooed Gray away from Wilde. In Hugh's life, religion and homosexuality had been carefully separated. He disapproved of Gray and Raffalovich, and wrote—rather angrily—to James of "immorality on stone floors." Hugh said he couldn't say more. James's rejoinder was a mixture of laughter and affection. "*There* was exactly an admirable matter for you to write me *about*," wrote the Master. Thus prodded, Hugh seems to have offered a fuller account. James was still not satisfied.

> When you refer to their "immorality on stone floors," and with prayer-books in their hands, so long as the exigencies of the situation permit of the manual retention of the sacred volumes, I do so want the picture developed and the proceedings authenticated.

Shortly after this exchange, in a note to Hugh the Master novelist writes "Raffalovich of Edinburgh ('immorality on stone floors!') comes on

Tuesday." And it was Raffalovich himself who told of an incident when James once called on the Beardsleys

> and Aubrey's sister (a beautiful and charming girl) pointed out to him on the stairs a Japanese print which shocked him. He called it a "disconcerting incident" and always afterwards fought shy of her, though the print on the stairs was nothing startling.

Clearly James's "puritanism" puzzled those who knew him: behind it there was the laughter of *What Maisie Knew.*

Years later Hugh, remembering himself when James met him "as filled with vitality as a merry-go-round at a fair," said that

> It was this vitality that attracted and bewildered him. How could I have so much eagerness, so much real curiosity about life, so much interest in so many *different* things and yet penetrate life so thinly? Why, if I wanted to know so much, didn't I see that I knew more? When I visited Lamb House I must give, in every detail, the full account of every adventure. There he would sit, listening, his head on one side like a stout and very well-dressed robin. But at the end of it I had omitted, it seemed, every essential.

In the year of his seventieth birthday James wrote a letter to Hugh, who had been telling him of the "high jinks" in which he had "wallowed" in town: "as if," said the Master,

> I ever remarked on anything but the absolute inevitability of it for you at your age and with your natural curiosities, as it were, and passions. It's good healthy exercise, when it comes but in bouts and brief convulsions, and it's always a kind of thing that it's good, and considerably final to *have* done. We must know, as much as possible, in our beautiful art, yours and mine, what we are talking about—and the only way to know is to have lived and loved and cursed and floundered and enjoyed and suffered.

Woman-About-Town

Another aspect of James's "puritanism" came to the fore in the year he met Hugh, when he found himself at the center of a pathetic minor comedy involving his old acquaintance of Winchelsea Ford Madox Hueffer and his friend Violet Hunt. Since the days at the turn of the century when he had waylaid the Master on his daily strolls, Hueffer had seen little of James. He had had a breakdown in 1903 and gone to Germany for a cure. James had written sympathetically to his wife. During his editorship of the *English Review* in 1908 and 1909 Hueffer published four of James's late tales, including "The Jolly Corner"; but the publication was arranged by James's agent and there was no contact to speak of between editor and author.

James had known Violet Hunt since she was a young girl. He had visited her father, Alfred Hunt, an Oxford don who at the urging of Ruskin had become a water-colorist. Violet had memories of a silken-bearded Henry James with "deep, wonderful eyes," who looked as if he might have worn earrings and been an Elizabethan sea captain. She wrote tales and novels, and in her youth possessed a certain Pre-Raphae-lite beauty. James occasionally invited her to Lamb House and listened to her sex-charged gossip. Her diaries show that he shied away from hearing about her love affairs. "He always wants my news," she wrote, "but never more than half of it, always getting bored or delicate." On one occasion she speaks of "drifting as I know how" in her "white Chinese dressing gown," into the Lamb House drawing-room. She had been un-well after dinner, and James was "all solicitude and I do believe pleas-ure"—but unapproachable. James's letters to her are coy and telegraphic. He poses as a "man-about-town" who will be happy to see the "woman-about-town" when he is in London. He called her his "Purple Patch."

The Purple Patch was almost fifty in 1909; Hueffer was not yet forty. They had become lovers; and the discrepancy in their ages made Hunt wish ardently for marriage. Elsie Hueffer, however, was unwilling to give Hueffer a divorce; in due course she sued for "restitution of conjugal rights." The case got into the newspapers. James happened to have writ-ten to Hunt on 31 October 1909, just before the scandal broke, inviting her to visit him at Lamb House. Two days later, with strange paragraphs appearing in the press, he apparently decided that it would be wise to avoid possible publicity. He may have had memories of Emilie Grigsby. He wrote to Violet Hunt:

> I deeply regret and deplore the lamentable position in which I gather you
> have placed yourself in respect to divorce proceedings about to be taken
> by Mrs. Hueffer: it affects me as painfully unedifying, and that compels
> me to regard all agreeable and unembarrassed communication between
> us as impossible. I can neither suffer you to come down to hear me utter
> these homely truths, nor pretend, at such a time, of free and natural
> discourse of other things.

Hunt understandably resented having the door of Lamb House slammed in her face. She told James he was passing judgment on her private life. James replied that her "relationship with Hueffer" was "none of my business at all." He had merely spoken of her "*position,* as a result of those relations." We may judge that by this he meant essen-tially the fact that she had got herself into the newspapers. He confined himself, however, to insisting that hospitality for Violet Hunt would involve him with Hueffer's and his wife's "private affairs, of which I wish to hear nothing whatever." To Hueffer, who wrote in remonstrance, James reiterated that he had not "pretended to judge, qualify or deal with any act or conduct of Violet Hunt's in the connection . . . that whole quantity being none of my business and destined to remain so."

Hueffer later went to Germany, claimed German nationality and pretended to get a divorce there. When Violet began to use the name of Mrs. Hueffer, Elsie Hueffer sued for libel. She was the only legitimate Mrs. Hueffer under English law, having no bill of divorcement. She won; and the effect was to involve Hueffer and his common-law wife in new scandal. James continued to correspond with Violet Hunt; and he saw both her and Hueffer in London on at least one occasion, in April 1912, for a note in his pocket diary records: "Met Violet Hunt and F. M. Hueffer and went home with them for half an hour."

In 1913, Hueffer brought out a book on James, the first "critical" study of the novelist to appear. "Mr. James is the greatest of living writers," Hueffer wrote in his introduction, "and in consequence, for me, the greatest of living men." The volume is discursive, like most of Hueffer's critical writing; but he showed his literary judgment by singling out the works in which James had developed his late techniques, notably *The Spoils of Poynton, Maisie,* and the tales he himself had published in the *English Review.* A few weeks after the book's appearance Archibald Marshall asked the novelist how he felt about it. James replied:

> I am vaguely aware that his book is out, but he has at least had the tact not to send it to me, and as I wouldn't touch it with a ten-foot pole nothing is simpler than for it not to exist for me.

The Velvet Glove

After his two visits, of 1907 and 1908, to the Parisian world of Edith Wharton, James incorporated her high life—of society, of literature—in a tale of such fine-spun allusion that few have recognized his elaborate joke and the deeper criticism it contains. Mrs. Wharton recognized the joke at once, but seemed to close her eyes to the meanings that might be read in it. The origin of the tale was more complicated than she knew. An agency in New York whose letterhead bore the Marxist slogan, "From each according to ability, unto each according to need," wrote to James saying that Mrs. Wharton had suggested he write an article about her. Apparently a socialist publication was interested in the discussion of labor-management relations in her new novel, *The Fruit of the Tree.* "She has indicated," the letter told James, "that if the leading opinion could be from your pen, it would be gratifying to her."

James did not believe Mrs. Wharton would, in this fashion, ask for a "puff" from him. She herself denied any knowledge of the matter. However she did say (James told his agent) "that she would be sorry to stand in the way of my writing the little—or *a* little article—if I am moved to it." He was tempted to use her new novel as a peg for such a tribute. Perhaps he felt that there was practically no other way in which he could reciprocate her extended hospitalities. He put the matter to her with candor. A seed had been dropped in his mind, he said, "by however a crooked *geste,*" and he was now conscious of "a lively and spontaneous disposition to really dedicate a few lucid remarks to the mystery of your genius." Mrs. Wharton asked Scribner's to send him *The Fruit of the Tree.* When he had read it he had no desire to write about it. The novel was simply not good enough. He said as much to Mrs. Wharton; while praising "the element of good writing in it," still, he said, "I don't feel that I can 'enthuse' over you in a hole-and-corner publication."

There was, however, an idea for a story in the incident. What if a great lady—of the world and the pen—did ask a great writer for a puff? How amusing the irony, to have her forget her goddess-state and invite, from a mere mortal, a particular tribute. James seems to have written the tale in an open spirit of mockery; his first title was "The Top of the Tree." In the end he called it "The Velvet Glove."

At a reception in Paris a young English nobleman approaches a novelist-playwright, John Berridge (perhaps an allusion to Walter Berry), author of "a slightly too fat volume" called "The Heart of Gold." The young Englishman is an intermediary—like the inquirer from New York; he asks whether Berridge wouldn't take an interest in a book by a friend of his. He would value his opinion. Berridge however happens to find life more interesting than literature. He is an outsider in society, a mortal on Olympus enchanted with the romances of the Olympians. (The word "Olympian" is sprinkled with great regularity through the pages of the tale.) When he meets the glamorous Princess, he is astonished, after admiring her elegance and beauty, to discover that, disguised as plain Amy Evans (a name as plain as Edith Jones), she is a writer of novels. He has read her recent novel *The Top of the Tree* in its "tawdry red cover" (*The Fruit of the Tree* and other fictions of Mrs. Wharton's were bound in red).

Berridge is delighted when this creature of magic suggests they leave the party together; she will take him for a ride in her "chariot of fire." In the cushioned vehicle Berridge feels himself carried on wings of Romance. It is a soft April night; they are hanging over Paris

> from vague consecrated lamp-studded heights and taking in, spread below and afar, the great scroll of all its irresistible story, pricked out ... in syllables of fire.

But the beauty so touching to Berridge seems not to touch the Princess. She pursues her purpose relentlessly. Her new novel *The Velvet Glove* would benefit greatly from a preface by John Berridge. It "would do so much for the thing in America." She says this "with the clearest coolness of her general privilege." And she also says, "of course I don't want you to perjure yourself; but—" and the Princess brushes him again with her "fresh fragrant smile"—"I do want you so to like me, and to say it all out beautifully and publicly." And Berridge had thought she valued him for himself and the successful play he had written!

In effect James seems to be saying that Princesses should not step off their pedestals for then they cease to be Princesses. Berridge replies to mere "Amy Evans" by kissing her hand; and then unceremoniously he presses his lips against hers. "You are Romance," he tells her with a show of gallantry. "Don't attempt such base things. Leave those to us. Only live. Only be. We'll do the rest."

There was something deeply mocking and hostile in the tale—not least in its incidental parodying of the prose of *The Fruit of the Tree.* Behind its verbal gauze is a suggestion of trust betrayed, of the mighty who cease being mighty when they scribble, of resentment against that *grand monde* James admired and studied but also criticized. In a letter to Grace Norton on the eve of his first visit to the rue de Varenne, he had spoken of getting news of the Nortons from Mrs. Wharton, adding, "so far as the Pampered Princesses of this world can, when very intelligent and very literary and very gracious, *ever* arrive at real news of anything!"

James seems to have been sure that his joke would not offend—he had perhaps noticed a sentence in *The Fruit of the Tree* about characters "blent in that closest of unions, the discovery of a common fund of humour." When the story appeared in the *English Review* of March 1909 Mrs. Wharton apparently told him it was "really good." Two periodicals had declined the tale, he replied—"which was a good deal *comme qui dirait* like declining *you;* since *bien assurément* the whole thing *reeks* with you." Years afterwards in her reminiscences Mrs. Wharton said the tale originated one night in Paris when she had taken James on a long drive "high above the moonlit lamplit city and the gleaming curves of the Seine." She was once asked about the tale, and rejoined with a smile, "Oh but I would never have asked Henry to write a preface for me." And— perhaps as a way of throwing dust in the questioner's eyes—she told of "a very beautiful young English woman of great position and unappeased literary ambitions" who had once tried to beguile James "into contributing an introduction to a novel she was writing—or else into reviewing the book, I forget which."

A Passion on Olympus

Henry James had spoken of Mrs. Wharton as being "almost too insistently Olympian." It is doubtful, however, whether he would have written "The Velvet Glove" had he known how troubled and difficult—and passionate—life had become on Olympus. Her high life of the intellect had been her way of escaping from a frivolous and imprisoning society, and from a stifling marriage with a good-natured easy-going man who felt ineffectual, particularly when faced with his wife's strong will and her ethical, moral and artistic intensities. Both husband and wife were usually depressed when they were together, for the marriage was sexually unsatisfying, and Teddy and "Puss," as he called her, were constantly in flight from one another.

For years Mrs. Wharton closed her eyes to her husband's indifferences. She took him for granted, and he let her go her own way without making demands. Then in 1908—when she was forty-six—she had had an illumination. Reading a book on heredity she was "struck by a curious and rather amusing passage" and held it out to her husband, saying "Read that!" Teddy dutifully looked at the page. "Does that sort of thing amuse you?" he asked. Such moments had probably occurred many times before. Now, however, she "heard the key turn in the prison lock," as she confided to a new diary which she began to keep at this time. "Oh, Gods of derision! And you've given me twenty years of it! *Je n'en peux plus.*" She had finally faced the truth of her marriage.

What revealed it was her having—after these many years—fallen in love. She was experiencing a kind of "quiet ecstasy" in the presence of Henry James's journalist friend Morton Fullerton. A lover of the life of letters, and of women—though he was capable of intimate male friendships as well—Fullerton had had passionate affairs ever since settling in Paris. Most of his friends did not know of his brief, unfortunate marriage to a singer at the Opéra Comique; nor of the French mistress—Henrietta Mirecourt—with whom he was deeply involved. By the time Edith Wharton met him, Fullerton was more French than the French. He wrote in French and French poetry was constantly on his lips; he was in every way an *homme de coeur,* a discriminatingly promiscuous Victorian-American. Fullerton had some of the stance of Edith Wharton's intellectual friend of many years, Walter Berry, but he was softer, more gentle; there was a touch of the feminine in his make-up to which Mrs. Wharton's long-deprived femininity deeply responded. She would write in her memoirs that Berry had found her "when my mind and soul were hungry and thirsty, and he fed them till our last hour together." Of Fullerton, who fed much more, though for a briefer time, there is no mention. The

uniquely passionate journal she devoted to this love affair of her middle
life was once thought to have been addressed to Walter Berry; but it has
now been shown that she was in reality addressing not the friend of her
mind but the lover of her body. Edith Wharton had suddenly become
aware that Eros lived on Olympus.

Henry James understandably did not have access to the journal, otherwise he would have known that the proud Princess was no longer on
her pedestal. "I am a little humbled, a little ashamed," she wrote, "to find
how poor a thing I am, how the personality I had moulded into such
strong firm lines has crumbled to a pinch of ashes in this flame!" She told
herself that she had endured her marriage "all these years, and hardly
felt it, because I had created a world of my own, in which I had lived
without heeding what went on outside." Henry James had spoken of this
to certain of his friends and had characterized it as the blindness of those
who have been too "facilitated." Now, bit by bit, James began to discover
new realities within the house of mirth.

Edith Wharton began to confide in the Master only after his second
visit to her in Paris, in 1908. He offered her the advice he had always
given his friends—that one must "live through" an experience and try
not to avoid it; that in life it was better to give way to tears than to hold
them back; and also that one had to continue with the everyday things
of existence—in a word, keep a hold on reality. He warned her against
acting impulsively. She must not, he said, let herself conclude anything
in a hurry.

Having had her conquest of Paris, Mrs. Wharton came to England
late in 1908—to English hospitality and rounds of country visits. She also
came and went in Lamb House. Writing to Walter Berry in Cairo, James
said she had been having

> after a wild, extravagant, desperate, detached fashion, the Time of her
> Life. London, and even the Suburbs have opened their arms to her; she
> has seen everyone and done everything . . .

He went on to say that with Edith's "frame of steel it has been remarkably good for her. But what a frame of steel and what a way of arranging
one's life!"

She seems by then to have told James frankly of her unhappiness in
her marriage; but she had as yet by no means fully confided in him. "I
suffer almost to anguish for the darkness in which I sit," he wrote to her
in April 1909, the month in which "The Velvet Glove" was published.
"You must have been living very voluminously in one way or another—
and however right it may serve me not to possess the detail of that, I have
to invoke a terrible patience—which precludes no gnashing of teeth." To
this Mrs. Wharton seems to have responded with greater candor, for in

his next letter James told her he now saw "with all affectionate participation" that her anxiety had been "extreme." He urged her to "live in the day—don't borrow trouble, and remember that nothing happens as we forecast it—but always with interesting and, as it were, refreshing differences."

From this point on, Fullerton's name begins to figure in the Master's letters to Mrs. Wharton. He now appears in company with her—they turn up at Lamb House together. James goes on excursions with them. Under 4 June 1909 James's date-book discreetly records: "Dine with Morton Fullerton and E.W. Charing Cross Hotel." It was the lovers' last night together before Fullerton went off on a brief journey to America. The next morning, James saw Morton off at Waterloo. He consoled Mrs. Wharton during her lover's absence. "Went by motor with E.W. to Guildford and thence by beautiful circuit to Windsor and Queen's Acre," where they spend two days with Howard Sturgis.

From 12 to 14 June James was at Cambridge, where his young admirers can scarcely have known he was at the center of a series of *liaisons dangereuses.* On the 16th: "Dine with Mrs. Wharton at Lady St. Helier's." He goes again to Queen's Acre on 26 June with Mrs. Wharton and motors the next day with her to see Mrs. Humphry Ward at Stocks; on 28 June he motors with her and Howard Sturgis to Hurstbourne. During the first week of July he is at the Reform Club and then retreats to Lamb House where on the 12th, "E.W. and Morton Fullerton arrived to dinner and for night." The next day Mrs. Wharton motors James to Chichester and en route they stop at Eastbourne for lunch with Jonathan Sturges. On 15 July, "Motored with Edith Wharton and Morton Fullerton to Folkestone and thence Canterbury where we lunched. They return to Folkestone for France—I returning to Lamb House by train."

What these bare entries do not reveal is a drama within the drama. While Edith Wharton was living out her crisis of middle age with Fullerton, the Gallo-American was working out a crisis of his own—with the intimate participation and help of his friends. Fullerton had finally broken a long reticence and told James late in 1907 of the complicated love affair he had been having with Henrietta Mirecourt in Paris. That he had rarely been available to come to Lamb House when the Master beckoned had been a source of chagrin to James. He had guessed at "complications" in Morton's life which he was "utterly powerless" to get at. The "clearing of the air," said James, "lifts, it seems to me, such a load, removes such a falsity (of defeated relation) between us."

But the plot was thicker than a mere love affair. Fullerton had been driven to speak to James because his mistress was blackmailing him. She had taken possession of some of his papers; Morton, as a "voice" of the august *Times,* felt himself vulnerable. The woman apparently could be bought off. But Morton had no money. He did not appeal to James for financial help—he seems simply to have conveyed to the Master his anguish and his dilemma.

James regarded the blackmailer as "a mad, vindictive, and obscure old woman" who was angry because Morton hadn't married her—or, we might observe, who was jealous of Mrs. Wharton. For the latter, it may have been a question not only of rescuing her lover from his mistress, but of rescuing her own love letters among his papers. Mrs. Wharton devised an intricate gambit. She had been asked by Macmillan to write a book on Paris; she now suggested to the publisher that he should give Fullerton a contract for this book, which she herself was too busy to do. Meanwhile James was to induce the publisher to give Morton a larger advance than was usual for such a book; she would give James the additional sum, which he would in turn pass on to Macmillan. Fullerton, of course, was to know nothing of this. Macmillan simplified matters by agreeing to pay Fullerton the additional £100 (a considerable sum at the time) provided James would act as guarantor. In telling Edith of this, James expressed the hope the blackmailer would not demand too much. By late summer of 1909 the two novelists could congratulate one another on their rescue operation, and Mrs. Wharton told James that Fullerton was a changed man. The journalist never delivered the book; but Macmillan apparently decided to forget about the matter.

In all this there was a side-plot as well. While Edith Wharton intrigued with James, and James intrigued with Macmillan, she was urging and helping Morton Fullerton to perform an act of friendship for Henry James. When the last volume of the New York Edition had been published, Fullerton wrote a long and full article on the Edition and on the significance of James's career in the history of the novel. He had no difficulty placing it in the *Quarterly Review,* where it appeared in April 1910. Mrs. Wharton tried to induce *Scribner's Magazine* to publish the piece in America; "I have had a hand—or at least a small finger—in the Article, and I think it's good . . . ," she wrote to the magazine. "I long so to have someone speak intelligently and resolutely for James." But *Scribner's* was not interested, and the essay was eventually reprinted in the *Living Age.*

James had been shown the article in manuscript; he said he was "embarrassed . . . fairly to anguish." It reads indeed as if the Master had inspired it: but he had talked often enough with Fullerton and Mrs. Wharton for them to have imbibed a great deal of his doctrine. James may have felt uneasy over the fulsome Fullertonian journalese. However, its genuine insights into his discoveries and his achievement make of the essay an important contemporary document, one of the few to speak of the high originality of James's work. Thus in an ironic way Edith Wharton reversed the situation of "The Velvet Glove" and secretly repaid James with kindness. If the Master hesitated to "puff" his acolytes, the acolytes could, with energy and sincerity, puff the Master.

2

THE

FINER GRAIN

The Bench of Desolation

The first royalty statement for the New York Edition had reached Henry James in October of 1908 when the final volumes were still in preparation. The figures knocked him "rather flat"—"a greater disappointment than I have been prepared for." James had not reckoned on the heavy permissions fees due to the other American publishers— Houghton Mifflin, Harper's, and Macmillan—who held rights in his work. His agent explained this to him. But the Master had had his shock. The gathering in of his work of a lifetime, which he had counted on to yield revenue for his declining years, showed signs of being a complete failure. His new fling at the theater moreover had as yet brought him no great returns. "The non-response of *both* sources," he told Pinker, "has left me rather high and dry."

It left him, emotionally, higher and drier than he knew. The effect, though delayed for a time, was as if he had faced a hostile audience again, and been told that his life work was vain and perishable. Re-reading the royalty figures he discerned that his first payment would total $211. "Mr. James depressed," Miss Bosanquet noted. "Nearly finished *Golden Bowl* preface—bored by it—says he's 'lost his spring' for it." Some of that depression crept into a letter to Howells on the last day of 1908. "It will have landed me in Bankruptcy," he said of the Edition. "It has prevented me doing any other work."

Early in 1909, little more than three months after receiving the royalty figures, James noted that he felt sharply unwell for the first time in six years. Miss Bosanquet's diary of 17 January says simply, "Mr. James unwell (heart trouble)." At least that was what he thought he had. There were some palpitations, a little shortness of breath, but no pain to speak of. The doctor in Rye, Ernest Skinner, prescribed digitalis. He found nothing ominous and urged James to take more exercise. The Master had become too fat. But Henry, writing to his brother and describing his symptoms, said he was "a little solitarily worried and depressed."

In due course, with increasing anxiety, Henry James wrote to Sir William Osler, who had examined his brother at the time of William's heart attack ten years before. The great doctor recommended that Henry see the renowned heart specialist of the time, Sir James Mackenzie. The novelist paid his visit 25 February 1909. The physician's notes tell us that he found the patient "stout and healthy-looking." His heart was slightly enlarged but "there is no murmur present." He prescribed exercise and moderate eating, and addressed himself to James's anxieties. Sir James Mackenzie later used the novelist as a case history in his book *Angina Pectoris* because he wished to demonstrate how he reassured a patient who imagined he had a heart condition. "You think," he told James,

> you have got angina pectoris, and you are very frightened lest you should die suddenly. Now, let me explain to you the real matters. You are sixty-six years of age. You have got the changes in your body which are coincident with your time of life. . . . It simply follows that if you be more judicious in your living, and give your heart less work to do, there is no reason why you should not reach the ordinary span of human life.

The doctor reported his patient was "greatly cheered by this," and that he remained in good health. But apparently James did not believe Sir James Mackenzie. He continued to speak of having had a "cardiac crisis." He had apparently decided he was as ill as his brother.

Still, he followed the doctor's orders and during the rest of 1909 found himself much improved. He worked, he entered into the casting of *The Outcry,* and he was preoccupied with the affairs of his Olympian friends. In October came the second royalty statement for the Edition. This time it yielded $596.71. He told his agent that in no year had he so "consummately managed to make so little money as this last." His earnings reported to the income tax that year were £1,020, as compared with £1,096 in 1908 and £1,309 in 1910—an income adequate for his bachelor needs, but offering him slim margin if his powers should fail.

One day, shortly after this, in a fit of sadness, perhaps prompted by fantasies of death, he gathered his private papers—forty years of letters from his contemporaries, manuscripts, scenarios, old notebooks—and piled them on a rubbish fire in his garden. "I kept almost all my letters for years," he wrote to Mrs. J. T. Fields, on 2 January 1910, "till my receptacles would no longer hold them; then I made a gigantic bonfire and have been easier in mind since."

His last effort to work off his depression occurred on 4 January when he began to make notes in pencil, in a large scrawl, for a new fiction which Harper's had asked him to write. It would be his last recorded invocation of

> all the powers and forces and divinities to whom I've ever been loyal and who haven't failed me as yet—after all: never, never yet! . . . *Causons, causons, mon bon*—oh celestial, soothing, sanctifying process, with all the high sane forces of the sacred time, fighting through it, on my side.

It seemed to him he was emerging from his recent "bad days" and "the prospect clears and flushes, and my poor blest old Genius pats me so admirably and lovingly on the back that I turn, I screw round, and bend my lips to passionately, in my gratitude, kiss its hand."

The "sane forces" refused to stay with him. Shortly after writing this supreme appeal to the Muse he collapsed. Some vague discomfort in the stomach: inability to take food, a certain amount of nausea. It was indeed difficult to swallow the fact that his work of a lifetime had not met with a greater reception and brought him the recognition he craved and the money that would have given him a greater sense of security. After some weeks he admitted to being attacked by "the black devils of nervousness, direst damndest demons."

His illness had been signaled just before the new year by two bad attacks of gout, first in one foot and then in the other. Now he lingered in bed mornings, dozing in a kind of withdrawal from his daily existence. His state was "obscure." He would announce improvement for forty-eight hours and then relapse. Miss Bosanquet was laid off for the time. Ernest Skinner still found nothing seriously wrong, but after some three weeks of recurrent illness he put Henry to bed and induced him to have a nurse.

"A digestive crisis making food loathsome and nutrition impossible —and sick inanition and weakness and depression," the Master wrote to Bailey Saunders. Dr. Skinner had him fed every two hours. Mrs. Wharton discreetly asked if he was in need of funds. He replied he was on a decent financial basis "with a margin of no mean breadth"; she made him promise that if he should be in need he would let her know, and once he was on a regular regimen she sent him great clusters of grapes. Henry wrote a full account of his illness to William and blamed his condition on his having for so long "Fletcherized"—the fad involving lengthy mastication.

Although Henry had cabled cheerfully to Irving Street, William James dispatched his son Harry to visit the novelist. Harry arrived at Lamb House on 24 February. Firm and managerial, he sized up the situation at once. Two things were required, he wrote to his father and mother: get James out of Rye to London; and have him thoroughly examined by an eminent medical authority. He turned once again to Sir William Osler.

Harry described his uncle as having been, on his arrival, on an "upward wave" but secretly Fletcherizing again. Then there was a new collapse. Harry found him in the little oak bedroom in a state of complete despair:

> There was nothing for me to do but to sit by his side and hold his hand while he panted and sobbed for two hours until the Doctor arrived ... He talked about Aunt Alice and his own end and I knew him to be facing not only the frustration of all his hopes and ambitions, but the vision looming close and threatening to his weary eyes, of a lingering illness such as hers. In sight of all that, he wanted to die ... He didn't have a good night and the next day the same thing began again with a fear of being alone.

When Harry announced he was writing to Osler, the Master "stopped panting and trembling, and from that moment began to revive." In the evening the "portentous invalid" was vivacious and jocular. Harry realized the great authority and solemnity of the Johnsonian dictator who co-existed with the death-haunted mortal lying there on his bed, as he

> watched him begin to stir a cup of beef tea with an expression like a judge about to announce an opinion, and a gesture by which he ladled teaspoonfuls eighteen inches into the air and poured them splashing back again.

Uncle and nephew came up to town together to Garland's Hotel in Suffolk Street, and on 14 March Sir William Osler gave Henry James the most complete physical examination he had ever had. He found nothing seriously wrong. The novelist's eating habits had done no damage to his stomach; heart, lungs, arteries were fine, and he said that Henry had "the pulse of a boy." William had written to Henry that perhaps he ought to recognize that what he had was something in the nature of a "nervous breakdown." The novelist, telling William of Osler's examination, denied this, insisting it was a stomach condition. Osler prescribed massage and walks, and a general routine intended to make James take an interest in everyday occupations.

Even before Harry James returned to America, satisfied with Osler's examination, William and Alice James had sailed to be with Henry. They had decided from Henry's letters that he needed family, distraction, company. William planned himself to take a further cure at Bad Nauheim, for his heart was troubling him again. They arrived in April and Alice took over in Lamb House. The date-book in which she wrote a daily sentence or two is a sad little document, recording William's increasing debility and Henry's constant changes of mood, from deep depression, to partial calm, and then a relapse into depression. An entry she set down in June is eloquent: "William cannot walk and Henry cannot smile."

In May 1910 Edward VII died; during the period of mourning, the London theaters were closed and this proved a death blow to Frohman's repertory and the impending production of James's play. Frohman paid James $1,000 forfeit as agreed. By this time Henry was indifferent to his work in the theater. William with his psychiatric eye judged his brother's case "more and more plainly one of melancholia, 'simple', in that there are no fixed or false ideas," apart from Henry's belief the cause had been diet. In due course, William and Alice convinced Henry that the best thing for him to do would be to return to America with them. William would go to Nauheim first. Alice would remain in Lamb House with Henry. They would then join William and travel in Switzerland. There seems to have been no realization on Alice's part that her husband was too ill for such a journey.

They carried out their plan. In Lamb House Alice tried to distract Henry. One day, when he could not read, and sat in glum despair, she tried to teach him to knit. He was beyond occupational therapy. Yet he was able to gather his most recent tales into a volume to be called *The Finer Grain*. He led off with "The Velvet Glove" and concluded with a long tale of passivity and despair called "The Bench of Desolation." Scribner's agreed to do the book, and Methuen in England; each paid him $1,000 advance. By now he was taking more food, and walking almost daily. In May Alice took Henry to visit Mrs. Charles Hunter, the hostess of Hill Hall and patroness of the arts. Sargent was there, and Percy Grainger, the pianist; there were assorted peers, and James sat for his portrait to Mrs. Swynnerton. But "I am unfit for society," he wrote to Goody Allen.

Early in June they made the trip to Bad Nauheim, where William was having the last of his "curative" baths. He had not benefited by the cure; he was much weaker. They stayed a while in Nauheim; they went on excursions. To his friends the Protheros in Rye Henry wrote, "I have really been down into hell . . . I keep hold of my blest companions, I intensely clutch them, as a scared child does his nurse and mother."

They went to Zürich, William dragging himself along, then to Lucerne, and the Geneva of their youth. Here the news reached them that Robertson James had died in America in his sleep of a heart attack. Alice told Henry and they agreed to withhold the news from William for the time being. "Dark troubled sad days," wrote Henry in his little date-book, recording an attack of gout. Early in July they reached London. Henry went to stay at the Reform Club; William and Alice stayed in a hotel. Henry began to note "William great source of anxiety." The elder brother had sharp attacks of chest pain and several times took to his bed.

On the morning of 21 July 1910 Henry James awoke in his room at the
Reform Club from a good night's sleep. He felt well again. In his date-
book he scribbled, "woke up in great relief." Then two months later, on
12 September, he wrote, "woke up with a return of the old trouble of the
black times, which had dropped comparatively, yet as markedly on red-
letter day July 21st with that blessed waking in my London room." The
date-books for that year contain certain mysterious markings from October onward, with James using red and black crosses in great profusion.
Thus on 24 October there are no less than fifteen red crosses instead of
his usual record of engagements, and on 25 October twenty-seven. On 31
October there are four black crosses and on 11 November they are alternately red and black. After 12 November, the markings are exclusively
red save on 21 November when there are four black ones. And so on, with
variations, until the end of the year, when the ritual is abandoned.

It may be that the red crosses marked the days on which James felt
comparatively well and the black his more depressed days, with their
number a key to the extent of his well-being or discomfort. Or the crosses
may be a record of pill-taking. The day of the splendid awakening in the
Reform Club may also have been the morning of that "most appalling yet
most admirable nightmare" of the Galerie d'Apollon in the Louvre which
he commemorated in *A Small Boy and Others.* It can only be conjecture,
but the dream was of the sort—in its components of fear, anxiety, and
frustration, and then its triumph—that might indeed have resolved his
long weeks of depression. Certainly from the time of that awakening,
recorded in so enigmatic a form, we may date his gradual recovery from
his severe illness of 1910. The dream of self-assertion, of putting to flight
a frightening other-self, may indeed have helped restore to James that
confidence and faith in himself which had crumbled when he received
the news of the Edition.

After their stay in London, Henry, William, and Alice went briefly to
Rye to enable William to have several days of complete rest before sailing. Henry noted "Poor—very bad, nights and days for William. Difficult
days—dreadful gloomy gales—but I feel my own gain in spite of everything. Heaven preserve me." Mrs. Wharton, accompanied by Walter
Berry, arrived with her motor; they took Henry to Windsor, to visit Howard Sturgis at Qu'Acre. "The dark cloud of William's suffering state
hangs over me to the exclusion of all other consciousness," Henry wrote
on 11 August.

The Jameses sailed on 12 August on the *Empress of Britain* for Quebec, Henry accompanied by Burgess. In his date-book he wrote, "extraordinarily peaceful and beautiful voyage with no flaw or cloud on it but
William's aggravated weakness and suffering." The voyage lasted six

days. At Quebec Harry was on hand to help his parents and uncle make the day-long journey to Chocorua. Billy James, who met the voyagers at North Conway in a car, was appalled at his father's weakened condition. The end was not in doubt. William James was suffering too much to want to live. On 26 August his younger brother wrote to Grace Norton, "my own fears are of the blackest, I confess to you, and at the prospect of losing my wonderful beloved brother out of the world in which, from as far back as in dimmest childhood, I have so yearningly always counted on him, I feel nothing but the abject weakness of grief and even terror." Grief made James reopen this letter after he sealed it to add: "William passed unconsciously away an hour ago—without apparent pain or struggle. Think of us, dear Grace—think of us!"

Notes of a Brother

William James died on a Friday and on Monday Henry rose at four-thirty and journeyed from Chocorua to Cambridge where in Appleton Chapel the Harvard University service was held. The philosopher was cremated and his ashes were placed in a grave beside his parents in the Cambridge Cemetery. "Unutterable, unforgettable hour—with those that have followed . . . all unspeakable," the son and brother wrote in his date-book when they were back in Chocorua.

In the setting of mountain and valley and lake, Henry and Alice, his niece Peggy and his nephews spent the following days. Henry's mourning was profound. He had loved his brother with a strong devotion and admiration in which he diminished himself in his belief in William's superiorities; "I was always his absolute younger and smaller," as he wrote, "hanging under the blest sense of his protection and authority." Henry James was now sole survivor of that branch of the James family which had given America two remarkable men; he was the last heir, the final voice; his would be the last word.

The letters Henry James wrote during these weeks were filled with an intense grief, a powerful emotion of helplessness but also of strength. "My beloved brother's death has cut into me, deep down, even as an absolute mutilation," the Master wrote to Edith Wharton. William's "extinction changes the face of life for me," he wrote to their oldest friend, T. S. Perry. It changed his life in quite another sense from that which Henry believed. He had always found himself strong in William's absence. Now he had full familial authority; his nephews deferred to him; his brother's wife now became a kind of wife to him, caring for him as she had cared for the ailing husband and brother. Henry had ascended to what had seemed, for sixty years, an inaccessible throne.

The novelist (and Burgess with him) stayed on and in due course moved with the others back into Irving Street, where Henry began to work again. He would spend the winter in America, he announced, to give support to his brother's family. There was another purpose in his remaining, for Mrs. William James had promised her husband that she would hold séances and try to communicate with his spirit. William's lifelong interest in extra-sensory and extra-human experience had prompted him to tell her that he would seek to continue research from beyond the grave. The matter was not kept secret. Somerset Maugham, who dined in Irving Street during that winter, was told that Henry and his sister-in-law were available for any spiritualist messages that might come. None came. When later Henry received a document describing a séance at which William's voice was heard, he denounced it as "the most abject and impudent, the hollowest, vulgarest, and basest rubbish."

In Irving Street James converted *The Outcry* into a novel and read the last proofs of *The Finer Grain.* He walked a great deal. He was bored. After a number of weeks it was a relief to hear "the silver steam-whistle of the Devastating Angel." Mrs. Wharton had crossed the Atlantic and was staying at the new and splendid Hotel Belmont in Times Square. Emerging from his period of retirement, the novelist took train for the city of his birth.

On 17 October 1910 John Quinn, the wealthy Irish-American lawyer, a lover of literary celebrity, was dining at the Hotel Belmont when he recognized Henry James, massive, slow-moving, awe-inspiring, at dinner with two gentlemen and a lady. Quinn would never know that he was witness to an unusual gathering. It was not so much James dining with these three, as Edith Wharton dining with three men of great importance in *her* life. With the Angel of Devastation at the Belmont were Walter Berry, on one of his holidays from his post in Egypt, and Morton Fullerton —and the Master, who was friend and party to those other friendships. Henry James had joined the others in hotel quarters "that were as those of the Gonzagas, as who should say, at Mantua." He was delighted that he had answered the summons of the Angel—"the being devastated," he wrote to Howard Sturgis, "has done me perceptible good."

He enjoyed Manhattan, although he would tire of it and say it was "the eternal Fifth Avenue." Still, it was infinitely more interesting than Boston, "so far as either of them is interesting." During this year in America, in which he avoided all publicity and refused to lecture, James kept Irving Street in Cambridge as his base and periodically came to New York, usually staying with Mrs. Cadwalader Jones off lower Fifth Avenue. He was given a guest membership at the Century Club and there among painters, writers, and amateurs of the arts he often lunched; he visited art galleries; he attended the business meetings of the American Academy. His nephew took him to visit the Rockefeller Institute, where he met the director, Dr. Simon Flexner, and certain of the research scientists. Harry was then business manager of the Institute. Dr. Peyton Rous, later a Nobel Prize laureate, remembered James's serious face and his "banker's eyeglasses." Dr. Flexner introduced Dr. Rous as in charge of cancer research. Henry laid a heavy hand on his shoulder and said: "How magnificent! To be young and to have divine power!"

In the spring James accepted an honorary degree from Harvard "with deference to William's memory." He visited his Emmet cousins in Connecticut. He revisited Newport. He was still in the hands of doctors. In Boston he consulted Dr. James Jackson Putnam, a Freudian, who had known William James; their discussion seems to have been about Henry's depression and ways of eating sensibly and walking a great deal. "You tided me over three or four bad places during those worst months," James wrote to Dr. Putnam. In New York he consulted the fashionable Dr. Joseph Collins, who later published an account of James's calls on him. Dr. Collins's conclusion was that Henry James had

> an enormous amalgam of the feminine in his make-up; he displayed many of the characteristics of adult infantilism; he had a singular capacity for detachment from reality and with it a dependence upon realities that was even pathetic. He had a dread of ugliness in all forms . . . His amatory coefficient was comparatively low; his gonadal sweep was too narrow.

James described Dr. Collins's therapy as "baths, massage, and electrocutions." He found Dr. Putnam more helpful.

He spent pleasant hours with Howells; he had long talks with Grace Norton. The early summer brought intense heat and Henry fled to Nahant, to the house of an old friend, George Abbot James. Mrs. Wharton was back at The Mount trying to decide whether to sell it or not and whether to part from Teddy. James spent a very hot weekend there. Electric fans, iced drinks, cold baths, didn't seem to help, but motoring did, and they drove across miles of landscape in search of coolness. Mrs. Wharton felt a great desire to pack James off to Europe on the next ship, he seemed so miserable. She got him a booking on a liner sailing from Boston but he had planned his sailing and wasn't going to change it. "Good God, what a woman—what a woman!" he exclaimed. "She does not even scruple to project me in a naked flight across the Atlantic."

James made his farewells in Irving Street, and sailed for England on 30 July 1911. Shortly before sailing he learned that Jonathan Sturges, "the little demon," had died in England. His older friend John La Farge had died while he was in America.

Aboard the *Mauretania,* the smooth ocean liner of the new century, James was lifted across the sea "as if I had been carried in a gigantic

grandmother's bosom and the gentle giantess had made but one mighty
stride of it from land to land."

Re-established in Lamb House, the Master promptly recognized the
realities of his situation. Rye had been splendid for the time of his big
novels and the retreat from London. But its loneliness had a great part
in his depression; and he found himself slipping again into despair. His
remedy was to leave at once, for his perch at the Reform Club. "Dear old
London and its ways and works, its walks and conversations, define themselves as a Prodigious Cure," he wrote. His problem was what to do with
his servants—and how to arrange his work. Miss Bosanquet was willing
to resume work on the old basis, but the Reform Club would not allow
him to have a female typist in his rooms. However, his amanuensis had
two rooms available at one end of her flat in No. 10 Lawrence Street in
Chelsea. There was a separate entrance. James found he could take a taxi
in the morning, and in ten minutes be at work. He came to call the rooms
his "little Chelsea temple, with its Egeria." Here he began dictating his
notes of a son and brother. He soon found himself writing instead the
story of his earliest years—*A Small Boy and Others,* the book that would
precede his tribute to William.

In a certain sense the "interrogation" of his past in that dim Chelsea
room, to the accompaniment of the familiar typewriter, ministered to
further physical recovery. He experienced release from discouragement
and depression as when, a decade earlier, he had written a series of
novels and tales about children. Now he drew directly on the experiences
of the little boy who had played in lower Fifth Avenue, traveled in the
river steamer to visit his grandmother in Albany and eaten peaches from
remembered trees in her large yard. There came back to him the London
of Dickens and Du Maurier, the Paris of the Second Empire and the first
visit to the Galerie d'Apollon. He saw himself and his brother as pious
little American "pilgrims" discovering the paintings of Delacroix, or
attending old melodramas in the Bowery. His memories found shape and
rhythm in the resonances of his style. One hears the personal voice in
every line of *A Small Boy and Others;* by degrees what is built up for us
is the development of an artistic sensibility and the growth of an imagination.

James wrote now in the voice of his father and his brother. When he
quoted from their letters he freely revised their texts, as if they needed
the same retouching given his own work in the New York Edition. When
his nephew Harry protested, after *Notes of a Son and Brother* was published, at this violation of William's words, Henry explained that he was
showing a marked respect. His goal was to make the documents (and his
own text) "engagingly readable"; but, he admitted, "I did instinctively

regard it at last as all my truth, to do what I would with." He subtly altered content as well. Part of the family history had to be written as art: this was why James blended two trips to Europe into one, and made his father write a letter to Emerson in stronger language than was in the original. The novelist's visual memory for detail was extraordinary: he calls up the size, shape, and appearance of objects; he remembers the essential physiognomies; he is aware of old smells and sounds, and when it comes to food he has all the taste of a hungry little boy. His "dive into the past" was hardly "free" association—but it was a return to a very old reservoir of experience, the buried emotions of his childhood.

A Small Boy took little Henry to his fifteenth year, when he had typhus at Boulogne-sur-Mer. James then embarked on a second volume, calling it at first "Early Letters of William James with Notes by Henry James." When Harry sent him from America letters of the elder Henry James, the novelist added a long section on his father, and in this fashion there evolved *Notes of a Son and Brother.* To his nephew, the busy uncle kept explaining that he was writing much more than he would use; that ultimately the "Family" book would be carved out of this material. In reality Henry James, in accordance with the imperious impulses of his ego, was taking total possession of the family scene. Harry James himself would ultimately edit his father's letters. But the Master's enterprise yielded two works of rare autobiography in his most original vein. James gave the volumes to the Macmillans in London, and in America to Scribner's. He was paid £500 in advance by each publisher.

Late in 1911 James found a solution for his "lonely" servants in Rye. His favorite nephew Billy married that autumn Alice Runnells, daughter of an affluent railroading family. The uncle very promptly offered them Lamb House as a honeymoon house. The young couple accepted with delight. James worked happily in London; and when the honeymooners came to the metropolis the uncle opened up for them all the avenues of English life. Billy, with his interest in painting, was taken to museums, to studios and to see the royal Holbeins at Windsor. The newest Alice in the James family—the third—enjoyed meeting James's writer friends. Long remembered by both the young Jameses was a weekend at Mrs. Hunter's in Hill Hall, with notables of art and music present, and George Moore at the dinner table insisting on the interest of adultery. The Master went for a walk with the Irishman, and said afterwards that he had never met—never in all his experience—anyone quite so "unimportantly dull" as George Moore.

James was extraordinarily active in that winter and spring of 1912. He was delighted that his old friend Edmund Gosse had become librarian of the House of Lords and had tea with him in lordly surroundings. At the beginning of 1912, dining at Gosse's, he met the young French writer

André Gide, "an interesting Frenchman," James noted. During that period he met May Sinclair, attended a reception at Sir Edward Elgar's, saw again his old friend Lady Gregory. He saw something of Lady Ottoline Morrell, who records their meetings in her diaries. On one occasion (8 May 1912) James noted that "she was very interesting; and also beautiful. But"—referring to her "window-curtaining clothes"—"I wish she didn't run so much to the stale, but a little more to the fresh, in costume."

On 26 June 1912 Oxford bestowed the honorary degree of doctor of letters on the Master. Attired in academic gown he heard himself described as "fecundissimum et facundissimum scriptorem, Henricum James," and may have remembered the dinner he had given years before in London to celebrate bestowal of that same honor on Turgenev.

He wrote during that year a long and warm letter of praise for William Dean Howells's seventy-fifth birthday to be read at one of Colonel Harvey's great dinners in New York, in which he surveyed Howells's work with affection and friendliness. The Master's date-books do not record his encountering at the Reform Club another American, young, with thick fluffy brown hair and a little pointed moustache and beard. Ezra Pound wrote home that he and Henry James "glared at one another across the same carpet" and years later in the *Cantos* set down a memory of "the great domed head, *con gli occhi onesti e tardi* | . . . drinking the tone of things / And the old voice . . . weaving an endless sentence."

"La Folie des Grandeurs"

The years had passed and Hendrik Andersen, now forty, had produced no professional work to speak of, certainly nothing that could be considered a masterpiece. James had had great expectations, for he endowed Andersen with his own feelings about the role of an artist; and from time to time, in his letters of love, he had admonished the sculptor to work within the realities of his "trade." After their brief meeting in America in 1905, James had written to him, "it's all pretty wretched, this non-communication—for there are long and weighty things about your work, . . . your building, on and on and up and up, *in the air,* as it were, and *out of relation to possibilities and actualities,* that I wanted to say to you." What American community, James wondered, "is going to want to pay for thirty and forty stark-naked men and women, of whatever beauty and lifted into the raw light of one of their public places. Keep in relation to the *possible* possibilities, dearest boy."

In 1906 Andersen sent James a photograph of a statue of two lovers in embrace. James said the work was the finest of the long "and interminable" series; but, he went on, "I don't think I find the *hands,* on the backs, *living* enough and participant enough in the kiss. They would be, in life, very participant—to their fingertips, and would show it in many ways." He urged Andersen to "make the creatures palpitate, and their flesh tingle and flush, . . . their bellies ache and their bladders fill"—thus the artist who had once described a parsimonious kiss in one of his famous novels, and had lately revised it in the sense in which he now wrote. In that same year he adjures the sculptor to "stop your multiplication of unsaleable nakedness for a while and hurl yourself into the production of the interesting, the charming, the vendible, the *placeable* small thing."

In 1908, after he had his reunion in Rome with Hendrik and watched him work in his studio, James resumed his warnings. He had seen the great impractical fountains, the lifeless nudes, *tutti bravi signori,* brave men, and beautiful women; and he remarked ironically, "we shall have to build a big bold city on purpose to take them in." James could not have put his finger more accurately on Andersen's vaulting fantasy, his mania of the colossal.

Early in 1912, Hendrik sent the Master plans, circulars, an appeal for funds, which he was distributing throughout Europe. He wanted to build a "World City," a "world centre of communication." The motto for it would be "Love—Equality—Peace." Hendrik envisaged a Paris-like metropolis: a long mall, resembling the Tuileries, with a Palace of Nations, like the Louvre, an Olympic athletic area at one end, a vast Palace of the Arts at the other, and a tremendous tower presiding over the entire fantasy. It was an architect's and sculptor's dream of a kind of permanent, super-World Fair. The plan, for which elaborate architectural drawings were made by forty architects, would later make specific every aspect of the city down to the central heating. Andersen's idea was that it could be placed anywhere; he had no particular site in mind.

The scheme was too much for the Master. James's reply on 14 April 1912 had a portentous beginning.

> Not another day do I delay to answer (with such difficulty!) your long and interesting letter . . . Brace yourself . . . though I don't quite see why I need, having showed you in the past, so again and again, that your mania for the colossal, the swelling and the huge, the monotonously and repeatedly huge, breaks the heart of me for you.

His only answer to this waste of money and time on "a ready-made City" was to "cover my head with my mantle and turn my face to the wall, and there, dearest Hendrik, just bitterly *weep* for you." He warned him of "dread Delusion"—medical science had a name for it, MEGALOMANIA, and Henry wrote it in capital letters, adding, "look it up in the Dictionary." He also gave it to him in French, *la folie des grandeurs.* The idea of a city built *de chic* filled the Master "with mere pitying dismay, the unutterable Waste of it all makes me retire into my room and lock the door to howl!" He would continue to howl, he said, until he heard that Hendrik had chucked the whole thing into the Tiber. He closed asking the sculptor to understand "how dismally unspeakably much these cold hard, desperate words, withholding sympathy, cost your ever-affectionate, your terribly tender old friend."

When Hendrik wrote again a year later, James had to recognize that "evidently, my dear boy, I can only give you pain." He repeated he did not understand "your very terms of 'world' this and 'world' the other." The Master went on to say that he would feel quite the same about such vague immensities "even if I were not old and ill and detached, and reduced to ending my life in a very restricted way." "The World," he said,

> is so far vaster in its appalling complexity than you or me, or than anything we can pretend without the imputation of absurdity and insanity to do to it, that I content myself, and inevitably *must* (so far as I can do anything at all now), with living in the realities of things, with "cultivating my garden" (morally and intellectually speaking), and with referring my questions to a Conscience (my own poor little personal), less inconceivable than that of the globe.

With the words of Voltaire, this curious friendship of the Master with the no longer young sculptor more or less came to an end. James referred again to "the dark danger" of megalomania, and signed himself "your poor old weary and sorrowing and yet always so personally and faithfully tender old Henry James."

In the inner world of the Master some deep dream of grandeur also existed—a dream of triumph amid the art works of the great world—as in the Galerie d'Apollon of the Louvre where he could defeat fear and feel the exaltation of power. It may be that Hendrik Andersen was James's "secret sharer" of those drives of craft and glory. James, however, had been able to control and channel his drive to greatness into the realities of his time and his world. Andersen's sculptured utopia was never built, but some of his unsold statues would be used, after his death in Rome, to adorn the buildings projected by another individual with a *folie des grandeurs*. The ornaments for an intended city of peace became part of the trappings of Mussolini's Rome.

A Browning Centenary

The Master had avoided public appearances during all the years of his residence in England. *Guy Domville* had been an exception and a mistake for which he had paid a heavy price. He had done nothing abroad comparable to his lectures on Balzac in America. Nevertheless, in the fullness of age, during that spring of 1912 in London, James faced a distinguished audience to deliver a commemorative tribute to Robert Browning, on the occasion of Browning's hundredth birthday, 7 May 1912. He called his paper "The Novel in *The Ring and the Book.*" The ceremony, under the auspices of the Royal Society of Literature, to which Henry James had been elected some years before, was held in an upper chamber of Caxton Hall. Edmund Gosse presided. The other speaker was Arthur Wing Pinero, the playwright, whose subject was Browning as a dramatist.

The playwright's address was long and loud, delivered with oratorical flourish and booming voice. "Pinero who thunderously preceded me," said James afterwards, "spoke twice as long as I had been told he was to; and this made me *apprehensive* and hurried and flurried and worried and faint through the sense that we were all *spent—* and the hall vast." It was too vast to carry James's voice when he let it fall, so that his talk was intermittently inaudible in some parts of the place. And yet the audience never became restless. As at the Balzac lectures there were bursts of applause; and when the Master came to a passage describing the sense of place—Tuscany and Rome—in Shelley, Swinburne, and Browning, a great stir and a great flutter greeted his words: "Shelley, let us say in the connection, is a light, and Swinburne is a sound—Browning alone is a temperature."

James's tribute analyzed *The Ring and the Book* to show how it might have been written as a novel—a novel, to be sure, by the author of *The Golden Bowl.* But he was clear throughout—as he expounded doctrine out of the New York Edition prefaces—that his was an act of homage to Browning. He singled out one quality in especial in the poet's work —"the great constringent relation between man and woman"—as the thing of which Browning's "own rich experience most convincingly spoke to him," and as the thing "absolutely most worth-while." But there wasn't a detail of the "panting" flight of Caponsacchi and Pompilia, the "man and woman" of the poem, over the autumn Apennines "that doesn't positively plead," he said, "for our perfect prose transcript."

The lecture had elegance; it had authority; it spoke for a powerful directing mind. James created seemingly impossible sentences and made them meaningful to the audience. Lord Charnwood, biographer of Lincoln, who had hitherto felt, "personally, sick when I see a page of Henry James in cold print," listening that afternoon found the paper "fascinating, soothing, elevating, even in parts intelligible to me when I heard it from the living voice of a quite living man." And Charnwood was struck by the way James left him aware, in his talk of Browning, "of one thing that might really satisfy a man's desire of life, namely to love a woman." When James stopped and sat down it seemed, said one account, "as if the applause would never cease."

He had richly paid his debt to the poet of his youth, who had taught him so much about "point of view." But now the audience of literary England, of his peers and of his readers, paid its homage to him, in a measure that perhaps James, in his flustered state, and high nervousness, did not appreciate—until he read the reports in the papers. James had begun by reading the expository part of the lecture rapidly; then he slowed down. His tone was conversational, his voice mellow. "All true charm is indescribable, and that of Henry James is more indescribable than most," one reporter wrote. "I noticed," wrote Filson Young in the *Pall Mall Gazette,* "that even the most experienced reporters gave it up in despair, laid down their pencils, and sat hypnotized . . . One merely listened to the voice of this charming old artist as though in the enchantment of a dream." Though that voice was not always quite audible, he went on,

> such was the magic of this dear old man's personality, and such were the affection and regard in which he was held by his audience, that not a sound or movement disturbed the silence of the room during the whole of that long and infinitely complicated address.

"It might indeed have diverted you," James wrote to Mrs. Wharton, "to be present at our Browning commemoration—for Pinero was by far the most salient feature of it . . . He had quite exhausted the air by the time I came on—and I but panted in the void." But he had "struggled through," he said—and he clipped Filson Young's comments and sent them to Cambridge, Massachusetts.

The Firebird

Billy and Alice James had remained in Lamb House throughout the winter of 1912. The couple returned to America in June, and James resettled in Lamb House. Summers were never lonely in Rye; it was the winters James feared. But the summer brought its own moments of terror with the "eagle pounce" of the Firebird—his new name for Mrs. Wharton and her Chariot of Fire.

James had hardly got back into Lamb House when he wrote a beguiling—and also a cunning—letter to Mrs. Hunter at Hill Hall. There had been some question of his visiting there with Mrs. Wharton and motoring in the surrounding countryside. He suggested tactfully that Mrs. Hunter should try to stay her hand a little "as regards marked emphasis or pressure" in urging Mrs. Wharton to come. If she came, there would be the motor, and he was busy with his writing. "Pleading with her to come does imply such a pledge—her motoring habits and intentions being so potent and explicit."

His plea didn't help. Little more than a fortnight later James was

wiring Mrs. Hunter that the Firebird was about to sweep "and to catch
me up in her irresistible talons." Dispatches were sent to Edith's friends
and his own, describing the inexorable advance of the authoress on
Lamb House. The first, dated "Reign of Terror, *ce vingt juillet,* 1912," to
Howard Sturgis, was a "sort of signal of distress" thrown out confiden-
tially

> at the approach of the Bird o'freedom—the whirr and wind of whose
> great pinions is already cold on my foredoomed brow! She is close at
> hand, she arrives tomorrow, and the poor old Ryebird, . . . feels his barn-
> yard hurry and huddle, emitting desperate and incoherent sounds, while
> its otherwise serene air begins ominously to darken.

What particularly troubled James was that Miss Bosanquet had gone
away for a holiday, providing a temporary substitute, Miss Lois Barker,
who would now collect pay while her employer had to go off with Mrs.
Wharton. "Oh, one's *opulent* friends," he told Goody Allen, "they cost the
eyes of the head."

The comedy of the Firebird resolved itself into a series of compromises. James sent her off alone; he promised to go with her to Howard
Sturgis and to spend four or five days at Hill Hall. "The horrible thing
about it is that it will be most interesting and wonderful and *worth while*
and yet even this won't solve effectually my inward ache." From Qu'Acre
they motored to Cliveden for tea, and promised their hostess, Nancy Astor
—whom James thought "full of possibilities and fine material—though
but a reclaimed barbarian"—to return. James's date-book recorded:

> July 30–31—Afternoon run to Cliveden. Three New Yorkers (*such*
> New Yorkers!) staying for night with Nancy Astor. Beautiful walk on the
> slopes down to and by river 6–8 with E.W. Americans left—day wet.
> Aug. 1—Agreed to stay over today Thursday . . . Second stroll with E.
> but had pectoral attack after lunch—through too much hurry and tension
> on slopes and staircase. Quiet till dinner—but second attack on mounting
> room 10:30. Lord Curzon at dinner.

Edith Wharton was understandably upset by Henry's heart flurries.
They left on 2 August and went back to Howard Sturgis's where they
lunched. Then she sent James back to Lamb House in her car. He went
straight to bed on arriving, and remained there the following day. Then
he renewed his long walks and experienced immediate relief. "The only
proper place for me is home," he wrote Mrs. Hunter.

Mrs. Wharton came to Lamb House early in August just before taking
flight for the Continent. "The firebird perches on my shoulder," James
wrote to Sturgis on 12 August. To Mrs. Cadwalader Jones he gave the
ultimate summary of "Edith's prodigious visit."

She rode the whirlwind, she played with the storm, she laid waste whatever of the land the other raging elements had spared, she consumed in fifteen days what would have served to support an ordinary Christian Community for about ten years. Her powers of devastation are ineffable, her repudiation of repose absolutely tragic, and she was never more brilliant and able and interesting.

Lois Barker, Miss Bosanquet's substitute, turned up at Lamb House each morning that summer, to be ushered by Burgess into the Green Room, and occasionally the Garden Room. James was often late. More than once on arriving she met him in the hall dressed only in pajamas, carrying a large bath sponge. He beamed at her reassuringly in his informality with his "large blue eyes." He dictated his autobiographies without notes, though occasionally he darted to a drawer to return with a letter or other document. As he wrote the passage in *A Small Boy* in which Thackeray admired the buttons on his boyhood jacket, he held in his hand the daguerreotype by Brady of the small boy wearing the jacket. Suddenly in the midst of dictating he left the room and returned carrying the original jacket, buttons and all.

A Determined Woman

One of the consequences of the Firebird's view of Henry James during the summer of 1912 was her growing belief that he needed money. He had complained to her once too often of his low royalties; his ironies about his unprincely scale of life were taken seriously. During 1912 Walter Berry sent James a beautifully fitted leather case lined with morocco. James had written an elaborate thank-you telling Berry how the handsome object—he called it "him"—made everything else in Lamb House seem poverty-stricken: "I can't live with him, you see, because I can't live up to him." James was in reality telling Berry with his customary irony that he didn't need so grandiose an article; but Mrs. Wharton, who saw this letter, must have received quite another message.

In the preceding year she had quietly mounted, with the help of Edmund Gosse in England and William Dean Howells in America, a vigorous campaign to obtain the Nobel Prize for Henry James. It had never been given to an American and would not be until 1930. The Swedish Academy was thoroughly apprised of the Master's supreme position in Anglo-American letters. But the northern judges of the world's literature had not read Henry James and had not read about him in the newspapers. He had been very little translated—indeed he considered himself untranslatable—and was not as "visible" as Kipling, who had received the Prize in 1907. It was much easier for the Academicians to award it that year of 1911 to Maurice Maeterlinck.

Edith Wharton was not to be deterred. Remembering the device by which she—and the Master himself—had provided much-needed funds to Morton Fullerton when he was being blackmailed, she entered into secret correspondence with her publisher in America—who was also Henry James's. She and Charles Scribner agreed that $8,000 could safely be diverted from her royalties to the Master's account without arousing suspicion. They could hardly falsify the earnings on the New York Edition. But James's agent had told Scribner's that the Master was working on a novel of American life—an allusion to *The Ivory Tower*, which he had sketched out just before his 1910 illness. Charles Scribner accordingly wrote to James: "As the publishers of your definitive edition we want another great novel to balance *The Golden Bowl* and round off the series of books in which you have developed the theory of composition set forth in your prefaces." If James could begin the book soon, Scribner said, he was prepared to pay him an advance of $8,000 (£1,500), perhaps half on signing the contract and half on delivery of the manuscript. The novel would then be added to the New York Edition.

James had never received so handsome an offer. It was settled that he would be given a 20 percent royalty; Scribner's would have world rights and would thus arrange publication in England. James would write the novel as soon as possible after the completion of the autobiographies, which Scribner's were to publish. The novelist's agent was not fooled. Miss Bosanquet's diary, after James's death, notes that Pinker "has been convinced by his recent communications with Scribner's that his guess as to Mrs. Wharton having subsidized the Scribner novel contract was quite correct." But the agent was discretion itself. Mrs. Wharton was disturbed that James handed the matter over to his agent, and caused Scribner to suggest to James that since the initiative had been the publisher's the agent was not needed. James, however, insisted that Pinker receive his usual 10 percent. The first installment of the advance was thus $3,600—which James happily pocketed, still puzzled, but also delighted.

Mrs. Wharton's initiative, while meddlesome and not required, helped to give James's morale a lift at a crucial moment. For in the autumn of 1912, when he seemed to have fully recovered from his depression and illness of two years earlier, he suddenly came down with the painful systemic virus disease known as *herpes zoster*—in a word, "shingles." James had a very bad case—it laid him low for the next four months and while he could have been ambulatory, he spent much time in bed since clothing irritated his skin. A consequence was that he did not get the exercise he required. His letters of this time betray his intense irritation and suffering. And yet he managed to do a considerable amount of reading and planning, and even dictation, so that *A Small Boy and Others* was completed, and *Notes of a Son and Brother* got under way. In February of 1913, his prolonged inactivity produced an accumulation of fluid at the bottom of James's lungs. As his breathing became more difficult, and his discomfort acute, alarms went out to his friends. The doctor brought in a nurse, whom the Master regarded as "a mild dragon." But once diagnosed, James's edema was readily treated and he rapidly recovered. "My vitality, my still sufficient cluster of vital 'assets,' " James wrote to his nephew Harry, "to say nothing of my *will to live and to write,* assert themselves in spite of everything." The prospect of doing a new novel for Scribner's, the handsome sum advanced, the progress of the autobiographies, prevailed over the ills of the flesh.

Shortly before the onset of the attack of shingles, James had found a flat in Cheyne Walk, in Chelsea. His room at the Reform Club had served him for more than ten years. With his intermittent illnesses and his need to have Miss Bosanquet available, and above all remembering how his "hibernation" at Rye bred loneliness and depression, he had decided to return to the metropolis. He would use Lamb House only in the summers. No. 21 Carlyle Mansions suited him in every way. It was an L-shaped apartment, with two large rooms hanging over the Thames; these could serve as study and dining-room. There were five bedrooms in all. The flat would cost him £60 a year more than his *pied-à-terre* at the Reform. He would have as a neighbor his old friend, Emily Sargent, sister of the painter. The front rooms gave him a great deal of sun, and the pompously embanked river offered him a walk all the way to Westminster. The view had been painted by Whistler. In 1869, during his first adult trip abroad, James had been taken to this area to visit Dante Gabriel Rossetti. He was again near his clubs and a new generation of friends. He now had a telephone; the days of "calling" and leaving cards were being supplanted by that device. Taxicabs were handy. He was ready to settle down to work again. But he knew—he felt—that this was his last harbor.

Since he was still ill in January 1913, when he took possession of the apartment, the move was made by his servants, who brought various pieces of furniture from Lamb House, and settled everything for the Master. It was probably soon after his arrival in Cheyne Walk that Desmond MacCarthy called, and was told by the diminutive "rock-faced" Burgess that the Master was unwell. MacCarthy turned to leave but James summoned him. He found him sitting in an armchair with a foot rest, his eyes half-shut. He seemed to speak with difficulty, MacCarthy wrote to Virginia Woolf, "as though whenever his lips closed, they were stuck together and the wheels of his mind turned with a ponderous smooth difficulty, as though there was not steam enough to move so large an engine." James asked MacCarthy not to smoke; he rang for tea. "If I take tea it will either kill me or do me good, what shall I do?" MacCarthy refused to take so momentous a decision. The conversation was labored.

> Gradually I became aware, however, that we were making progress. We began to talk about the power to visualize memories and imaginary scenes. He seemed to think that a novelist's power depended on it. I admitted that in his own case the dependence was masked. . . . Then we went through the novelists with this idea in our heads, and he read to me. All the time he was getting brisker and brisker till at last from a semi-comatose condition he began to grow positively lively—shoveling on coal and eating cold tea cake and sweet buns. I enjoyed my afternoon extremely.

The Master at Seventy

Late in 1912 or early in 1913 Edith Wharton caused to be circulated among leaders of society and finance in the United States a form letter proposing that a substantial sum be raised in honor of Henry James's seventieth birthday, on 15 April 1913. The letter named a bank into which contributions should be paid. Mrs. Wharton evidently regarded the secretly diverted royalties as a stop-gap; she wanted the Master to receive a large purse. One of her thoughts seems to have been that James might purchase a car from the proceeds of this subscription.

While the appeal was private, word of it reached James's nephews, and Billy cabled his uncle at once. The reply could not have been more prompt. "Immense thanks for warning taking instant prohibitive action. Please express to individuals approached my horror money absolutely returned. Uncle." This was followed by a letter saying, "A more reckless and indiscreet undertaking, with no ghost of a preliminary leave asked, no hint of a sounding taken, I cannot possibly conceive—and am still rubbing my eyes for incredulity." The money was returned. The chances are James said not a word to Mrs. Wharton about this. Their friendship continued unchanged; however misguided the attempt, her motive had been generous.

James's friends in England had quite another scheme. A small informal committee issued an appeal to the Master's friends and admirers. His seventy years of art and distinction should be honored, and in a fitting public fashion. James got wind of this initiative and asked very promptly that it be stopped. He explained to Miss Bosanquet he didn't want it bruited abroad "that I'm a fabulous age when I'm trying to put forth some further exhibition of my powers." Lucy Clifford flatly told him he was "cold, callous and ungracious." He capitulated. Nearly 300 persons subscribed to the fund, to which no one was allowed to contribute more than £5, and with £50 of the proceeds, a silver-gilt Charles II porringer and dish was purchased to be presented to the author of *The Golden Bowl.* The balance was offered to John Singer Sargent to paint a portrait of the Master. Sargent, as a friend of many years, refused the honorarium; and the sum was used to commission a bust by a young sculptor chosen by Sargent, Derwent Wood.

In this way, and with all the niceties observed, the Master awoke on 15 April to discover himself, at least for a day, a great public figure. The bell at No. 21 began to ring early; the apartment was filled with flowers; cables and telegrams arrived from everywhere. The golden bowl was presented and accepted by James with his customary elegance: inscribed on it were the words "To Henry James from some of his friends." He announced he would sit for the portrait (and later consented to sit for the bust) but he would not accept the painting, which belonged to his admirers. He agreed to be its custodian and publicly willed it to the National Portrait Gallery, where it hangs today.

He had felt so many times in his life that the world did not want his art and did not recognize his genius. But on this day he was given a full measure of the world's affection. Opening the *Pall Mall Gazette* the Master found in it an editorial entitled "Henry James," which spoke of his "immense achievement" and the appearance at this moment of *A Small Boy and Others.* The editorial expressed the wish that "this keen observer, very great artist, and brilliant and generous critic of men and manners, may, in the best of health and the fulness of power, enjoy many more birthdays."

The name of Edith Wharton was not in the list of subscribers to the birthday tribute. The committee had known of her separate initiative and had not approached her; but James added her name afterwards and that of Walter Berry, along with the names of a few others to whom he wished to send a formal letter of thanks. "Dear Friends All," he began the letter, "let me acknowledge with boundless pleasure, the singularly generous and beautiful letter, signed by your great and dazzling array and reinforced by a correspondingly bright material gage, which reached me on my recent birthday, April 15th." It was so wonderful, he said, to count over "your dear and distinguished friendly names, taking in all they recall and represent, that I permit myself to feel at once highly successful and extremely proud." The list of names was a roll call of splendor in the annals of the arts, politics, and the social life of the time: it took in the nobility of England and the Rye neighbors; James's physicians; the personalities of the stage; a great many novelists; his French friends.

James posed that spring for Sargent in his studio in nearby Tite Street. Sargent painted him in a characteristic pose, his left thumb catching his striped and elegant waistcoat. He is wearing a bow tie and starched collar, and a watch chain dangles across the ample embonpoint. On the strong hand holding the waistcoat may be seen the topaz ring James had worn for many years. For the rest, the picture fades into chiaroscuro; the full highlight accentuates the great forehead, the eyes half closed but with all their visual acuteness; and the lips formed as if the Master were about to speak. James is caught in one of the moments of his greatness—that is, a moment of "authority." He felt as he saw himself take form on the canvas that he looked more and more like Sir Joshua's Dr. Johnson, and others had the same impression. To Rhoda Broughton, James wrote that the picture was "Sargent at his very best and poor old H.J. not at his worst; in short a living breathing likeness and a masterpiece of painting."

James greatly enjoyed his sittings in Sargent's high cool studio which opened on a balcony and a green Chelsea garden. He was a patient sitter, but Sargent had him invite friends to talk to him and distract him while he was being painted "to break the spell of a settled gloom in my countenance." Jocelyn Persse was summoned; and also the young Ruth Draper, freshly descended on London from America to do her inimitable monologues in some of the great houses. "Little Ruth is a dear of dears," James wrote, "and her talent has really an extraordinary charm." Inspired by her work, he wrote a monologue for her—which, however, she never performed, for she always created her own.

Since the picture had been commissioned, in effect, by some 300 persons, Sargent held a private showing of it in his studio in December 1913. The donors flocked to see the portrait and "I really put myself on exhibition beside it," James wrote to Gosse, "each of the days, morning and afternoon, and the translation . . . visibly left the original nowhere." It had been an "exquisite incident . . . most beautiful and flawless."

The incident had a sequel the following spring, when, early in May 1914, an elderly white-haired woman, placid-looking and wearing a loose purple cloak, entered the rooms of the Royal Academy in London on the opening day of the spring exhibition. She walked from room to room until she came to Room III, where the Sargent portrait of James was hung. Suddenly there was the sound of shattering glass. The peaceable-looking lady was wielding a meat-cleaver she had concealed beneath her cloak on Sargent's masterpiece. Several women pounced on her—but she had already cut three ugly gashes in it, through the left side of the head, the right side of the mouth and below the right shoulder. A man who attempted to defend the lady from the irate women had his glasses broken. The police arrived promptly.

At the station the woman, who gave her name as Mrs. Mary Wood, said she had never heard of Henry James. A militant suffragette, she had read that the Sargent picture was valued at £700. A woman painter, she said, would not have received anywhere near such a sum. She had wished "to show the public that they have no security for their property, nor for their art treasures, until women are given their political freedom."

"Academy Outrage," the newspaper headlines screamed. "Most gentle friend," Henry James wrote to Goody Allen after the onslaught, "I naturally feel very scalped and disfigured, but you will be glad to know that I seem to be pronounced curable ... The damage, in other words, isn't past praying for, or rather past mending." His table was strewn, he said, with 390 kind notes of condolence. The suffragette had only caused him to receive, hardly a year after his seventieth birthday, still another ovation. To Howells, James was less urbane. "Those ladies really outrage humanity, and the public patience has to me a very imbecile side." The Sargent portrait was repaired before the end of the month and exhibited under watchful guard.

The Ebbing Tide

Henry James remained in London until late in the spring of 1913 in order to pose for his bust. A few days before his scheduled departure for Rye, he felt ill, went to bed, and lost consciousness. He had never had a fainting spell and it frightened him. "I was *consciously* sure I was dying," he said. His doctor brought in a nurse; within twenty-four hours the Master—after a "wretched time"—was able to have lunch at home with his nephew Harry; Peggy James and Fanny Prothero came at once to give him support. His specialist, Dr. Des Voeux, was "very reassuring and interesting," James noted in his date-book. He said the novelist had *"very* great powers of recuperation." Heartened, James left as he had planned for Lamb House, accompanied by his niece.

He had begun to restrict his activities even before this brief illness. "The evening of life is difficult," he wrote. He tried to see it "as much as I can by exemptions and simplifications." In Rye he maintained his old way of life. He spent his three hours in the Garden Room every morning; with his niece he took his long walks in the afternoon, even if the pace was less lively.

Toward the end of the summer, Peggy James, now twenty-six, became mildly critical of her uncle—he seemed to her for the first time "a thoroughly *unreal* person. All that he says, and his manner of saying it, is pirouetting and prancing, and beating the air, very charmingly, but still once in a while you crave a strong simple note. And yet strong it certainly is too." She was echoing her father. Her uncle, perhaps sensing her feelings, said to her, "I hate the American simplicity. I glory in the piling up of complications of every sort. If I could pronounce the name James in any different and more elaborate way I should be in favour of doing it."

At Lamb House that summer visitors came and went. Peggy met Mrs. Wharton and Mrs. Cadwalader Jones and found both "formidable." Amy Lowell, representative of the new poetry, came in her massive weight, smoked her cigars and was "very noisy and amusing." Logan Pearsall Smith had a week-end at Lamb House. "The tide of gossip between us rose high, he being a great master of that effect," said James. Logan was to be especially lurid in his later reminiscences about the elderly Constance Fletcher and her adventures in a bath-tub in Lamb House from which, because of her girth, she could not extricate herself. Other visitors that summer were Joseph Conrad, "poor queer man," who came to Lamb House for lunch, and Bernard Shaw and Granville-Barker. James shocked Shaw by kissing him on both cheeks.

Wells's new novel *The Passionate Friends* arrived and James read it. His letter of criticism was as sharp as ever. Objecting as always to Wells's use of the autobiographical form, James said he found him "perverse" and "on a whole side, unconscious, as I can only call it"; but "your talent remains so savoury and what you do substantial. I adore a rounded objectivity." Wells, whether in irony or truth, replied that

> my art is abortion—on the shelves of my study stand a little vain-gloriously thirty-odd premature births . . . But it is when you write to me out of your secure and masterly *finish,* out of your golden globe of leisurely (yet not slow) and infinitely *easy* accomplishment that the sense of my unworthiness and rawness is most vivid.

To Walpole James said that this reply showed Wells "profusely extravagantly apologetic and profoundly indifferent." He added that artistically Wells had "gone to the dogs." Earlier, in a lecture on "The Scope of the Novel," Wells had denied that the novel could be an aesthetic and artistic end in itself. And when, shortly after this, James had insisted at the Royal Society of Literature that Wells be elected, the younger writer, to James's surprise, declined the honor: he wasn't going to allow himself to be voted into the Establishment. After a private talk with Wells, James wrote to Gosse that Wells "has cut himself loose from literature clearly—practically altogether."

James had a fairly decent winter in 1913–14. The young continued to come to him; and he took so much pleasure in Compton Mackenzie's *Sinister Street* that he made Hugh Walpole jealous. Then the second volume came out and James had to climb down. But he continued to write affectionate letters to young "Monty" Compton (his real name), the son of Edward Compton the actor, whom he remembered as a boy. In his late years Mackenzie, like Pearsall Smith, like Hueffer, like so many others, had his hoard of cherished and embellished anecdotes to build the "legend" of the Master.

In the spring of 1914 James showed an active interest in the plight of Robert Ross, Oscar Wilde's executor, who had, in the years since Wilde's death, slowly rebuilt the reputation of his friend. Ross was now suing Lord Alfred Douglas for libel, a repetition as it were of the Wilde case itself, but in a new and less exercised age. Behind the trial there were old animosities and old jealousies, but James felt haunted by Ross's "demoralized state." The thing was, he wrote to Hugh, "to try to help him to keep his head and stiffen his heart."

Early in 1914 James went to lunch with A. B. Walkley, the drama critic of *The Times,* to meet Henry Bernstein, the French dramatist. Bernstein talked to James of a new writer named Marcel Proust and of his novel *Du Côté de chez Swann,* just published. Edith Wharton later sent James a copy of the book, but we do not know whether he read it or not.

James had dispatched the manuscript of *Notes of a Son and Brother* before leaving Rye late in the fall of 1913. This left him free for other work. He had promised Bruce Richmond, the editor of *The Times Literary Supplement,* an article on "the new novel" and this he now wrote. "The Younger Generation," which appeared in two installments in the spring of 1914, revealed the old and vigorous James, but for the first and only time in his long critical career he had not read carefully all the novels he dealt with nor surveyed the entire horizon. His most remembered lapse was his dismissal of D. H. Lawrence's *Sons and Lovers;* but the entire article shows a failure in discernment if not in power. He began by wanting to say publicly why he disliked Wells and Bennett, whose money-opportunism he deplored; he wanted to say something about Conrad's *Chance,* and he had at last an opportunity to praise Mrs. Wharton, for he had liked *Ethan Frome,* and commended *The Reef*— writing her a letter comparing it to Racine—and had been delighted by the satire of *The Custom of the Country.* Then he wanted to be nice to Hugh, in his old way, and to pat young Monty Mackenzie on the back. The mixed motives of the article made it a grab-bag of comment; the old lessons of the master are repeated, but the attack is principally on the *saturated* novel, of which Tolstoy was the supreme example. Wells and Bennett were lesser English counterparts, whom James described as squeezing "to the utmost the plump and more or less juicy orange of a particularly acquainted state." Just as there was no "centre of interest" or sense of the whole in *War and Peace* so there was none in *The Old*

Wives' Tale or *The Passionate Friends.* The reader was left with the simple amusement of watching the orange being squeezed.

We have already seen how deeply Conrad, no longer young, was disturbed by the passages in the article devoted to him. Hugh, whose youth rather than his work was praised, felt that he had got off lightly; the other young men were pleased to have some notice, and Mrs. Wharton could not but derive satisfaction at having finally had public acclaim from the man she so intensely admired. All the English novelists of the time read the article and many felt themselves ignored; the Master, undisturbed, had had his say. He revised the article and gathered it in with the definitive essays he had written earlier in the century on Balzac, Flaubert, Zola, and George Sand. The book was his last critical collection. He called it *Notes on Novelists.*

"The Ivory Tower"

Publication of *Notes of a Son and Brother* on 7 March 1914 was the occasion for many new tributes to Henry James and letters from old friends. All were moved by the pages in the book devoted to the memory of Minny Temple, the long-dead cousin who had been James's "heroine of the scene." A note Harry James made in his own copy of the book observes that everything Henry James had said about Minny seemed to his nephew

> to be as appropriate as possible to W.J. allowing for differences of sex. They were clearly chips off the same block. It is as if time and distance had enabled H.J. to see in her and to describe the traits conspicuous to me in W.J. which he doesn't refer to in his allusions to his brother.

We might speculate that the love that Henry had for William—but could not offer or express—found its expression in the book of memory: there was also in Minny something boyish, vigorous, passionate. She had been for Henry long ago cousin, brother, sister, sweetheart, all in one. Now he had placed her at the very center of his and his brother's early lives. He had offered his genius to her memory—and in doing so offered it also to his brother.

Henry Adams, reading the book, which James sent him promptly, had other feelings. His wife, Clover Hooper, had belonged to that period of the James brothers' lives. "I've read Henry James's last bundle of memories which have reduced me to a pulp," Adams wrote to Mrs. Cameron. "Why did we live? Was that all? . . . Poor Henry James thinks it all real, I believe, and actually still lives in that dreamy, stuffy Newport and Cambridge, with papa James and Charles Norton." Adams seems to have embodied these melancholy feelings in a letter to the novelist. James's reply was an expression of the new-found emotional energies of his old age. In spite of illness and reduced activity, he wanted to live; he was determined to take from life all that it would offer him. *"Of course,"* he wrote to Adams,

> we are lone survivors, of course the past that was our lives is at the bottom of an abyss—if the abyss *has* any bottom; of course, too, there's no use talking unless one particularly *wants* to. But the purpose, almost, of my printed divagations was to show you that one *can,* strange to say, still want to—or at least can behave as if one did.

He went on to say that he found his consciousness still interesting "under *cultivation* of the interest."

> You see I still, in presence of life (or of what you deny to be such), have reactions—as many as possible—and the book I sent you is proof of them. It's, I suppose, because I am that queer monster, the artist, an obstinate finality, an inexhaustible sensibility. Hence the reactions— appearance, memories, many things, go on playing upon it with conse- quence that I note and "enjoy" (grim word!) noting. It all takes doing— and I *do.* I believe I shall do yet again—it is still an act of life.

Old, tired, Henry James continued to perform the acts of life and nothing showed this more than his last writings. *The Finer Grain,* his volume of tales of 1910, and the novel he was trying to write, subsidized by Edith Wharton, which he called *The Ivory Tower,* contain new subjects derived from his two visits to America. The stories, nearly all set in New York, and the fragment of the novel set in Newport and Manhattan have recurrent themes, to the effect that certain of the American wealthy had too much wealth; that this wealth was corrupting—and corruption; and that he, James, had been robbed of his national birthright. The anger in some of the stories in *The Finer Grain* was more fully expressed than in earlier works. Thus the story "Crapy Cornelia" contains James's vision of America (and of Mrs. Wharton):

> This was clearly going to be the music of the future—that if people were but rich enough and furnished enough and fed enough, exercised and sanitated and manicured and generally advised and advertised and made "knowing" enough, . . . all they had to do for civility was to take the amused ironic view of those who might be less initiated.

The women particularly in these tales are devoid of all sympathy; fat, ugly, rich, cruel, they seem to have lost the meaning of kindness. What one can read above all in these final stories is a picture of the crass money side of Edith Wharton's world—in effect a sense of America's betrayal of its own original high civilization.

The Ivory Tower was to have been written in ten books, each section devoted to a different character, and the whole designed to illuminate the central situation. The parts of the novel James completed show no sign of old age save that the images are over-weighted and the prose is heavy and "difficult," shot through with symbolic imagery. *The Ivory Tower* combines elements from James's last three novels—the American innocent, called here Graham Fielder, who, however, returns to America rather than live in Paris; the couple in love who cannot marry and plot to obtain the millions Fielder inherits from his uncle. In the opening scenes two former business partners are both dying—of their millions— full of guilt and unforgiveness. Possessed of the riches of their lives, Abel Gaw and a character called Betterman, the Cain figure, seem adumbrations of William and Henry James at the end of time, with their intellectual and artistic capital.

If the ingredients of the novel are familiar, the background is new. The novel would have been the story of a year, like Henry's own year in America in 1904–05. From Newport it would move to New York and later to the world of Edith Wharton at Lenox. What James intended to bring into this novel was the "money-passion," the spirit of "ferocious acquisition." The central symbol is the ivory tower, an *objet d'art* in which Fielder chooses to place an unread document left him by Gaw, the better man's rival. The tower is represented as "the most distinguished retreat" —from commerce, from sex, from all the turbulence and passion of this world. The pagoda of *The Golden Bowl* was a symbol of innocence and escape from reality; the ivory tower is a symbol of conscious withdrawal from reality looked in the face.

James's last novel was emerging as an apologia for his own life; it would have denounced, with all the delicacy and subtlety of his style, the world he had seen, at Biltmore, at Lenox, in the great houses of New York and at Newport. He had reclaimed his American heritage, but he seems to have felt it wasn't worth reclaiming. "You seem all here so hideously rich," says his hero. *The Ivory Tower* re-created the old myths of Henry James's life. In what would have been a dense and powerfully conceived work, James was drawing upon the oldest material he possessed—tales of treachery and fraternal humiliation. And the crowning irony was that as he worked innocently on this book, he could not know that it had been secretly subsidized by the very kind of wealth—and treachery—he condemned.

James wrote to Howells, who urged him in May of 1914 to pay still another visit to the United States, "I don't like to frequent the U.S. . . . weigh *prosperity* against posterity . . . That autumn, winter and spring (1910–11) which I spent in Cambridge and New York—well, I shall go down to my grave without having breathed to another ear what I went through with then."

James could, at the last, in the same vein, confess to his sister-in-law the deepest truths of his old stress-filled ties with Quincy Street—the tightly-drawn silver cords knotted and tangled which he recognized as "strange inevitable tentacles." They had been inevitable, as in all family constellations, and had tied him to his seemingly pliant yet rigid mother and his euphoric eccentric yet demanding father. His sister Alice had not escaped; her emotional imprisonment had resulted in her life's invalidism. William James had stood his ground, but could find his way only after his father's death. The younger brothers escaped into improvidence and alcohol. Henry had accepted exile from home and homeland; and his avowal of his total alienation from Boston—and America—modifies the euphemisms of his autobiographies and the sentimentalities visited upon the discordant family by literary historians. James had fled to save himself—and his art. He pledged a kind of allegiance to cosmopolitanism; and he too paid a price, the kind of malaise he described in his notes for *The Sense of the Past,* his unwritten international ghost story—the "scared" American figures "in search of, in flight from, something or other." Such had been the great compromises of his life on the secure battlements of his art.

3

OVER

THE ABYSS

A Wreck of Belief

The year 1914 had begun for James with the extraction of most of his teeth, "the wounds, the inconvenience, the humiliations," not to speak of the effects of the anaesthetic. He relied now on nitroglycerine tablets for his heart; he spoke frequently of his "desiccated antiquity." However, he was vigorous enough that spring to welcome again and entertain his niece and his youngest nephew, each with an American companion of whom the uncle was highly critical. James discoursed at length about the cultural environment William James had created for his young and the environment from which these other young Americans had come. They had affluence, a large measure of it, but no enlightenment.

For the rest, he kept up his social life, and Peggy noted the general level of his strength was better than the previous year. His date-book of the spring of 1914 shows him as active and as observant as of old. A note of 3 April records however,

> Bad days: climax of the long effect of privation of exercise—more intense demonstration of imperative need of sacrificing *everything* to this boon ... Long resolute walk from Piccadilly Circus down to Westminster and thence all along the Embankment to the corner of Chelsea Barracks and Hospital Road. I was more than three hours—nearer four—on foot—the length of the effort was the effective benefit—and this benefit was signal.

His niece provided him with company for his walks. They went to the cinema and to the Royal Academy, where Peggy saw the Sargent portrait and teased her uncle for wearing "exact clothes ... watch chain, waistcoat and tie, so that every eye ... was rivetted to him." They dined at the Philip Morrells', Prime Minister Asquith being present. The uncle took Peggy and her companion to the House of Commons for the third reading of the Home Rule Bill, the government obtaining a majority. "Rather historic occasion," he noted.

The Master stayed in London into July and on the 14th he went to Lamb House. A long entry in his appointment book of 30 July notes, with some minuteness, all his comings and goings of that summer but breaks off in the middle. There is no further entry until 4 August. On that day he scrawls: "Everything blackened over for the time blighted by the hideous Public situation. . . . horrible suspense and the worst possibilities in the air."

The coming of the Great War was, for Henry James, "a nightmare from which there is no waking save by sleep." The letters which he wrote during the early days of August 1914 are among the most eloquent of his life. He believed civilization had collapsed totally into barbarism and that this had turned his life into a gross lie. "I write you under the black cloud of portentous events on this side of the world, horrible, unspeakable, iniquitous things—I mean horrors of war criminally, infamously precipitated." Thus to his old Newport friend Margaret La Farge. To Edith Wharton he wrote (on 6 August) of "this crash of our civilization. The only gleam in the blackness, to me, is the action and the absolute unanimity of this country."

However, it was to the old, irascible and undividedly British Rhoda Broughton that he poured out his deepest anguish.

> Black and hideous to me is the tragedy that gathers and I'm sick beyond cure to have lived on to see it. You and I, the ornaments of our generation, should have been spared this wreck of our belief that through the long years we had seen civilization grow and the worst become impossible. . . . It seems to me to *undo* everything, everything that was ours, in the most horrible retroactive way—but I avert my face from the monstrous scene.

He could not avert his face. He had always lived too close to the realities behind human illusion. The "shining indifference" of nature chilled his heart. James awoke each day to find the same light, the same air, the same sea and the sky, "the most beautiful English summer conceivable." This was "the sole, the exquisite England, whose weight now hangs in the balance." He had remained an American all his years. Now he began to speak of "we" and "us."

Mrs. Wharton was in Paris when Belgium was invaded; she came over to England and visited James briefly at Rye. The Master felt unwell; he had a spell of illness in late August. He ate little; his nerves remained on edge. But he summoned all his strength and in September began to speak of returning to London. He couldn't work. He found it difficult to read. He wanted to be nearer to some source of information and contact.

In the days before his departure, his restlessness was increased by the war activities in Rye: the local enlistments, the drilling of recruits. Burgess announced he was joining up. His master gave him his blessing. "It's like losing an arm or a leg," James wrote to Mrs. Wharton, who promptly sent one of her menservants, Frederick, to help James for the time being. Burgess's job would be kept for him. "If it's *socks* you will throughout most want, I will keep you supplied," James wrote to him in his most maternal vein.

Two or three nights before his departure from Rye the first Belgian refugees arrived; James had offered his Watchbell Street studio as a gathering place. In the evening a sound of voices made the Master go to his door at the top of the winding street. Over the grass-grown cobbles came the procession of the homeless. "It was swift and eager," James would write, with "scarce a sound save the shuffle of mounting feet and the thick-drawn breath of emotion." He saw a young mother carrying her child. He heard "the resonance through our immemorial old street of her sobbing." History had reached his doorstep.

Soldiers

Even before he left Rye, James heard from Hugh Walpole that he was leaving for Russia. He had been turned down by the Army because of his poor eyesight, and was to be a war correspondent on the Eastern Front for the *Daily Mail.* "Think of me as I cross the North Sea," Hugh wrote. James replied that Hugh was showing "the last magnificence of pluck, the finest strain of resolution." From Jocelyn Persse came word almost at the same time. He had joined the Royal Fusiliers and was in a camp in Essex. Desmond MacCarthy was among the early callers at Carlyle Mansions once the Master was reinstalled. He had joined the Red Cross and was leaving for France. This would give him much experience, said James, and "can only contribute hereafter to his powers of conversation."

"We must for dear life make our own counter-realities," James wrote to Lucy Clifford. Having all his life declined to serve on committees, he immediately threw himself into Belgian relief, which had its headquarters at Crosby Hall in Chelsea; and when it was suggested that he visit Belgian wounded in St. Bartholomew's Hospital because he could speak French to them, he went eagerly. Presently he was moving from bedside to bedside talking to the English wounded as well. His date-book provides a record of constant hospital visits and of aid to individual soldiers. "Took three maimed and half-blind convalescent soldiers from St. Bart's to tea 24 Bedford Square," where the Protheros lived, "and delivered them home again." The next day he "telephoned Dr. Field inquiring about his attending to Private Percy Stone who has practically lost an eye." He sends a pocket comb to one soldier, cigarettes to others. On leaving hospital, a sapper of the Royal Engineers was invited to the Master's flat for meals; presently James arranged for him to have his teeth taken care of "at very reduced military rates." Friends of the Master wondered how the soldiers reacted to his subtle leisurely talk—but he seemed quite capable of entertaining and comforting them. He likened himself to Walt Whitman during the Civil War. It made him feel less "finished and useless and doddering when I go on certain days and try to pull the conversational cart uphill for them."

The sense of power and glory in James made him an admirer always of the soldier—"such children of history." He stopped soldiers on the street and astonished them by emptying his pockets of small change for them. He couldn't keep away from the windows of his flat if he heard the sound of a bugle, or the skirl of the bagpipe. Saturated reader of Napoleonic memoirs, admirer of the kind of action he himself had never had, he interrupts a letter to his nephew

> to watch from my windows a great swinging body of the London Scottish, as one supposes, marching past at the briskest possible step with its long line of freshly enlisted men behind it.

He left a record of his visits to hospitals in an essay, "The Long Wards," which shows the precise nature of the relations he established. James came to the soldiers not as a great writer or an admirable intellect of the age; the men probably didn't know who he was. What came through to them was his kindness, his warmth. His portly presence, quiet, authoritative, composed, conveyed almost in silence admiration without condescension, trust without question, an air of acceptance. All his life he had preached the thesis of "living through" and of "infinite doing." Now he practiced it in full measure. It gave him new reason for existence; and through the rest of 1914 and well into 1915, until recurrent illness slowed him up, he surrendered himself to the soldiers.

James enlisted himself in the same way in the service of a particular American activity that arose in England during the early days of the war, accepting the chairmanship of the American Volunteer Motor-Ambulance Corps in France. Richard Norton, son of his old friend Charles Eliot Norton, had thrown himself into this work, and James and Mrs. Wharton were committed to help. At first tentative and experimental, the Corps grew rapidly in importance; in Russia, Hugh Walpole, tired of inaction in Moscow, enlisted in the first hospital units on that front and saw action in this way.

With the pain—and resolution—of helping the wounded and the victims, James experienced the anguish of the wives and the widows. Clare

Sheridan, daughter of Moreton Frewen, his neighbor at Brede, wrote to James of her loneliness when her husband went off to the front. James's reply spoke for his own pain as well as hers.

> I am incapable of telling you not to repine and rebel, because I have so, to my cost, the imagination of all things, and because I am incapable of telling you not to feel. Feel, *feel,* I say—feel for all you're worth, and even if it half kills you, for that is the only way to live, especially to live at *this* terrible pressure, and the only way to honour and celebrate these admirable beings who are our pride and our inspiration.

At the end of August 1915 he went to lunch with Wilfred Sheridan, who was going "back to front after a week's leave; he splendid and beautiful and occasion somehow such a pang—all unspeakable." Sheridan was killed three weeks after this entry, and James wrote his widow, "who can give you anything that approaches your incomparable sense that he was yours, and you his, to the last possessed and possessing radiance of him?"

The first elation and tension of the war, with the seizing at any and every rumor, the passing on of "inside" information gleaned out of thin air, gave way in James to an overwhelming sense of the loss of youth— "the destruction, on such a scale, of priceless young life." He was writing two months after the death of Rupert Brooke—the shining youth of his 1909 visit to Cambridge, who had died of blood poisoning after serving with the Royal Naval Division in the Dardanelles. "He isn't tragic now —he has only stopped," James wrote to Edward Marsh. He foresaw "a wondrous romantic, heroic legend will form." James agreed to write a preface to Brooke's posthumous book, *Letters from America.*

Closest of all perhaps, because it touched him intimately, was the army experience of his man Burgess, to whom James wrote as a father to a son, letters of the greatest simplicity and concreteness.

> What things you are seeing, and perhaps will still more see, and what tremendous matters you will have to tell us! . . . I think it wonderful for you to be able in the midst of such things to write to us at all, and we are very grateful.

Burgess was wounded early in his service. In mid-1915 he was back in England in a Leicester hospital with thirty shrapnel wounds, none of them serious. But the exploding shell had deafened him, as it turned out, for life. "You have clearly been very bravely through very stiff things, but have paid much less for it than you might," James wrote him. "Keep up your heart—there are many so much worse." Burgess was ultimately invalided home. Later by special dispensation he was allowed to remain in James's service.

Statesmen

James had had a last meeting with Henry Adams in the opening weeks of the war. Adams crossed from Paris, and remained in England until he could sail to America. James wrote to Mrs. Wharton that "Henry, alas, struck me as more changed and gone than he had been reported, though still with certain flickers and *gestes* of participation." The historian had had a stroke a few years earlier. He would return to Washington and there outlive Henry James.

The novelist saw other Americans in London; for he fell into the habit of periodically calling on Ambassador Walter Hines Page, and discussing with emotion America's failure to come to the aid of the Allies. He waited eagerly for news when Walter Berry went to Berlin on a mission. Berry was not reassuring. German morale was too high. James's nephew Harry also came abroad on a Belgian relief mission and brought back to his uncle some eye-witness experiences which the latter seized upon eagerly. Finally he had accounts from Mrs. Wharton of her visit to Verdun, and other fronts. John Bailey, an English critic who visited James in October of 1914, reported that "He is passionately English and says it is almost good that we were so little prepared, as it makes our moral position so splendid. He almost wept as he spoke."

Among those who heard the "trumpet note" of Henry James at this time was Margot Asquith, wife of the Prime Minister, Herbert H. Asquith. James had known both in earlier years—Margot when she was the young and marriageable daughter of a Scottish Liberal baronet. An accomplished hostess, Margot lost no time in having James to lunch at No. 10 Downing Street. Her luncheons were casual; prominent figures turned up and the Prime Minister, coming from his morning's conferences, never knew whom he would find at table. He found again, after some years, Henry James.

In December 1914, at one such luncheon, the Master chatted with General Sir Ian Hamilton; and it led to his dining with Viscount Haldane, the Lord Chancellor, in the company of Ambassador Page and Winston Churchill, First Lord of the Admiralty. Churchill was at the top of his younger form when James met him. He breathed war and action with wit and eloquence. James's comment after this occasion was simply that he found in the war leadership "no illusions, no ignorances, no superficialities"—and "deep confidence."

In the depth of that winter, early in January 1915, the Asquiths invited James to Walmer Castle, in Kent, near Deal, for one of their week-ends. The castle is a thick-walled machicolated old fortress with embrasures twenty feet deep. A halfway point—Dover was nearby—to the Western Front, it served symbolically to make the war leaders feel they were near their fighting men. Miss Bosanquet noted in her diary: "Mr. James being away weekending with Mr. Asquith and his daughter, Elizabeth, who is decidedly cultivating him, I had a free morning." Both Asquith's daughters, Violet, later Lady Violet Bonham-Carter, and Elizabeth, then a precocious seventeen but already a lively companion to her father, liked James; and he found them charming. "I don't do things easily nowadays," James wrote to his nephew on the day he made the trip to Walmer Castle. "But I thought this, in all the present conditions, almost a matter of duty, really not to be shirked." More than "duty," it was an occasion to assuage curiosity about the conduct of the war, the personalities involved, the social fabric in which England's leaders moved in a time of high stress. The "great Winston" was expected and other important guests.

The day was bright and cold. Walmer Castle was picturesque—a great terrace over the Channel—and James was thrilled to see the ships of England "going about their business in extraordinary numbers." Before dinner, writing to Edith Wharton to tell her that without the aid of her borrowed servant Frederick he would not have been able to accept this invitation, James said that "the sentiment the place makes one entertain in every way for old England is of the most acutely sympathetic." There seems later, however, to have been a collision between the First Lord of the Admiralty and the Master—the two most articulate men present on the occasion. Churchill, full of pride, confidence, faith, and swagger, accustomed to having the center of the scene, found Henry James at that center. The First Lord had never read James; he was impatient at the deference shown this old man who was so slow-spoken, even though his rhetoric was so remarkable—when he finally got it out. Churchill disregarded the Master; or he interrupted him. He showed him "no conversational consideration." He used a great deal of slang, some of which apparently grated on the novelist. The encounter was not a happy one for the Asquiths, who were very fond of Henry James.

When James was about to leave, at the end of the week-end, he said to Violet Asquith that it had been a very interesting, "very encouraging experience to meet that young man. It had brought home to me very forcibly—very vividly—the *limitations* by which men of genius obtain their ascendancy over mankind. It," said the Master, fumbling apparently for a bit of *argot* in the Churchill manner, "bucks one up."

James lunched again with the Prime Minister late in March of 1915 —"on the chance of catching some gleam between the chinks"—but had to content himself with the same rumors as everyone. The indefatigable Margot had sent James her diaries and he read all the old gossip with great relish. He was probably being ironic, however, when he wrote her that she was "the Balzac of diarists." The diaries had created "an admirable portrait of a lady, with no end of finish and style . . . if I don't stop now, I shall be calling it a regular masterpiece." He stopped.

He worked hard at this moment on an interview he had agreed to give to the *New York Times* on behalf of the American Volunteer Motor-Ambulance Corps. "H.J. finding," as Miss Bosanquet put it in her diary, that

> the Copy produced . . . wouldn't do at all from his point of view, has spent the last four days redictating the interview to the young man who is, fortunately, a good typist.

The result was published in the *Times Magazine* of 21 March 1915. It is doubtful whether the reporter was allowed to write a single sentence of his own. James artfully introduced sections on style, achievement, revisions in the New York Edition; but he focused mainly on the courage of England at war and the appeal for funds on behalf of the Volunteer Ambulance Corps, writing: "It is not for the wounded to oblige us by making us showy, but for us to let them count on our open arms and open lap as troubled children count on those of their mother."

In the interview James used a phrase which, during the Second World War, made its way into one of Churchill's major speeches: this was his allusion to the British—"this decent and dauntless people."

Treacheries

One day early in July 1915, James stopped at the Reform Club and was handed a parcel which had lain there unforwarded. The book it contained had an elaborate title-page: *Boon, The Mind of the Race, The Wild Asses of the Devil,* and *The Last Trump,* and purported to be "a first selection from the literary remains of George Boon." It was edited by one Reginald Bliss and "An Ambiguous Introduction by H. G. Wells" ended with the statement that "Bliss was Bliss and Wells is Wells. And Bliss can write all sorts of things that Wells could not do."

The book, it soon became clear, was a long and witty joke; it poked fun at many things and named many writers, not least Henry James, who was indeed the very center of the joke. Wells himself could not sign such a book; the little boy with the pea-shooter behind the prophet, seer, scientist-journalist-historian was treating himself to a lark. In "Chapter the Fourth," entitled "Of Art, of Literature, of Mr. Henry James," Wells constructed a dialogue on the novel between George Moore and Henry James, in which he let loose all his bottled-up anger against James's recent essay on "The Younger Generation" and the many unsolicited reviews of his novels the Master had sent him in their private correspondence. James had called Wells "cheeky" once too often; Wells now proved his cheekiness. "In all of his novels," Wells wrote of James,

> you will find no people with defined political opinions, no people with religious opinions, none with clear partisanships or with lusts or whims, none definitely up to any specific impersonal thing. There are no poor people dominated by the imperatives of Saturday night and Monday morning, no dreaming types—and don't we all more or less live dreaming? And none are ever decently forgetful. All that much of humanity he clears out before he begins his story.

A crucial passage in the dialogue, which would be quoted across the years, characterized a James novel as

> like a church lit but without a congregation to distract you, with every light and line focused on the high altar. And on the altar, very reverently placed, intensely there, is a dead kitten, an egg-shell, a bit of string. . . . It is leviathan retrieving pebbles. It is a magnificent but painful hippopotamus resolved at any cost, even at the cost of its dignity, upon picking up a pea, which has got into the corner of its den.

The character Boon then starts to write a novel in the James manner, an elaborate parody of *The Spoils of Poynton* interlarded with echoes from "The Turn of the Screw."

James read the chapter with bewilderment. He had always considered himself Wells's friend, and he wrote to him now with great simplicity, but also clearly in pain:

> It is difficult of course for a writer to put himself *fully* in the place of another writer who finds him extraordinarily futile and void, and who is moved to publish that to the world—and I think the case isn't easier when he happens to have enjoyed the other writer enormously, from far back; because there has then grown up the habit of taking some common meeting-ground between them for granted, and the falling away of this is like the collapse of a bridge which made communication possible.

He concluded by saying that "my poetic and my appeal to experience" rested upon *"my* measure of fulness—of fulness of life and of the projection of it, which seems to you such an emptiness of both."

Wells replied by being contrite. James had written "so kind and frank a letter after my offences that I find it an immense embarrassment to reply to you." There was, he said,

> a real and very fundamental difference in our innate and developed attitudes towards life and literature. To you literature like painting is an end, to me literature like architecture is a means, it has a use. Your view

was, I felt, too dominant in the world of criticism and I assailed it in tones of harsh antagonism.

But, he confessed, *Boon* was "just a wastepaper basket." He had written it to escape from the war. Wells ended, "I had rather be called a journalist than an artist, that is the essence of it, and there was no other antagonist possible than yourself." He signed himself James's "warm if rebellious and resentful admirer, and for countless causes yours most gratefully and affectionately."

James in his answer to Wells, his last letter to that writer, began by saying that he didn't think Wells had made out any sort of case for his bad manners: one simply didn't publish the contents of waste-baskets. He went on: "I live, live intensely and am fed by life, and my value, whatever it be, is in my own kind of expression of that. Art *makes* life, makes interest, makes importance," adding that he knew of no substitute whatever for "the force and beauty of its process."

Years later Wells in his autobiography, apparently still feeling some guilt over his behavior, sought to justify his attack on James. In reality his reminiscences were a renewed attack. Thus, where other writers are described—the brilliant fire in Conrad's eyes, the deportment of Shaw, the aspect of Crane—Wells could paint only the formal side of James: his habits and rituals, the special hats he wore for different occasions, the matching canes. But just as Wells had over-dressed himself for the first night of *Guy Domville,* compared with Shaw, so he singled out as formality those very objects which made James in reality look informal: his peaked cap, his colorful waistcoats, his varied walking sticks. James had come to represent for Wells the sovereignty and established power of the aristocracy and no matter how genial and accepting the American was, Wells faced him with an under-edge of hostility. "He saw us all as Masters or would-be Masters, little Masters and great Masters, and he was plainly sorry that *Cher Maître* was not an English expression," Wells wrote.

In the end he would try to excuse his attack by calling James "a little treacherous to me in a natural sort of way." Certainly there had been no treachery in James's attempt to have him elected to the Royal Society of Literature. But the Master had criticized his work—those proliferating social novels now judged obsolescent—with too much candor.

Loyalties

Early that summer of 1915, Henry James, friend of the Prime Minister, a singular figure in England's literary establishment, incessant worker among the wounded and the refugees, discovered to his deep chagrin that he was considered still—officially—an alien. When the time came to plan a summer at Rye, he was told he would have to report to the police. Rye was a forbidden zone. Aliens—however friendly—had to have permission to go there.

This gave James some troubled hours, the upshot of which was his writing to his nephew Harry, telling him he had decided to become a British subject. He had felt he should do this ever since the war began. He wanted now to take the only logical step that would "rectify a position that has become inconveniently and uncomfortably false."

> I have spent here all the best years of my life—they practically have *been* my life: about a twelvemonth hence I shall have been domiciled uninterruptedly in England for forty years, and there is not the least possibility, at my age, and in my state of health, of my ever returning to the U.S. or taking up any relation with it as a country.

He was telling Harry this simply to let him know; his mind was made up and he hoped his nephew would understand why he had taken such an important decision.

He did not wait for Harry's answer. He found out from his solicitor that all he needed to apply for British citizenship was to surrender his American passport, and have four persons testify—it amused him greatly —to his literacy as well as his good character. He turned to Gosse, in his exalted position as librarian of the House of Lords. And then it occurred to him that he could call on another excellent witness. There went forth on 28 June a letter from Henry James to Herbert H. Asquith at No. 10 Downing Street:

> I am venturing to trouble you with the mention of a fact of my personal situation, but I shall do so as briefly and considerately as possible. I desire to offer myself for naturalization in this country, that is, to change my status from that of American citizen to that of British subject.

He wished "to testify at this crisis to the force of my attachment and devotion to England and to the cause for which she is fighting."

> I can only testify by laying at her feet my explicit, my material and spiritual allegiance, and throwing into the scale of her fortune my all but imponderable moral weight—"a poor thing but mine own." Hence this respectful appeal.

Would the Prime Minister bear witness to Henry James's "apparent respectability, and to my speaking and writing English with an approach to propriety?"

Prime Minister Asquith was delighted. He went beyond the act of bearing witness to ask the Home Secretary Sir John Simon to facilitate the Master's desire to become a subject of the King. The application, to which Asquith, Gosse, George Prothero, and J. B. Pinker were witnesses, went through in record time. It contained the following statement:

> Because of his having lived and worked in England for the best part of forty years, because of his attachment to the Country and his sympathy with it and its people, because of the long friendships and associations and interests he has formed there these last including the acquisition of some property: all of which things have brought to a head his desire to throw his moral weight and personal allegiance, for whatever they may be worth, into the scale of the contending nation's present and future fortune.

At 4:30 P.M. on 28 July, having some weeks before surrendered his American passport, Henry James took the oath of allegiance to King George V. *"Civis Britannicus Sum,"* he proudly announced. He added: "I don't feel a bit different."

The news was formally proclaimed by *The Times:* "Mr. Henry James. Adoption of British Nationality." "All lovers of literature in this country," said the newspaper,

> will welcome the decision of this writer of genius, whose works are an abiding possession of all English-speaking peoples, and they will welcome it all the more on account of the reasons which Mr. James gives in his petition for naturalization.

The Master had expected the avalanche of mail that descended upon him from all parts of England. What he had not expected was the acute American resentment. To many Americans his swearing allegiance to the English King seemed a confirmation of the legend that he was "anti-American." James in the end simply shrugged his shoulders. It seemed to him highly irrational of a country which measured its own aliens by the speed with which they became naturalized Americans.

He could now go and come freely. But his health was poor and his life had become constricted. He was learning to take for granted, he said in a letter to Edith Wharton, "that I shall probably on the whole *not* die of simple sick horror—than which nothing seems to me at the same time more amazing. One aches to anguish and rages to suffocation, and one is still there to do it again, and the occasion still there to see that one does." He lived in a world of death: everyone is killed, he remarked, who belongs to anyone, and one was getting the habit of looking "straight and dry-eyed, hard and arid, at those to whom they belonged." However he mustered sufficient strength to be entertained by the Prime Minister on the day of his naturalization. It was one of the last dinners James attended in London.

The Mulberry Tree

In January of 1915 James received word that the large mulberry tree in his garden at Lamb House had been toppled by a violent storm. To Mrs. Dacre Vincent, a Rye friend who sent him these tidings, he answered in personal terms—

> He might have gone on for some time, I think, in the absence of an *inordinate* gale—but once the fury of the tempest really descended he was bound to give way, because his poor old heart was dead, his immense old trunk was hollow.

James had hoped to go to Rye shortly after his naturalization in the mid-summer of 1915. But he was ill throughout August and with effort finished his preface to Rupert Brooke's *Letters from America.* The prose of that essay shows, however, little strain; it is a beautiful eulogy and was James's last piece of writing. Long before, he had stopped work on *The Ivory Tower.* That novel was too actual; the war seemed to make it obsolete. Instead he turned to *The Sense of the Past,* which he had set aside in 1900, and worked intermittently on this, but half-heartedly. Its subject had always been too difficult.

He did not go to Rye until 14 October. During the year he had been away he had loaned Lamb House to various persons who needed temporary housing, and he was turning it over to still another tenant. Mrs. William James later said that while he was there this time "he burned up quantities of papers and photographs—cleared his drawers in short." In the midst of this he developed acute symptoms and sat up for three nights breathing with difficulty. Ernest Skinner told him there was a change in his heart rhythm—he seems to have had intermittent tachycardia or auricular fibrillation—and prescribed digitalis. He was able to return to London, where Sir James Mackenzie confirmed the diagnosis. In November James wrote to Rhoda Broughton, "Bustling is at an end for me for ever now—though indeed, after all, I have had very little hand in it for many a day." Hugh returned from Russia at this time and talked to the Master over the phone from Cornwall. James wrote to him tenderly: "Do intensely believe that I respond clutchingly to your every grasp of me, every touch, and would so gratefully be a reconnecting link with you here." "Delightful letter from H.J.," Hugh wrote in his diary; "—one of the most truly affectionate I've ever had from him."

Mrs. Wharton had been in London a few weeks earlier and had telephoned James, wanting to drive him to Qu'Acre to see Howard Sturgis. He told her he was too ill. She then asked him whether he could lend Miss Bosanquet to her for the day. Miss Bosanquet, as she later recorded, "made a rather flurried way" to Buckland's Hotel in Brook Street, where she found the lady novelist in an elegant pink negligee, with her arms "very much displayed." The central heating was turned up too high for Miss Bosanquet's comfort.

"Of course," said the Firebird, "I didn't really want you to come here to write letters for me, but just so that we might have a quiet talk." Miss Bosanquet, knowing the closeness of Mrs. Wharton's relation to the Master, spoke candidly of his ever-increasing illnesses. The doctors now considered that James had a real, not a psychological, heart condition. Thus Mrs. Wharton established a link within the Master's household, which would enable her to act, if some emergency occurred.

Early in the morning of Thursday, 2 December 1915, James's maid, Minnie Kidd, came to Miss Bosanquet's flat in nearby Lawrence Street and told her that Mr. James seemed to have had "a sort of stroke." The maid had been in the dining-room at eight-thirty and heard the Master calling. She entered his bedroom. He was lying on the floor; his left leg had given way under him. She called Burgess, and between them they got James into bed. Miss Bosanquet came at once to Carlyle Mansions. James was open-eyed and calm. He had had, he told her, a stroke "in the most approved fashion." The most distressing thing, he said, was that in wanting to ring for his servants he had found himself fumbling with the electrical wiring of the bedlamp. He had then called for help. Edith Wharton reported he told Fanny Prothero, after the first stroke, that in the very act of falling "he heard in the room a voice which was distinctly, it seemed, not his own, saying, 'So here it is at last, the distinguished thing.' "

Dr. Des Voeux arrived promptly and confirmed that it was a stroke, a slight one. The Master then dictated a cable to his nephew: "Had slight stroke this morning. No serious symptoms. Perfect care. No suffering. Wrote Peggy yesterday." In the long letter James had written the previous day to his niece, he had recounted his recent illnesses, described life in London, complained of his sleepless nights. He told Peggy of Burgess being back on extended leave from service. Then he felt tired and ended his letter with the words "the pen drops from my hand!"

It had indeed dropped, and for all time. Mrs. William James cabled that she was sailing at once; she had promised her husband she would "see Henry through when he comes to the end." Miss Bosanquet meanwhile took charge. On the second day, Dr. Des Voeux announced that James had had a second stroke. The paralysis of his left side was more complete. He called in Sir James Mackenzie. They pronounced the novelist to be in grave condition, and that night his neighbor Emily Sargent and her sister Mrs. Ormond stayed up in the flat in case they should be wanted. The doctor brought in two nurses. Miss Bosanquet sent a second cable to Harry James and also telegraphed Mrs. Wharton, who was at Hyères. Within twenty-four hours, the patient had rallied and was calling for a thesaurus to discover the exact descriptive word for his condition. He didn't think "paralytic" was right.

A Terror of Consciousness

Two diaries were kept during Henry James's last illness. Miss Bosanquet's records with some minuteness the comings and goings, the daily reports of the doctors, and such talk of the Master's as she heard. Mrs. William James began a diary shortly after her arrival, in which she wrote down certain remarks made by James. These reveal that he was from the first disturbed about his "sense of place," and then, as he struggled to orient himself in the scale of his mental wanderings, he experienced a strange terror. He began to think he was mad—and that his visitors would notice he was mad. There had apparently been some brain damage from his second stroke.

This condition went at first unnoticed; he seemed simply to be rambling. On 10 December Miss Bosanquet recorded "mind clouded this morning and he has lost his own unmistakeable identity—is just a simple sick man." He was running a temperature; the doctors found he had a clot in his lung. In this condition, James spoke to Miss Bosanquet very strongly and clearly about wanting to take Burgess to Lady Hyde's with him. He would then send Burgess back. "Where am I?" he asked. "What is this address?" When Miss Bosanquet told him it was 21 Carlyle Mansions, he answered, "How very curious, that's Lady Hyde's address too." On the next day he spoke of himself as being in a strange hotel far away from London. On 13 December he wanted to know where certain manuscripts were; he thought they had gone to Ireland. In the latter part of the day he spoke of himself as being in Cork. Mrs. William James arrived that evening, 13 December, after a stormy crossing. James seemed glad to see her. He patted her hand and said, "I don't dare to think of what you have come through to get here." Then he began to speak of being in California, probably because Mrs. James had been there with Peggy during the preceding summer. He complained that he was constantly surrounded by women. "The absence of the male element in my entourage is what perplexes me."

The confusion returned on 16 December when the barber came to shave him. Later James told Miss Bosanquet it was "most painful and distressing" to be spoken of as if he were in London. Even the barber was in on the conspiracy. "When I asked him this morning if he'd been in London recently he actually said he was here now." After tea on this day he wanted to know whether someone could help clear up his mystification. "I have a curious sense," James said, "that I'm not the bewildering puzzle to all of you that you are to me." He again spoke of the absence of males with the "negligible exception of Burgess and the doctor."

The next day James again said he was in Cork. His return again and again to that city may have been a memory of the death of his mother. He had been in Cork only once—on his journey back to England after Mary James died.

On 21 December when Miss Bosanquet came into the bedroom, James said: "This place in which I find myself is the strangest mixture of Edinburgh and Dublin and New York and some other place that I don't know." Miss Bosanquet mentioned Mrs. Wharton, and James asked: "Does she seem at all aware of my state?" James may have been talking of his mental state; Miss Bosanquet believed he was referring to the state of his illness. On 22 December she noted that

> he looked desperately ill—his face all drawn and wasted and unshaved, head falling right over to the paralysed side, and his body barely covered by a brownish Jaeger blanket—his feet sticking out beyond it at the bottom . . . If ever a man looked dying, he did.

During Christmas James suddenly became restless. He was moved into the drawing-room and then from one chair to another. "He was furiously angry with everyone who tried to reason with him." In the afternoon the whole household was prostrate, "Kidd and Burgess flat in the kitchen, the nurse hysterical in the passage." The next day some movement seemed to have returned to James's arm and leg. He was again moved into the drawing-room, where Miss Bosanquet found him looking "a complete wreck of his former self now, and his eyes have a strained, wandering expression—they don't look intelligently at one a bit." The following day he was profoundly depressed. He kept saying good-bye to each member of his household.

During the early days of January there seemed to be some improvement and on 12 January he asked if he mightn't go to Rye. Then he seems to have made the journey in his mind, for he spoke to Burgess of how nice it was to be back in Lamb House. He showed an increasing concern about the effect he was having on other people. He asked Burgess whether his muddled condition of mind didn't make people laugh. Mrs. James intervened defensively, "Never, Henry, no one wants to smile." The Master fixed her with his right eye—the left eyelid was drooping because of the stroke: "What is this irrelevant voice from Boston, Massachusetts, breaking in with remarks in my conversation with Burgess?"

On another occasion he seems to have been imagining one of his plays was being produced. He asked Mrs. James, "What effect will my madness have on the house?" Then he waved to Mrs. James "not to speak before them," meaning the nurses. He indicated he wished to conceal his "madness" from them.

Read in their fragmented form, these partial records of James's mental confusion suggest a kind of heroic struggle to retain his grasp on reality in the midst of his death-in-life. The Master may have been living out that "terror of consciousness" with which he had sought to endow his hero in the unfinished novel *The Sense of the Past*. He had actually turned over some of its pages on the evening before his stroke. In his notes for this novel James had spoken of his hero, walking into the year 1820 with his knowledge of the future, as being "in danger of passing for a madman." He feels "cut off . . . and lost." In his sense of being cut off from those around him, in the grim comedy of confusing London and Cork, James was apparently living out a part of his fiction. Shuttling in his confused memory between the cities of his pilgrimages—the Ireland of his father and grandfather, the London, Rome, Edinburgh, of his own experience—he had a sense of being in two places at once. Memory became actual; the actual of the sickroom intruded on memory. And the danger of his being thought mad was a terror imposed on the terror of death.

Final and Fading Words

During the first period of his confusion, before the arrival of Mrs. William James, when his fever was high, Henry James had wanted to write. He kept asking for paper and pencil. When he got it, his hand would make the movements of writing. Then he wanted to dictate. The typewriter was brought into the sickroom. The familiar sound pacified him. "I find the business of coming round about as important and glorious as any circumstances I have had occasion to record, by which I mean that I find them as damnable and as boring," he dictated to Miss Bosanquet. The sentences that followed were spoken slowly and with many pauses, as if he were making a great effort to mobilize his thoughts. "Such is my sketchy state of mind, but I feel sure I shall discover plenty of fresh worlds to conquer"—and he added, "even if I am to be cheated of the amusement of them."

The Master's mind was disintegrating; but it still had its moments of logic. On 11 December, he called once more for the typewriter and dictated words about touching "the large old phrase into the right amplitude . . . we simply shift the sweet nursling of genius from one maternal breast to the other and the trick is played, the false note averted." Then he exclaimed: "Astounding little stepchild of God's astounding young step-mother!" There followed a passage that seemed to recall the war, but it became confused with his reading of Napoleonic memoirs. Sometimes

Miss Bosanquet missed a word; sometimes his thought was discontinuous.

> . . . on this occasion moreover that, having been difficult to keep step . . . we hear of the march of history, what is remaining to that essence of tragedy, the limp? . . .
>
> . . . mere patchwork transcription becomes of itself the high brave art. We . . . five miles off at the renewed affronts that we see coming for the great, and that we know they will accept. The fault is that they had found themselves too easily great, and the effect of that, definitely, had been, within them, the want of long provision for it. It wasn't why they [were] to have been so thrust into the limelight and the uproar, but why they [were] to have known as by inspiration the trade most smothered in experience. They go about shivering in the absence of the holy protocol—they dodder sketchily about as in the betrayal of the lack of early advantages; and it is upon *that* they seem most to depend to give them distinction— it is upon that, and upon the *crânerie* and the *rouerie* that they seem most to depend for the grand air of gallantry. They pluck in their terror handfuls of plumes from the imperial eagle, and with no greater credit in consequence than that they face, keeping their equipoise, the awful bloody beak [of] that vindictive intention, during these days of cold grey Switzerland weather on the huddled and hustled after campaigns of the first omens of defeat. Everyone looks haggard and our only wonder is that they still succeed in "looking" at all. It renews for us the assurance of the part played by that element in the famous assurance [divinity] that doth hedge a king.

During recent months James had seen his old Roman friend Count Primoli who was a Bonaparte and Princess Victor Napoléon of Belgium. Perhaps some recollection of this caused him to dictate on the next day —12 December—the sentence, "the Bonapartes have a kind of bronze distinction that extends to their fingertips and is a great source of charm in the women." He went on to say, "therefore they don't have to swagger after the fact; fortune has placed them too high and anything less would be trivial." He rang in a change: "There have been great families of tricksters and conjurors; so why not this one, and so pleasant withal?" That he was moving in consciousness from the Napoleonic family to the James family is suggested by the sentence immediately following: "Our admirable father keeps up the pitch. He is the dearest of men." Then he went back to the Napoleonic legend:

> I should have liked above all things seeing our sister pulling her head through the crown; one has that confident . . . and I should have had it most on the day when most would have been asked. But we jog on very well. Up to the point of the staircase where the officers do stand it couldn't

be better, though I wonder at the *souffle* which so often enables me to pass.

We are back from . . . but we breathe at least together and I am devotedly yours . . .

The sudden transition suggests that James was thinking of himself as dictating letters.

"After luncheon," Miss Bosanquet noted (still on 12 December),

he wanted me again and dictated, perfectly clearly and coherently two letters from Napoleon Bonaparte to one of his married sisters . . . After he had finished the second letter he seemed quite satisfied not to do any more and fell into a peaceful sleep.

Actually the first letter was the Bonaparte letter, and James signed it with the original Corsican form "Napoleone"; the second letter, no less Napoleonic in its sharpness of tone and military eloquence, was signed with his own name, and sounded as if he had gone out into the world and had conquered, and was allowing William and Alice to share in the spoils. The first began:

Dear and most esteemed Brother and Sister,
    I call your attention to the precious enclosed transcripts of plans and designs for the decoration of certain apartments of the palaces here, the Louvre and the Tuileries, which you will find addressed in detail to artists and workmen who are to take them in hand. I commit them to your earnest care till the questions relating to this important work are fully settled. When that is the case I shall require of you further zeal and further taste . . .

And the second read in part:

My dear Brother and Sister,
    I offer you great opportunities, in exchange for the exercise of great zeal. Your position as residents in our young but so highly considered Republic at one of the most interesting minor capitals is a piece of luck which may be turned to account in the measure of your acuteness and your experience. A brilliant fortune may come to crown it and your personal merit will not diminish that harmony. . . . I have displayed you as persons of great taste and judgment. Don't leave me a sorry figure in consequence but present me rather as your fond but not infatuated relation, able and ready to back you up, your faithful Brother and Brother-in-law,   Henry James.

Some other passages of dictation were taken down at various times in longhand by James's niece. One of them comes close to modern "stream of consciousness" in its fragmentation and discontinuity:

across the border

all the pieces

Individual souls, great of . . . on which great perfections are If one does . . . in the fulfilment with the neat and pure and perfect—to the success or as he or she moves through life, following admiration unfailing . . . in the highway—Problems are very sordid.

On a day of sore throat and much malaise, he seemed to show an awareness that he no longer could command his old coherence. "These final and faded remarks," he dictated, "have some interest and some character —but this should be extracted by a highly competent person only—some such whom I don't presume to name, will furnish such last offices." Implicit in this was the lingering of an old curiosity, his sense that all of life, even the act of dying, had interest, to be discerned and recorded. The rest of the passage, however, has in it a note of despair and then of resignation:

invoke more than one kind presence, several could help, and many would —but it all better too much left than too much done. I never dreamed of such duties as laid upon me. This sore throaty condition is the last I ever invoked for the purpose.

The Distinguished Thing

Lord Morley, later Viscount Morley of Blackburn, statesman and man of letters, had always regarded Henry James as a superficial and trivial person. Almost forty years before, he had told the Macmillans he found James's essays on French poets and novelists simply "honest scribble-work." Late in 1915 Prime Minister Asquith told Morley that he was thinking of recommending James for the Order of Merit, the greatest distinction conferred by the Crown on civilians. As a British subject James was now eligible for this honor, held by two other novelists, Thomas Hardy and George Meredith. Morley objected. What had James done but write of the idle rich, as compared with Hardy's personages? Asquith wavered. He was fond of Henry James. He knew that he was gravely ill. And the New Year's honors list was almost ready.

Edward Marsh, who had served as Winston Churchill's secretary, was now attached to the Prime Minister's office. On 18 December he wrote to the Prime Minister "in the hope that the question of the Order of Merit for Henry James has not been irrevocably set aside." There was, he argued, little doubt of James's right to stand beside Meredith and Hardy. If they had qualities not in James, it was equally true James had qualities which they did not possess. "It has been said," Marsh went on, that the great French novelists are conscious artists, the English inspired amateurs. Henry James is the exception. No writer of his time gives the same impression of knowledge and mastery in the architectural structure of his works, and in the gradual building up of atmosphere, character, and situation.

Marsh mentioned the prefaces to the New York Edition, "a uniquely illuminating account of an artist's creative processes." He pointed to James's influence on other writers—listing Bennett, Wells, Mrs. Wharton. He invoked Stevenson's regard for James; he mentioned Edmund Gosse. He said he was certain "the profession of letters as a whole would warmly welcome this appointment." There were two extraneous considerations. One was James's generous and impressive gesture of adherence to England's cause. And the other was that the United States would appreciate the compliment to an American-born writer such as James. "I understand Lord Morley is against the proposal; but with the greatest respect for him I could wish that some opinion might be taken which would be representative of a later epoch in taste."

Asquith needed just such arguments to stiffen the case for James against Morley. Two days after Marsh submitted the memorandum, a message came from Buckingham Palace, signed by the King's secretary. "The King, acting upon your recommendation of the case, will be prepared to confer the Order of Merit upon Henry James."

On New Year's day, a great pile of telegrams and letters descended on Carlyle Mansions. One was a note from George Alexander, who said that he was proud to have produced *Guy Domville* even though it had not been a success. Lord Bryce brought the insignia of the order to James's bedside. The distinguished invalid seemed pleased although he was vague and his mind wandered. Mrs. James read him some of the telegrams and he said, "what curious manifestations such occasions call forth!"

Things became a little easier during the first days of the new year. Peggy after a rough wintry voyage reached her uncle's bedside. James's mind seemed clearer; he signed a power of attorney for Mrs. William James to allow her to take care of all the servants and the bills. But at this time Miss Bosanquet found a note written by Peggy criticizing her for having taken too much upon herself and that she had seemed to be getting pleasure "managing things in a heartless sort of way." In a letter to her oldest brother, Peggy said the amanuensis had been "getting a bit above herself." In reality the trouble was that Mrs. William did not like Miss Bosanquet's writing about James's condition to Mrs. Wharton—she so disliked Mrs. Wharton, whose morals, Peggy had told her mother, "are scarcely such as to fit her to be the companion of the young and innocent." From this time on Miss Bosanquet found herself more and more excluded from 21 Carlyle Mansions. She came daily to inquire about her employer but stayed only if asked to do a specific bit of work. Deeply hurt, she was unaware that New England puritanism as well as bourgeois morality had played a large role in her banishment.

In January, James's nephew Harry arrived. "He has a tremendous chin—the most obstinate-looking jaw," Miss Bosanquet noted. Preparing himself to be James's executor, Harry asked her to go through the unfinished typescripts and make lists. He went to Rye and had inventories made of the furnishings and the books. Mrs. William wondered which furniture to take back to America from Lamb House. In the midst of these preparations for the novelist's death, it began to dawn on her that Henry James was a great and important figure; that the English stood in awe of him. She had for so long accepted the idea that he was simply William's artistic brother, a kind, amiable, gentle, idiosyncratic man.

Some of her letters to her sons in America are touching in their picture of the Master finally at bay:

> He seems like a tired child but tranquil, comfortable, enjoying his food and the sitting on a big lounge in the window whence he can look out at the river, with the ever-creeping barges and the low-lying clouds. He thinks he is voyaging and visiting foreign cities, and sometimes he asks for his glasses and paper and imagines that he writes. And sometimes his hand moves over the counterpane as if writing. He is never impatient, or contrary or troubled about anything. He still recognizes us and likes to have us sit awhile beside him. He very especially likes Burgess—"Burgess James" he called him yesterday. It is a touching sight to see little Burgess holding his hand and half kneeling in the chair beside him, his face very near to Henry, trying to understand the confused words Henry murmurs to him.

James thought, as he watched the boats on the Thames, that he was on a ship. When he asked for Burgess on one occasion, Mrs. James said he was out on errands. "How extraordinary that Burgess should be leaving the ship to do errands!" he exclaimed. To Peggy he turned one day and said, "I hope your father will be in soon—he is the one person in all Rome I want to see." And again, "I should so like to have William with me."

The Master continued on this plateau until the last week of February. On the 23rd when Mrs. William came into the sickroom he said to her, "Beloved Alice," and then told her to tell William he was leaving in two days. Two days later he was seriously ill. On the 24th he spoke of "a night of horror and terror." On the next day, "stay with me, Alice, stay with me." He lapsed into unconsciousness on that day. On 27 February the nurse summoned Mrs. William. The novelist was breathing hard and trembling. She sat beside him till the symptoms passed and he slept. His pulse and temperature were normal. He tried to speak during the day but his words were unintelligible. On 28 February he could take no nourishment. At four that afternoon the doctor said, "This is the end." James was breathing in short gasps. At six he sighed—three sighing breaths, at long intervals, the last one, Mrs. William James noted, "very faint." She wrote, "He was gone. Not a shadow on his face, nor the contraction of a muscle."

Henry James O.M.

Miss Bosanquet, arriving at Carlyle Mansions that evening, met Emily Sargent in the hall and learned the news. She left a note for Mrs. James and then wired Edith Wharton, who wrote to her that James had been "one of the wisest and noblest men that ever lived." On the 29th Miss Bosanquet asked if she could be of help; she was assured that "everything had been provided for." There was talk of a service in Westminster Abbey; it was however not feasible and Mrs. William decided in favor of a funeral in Chelsea Old Church. The body remained in Carlyle Mansions. Burgess gave his master his last shave. The coffin was brought and James was placed in it.

Miss Bosanquet returned on 1 March and was taken into the drawing-room by Minnie Kidd. Henry James O.M. lay in his coffin. It was covered with a black pall and there was a white square over his face which the maid folded back. The face was bandaged to keep the jaw from falling. "It looked very fine," Miss Bosanquet wrote, "a great work of art in ivory wax. Perfectly peaceful, but entirely dissociated from everything that was his personality."

She went back and viewed the body on the next day. The Master looked more like his living self because this time there was no bandage around his face. "Several people who have seen the dead face are struck with the likeness to Napoleon which is certainly great."

At the outbreak of the war James had inscribed *Notes on Novelists* to Edmund Gosse with the words "Over the Abyss." In a letter to *The Times* on the day after the funeral, Gosse conveyed the emotion of the mourners who overflowed Chelsea Old Church.

> As we stood round the shell of that incomparable brain, of that noble and tender heart, it flashed across me that to generations yet unawakened to a knowledge of his value the Old Chelsea Church must for ever be the Altar of the Dead.

To the old church, which had seen much literary history, there came, in the midst of war, those who had known Henry James and cherished him —Kipling, Gosse, Jessie Allen, Lucy Clifford; representatives of the Prime

Minister and the war group James had met. Dickens's daughter, Mrs. Perugini, was there, and Howard Sturgis, the Colvins, the Pollocks, and many others including Ellen Terry. Mrs. James, Peggy, Sargent and his sister sat in the front pew; the servants sat on the opposite side. Fanny Prothero wandered in and found herself a seat far back. The service was conventional—the lesson from I Corinthians and two hymns, "For all the Saints" and "O God, our help in ages past."

A plaque honoring James and speaking of "amenities of brave decisions" hangs on the wall of the church. Sixty years later England paid its ultimate honor by unveiling a memorial stone to James in the Poets' Corner of Westminster Abbey.

The body was cremated at Golders Green. Mrs. James took the ashes back to America. She smuggled them in; it was wartime and she took no chances. The urn was buried beside the graves of Henry's mother and sister, where he had stood in 1904 and looked at the "Medusa face of life" and cried *Basta! Basta!*

James left all his property to Mrs. William James and after her to her children. His estate was valued at less than £9000—exclusive of his share of the James properties in Syracuse. Harry received Lamb House, valued at £2100, and its contents. Peggy got his insurance. James bestowed gifts of £100 on Jocelyn Persse, Hugh Walpole, and Lucy Clifford. All the servants were provided for. There were gifts to various nephews and nieces, children of his younger brother, but a codicil withdrew the gift from his nephew Edward Holton James, because he had written an anti-royalist pamphlet which had embarrassed his uncle.

The obituaries—in newspapers filled with the war—were of great length. One newspaper inquiring into the status of James's works found that very few of the Master's novels were in print, and the late ones were expensively available only in the New York Edition. James would indeed sink from sight; swallowed up by the war, his would be among the forgotten reputations of the 1920s, although an occasional subject of controversy, mainly about his expatriation. When the Second World War came he was, however, remembered and read, and by the mid-twentieth century his books were in print in great numbers. Long after his death, he was constantly quoted—certain of his phrases reverberating into modernity. The secret of his enduring fame was simple: he had dealt exclusively with the myth of civilization; he had written about men and women in their struggle to control their emotions and passions within the forms and manners of society. He understood human motive and behavior and was the first of the modern psychological novelists. He had carried his art into a high complexity and he had endured because he had fashioned a style. He had had great ambitions; he had sought power in craft and had found it; he had shown how artists take the chaos of life and shape it into forms that endure. Younger men would find him a signpost, a guide, a vast encompassing intelligence. Ezra Pound would speak of him as a Baedeker to a continent. His influence was pervasive—the entire "modern movement," from Joyce to Virginia Woolf, drew upon his explorations of subjective worlds. Correspondents kept his letters; several thousand survive, in his expansive mandarin style. Those of his later years speak with considerable freedom of his feelings and express his complex humanity: many, filled with his characteristic gentleness and tenderness, his ability to enter into other people's lives, are regarded as highest examples of the epistolary art. The memory of his wit also remained, and of his courage. His eulogy of Jeffrey Aspern might have been written of himself:

> ... at a period when our native land was nude and crude and provincial, when the famous "atmosphere" it is supposed to lack was not even missed, when literature was lonely there and art and form almost impossible, he had found means to live and write like one of the first; to be free and general and not at all afraid; to feel, understand and express everything.

Long before, he had urged young novelists to "be generous and delicate and pursue the prize." The prize for him had been always the treasure of his craft. He felt powerful because he knew that his imagination could transfigure life. He had written some years before his death an essay, "Is There a Life After Death?" If one meant physical life, James believed there was none. Death was absolute. What lived beyond life was what the creative consciousness had found and made: and only if enshrined in enduring form.

In one of the last sentences of the essay he wrote: "I reach beyond the laboratory brain." This was his final word to the new age.

ACKNOWLEDGMENTS

I am indebted to Alexander R. James, grandson of William James, and to various members of the James family for certain priorities given me long ago in the family papers. The children of Robertson James also provided documents, including the diary of Alice James. The libraries and librarians at the time of the writing of the original biography and editing of the letters have had my thanks in earlier publications. The greatest single collection of documents relating to Henry James is in the Houghton Library at Harvard; other papers and letters will be found in the Bancroft Library, Berkeley, the C. Waller Barrett Collection, University of Virginia, the Berg Collection in the New York Public Library, the Morgan Library, the Miller Library of Colby College, the Humanities Research Center at the University of Texas and the Beinecke Rare Book and Manuscript Library at Yale. A list of holdings of Henry James letters appears in the final volume of my edition of the letters.

The present volume benefits from interviews I conducted earlier in the century with Clive Bell, E. F. Benson, Bernard Berenson, Henri Bernstein, Theodora Bosanquet, Alvin Langdon Coburn, Mrs. Edward Compton, Lucien Daudet, Mary Robinson Duclaux, Sir Johnston Forbes-Robertson and his wife Gertrude Elliott, Ford Madox Ford, W. Morton Fullerton, David Garnett, Harley Granville-Barker, Ambassador J. J. Jusserand, Gertrude Kingston, Gaillard Lapsley, Percy Lubbock, Katherine Lewis, Maurice Maeterlinck, Urbain Mengin, Margaret Perry, Elizabeth Robins, George Bernard Shaw, Countess Ursel de Sartiges, Logan Pearsall Smith, Allan Wade, H. M. Walbrook, Dorothy Ward, Peter Warren and Edith Wharton.

Among recent debts incurred I wish to thank Louis S. Auchincloss, Alan Bell, General Marius Daille, Richard Garnett, Phyllis Grosskurth, Mrs. Paul Hammond, Sir Rupert Hart-Davis, Mrs. Stanley Hawks, Frederica and Harold M. Landon, Anita Leslie, Sir Compton Mackenzie, Robert Mengin, Simon Nowell-Smith, S. Gorley Putt, Dr. Gordon N. Ray, Roger Senhouse, Stephen Spender, Patricia Curtis Vigano, Sir John F. B. Watson, Dr. Octavia Wilberforce. I am particularly indebted to Adeline R. Tintner and her husband Dr. Henry D. Janowitz.

NOTES

The notes which follow are intended as a general guide to the sources from which this edition is drawn. Most of the notes are confined to the new material and to the revised or rewritten sections. Initials are used for the principal figures: HJ Sr., HJ (the novelist), WJ (William), and AJ (Alice); HJL (*Henry James Letters,* four volumes, issued by Harvard University Press, 1974–84). Researchers will find annotation in the five-volume edition, New York and London, 1953–72.

PART ONE: The Untried Years, 1843–1870

page

20   *Notes on a Nightmare:* A nightmare similar to the one James describes in *A Small Boy and Others* (1913) is recorded in Ottoline Morrell's *Memoirs,* ed. Gathorne-Hardy (1963), pp. 171–72, as well as another dream containing similar content.

56   *An Obscure Hurt:* Ernest Hemingway was the creator of the legend that James was impotent. Hemingway's version was that it was caused by a bicycle or horseback-riding accident. He incorporated this in *The Sun Also Rises* (1926) in Chapter XII but Maxwell Perkins, his editor at Scribner's, induced him to remove the name James and simply use Henry. Hemingway wrote Perkins it was "generally known to have happened to Henry James in his youth." See Hemingway, *Selected Letters,* ed. Baker (1981), pp. 208–9. The novelist appears not to have read HJ's autobiography *Notes of a Son and Brother* (1914) but developed his fantasy from Van Wyck Brooks's *The Pilgrimage of Henry James* (1925) which appeared while he was writing his novel. Brooks wrote that HJ had been "prevented by an accident from taking part" in the Civil War. See also *Correspondence of F. Scott Fitzgerald,* ed. Bruccoli-Duggan-Walker (1980), p. 170. Fitzgerald writes to Brooks that he had just read *Pilgrimage* and "so did Zelda and Hemminway [sic]," adding, "Why didn't you touch more on James's impotence (physical) and its influence?"

Chapter XII in *The Sun Also Rises* has a conversation between the impotent Jake Barnes and his friend Bill Gorton. After Barnes refers to his First World War "accident," Gorton says: "That's the sort of thing that can't be spoken of. That's what you ought to work up into a mystery. Like Henry's bicycle." Barnes replies it wasn't a bicycle, "he was riding horseback." The Hemingway fantasy was accepted by R. P. Blackmur, who equated the accident with Abelard's castration (*Literary History of the U.S.* [1950] II, p. 1040); F. O. Matthiessen, *The James Family* (1947), who raised the question of impotence; Lionel Trilling in *The Liberal Imagination* (1950), p. 169—"only a man as devoted to the truth of emotions, as Henry James was, would have informed the world despite his characteristic reticence of an accident so intimate as his." See also *Hound and Horn* (April 1943), p. 522, in which Glenway Wescott speaks of "expatriation and castration." Stephen Spender in *The Destructive Element* (1935), pp. 36–37, alone among critics called the idea of HJ being castrated "exaggerated and improbable." See also Saul Rosenzweig, "The Ghost of Henry James," in *Character and Personality* (December 1943) and Adeline R. Tintner, "Ernest and Henry" in *Ernest Hemingway: The Writer in Context,* ed. Nagel (1984).

79   *Jacob and Esau:* For "twinship" and individuation, see Howard M. Feinstein, *Becoming William James* (1984), pp. 138–39, 223–35, 322–23, 345–45. The passages dealing with James's tales of this period have been rewritten.

97   *The Dishevelled Nymph:* Although in *A Small Boy* (1913) HJ speaks of his typhus in Boulogne as the gravest illness of his life, he tended in later years to treat his "obscure hurt" as inaugurating a state of "invalidism" which most of his early critics accepted. Given James's active pursuit of his career and his travels, the word *invalidism* seems hardly appropriate. Jean Strouse, *Alice James* (1980) and Feinstein have enlarged our picture of James family illnesses by showing how "invalidism" in the James family was in reality at certain times a way in which the children manipulated their parents. AJ's invalidism became her way of life. In the case of HJ and WJ —and especially with HJ—it seems to have been psychosomatic. HJ's constipation, described by him in a series of unpublished letters to WJ from Florence in 1869 (Houghton Library, 7, 16 and 26 October), relate his condition to his back injury during the Newport fire. This seems the only time during which he was thus troubled. In one of these letters HJ describes a rectal examination by an Irish doctor in Florence who was able to reassure him that there was no "palpable obstruction" and no hemorrhoids had developed. His illnesses of this period seem to have been of the same order as his migraines, which usually accompanied situations of frustration and suppressed rage—some due to financial pressures from Quincy Street.

104   *Minny Temple:* Her letters to John Gray were apparently copied out for HJ's use in *Notes of a Son and Brother* by Mrs. WJ.

PART TWO: Years of Saturation, 1870–1875

117   *The Precious Wound:* The "tentacles" of Boston and Cambridge, HJL IV, pp. 657–58, 1 April 1913.

155   *William:* For a detailed account of WJ's troubled relations with his parents see Feinstein.

163   *The Palpable Present:* Literary reference and "the museum world," see Edel, the HJ issue of *Revue de Littérature Comparée,* July-September 1983, "The 'Felt' Life of Henry James," pp. 269–73. Adeline R. Tintner's numerous papers have illuminated the "museum world."

page
171   *A New York Winter:* HJ's letters to Arthur George Sedgwick were made
      available to me by his daughter, Mrs. Paul Hammond.

PART THREE: The Conquest of London, 1875–1881

199   *In the Provinces:* Visit to Le Perthuis. See *Portraits of Places* (1883), "From
      Normandy to the Pyrenees," pp. 165–73. HJ's letters to Childe were made
      available to me by the Countess Ursel de Sartiges.
229   *The Bachelor of Bolton Street:* I have extended this chapter to include a
      certain amount of speculation about HJ's sexual reticences.
244   *A "Divorce":* This chapter replaces an earlier account of the effect of WJ's
      marriage on HJ. See Richard Hall, "The Sexuality of Henry James" in *New
      Republic,* 28 April 1979, pp. 26–29, and 5 May 1979, pp. 25–29, for a discussion
      of HJ's "unrequited" love for WJ. Hall calls HJ's love for WJ "the central
      emotional experience" of HJ's life and argues that this had been "blocked"
      in their adolescence and so frustrated "the adult realization of his passions."
      Hall argues that HJ's emotions might be called "incestuous" rather than
      homosexual. The homoerotic motif in certain of HJ's novels—that between
      Rowland and Roderick, Newman and Valentin, Muniment and Hyacinth,
      seems more brotherly than "gay." Feinstein's discussion of "individuation"
      throws light on this, pp. 223–30.
295   *Castle Nowhere:* Four letters from Fenimore to HJ were found by me among
      the WJ papers at Harvard and have been published in HJL III, pp. 523–62.
      The HJ-Benedict correspondence is printed in an appendix to Jorg Hassler,
      Switzerland in the Life and Work of Henry James (Basel, 1966), pp. 136–62.
      AJ on Fenimore and HJ, Ruth Bernard Yeazell, *The Death and Letters of
      Alice James* (1981), pp. 124, 149.

PART FOUR: The Middle Years, 1881–1889

315   *The Peacock and the Butterfly:* For the genesis of this chapter see Edel,
      Writing Lives (1984), pp. 237–47. HJ's letters to Montesquiou are in Philippe
      Jullian, *Robert de Montesquiou, Un Prince* (Paris, 1965), p. 128.
341   *Palazzo Barbaro:* Patricia Curtis (Vigano) kindly provided access to the
      Palazzo and its library.
355   *The Gallo-Romans:* For a full account of Urbain Mengin see his son's book,
      Robert Mengin, *Monsieur Urbain* (Paris, 1984), particularly pp. 114–18. Bour-
      get's executor, General Marius Daille, gave me access to HJ's letters to Bour-
      get: the latter's to James are in Houghton.

PART FIVE: The Dramatic Years, 1890–1895

370   *A Divine Cessation:* See Strouse and Yeazell. The quotation from Dante is
      from *Paradiso* Book X, pp. 128–29.
373   *The Wheel of Time:* My description of W. Morton Fullerton is based on three
      meetings with him, two when he was still at *Le Figaro* in the 1930s, and the
      last in 1944 after the liberation of Paris. See also HJL IV, pp. xxiii–xxiv.
406   *"Saint Elizabeth":* I met Elizabeth Robins twice in 1937 and corresponded
      with her. Her friend, Dr. Octavia Wilberforce, supplied many details, after
      her death. The Robins papers are at New York University; some are in the
      Humanities Research Center, University of Texas.

page

PART SIX: The Treacherous Years, 1895–1900

437   *A Squalid Tragedy:* See *The Memoirs of John Addington Symonds,* ed. Gross-
      kurth (1984).
440   *The Two Romancers:* Daudet's letters to Theodore Child contain his praise
      of HJ's French. Lucien Daudet, son of Alphonse, originally made HJ's letters
      to his father and mother available to me. They are now in Houghton and
      Morgan. He also gave me information about the friendship with Meredith.
450   *Houses and Old Things:* In *The Spoils of Poynton* (Chap. vii, 77 [The Bodley
      Head James, London, 1967]) James writes: "In the watches of the night, she
      saw Poynton dishonoured; she had cherished it as a happy whole, she rea-
      soned, and the parts of it now around her seemed to suffer like chopped
      limbs. To lie there in the stillness was partly to listen for some soft low plaint
      for them." HJ, in addition to sustaining his symbolism of "amputation,"
      seems to be invoking a memory of Dante, *Inferno* XIII, 22–43.
463   *The Little Boys: Frank Leslie's New York Journal of Romance, General Liter-
      ature, Science and Art* was founded by Frank Leslie (1821–1880), an English-
      born engraver and publisher who published illustrated journals from the
      time of his emigration to New York in 1848. His use of illustrations was
      extensive and popular. Tom Taylor (1817–1880), educated at Trinity College,
      Cambridge (of which he became a Fellow), was editor of *Punch* from 1874
      to 1880. Long before achieving that position he was known for his popular
      plays, some in collaboration with Charles Reade, based on plots by earlier
      writers. His best known in the U.S. were *Our American Cousin* and *Still
      Waters Run Deep,* which HJ saw. He edited Haydon's autobiography in 1853
      and wrote a number of pot-boiling cliff-hangers for popular journals. *Temp-
      tation* appeared in the "New Series" of Leslie's journal, Vol. I, Part I, the
      installments running January, pp. 1–12; February, pp. 65–76; March, pp. 129–
      44; April, pp. 193–209; May, pp. 257–72; June, pp. 321–76, and in Vol. II, pp.
      33–108. HJ's account of his readings in New York is given in his essay on
      George Du Maurier, *Partial Portraits* (1888), and in various chapters of *A
      Small Boy and Others.* I am indebted to Adeline R. Tintner for assistance in
      obtaining the *Temptation* serial.
484   *L'Affaire:* For Mengin's description of HJ's visit to the Bourgets, where he
      was also a guest, see Mengin, p. 216 *et seq.*
494   *A Young Sculptor:* HJ's letters to Andersen are in the Barrett collection
      (Virginia). Corrupt typewritten texts exist in the British Library and the
      Library of Congress. On pp. 290–91 of Mengin's book, there is a discussion of
      whether James was a homosexual between Mary Robinson Duclaux, the
      British poet, and Urbain Mengin. Both knew James from the 1880s to his
      death. The question was raised by Mme. Duclaux. Mengin recalled that
      James considered Oscar Wilde an "unclean beast" and that he was "like
      myself never shocked to read about the customs of the Greek and Latin
      poets." "But try to imagine," Mengin continued, "HJ submitting himself—
      yes, we must use the word submit—to such customs. It's like my trying to
      imagine you, Mary, under my very eyes, giving yourself a shot of heroin."
      Mengin said it was necessary to recognize that for HJ homosexuality wasn't
      a question of morality but of sensibility. Within his sensibility "HJ would
      have a horror of the physical act. . . . Certain of his friendships, leanings,

gestures, could, I know [said Mengin], make one think he was capable of submitting himself . . . but those gestures were in themselves a signal, and I'd say a proof, that he wasn't capable of this kind of surrender. His affectionate manner of grasping your arm, or of patting you on the shoulder, or giving you a hug—he would never have done this if these gestures had, for him, the slightest suggestion of a pursuit of physical love. He was too refined, . . . and by the way how much more refined, intelligent, how much more the artist, and more puritanical than his brother William."

PART SEVEN: The Illusion of Freedom, 1900–1905

538 *A Poor Ancient Lady:* The papers of Margaret Mary James (Peggy) are in the Bancroft Library at Berkeley, California. HJ's letters to Marie Souvestre are in Morgan.

559 *The Real Right Thing:* See Appendix iv, HJL IV, p. 805 for HJ's testamentary remarks to his nephew Harry. HJ's *The Tempest: Essays on Literature* (The Library of America, New York, 1985), pp. 1205–20.

566 *A Queer Job:* I am indebted to the late Harold Morton Landon and his wife Frederica Rhinelander Landon for material relating to William Wetmore Story.

573 *An Exquisite Relation:* Aside from Hugh Walpole's claim that HJ was "madly in love" with Jocelyn Persse, we know very little about the latter. He led a quiet life, was much interested in the theater, and married after serving in the First World War. Sir Shane Leslie described him briefly in *Horizon* VII, p. 42 (June 1943). Walpole refers to him occasionally in his unpublished diaries. I have never been able to find a photograph of him. We corresponded briefly in the 1930s.

579 *An Agreeable Woman:* HJ's letters to Mrs. Wharton are at Yale, in the Wharton papers. I have also drawn on my conversations with her in 1931 and 1936 as well as on talks with Frederica Landon, Aileen Tone, Nicky Mariano, Louis Auchincloss, and earlier those who knew her in Paris.

613 *The Brothers:* WJ's letter about HJ to the American Academy of Arts and Letters is in HJL IV, pp. 787–88.

PART EIGHT: The Master, 1905–1916

629 *The House of Mirth:* HJ's letters to Berry were published in 1928 in Paris by the Black Sun Press but are transcribed inaccurately. See also Edel, "Walter Berry and the Novelists: Proust, James and Edith Wharton," *Nineteenth Century Fiction* 38:4, pp. 514–28.

709 *Final and Fading Words:* See HJL IV, pp. 808–12, for the complete text of HJ's deathbed dictation.

BRIEF BIBLIOGRAPHY

James Family: Katharine Bagg Hastings, *William James of Albany and His Descendants* (New York, 1924); F.O. Matthiessen, ed., *The James Family,* anthology of writings (New York, 1947).

Henry James, Sr.: WJ, ed., *The Literary Remains of the Late Henry James* (Boston, 1884); Austin Warren, *The Elder Henry James* (New York, 1934).

William James: Gay Wilson Allen, *William James* (New York, 1967); Howard M. Feinstein, *Becoming William James* (Ithaca, N.Y., 1984); Ralph Barton Perry, *The Thought and Character of William James* (Boston, 1936); J, ed., *Letters of William James* (Boston, 1920).

Alice James: Edel, ed., *The Diary of Alice James* (New York, 1964); Jean Strouse, *Alice James* (Boston, 1980); Ruth B. Yeazell, *The Death and Letters of Alice James* (Berkeley, 1981).

Henry James: Edel and Dan H. Laurence, *A Bibliography of Henry James,* third edition, revised with James Rambeau (Oxford, 1982); Edel, ed., *Henry James Letters,* four volumes (Cambridge, 1974–84); Percy Lubbock, ed., *Letters,* two volumes (New York, 1920); Edel, ed., *The Complete Tales* (New York/London, 1961–64); Edel, ed., *The Complete Plays* (New York/London, 1947); Edel and Edmund Wilson, eds., *The Critical Writings,* two volumes, Library of America (New York, 1984); Frederick W. Dupee, ed., *Autobiography* (New York, 1984); F. O. Matthiessen and Kenneth B. Murdock, eds., *Notebooks* (New York, 1947); S. Gorley Putt, *A Reader's Guide to Henry James* (New York, 1966).

INDEX

This index lists persons and data likely to be sought by a reader. It does not include passing allusions to them. Initials are used for the James family and for repeated names like Lamb House (LH), De Vere Gardens (DVG), or Miss Woolson (CFW), etc.